ADVANCE PRAISE

Henry has written a devastating and powerful first-hand account of a remarkable life, a tale of strength and survival, of the bright light of humanity that shines through the darkest days and reminds us why it is so important to resist the forces of oppressive intolerance and discrimination, whatever the source or direction.

A book of impregnable power that deserves the widest audience.

–Philippe Sands, Author East West Street.

Being a child of the Holocaust, I am very familiar with its narrative. However, rarely have I read a more riveting account of surviving the odds, as Henry Reiss's Book *The Engineers*.

The brilliant hour-by-hour suspense portrays the penultimate combination of man's will to survive and the ingenuity of finding ways to do so. It displays the brush stroke of a potential literary giant, painting the very worst of humanity, with the occasional glimpses of the very best in humanity, and the immeasurable consequences that unfold.

We witness through his eyes the juxtaposition of Vienna 1988, with restaurants full of people eating, drinking, singing, and Vienna 1938...

Hitler had annexed Austria, and the Viennese were celebrating the Nazis rise to power and the spilling of Jewish blood.

The indomitable spirit of Henry Reiss, during the roller coaster of emotions, combined with the back drop of history keeps one enthralled at all times.

–Eva Fischl OAM, President The Joint Distribution Committee (Australia).

I was six years old at the outbreak of war. Henry knew me even before I was born. I remember much of what Henry tells here as my family joined the Reiss family at critical times in their survival. The Reiss' and Habers' lost almost all of their extended families in the Holocaust but it gives me joy that we remain connected.

–Richard Haber, Author of *Still Here*.

THE ENGINEERS

A MEMOIR OF SURVIVAL THROUGH WORLD WAR II IN POLAND AND HUNGARY

HENRY REISS

ISBN 9789493322370 (ebook)

ISBN 9789493322363 (paperback)

ISBN 9789493322387 (hardcover)

Publisher: Amsterdam Publishers, The Netherlands

info@amsterdampublishers.com

The Engineers is part of the series Holocaust Survivor Memoirs World War II

Copyright © Christine (Krysia) Hill, daughter of Henry Reiss, 2024

Cover image: Ilana Bodenstein, great-granddaughter of Henry Reiss

Corresponding editor: Miriam Levy, granddaughter Miriamngj@gmail.com

All Rights Reserved. No part of this publication may be reproduced or transmitted in any form or by any means, electronic or mechanical, including photocopy, recording or any other information storage and retrieval system, without prior permission in writing from the publisher.

CONTENTS

Introduction	xi

PART I
CHILDHOOD, SCHOOLS, STUDIES, AND FAMILIES

Kraków	3
Galicia	9
Annexation by the Soviet Union	17
Early Years	25
Return to Budynin	32
High School: Oserdów and Sokal	38
Summer Holidays in Oserdów	42
Lwów Polytechnic	45
Judenfrei	49
Wedding and the Anschluss	54
Who would survive?	59

PART II
UNDER SOVIET OCCUPATION IN POLAND

Lwów under the Red Army	65
The Government Mills Trust	71
Nationalization	79
Passportization and the perfidy of the NKVD	85
A court case and a spy	93

PART III
UNDER GERMAN OCCUPATION

Call-up to the Red Army	109
German Army arrives	116
Working for the Gestapo	124
Surrendering the Jewish furs	131
Actions and the Jewish Star	143
Action against my mother	153

PART IV
UNDER GERMAN OCCUPATION – AS AN ARYAN

Planning our escape	167
Moving to Warsaw	175
First steps as Daraż	185
Critical need for employment	192
Lusia blackmailed	202
Warsaw Ghetto Revolt	214
Only with an Ausweis	227
Accused	237
Lusia blackmailed again	245
Planning an escape	255
The Gestapo take Lusia	262
Elżunia at the Gestapo	270
Leaving Legionowo	278

PART V
UNDER GERMAN OCCUPATION IN HUNGARY

Polish Guides – German Police	285
Slovakian Latkes	291
Waiting at Kassa, Hungary	300
Camp Kadarkút for Polish families	306
Yellow Star for Hungarian Jews	313
The medical examination	320
Taszár Airfield employment	329
Arrested by Hungarian gendarmes	338
Escape	344
Habers deported	353

PART VI
UNDER SOVIET OCCUPATION IN HUNGARY

Life with the Soviets	365
A German spy!	386
German counteroffensive	394
Crossing the Danube	409
Leaving Taszár	422
Capitulation	429
The Yugoslav repatriation mission	435
Watch smuggling	440

Stamp smuggling	456
New Life: May 1946	465

PART VII
AFTER THE WAR

Emigration	475
Poland revisited: 1967	481
Sentimental journey: 1988	492
My thoughts on Antisemitism	502
Kindness	513
Notes	517
Photos	522
Acknowledgments	528
Amsterdam Publishers Holocaust Library	531

Dedicated to the memory of Lusia

*whose extraordinary courage
wisdom and determination
were decisive in our surviving
the HITLERITE MADNESS*

INTRODUCTION

I began writing this memoir a few days after leaving Soviet-occupied Budapest and arriving in the American Zone of Germany in July 1946. We were staying in a camp for displaced persons, in the small German town of Ulm on the Danube. Since then, whenever I've had a peaceful moment in a quiet corner, I tried to put on paper some of those nightmarish years, still so vivid in my mind.

With this story, I also wanted to answer the questions, asked so often, how it happened that we were among the few survivors of the 6 million European Jews who perished in the Holocaust. Our surviving family unit consisted of me, my wife Lusia – both of us 39 years old – and two children, Elżunia, aged eight years, and a baby girl, Krysia.

Like many other displaced people, we had neither documents nor money and possessed no visa to another country: no knowledge of any overseas language, even the name we were still using was false, for we felt it was too early to revert to our real name.

If the reader wonders why, with so many disadvantages, we chose to become immigrants instead of returning to our country, Poland, particularly when the Polish government had offered us attractive positions within our profession as qualified engineers in the reconstruction of the war-torn country, the answer can best be understood by the story related in this book. The reasons go back to my childhood.

I was born in Kraków in 1907, when this beautiful town was still part of the Austro-Hungarian Empire. The first words I would listen to and the first words I uttered were Polish. I attended Polish schools, learned and loved Polish romantic literature, admired the country's great history, and became deeply attached to the Polish landscape, the soil of my fatherland. I considered myself Polish and was proud to belong to this great and once powerful nation. Proudly I joined in the singing of Poland's national anthem: *Nie damy ziemi skad nasz ród* [We shall not surrender the land of our ancestors].

But there was another side to my life: My Polish home was also a Jewish home. My parents, grandparents, and great-grandparents were Jewish. That factor was to weigh heavily over my existence. In prewar Poland, I was confronted with a Polish-Jewish conflict that intensified throughout World War II. I survived only because I changed my identity to Piotr Daraż, a Roman Catholic Pole. As Henryk Reiss, I would have perished, together with my wife and child.

When the war ended, we were in Hungary. Poles, including a few Jewish survivors, were returning home to Poland. But where was our home? It was an existential dilemma. To return to our true identity, with the name of "Reiss" and potentially be exposed to the Polish-Jewish conflict, or to continue as Christian "Daraż," detaching ourselves and our children from the Jewish nation.

The heroes of the Warsaw Ghetto had fought against impossible odds, not even for survival but for an honorable death. Young Jewish boys and girls gave their lives so that we, the survivors, could be proud of our heritage and tell future generations of the horrible suffering of their people. How could I fulfill my part in telling that story without renouncing my false identity "Piotr Daraż"? We made up our minds. We would venture as the Reiss family into an unknown world, hoping to find a place under the sun but far from the scenes of our people's martyrdom: a place where we would not be hated by our neighbors, where our children would not be held responsible for the crucifixion of Christ.

The writing of this story has had many interruptions since we made that momentous decision. The inevitable problems confronting newly arrived immigrants consumed much of my time and energy, dissipating the concentration needed to recall those turbulent years. After the death of Lusia, my unforgettable companion in our struggle,

I again took up this story. Once again, I relived those years of war by recalling our unbelievable experiences. I have tried to reflect on those whose lives intertwined with ours: those whose bravery and nobility led them to give us a helping hand, often at the risk of their own security; as well as those whose prejudice and hatred could have destroyed us. With eternal gratitude, I shall cherish and respect the memory of the former, the latter are left to God's judgment.

Henry Reiss, Cremorne, Australia, 1991

My grandfather spent many years working on his memoir, originally in Polish then translated and self-published just before his death in 1991. It was available for his family and friends shortly thereafter. In his life, Henry rarely mentioned the events in this book for reasons that I imagine but do not know. This memoir is illuminating for his family, but its value is much broader.

Growing up in Sydney, I attended a Jewish school where many of my friends were children of survivors. I found it particularly hard to comprehend how Hitler's Final Solution had been executed in plain sight. Henry's memoir illustrates how fear, hate, jealousy, or necessity meant individuals facilitated, witnessed or simply ignored what was going on. In fact, the prewar relationships between Ukrainians, Poles, and Jews in the region of Galicia may have informed the responses to the evolving genocide. This understanding also helps to contextualize the current Russian-Ukrainian conflict.

Importantly, Henry's memoir is a testament to those who, with acts of kindness, determined his family's survival and thus my existence. For these reasons, despite the sadness, it is inspiring and remains relevant.

Miriam Levy, Sydney, Australia

PART I

CHILDHOOD, SCHOOLS, STUDIES, AND FAMILIES

1907-1939

KRAKÓW
SEPTEMBER 1939

For the past few months, we had lived under great strain. Having swallowed the Rhineland, Memel, Austria, and Czechoslovakia, Nazi Germany had turned its covetous eyes upon Poland. The cafés in Kraków were swarming with self-appointed politicians. The mood was grave, everyone sensing an approaching storm. Posters on city walls announced a general mobilization.

Each day brought new rumors, fueling new fears. The Polish foreign minister, Colonel Józef Beck, flew to Paris and London. Hitler summoned the German ambassador of Poland. Germany's foreign minister, Joachim von Ribbentrop, flew to Moscow, where the airport had been decorated with swastikas. With a friendly smile, the perfidious Vyacheslav Molotov, the Russian foreign minister, greeted this representative of Germany and archenemy of the Soviet Union. Meanwhile, France and England guaranteed the independence of Poland within its existing borders. Polish radio affirmed the invincible strength of our army over and over. Marshal Edward Rydz-Śmigły, our commander-in-chief, proudly declared he would never surrender Gdansk, nor the Corridor. "A battle on two fronts will end in swift humiliating defeat for the enemy!" "We shall repeat Grunwald!" chanted the crowds, gathered around the monument of King Jagiełło He had been the victor over the Teutonic Knights at the Battle of

Grunwald in 1410, one of the greatest military triumphs in Polish history.

Lusia and I were listening to patriotic speeches, sharing the enthusiasm of the crowds, singing the national anthem as one: *Jeszcze Polska nie zginęla* [Poland has not perished yet]. We returned home very late, tired, and apprehensive.

The night was hot and humid, with windows open. I tossed restlessly, finally falling into a deep slumber that lasted only until the early hours when a deafening noise suddenly woke me. It sounded as if an infernal machine was about to break up midair and over our very heads. The roar intensified, coming closer and lower.

I jumped out of bed and ran to the open window. Just above our roof, a powerful plane was furiously spitting machine-gun fire. I could actually see the pilot's head amid the clouds of smoke, and with horror I recognized the Teutonic Cross on the plane's body and wings, the black emblem of the German Luftwaffe.

It was 5 a.m. Friday, 1 September 1939. The uncertainty was over; the Germans had treacherously attacked Poland and the Second World War had begun.

I woke Lusia (all her life she enjoyed sleeping in) and she had neither heard the roar of the plane nor the firing of the machine guns. Quite recently, she had completed a course in civil defense and joined a voluntary national organization. In the event of an air raid, she was to be at the rallying point without delay. Hastily dressing but still drowsy, she ran from the house.

I dressed quickly and went down to the street. The planes had gone. Slowly, sleepy people were emerging from their homes, some had heard the roar of the planes but had not seen them. There had been Polish planes over Kraków in the last few days and people presumed these were Polish, too.

In our block of flats lived a major of the Polish army. On the street in his smart uniform, he was waiting for his car. He regarded my account with disbelief and visible resentment. He advised me not to spread this news suggesting that I was mistaken. I could see what he was thinking; how could a civilian, a Jew at that, recognize a German warplane?

People were getting ready for work. Trams and buses appeared in the streets. Lusia returned from the rallying point when no one else had turned up. We switched on the radio: morning music as usual. It was as if nothing had happened. Was it only a nightmare?

We telephoned our friends, the Herzhafts. They confirmed my observations. Not only had they heard the planes, they could actually see the devastation of an aircraft attack. A three-story building just opposite their house had been hit and reduced to rubble.

By noon there were no doubts. German radio broadcast Hitler's speech: "We will put an end to Polish provocations. The German army has stopped the attack by Polish criminal gangs. *Heute Morgen haben wir zurückgeschlagen* [This morning we hit back]." In truth, Hitler had ordered a group of German criminals to be taken out of jail, dressed in Polish army uniforms, and shot, their bodies left on German soil at the Polish border. A charade of Polish "aggression."

At nine o'clock, as I always did, I went to the office. The mood was grave. Foreman Borowiec arrived. We were supposed to start a new building project on Monday and were awaiting instructions. He told us the roads were packed with soldiers; many wounded and large numbers of refugees were fleeing. I was stricken with panic. What should I do? This question I would ask myself innumerable times over the years to come. Nevertheless, I decided to do nothing different and the day passed without incident.

On Sunday though, the frightening roar of approaching planes returned. Squadrons of German bombers attacked our beautiful Kraków. Luckily, Lusia and I were on our own. In July, we had taken the precaution of sending our little daughter Elżunia, then 15 months old, with her nanny Zofia to our country property, Oserdów. The property was managed by my brother, Ludwik, and my mother. It was situated in a quiet village in the eastern part of Poland, far from the German border. We felt certain the German attack would be halted before it could get there with the assistance, as promised, of the French and English. We were confident the aggressor would be defeated. The nights in Oserdów would be peaceful for Elżunia: no fear of air raids, bombardments, or terror.

Perhaps we should go east to Oserdów too? But how? Going by train was out of the question. The railways were already in chaos. A few days earlier, Lusia had managed to take some of our most precious possessions by train to Lwów where her parents lived. She took some Persian rugs, silver cutlery, and my stamp collection. She had returned to Kraków on the last train and recounted a terrible journey as carriages were already bursting with people who had the same idea to flee. There were lost children and hundreds of suitcases abandoned on station platforms. There were even rumors that Kraków station had been bombed.

We decided to flee to Oserdów immediately and Lusia began to pack a few essentials. I ran into the street to find a taxi, although I held little hope. Too many people had the same idea and, in any case, the army had requisitioned most vehicles. Luckily, I did find a driver who agreed to take us to Jaroslav, a small town some 200 kilometers away, for 400 złoty, then a considerable sum. From there, we could take a night train to Belz, the nearest railway station to Oserdów.

Our small suitcase was packed. It was almost time to leave when the taxi driver appeared at the door breathlessly advising that his taxi had been requisitioned by a Polish officer. He promised that as soon as he was free, he would return to get us. Four hundred złoty was a fortune to him. We could think of no other way, so we just had to wait.

The minutes passed slowly. An hour went by. Should I try and find another taxi or would he come back? There was mincemeat in the ice chest. Lusia mixed it with eggs, onions, and breadcrumbs. She was melting butter in the frying pan when he reappeared. We left immediately. In the last seconds, Lusia switched off the gas. I can still picture those beautifully shaped hamburgers which remained uncooked. We locked the door of our beautiful apartment and the first chapter in our life together had ended. A life that began on our wedding day, 24 June 1934. We left behind professional success and personal happiness, uncertain of what lay ahead.

We were leaving Kraków, a city where my mother's family, the well-known and respected Tilleses, had lived for several generations. My mother, my grandmother, and my great-grandmother, as well as myself and our daughter Elżunia, had all been born there. An ancient and beloved city with its green parks, where pensioners sat on sun-drenched benches, where red train cars could barely squeeze through the Florian Gate – Kraków, with its historical Sukiennice and St. Mary's Cathedral, whose traditional fanfare from the tower had once been cut off by a poisoned arrow shot by Tata invaders. Once again, the alarm signal from the church tower warned the townsfolk of a new invader whose poison arrows, it transpired, were aimed at millions of innocents. We left it all, in a taxi avoiding the central thoroughfares and using side streets to reach main roads that were already crowded with refugees, themselves burdened by bundles and children in tow. They were on foot, on horseback, and in cars, all moving eastward.

We reached Tarnov, 100 kilometers from Kraków. A volunteer committee welcomed us with hot soup, bread, and drinking water. Behind the trestle tables, women stood – old and young, some wrinkled by age and toil, others delicate, well-presented socialites. Some had distinct Polish features and others were obviously Jewish – their faces drawn with fear.

The majority of the refugees were Jewish. The Jewish women among those offering food wanted more information than they had. What did we think was going to happen? They, too, would be grabbing their bundles and running soon, although they didn't know that then.

We ate their hot soup ravenously. It was the first time in our lives that we had relied on a soup kitchen. It was Sunday and the shops were closed. Suddenly we heard a low, threatening growl of engines. Everyone looked up, searching for planes. There was no time to lose. We jumped back into our taxi and sped from the town center onto the highway. Our driver was forced to slow down for potholes, but there were also many cars on the road, and overtaking other vehicles was impossible. A second wave of growling approaching fighter planes could be heard. It did not occur to us for one moment that we could be an actual target. We watched them as they flew high above us. Then, one plane left the formation and dived right over the top of the stream of refugees. Did the pilot want to observe us close-up or photograph the exodus? Then the unbelievable happened: Machine-gun fire swept our slow-moving column of refugees. There was a terrified panic. Our taxi driver managed to reach and stop under the protection of a roadside willow. Leaping out, we flung ourselves to the ground. The plane came again spitting a salvo into a group of carts. Horses stampeded and carts full of people and possessions overturned into ditches. We could hear cries of pain mingled with prayers and curses, the fading staccato of machine guns, the whining of crazed and wounded horses.

We pressed our heads hard against the ground, holding our breath.

The frightening rumble of the low-flying plane came again and more machine-gun salvos tore through the air. Were we hit? Somebody next to us cried out "Gas!" Was it a gas attack? We had been taught if that happened, one should cover one's mouth and nose with a urine-soaked handkerchief. Easy enough to find a handkerchief, but urinating in such a panic was out of the question!

The "heroic" pilot reappeared and unloaded another burst of ammunition. Somebody nearby shrieked in pain. We could hear children sobbing. After a time, the sound of the plane subsided and faded away completely. People crept out of ditches and collected their bundles. Others lay where they had fallen. Quickly we climbed back into the car, but our driver refused to go on. "I've had enough," he exclaimed. "I'm going home."

I was not surprised. Like everybody else, the poor fellow was paralyzed with fear. The thought of having to continue our flight on foot was terrifying. We had with us a small bottle of vodka. I proffered it to him. After two gulps, the color returned to his cheeks. The alcohol plus promised bonus, if he could just get us to the railway station at Jaroslav, achieved the desired result.

To our surprise, the Lwów-Sokal train, which I had often taken on journeys from Kraków, was leaving on time. We were surprised that it was quite empty. The ticket controller passing through the darkened carriages punched our tickets as if nothing was amiss and, listening to the familiar rumbling rhythm of the train as it moved through the darkness of the night, we relaxed and rested.

We arrived at Belz at two in the morning. I had messaged my brother, Ludwik, who was waiting with a carriage and another horse-drawn wagon for our luggage. My family in Oserdów had no idea that we were lucky to escape with our lives and just one small suitcase, nor that we had passed through a baptism of Luftwaffe fire!

My mother was waiting with a prepared dinner. She looked anxious. Elżunia was safely asleep in a white cot in which I too, had slept as a small child. While Mother held the kerosene lamp, Lusia gazed into the face of our sleeping child. Tears rolled slowly down her cheeks.

GALICIA
EARLY SEPTEMBER 1939

Oserdów had been in my family since before 1880 when my grandfather, Nuchim Reiss, owned the farm there and in the neighboring property Budynin. When he died, Oserdów was left to my father, Philip, and his brother, Joshua, a physician in Lwów. My father leased his brother's share and my family worked very hard on the farm to make ends meet.

According to the terms of the Treaty of Brest-Litovsk, the Russians had withdrawn from Poland and recognized the independence of Ukraine and other regions in late 1918, the end of World War I. Upon their departure, the Russians had burned down our farmhouse, stables, sheds, and barns and it was only with great effort and industry that Oserdów was rebuilt. Trees were planted, a vegetable garden established, and a fishpond dug. The barn was rebuilt and livestock numbers increased over time to at least 20 horses and 30 cows. A dairy and piggery were built. Butter and cheese were processed and sent daily by night train to Kraków. We developed sugar beet crops for the sugar refinery and supplied fruit to the local market. The income, despite ceaseless hard work, was modest. Farm products support only low prices and the fiscal policy was merciless toward the Jewish taxpayer.

I was always enchanted by the beauty of the family property. Its meadows and grasslands, fields of rye and wheat, the fragrance of freshly mown grass or clover, the warmth of July afternoons, the freshness of spring mornings, the aroma of freshly plowed soil after the rain were some of the things I loved.

In Polish literature, much has been written about the peasant's love for his soil; this love is complete, strong, and eternal like no other love. Poets have described it. Boryna, a character in the immortal Nobel prize-winning *Peasants* by Reymont, dies in his field while sowing "till his last breath." Such love cannot be fully comprehended by those born and raised in towns, for whom bread is purchased in a bakery and milk supplied in a bottle.

In Oserdów, I felt happy holding a pitchfork, shovel, or hoe captivated by the gleaming blackness of a ridge of soil freshly exposed by the sharp edge of a plow, evenly driven by steady well-matched, well-fed horses. My father's horses, our horses! I liked to walk behind a row of harrows with a stick and smash the larger lumps of earth overlooked by sharp teeth. I followed the sowing machine, watching the grains of wheat and rye disappearing in the fresh soil. I would wait with eager anticipation for the moment when young plants pushed through the earth's crust, in beautiful, even rows like miniature schoolchildren in green uniforms.

I adored harvest time. About mid-July, elderly women and young girls would take up their positions in a row in front of a field of ripened rye, ready and waiting. I remember as if it were yesterday – Father approaching one of the older women asking for her sickle. All chatter stopping and in total silence except for the singing of larks and buzzing of insects. I recall watching my father bend in a slow but dignified way, grasping a handful of rye and cutting it with an experienced stroke. Watching him, the harvesters waited. Father straightening, in his left hand the bundle of rye, in his right the sickle. In a loud voice, addressing the harvesters with "May the Lord bless you with good health and good luck!" the harvesters replying in unison "May God bless you too!" so harvest could begin. Backs bent, moving slowly along the field, they left behind tightly bound sheaves.

By evening, hemispheric stacks of the new crop stood in evenly spaced rows like soldiers on parade. The harvesters left the field with slow, tight steps, yet with a song on their lips. The sinking sun bade them farewell till tomorrow. Listening to their songs, I joined them, young but deeply moved by the beauty of those solemn yet joyful moments.

All through my life I have returned many times in my mind to the fields of Oserdów, to the silence and solitude along a narrow bank between the walls, silence broken only by insects or hummingbirds singing beside the golden wheat, ripening rye, the poppies, and cornflowers in the setting sun.

It was to this beloved Oserdów that I escaped the madness of the third day of the war, a madness the extent of which I could never have predicted, one that would threaten my life and take the lives of many in my family and of millions of men, women, and children.

We had returned in the hope that provenance would permit us to stay in relative quiet until the time when the Polish army, aided by our Western allies, mounted a successful counterattack.

We listened to the radio which relayed messages in code, relating movements of the enemy bombers: "*Uwaga, uwaga, nadchodzi, nadchodzi, czekolada* [Attention, attention, coming, coming, chocolate]" followed sometime later by "*Uwaga, uwaga, odchodzi, odchodzi, papier* [Attention, attention, going, going, paper]." We understood chocolate implied bombs and paper empty. Polish radio announced: "We have bombed Berlin; all our planes returned safely to their bases." Our spirits rose. Then again: "Attention, attention! Coming, coming, chocolate" and "Attention, attention! Going, going, paper."

It was early September. The threshing machine was busy. On the top platform, a girl stood cutting one sheaf after another, feeding them into its powerful mouth. Heaven forbid that a leg or hand should come in contact with those blades! Golden grains of wheat, sorted according to size, fell into sacks. Stalks of straw denuded of grain were cast out onto an elevator that carried them to the top where farmhands grabbed them, spreading them evenly into a huge steadily rising stack. Husks, shafts, and weeds found their places beneath the machine.

Samko Mackiewitz, the mechanic who had been looking after the thresher for years, wandered about with oil can in hand, watching, checking, and oiling, a serious expression on his grimy face. The machine turned rhythmically, and the driving belt regularly rotated the main drum of the thresher, occasionally faltering when chaff was too big or insufficiently spread out. It was as if no war had broken out.

Then suddenly, the gentle hum of farm machinery was drowned

out by a thunderous roar from high above us. What was it? Everyone stared, frozen, as two huge black German fighter planes, like birds of prey, tore through the sky in pursuit of a small Polish plane that was trying desperately to evade them. We all stared at the sky spellbound, holding our breath, until a cloud veiled our view. We could still hear their roar. Moments later, low overhead, the small Polish plane with white and red signs emerged from the clouds heading straight toward us and the thresher.

The pilot lifted just in time, seeming to pass only centimeters above the heads of those on the thresher platform, and landed about ten meters away. The young pilot jumped out running and gesturing frantically to keep clear, anticipating that the German planes would come down to destroy his machine. Yet the low cloud protected us and did not disperse. The German planes circled for some time but, unable to see the little Polish bird, they gave up and roared away.

I rushed toward the pilot welcoming him into our house. He declined; he was in a hurry. "I'm from Kraków," he said. "Is there news?" I begged to know. He told me Kraków had fallen, that the German army was moving very fast – the situation was serious. He asked for help to restart his plane. The sky was now clear and in a few minutes he had disappeared. A grim reality confronted us. The dream of escaping the war in the haven of Oserdów was shattered.

It was not too long after that groups of refugees began to arrive. Desperate people, in or beside their carts pulled by tired horses, streamed in. Women, children, old men, and Jews with beards came, mostly walking while carrying bundles, eiderdowns, pots and pails, teapots and stools and occasionally with a dog or goat on a string. Their destination was unknown.

With the refugees came news from the occupied territories. The Germans were behaving badly. Young men, mostly Jews, were being rounded up and taken into forced-labor camps. Did a similar fate await us? What to do now?

Polish radio Warsaw made itself heard. Colonel Roman Umiastowski read the order of the commander-in-chief: "All men capable of bearing arms are to withdraw immediately to the east." There were no details from the front, no information, only the constantly repeating demand that "all men are to withdraw immediately to the east."

We suspected the high command had hopes of holding the German offensive and needed soldiers to fill the gaps. Or perhaps they wanted to prevent the Germans from obtaining more forced laborers. Whatever the motive, an order was an order, and we began to prepare our "withdrawal."

Since the order of the commander-in-chief related solely to men, capable of bearing arms, what to do with the women was not clear. It was obvious to us that young men, particularly Jews, should not fall into the hands of the Germans. At the time it did not occur to anyone that Hitler's diabolical plans included women and children as well. We understood that we had to split up. Someone had to remain on the farm. Harvest was just finished, the threshing underway; the autumn plowing needed to begin. Potatoes and beet were still to be harvested. Cattle in the barn needed attention, the dairy was in production – there was an endless number of tasks to be carried out. It was out of the question that all of us could leave. Besides, how could we venture into the unknown with a baby of 18 months?

We decided that my brother and I would retreat eastward and Lusia would accompany us until we joined with the armed forces. She would then return to Oserdów where she and my mother would run the farm. Knowing Lusia's determination, common sense, and knowledge of German she would be able to deal successfully with the military occupation. We reasoned that the German authorities would need agricultural establishments to continue production. The Germans would not harm a single woman with a small child. We had to believe that.

A farm supervisor, Moshe Bear, and another young Jew from the village, David, joined us. We took two vehicles: a smart coach with a beautiful pair of horses, driven by Ludwik, with Lusia and me in the passenger seats along with a cart pulled by draft horses for the other two. We tried to avoid the main roads as much as possible. We had a map and were guided by information from helpful strangers. Those roads were clogged with refugees, military units, cars, and lorries. We were afraid of air raids and the possibility that our vehicles might be requisitioned by the military. We planned to head in the direction of the Tarnopol district where we had relatives and could stop for a few days, waiting for the military situation to clarify itself.

We received our first news of the catastrophic situations of our

Polish defenses from one of our hosts along the route, a Mr. Waldman, who was a native German. He was very well informed, being able to listen to the German broadcast. He enumerated all the occupied Polish towns, it seemed to us, with some glee. The Polish government had left Warsaw, which was surrounded and being heavily bombarded. The Polish army was in retreat. Nearing the Tarnopol region we reached Cecowa, a farm managed by Uncle Jacob Weissglass and his wife, Amalia (Ciocia Malcia), my father's sister. We were warmly welcomed, though pleasure was mixed with sadness. What would they do? For them to leave their farms was unthinkable. The autumn plowing was in full swing, the winter corn was being sown. Uncle Jacob was on his feet from early morning until late at night.

"It's our duty to sow. If we leave, who will harvest next year?" he asked despairingly. Aunt Amalia was busy preparing food for the next part of our journey.

Just as we were ready to go on, we struck trouble with our horses. Not being used to long distances, we could see they were unfit to continue. I asked my uncle for replacements and he kindly agreed, giving us a pair of small but lovely steeds. We felt much safer with these modest farm horses. We were young and presentable, which had already drawn unwanted attention. We had noticed many suspicious gazes especially when passing through Ukrainian villages.

We continued on the road where the chaotic remnants of the Polish army's retreat were evident. Odd groups of soldiers mingled with refugees. There were abandoned cars, already robbed of seats and seat coverings. It seemed miraculous that we were journeying without harm so far. We had to cross the water of the river Dniester since the bridge was closed to civilians. Before the Romanian border, we decided to stay overnight at the village of Podwysoka in the hope that a Jewish property owner might assist us. The name Reiss was well known among the Jewish farming community and we were welcomed.

We arrived in the evening of 16 September but found the Weich's country home crowded with high officials from Warsaw, including the Chief of Office of the President of the Republic, Professor Ignacy Mościcki. Despite the excitement and general chaos, Mr. Weich managed to feed us and our horses but could not accommodate us, though he arranged lodgings in the house of a poor Jewish villager. He assured us his guests would be able to inform us in time when we needed to cross into Romania.

Rising early after a restless night, we went up to the house to seek the latest news. It was immediately obvious that something had happened. The house was deserted and all cars and carriages gone. The entrance doors were wide open. There was no response to our knocking. On entering, a great picture of destruction confronted us: broken furniture, scattered articles, fragments of smashed glass, and porcelain; there were no carpets and not a living soul to be seen.

Bewildered, we searched the rooms and finally found Mr. Weich in a nook next to the kitchen hiding, deadly pale and greatly agitated. After receiving a telephone message the previous night, his Warsaw "guests" had left in panic heading toward the Romanian border. The Soviet army had crossed into Poland along the frontier. Sometime later, around midnight he thought, he had been woken by the sound of breaking furniture.

A Ukrainian gang was raiding the house. Terrified, he jumped out of the window and in the darkness jumped into a fishpond, up to his neck in water. He remained there until daybreak hidden by the reeds. The gang had searched the whole property. Perhaps it was only a personal vendetta, being settled in the current state of upheaval, yet he advised us to leave as quickly as possible. He would go to Horodenka, a town a few kilometers away. He could not face another night on his property.

We were stunned. By chance alone there had been no room for us in Weich's home. How those uninvited guests would have dealt with us we could only guess. We had to reassess. The situation had changed suddenly again. Simultaneous with Germany's invasion of western Poland, the Red Army had invaded the east. The Soviet-Polish Nonaggression Pact of 1932 was unilaterally broken by the Soviets. It transpired later that a secret protocol, the Molotov-Ribbentrop Pact between the Germans and the Soviet Union was being realized, shocking us and the world. Poland was divided in two, just like that. Germany would stay on their side of the line, and for us now, we had suddenly become part of the Soviet Union. The question was: "What were Moscow's intentions?"

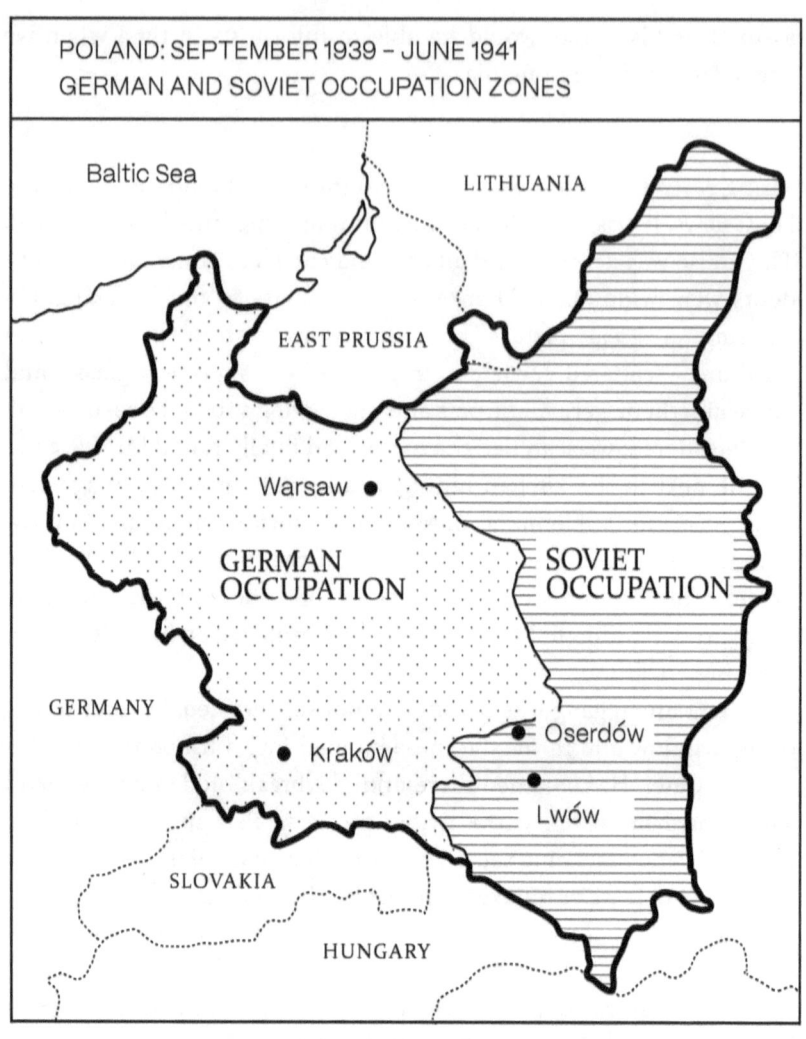

ANNEXATION BY THE SOVIET UNION
16 SEPTEMBER 1939

Whatever plans the Soviet Union had for Poland, at least the danger of falling into the hands of the Germans had been warded off. My mother and Elżunia were in Oserdów and all of us were within the Soviet-controlled zone. We realized that while conditions might change under the Soviets, surely this would be true for everybody, not just for the Jews. There should be work for Lusia and me. The Russians would probably take Oserdów away from us, but was life as landowners so easy? Besides, Oserdów, like so many other Jewish-owned properties, was already listed by the Polish government for resumption and forced sale to Polish settlers. Ludwik would find a job with his extensive experience in agriculture. With the three of us working, we should be able to take care of my mother and our child.

Antisemitism might lessen, too. No longer would we be treated as second-class citizens as we had been under the Polish government. Poles, Ukrainians, and Jews should now be equal. We were hopeful!

We would return immediately to Oserdów. But while collecting our belongings, the door flew open and a young man, wearing a red armband, stood blocking our exit with a rifle aimed straight at us. To our horror we heard "Hands up!" ordered in Yiddish. He was rambling about exploitation of the working class by parasites such as ourselves. Our carriage must have suggested a social status that wasn't acceptable to this revolutionary; we saw the glare of hatred in his eyes and wondered what to do. Luckily our host returned just in time, slapped the man over the head with his cap several times, took his rifle, yelling abuse in Yiddish, and threw him out "*Gey, gey meshugener* [Go, go, you madman]!"

He was a village simpleton. Poor and unemployed, the lad had become embittered by capitalism and antisemitism and had thought the time of reckoning had arrived. Mr. Weich advised we leave immediately though, for our safety and his.

As we left, we noticed from the windows of wooden, thatched cottages we passed, small flags waving; yet only a few were red to welcome the Soviets. The majority were yellow and blue – the colors of the nationalistic Ukrainians who harbored an intense hatred of the Poles but also a centuries-old hatred of Jews. As our carriages rumbled past, young men in groups outside their houses stared at us with open hostility. We moved along quickly, fearing they may decide to deal with us by old methods – those of the Khmelnytsky Cossacks.

We were reaching the outskirts of the village when we heard shouting, demanding us to stop. Looking back, a group of young men were pursuing us. We whipped our horses and sped on, and fortunately our would-be persecutors disappeared. In half an hour, we reached the Romanian-Polish border town of Horodenka.

The town was in a festive mood. Soviet tanks stood in the marketplace surrounded by a seemingly friendly crowd, men and women of all ages, mostly Jews, but some Ukrainians and Poles as well. But it was the Jewish people who warmly welcomed the Red Army. The Poles traditionally hated the Soviets, particularly after the stab-in-the-back breach of their mutual nonaggression pact. The Ukrainians were the most upset. They had hoped that Hitler would give them an independent Ukraine (and perhaps a free hand against the Jews). Only the Jews were relieved, avoiding the terror of Nazi occupation and the possibility of a bloody Ukrainian pogrom. The Jews believed the Soviet regime would provide equality and fair treatment. The antisemitism of the Poles and the Ukrainians might be overruled.

Since 1918, the time of Poland's independence and release from the Austro-Hungarian Empire at the end of World War I, Jews were regrettably exposed to antisemitism by diverse sections of the population with the silent approval of the authorities and sometimes open incitement by the church and state. Government, as well as municipal positions, were inaccessible to Jews. A Jew could neither become an employee, nor even a cleaner, in a public institution. A Jew could not become a tram guard, railway guard, engine driver, policeman, postman, gasworks employee, post office employee, power plant worker, and so on. Apart from the professions, a Jew could only be self-employed: a tradesman, merchant, or farmer. The tax authorities squeezed him with special taxes. Simultaneously, propaganda slogans such as *Nie Kupuj u Zyda* [Don't buy from a Jew] made existence even harder.

The Jewish populations of small Polish towns were composed mainly of poor people, struggling to survive often under extremely difficult economic conditions. They had little to lose from the Red Army and greeted the Soviet soldiers enthusiastically.

We stopped in the marketplace in Horodenka and joined the crowd near one of the Russian tanks. A young soldier in a shabby uniform was addressing them. He spoke fluently, praising life in the Soviet Union, describing the wonders of their industry, the big cities, the high quality of agriculture, and other achievements. He proudly affirmed the Soviet equality of the sexes, equal rights for everyone to study, and jobs for all, "thanks to our leader and a great builder of the Soviet Union and father of the nation, Comrade Stalin!" The crowd applauded, delighted with this portrayal of happiness in a socialist land. There were many questions. The Russian soldiers were very friendly, entering willingly into conversation with civilians. One of them, a young Jewish soldier, seemed to answer with irony: "If you manage to get a kilo of sugar, you will be happy. If you get a cut of meat or a piece of butter, you'll be very happy, and if you obtain a pair of boots, you'll be blissfully happy." Later in Lwów, we came to better understand the Soviet reality.

That return journey to Oserdów was entirely different from the one just a few days before when we rode over Polish soil under Polish control. Despite the chaos and confusion, we had felt some sort of authority and order. At road crossings, traffic had been directed by Polish military police. Now there was no trace of the Polish army. The Polish police had disappeared. We saw only small groups of soldiers returning to their homes without arms. Rifles had been thrown away or, according to orders, handed over to the Red Army. Yet they looked happy, and why not? For them the war was over. They were free, going home to their families.

We continued our journey with apprehension, fearful that sooner or later some intoxicated group might feel empowered by this change and try to take away our carts. We gave lifts to soldiers, thus discouraging others from molesting us, and time passed quickly as we listened to their songs and stories.

We were approaching Cecowa, where my uncle had exchanged our horses. We wanted to retrieve ours. We rode alongside fields that had been bustling just a few days ago with harrows, sowing machines, slowly moving horses, and scores of busy farmworkers – the atmosphere of farming life. And now? Not a person in sight. We approached the farm buildings and saw no activity at all. At the homestead, a country girl appeared and told us in Ukrainian, "They are not here. They went to Zborow."

"Everyone?" we asked.

"Everyone," she answered.

She was reluctant to talk but shared that two days earlier the Weissglasses, my uncle and aunt, had gathered what they could and headed to the small Jewish shtetl of Zborow. Landlords of Cecowa were considered the enemy of the working class and they must have been frightened to stay. We reached them in the shtetl and found them very depressed, sheltering with a friendly Jewish grain merchant they knew.

We drove on, downhearted and apprehensive. It was painful to confront these sudden changes. A little way further along, we ourselves were chased and then confronted, threatened, and searched under suspicion of being landed gentry. Luckily, a member of the village revolutionary committee rescued us. Although he was elderly, he convinced his colleagues that we were not responsible for the wrongs that they had suffered. After this experience, we decided to change our travel arrangements, no longer riding in our carriage but taking the cart. Lusia wore a kerchief on her head and Ludwik took off his spectacles to appear more peasant-like. Where possible, we avoided villages and large farm properties. Along the way, we learned that many Jewish landowners had abandoned their properties. Some were evicted and others ran away fearing both revolutionary committees and roaming Ukrainian gangs who had turned this new order into an opportunity.

Even our hospitable German, Mr. Waldman, had disappeared one night, taking everything – his horses, carts, machinery, furniture, as well as the freshly threshed corn in a caravan of vehicles, to the Poland occupied by Germany.

We reached Oserdów, uncertain what to expect. Despite our good relationship with the villagers, who were relatively well to do, we knew they harbored strong national Ukrainian sentiments and we worried that losing the dream of an independent Ukraine, one the approaching German Army had rekindled, might leave them angry and resentful.

We approached our fields late in the evening. The trees of our orchard, the driveway flanked by hazelnut bushes, and our house appeared before us. On the veranda, the door opened and Mother ran out. She reported that all had been quiet. The girls milked the cows and beat the butter as usual. The jobs in the fields were performed normally. The Red Army and the revolutionary committees had not appeared.

Some Jewish refugees were slowly returning to their homes in Belz. The horror of Hitler's occupation had been warded off. We came upon a small detachment of Red Army soldiers and I tried to pinpoint the officer, but they all wore the same uniform. One of them, however, looked a little different and I invited him to join me on my cart. He was in charge and advised he had orders to stay overnight in Oserdów in our house! His manner was quiet and polite – he was a teacher in private life. We chatted about our lives and our Jewish problems. We were grateful to be liberated from the dangers of fascism and established a cordial relationship. He advised us to leave the village for a big city. "You would find engineering jobs there easily," he said.

"But what about our farm, my mother and brother?" I asked. "What would happen to them?" and he confessed he did not know.

On reaching Oserdów, we fed the soldiers and their horses and put half our house at their disposal. Beds were made up with freshly laundered sheets. The next morning after they had gone, we found that none of the beds had been used. They had all slept on the floor, the officers as well as the soldiers.

Lusia and I decided that although we had just arrived back in

Oserdów, continuing here made no sense. There were too many risks. We decided to leave for Lwów and join Lusia's parents. Mother and Ludwik felt compelled to stay. How could they leave the farm, the employees, the horses, cows, and pigs; the sowing was in full swing. If the new authorities would take over the property, maybe they would be retained as management. Our property was small and modest and perhaps it would be treated differently from the larger estates. "Let's wait and see," Mother said.

The only possible way of traveling was by cart, yet we needed someone to drive us. There was only one choice – our coachman, Ivan Gruntas. Ivan had worked for us for many years. He was an excellent driver and, being familiar with many types of agricultural machines, had a better position and pay than most workers. I felt I could trust him despite, or perhaps because of, a past episode when I had caught him stealing from us.

Many years ago, we were often surprised to discover grainless sheaves of corn in our barn. During the night, somebody must have crept into the field, threshed grain, and returned the bare sheaves to the stacks. Theft of corn from the field was rare as, if captured, the thief could be very severely punished by law. Although I was quite young, I decided to investigate and discovered Ivan threshing the corn in the middle of the field by moonlight. I could have reported him and he knew I had seen him, yet I decided to forget the incident. I felt for him and became more considerate. I asked Father to increase his pay. I took care that he was given lunch whenever he drove me in the neighborhood and I gave him generous tips, second-hand clothes, and sweets for his child. We saw to it that he always had a warm sheepskin when we drove in winter and Mother made sure he had plenty to eat.

Years passed since that incident, but now I was depending on his goodwill. He was the only one who could take us to Lwów. He knew the way since he drove a cart there often and he knew too how to repair the cart if necessary. When he came to work in the morning, I asked him. Both of us knew the time for orders was over: he was free to say yes or no. With a friendly look, he answered, "Of course!"

We left home very early, Lusia, myself, little Elżunia, who was now 17 months old, and her nanny, Zosia Janicka. Gruntas drove. The road was bad and the cart jolted all the way. We made only slow progress. We were tense. Refugees were returning to their homes. Bands of "desperados" were loitering about. After five hours, we reached the town of Zolkiew. At the tollgate, there were Red Guards with red bands on their sleeves. We had encountered such guards before and they had always let us pass. We explained we were returning home to Lwów, like many other refugees. These revolutionary citizens apparently didn't like the look of us because they ordered us to report to the town's revolutionary command. Perhaps because we did not appear as impoverished as other refugees, had good horses, a cart, and driver. We did have a lot of goods with us including a sack of flour, potatoes, onions, apples, meat, and butter.

Escorting us to the town hall, the headquarters of the new command, the building seemed empty. On the ground floor, behind open doors, I could see overturned desks and chairs. Shelves were pulled down and files were strewn on the floor. On the first floor, we stopped in front of an imposing double doorway. The guard knocked. We entered a magnificent office. In the middle of the room was a large desk and behind it sat the town commander, an impressive-looking man. The guard ordered me to wait near the door. He approached the official behind the desk with his report. The chief nodded and my escort motioned me to approach the desk and then he left. I was intimidated. He asked my name, where I had come from, where I was traveling to, and who my companions were. The town commandant spoke very poor Ukrainian with a Yiddish accent. I told him we had fled Lwów to escape the Germans, but now that the city had been liberated by the Red Army, I was returning. My Ukrainian was fluent but my accent was undoubtedly Polish. When I told him my family name, his expression softened. "A *yid* [A Jew]?"

"Naturally," I answered in broken Yiddish. "Otherwise, why would I escape to Lwów?"

He released me immediately. Before leaving, I asked him to give me some kind of pass to document that the bearer was returning home to Lwów and his identity papers had been verified.

After a moment's hesitation, with some embarrassment, he asked me to write the document myself. I wrote in Polish and Ukrainian. After applying a seal, he signed it in crooked, almost illegible handwriting. In this way, I received my first personal document from the new rulers, signed by a Jewish member of the Communist Party, the town commandant, an uneducated and probably illiterate man.

The pass proved very helpful, and within hours we reached Lwów without encountering more obstacles.

Lusia's parents were surprised but exceedingly happy to see us. Polish communication systems were in chaos; the country was without mail, telephones, railways, and buses.

Gruntas had sufficient food and fodder for the horses for his return journey. We shook hands and I felt tears well in my eyes, and so I could see in his. I wondered if I would ever return to Oserdów. It was late September 1939.

EARLY YEARS

My great-grandfather Moshe was born in Russia, and there, compulsory army service could last for 25 years. To avoid this, together with his two brothers, he escaped into the Austrian partition of Poland, where he had been attracted to their liberal policy toward the Jews. He adopted the name of Reiss and settled in the village of Tudorkowice near Krystnyopol, a few kilometers from Belz.

Moshe Reiss became well known for his piety and wisdom. He had three sons – my grandfather Nuchim, Leib, and Izaak. From a very early age, he transported goods from place to place in a horse-drawn cart. Living mainly on bread and milk, he saved every cent from his meager earnings.

Moshe had a small farm. With his three sons, they learned the skills of and became competent farmers. While Jews more often lived in cities and small towns, earning their living as shopkeepers or artisans, Jewish farmers did exist. With hard work and modest lifestyle, they would lease farms from their Polish owners and later, if the opportunity arose, purchase them.

Polish nobility, who had inherited their properties from their forefathers, had neither the ability nor the interest to run their farms personally. They would engage an administrator, though if the property did not produce a sufficient yield, or was too much trouble, offers of cash by Jewish administrators to lease the farm and purchase stock and equipment would be considered, providing a handsome annual income without effort or risk.

Jews had been living in peace and freedom under the Habsburgs and some had made good progress in the field of commerce. Many had become prosperous. One such wealthy man in the small shtetl of Belz was David Laib Taube. My grandfather, Nuchim, was strong, handsome, and intelligent and had gained the respect of the rich merchant who entrusted his daughter, Chaja, to him in marriage. Nuchim could read and write fluently in Polish, Yiddish and German. I can only remember Chaja as a small, wrinkled, somewhat ugly woman, clad in a long dark frock with a black kerchief on her head. She spoke Yiddish with her Nuchim and their children and Ukrainian with the peasant girls who worked for her in the vegetable garden and fowl houses.

Perhaps with help from David Laib Taube, my grandfather Nuchim succeeded in securing a lease of Budynin in about 1880. The property was beautiful, the soil rich, the buildings in good condition with three big stables, sheds for carriages, barns for corn, a huge three-story granary, a distillery with quarters for the *gorzelnik* [distiller], and a few houses or *czworaki* for the farm workers. The property had three fishponds, a very large orchard, and a vegetable garden. The house was a gracious old Polish manor house, shingle roofed, and L-shaped with a whitewashed veranda that ran the length of the building. There were stylish colonnades, four separate entrances, 11 rooms, two kitchens, and a spacious and impressive ballroom. I remember very clearly the magnificent flowerbeds, including beautiful long-stemmed rose shrubs bound to stakes formed by glittering, colored glass balls in red, blue, yellow, silver, and gold. At the rear of the house was a circular lawn surrounded by an evergreen hedge with a giant maple tree in the center. A gravel driveway edged by white-and-yellow daffodils, red pansies, white lilies, and blue irises presented a multicolored ribbon of flowers to greet guests arriving in their splendid carriages.

My grandfather and his sons labored at least 12 hours a day, seven days a week. He had, I believe, 14 children, of whom six sons and five daughters survived their infancy. The vegetable garden, the chickens, geese, and ducks were the responsibility of my grandmother and her daughters who were also in charge of the kitchen, bread baking, and cooking for family and servants.

Farm chores including care of the stables, cattle, and horses, the cultivation of land, the administration, bookkeeping, and finance were distributed among the sons. Two studied – Salamon, law, and Joshua, medicine. In 1890, the owner of Budynin decided to sell the property and my grandfather bought it. A few years later, the neighboring property of Oserdów belonging to Count Grocholski was also purchased. He owned over 1,000 acres of excellent, arable land; many properties contained magnificent buildings, livestock, machinery, equipment, and a large distillery.

The lives of my grandfather Nuchim's brothers, Laib and Izaac, had taken a similar turn. Their many children therefore became landowners or married into landowner families. Of my grandfather's 11 children, five girls had married Jewish landowners. Altogether, the Reiss family, including relatives by marriage controlled some ten large farming properties. They were prosperous, well known, and respected as leading landowners in the district of Galicia. Some ten percent of the best farming properties in the area had been transferred from the Polish aristocracy into Jewish hands in this way since 1848. Prior to this, Jewish ownership of land had not been permitted.

In contrast, my maternal grandparents, Emanuel and Amalia Tilles, lived an entirely different, middle-class urban life. I do not recall many details about them as immediately after marriage to my father Filip, my mother, Rudolfina, left the Tilles family home in Kraków to settle in Budynin and then Oserdów. The Tilleses owned number 36 Grodzka Street; a four-story apartment house situated in the heart of Kraków. Grodzka Street was considered one of the most beautiful streets in Europe. Emanuel was a well-respected alderman of the city council. He spoke excellent Polish, as did many Kraków Jews, as well as equally good German and not one word of Yiddish. They had many children, and I know that 11 – four sons and seven daughters – survived infancy. Emanuel owned and ran a liquor store from the ground floor of his property. Two of his brothers were well-respected lawyers in Kraków. During World War I, when war between Russia and Austria had broken out, Polish patriots hoped a Polish state would be once again recreated. Józef Pilsudski, the future Marshal of the reborn Poland, created a military organization to fight Russia. Polish youths joined the "Polish Legion." Many Jews regarded themselves as Poles and were prepared to fight and die for Poland. A younger brother of my mother, Dr. Joseph Tillis, rose to the rank of an aide-de-camp of General Wladyslaw Sikorsky.

Filip, my father, was employed by his father on the farm at Budynin. Filip was tall, lean, and – from my memory – handsome. He wore a small mustache and had a fine sense of humor. He was quick tempered but well liked. Despite a lack of education, he was still considered an excellent farmer. The huge orchard of apple and pear trees was his proudest achievement. The three fishponds, abundant in carp, were also a special pride. At 29, he married my mother, Rudolfina Tilles, who at age 19 was the youngest daughter of 11 children.

My father's eldest brother, Samuel, was already married to Rudolfina Tilleses older sister Rosa. In keeping with the custom, these marriages were arranged by a matchmaker. My parents, Philip and Rudolfina, had married in Kraków on 22 January 1907 and I was born on 25 October, exactly nine months and three days later, in the home of Rudolfina's parents in Kraków.

I was given the name of Henryk after one of my forefathers. Six of my cousins also bore this name. My mother's name, Rudolfina was in honor of Crown Prince Rudolf Habsburg, who was very popular and loved by the Kraków Jewry. A few days after, my birth mother returned with me to Budynin and I was put into the arms of Katerina ("Kaska"), a young Ukrainian peasant woman and wet nurse.

My mother had an excellent command of Polish and German, even some French, and she played the piano and liked to sing in all three languages. She read romantic literature and couldn't understand a word of Yiddish, the everyday language of her husband's family. Adjustment to rural life may have been difficult. Life on the farm was very busy; my father worked long hours managing such a large property. My mother managed a large brood of chickens and the household. I recall newly hatched fledglings spending one cold spring in our kitchen and larder, noisily clucking, pecking, and likely defecating.

At the outbreak of the First World War in August 1914, when I was seven years old, my father was conscripted to the army. With no radio or television, not even a telephone, and given that most conscripts did not know how to read and there was no newspaper anyway, news of mobilizations often came via a small police detachment, who, when the need arose, came and collected the conscripts. When such a policeman arrived on foot, my grandfather Nuchim put a cart and horses at Filip's disposal. I remember the sad leave-taking very well. Mother and Grandmother cried and my always stern grandfather stood there with a worried expression.

News from the battlefield was bad, with fears of a Russian invasion from the east. There was fear of pogroms if the Cossacks (special detachments of the Russian army infamous for their murderous anti-Jewish activities) arrived. Many Jewish families abandoned everything and fled to Vienna. We, too, left on an overcrowded train. I remember the air was oppressive, the train overcrowded, mainly with women, children, and old men. Many of the passengers were dirty and smelly, likely to be Jewish refugees from small poor villages and shtetl.

In Vienna, in the 20th district Brigittenau, at 8 Heinzelman Street, we lived with Mrs. Gruber. Her husband was in the army, too. She let one room of her two-room flat to us. Other members of the Reiss family were also in Vienna: Grandfather Nuchim, Grandmother, Uncle Samuel and Aunt Rosa and their four children, of whom the youngest Józek was my age. My father's youngest brother, Joshua, whom we called Szyiko, was also in Vienna, finishing his medical studies at the University of Vienna.

There was compulsory schooling, so Mother enrolled me at Greiseneckergasse, about ten minutes' walk. I didn't know a single word of German. The back seat in class was the privilege of the worst students; they called it *Esel Bank* [the asses' bench] where I sat. Refugees were resented. Reason enough: They ate up the modest food reserves of the Viennese. Nevertheless, in time life became more normal; my brother and I started to speak German.

Obtaining food was difficult. The bread was yellow, based on corn; milk was watered down. In the mornings before school, when it was still pitch dark and often freezing cold, my brother and I queued up for milk. I had our ration ticket and Ludwik had Mrs. Gruber's. As we already spoke some German, people came to know us. Children were permitted to move to the head of the queue so that we would be on time for school.

In the second year of the war, our teacher appealed to all

schoolchildren to place some sweets and other tidbits into a small parcel, which the school would send for Christmas to the soldiers at the front line. The teacher told us about the heavy fighting and that it was our duty to share some warmth and gratitude in the form of gift parcels. Thinking of my poor father, I saved every cent, stopped going to the Sunday movies, and instead purchased sweets, chocolates, small packets of tobacco and cigarette papers, and matches. Mother gave me a bobbin thread, a few needles, buttons, and some magazines. I took the parcel to school a few days before Christmas and was the only one in class who did so. Still, it was too late as parcels had been sent to the front already. I wanted so much to contribute to the defense of the Fatherland and the Emperor whom I adored; his benevolent countenance looked down on all of us from the wall in every class. He had such a friendly, fatherly face. The teacher suggested I gift the parcel to the one in the class who, in my opinion, was most deserving. There was a small, shabbily dressed boy who appeared to be always hungry. The teacher had the same idea in her mind and praised me highly. This act may have softened her attitude toward me but not that of the other boys. Most remained unfriendly and often teased me, saying *Reiss-Scheiss-Paradeiss, Zwetchken Knodel, Eierspeis* [Reiss-shit-tomatoes, plum dumplings, scrambled eggs].

On Monday, we received shattering news: Father was wounded and hospitalized in Vienna. For two years, he had fought valiantly in a war, but for whom exactly and why, I doubt he really knew. He had shot equally innocent and ignorant Russian soldiers, probably some Jews among them. He had fought in defense of the Kaiser and the Austro-Hungarian *Vaterland* until a bullet pierced his chest and stuck there. We visited him, but the hospital was far away from the city center. When his wound healed, he was dispatched back to the battlefield. My mother wept bitterly.

Then more sad news. In November 1916, the beloved Emperor Franz Joseph died. All schoolchildren attended the funeral. It was beautiful and made a deep impression. The brass band marched slowly to the *Trauer march*. Behind the hearse bearing the coffin, the Emperor's horse followed. Crowds lined the streets; many people were crying. He had been much loved by his people.

The Young Archduke Karl ascended the throne and became the

new Emperor of Austria, looking very handsome in his officer's uniform, with his small mustache. At school, they took down the portrait of the old Kaiser and hung a photograph of the new one with his wife, Zita, and their small son, Otto, but it was a short-lived rule. The war was over, the Empire collapsed.

RETURN TO BUDYNIN
1918

After living in Vienna for four years, in May 1918, my mother packed our few belongings and we returned to our home. In Budynin, the buildings were greatly damaged, our livestock, horses, and cows, as well as carts and agricultural equipment removed, partly by the Russians and partly by neighboring villagers and, we suspected, our local peasants. At Oserdów, the Russians had completely burned down all the buildings, homesteads, cottages, furniture, and barns and apparently taken our livestock and equipment back to Russia. To my brother and me, the neglected and overgrown orchard was an opportunity for an exciting adventure. I was 11, my brother nine. After Vienna, where our playground was the pavement in front of our house for hopscotch and leapfrog, we now looked at Budynin, with everything green and the orchid in the full bloom of spring, as a beautiful paradise. The air was filled with sweet scent from the apples, pears, and cherry-tree flowers. Half-wild margarites, yellow buttercups, and dandelion clocks flew in all directions at the slightest puff of air. I had only seen violets in flower shops but could not recall ever seeing them actually growing. Here, violets were plentiful, and I picked and triumphantly presented a bunch to mother. She was delighted. Happy memories of that time arrest me even now when I encounter beauty or fragrance.

Slowly we were settling back in. Peasants brought gifts: bread, butter, eggs, cheese, and even live chickens and geese that formed the beginnings of a renewed farm stock. We established a big vegetable garden and Father brought a few cows, so we had milk. The government provided a few demobilized army horses, old, sick, and feeble, but still of some help. In this way, we began to fill our stable once again, and under Father's care, even the ex-army horses gradually regained their strength.

Yet we had no means to purchase seeds or farm equipment or hire labor. We entered into partnership arrangements with the local peasants; we supplied land while they supplied everything else. After harvest was completed, the crop was divided into two equal parts, one taken by the peasant-partners, the other delivered to our yard. Father worked very hard. Fortunately, some peasants returned a few horses and cows and equipment they had taken in our absence. The bank started to give us credit and the farm began to recover. We looked towards the future with hope.

Regrettably, this peaceful life did not last long. In November 1918, the Armistice was negotiated and the following year saw the signing of the Peace Treaty of Versailles, leading the way, after 123 years of lost independence, to the recreation of an independent Polish state, reclaiming parts of Austria, Russia, and Germany. So began the Second Polish Republic.

Yet this brought new problems. Like many villages in Galicia, our district was largely a Ukrainian community with only two other Polish families, Wojciech Wilczek, his wife and five sons, the youngest of whom Stanislaw was my playmate, and Ludwig Mazurek from the Polish province of Mazury. Ukraine had once been an independent state and its nationalistic aspirations for self-determination, for a state of their own, went unrequited in the Armistice negotiation.

New Poland included lands with seven million Ukrainians. Lwów had, in fact, once been a Ukrainian town called Lviv after its founder, Lew, a Ukrainian prince. The Ukrainian people hated both the Poles and the Jews and resisted their inclusion into the Polish state. Rebel Ukrainian bands attacked Polish and Jewish estates, burning their houses and crops, targeting those like us living on isolated farms. Ukrainian militia units took control of Lwów and claimed sovereignty over the region. The fighting was particularly intense between the Ukrainian and Polish forces concentrated around Lwów, mostly fought by Polish World War I veterans against the Ukrainian militia forces.

My mother was unused to this turmoil and, pressed by her, my father agreed to leave the village. A sleigh with two strong horses was loaded up with necessities and food. On one bitterly cold morning in the winter of 1918-19, we headed toward Stanislawów some 200 kilometers away. Rudolfina's elder sister, Teofila, lived there with her husband Ephraim Seinfeld, a wealthy businessman. We did not have a plan.

We traveled for several days in constant fear as Ukrainian militiamen often stopped us to search for arms. Father was fluent in Ukrainian, which helped, and a supply of cigarettes came in handy. Ukrainian villagers we passed looked at us with disdain and often open hostility. After a few days of traveling, we reached Stanislawów, which was at that time the capital of the newly proclaimed Ukrainian Republic (*Ukrainska Zapadna Narodnaya Republica*).

The Seinfelds lived on Halika Street next to a marketplace and had a large hardware shop on the ground floor. The house had belonged to the family for more than a century. We rented a small flat in Lipowa Street, just one room with a kitchen, no bathroom, modestly furnished using the money from selling our horses. I was 11 years old and my mother decided my brother and I would have private tuition, as the language at school was Ukrainian, which we did not know well. Our neighbor, Mr. Folgier, a high school teacher, agreed to teach us mathematics and nature studies, which were the subjects he taught at school.

I still remember the time he picked from his well-kept vegetable garden a flower from a pea plant and explained the mystery of its development from flower to fruit. He had two children, a boy and girl more or less our ages with whom we played. Other children from the neighborhood joined us in our favorite game, "shopkeeping." From our homes we would secretly take bits of various food: lumps of sugar, marmalade, cheese, cake, and so forth, and draw lots to see who the shopkeeper would be. The rest of us would be customers. The game would end with us eating all the merchandise. The "shopkeeper" had the privilege of extra helpings. Why do I describe in such detail a seemingly unimportant event of my childhood? One of these children, Lusia, was to become my wife.

Poland was ultimately victorious in the Polish-Ukrainian conflict and Ukrainian rule ended in Stanislawów on 19 May 1919. This war, fought heavily in eastern Galicia and around Lwów, was over, but before leaving, Ukrainians ransacked Jewish shops and beat Jewish people. Our family locked themselves inside for several days until the last Ukrainian soldier had left town.

When the Polish army returned, it was a beautiful day and I recall streets were lined with excited crowds. The first ranks appeared, bearing standards, the cavalry in the lead, handsome youths in colorful uniforms on beautiful horses. Young girls handed bouquets to the officers and more flowers rained down from balconies and roofs.

The atmosphere was one of excitement, yet for us, some uneasiness. What stance would the Polish authorities take toward the Jews? Almost half the population of Stanislawów was Jewish. We had the answer that same evening. Groups of Polish soldiers marched in, looting several shops, smashing windows, and cutting the beards of a number of Jews. Several of them, bleeding, were taken to hospital.

The cutting of Jewish beards by Polish soldiers was not a new game. In 1918, General Joseph Haller's army formed during World War I liberated the city of Poznan in the western part of Poland.[1] Clad in their splendid blue uniforms, the *Hallerczyki* [the Haller boys] entertained themselves by cutting the beards off any Jew they found. This time, the Polish soldiers claimed it was done in revenge, accusing the Jews of pouring boiling water from their windows over the Polish army when they had entered town, a stupid fabrication, physically impossible because of the distance from window to street, and also unlikely as the sentiment of welcoming the Poles did not match this accusation. It took some time for order and stability to return, for Jews to feel safe to go out and reopen the shops. Life returned to normal.

At the time, I had been preparing for an examination before the Ukrainian board of examiners, but now I had to prepare for the Polish examiners. Thanks to my mother, my knowledge of Polish was good, but I knew nothing of Polish history and had to learn about the kings, famous battles, and important dates. I studied intensely and passed, qualifying to attend the second year of high school.

As Budynin was now under Poland, once again we decided to return. The high school closest to our village was in Sokal, a township of about 3,000 inhabitants and some 30 kilometers from Budynin, which by horse-drawn carriage was too far. Mother thought it best that she and the children move to Sokal. Father visited us every Sunday, laden with fresh vegetables, fruit, eggs, chickens, cheese, and other provisions.

I excelled in Polish and became a favorite of our teacher, Marion Baranski. I felt very proud when he invited me to his home one Sunday morning. I was surprised to find him still in bed and the whole flat reeking with a strange odor. He asked me politely to bring the milk in from outside, empty the chamber pot from under his bed, and bring him some water from the barrel on the veranda for the wash bowl. He asked me to return next Sunday. He was running a small private lending library, and for a monthly fee of two-złoty, mother could borrow books. I enrolled my mother and took two books for her. She loved reading and Professor Baranski, being fond of drink, needed some extra income. There were 25 pupils in my form, including five Jews. The Poles stayed with their group, the Ukrainians with theirs, and my playmates were the children of my mother's friends from neighboring Jewish country properties.

Mother had arranged private lessons for us in French and in Hebrew. I also joined a group of Hashomer Hatzair. On Sundays, we would hike to the nearby forest and spend the day practicing, marching armed with sticks instead of rifles, singing Hebrew songs, eating bread and hard-boiled eggs, and drinking clean spring water. This was our first paramilitary training, the first lesson in Zionism. Our activities were, as far as possible, secret.

I finished second grade of high school with excellent marks and returned home for the summer. To be in Budynin during harvest was a joy, but the happiness was short lived. It was now 1920 and new clouds of war threatened our peaceful existence. After the Russian Revolution, the Bolshevik Party had taken over. A huge Red Army was amassed on the Polish-Soviet border ready to propagate their revolution. Terrifying rumors were spreading of Red Army Soldiers killing property owners, burning their farms, and raping women. Ukrainian "patriots" saw this opportunity and were also gleefully waiting for an opportunity to confront the Poles and, as usual, the Jews. Although the Bolshevik Army was still far away, Mother once again decided to pack a few belongings and took the children to Kraków, where her sister Andzia Beckman lived. They squeezed us in with them in their modest flat.

Kraków was far from the front line and life was quiet. Mother immediately enrolled both Ludwik and me in St. Anne's high school. The scholastic standard was very high and I did not find the work easy, particularly Latin and Greek. The other boys had already a year of Latin behind them. I knew very little; one year in Stanislawów and another in Sokal had given me a basic grounding only. We struggled but worked hard.

Meanwhile, the war situation had changed dramatically. The Red Army had approached Warsaw and the Polish army was on the verge of disintegration. Pilsudski, commander-in-chief of the Polish army, had concentrated a considerable number of troops along the river Wisła (Vistula), determined to defend the crossing. In brilliant maneuvers, remembered in history books as "The Miracle on the Wisła," the Polish army defeated the much stronger Red Army, so crushing them that the invaders were forced to retreat and ultimately be defeated in this Polish-Soviet war. Poland, and perhaps the whole of Western Europe, was saved from the hunger, chaos, and economic ruin expected from communism, the dreaded consequence of Soviet victory.

We stayed in Kraków until the end of the school year and I finished third year with gratifying results. I was 13 years old, had changed school four times, and was fluent in three languages: Polish, German, and Ukrainian, with beginner's knowledge of French and Hebrew. For seven years, Ludwik and I had been without a stable home and close, permanent friends. We had lived through three wars: World War I, the Polish-Ukrainian war of 1919, and the Polish-Soviet war of 1920.

Unsurprisingly, my 13th birthday, my bar mitzvah year, was not marked by particular celebration. My uncle, Zygmunt Beckman, said a short prayer, took *tefillin* [phylacteries], and showed me how to put them on. Without a synagogue, without a rabbi, without guests and most of all without my father, who was far away and likely lonely maintaining the farm in Budynin.

HIGH SCHOOL: OSERDÓW AND SOKAL

1921-23

After three successive wars, the frontiers of Poland were established and slowly the country began to rebuild and recover. The wounds of war were healing. We returned home from Kraków and moved into my grandfather's large country house in Budynin. A private tutor would live with us and home-school Ludwik and me for the yearly examination in Sokal.

A Jewish tutor, Mr. Joseph Adler, about age 30 and unable to find work in Lwów, accepted the position with full board and a small salary. With his help, I did my fourth and fifth years of high school from home. This wasn't easy, lacking school discipline and competition from fellow students. Our Jewish origin was an additional disadvantage. I recall once facing a teacher's plot at the final examinations so perfidious that it almost cost me a year of studies. In Budynin, Ivan Sokil, the son-in-law of the Greek Orthodox priest, Krawczyk, was a high school teacher of physics and mathematics in Sokal. The Greek Orthodox Church in Poland was the centerpiece of Ukrainian nationalism and priests and teachers had tremendous influence over the mostly illiterate masses. Many of them abused their position by propagating in the churches and schools their profound antisemitism, which was unchallenged.

During the short existence of the Western Ukrainian National Republic, Ivan Sokil had been an officer in the Ukrainian army. The collapse of the republic meant the end of his political career. At the end of my fourth year in high school, when he was examining me in physics, Mr. Sokil asked me several questions that I was able to answer quite well. He then took from the cupboard an instrument I had never seen before. It was a cone with three small weights attached to its curved surface. It rested easily on its apex. Yet the moment the weights were removed, the cone toppled over, I was asked to explain. I had studied physics from books but I had never seen any experiment and, although I was fascinated by this unusual structure, I could not explain the phenomenon. The answer was, of course, quite simple. The cone with the attached weights had its center of gravity below the support, hence it was in a stable equilibrium. When the weights were removed, the center of gravity was above the support, hence the structure collapsed.

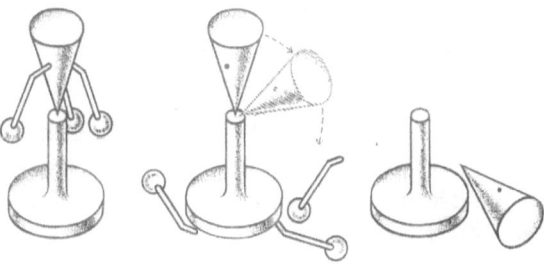

I knew he had failed me. In the next examination, mathematics, I could not think clearly. The teacher was unfriendly, and although my reasoning and methods were correct, he stopped the examination. If I failed this exam as well, I would have to repeat the year. In the following subject, nature study, I was upset and confused and I mixed up the number of flowers, which was sufficient to fail in that subject. My mother and Mr. Adler were in despair. I was a good student, and to make me repeat the year would have been unfair and likely discriminatory. Luckily, Mr. Adler advocated for me and was successful in gaining permission for me to repeat exams in critical subjects in which I then did well. Professor Sokil was apparently furious when, as a result, I was passed for the year. The nature study teacher admitted to me in a private conversation that she had been persuaded to fail me by Professor Sokil in the first place. He was likely a man who had grown up listening to Russian and Ukrainian slogans such as "*Bey zyd, spasay Rosseyu* [Beat the Jew, save Russia]."

My mother and tutor decided it would be better if I attended school, and thus for year six until eight, I attended school in Sokal with my cousin Józek whose father (my uncle) had joined my father to assist in the management of Budynin and Oserdów properties.

In year six, students at Sokal could choose between a so-called Classical course (Greek and Latin) or Science stream: math and science together, with singing and drawing as new subjects. My favorite subject was Polish; I loved Polish literature and was reading a lot. I was good at drawing but felt particularly relaxed in the singing lessons where the animosity of our peers dissipated. We sang folk songs, Christmas carols, and religious songs – all with feeling. We did not participate in studies of the Catholic religion, using the time to study or play. As part of a humanitarian action after the wars, under the American Relief Administration (ARA), founded and led by Herbert Hoover, food and other aid were provided to Poland during this period of difficult recovery. I recall the American YMCA donated hot food for schoolchildren's lunches. Every day, a horse-drawn cart would deliver big containers of warm food – beans, cocoa, or rice. We often helped the driver unload it in our free time. The aromas were enticing but the smell and sight were all we received. The food was for Christian students only.[1]

Our relationship with our peers was on the whole cool. Each group remained separate. Polish students were seen and heard in the streets of Sokal. Ukrainians neatly dressed were seen in front of the church on Sundays but otherwise kept to themselves. Józek and I were the only two Jewish boys in our class. We kept to ourselves. Ludwik and I stayed with a Jewish family, the Honigs, and Józek lived nearby with another Jewish family. There was no secondary school for girls in Sokal, thus we had three girls in our class. Two were Jewish and not too "attractive" and one was a Polish girl, Danusia, who was beautiful. I had quite a crush on her. I was not alone in liking Danusia and was proud when I suspected she liked me, too, although we were never alone.

One evening, I decided to take a risk and entered her neighbor's property standing at the dividing fence, hoping that she might appear, which she did. She was shocked to see me and was afraid that the neighbors would discover my presence and that I would be treated as an intruder or thief. The next day, she was angry and wouldn't look at me at school. The next evening and the next I persisted at her fence, signaling with my torch. Finally one evening, she approached the fence and we kissed! I was overjoyed with the victory and proud that the most beautiful girl in Sokal was mine! There were many visits to the fence until her mother discovered us and angrily brought an abrupt end to the "affair." Life could be cruel.

I did finish the year successfully with "good" and some "very goods" marked on my report. One of my teachers confided in me that the principal had insisted he mark my score down. Distinctions would not be acceptable for a Jewish student.

SUMMER HOLIDAYS IN OSERDÓW
1921-23

We spent our school holidays, as well as all Christian and Jewish religious holidays, on the farm. All four seasons had their attractions and every moment spent on the farm gave us great joy and happiness.

Did we play like other children? My brother and I had no playmates. The peasants' children who went to the local Ukrainian school from an early age had to help their parents around the farm. They had no time for play; their life was very hard. Even a three-year-old might take care of the flock of geese, leaving at dawn to graze in a ditch nearby. He carried a stick that constituted his weapon and his authority. Young geese were afraid of him, yet the poor child was often terrorized by the gander that would attack him. Aged four, a child was promoted to mind a calf, and by age five, he controlled a cow with his string. His responsibility was to stop it from getting into the landlords' fields with their tempting fresh shoots of young wheat or rye. By age ten, he could do almost anything required in the field or garden. The girls also had to work very hard. These peasants depended on their children's help and could not send them to school. Consequently, one-quarter of Poland's population was illiterate.

I also helped on our farm. I recall helping with crop rotation. Corn was easily solved. However, potatoes presented a problem, the price being low at times (two to three złoty for 100 kilos) and transportation costs to town prohibitive. Our solution in Budynin was with a distillery producing spirits from potatoes that were sold to the Polish spirits monopoly at a comparatively high price.

In Oserdów, we found a different solution: converting potatoes into meat. At the end of autumn, we would purchase about 100 cows that were no longer fit for producing calves or milk and fed them leftover potatoes for 100 days. After this period, they were unrecognizable, their coats shining, their bodies filled out, and they had a contented glow in their eyes. The poor things were destined for the slaughterhouse, but from our point of view we were not only making profitable use of our potatoes, but the rich manure was increasing the fertility of our soil as well.

Our dairies' waste production of whey and buttermilk was also repurposed. We used it to feed our pigs for the bacon industry. We erected a pigsty and bought 150 to 200 newborn piglets from the market and fed them for three or four months with the byproducts of the dairy. Once the pigs were 60 to 70 kilos in size, they were loaded into sleighs and delivered to a meat factory, where they were slaughtered, processed, and exported to England.

My Uncle Salamon often traveled to the estates of Polish aristocrats, and I recall one day when he returned with a handful of ears of wheat and rye that he had plucked from one of the farms. They were exceptional. The wheat, instead of just one ear, had three fully grown ears on a single stalk, which meant an unbelievable triple crop from one seed. Although the rye was still bearing one single ear, it was unusually large, long, and full of grain, thus twice the normal size. We experimented ourselves with growing this new grain from seeds threshed by hand from those ears. It was a success and word spread through the district.

I learned much of the complexity of farming during this period. Timing and the method of planting, including the density as well as the method of harvest, could greatly influence the success of the crop. The end of each harvest was celebrated joyously with a *Dozynki* [harvest festival]. Women and girls, festively dressed in richly embroidered colorful skirts, approached our house singing. On their heads they wore garlands made of wheat, rye, barley, and oats, interwoven with cornflowers and red poppies. Girls were followed by men, the mowers, all marching slowly and with dignity.

Father, Mother, my brother, and I would stand on the veranda, awaiting the procession that halted in front of us. One of the women would say a few words of thanks and best wishes for the master, mistress, and young masters. After thanking them for their hard work and wishing them God's blessing and protection for the coming year, Father approached the women harvesters and removed the garlands from their heads. We hung them on the walls inside the house, where they would remain for several months until they had shed their grain.

Then Father would invite the harvesters to the table. A bottle of vodka would appear. Shyness would disappear and for an hour or so, everyone relaxed, ate, and danced on the lawn. Happy and exhausted they would go home.

Our orchards also formed an important part of our farm. There were hundreds of trees, many very old that were bearing fruit in abundance. The majority had been planted by previous owners, obviously knowledgeable and keen gardeners. My grandfather and father made improvements by planting and grafting new varieties of winter fruit.

I recall that Jewish men took many occupations in the area. The *Sadownik* [orchardist] examined a crop while still on the tree to estimate the future season's production in exchange for a payment. Another little-known Jewish occupation was a *Rymarz*, a person producing leather harnesses suitable usually for workhorses. Many occupations connected with the building trades were also in Jewish hands, including bricklayers, carpenters, roof coverings (*Schindlers*), glazers, locksmiths, and painters, and often the Jews working in our district came from Belz. These workers typically spoke only Yiddish, a little Ukrainian, and hardly any Polish. My knowledge of Yiddish is thanks to them. I enjoyed watching them work.

I spent quite a lot of time with the animals. I loved watching the tender way little pigs were fed and cared for by their mother. I fed the hens, roosters, chickens, and turkeys and enjoyed seeing them gathering around from near and far fighting over the golden grains. These were the pleasures of my childhood. Study and books were duty, and real joy began when books were closed and the door opened onto the green of our orchards, gardens, and fields.

LWÓW POLYTECHNIC
1926-32

I decided to apply to study civil engineering, though not for any particular interest in this field but because as a Jew there was a chance I would be accepted. Enrollment in medical or law faculties required influential connections that my parents, having spent their lives in a small village, did not possess. A *numerus clausus* restriction also meant only ten percent of students admitted could be Jewish. This figure was in proportion to the number of Jews within the 3.5 million total population of Poland. No Jews were permitted within the faculty of agriculture and forestry *(numerus nullus)*, although that was my true love.

In the mechanical, chemical, and electrical engineering departments, the capacity of the laboratories was limited and, therefore, restricted for Jews. Civil engineering offered many more positions in the field of building roads, railways, and bridges.

I studied at the Lwów Polytechnic with the help of family connections in Lwów. My Aunt Pauline (Ciocia Pepcia) provided bed and board, and I had lunch and dinner with an uncle, solicitor Salomon Reiss. I coached other students, preparing for them projects that they would present as their own, and thus could pay for my university fees, technical books, drafting materials, and clothes.

Knowledge of a subject was not sufficient to pass examinations. Sometimes open antisemitism could risk success. In my first year of engineering, studying geology, taught by an elderly professor, Dr. Eng Theisseyre, I noticed he wrote the word *Zyd* [Jew] next to the names of certain students.

One professor, Dr. Bryla, was my examiner on "bridge construction." I sat opposite him at his desk. Staring at me, he asked me to prepare a draft design of the bridge for a first-class road over a river where one bank is 30 meters higher than the other and the river is 300 meters wide. It was a very unfortunate configuration of the terrain for a first-class bridge, for the fall, according to regulations, must not exceed five percent. I began to sketch the alternatives, but he didn't like any of them. "Apply the solution adopted at the construction of the Sandomierz bridge," he said. "I have lectured on it." Not having the slightest idea what had happened at Sandomierz, I tried more far-fetched solutions. "I have lectured on it," repeated Professor Byrla, hinting at the fact that I mustn't have attended his lectures. I had no answer, but as he was about to give me the next question, I collected all my courage and asked: "I realize that I have failed but am greatly interested to know. What is the right solution to the problem?"

"The solution is very simple," he replied. "Not to build the bridge at the suggested spot, but to move it elsewhere. Such was the Sandomierz decision." Stunned, I remained silent.

The second question concerned the use of concrete for a reinforced concrete structure in subzero temperatures. This was a standard question, and I started enumerating the methods exactly by the textbooks: "To boil the water!"

Bryla shook his head.

"Heating the gravel?"

"No."

"Warming the mixture while setting the concrete in its forms?"

"No."

"After pouring the concrete, cover up the construction with a tarpaulin and heat underneath for 30 days?"

"No!"

"Watering with hot water?"

"No! No! No!"

At last, I lost my self-restraint and blurted out: "Not to pour concrete at all, postpone until the spring!" He looked at me sternly and asked for my identity book. I realized I had nothing to lose, so collecting my courage, I said, "Postponing the pouring of the concrete to the spring is as good an answer as moving the Sandomierz bridge to another spot." He didn't reply and I saw that he was writing a long word in my record book. I felt sure he was writing *niedostateczny* [unsatisfactory].

He shut the book and, handing it over to me, said, "Sometimes one word decides the result of an examination." Taking the receipt for six złoty, he turned on his heel and left without another word. I was furious. Not only had he failed me, but he had taken the six złoty, too! In the corridor where a group of curious friends waited, I opened the record book and with astonishment read: "distinction."

Professor Bryla was supported by a senior tutor, Venceslaw Poniż, a talented Yugoslav. Poniż spoke Polish fairly well with a strong Yugoslav accent and was relatively friendly toward the Jewish students. Often, when I was entertaining colleagues with my mischievous wit in the university hallways, Mr. Poniż would listen and be doubled up with laughter. He often tried to cheer us up before exams, realizing that our life at the university was far from easy. Always very helpful and understanding, we all liked him very much.

My relationship with Poniż became close while I was doing my vocational practice. Such training was obligatory and organized by the university. I had been delegated to work for the Department of Main Roads in the locality of Turka by the river Stryj. It so happened that Mr. Poniż wanted to take his family to visit the mountains. He had arranged a job for himself as supervisor of bridge construction in the beautiful mountain village of Jawora, just one railway stop from Turka. I was rather lonely and as the Poniż family was also cut off from the rest of the world, I visited them every Sunday and was warmly welcomed in their farmer's cottage.

In the district of Turka, many watermills were scattered throughout the mountain villages belonging to poor Jewish families, passed down from generation to generation. The families could mill the rye or barley in their own homes. In recent times, river waters flooded by heavy rain were damaging fields and local farmers complained to the authorities. This prompted the authorities to require millers to have a license for their mills, complying with building and water regulations approved by the water board. Such plans requiring a qualified engineer were costly for the poor Jewish millers. Thus, during my vocational training, I found an opportunity to earn some income on the side. News of a young Jewish "engineer" had got around the small town of Turka. I was able to visit the mills, carry out on-site measurements and prepare drawings, presenting them to Mr. Poniż , the qualified engineer, to sign and submit to the water board. For ten fantastic days, I wandered from village to village in a most beautiful part of the Polish mountains, enjoying every minute, helping poor villagers and ultimately earning 800 złoty, which was the equivalent of two months' salary.

My relationship with Mr. Poniż was excellent, but I never imagined then how helpful he would be to me much later.

JUDENFREI
1928-1931

At the Lwów Polytechnic, Jewish students clung together as one united group, separated from the main body of Polish students by their manifest hostility and from the Ukrainian students by a wall of cold indifference.

We had in our group about ten male and three female students; the latter were Edda Fishler, Lola Majblum, and Lusia Herman. Lusia was not the first to get my attention, but while recovering from the unrequited love of Edda, I began to notice Lusia. I recall one day, sad and disappointed by rejection from Edda, stopping at the Polytechnic without any particular purpose. I didn't expect to find anyone in the drawing room, which seemed empty until I saw, in the far corner, Lusia leaning over a drawing board. I sat down and we talked, or, rather, I talked and she listened. Lusia was a wonderful listener – wise, understanding, friendly, and warm. I began to see her regularly especially since she had transferred from pure mathematics to civil engineering. From then, until the completion of my studies, we met every Monday in Lindego Street, a quiet lane five minutes from my Uncle Salamon's home where I used to dine. Sometimes we went to the cinema, sometimes for a walk to Stryjski Park. We were relaxed, happy, and comfortable together.

The conditions under which Jewish students attended university lectures were always difficult, but sometimes our lives were in danger.

Anti-Jewish riots would repeatedly flare with minimal or no provocation and then calm again.

1928 was an election year for the Polish *Sejn* [parliament]. In Lwów, we had to elect four representatives. The population of Poles, Ukrainians, and Jews was more or less equal in number. Dr. Emil Sommerstein, a well-known lawyer and leader of the Jewish parliamentarians, headed the Jewish list (number 17). It was enormously important for Polish Jewry to ensure the reelection of Dr. Sommerstein. Thus, the Jewish youth of Lwów, using horse-drawn carriages, taxis, and even stretchers for the sick, dragged all registered voters to the poll. The result, totally unexpected, was that two Jewish candidates gained seats in the parliament, as did two Ukrainians. The Poles gained none.

Fury seized the Polish university students, particularly the veterinary students and those from the Polytechnic. Armed with walking sticks embedded with razor blades in their ends, iron rods, and metal pipes, they attacked Jews who cross their path, irrespective of sex and age. They shouted, "Long live Polish Lwów," and the Jews had to run and hide to escape. A bloodthirsty crowd followed them, dragging them out and beating them. Walking the streets was dangerous – people stayed home. Those riots lasted several days, but the police looked the other way. Their sympathy was undoubtedly with the demonstrators. There were no arrests despite many injuries and broken shop windows.

A turning point occurred when a Jewish butcher, in self-defense, killed one of his assailants with a knife. The student's funeral developed into a huge demonstration. There were plans to march into the Jewish district and avenge the death of their "martyr." Fear seized the Jewish population. Fortunately, the police did step in and dispersed the students.

At the time of those riots, Jewish students did not attend lectures as it was too dangerous to walk the streets. Lusia did not have a telephone and I was unsure if she intended to meet as usual on a Monday evening. I worried she would come despite the risk as she lived in a quiet district and might be unaware of the situation in the center of the city. I decided I would go to meet her. It seemed the situation had calmed down. I was just ready to leave when the phone rang. Lusia? I hoped and picked up the receiver. "Henek!" I recognized the loud, excited voice of my cousin Joseph Kristianpoler. "I have been attacked, I have a bad head wound, and I am at the doctor's surgery. I'm afraid to go home alone. Please come and help me get home as the doctor wants to close the surgery." He gave me the doctor's address and hung up. What to do? Lusia had not phoned, which meant she may be strolling up and down Lindego Street waiting for me. How could I leave her, yet my wounded cousin was waiting at the doctor's. I was afraid for myself, too. There were even cases of crowds stopping taxis and dragging out Jews for a beating.

The call of duty won. I retrieved Joseph from the doctor's surgery. In the taxi on the way home, we were suddenly surrounded by an angry crowd. Students approached and we were forced to slow down. The taxi driver and we were pale with fear. Moved by an instinct for self-preservation, I opened the window, put my head out, and loudly shouted, "Long live Polish Lwów," the battle cry of the mob. It worked: the crowds parted, the driver accelerated, and we drove away.

It was already 8:20 before I could leave Joseph. Would Lusia be waiting for me? I asked the driver to take me, but he refused. He had enough and I could hardly blame him. I decided to walk, using side streets and listening carefully for the noise of rioters. I arrived at Lindego Street at nine o'clock. There was not a soul in sight. Then I saw Lusia! She had walked calmly from one end of the street to the other and had waited for me for over one-and-a-half hours, confident that I would come. She hadn't run away in panic; she wasn't afraid. This remarkable woman's courage, perseverance, and determination were to surface again in a future that would present even greater challenges.

Compulsory military service in Poland meant that every male age over 21 had to appear before a conscription committee, where it was decided who was "A" category (fit for military service) and who was "C" category (unfit for military service). Graduates of secondary schools were directed to military academies to be trained as officers. At the time, Jews were not considered to be suitable material for the officer class and most were classified "C" category. Also, a university student's conscription was usually deferred until the end of their studies. My cousin Józek lost the right to deferment. In response to the riots, he had made a stink bomb in the laboratory to use in his defense and had been denounced when this caught the attention of other students. He was suspended from the university for six months. The consequent enlistment would ultimately have disastrous consequences for Józek.

During my university years, I was a member of the Union of Students of Civil Engineering at the Polytechnic, which had existed for many decades, accepting all students irrespective of nationality or religion. Membership was voluntary, but every Jewish student belonged. At the end of each year the union organized an excursion abroad, joined also by professors and tutors of our faculty.

This year's planned excursion included Czechoslovakia, Hungary, Yugoslavia, Bulgaria, and Turkey. In total, 36 students had enrolled among them three Jews: Lusia, Edda, and I. The trip was nearing and then unexpectedly, the Polish students wrote a memorandum to the University Senate, protesting against the inclusion of Jewish students on the trip, suggesting "they could not and should not represent Polish youth abroad." We decided to fight this as the constitution guaranteed our rights and our parents paid taxes, so we appealed to the university authorities. We had the law on our side. After many meetings, our "revolt" succeeded, but not in the way we had hoped: the excursion was canceled. Of course, this did not endear us to our Polish colleagues.

Not long after, reactionary nationalists won mastery of our Students Association and were successful in changing a statute to read that: "Only a Christian or an Armenian may be a member of the Association." The anti-Jewish motion was thus passed. The Association of Students of Civil Engineering was not the only one to be *Judenfrei* [without Jews]. Jews had been years ago expelled from *Brateniak* [brotherhood] founded to assist students. This organization, subsidized by the government, ran a cafeteria serving cheap meals to all students except Jews. There was also a brotherhood shop, which sold writing and drafting materials at not-for-profit prices – also not to Jewish students.

In the following years, Polish students decided not to sit next to Jews in lecture rooms. Five minutes prior to the beginning of a lecture, at a given sign, Polish students would ostentatiously vacate seats next to Jews, moving to the back of the hall, leaving a few empty rows between Jewish and non-Jewish students. These "ghettos" within a classroom were condoned by the lecturers.

I completed my studies in October 1932 with the results of my final examination being just "pass." The intention of the examination board was plain; even the brightest Jewish graduates found it difficult to get positions as engineers and the basic pass was an additional obstacle.

Some Jewish people became interested in communism as a solution to a seemingly hopeless future. Lusia's brother Edzio and his girlfriend Rosa were smuggled by the Communist Party out of Poland and into Russia. Some became Zionists and left for Palestine, including three of Józek's siblings: my cousins, Ludwik, Cesia, and Stepha, who were pioneering founders of Kibbutz Beth-Alpha, and Ramath Jochanan. Two other cousins, Ludwik and Fela, children of Uncle Lazar Ecker, also left for Palestine.

Not all our professors and tutors took part in the unjust and malicious behavior. I pay tribute to the many professors who helped us or who had the courage to oppose the majority or sometimes spoke publicly in our defense. I pay tribute to Professors Stanislaw Brzozowski, Karol Warotek, Kazimierz Bartel, Adam Kuryllo, Tadeusz Obminski, Stephan Bryla, Emil Bratro, Karol Zipser, and Antoni Lomnicki. A tribute to those tutors who helped us with friendly advice: Venceslaw Poniż, Kazimierz Bartoszewicz, and Jurek Preiss, and to those few of the 180 students in our faculty of civil engineering who were willing to support us.

I do remember a student colleague, Biedronski, a tall blond fellow with a magnificent voice, courageous like a lion who battled for our rights: a lonely, hopeless battle. I remember Felix Szwed, who had been a devoted friend for three years but ultimately, when threatened by Polish colleagues, of total social and professional isolation, was forced to sever his relations with us. I wonder whether you survived the war, dear Felix? How good it would be to meet you, shake your hand, sit down, and talk.

WEDDING AND THE ANSCHLUSS
1934

I graduated in 1932 and spent a few months in Oserdów, writing many job applications without success. I finally landed a job in the construction of a railway line in Kraków thanks to my family connections.

It was while staying in a furnished room in Kraków that I made up my mind. Although I had many relatives and friends there, I felt lonely. I was missing Lusia. I proposed to her and her parents. Lusia later told me how thrilled her family was. I was her mother's favorite.

My family received the news with mixed feelings. My parents never questioned my decision, but my more distant relatives, particularly aunts who adored me, were disappointed. Not with Lusia herself but with the fact that she was not well off. Our wedding was to take place in Lwów.

Lwów had been the capital of the region, Galicia, previously part of the Austro-Hungarian Empire and now Wschodnia Malopolska (eastern Poland) since the independence of Poland. It was a beautiful city of over 200,000 inhabitants. Most of my and Lusia's families had lived in this area all their lives. Lusia settled all the formalities and sent me a few wedding invitations for my relatives in Kraków. I gave one to my employer, Mr. Freund, a wealthy builder. The Freunds had an adopted daughter, a very pretty girl in her early twenties. Maybe they were looking for a suitor for her, as on presenting my invitation I felt only displeasure. Perhaps without coincidence, when my contract expired soon after, it was not renewed.

I worked as usual on the Saturday before my wedding until midday and caught the next train arriving at Lwów at midnight. I was expected at the station by one person only, Lusia. The next day we were to marry. It so happened that Lusia was late for her own wedding. She had a reputation for lateness, but this time the reason was more sinister. It was Sunday and all the shops were closed. While Poles and Ukrainians went to church, Jews would secretly keep the back doors of their shops open. Police would patrol the streets, keeping an eye on the Jewish shops. The fines for trading on Sunday were high and included the loss of license. An observer was often employed to warn Jewish shopkeepers of patrolling policemen. That was the case at the Jewish hairdresser where Lusia went that Sunday morning. She was just ready to leave when a warning signal came. Doors were shut and locked and no one was allowed to leave. Time passed and Lusia was getting very upset. It was a long way to Rabbi Lewin's apartment, but the hairdresser was afraid of losing his license and refused to let her out. Finally, in desperation, she jumped through a rear window, luckily without accident or discovery.

Our wedding ceremony on Sunday 24 June 1934 was performed by the rabbi and his wife along with our closest relatives in attendance. It was a small affair. We had no wedding reception so as to spare our family expense.

We returned to Kraków, where I had redecorated my small sparsely furnished bedroom at my aunt's flat, which we shared with her family of four. On Monday, I was back at work again.

Lusia tried to find a job in her profession, but all doors seemed closed. An Uncle Dudzio had attended school in Kolomyja with Malaszynski, who now occupied the position of chief engineer in the Department of Public Works in Kraków. Although 20 years had passed since they were at school together, out of respect for the connection, Malaszynski helped Lusia and gave her a job. This happened just after a disastrous flood destroyed about 50 bridges within the *Wojewodshaft* [district] of Kraków. Lusia was to be in charge of the reconstruction of a wooden bridge in Wadowice, some 30 kilometers from Kraków. She was the only woman engineer in the entire Kraków region. After three months, the bridge was rebuilt in good time, but once done, the contract expired and Lusia returned to Kraków without work. Soon afterward, my contract with Mr. Freud also came to an end. Our savings could not last long, and without jobs, we decided to return to Oserdów in 1935 for the time being.

I loved Oserdów and had been looking forward to living and working on the farm, but Lusia was not so keen on it. A city girl, she would have preferred to live in Lwów. Yet my father had died recently and my mother and brother were keen to have us. Food was no problem and Lusia understood and accepted.

We had packed our belongings and were ready to leave Kraków when Uncle Jozef Tilles advised us that a client of their bank was looking for an engineer. The company specialized in the design and construction of small power stations, industrial furnaces, and high factory chimneys, work totally outside of my education and experience. The owner of the company was Jozef Elsner, a Pole of German origin. He received me pleasantly and told me that I was going to replace two engineers who had been working for him for many years but had decided to set up their own business. Both Lusia and I were delighted. We could hardly believe our luck. My first salary was 250 złoty per month, but after a short time it rose to 300 złoty.

Soon the company was overloaded with work and we were looking for part-time staff. At my request, Mr. Elsner agreed to have Lusia do some design work on the industrial furnaces. She quickly became familiar with this new field of engineering and became very good at it. In 1937, my work took us to Warsaw to develop a power station for the Polish Skoda works. We stayed in this beautiful capital of Poland for over eight months, renewing old and establishing new friendships. We met and became friendly with Engineer Moses Eisner, from whom I ordered steel structures for this power station. Mr. Elsner, my employer, was congratulated by the governing director of the Skoda works for my efficiency, but with a sting: "What a pity he is Jewish." Moses Eisner, who supplied the steel, left for Australia early in 1939.

Life was good, we had friends, played bridge, and sometimes even dined out. Since our financial situation had improved, we left our little room, moving to a pleasant and modern one-bedroom apartment. We designed our own furniture and had it made by a reputable furniture company. It was elegant and beautifully finished. The bedroom suite was made of California birch, while the lounge dining furniture was of

Brazilian rosewood. Lusia and I were excited and happy, and we were expecting our first child. We had thought that with my permanent and well-paid job, as well as Lusia's extra earnings, we could afford a child. At the time, our friend, Henio Haber, had accepted a position in Warsaw. He worked as an architect but had been the Kraków representative of Isteg, a firm manufacturing special reinforced concrete floor structures according to an American patent. Henio offered this work to Lusia on a profit-sharing basis, which she eagerly accepted.

Thus, we both returned to Kraków with employment. Lusia settled down to her new job with great enthusiasm. She supervised several construction works even when her pregnancy was well advanced. Our child was due in April, but in March, Lusia was still running on scaffolding, slippery from frost and snow, and our concerned foreman personally had to take her off the construction site.

Lusia's first labor pains began while we were playing bridge with the Habers, who were visiting. Despite the contractions, she had to finish the game. She had such a great hand; how could she interrupt the rubber? She eventually withdrew and we went to the private hospital. Lusia's mother arrived from Lwów for the event. The labor lasted many hours, but eventually Elżunia was born in the early morning of 17 April 1938, weighing 2.65 kilos and looking beautiful with blond hair and blue eyes.

Lusia remained in the hospital for seven days, during which time I successfully negotiated a great price on the rental of a residence that Lusia had been very keen on but for the cost. I packed all our "wealth" into huge boxes, organized movers, and moved into the new apartment. Proud and happy, I surprised her on her return home from the hospital. We were very happy with a lovely home, a beautiful baby, and a steady, promising, interesting, and well-paid job. Lusia would continue working, and before long, we employed a nanny for our baby and a housekeeper, who was also an excellent cook. We were both young, healthy, and eager to work hard.

But everything was changing around us. In 1934, Engelbert Dolfuss, the chancellor of Austria, was assassinated by the Nazis. The Anschluss, or annexation of Austria into Nazi Germany, followed in March 1938. Austria ceased to exist. Adolf Hitler declared the Sudetenland to be annexed to Germany and declared it his last territorial claim in Europe. British Prime Minister Neville Chamberlain believed him. The ink on the signatures of the famous Munich Agreement, designed to appease Hitler and prevent major war on the continent, was still wet when Czechoslovakia was overrun by the German Wehrmacht.

Poland had also taken part in the dismantling of its sister republic; with Hitler's blessing, the Polish army entered the tiny, once-Polish province of Cieszyn. It was beyond belief that Poland's responsible government would so shortsightedly accept such a gift from Hitler.

Finally in November 1938, when a Jewish young man Herschel Grynszpan assassinated Ernst vom Rath, the secretary of the German Embassy in Paris, in protest against the inhuman action of the new Germany against Jews, the infamous *Kristallnacht* [Night of Broken Glass] followed.

The beginning of the end of our happiness was heralded by those tragic events. Less than a year later, on 1 September 1939, German bombs woke us, heralding the beginning of our own personal nightmare.

WHO WOULD SURVIVE?

Lusia and I both had many relatives who lived in Lwów. Most did not survive. Each, had they survived, would have had a unique story of their experiences during this period. I cannot write my own story without at least honoring their names here and sharing a few details of their lives.

My father's oldest brother, Salomon Reiss, studied and lived in Lwów. He was a successful lawyer, a man of high repute, and a member of the examination board for admission to the Law Society. He and his wife, Rosa, had two sons – Bruno, who was the same age as me, and Edek, who was a few years younger.

My father's youngest brother, Joshua Reiss, a physician, was known in the family as Uncle Sheyko. He resided in Kosciuszko Street and was married to a beautiful woman, Mina, with one daughter, Joanne. He looked much younger than his age and was full of fun. We adored him.

My father's oldest sister, Pauline Francos, or Ciocia Pepcia, lived with her husband, Uncle Jacob, with whom I had lodgings during most of my university days. Their door was always open for family at any time. Our grandparents, Nuchim and Chaja Reiss, lived with them until they died. Grandfather Nuchim died in 1927 at the age of 72, and Grandmother a few years later aged 88.

My father's oldest sister, Salomea Kristianpoler, Aunt Salcia, also lived in Lwów for many years. She had six children – three lived outside Poland, and the other three, Dolek, Joseph, and Andzia, lived with their mother. They all struggled for a living.

Father's other sister, Antonina (Toncia) Ecker, lived in Lwów, too. She was self-educated, well-read, and an extremely intelligent woman nicknamed Langensheidt after a popular German dictionary. Her late husband, Dr. Lazar Ecker, was a public notary in Zborow. Their three children left Poland before the war.

Another older brother of my father, Ignacy, lived in Budynin. He was an accountant and was run over by a cart, after which his back was hunched. He and his wife, Antonina, had a daughter, Helene. After Ignacy's death, they sold their share in the Budynin property to Uncle Salomon and lived in Lwów thereafter.

Father's sister, Cecily, with her husband, Simon Ecker, and her two daughters, Frania and Ludwika (Wisia), lived and worked on their property in Waniow, which had been in their family for three generations.

Uncle Herman Reiss, father's youngest brother, leased Potoki at Rawa Ruska, a huge property owned by Laib Reiss, grandfather's brother. As a result of the Soviet Revolution, he and wife Berta had to leave their property and arrived in Lwów and, of course, stayed with Aunt Pepsi, as did Aunt Amalia, my father's youngest sister, with her husband, Jacob Weissglass, and their son, Adolf. Many of these property owners abandoned their properties, as we did, moving to Lwów with children and sometimes grandchildren.

There were many of my father's cousins in Lwów as well. I recall my father's first cousin, Hela, who went to school with Lusia. She was married to Dr. Jechezkel Levin, a well-known chief rabbi in Lwów. They had two children, Kurt and Laib, the latter named after Hela's father, who had been killed before the war by one of his Ukrainian farmhands.

Some of my mother's family were also in Lwów, including her sister, Edda Bombach; her husband, Philip; two sons, Norbert and Henry; and a married daughter, Zofia, who had two small children. My mother's brother, Ludwik, also had to leave Oserdów and joined us at Chmielowskiego Street.

Lwów was the hometown of Lusia's family. Unfortunately, I have little information about them. Her father, Professor Simon Herman, had been a high school teacher during the time of Austrian rule. After the outbreak of the 1914 war, he found himself in Vienna with his family and thousands of other Jewish refugees. Here he became the founder and headmaster of the *Gimnazium,* the only Polish secondary school. This school was founded for the Polish-speaking, mostly Jewish schoolchildren; his parents had escaped the Russian invasion. After the war, he returned to Stanislawów and worked in the school. Due to the ongoing (1918-19) Polish-Ukrainian war, Stanislawów had become the capital of independent Western Ukrainian National Republic, and Ukrainian was the official language in the schools. Professor Herman was dismissed after the liquidation of the short-lived Western Ukrainian state when Stanislawów became Polish again, out of favor because of his "collaboration with the Ukrainians." He subsequently worked for a private school in Lyon and other places where enrollment had become popular as affluent Jewish people enrolled their children to avoid the growing Polish antisemitism. Of Lusia's grandparents, Simon Herman's parents, I only know that they lived in Kolomyja running a general store. They raised three sons and a daughter. Simon was the eldest, a brilliant mathematician. I suspect Lusia inherited his genes.

Of Simon's siblings, I know of Emanuel, an enterprising pharmacist, David (Dudio), who was a post office employee in the Austro-Hungarian and subsequently Ukrainian state. He, too, was dismissed by the Polish state and had great difficulty obtaining another position. There, sister Hilda and her husband assisted in running the store.

Lusia's mother, Regina, came from Brzezany, some 200 kilometers from Lwów, where her father, Mr. Karp, was a well-known personality who owned a private bank and some properties. Regina was one of three daughters and two sons. She was a small woman, loved music, played the piano, painted, embroidered, and knitted beautifully. She was a typical daughter of the middle class and lived with the children in Lwów while her husband Simon worked in distant places, spending school holidays with the family.

The youngest of Mr. Karp's children was Dr. Adela Carp-Fuchs. Unable to obtain a position in her profession, teaching, she established her own private school in Lwów. Starting from one rented room, a secondary school grew, catering to 400 girls from Lwów and the surrounding district. Graduates of the school are spread all over the world, including our friend Dora Horowitz, who now lives in Australia and attended the same class as Lusia.

Adele married Dr. Zygmunt Fuchs, a tutor at the Lwów Polytechnic, who lectured on the strength of materials and hydraulics. Very gifted in his field, he was offered a professorial chair on the condition that he agree to be baptized. He declined and remained a lecturer until the Soviet occupation, when he was nominated University Professor. Lusia's younger sister, Fela, then in her early twenties, a part-time secretary, lived with her parents.

I know little about Lusia's uncles. One, Salo Karp, lived in Lwów with his wife and two children; he owned a button factory from which he made a meager living.

It was September 1939 and tremendous changes were taking place. After 20 years of independence, Poland was divided again between Germany and the Soviet Union. There were at least 150 members just of my family, of all ages, from all walks of life – landowners, property owners, engineers, doctors, solicitors, bankers, teachers, a rabbi, shopkeepers, businessmen, academics – whose lives were all suddenly overturned. Many arrived in Lwów having lost their properties, businesses, and jobs, some even losing the roofs over their heads. They found themselves in the grip of a totalitarian system, controlled by a "party of workers and peasants" and acting under the slogan "proletarians of all nations unite." This party was not friendly toward people unless they were workers, peasants, or proletariat. How were these individuals to manage in this new order? How many would survive?

PART II
UNDER SOVIET OCCUPATION IN POLAND

SEPTEMBER 1939-JUNE 1941

LWÓW UNDER THE RED ARMY

In contrast to the chaos in Kraków, Lwów remained almost untouched by the war. The main railway station and a few factories had been hit by bombs, but otherwise no great damage was noticeable. The majority of shops were shut, though, and there was a shortage of food, with queues for everything, even bread and milk. Fat and sugars were luxuries pursued almost at the risk of life itself. One day, both Lusia and I went in search of sugar. I joined one queue and waited patiently while Lusia joined another, which had formed at a second entrance. A maximum of one kilo was being sold per person. The queues were slow and long. I was standing close to the shop window, people surrounding me on all sides, pressing hard until I was squeezed too hard against the glass. I called out, begging the crowd to retract. Too late! I heard the cracking and then felt the crash of glass crumbling away from me, and I fell forward with it. I was lying on the floor, inside the shop, bruised and cut, hands and face bleeding while the crowd surged forward to the counter pushing for their places. Lusia was one of them! She was horrified to see me on the floor but realized I was okay, so she continued valiantly to defend her place in the indoor queue and eventually be rewarded. A militiaman stopped those trying to enter through the broken window. He ordered that I be given my kilo of sugar, and thus Lusia and I returned home elated. This was sufficient for a considerable time.

The city was stripped of essential commodities by officers and soldiers of the Red Army, looking poor and sad in their long, unhemmed army coats. They queued regularly in front of every shop. They purchased shoes, leather goods, textiles, clothes, underwear, watches, and chamber pots – everything they could lay their hands on, in fact.

We had seen this phenomenon before. On the first day of the occupation, we observed that Russians did not break into the shops to rob or plunder but stood quietly in queues, paying in rubles without bargaining even though the merchants raised their prices. The rate of exchange was very favorable for the occupiers, though, as one ruble equaled one złoty.

A story went around about one Russian officer who entered a shoe shop and asked for a pair of shoes. The shopkeeper asked which size, but the officer simply pointed to the nearest pair and asked the price. The shopkeeper told him they were 30 złoty a pair (their normal price was 22). "Give me 200 pairs," the officer told the astonished merchant. When asked why he needed so many pairs of identical shoes, the officer replied that in civilian life he was chairman of a kolkhoz and wanted them as a gift for every member. In reality, the Russians were likely selling the cheaply acquired goods on the black market back home. I tried to chat with the soldiers in the queues about their purchases. Embarrassed, they seemed to want to avoid the discussion. When I asked why they purchased so many, "*Unas wsio yest* [We have plenty of everything] and only buy presents for relatives and friends" was always their story.

Cinemas and theaters were full. Tickets were cheap, although one had to queue. We did not have the energy for that as we were forced to concentrate on acquiring daily necessities. Yet on one occasion we did see a movie – a Soviet film presenting the Cossack leader Bohdan Chmielnicki as a national hero and a great revolutionary. We understood that he and his Cossacks were responsible for the murders of hundreds of Jews during infamous pogroms in Ukraine in the 17th century. We were afraid to leave before the film ended, not wanting to face the stares from militiamen sitting at the entrance. The second film depicted life in prewar Lwów, presented as a documentary. In it were depicted long queues of poorly dressed people; as snow was falling, people were shivering. In the film, smartly dressed Polish officers forced their way through the crowd loading themselves up with packages. These images were not representative of anything we had experienced and were presumably examples of Soviet propaganda.

One day, to my great and joyful surprise, I met a very good friend from Kraków, Henio (Henry) Haber. Our friendship had begun in 1926 at the Lwów Polytechnic when he was studying architecture and Lusia and he attended lectures together in descriptive geometry conducted by Professor Kazimierz Bartel (later the prime minister of Poland). We had spent many a Sunday afternoon with Henry and his wife, Irka, playing bridge. It was good to meet him again on the streets in Lwów. Henio had also left in September 1939 upon the order of the chief of the Polish armed forces: "All men able to carry arms are to withdraw to the east." Homeless in Lwów, not knowing anyone, I took them to Lusia's parents, who welcomed them warmly. They slept together in one small bed for several weeks.

At that time, the news coming from Kraków under the Germans was reportedly not as bad as expected and life in Lwów was very hard; thus, Henio Haber and his wife decided to return to Kraków. He had to cross the border illegally on the river Styr. He crossed on horseback – his first and last time on a horse!

Living in the flat belonging to Lusia's parents, at number three Chmielowskiego Street, I was unsettled. The routine of my life had been broken. I had been driven out of my profession and my home. Surviving without work or income and with only a meager food supply to feed a family of six plus Zosia, Elżunia's nanny, was not easy.

We received bad news. My cousin Joseph, son of Uncle Samuel and Aunt Rose, had been arrested by the Russian secret police. Józek was my childhood playmate in Vienna, where we lived during World War I, and subsequently in the afternoons in Budynin and again in Sokal, where we attended high school together. He had been conscripted into the Polish military during his suspension from the Polytechnic. He ultimately completed his degree in industrial chemistry and assisted his family in the management of the Budynin property. After five years of unemployment, he had found work in a bacon factory in Złoczów. Yet when the Polish military action of WWII occurred, he had been mobilized to join, although the Polish army collapsed, invaded on both sides, after only 16 days.

The Soviet authorities had issued orders that all employees of factories and offices must return to their place of employment and officers of the late Polish army must register immediately with the Soviet secret police. Joseph reported and was instantly arrested.

At the time the methods of the NKVD, the Naródnyi Komissariát Vnútrennikh Del, or People's Commissariat for Internal Affairs, which was effectively the secret police, were unknown to us. We felt compelled to assist him. Józek was a worker, an employee of a factory, not really a soldier. My family unanimously suggested I go, since I was enterprising and able to argue logically, in the hope that I would convince the Soviets to release Józek. Lusia insisted on accompanying me. First thing the next morning, we proceeded to the entrance at the Tarnopol Tollgate hoping for a lift on a Soviet truck to Zloczów. We had heard they took civilian passengers willingly, including refugees, speculators, demobilized Polish soldiers, Jews, Ukrainians, Poles, youngsters, women, and children. We got a lift, but by the time we arrived at Zloczów, the arrested Polish officers had been deported further east in the direction of the Soviet border. We were obliged to keep following even though the mood of travelers was gloomy. They spoke of raids on returning Jewish refugees and even murder of a whole Jewish family by Ukrainian gangs.

In Zborow, we were again too late as the transport had moved on to Tarnopol. We were not sure if further pursuit made any sense. Perhaps it was too dangerous. The last leg of the journey was particularly nerve wracking. We were joined by some Ukrainian youngsters whose looks implied hatred and who stared at our comparatively good clothes, shoes, rucksacks, and wristwatches covetously. In the oncoming darkness, Lusia and I sensed danger. One slash with a knife would have been sufficient. The speeding driver wouldn't have noticed a thing.

Despite the ominous mood, we arrived safely in Tarnopol, a city of some 60,000 inhabitants. We knew a Dr. Weissglass who lived there and located his house. There was warm hospitality but bad news. The officers' transport did stop in Tarnopol for a day camping on the tennis court surrounded by NKVD guards. But they had left Tarnopol, again in the direction of the Soviet border, just one day before our arrival, and we estimated they would be in Russia by now.

As a last resort before our return to Lwów, I decided to contact the local NKVD and make inquiries. The soldier and guard looked at me with astonishment when I explained the situation of my cousin, speaking slowly and politely to the commanding officer. He listened carefully and then explained.

If my cousin, a Jew, could become a Polish army officer, he must be a fascist, since the entire Polish officer corps was fascist. If my cousin, an engineer, was able to exist unemployed for several years, his father must have been a capitalist. The Soviet Union was in a state of war against fascists and capitalism, irrespective of whether they were Jews or Poles. If the Soviet authorities decided to arrest my cousin, they most certainly had reasons. If after an inquiry into his case it transpired that he was innocent, the authorities would release him. He warned that as a cousin of the arrested officer, I, too, could be suspected of fascist tendencies and a capitalist background. He advised me to disappear.

We returned to Lwów despondent. The first and only message from Joseph arrived not long after our return. The address given was a Polish prisoner-of-war camp in Smolensk in the Soviet Union. He wrote that he was well, the air was brisk, and perhaps could he have some winter clothes. The family sent a parcel, but its arrival was never confirmed. We found a Soviet lawyer who claimed to have connections in Moscow and asked if he could, perhaps, construct an argument for Józek's defense if we made several payouts to him, each of 100 rubles. As the payouts continued, their size increased, including the last request of 1,000 rubles from me and several others with similar problems, without any signs of progress. We realized this was just a scam and gave up.

There were disturbing nights during this time. Nights where lorries, trucks, cars, and horse-driven carts could be heard in the streets outside, stopping in front of flats or houses. NKVD soldiers might suddenly enter demanding identity checks against a prepared list. Irrespective of gender, age, religion, or health, people were loaded onto transports to the railway station where long rows of empty freight trains stood waiting. Deportations to distant districts of the Soviet Union were occurring without notice. The entire population was in a panic.

There was a pattern. One day, Józek's old father and sick mother were taken away. It turned out that the NKVD had permitted deported officers to write short notes to their next of kin, and it was with these addresses that the next enemies of the Soviet Union were identified. Józek's parents were deported. All of this happened upon the making of a harmless stink bomb for some self-defense against antisemitism.

The NKVD soldiers were not brutal, though. There were no beatings, no shouting, no looting, and there were many instances of compassion that I remember. They helped carry bundles, loaded them onto the carts and lorries, and comforted their distressed victims. These 20-year-olds had been obeying orders which appeared cruel to us, but making night arrests and carrying out deportations seemed, to them, a natural occurrence.

"*Privyknesh* [You will get used to it]," they consoled us. If not, "*Zdochnush* [You will perish]." Another indication of our future was "*Zyet budesh a yebat nye zahochesh* [You will live, but you won't want to make love]."

THE GOVERNMENT MILLS TRUST

By 1940, the city of Lwów swarmed with many thousands of refugees from the German-occupied territories. The great majority of them were Jews, the men haggard and often homeless without means to support themselves and without opportunities for work.

Yet, "the Soviet authorities do not recognize unemployment" and "unemployment is an invention of the capitalist system" was the new doctrine. *Nie budiesh rabotat, nei budiesh kushat* [You don't work, you don't eat] was the motto of the new order. When huge posters were displayed on the walls of the town, summoning people to the Labor Exchange, thousands, including Lusia and I, registered.

The posters invited young men to volunteer for work in the Donbas region. Some Jewish idealists entered this "Workers' Paradise" wanting to contribute to its development. After registration they were taken almost immediately to the coal basin on the River Don and put into brigades to work in the coal mines. Such work was not even hinted at during the registration in Lwów. Idealists suddenly found themselves working in a Soviet coal mine. This was something even the Russians would have tried to escape if they could. It was unsurprising that authorities recruited laborers from newly gained territories who had no notion of the conditions.

We felt agitated without work. Prices were rising. Residents of Lwów lived by selling their clothing, linen, shoes, or anything they could spare. Those with foresight did well as the black market flourished. Prices of foreign currency jumped with people purchasing US dollars with plans to escape. Some speculated, making quick money by exchanging rubles for dollars and vice versa. One US dollar reached the price of 300 rubles, or 300 złoty, which was fantastic compared to the official prewar rate of exchange of 5.3 złoty for a dollar. But who of us had dollars to sell?

Lwów's banks were instantly nationalized and all accounts closed. It was possible to withdraw a maximum of 300 rubles in total, irrespective of total savings, and the remainder was forfeited. In this manner the Soviet government appropriated the savings of rich and poor alike. The non-working man was under suspicion – "probably a capitalist with enough money to live without work" – and in danger of deportation to the Asian interior or the *Lagery*, the forced-labor camps. Each citizen was under scrutiny, and each had a file with the NKVD.

Blocks of apartments, regardless of size, were nationalized. The janitor was retained with the official title of *uprawdom*. A simple man, often illiterate, was thus granted the management of several flats or houses and was at the beck and call of the NKVD. His duty was to know as much as possible about every tenant in his block and to report their movements. The secret police would easily know whether a citizen was working or not. People were naturally frightened. Those with independent means would purchase a kind of falsified work certificate. Such a document, along with a bottle of vodka for the janitor, would safeguard an illegal existence most of the time.

Our family name, Reiss, was well known in Lwów. My uncle, Dr. Salamon Reiss, was a prominent solicitor and known to be a wealthy man. Many Reisses were known to come from landowner heritage. I must never admit to being part of a family who, according to Soviet beliefs, was an enemy of the system. I was relieved then, to receive a card in the mail asking that I report for an interview at OBL-MEL-TRUST District Mill Trust.

The director of the trust was Comrade Litovczenko, a handsome man about 30 years of age sent from deep inside the Soviet Union. He was rather poorly dressed in the standard Soviet black suit and once-white shirt. I handed him the postcard that I received from the Labor Exchange and completed a lengthy questionnaire. Some of the questions were difficult to answer, such as those to determine my social background. My father's profession or occupation was particularly tricky. How to avoid the truth without lying? I wrote "farmer," which was true. My father should not be considered a *pomieszczyk* [landowner], since the farm he owned was not a very large one. Later I realized that the simplest and best answer would have been a lie. From the first moment they crossed the Polish border, one often heard lies from Soviet soldiers. This is what experience had taught them. To survive the Soviet system, one must at times be able to lie and steal, and at others, to not hear or speak.

Director Litovchenko directed me to the chief engineer, a young intelligent-looking fellow with black curly hair and sparkling eyes. "I am Lazar Mojsiejewicz Kofman," he introduced himself politely.

"*Da*," I said.

"Jewish?"

"*Da*," I answered.

The name of the chief engineer left no doubt as to his religious identity. I left the question about nationality unanswered. I didn't know if it was better to be Polish or Jewish.

Before September 1939, I considered myself to be of Polish nationality and Jewish religion. For me, raised on Polish soil with my education in Polish history and literature and a Polish mother tongue, my nationality was most certainly Polish. In religion, I had not been active and I had little in common with Judaism. The thing that bound me to my Jewishness was the ill will of most Poles and Ukrainians. Our complete assimilation was prevented by Polish government policy and the enmity of the Polish people. The violence of our university colleagues had cemented the divide. We wanted to be Poles, but the Polish nation didn't want us.

In contrast to Poland, in the Soviet Union, being Jewish as a nationality rather than a religion was acceptable. In fact, we thought it might be an advantage. The Soviet Union did not trust the Poles, particularly so soon after sticking a knife into their Polish backs in September 1939. The Polish government exiled in London appealed to its nationals not to cooperate with the Soviet Union. The Russians also could not trust the Ukrainians, who had long dreamed of an independent state, not a Soviet version of Ukraine. Certainly, the Jews welcomed the Red Army as a savior from a Nazi onslaught, but we also considered them as a relief from Polish discrimination and Ukrainian animosity. So it was comparatively easy under the Soviets for Jews to obtain jobs.

Engineer Kofman engaged me on the spot as a building engineer at a salary of 650 rubles per month, fixed according to the profession and function of the trust.

In 1940 there were about 50 mills in the Lwów district. The trusts had taken over their management. The headquarters of all trusts *Glav-Muka* was in Kyiv, the capital of the Ukraine Soviet Republic. The Lwów trust had its central office in the Sprecher house in the fashionable street of Lwów, the Akademicka, in a most splendid office building. The office was divided into departments, and I was allocated a desk in the technical department. Slowly, the various sections were established in this Nationalized Trust of Mills: mechanical engineers Katz, Aptowitz, and Wojcik; chemical engineer Klajnerman; electrical engineer Kahane; milling engineers Neuman, Meyr, and Isacc Kreppel; hydraulics Rubinek; and myself a civil engineer.

It felt strange to see that all the engineers were Jews except Wojcik and Rubinek. The director of the technical apartment was a Ukrainian engineer Sekonda and his deputy was Isaac Kreppel. In our room was also the purchasing department managed by Borowski, a well-dressed Warsaw Jew who had full command of Russian.

The planning department was run by two ex-solicitors, Alexander Faul and Moses Grunfeld. Leo Lonker, his son and son-in-law, were the bookkeepers. The driver for the management was Segel. Again, all Jews. Only the management of the trust was purely Russian: Director Litowczenko, well-mannered but a drunkard, and his deputy, Comrade Borszcz, a Soviet simpleton.

In fact, over 90 percent of the employees in our trust were Jews, and a similar situation prevailed in other trusts and cooperatives in the Lwów area, embracing all branches of industry, production, and commerce. Mystifyingly, the whole of the technical staff sat at their desks with nothing to do. The mills had not yet been taken over by the trust and might not have even known of our existence, trying as before to solve problems by themselves. I sat at my desk and copied articles from *Pravda* and *Izvestia* to brush up on my Russian.

The first task given to me was to "prepare the requirements of all building materials for all of the mills of the trust for the whole of

1940." I was stupefied. How could I foresee what building materials would be required, not knowing the condition of the existing mills, what alterations or repairs were required, or what new constructions or additions were planned? I hadn't even seen any of the mills yet. I approached Engineer Kofman for an explanation. He smiled indulgently. "The Soviet Union is governed as a planned economy," he explained. "Each year, the Moscow Ministry of Planning receives from the entire country the requirements for the building materials for the coming year. On this basis a production plan is prepared and supplies are distributed among the factories for production." He advised me not to worry unduly and only to complete an estimate to the best of my ability and knowledge. He hinted that I should not expect the requirements in my list to be met.

I decided to delegate the request to the mill's managers. They ought to know best. I ordered 50 large sheets of paper, a few sheets of carbon paper, and some hard pencils. I drew up a questionnaire, listing all of the required building materials. There was no carbon paper, so I made each copy by hand. It was a peaceful occupation, looked on with envy by my idle colleagues. Once the questionnaires were dispatched and replies began to arrive, I could see that Director Litwoczenko was impressed. The Soviets loved planning.

The new "owners" of the mills didn't quite know what this request was all about and came to Lwów for clarification, and, consequently, I received nearly all of the estimate forms, enabling me to compile a more accurate summary of requirements for Kofman. Nevertheless, as he examined the document, he suggested I double or triple some of the figures, tolerating with a patronizing smile my naivete.

After many months, some meager supplies did start to arrive. The most needed did not arrive at all. Nails, ordered in a variety of sizes, arrived in only one big and unsuitable size. I now understood the meaning behind Kofman's smiles when he first examined my list of building requirements.

I began to notice my engineer colleagues who were traveling to the countryside to inspect the mills were absent for a few days. As I had never visited a mill and had no notion of its construction, I thought this would be useful for me, too. At my request, Kofman provided me with a *kamandirowka* [traveling order] to the town of Bóbrka. My more experienced colleagues told me I should not rush this trip, so I spent a few hours at home the afternoon before I left. Early the next morning at the railway station there were many waiting for the train. A Soviet female conductor was shouting "*Nyet miesca* [No room]!" She ignored my official traveling order. I could see others pushing their way in passing a banknote into her hands as they proceeded. I had no notes, but eventually she let me board the train. To my amazement it was almost empty and the young Russian conductor smiling innocently. Obviously, she had ways to improve her income. The same scene was repeated at each station.

I found my way to the mill easily. The previous owner had been removed and the former manager was appointed as director. He knew me from the trust and I gave him my *komandirowka*. He agreed to apply the dates as had been suggested to me by my colleagues, signing off that I had arrived the day before and intended to leave the day after even though he knew perfectly well that I was only there for that day. He was already familiar with the procedure and, I realized, was becoming familiar with the principles of the Soviet system.

I inspected the mill and, in so doing, tried to understand the milling process. I understood about flour and grain from my Oserdów experience. I could tell different grain qualities and knew the weeds by name. The new director was impressed and we discussed the mill's problems and future rebuilding plans. I made a list of all required building materials and he signed off on them. He was pleased, hoping he would receive the required material in the near future. This was unlikely to ever happen.

The family provided me a home-cooked lunch, reminding me of prewar times. As I was ready to leave, he held out his hand and asked, "*A panski woreczek* [And your little bag]?" I stared at him, bewildered, but I ran with it and slapped my forehead, "Ah, the pouch! In my hurry I left it at home." He offered to lend me his bag, which he hoped I would return given it was so difficult to obtain linen now.

To my surprise, he left and returned shortly with a good size white linen bag full of beautiful flour of a quality not available in Lwów. He placed it in an old sack for protection and I sat on the sack all the way home. This parcel contained 20 kilos of beautiful white flour. My family was delighted. I slept till late the next morning as theoretically I was still at Bóbrka. I was reimbursed the equivalent of 100 rubles for the expenses of my journey, documented as two days and two nights lodging (they didn't even ask for receipts), and the railway fare plus local transport boosted my monthly salary of 650 substantially. In the future, I was better prepared. Once, a young director of a mill in Gródek, Jagie Honski, advised me that there was a cork in the knapsack I had provided. When I got home, I discovered a bottle of champagne hidden deep in the flour.

A real windfall landed in my lap when our trust decided to erect a stand at the first yearly district exhibition of the food industry. My "artistic" talents must've been known to management since Engineer Kofman informed me I had been appointed director of our stand, responsible for the design, construction, and presentation of the colored graphs displaying the impressive data on the execution of our yearly plan.

The Soviet system liked to boast about its results. The simplest achievements were boldly advertised in posters, graphs, and articles in newspapers. On the front page of the Soviet newspaper, one would find the photograph of the peasant girl who, during the previous year, had milked so many thousands of liters. Next to her stood the "heroic" cow. News from abroad, particularly about the war or political events in France or England, was found on the last page in a few brief lines only. Who was interested? Obviously, the big story of the extraordinary milk-producing cow was more interesting and important than a capitalist war.

Reports from general meetings of various state-owned factories were indigestible, comprising figures of attained production increases compared with the previous figures, ambitious plans, and fantastic projections anticipated for the coming year. How the projections compared with the results were something I discovered in our mill trust, where projections were constantly adjusted in order to synchronize them with the actual production results. By the end of a year, the execution of the plan was usually at a rate of 100-105 percent, triumphantly achieved and celebrated. All of this planning was senseless. The mills would process only that quantity of grain that was supplied by the peasants and not one kilo more. The plans did not improve or in any way affect production.

I pondered about the flour that the mill directors and many others gave us and other engineers who visited them. How was this accommodated in their calculations? I discovered that the Soviet authorities had introduced a new word into the milling vocabulary – *Rozkurz* [flour drift]. In theory, 100 kilos of grain should give, after milling, approximately 100 kilos of product. In practice, a certain percentage of flour drift was deducted, attributed to the quality of the grain and the extent of its dampness. This meant the peasant was regularly robbed on the scales. In addition, when his grain was weighed in, one to two kilos were deducted for the sacks. Thus, the mills of the socialist state robbed the peasants of about five percent of their product. In a country of permanent scarcity, such a surplus constituted a fortune.

NATIONALIZATION

Although these trips were profitable, they were not always pleasant. We were charged by the trust to visit a mill and ask all the employees to attend a meeting. We would announce that their mill now belonged to the trust. The existing owners would be replaced by an elected new director. This would have been rewarding work for a communist who subscribed to the infallibility of the Soviet system, but neither I nor any of my colleagues belonged to this category. How could I enthusiastically deprive people of their property, people who with great effort over generations had built their mills and created a livelihood for themselves and others? That I was from a similar background made the execution of such inhumane and unjust laws abhorrent. I tried to mitigate the damage as best I could, allowing opportunities for coexistence between the newly demoted owner and the mill staff where possible.

I recall visiting a mill in Zloczów, owned by a Mr. Stern. The mill had been built many years before by his father, and the two had worked seven days a week, often late into the night, to build the mill and get it working. I managed to assist him in choosing a friendly director who had been a devoted employee until then. I handed the mill over to this new management, including a newly appointed deputy director (Ukrainian) and bookkeeper (Jewish), while publicly "appealing" to the ex-owner to assist them. I later learned he had bought a cart and horses and was transporting goods between Lwów and Zloczów, allowing him to at least continue to make a living.

We had to forcibly take over one mill from a poor Polish settler. He had bought a small piece of land and, with his own hands, worked 16 hours straight each day to build his mill. He made the planks from logs himself, used recycled materials such as old foundation bricks, slaked the lime himself, and, as he was illiterate, had built his mill without plans, relying on his memories of years working in them. He purchased junk tin sheets for the roof, patching holes himself. In a scrap yard, he located a fire-damaged steam engine that he brought home with the help of his neighbors and their loaned horses. He used scrap rollers and ultimately produced a mill that, despite being non-standard in every way, functioned sufficiently well. He served his community, often milling for small fees or in exchange for a little grain, or sometimes for nothing. The surrounding villagers loved him. When I visited this mill, I discovered that the miller and his wife had been taken away one night by the NKVD for reasons unknown. I relayed all of this to my supervisor in the trust, who seemed embarrassed at the story yet remained silent. I suggested no external director would be able to manage this small mill, which was continuing to operate with the work of the local community and asked that the trust make the final decision.

Soon after, it was reported back to me by the same supervisor that my story of the small mill had been relayed back to him by the NKVD head office. He glanced significantly at my colleague Osyp's empty chair. I was panic stricken! How often had I voiced critical, sometimes even sarcastic remarks about the "new order" in front of Osyp? Perhaps all of this had been meticulously noted in my secret police file? Good God! It seemed likely that our colleague Osyp was an NKVD informer. For now, we must only communicate in his absence. I warned all colleagues to be on their guard and I kept my tongue under control – hopefully not too late.

Some months later, I happened to meet Osyp face-to-face. It was on the main street, Akademicka, one lovely Sunday morning when he stopped and greeted me most amicably. He proposed a short walk. I considered that sooner or later he had to write something about me and I was prepared. In a friendly way, he asked if I had relatives in Lwów as he thought my name sounded familiar. I explained calmly that I had been a resident of Kraków and until the outbreak of war had been employed in a Kraków engineering firm. We were in Lwów because my wife and her parents lived here and we both had work as engineers. Osyp inquired tactfully about my family. I recalled that in my questionnaire I had made a silly mistake, stating that my father's occupation was farming. I was nervous. I shared that my father worked as an agronomist but had died early, before I was old enough to remember details of his working life.

He was interested in my opinion about the Jewish refugees who seemed to want to return to German-occupied Poland, perhaps dissatisfied with the new order in Lwów. What was my view? I hesitated. An enthusiastic uncritical answer could raise suspicion that I had unmasked him as an NKVD spy. My answer must be credible but not uncritical.

"Before I answer your question, Comrade Osyp," I said, "I'll have to tell you something of my prewar experience. I studied at the Polytechnic here in Lwów. These were times of anti-Jewish actions. We were afraid to attend lectures; our colleagues hated us, often attacked us. Nobody stood in our defense and sometimes we were beaten. Our colleagues created a ghetto in the lecture rooms. The university authorities ignored the situation. After graduation none of my Jewish colleagues obtained a government appointment. I was fortunate enough to get work with a Kraków firm only because of my good knowledge of German. My wife and many others failed to obtain a position in their profession, taking all kinds of occasional jobs like drafting or tutoring. My father-in-law, a retired schoolmaster and elderly man, was heavily beaten up during those student riots. His brother, an ex-post office employee, lost his job and could only survive thanks to help from my father-in-law, a pensioner himself. My wife's sister, being Jewish, was not even accepted at the university.

"When you ask me how I feel about the present and how other Jewish people feel, what do you think? I obtained employment in my profession in our trust. My wife works at the NKVD in the Department of Railways as a design engineer. My father-in-law is receiving an old-age pension and pays little rent, receives medical treatment free of charge, and is not afraid to stroll in the street. His brother works at the post office and is happy. My wife's sister studies at the university at the state's expense. There is no ghetto or danger of being beaten up by colleagues. We Jews, once second-class citizens, are now citizens with full rights. Does that answer your question?"

Osyp listened in silence. If I was to convince him that my comments were authentic, I would have to make some criticism as well.

"Naturally, there are some shortcomings," I said. "The Soviet Union took over huge territories in a state of war and confusion. People complain that there is no salt. They forget that the salt mines are on the German side, and bringing salt from Russia, from behind the Urals, is not so simple. Only shortsighted people see nothing but the deficiencies of a new system. I am not one of them. Should you ask me whether I see some mistakes committed by the system, I will answer in the positive. I believe it was a mistake to throw out big mill owners immediately. They ought to have been retained until the mills were repaired by them, damages caused by war removed, and the mills resumed normal operation. They would have solved all of the problems better and more quickly than the trust could, and perhaps the town would have had bread sooner. We could have then removed the owners more efficiently, taking over production. Small and distant mills should have been left with their previous owners appointed as directors, allowing them to work for the local population. More of such mistakes will be committed, but in what system are the authorities not subject to errors, human errors, not mistakes of the system or a concept?"

Had he believed me? Would I be a candidate for deportation to Siberia or put in a concentration camp? I would have to wait and see. Certainly, arrests and deportations were routine occurrences. People were taken from their homes at night for no obvious reason. There was a saying in the community that Soviet citizens fell into three categories: those who had been imprisoned, those who were actually in prison, and those who were expecting to be imprisoned sooner or later. One unfavorable remark by Osyp, one single denunciation to the NKVD by anyone, would be sufficient to be placed on the list. Many times at night, I would wake up imagining that I heard knocking on the door. Sudden visits by the secret police were a nightmare for the whole population – Poles, Ukrainians, and Jews.

The room in Aunt Pepcia's flat (vacant after the deportation of Uncle Samuel and Aunt Rosa) had been allocated to a Soviet couple.

She was employed by the NKVD and her husband was employed as an accountant in my trust. My Aunt Pepcia and Uncle Jacob Francos were very wealthy and their spacious flat was appointed with luxurious furniture, Persian carpets, and paintings. Undoubtedly, the Soviet tenant appreciated their social status. I was worried my colleague had noticed me visiting my aunt. I stopped visiting immediately.

Uncle Jacob had heart trouble and news of his death was brought to me one day by none other than my Soviet colleague Osyp. He approached my desk and whispered the bad news. He therefore made it very clear that he knew who I was – a relative of this wealthy couple. I suddenly felt unsafe within the trust, yet the meeting for my election to the *prof-spilka* [trade union] was approaching. Every employee in the Soviet Union must be a member of a *prof-spilka*. Without a membership card, he cannot be employed.

The procedure for acceptance of new members is laid down by party authorities, usually taking the form of a public hearing, and requires unanimous acceptance by the general assembly. A candidate must get up and relate the history of his and his father's life. Any black spots in his past might result in rejection and therefore any chance of employment. A capitalist, an ex-Polish army or police officer, or a landowner and his family could not be accepted. They were enemies of the nation. Greatly apprehensive, I stood up before a general assembly to tell my life story, omitting all the "black spots," having quite a few of them. I painted a picture of myself and my family as typical members of the working class. The general assembly listened, and when the chairman opened the discussion, there were no embarrassing questions. I could see my Soviet colleague standing in a corner, smiling. He had voted for me with his hand prominently raised, although he knew who I was. I was unanimously accepted into the union.

My professional duty to visit the many mills did pose the danger of being recognized as a member of the capitalist Reiss family. Some of the mills were situated close to our hometown such as in Rawa Ruska, where at a nearby large farmstead, Potoki, my father's brother, was the leaseholder. I feigned illness to avoid visiting that area but could not avoid going to Uhnow, a small town at the new German-Soviet border. Uhnow was very close to a small town, Belz, which was then only a few kilometers away from Oserdów.

It was so nostalgic for me, as I stood on the banks of the Solokija. I could imagine the smoke I saw was from the chimney of our house in Oserdów. On one visit to a small Jewish shtetl of Mosty Wielkie, I was talking to a Jewish accountant when a tall young Jew entered smiling broadly, stretching out his hand. It was young Lieberman, son of Chaim Lieberman from Belz, who for many years had purchased grain from us in Oserdów. I was unmasked. After the initial shock, I calmed down and felt their warmth. I inquired about the fate of his family.

At the outbreak of war, the Russians had occupied Belz. Yet the Soviet-German line of demarcation had cut Poland so that Belz was to remain on the German side. The Jews, who constituted 95 percent of Belz's population, panicked. The majority packed their meager possessions and moved toward the Soviet border, a few kilometers away. On arrival, they were told by the guard that they had no permit to cross and would not be allowed into the Soviet Union. They refused to return to Belz and camped on the border. They begged, prayed, and cried in vain. After many days in cold and rain, the compassion of a Soviet guard overruled his country's orders. "*Haj ubiut, ja nie mogu smotri!* [Let them kill me, I cannot watch any longer.]" He lifted the border rail and let everybody in.

I impressed on Chaim that I was depending on his and his brother-in-law's discretion. They appreciated the situation. I had to trust them. I had no other choice.

PASSPORTIZATION AND THE PERFIDY OF THE NKVD

Osyp's reproach that Jewish refugees preferred returning to the German side of Poland rather than living in the Soviet Union was justified. Refugees were receiving letters from home saying the situation under the German occupation was not as bad as they had feared. Although some quality flats had been requisitioned and their owners evicted, on the whole Jews were permitted to continue to live in their apartments. Food rations were half those of the Poles, but people somehow managed. Work was compulsory, but no one complained. They worked in private businesses for the German authorities, and work permits protected them from forced-labor camps. In contrast, in Lwów, many refugees from Kraków were without proper homes or money and lived in fear of being deported to the Far East. Letters were arriving suggesting to "come back home!"

Meanwhile early in 1940, the Russians ordered the "passportization" of the whole population. Every citizen in the Soviet "liberated" part of Poland was provided with a so-called "passport" – an identity card with a photograph. In the Western world, passports were issued for traveling abroad. In the Soviet Union, where citizens were not free to leave, everyone had to have a passport. To obtain one, proof of registration was required. Applicants residing in Lwów before 17 September 1939 (the date of the Red Army's entry into Poland) had an automatic right to a normal passport. Those registered after 17

September were considered refugees and thus not entitled to a normal passport, but one with a so-called "paragraph 11." They had usually been reserved for untrustworthy elements: convicts, criminals, speculators, social parasites, or general citizens who did not enjoy the trust of the authorities. A holder of such a passport would not be allowed to live in a capital city, or within 100 kilometers of the Soviet Union border.

As almost all refugees appeared in Lwów after 17 September 1939, they had no right to normal passports and consequently would have to leave. That meant giving up newly acquired positions and their means of livelihood and moving to the provinces where there would be few possibilities for thousands of strangers to find accommodation or work. It was no wonder refugees preferred to return to the German-occupied zone.

Yet, it was uncertain how these thousands of men, many with wives and children, could cross back across the heavily guarded Soviet frontier. This question was suddenly answered when, one day, a German military delegation arrived to regulate, jointly with the Soviet authorities, the movements of people uprooted as a result of the war and the subsequent division of Poland. In contrast to the shabby gray appearance of the Soviets, the young and smartly dressed German officers in their sparkling cars caused a stir on the streets of Lwów.

Public notices were displayed in three languages: Russian, Polish, and German, and a combined German-Russian commission started to register all citizens of former Poland who wished to return home. Zosia, our child's nanny, who had family in Kraków, applied, as did all Polish and most Jewish refugees. It was quite a sight. From early morning, long queues of anxious people formed at the entrance of the building. They submitted documents proving they belonged to the "General Government," as the Germans called their Polish-occupied territories. The officers studied these applicants patiently, asking polite questions, and registered the candidates, issuing passports with serial numbers. Next to a German sat a Russian officer who registered the candidates in Russian, and next to him an interpreter. Everything was conducted quietly, politely, and in a friendly fashion.

There were no religious restrictions. All applicants were registered and promised that in due course they would be informed in writing when the transfer to the General Governorship would take place.

People returned home full of hope and happy that they would return to their families, perhaps soon.

"Passportization" did not create major problems for us. Lusia, Elżunia, and I had arrived in Lwów only a few days after 17 September and the house administrator had issued us (thanks to my father-in-law's intervention and a bottle of vodka) a predated document of registration. We were thus able to obtain our passports. Not everybody was so lucky. It was particularly disastrous even for people born and living in Lwów but caught at the outbreak of war in parts of Poland now occupied by the Germans. Despite having parents and families in Lwów, if they returned home after 17 September, they were not entitled to normal passports. People presented documents proving they were born in Lwów and had attended schools, and universities, and worked there. Even if only a few months before the war they had left, they were now forbidden to live in Lwów, becoming second-class citizens. A tragedy!

A difficulty arose with my mother's passport. She had arrived in Lwów a few months after 17 September and the house administrator could not issue her a predated registration card. At the time, I did not consider the card essential as she was elderly and I was supporting her. It seemed reasonable that since Lusia and I were both working full time, the mother had to care for our child, and therefore the issue of a normal passport should not create difficulty. What appeared logical to us was not necessarily logical to the Soviet authorities. My application was rejected, my mother was forbidden to live with us, and she had to leave Lwów as soon as possible. She would receive a passport marked with "para-11," a passport for a second-class citizen. I was shattered. I could never permit my mother, an elderly woman without a profession or a single relative or friend outside of Lwów, to be exiled. Full of indignation, I requested to see the head of the NKVD. He was bound to understand me and reverse the decision.

After three evenings of queueing, I appeared before him. He listened, nodded his head, and told me to return two days later. When I arrived at the stated time, he was not in the office. The secretary advised me to return two days later. I realized that if the matter dragged on, Mother was neither safe in the street nor at home since her presence in Lwów was illegal. I decided to ask Lusia for help. She excelled in diplomacy, knowing how to persuade quietly and logically.

In addition, as she worked as an engineer in the railway department of the NKVD, she perhaps would have some more influence. Besides, she had by now acquired an excellent command of Russian.

After three hours of waiting, we were admitted to the officer in charge. He listened half asleep, obviously bored and completely indifferent. No wonder! He had to listen to many similar requests daily. He explained that he acted according to instructions, but many people live in the provinces and that no exception would be made in my mother's case. Nonetheless, he promised to study the case and told us to come back in three days. After those three days, we returned and were told again to come back, and so on it went. As my mother had no identity papers whatsoever, having lived all her life in the village, I now prepared a number of documents for her including:

- Certificate of my employment with the Mill Trust
- Certificate of Lusia's employment with the railway NKVD
- Certificate confirming that Elżunia, aged two, was our daughter
- Certificate stating that our mother, as per fixed photograph and identified by two additional witnesses, lived with us
- My undertaking to support my mother, certified by the *Upravdom* [manager of the house]
- An identical undertaking, signed by Lusia
- Certificate that I was a member of the trust *prof-spilka*
- Medical certificate stating that my mother was suffering from an eye disease and needed close contact with the Lwów ophthalmic clinic
- Witnessed statement signed by Lusia and me declaring that Mother was looking after our two-year-old child while we were at work.

The preparation of these documents required great effort and much time, yet they were to no avail. It was like talking to a wall: neither "yes" nor "no," just waiting for hours in front of the NKVD building week after week.

Finally, my patience gave out. One evening, I reached the desk of the officer in charge of the passport department, in barely concealed anger put the whole pile of documents in front of him, and declared that either he settle my request positively now or I would write to the head of the NKVD, accusing him of injustice toward a Soviet citizen, which was against the Soviet constitution. I thrust my Soviet passport in front of him.

He looked as if he were noticing me for the first time and asked me to come back the following day. I returned the next evening and obtained for my mother a normal passport without the para-II. After many weeks of struggle against Soviet perfidy, I had raised my voice and won! It was a lesson on how to approach the Soviet bureaucracy, if necessary, by attacking. This lesson was to stand me in good stead later.

Registration of those wanting to return home now completed, the German delegation left Lwów and the waiting began. The refugees were unsettled and nervous, some working, mostly just waiting from day to day. But they didn't have to wait too long.

One day, some young men did not report to work. Single men had been taken by the militia during the night. Only refugees were affected, none of the local residents. Militiamen arrived at night, with a personnel list: name, address, and age. Nobody knew why the Soviet authorities kept silent. The following night, they took some more people. Once again single men only. Those taken away had no passports but were on the list for repatriation. Panic befell the bachelors and single men. They started hiding, not sleeping in their homes. Married men with families were not touched. People were guessing. Perhaps there were German spies among the single men, and since they could not be identified, they arrested them all. The married ones relaxed; it would have been a poor spy who would burden himself with family and children.

Quiet was restored but only for a few days. One night, carriages, military trucks, peasant carts, and all sorts of transport reappeared. The population froze. Who will they take this time? Ex-capitalists? Speculators? Ukrainian Nationalists? Wealthy Jews?

This time, the victims were the refugees – those who registered for the return home. The NKVD had an easy job. The refugees themselves had provided their names and addresses. With this list, the militia attended the stated addresses, checked documents, and took them all irrespective of age or health, and loaded them onto the trucks and to the railway stations. Our Zosia Janicka was also on that list.

We heard the frightening knock at the door and hid her at the last moment in a cupboard. Standing in front of it, I talked to the militiamen, explaining that she hadn't lived with us for quite some time and had left without giving her new address. They searched the whole flat, even looking under the beds, but luckily didn't open the cupboard.

At that time, also living with us was my mother's youngest brother, Dr. Joseph Tilles. Before the war, he had worked as a deputy manager in the Weiner Bank Verein, the Kraków branch. It was thanks to his recommendation that I obtained my last job in Kraków. Escaping from Kraków like many others, he found us in Lwów and stayed with us until I managed to get him a position as an accountant in Bóbrka, a town some 60 kilometers from Lwów. In connection with this work, he came to Lwów from time to time and stayed with us.

It was most unfortunate our trust had requested him for a conference at that particular time. Militiamen checking passports found that Uncle Joseph did not have one. He had considered himself a Pole, not any Pole but a Polish patriot; he would not accept a Russian passport.

The NKVD man did not lose much time deliberating. They took Uncle Joseph, who had come to Lwów for just one day, and put him on a truck. His few meager possessions were in Bóbrka. It was a tragedy. We all liked him very much and were greatly upset. My mother burst into tears. He went quietly as if to his execution. What could he do?

Lusia didn't give up. Immediately she located the officer in charge and spoke out, insisting that he was not entitled to take away somebody not on his list and that he was under the jurisdiction of the NKVD in Bóbrka, not Lwów, and since passportization was incomplete in Bóbrka, Comrade Tilles had no passport. Should the Bóbrka NKVD consider that he had to be deported, continued Lusia, then they could make that decision. Lusia spoke to the officer in a determined tone in perfect Russian. "Apart from all that," she added, "Comrade Tilles is an accountant at Bóbrka Mills and had just been called by a telegram to report to the Mills trust in Lwów, and that is why he is here."

Taken by surprise, the officer listened and asked to see the telegram, which Uncle Joseph fortunately had with him. After carefully studying it, he issued an order to release Joseph before the trucks had driven away.

We could hardly believe it. Lusia's courage and quick grasp of the situation, her resolute way of acting, and her perfect Russian had saved Uncle Joseph from deportation to the "white bears country," as it was known at the time. The night intruders left, the doors were shut, and the trucks drove away. Zosia crawled out of the cupboard, almost asphyxiated. We were all emotionally exhausted. Lusia made some tea and we drank a toast to Zosia, Uncle Tilles, and, of course, to Lusia, the heroine of the night.

We had many friends among the refugees, and the next morning we ran to the Uberalls' apartment. We had been friends since our student days sharing a love of bushwalking in the Carpathians. They had studied law at Kraków University and were married with a little girl, Magda, a year older than Elżunia. Magda's nanny, Danusia, and our Zosia were sisters. They had tried to escape Kraków like us and headed toward the Romanian border, unsuccessfully. They had returned and, like us, headed to Lwów. We kept in close contact.

When we arrived to see how they had fared that night, we found with great sorrow their flat empty. Lusia, Zosia, and I rushed to the main railway station. It was an exceptionally hot June and there were long freight trains full of families, elderly folk, and small children. How to find the Uberalls? We and others were calling out trying to locate relatives and friends. By sheer luck, we spotted them and gave them some bread, milk, water, and marmalade that we had gathered at the last moment.

They had with them a few kilos of semolina and thanks to those groats, as I was told years later, little Magda survived their long weeks of travel. We could not stay long because the guards were chasing us away. I noticed a familiar face in a carriage outside the station and recognized Mr. Freud, the owner of the firm I had worked for in Kraków. He was waiting for permission from the NKVD to join his wife, who was among those already taken for deportation. He had not been home the previous night, but on returning in the morning found his wife gone. His request to join her was refused! He had to apply in writing to the chief officer of the NKVD and sign a declaration that he was willing to join the transport of his own free will and at his own risk. What a perfidy! She was already taken, but her husband was required to apply for permission to be deported.

We did at last receive a letter from Uncle Samuel and Aunt Rosa.

After a long and tiring journey in cattle trucks, they had arrived in the Kolkhoz Min-Bulak in the Semipalatinska region of the Soviet Republic of Kazakhstan. Aunt Rosa described their experience in colorful language. They had been allocated to a poor Cossack shepherd's family. Living in a small house with clay flooring, they slept on a bundle of straw in the corner of the only room. Food was cooked on a primitive hearth heated by animal dung that Aunt Rosa collected. The area was desolate, with no trees or shrubs, only some spare tufts of grass. They lived on a small bread ration and goat's milk. The summer was hot and she toiled in the scorching sun without any shade or the slightest breeze. No one made her do it; she just wanted to assist the shepherds. My wonderful Aunt Rosa.

We regularly sent them parcels. Clothing was bartered for food. Once, after standing in a long queue, I was lucky to obtain a box of chocolates filled with sour cherries, which I added to the parcel. Such parcels were joint family arrangements and included food such as grits, buckwheat, white flour, and some clothing. The parcels took months to reach their destination but were greatly appreciated. It was my job to wrap the packages as there were special rules. The weight was limited to ten kilos and the parcel had to be wrapped in white linen with the address in an indelible pencil. The parcel wrappings were reused as foot coverings, so-called *onouce,* as no stockings were obtainable. Every piece of material was valuable.

A COURT CASE AND A SPY

From the moment the Soviet army entered Lwów, the authorities started their expropriation. This action was directed not only at the rich and very rich, but also, and with similar ruthlessness, the middle classes, and even the poor. The first strike was to nationalize banks. Accounts with an excess of 300 złoty per person were closed, leaving many with no cash or possessions. Next were property owners.

Blocks of flats were expropriated regardless of size. People who had invested their life savings in a small block of, for example, four apartments, usually rented to poor tenants at low rentals, were left without means of livelihood or the right to government pensions since they were considered to be bourgeoisie and exploiters of the working class.

Shopkeepers were severely hit. On our street, there was a small grocery shop that had catered to the everyday needs of the local population. An elderly Jewish couple ran the shop on their own, on their feet from early morning till late at night. The Soviet authorities imposed high taxes on them, which they paid with great effort. They believed their small shop would somehow hold its own, allowing them a modest living. They never foresaw the day when they would have no goods for sale. Wholesale supplies of coffee, tea, sugar, rice, and many similar items ceased to exist. Flour and other grains were not obtainable. They sold their modest stock till their shelves were empty.

Potatoes, cabbages, cucumbers, and onions were delivered in small quantities by peasants who had known them for years. Finally, they sat in an almost empty shop and waited. Perhaps the situation would improve? Surely it could not last! They didn't have to wait for the next tax invoice to find this time it was higher. They had nothing of value to sell and, helpless, they were forced to close their shop. For non-payment of taxes, the punishment was severe. Shopkeepers were blacklisted as speculators and many poor and often elderly people lived in fear of deportation. The taxman kept demanding the payments, and some ruined shopkeepers, finding themselves in such a hopeless and tragic situation, chose suicide.

Ex-owners of real estate were in an equally tragic situation. Properties usually were purchased with long-term loans, not cash. When authorities took over the properties, the banks and credit accounts continued demanding repayment of the loans, with interest. Lenders did not care that the properties had been nationalized or that their ex-owners had no income. All debts, they said, must be settled. Hours spent in government offices explaining, crying, and begging, were without use. Debtors were put on a blacklist and sooner or later arrested or deported. Many perished. Suicides increased.

After weeks of frustration my Uncle Joshua, a well-known physician in Lwów, obtained a position as health inspector for the Restaurant Trust, which controlled all restaurants – probably more than 50 – in Lwów. Russians liked to eat out, particularly as many had arrived without their families and ate heartily after their lean years in the Soviet Union. I was told by a tearoom owner that a Russian would order a three-egg omelet plus four additional omelets for his table at the same time. When the astonished waitress inquired what had happened to the friends for whom he had ordered the other omelets, the Russian replied, "It is for myself, in case you run out of eggs." Cooking at home was difficult as many items were in short supply, but state restaurants had priority. As restaurant prices were very reasonable, they were well patronized by Russians and the well-to-do new aristocracy – the speculators.

My uncle's duty was to control the standard of hygiene in the restaurant kitchens. As they were scattered all over town and public transport was overloaded and unreliable, the poor fellow had to walk from one restaurant to another. It was difficult to assess the cleanliness of each kitchen. As a well-known physician of many years standing, he must have been resentful. But the work certificate, salary, and free meals might have been a relief at this difficult time.

Then one day, a special health commissioner from Kyiv, during an inspection of one of the restaurants, noticed a mouse running across the kitchen floor. My uncle, who was responsible for the hygiene of the kitchen, was suspended from his duties and ordered to appear before the "People's Court." A special prosecutor, a young Jewish woman delegated from Kyiv, charged him with sabotage.

Investigations and interrogations began, and my uncle's bourgeois capitalist origin was uncovered. The enthusiastic young prosecutor prepared a charge of subversion. Uncle engaged lawyers for his defense. Witnesses were called. Being well liked by the managers, cooks, and waitresses, many gave evidence in his favor and the court found him not guilty of the charge of subversion. He was, however, convicted of negligence in fulfilling his duties and lost his position. He fell into a state of severe apathy soon after and lived only a few months longer under the protective wings of his loving family. He died a broken man.

There was another, though maybe less menacing, trial before our trust's *prof-spilka* in which I, or rather my spiteful tongue, was the accused. The Soviet system was built on the fulfillment of the norm. The success of every employee depended on the extent to which they fulfilled that norm. The head of our Personnel Department, Irena Tolloczko, was married to a high official in the Russian food industry. One morning, apparently in a bad mood, Comrade Tolloczko addressed me and some colleagues in a rather unpleasant manner, for no apparent reason. I remarked that perhaps last night her husband, Comrade Director Jamczenko, had not fulfilled his norm. My colleagues laughed and we returned to work.

Unfortunately, a spiteful flatterer had repeated my remark to her. She seethed with rage. Being the head of our *prof-spilka*, she invoked a general meeting at which she launched a tirade against the comrade (not mentioning my name) who had dared to express malice and disrespect toward her husband, the chief of the food industry in Lwów – a member, she reminded us, of the Central Communist Party and a most important and powerful person. If this comrade (and she indicated she knew who it was) would come forward, confess, and beg her forgiveness in the presence of the full assembly, she might refrain from reporting him to her husband, who would certainly find a way to deliver an appropriate lesson. She called for a further General Assembly in a week's time, giving me time for consideration.

I was very upset. My stupid, malicious tongue! I was furious with myself. I could not contemplate appealing before the General Assembly on bended knees, asking such an arrogant woman for her forgiveness. Never!

The *prof-spilka* had a so-called "court of honor." Ex-solicitors Moses Grunfeld and Alexander Fall were honorary judges and I entrusted them with my case. They approached the offended "lady," expressed in my name my regret and repentance, and explained it had merely been a silly joke. This was in vain. She insisted I must present to the General Assembly, publicly admit my guilt, and beg for forgiveness. Both judges advised me to comply. Why fuel her hostility? She could cause me grievous harm. They reminded me how in the infamous Moscow trials of 1934, great communists, including some Fathers of the Revolution and members of the Comintern, had been forced to bend their knees and confess crimes they had never committed. With my family to consider, I had to agree. The General Assembly took place. I had prepared my speech carefully. In it, I underlined the great merits of Comrade Tolloczko, confessed regret from the depth of my sinful heart for the crime I had committed, admitted my unjustified, spiteful behavior toward such a magnanimous and beautiful person, and then asked for forgiveness.

Comrade Tolloczko radiated. She addressed the Assembly sharing that it was not merely her, but the whole *prof-spilka* that had been offended, and thus the Assembly, must decide if I deserved forgiveness. "All in favor raise their hands," she ordered. Everyone raised their hands. I went home with relief. After so many disturbed nights, I could sleep peacefully. I vowed from then on to keep my tongue under control.

The winter was severe that year. I caught a cold on one of my travels and had to remain in bed. Lusia notified Tolloczko and rang the polyclinic (the district's health center), asking for a doctor to visit me. It was not acceptable to report sick without producing a doctor's certificate. There were no private doctors, only those attached to the polyclinic's. They reported for work in the mornings, some treating patients in surgery, while others received a list of home visits. Their pay was miserable, but medical care under the socialist system was free.

Around midday a doctor arrived and, still standing at the door, asked loudly, "Do you have a temperature?"

"It's 38 degrees and I have a slight chill," I answered.

He told me to take aspirin and remain in bed for three days. He left, leaving behind a pre-prepared prescription and a signed certificate with my name and the date already filled in. My mother, who was at home, offered him a cup of tea. Standing at the door, he told her he couldn't afford the time as he had 30 patients whom he was required to visit that day. He had to walk because it was impossible to rely on public transport, so he could only give two minutes to each patient.

Soon after, someone knocked on the door again. To our surprise, two women entered: Irena Tolloczko, in her capacity of chief of Personnel, and her Russian secretary. "Worried" by my illness, they had come to see if they could help. More likely, they did not believe I was really sick. People often took a few days off feigning sickness. They were all public servants and working for the socialist Fatherland was not very dear to their hearts. The authorities tried to combat the absenteeism, calling it *pryhul* [absenteeism under false pretenses]. Consistent absenteeism or phony sick leave was justification for a court case, and malingerers were in danger of losing their jobs. Irena Tolloczko had hoped to find me not at home and had brought a witness along. What a joy it would have been to her! Instead, she found me in bed with a thermometer in my mouth. What a disappointment.

There was another day I was absent from work but only for a few hours. We had received a letter from Charkow from Lusia's sister-in-law, Rose, advising that she was on her way to Moscow where it would be easier, she thought, to continue her search for her husband, Edek, who had been arrested. Hoping that Edek was still alive, she was determined to obtain his release from prison. They had a three-year-old son, Felix, whom she wanted to leave with us. Some of her friends were traveling to Lwów and agreed to bring the child. We were informed of the exact date and hour of their arrival.

I had shown the letter, written in Russian, to Koffman and Irene

Tolloczko and was given release from work for half a day. Felix Smirnow, a charming pale little boy, alighted from the train. He had been born in Charkow, USSR. His father, an active communist, many times imprisoned in Poland, was now in Moscow, a victim of Stalin's purge of the communists of Western Ukraine.

As we climbed onto a tram, Felix had tears in his eyes. "I've come to live with you, Uncle," he said quietly in Russian, as his mother must have taught him. He was quiet and very well behaved. Dressed in a small brown fur coat, which God knows at what expense his mother had obtained for him, he carried a small suitcase with the rest of his meager belongings. As he looked at me sadly with deep, intelligent eyes, wavering between fear and yet some instinctive confidence, he fought back tears. My eyes were not dry either. At home, I handed him into the loving embrace of Lusia's mother – her grandson, the child of her greatly beloved and only son.

None of us could guess what was in store for this charming boy. My concern for poor Felix was soon pushed aside by another anxiety. I had noticed that Lusia was not her usual self. She seemed sad and troubled but refused to answer my questions. She claimed only to be suffering from headaches. It was the first time Lusia had hidden something from me. For days, she was silent despite my pleas. I was greatly concerned.

One evening, she went out again without answering my question as to where she was going. She returned after two hours, more upset than ever but stubbornly remaining silent. She begged I desist from demanding explanations. She assured me that she would tell me in due time.

After two more mysterious evening excursions, when I opened the door to let her in, Lusia broke down and revealed her secret. Working as a design engineer for the railway department of the NKVD, she worked with her usual conscientiousness and her superiors were satisfied. She had even been recommended for a special "Stalin reward" in the form of a watch made in Russia.

Subsequently, she had been called into the office of the chief engineer and introduced to a stranger. The man advised her that the NKVD had decided to employ her as an "observer." Her task was to observe two of her colleagues and report weekly on their movements and conversations.

Lusia recoiled at the prospect of becoming an informer, but she had no choice. The NKVD man emphasized she would be rewarded and subtly indicated that such a position might be very useful both for herself and her husband. He advised her to consider it very seriously before rejecting his proposal. The mention of my name by the NKVD terrified Lusia. Maybe they knew something! Maybe they were aware of my capitalist background! Many colleagues from the Lwów Polytechnic knew me, and there was no lack of informers around. She had no alternative but to agree.

The condition of her engagement was to liaise regularly and discreetly with an officer of the NKVD and maintain absolute silence at home. She had been tormented by the puzzled sadness in my eyes but had to keep silent, afraid not so much for herself and her parents but for me. She also had a problem with the reports. Both victims selected for her were colleagues from the Polytechnic – Jewish students, diligent, hard-working, and loyal. What could she write about them? Lusia had prepared two reports describing conscientious work and punctuality. Her reports were flattering but objectively honest. She delivered the reports in the evening at a shady corner of the side lane to her contact. It was like a second-rate spy movie. Lusia was disgusted with the task imposed upon her, but her employers were even less delighted with her reports. They had expected some accusations and negative comments, not praise. After a few more worthless reports, the NKVD authorities relinquished Lusia's cooperation. She relaxed and home life returned to normal. We never knew, though, who had taken over her function and now who spied on her or me.

There was no similarity between Lusia's job and mine. Lusia worked purely professionally, executing and checking drawings in an engineering office. She earned 700 rubles a month whereas I earned only 650. I did have "payment in kind," which was at least double the value of my salary, not to mention the cash refunds for my traveling "expenses" and some extra free hours. My professional work, however, was of little real value for my country, and the trips had only a political character – the expropriation of the owners, taking mills, and establishing "red corners" (a room for meetings and lectures on political education) and a "wall newspaper."

Once, however, I was commissioned to perform a responsible

professional task. One of the largest mills in Lwów had broken down. The internal brickwork of the boiler had burned through and the chamber of fireproof bricks had collapsed. The mill came to a sudden halt. Immediate repair was not only a technical but political task. Engineer Kofman and I had been summoned by the trust director. The instruction was short: "Tomorrow, the boiler must function at any cost, or else." The head of the Food Industry had made the trust director, Comrade Livtoczenko, personally responsible. He in turn passed the responsibility onto Engineer Kofman and myself.

Luckily, I had a good understanding of the problem from my work in Kraków, where I specialized in industrial structures, particularly in the construction of brick enclosures for all types of boilers. True, I had never crept into a boiler or inspected a fire-resistant brick enclosure. There were master bricklayers who specialized in such work. I didn't know, however, that those special fireproof bricks must be placed in special fireproof mortar and that the gaps between the bricks must be so narrow that a razor blade could not pass between them.

In a pair of overalls, slowly and with difficulty, I crept into the fire chamber, reaching the spot where the breakdown had occurred. The damage was total: The walls were burned through, the arch had collapsed, and the brickwork was in ruins. Naturally, the boiler was out of action. I inspected the damage and slowly crept out, covered in black dust like a chimney sweep. Waiting for my report were both the director of the trust and the director of the mill. I asked for the person in charge of maintenance and repairs of the fire chamber. They did not know of the existence of such a person. I asked whether fire-resistant bricks and mortar were available and what quantities were there. They didn't have the slightest idea. The director of the mill was a Russian who obviously knew how to "manage" flour for himself and his friends but was not greatly interested in the running of the mill.

I advised the two gentlemen that without bricklayers and suitable bricks I was helpless, for regrettably with my bare hands nothing could be accomplished. But I was wrong. Under the Soviet system, there is a very important word: "responsibility." Consequently, my director, without any lengthy deliberations, said sharply, "You are the building engineer of the trust. You are responsible for the mill being set in motion no later than tomorrow morning. The mason and the required material are your problem and your responsibility. If the repair job is not completed in time, the district NKVD will become interested and you will have to justify your case to them. I'm sure you realize the consequences."

I was familiar with accusations in such circumstances: "sabotage and counterrevolution." I realized I must find a solution. Searching through the boiler house, the storerooms, and all the dark corners of the mill buildings, I found a small quantity of white and red bricks. The white looked to me as if they were fire-resistant, but they could just as well have been white building bricks. The fire-resistant mortar comes in the form of a white powder in paper bags like cement does. I hadn't found such bags anywhere. One of the mill workers I spoke with suggested that the previous owners had regularly inspected and repaired the boiler, but the new management had totally neglected it. I inquired about a mason or laborer who had some experience in bricklaying and I was lucky; there was a man who before the war worked as a mason who was now working in the mill, where it was warmer and there was some free flour to be had.

That very day, the two of us crept into the boiler and cleared the collapsed ruins, removed all the broken and burned bricks, and began to rectify the wall without mortar. We worked hard to ensure each brick was smooth, without gloves, which after hours of work left the skin on my hands quite raw. At midnight, the battery of our electric torch gave out and I crept out, happy at last to stretch my aching back. We had been working for hours on our knees with our heads bent in a tight space. I went to the director's office, which was brightly lit, and knocked on the door. After some time, the door slowly opened and I found the director of the mill and the director of the trust inside. Both were completely drunk. I controlled my anger and asked for a new torch battery. They seemed barely to comprehend and were unable to help.

My bricklayer had a few candles at home, and he agreed to fetch them while I waited in the cold. After an hour, he returned, and by candlelight we finished our work. Director Livtoczenko graciously permitted me to go home and rest for a few hours. Kofman praised me for my "Socialist enthusiasm."

In my work, I was challenged by technical as well as financial problems. The construction of a new building or alterations to an old one required a lot of formalities. Plans, specifications, and estimates of cost had to be carefully prepared. Similar to Western practice, it was the banks that financed such expenses. In the Soviet Union, there was only one bank, the State Bank, which kept close control of each enterprise. The bank reviewed the plans, specifications, and estimates and approved or rejected the release of the required funds. Therein was the problem. When one of the mills in Lwów decided to erect an additional grain storage building, it was my role to complete the plans and budget. There were teams of building tradesmen in Lwów who acted as subcontractors tendering for building works. I was astonished when their quotations were three times higher than my estimates, which had been derived from the Soviet Encyclopedia of Norm of Work and Prices [*Yadynore Normy Wyrabotyky I Rascenky*].

This encyclopedia, whose size resembled the *Encyclopedia Britannica*, was very precise, setting norms and prices for all building tasks, labor materials, and transport for every element of building work. The difficulties of prescribing costs in this way were manifold. Many volumes were actually not available, thus all trades were not covered. One could also not possibly cover every type and size of material required. The time lost on locating substitutes for unavailable materials, time spent on repairs and correcting mistakes, and time wasted in tea breaks and deliveries, had not been allowed for. Also, the information regarding output per hour was based on totally unrealistic assumptions. Finally, the basic accepted wage was three rubles per hour, whereas no trained worker would accept less than six or seven rubles. Engineer Kofman agreed that the norms were absolutely unrealistic and suggested that one must arrive at a realistic price in another way. The bank was only capable of measuring construction above ground, and thus one might have to "adjust" the extent of construction below ground, such as by increasing the depth of foundations, pumping of nonexistent underground water, and so on. Fictitious work would provide additional finance and cover the real building costs.

I expressed my apprehension at attempting to falsify the estimate, as the bank engineer could inspect the trenches and find out there was no underground water at all or that the foundations were not at the depth described. Kofman reassured me that the bank realized only too well that the norms were unrealistic and, as a rule, would not inspect the buildings at the early stages. I rearranged the drawings, deepened the foundations, and obtained sufficient financing for the completion of the building. Indeed, the first inspection by the bank's engineer took place only after the completion of the foundations.

Not everybody was so lucky. My colleague Anatol Kahane, the trust's electrical engineer, was responsible for electrical installations. A burned-out motor had to be rewired in the trust's workshop. The required quantity of copper was not available in our trust store or the workshop. To order wire from Soviet Russia was useless because it would take months to be delivered, if ever. Kahane applied to the trust for instructions. The NKVD insisted the mill be reactivated without delay, threatening that each day's delay would be considered sabotage and counterrevolution. The managem.ent authorized him to purchase wire on the black market, which he did. He worked many hours until the motor was repaired, tested, and reinstalled. The mill was reactivated and Kahane was proud of his success. But his joy was short lived. Somebody denounced him to the NKVD and a charge of purchasing material on the black market was lodged. Deliberations on the charge were ongoing, but fortunately in June 1941, midway through these hearings, the tides of war were to change, saving him from a 20-year "holiday" in a Gulag "retreat camp." The NKVD, Soviet court, and mill trust bosses suddenly retreated eastward.

We were always unsettled. I recall a sharp knock at our door one evening. How we feared those unexpected visits! It was a Soviet soldier and he entered without a word, walking through the hall directly into our sitting room, where the whole family was having their meal. My father-in-law asked him politely what he wanted. "*Posmotryt* [To look around]," he replied. He looked around all of the rooms. We offered tea, but he refused and left without a word. We sighed with relief when the door closed behind him but discovered a wool scarf belonging to Lusia's father had disappeared. This was not an isolated occurrence. These were thieves masquerading in military coats. No one dared to challenge.

While Lwów seemed peaceful, we noticed changes suggesting the opposite. Small posters, unobtrusively displayed on city walls, advised by order of Lwów City Council that existing air raid shelters be kept in good condition, destroyed shelters be rebuilt, and blackout material such as large sheets of deep dark paper and blankets be kept in readiness. Anti-aircraft shelters in a Soviet Lwów? Who would bombard Lwów? Not the Germans, with whom Stalin had concluded a peace treaty. Not the Russians, who feed us to the disadvantage of their own population. Not the British, who suffered such heavy losses on the Western Front, scarcely saving the remnants of their army. Who was going to attack us, the powerful Soviet Union herself?

I inquired if Kofman would share any information. He refused to talk. Rumors began to appear, and encoded messages arrived from the German side of Poland. In letters to Lwów, relatives and friends in Kraków wrote about German transports going to the east. Smugglers, flourishing across the German-Soviet border, brought information about a heavy concentration and movement of military material along the German side of the Soviet-German border. Along the Soviet side, our side, total silence.

Once again, Engineer Mandeblatt, the milling specialist from Kyiv, arrived. I thought he might be better informed than our local dignitaries and invited him for dinner. To my astonishment, he declined, politely explaining that he made it a rule not to receive anybody at his home and not to visit others. He avoided contact with people on the streets and in restaurants. He advised me, as a friend, to adopt a similar attitude. "You never know who is watching you and what kind of report he will write," he said. "As long as you sit alone at your table, it is difficult for anyone to invent something about you, but if you sit with somebody and talk, you run a risk." Was this the system we would have to live under for the rest of our lives?

I recalled some unbelievable stories that would reach us about life in the Soviet Union before the war: children being trained in school to spy on their parents and inform the teachers or the NKVD, and parents being afraid of being overheard by their children. People who were frightened to express even the slightest criticism about the system in their own homes.

The political tension we felt increased daily. There were rumors about single German planes flying over Soviet territory, supposedly on reconnaissance missions. Several had apparently been shot down.

It was rumored that in western Ukraine about 100 new airfields were being built. Why was the Soviet Union building so many airfields? New regulations reinforced concerns. The military command had begun to register all men of military age, me included.

Then in the Soviet newspaper of 14 June 1941, a notice appeared by the Russian News Agency TASS: "In the Western world, rumors suggest that Germany has submitted territorial demands against the Soviet Union and a war between Germany and the Soviet Union is imminent. This is false propaganda by powers hostile to the Soviet Union.

"The TASS agency is therefore authorized to state the following: Germany has not submitted any territorial claims to the Soviet Union. Germany fully respects the nonaggression treaty and so does the Soviet Union. Rumors about a planned attack on the Soviet Union are without any foundation. In accordance with its peaceful politics, the Soviet Union shall continue to respect the German-Soviet treaty and that all rumors about military preparations for war by the Soviet Union are manifestly absurd. The current Red Army maneuvers have no purpose other than the training of reservists and, as everyone knows, such exercises take place every year."

I had the uneasy feeling that we were on the eve of a German attack. I did not imagine how the Soviet military machine could withstand such an attack. My friends thought I was too pessimistic.

A week later, on 22 June 1941, the scream of planes and falling bombs once again woke us from a deep sleep. A Soviet-German war was no longer hypothetical but a horrible reality. How this war was to influence our destiny, we could not then have imagined, not even in our worst nightmares.

PART III
UNDER GERMAN OCCUPATION

JUNE 1941-AUGUST 1942

CALL-UP TO THE RED ARMY

On Monday, 23 June 1941, I went to the office as usual. Everyone was there – the Russians, the few Poles, a Ukrainian man named Sekunda, and the Jews. The atmosphere was tense. Just silence. We sat at our desks staring into space, waiting. For what? Nobody touched the papers stacked in front of them. The machine of the trust had stopped.

Breaking the silence, the phone rang, summoning Chief Engineer Kofman to Director Muraview's office. He returned with instructions: "War is war, but we are not in the army. We have to work with double energy and triple productivity. The mills must produce. The flour will be required for the army, and this is the duty of the trust to take care of the smooth functioning of the mills, now and especially after the harvest starts in three weeks' time."

Silently, we looked at one another and then at Kofman. Didn't they realize that in a few hours or days at the most, the Germans would be in Lwów? But Kofman had asserted himself as Chief Engineer and had begun issuing detailed instructions. Each of us was given a task. The store must be replenished with materials normally difficult to obtain. Our *snabzency* [buyers] were given a free hand to purchase on the black market: millers' gauze, copper, wire, oil, grease, and so on. Poor Rotstein stared. Under normal conditions these were almost unavailable, and now, under bombardment by German planes?

We, the engineers, received our instructions, too. Some of us were to go to the country to visit mills. The deputy head engineer, Sekunda, was instructed to compare the production of all our mills in the last six months with the planned production. He was speechless. I received instruction to go immediately to Gródek Jagielloński, a small town about 20 kilometers from Lwów. Waiting for the right moment, I approached Kofman. After all, we had been on friendly terms. I politely asked him if we weren't wasting our energy with the Germans apparently so close. He stared at me and I saw confusion in his eyes. "These are the orders from the authorities and that is that!" he said. He hurried away to the director's office.

The next morning, I set off for the railway station as instructed. I was afraid to leave Lwów and possibly be cut off from my family. The railway station would surely be the first target for bombardment. Yet I was too frightened to disobey the order. I reached the station with difficulty. Thousands of Russians, mostly families with children, were trying to leave. Ticket offices were besieged, with platforms crowded with frightened women and crying children. It was absolute chaos. Pushing through with my elbows, I reached my carriage and boarded the train. It was not far to Gródek, barely a few stops, but the train moved slowly. I was struck by the freight trains loaded with cattle, hay, and crude oil, all moving steadily toward Germany, just as they had for months. Why? Had the railway authorities not been informed of the outbreak of war? Were they also continuing business as usual?

At some stations, however, the cattle wagons were standing on the sidings. June had been a particularly hot month, and yet it appeared the railway employees had run away and left the wretched animals unattended. Some cattle had managed to break the barriers and jump the wagons and were struggling along the sidetrack, derelict and weak. Others that could not escape were bellowing plaintively so that one's heart ached to hear them.

I found the Gródek mill in disorder. The Orthodox Jewish bookkeeper had remained at home, wrapped in his old prayer shawl praying, his belief unshaken. With arrogant self-assurance the Ukrainian workers sat on a bench outside the mill awaiting the moment when the hated Soviet bosses would load their belongings on trucks and retreat to the east, leaving the mill and its stock behind. They stared at me with obvious resentment.

The manager, a Pole, was in his office. The mill was idle; there was no grain. These were the last weeks before the harvest. We talked in a friendly way. He was worried and especially afraid of his workers but not brave enough to leave the mill while the Soviet authorities were still in power. Therefore, he, too, sat, just waiting.

I gave him my bag as usual. Without a word, he filled it to the brim. I could barely carry it back to the station. The train to Lwów was almost empty as regular passengers had stayed home. I arrived home barely managing to carry my treasured 20 kilos of flour. Normally my mother-in-law took care of my "trophy," but this time I handed the bag over to Lusia. It was 24 June, our wedding anniversary, and this was my gift to her. She smiled wistfully but was unable to share the humorous aspect of a wedding anniversary gift of flour!

I blessed that Polish miller, not only for the flour stolen from the Soviet Empire but also for his assistance in getting me out of the mill without attracting the attention of the Ukrainians. He had led me through the back door with some personal risk. On the next day, the fourth day of this war, German aircraft were again flying over Lwów and dropping bombs. Salvos of anti-aircraft artillery could be heard. Here and there, fires broke out, black plumes of smoke rising from the vicinity of the central railway station. How lucky I had returned in time. Several bombs hit the station building – some were killed and many wounded.

The next morning, I went to the trust office again. There was chaos. Director Muraview and his deputy, Borszcz, had not turned up. They together with their driver and car had disappeared. Engineer Kofman rushed from desk to desk, answering one telephone and the next. My old antagonist, Irena Tolloczko, sat at her desk ready to burst into tears. It was whispered that her husband, Comrade Jamaczenko, had abandoned her, being ordered to Kyiv. Her self-assurance had disappeared.

We sat in the technical office gloomy and despondent. All we talked of was war. From north to south, the German border had run along the River Bug and River San about a hundred kilometers west of Lwów. We expected the Germans within two or three days and could not imagine the Russian troops being able to hold off the attacking tanks.

Around midday, Director Muraview and Deputy Borszcz returned rather unexpectedly – dirty, unshaven, and looking exhausted.

Muraview summoned me to his office immediately. He needed some reports, and I was good at preparing graphic statistical diagrams. He asked me to hurry. Still in his office, his telephone rang. Apparently, someone from high authority had been trying to get in touch with him all morning. The sharp voice could be heard far from the receiver. Muraview stammered awkwardly in reply, weakly denying some reproach, and was clearly frightened. He insisted he had left early only to inspect some mills. It appeared that the explanation was not being accepted. His driver "in confidence" had shared that the bosses left at daybreak heading toward the Soviet border. After three hours of driving, they had been stopped by military police on the Tarnopol Highway and their identities checked. Without current travel permits certified by the NKVD, they were ordered back. Numerous Soviet officials had panicked similarly, and on return to Lwów, questioning by the NKVD began. Poor Muraview.

Nevertheless, it was apparent that Soviet dignitaries were packing. Families were leaving, and official papers were sorted, packed, or destroyed. Trucks laden with bags, furniture, bedding, and women and children were heading eastward toward the old Soviet frontier.

Lusia's office had started packing up, too. She was well liked and respected and they invited her to go with them. They even offered a truck for her family and things. We talked for hours over the proposal. Could we leave everything and go to the Soviet Union? Her parents were too old, ill, and tired to undertake such a trip. Both had diabetes and needed insulin injections and a special diet for their survival. Her mother had poor vision, and the risk for them was greater than for us. Lusia's Uncle Jozef had nursed a hatred of Russia since World War I when as a volunteer in the Pilsudski Legion he fought against Russia. Elżunia's nanny, Zosia, had family in Kraków and did not want to leave. The German occupation did not threaten her anyway as an Aryan. Neither did my brother, Ludwik, nor Lusia's sister Fela want to go. So, it was out of the question. Our decision was also influenced by the information from Kraków, thus far, which had been under German occupation for two years. Nothing menacing appeared to have been happening. True, Jews had been moved from various districts of Kraków and resettled in the ghetto. Obviously, they had suffered great material loss. Our friend Henio and his wife, Irka, had returned to Kraków from Lwów. He had a job with the building firm as an architect and she in a bookshop that had belonged to her father until overtaken by a *Treuhander* [trustee] appointed by the Germans.

Under Soviet rule things had not been blissfully happy anyway. A visit from the NKVD and deportation were often threatened. Also, we did not believe Germany could win a war on two fronts. Hitler had said so himself in *Mein Kampf*. When Allied victory came, we had no wish to find ourselves in the depths of Asia in the clutches of the Soviets. As Soviet citizens with Soviet passports, perhaps we would not be permitted to return home. We remembered Lusia's brother Edek, who perished in the cellars of Moscow Lubianka prison despite his wife's devoted efforts to have him released.

These thoughts, plus the firm refusal of Lusia's parents to leave Lwów, determined our final decision.

The next couple of days, I continued to go to the office. One day, I returned home to find Lusia waiting for me looking dejected, my mother red-eyed and my mother-in-law even more upset. We had a modest meal together and only then was I let into the news. "I have bad news, Heniu," Lusia told me. "You have received a *powiastka* [call-up to the Russian army]." I looked at her with disbelief. She handed me the paper with my name, address, and instruction in violet ink to report immediately. Now there were tears in Lusia's blue eyes. My mother left the room. They had been so kind earlier despite their own worries, allowing me to finish my meal before giving me the news.

I was shocked. Although some months ago all men were made to register with the Department of Defense, I had never seriously considered the possibility of being called to the Red Army. I was 34 years old and never had military training. To find myself in the ranks of the defenders of the Red Empire? Leaving Lusia and our child, the whole family who were so dependent upon me?

The Russian expression *niemiedleno* [immediately] was well known to me. In the course of my work, I learned that although it literally meant "instantly," it was often interpreted as later, or tomorrow, or sometimes even the day after. One doesn't rush in the Soviet Union. I decided to delay presenting myself until the following day. There was no proof that I had received the notice. A young boy had delivered it, but no one had signed for it.

Yet I hardly slept that night. The next morning, someone knocked on the door. Before me stood a young lad who handed me a copy of yesterday's call-up, written in the same violet ink. This could not be ignored. Tomorrow it might be the military police at our door. It was time to go.

I was instructed on the notice to bring food enough for three days. With a loaded knapsack but a heavy heart, I parted from my family. Mother cried, as did my mother-in-law. My father-in-law, Uncle Joseph, and Zosia looked at me with sorrow. Lusia accompanied me to the assembly point where a soldier examined my papers and then opened the gate. A last embrace and then I entered – the iron gate closed heavily behind me.

I found myself in a huge schoolyard full of young men. There was no shelter from the hot sun, no clouds in the sky, and not the faintest breeze. I sat near a group of young men, leaned on my knapsack, and waited. Streams of recruits were arriving and we were made to squeeze closer and closer together. I could see many were Jews. Most had been sitting from early morning without a drop of water. Some had been sitting through the previous night. A large military transport had left the previous evening and we were waiting for the next convoy. Too nervous to eat properly at home, I sat eating my boiled eggs and bread. There was no water.

At dusk, we could hear German planes approaching, and now circling, above our heads. What a target we were, this concentration of men. There was nowhere to hide or even move. One of the planes flew lower and the second followed, probably observing. I pressed my head into my knapsack, shut my eyes, and listened to the roar of the motors. What will be, will be! Suddenly we heard fire from anti-aircraft guns. We could see shells exploding against the sky, but the planes flew higher than the shells, then changed directions and flew low to drop their bombs. I heard once again that penetrating, blood-curdling screech I remembered so well from 1939, a sound followed quickly by explosions. More screeching, whistling blood-curdling sounds and more explosions followed, and then only silence. The Soviet anti-aircraft artillery had obviously been hit. The plane circled and then flew away. Smoke and licking flames could be seen on the horizon. Eventually we all fell asleep.

Deep in the night, there were movements. Somebody had come out of the buildings giving orders. No further transport was available and we were ordered to go home. When they needed us, they would send again. I did not walk home, but I ran. Mother opened the door and embraced me, trying to control her sobbing.

At the Mill Trust, Comrade Borszcz personally took leave of everyone, shaking hands all around. Kaufman rushed from one to the other, obviously moved. Muraview and Mme. Tolloczko didn't bother to show up. And then they were gone.

Few were sad to see the Russian exodus. The Soviet occupiers had not known how to win the goodwill of the people. The Ukrainians, both the peasants and intelligentsia, were delighted. The Ukraine that the Soviets had created was not the free Ukraine the people had dreamed of, but one of hard and forced labor, deceit, NKVD, collectivization, and the kolkhoz [the collective farms]. The Poles were also glad of their departure. They would not easily forget the treacherous stab in the back of September 1939. Since their loss of independence 150 years prior, they had constantly struggled for freedom.

One might think that the Jews would also have wanted the departure of the Russians. Businesspeople and landowners were pleased to see them go, as were professionals such as doctors, engineers, and academics. So too, were religious Jews and even some disillusioned communists. Only the least privileged strata of Jewish society, the manual workers, and the struggling poor had gained social and economic benefits under Soviet occupation and were sorry. At that stage, few had reason to fear the German occupation. Some considered that Hitler might be influenced by the Allies to revise his anti-Jewish philosophy. No one imagined what was actually to come.

GERMAN ARMY ARRIVES

The moment the Soviets left Lwów, Poles and Ukrainians rushed to the prisons where the NKVD kept anti-Soviet elements – mostly nationalist Ukrainians. Discovering their fathers, brothers, and friends brutally murdered by retreating Soviet security forces, the Ukrainian mob turned their rage on the Jews, somehow blaming them. Jewish men, women, and children were viciously attacked on the streets, in the trains, and even at home. The beatings were brutal and the pogrom did not abate after the German army entered. A voluntary Ukrainian militia was immediately organized, and this black-uniformed bloodthirsty scum joined the mob in a bloody onslaught against the Jews.

No one in authority made any attempt to end the slaughter. The German gendarmes shut themselves in their barracks, leaving a free hand to the murderous Ukrainian gangs. The chief rabbi of Lwów, Dr. Jechezkel Levin, dressed in his clerical garb, and Dr. Henry Hescheles, the editor of the Jewish daily *Chwila* [the Moment], disregarded the danger and went to the Metropolitan Szeptycki, the head of the Greco-Catholic Orthodox Church, to ask for support. He was a greatly respected and noble leader in the community. Perhaps he could address his flock from the pulpit and condemn these frightful acts of barbarism waged against innocent people. On their way home, the rabbi and his partner were attacked and brutally murdered.[1]

Living as we did in a predominantly Polish district; we did not appreciate the extent of the violence in the Jewish district. Rumors of the riots had reached us at our home and, frightened, we did not dare venture out. One evening, there was an urgent knock on our door. Opening it cautiously, we saw Dudzio, Lusia's uncle, his eyes dazed. He ran to our bathroom from where we could hear the wails of a man crying. After some time, he joined us and told his story.

He lived in the area of the pogroms. Ukrainian militia had caught and driven him to the prison on Kazimierzowska Street. The courtyard was full of seriously wounded and brutally murdered Jews along with some others, and Dudzio was ordered to stay. He described witnessing Ukrainians using the butt ends of rifles to smash the heads of Jews who were injured but still alive. Blood and brains covered the walls and floors of the courtyard. Dudzio was forced to load corpses onto trucks that drove away – to where, no one knew. For the survivors, conditions were terrible. Dudzio and his coworkers were repeatedly beaten and driven to work faster. Once all the corpses were taken away, they were released. He attributed his escape to the fluent Ukrainian with which he was able to address the militiamen. It was from him that we learned of the murder of Rabbi Levin. He was so upset, spasmodically weeping and unable to speak, we had no reason to doubt the story's accuracy.

The Germans drove the Ukrainian militia back to their barracks. Order seemed to have been reinstated and the population calmed. Perhaps the discipline described by Jews of German-occupied western Poland would support an improvement. Still the Ukrainian police had power and their antisemitism was profound. The identity documents (passports) provided by the Russians defined our nationality as *Jewrej* [Jewish in Russian], identifying us as a target. With the help of a razor blade, I was able to falsify our passports, carefully removing lines and changing letters, altering *Jewrej* into *Polack*.

The first test was on Ludwik's passport. He was intercepted by the Ukrainian police, but his papers passed and he was released. So, I falsified documents for our whole family and many friends. The city walls held notices ordering employees to report back to their normal workplaces. I returned to the trust office. A new order had already been introduced. The Ukrainian, Sekunda, was now the master, self-appointed and sitting at the director's desk. He produced a list of workers who were to be kept; none of the Jewish employees except one, Rotstein, were on the list. I went home depressed. Staying home was dangerous, but without a work certificate, the streets were worse. Germans were picking up Jews on the streets and conscripting them into forced-labor gangs, where they worked under the whip of the SS men. Many stories emerged of Jewish workers never returning home. Rumors abounded that the SS shot them.

For many days, I stayed indoors, nervous and edgy, wondering what I should do. A family friend was organizing a building gang and was looking for more workers. A job, any job, was critical for the work certificate and security it provided. I accepted his offer. My task was to load slaked lime onto a cart. Standing all day in lime pits with a big shovel, separating layers and loading them, was hot, hard work, compounded by offensive smells and air so thick that breathing was difficult. Nevertheless, I was greatly relieved to have work. I did not leave the pit during the day. To be caught at home risked a visit by Ukrainian militia who might take any young men they found.

The Germans introduced regulations discriminating against the Jews. The use of public transport, parks, public toilets, and theaters was prohibited. The most frightening and painfully degrading order was to wear a white armband with a blue Star of David. The punishment for a Jew caught on the street without one was death. Lusia's mother took an old sheet and Lusia cut it into even strips. I located a piece of thick rubber shoe sole, cut out a Jewish star, and, using blue ink, pressed it onto the white material. The whole family was soon equipped to the satisfaction of the new masters. Street peddlers sold such "decorations" for ten złoty.

The first victim of the new order was Lusia. The Ukrainian militiaman caught her one morning and marched her and a few other Jewish women to a former Soviet barrack, where a German soldier assigned her to a job of cleaning toilets that had been left by the Soviets in an indescribable condition. Late in the evening, she returned home exhausted but happy at least that a German soldier had been pleased enough with her work to give her a loaf of bread. It took hours to rid herself of the stench. The next victim was Lusia's mother. She generally stayed home, too frightened to venture out, but she had not seen her sister for many months. It was cold. She wore her Persian fur coat with the Jewish armband on the sleeve. On the way, an unknown Polish woman attacked her furiously, scratching her face till it was covered in blood. Lusia's mother rushed home in tears.

The Germans established a Jewish Council, a *Judenrat*, as well as a Jewish militia, the *Ordnungsdienst*, known as the OD. I was on my way to work one morning when a car stopped in front of me and an OD man jumped out. He demanded my *Arbeitsausweis* [work certificate]. He examined it with contempt and opened the back door of his car, leaving me no choice but to get in. An SS man sat behind the wheel, which terrified me. Another man sat in the back seat, tall and good looking. He was, I later discovered, a violinist and music teacher. Not knowing where we were being taken, we sat silently, too terrified to talk. Arriving at Stryjski Park area, Lwów's most affluent district, the car pulled up outside a magnificent villa. The elegantly dressed SS officer led us toward the shed. Handing me a saw, which he had taken from the car, the German pointed, and we understood he wanted us to saw the logs. I felt relieved, as in our home village I had cut and chopped wood for many years of winter fires. I actually enjoyed it. So did ex-Kaiser Wilhelm II after losing World War I and retiring in Holland.

The saw I had been given was useless, however, with a handle at one end only, while on the other hung a piece of string. It was absolutely blunt. I summoned my courage and followed the SS man who had gone into the house already. After a while he opened the door. What did I want? "The saw is useless," I told him. "But if you would give me permission to leave the job, I could probably procure a better one." On condition that I would leave my colleague as a hostage, he agreed I could go.

Taking the useless saw with me, I hurried home to tell Lusia where I was and arrange for someone to go and inform the musician's family, because we didn't know how long we would be detained or what would happen to us later. The most difficult challenge was locating a new saw. Neither we nor any of our neighbors had one, and there was no possibility of buying one. My only chance was Rotstein, who was in charge of the store at the trust, as Sekonda had generously retained him.

I hurried to my old office and was lucky to find Rotstein at his desk. Still rosy cheeked and chubby, perhaps 22 or 23 years old, he was glad to see me. I had always been nice to him, liked him, and talked with him on a personal level. He was proud of our friendship. Showing him my saw, I explained my problem. Hadn't there been a new saw in one of the back rooms? Luckily it was still there, but he was conflicted and afraid of Sekunda. He trusted my promise to return it and mustered the courage to agree. I returned in triumph to my concerned and very anxious musician.

I found a trestle in the shed, set a log upon it, and asked the violinist to hold the handle and pull. The poor man did not know what was required. He could not catch the rhythm, and instead of pulling the saw, he pushed it, hampering my efforts. He had the beautiful, delicate long fingers of a violinist, born to play music, not to saw timber. Slowly, I explained that there was a certain similarity between the movements of the saw and the bow, both motions needing lightness, a rhythm without jerking. After a while, we were harmonizing well and the saw bit the timber effectively. After sawing a few logs, he sat down totally exhausted. I let him rest and chopped the wood into smaller pieces. The SS man came to inspect our work, asking why the violinist wasn't working. I explained we only had one axe, thus he was piling up the chopped wood.

The work lasted for over a week. Since the productivity of my partner was negligible, I had to work for both of us. The German scoundrel for whom we worked didn't even throw us a crust of bread. We brought food from home after the first day. Returning home each day, I would carry the old saw as proof of my employment. The new saw I hid well beneath the logs. I didn't allow the violinist to touch my axe. He tried once and almost injured his knee. To restore his self-respect, he told me of his musical successes and tried to explain the theory of music. To his disappointment, I did not show any interest.

I finished the job alone, putting the chopped timber in neat piles along the walls in several rows. I heaped some chips for kindling in a corner, swept the shed, and invited the SS man to inspect. Instead of praise, a loaf of bread, or thanks, all I got was a bark: "Scum, you dirty Jew." At the end of the job, I returned the saw to Rotstein, who was getting worried about its return. I took the old saw and never went out without it, finding it excellent protection against roaming Nazis and Ukrainian police.

Increasingly, food became scarce. We were required to queue for food. Rations for Jews were half the Polish rations, which were in turn smaller than those for Germans. A loaf of bread on the black market was ten złoty, an amount nearly impossible to earn. Milk for children was scarce. Lusia's father queued from dawn, often returning home empty-handed.

One day, I befriended a fellow in a bread queue who had means of buying fresh milk. As he was leaving Lwów, he told me the source. I decided to accompany him on his last trip. I took my armband off (a move punishable according to German order by death) as the woman selling the bread would not deal with anyone wearing a Jewish star, and we walked about an hour from town. She was a good woman, living in an isolated little house, and she owned one cow. She filled our milk containers with warm milk, and we returned to town. I put the armband back on as we approached. It was a relief when I got safely home. Each day that I took this walk, without the armband and with the container in my hand, I was very afraid.

During the 20 months of Soviet occupation, Lwów Jewry had been economically devastated. The once-affluent class had been dispossessed, and the poor were poorer than ever. The Nazis, in addition to their constant and targeted cruelty, imposed a levy of 20 million rubles on Lwów Jewry. To ensure that the money (an enormous sum under prevailing conditions) would be paid in time, the Germans took ten leading members of the community as hostages. Under this pressure and in the hope that by raising the ransom they would be left in peace, the Jewish population organized an unprecedented effort to collect the money. As a volunteer, the collection committee gave me a list of addresses to call on. Poor people gave what they could. I recall one woman wanting to give me the only valuable thing she possessed – a feather pillow! People sold their belongings and Poles and Ukrainians took advantage, obtaining goods at ridiculously low prices. Sadly, some prosperous people on my list claimed they had no cash, asking me to call again. A well-known jeweler from Kraków was expected to contribute a thousand at least. After three visits to his beautiful apartment, and only with great persuasion on my part, could I extract a mere 100 rubles. A not uncommon experience with the wealthy.

Within the newly established *Judenrat*, an *Arbeitsamt* [Labor

Exchange] was formed to supply Jewish workers for the various branches of the German occupation authorities. All Jewish citizens between the ages of 14 and 60 had to register. Some of the workplaces they were sent to were tolerable, yet most were unbearable. Where one was sent was a matter of luck or the right connections. It was possible, however, for the amount of ten złoty per day (the price of a loaf of bread), to employ another to work in one's place. A few times, I did pay this fee, but having no job and not too many rubles left, I decided one day to join the forced-labor force, hoping for the best.

A Jewish militiaman ordered us to get into line like soldiers and march. A wretched Jewish "army." Men of all ages, sometimes emaciated or at least hungry and pale, sometimes dragging their feet with difficulty, slowly trudged some seven kilometers right into the command of an SS guard within the gates of the now infamous Janowska camp.

Our task was to build a railway siding. Some had to carry gravel to form the ballast; others carried wooden sleepers, placing them in position while my group carried the rails. The work was exhausting as the rails were heavy and many in our group were weak and unsuited for such work. Sometimes when one would grip a rail firmly, it would slip from the hands of others. The supervising SS officer would lose his patience after shouting and lash out with his riding whip. "Offenders" who caught his eye – and he missed very few – immediately felt the searing sting of his whip. I worked unrelentingly, determined to give no cause for punishment, but late in the afternoon I, too, felt that whip on my back several times.

"*Los! Los!* [Come on! come on!]" the SS bully shouted, but there was no way anyone could work faster, their strength depleted and backs bent under heavy loads. At five o'clock, the work stopped. I don't know how I managed the two-hour walk home. The trams were running, but not for Jews. I would not go again, deciding in the future I would pay my ten złoty to another man. A few days later, the Janowska camp was closed, although Jewish workers who were there at the time were detained, and most ultimately perished from hunger or exhaustion. The SS were generous with their bullets and many workers were shot where they stood. Few escaped.[2] I worked in that camp for scarcely eight hours, yet in my thoughts, I often return to that hell on earth. The memory of those poor wretched men, good simple people, working class or educated, intelligent, sensitive, or dumb, ugly or simple, all unified by a profound fear. Every man's eyes fearing a bullet from an SS guard, who was safe in his uniform with a belt buckle carrying the inscription "*Gott mit Uns*" (God with us).

WORKING FOR THE GESTAPO

Early one morning, somebody knocked on the door. It was again Lusia's uncle, Dudzio, this time smiling brightly as he entered. "Dress quickly!" he said. "I have landed a good job and we need a few more laborers. Join me before they get some others. A German truck is waiting outside."

We hurried – my friend Anatol Kahane, who was staying with us since he was thrown out of his flat, Ludwik, and me. Outside, a German soldier sat at the steering wheel, and next to him a lieutenant of the German army, a Silesian, who spoke excellent Polish. We were driving to a German base in Raclawicka Street, a most elegant district of Lwów. Entering a big house, the lieutenant ordered a real feast of a breakfast for us: rye bread, butter, marmalade, and coffee. He was talkative and very polite. He was sorry, he said, that he had to make us work but assured us he would make every effort to see we were satisfied. He gave the impression of being a decent person despite his German uniform.

We worked on this job for many weeks. Every day after breakfast at Raclawicka Street, we would be driven off in a lorry, Dudzio, Ludwik, Tolek myself and one or two other young jews occasionally picked up in the street. We would drive to a Jewish apartment from which the owners presumably had been taken the night before by the Gestapo. We loaded their furniture and other contents into a truck and unloaded it at another address. We were the official furniture removers for the Gestapo! Ludwik and Tolek were strong and efficient and carried the heavy items. I tackled the lighter furniture. Dudzio was exceptionally clumsy, so we gave him bedding, curtains, and quilts. The Germans watched us closely, shouting "*Los, Los! Schnell! Schnell!*" From time to time, somebody would be hit on the back, but on the whole, we had no reason to complain. We knew it could be considerably worse.

At lunchtime, we would return to base, where the Germans employed a Polish cook. She was a plump, friendly woman of about 50 who showed us much sympathy, cooking us a good thick pea soup served up with some stale bread that the Germans wouldn't eat. Worn out, we sat on the kitchen floor eating every last morsel, even licking the bowl! As soon as we finished, another job required us. The lieutenant was a cool customer, rather polite, but he treated us comparatively well. The fact we spoke German was in our favor. He appeared somewhat embarrassed when he learned that Kahane was also an electrical engineer. Nevertheless, relaxation after the meal could not be allowed and, although dog-tired, we had to hasten to the next task.

One day, after driving us to a vacant apartment, the Germans entered first as usual and after a quick look called us in. The flat was still "warm" – we could tell someone had only recently slept in the bed, leaving sleepers beneath it. They had clearly taken the owners early that morning, suddenly and presumably unexpectedly. While shifting furniture, we heard the cry of a child and saw a boy of six or seven standing on the footpath just outside the window. He was weeping, calling out, "Mummy, mummy, mummy?" I was packing the contents of the cupboards into the crates and paused, taking two chairs outside to place in the truck. While the Germans were not watching, I asked a neighbor I could see looking from the window what happened. Full of terror, the neighbor told me how very early that morning the Gestapo had arrived, had taken the family, but had left the boy. The poor child had been standing at the window crying ever since. I hurried over, picked up the child, still crying for his mother, and handed him to the compassionate neighbor through the window.

Returning to the flat, I found our two young coworkers taking the beds to pieces. Under one of the beds, they had found a 20-kilo bag of flour, which they were trying to sneak through the entrance. I was in time to stop them. The soldier on guard looked humane. The cries of the child could still be heard. I braced myself before appealing to his conscience. "The parents have been taken and the child has been left without any means," I said. "The neighbors will take care of him. Would you agree that this bag of flour be given to them so they can feed the child till his parents return?"

He did not hesitate. "Of course, why not?" he said. I picked up the bag, ran out into the street, and gave the flour to the neighbor, who on receiving it quickly disappeared from the window.

The loading of the furniture complete, the Germans sealed the door. The Quartermaster General's Office would assign apartments stripped of Jews and furniture to newly arriving Germans. All furniture and other contents such as carpets, crystal, porcelain, and silver, often valuable, were the spoils of the Gestapo.

In the afternoon, we moved on to another job, but the cries of that poor child haunted me for many nights.

Occasionally, we had to collect confiscated Jewish furniture from a general store and install it for German use in ex-Jewish apartments. First, we had to disinfect the flats. This required sealing the windows tightly with wide adhesive tape. Then, the Germans would spray insecticides in the apartment and hastily leave, closing the doors firmly behind them. After a while, we had to rush in to unseal and open the windows. Sometimes, the windows were stuck and we could not avoid inhaling some of the poisons, which left us coughing for a long time afterward. At that time, of course, we had no knowledge of the existence of gas chambers.

Our life was difficult but bearable. For six days a week, we were occupied. We had become an efficient team of furniture removalists. As long as we worked under the supervision of our Germans, things were not too bad. When they "lent" us to the Gestapo, as they sometimes did, we never knew if we would get home safely or be shot on the spot.

Members of the Gestapo insisted on having only the best-quality furniture and had considerable expertise in this area. As a result, Jewish families occupying beautiful or well-furnished apartments lived in greater-than-average danger of arrest. There were informers –

even some Jews among them – who knew people or addresses and passed on such information to save themselves.

Our work was hard and often the riding crop was applied. I received a thrashing once. The Gestapo had led us to a beautifully furnished apartment on the second floor. There was a heavy antique wardrobe and the Gestapo man ordered me and another worker to take it down. With difficulty, we managed to move it onto the landing, but lifting and carrying it down was extremely difficult. I grabbed the front, the other took the back, and we started to descend. The piece was very heavy, but we managed to move it carefully so we would not scratch it. The Gestapo man was descending ahead of me, watching my every move. But the huge robe was beyond my strength and I could feel it slipping from my hands. I knew if I let that happen, it would be the end of me. I was covered with cold sweat as the Nazi roared at me, "Los! Los!"

Suddenly my partner broke down and his end of the wardrobe crashed onto the stairs. The Gestapo man jumped toward the poor fellow, but as I was still holding the wardrobe, I was blocking his way. Being the nearest victim, he dealt me a terrific slap on the face, then another, till I felt dizzy, but still, I did not let go. Ludwik, who had been watching tensely, jumped and grabbed the rear of the wardrobe while Kahane took hold of the center, and the three of us managed to get a hold of it and load it on the truck. The Gestapo bully calmed down while we carried the remaining furniture downstairs. I returned home with a swollen face, but alive!

Any jobs carried out by Ludwik, Kahane, and me were accomplished quickly and efficiently. The Germans seemed pleased with us. Problems arose whenever additional Jewish workers joined us. Then there was shouting, cursing, and sometimes beatings.

The German-created *Judenrat* had gradually developed into a large organization controlling all aspects of life in the Jewish community. It was like a miniature Jewish state with its own government, police, and various departments but ultimately answerable to the German authorities. About 4,000 of the 150,000[1] Jews in Lwów were employed as clerks, laborers, and policemen, with some 700 Jews in the last category.

Many well-known and respected Jewish citizens were participating in the Judenrat. One of them was Dr. Zarwincer, who had once been employed as a senior solicitor in my uncle's law office. I knew him well. During a chance meeting in the street, he told me that Jewish public figures, including himself, had only reluctantly agreed to work for the Judenrat. The Germans had threatened that unless they agreed to serve, unscrupulous characters would be appointed instead who would surely cause greater harm. The elite of Lwów's intelligentsia therefore agreed. All of them spoke excellent German, and it was assumed this would afford them some respect. In addition to the labor exchange, departments were established for maintenance, health, social services, provisions, and housing.

The Judenrat was considering the establishment of a building department that would deal with the maintenance and repair of buildings assigned to the Jewish Quarter. Dr. Zarwincer offered to move my nomination to head this department. Apart from the salary in cash and assured food rations, the employees of the Judenrat had a "bulletproof Ausweis" for themselves and their families that would protect them from all kinds of German chicanery. Dr. Zarwincer promised to let me know, but luckily for me, the offer never came through. Maybe I would have let myself be persuaded by the excellent conditions, but I am sure I would have perished, as did almost all functionaries of the Judenrat, including Dr. Zarwincer.

I was not the only furniture removalist among the Jews. I returned home from work one evening to find that our chairs were gone. The family told me that a Jewish policeman had called and taken them away to the German stores. My distress was not so much for the loss of the chairs but the 50-dollar banknote I had hidden in the upholstery of one. I had been keeping the money for an emergency, as lives often depended on having some money on hand. I was very upset.

I decided to locate the chairs. Through careful inquiries, I found the address of the store where the last day's "catch" had been unloaded. The official director of the store was a German, but a young Jew was actually managing it. When I told him my problem, he led me to the German director, a fat, jovial man who was just having his breakfast. "*Herr* Director," my young friend addressed him, "this man has come to see if any of yesterday's furniture requires any repairs. Shall I take him to have a look?"

The fat man nodded his approval. I was amazed at the enormous quantity of goods. There were dining room suites, bedroom suites, children's furniture, writing desks, leather armchairs, office furniture, stacks of mattresses, mountains of chairs, and other items all carefully arranged. I doubted that so much expensive furniture had ever been amassed in one building anywhere in all of prewar Poland. I was lucky. Our chairs were right in front. I soon picked out the one I was seeking. The $50 banknote was still there! My Jewish companion smiled. I thanked him heartily, offering him a box of cigarettes, which he refused. He was glad, he said, that we had succeeded. He did not ask the value of my treasure.

In October 1941, the Germans ordered all Jews in German-occupied territories to be "herded" into ghettos. The Lwów Ghetto was to be separated from the rest of the town by a closed railway line. Over each of the four streets leading to the Ghetto was a bridge, but only the one at Peltewna Street was to remain open for Jews. It became known as the "Bridge of Death." The German gendarmerie and the Ukrainian militia would guard the bridge. And so Jews began slowly streaming into the ghetto. In carts, wheelbarrows, prams, suitcases, knapsacks, and bundles, they carried the pitiful remnants of their possessions. At the checkpoint under the bridge, the guards stopped each person, letting the healthy and able pass but separating the elderly and ill, among whom were many women and children. Documents were checked, and those lacking a valid work certificate were piled onto trucks and sent to the Janowska Street concentration camp. Several thousand victims would perish there.

    The order to move into the ghetto paralyzed our family with fear. We had been living more or less comfortably at Chmielowskiego Street in the Aryan district. The thought of transferring the whole family, our elderly and ill parents, and the small children, Elżunia and Felus, to the dirt, stench, and misery of a ghetto filled me with horror. We decided not to move until forced. Although Ludwik and I were working, money to buy adequate food for the family was still a big problem. We decided to sell some of our "treasures".

    I inquired around and found a young Jewish woman who, with the help of her boyfriend – a German army truck driver – was trading Persian carpets. She bought two of our best at an absurdly low price, but I was glad to be able to sell them. She also bought our silver cutlery, offering very little. Lusia's beautiful grand piano, a Blüthner, had already been sold for next to nothing some months ago.

I had one thing left that would fetch a reasonably good price: my greatly cherished stamp collection. Many Germans were passionate philatelists, so gradually and reluctantly, I sold my whole collection. I had the help of a Pole, who had the contact and who likely took the lion's share of the sale. Gradually having sold all our valuables, we looked with great concern into a dark future. We lived from day to day.

SURRENDERING THE JEWISH FURS

The summer had long since passed and the chill of autumn warned of the approaching winter. My family was still together and we had not had a single visit from either the Ukrainian militia or the German gendarmes. The Hitlerite bestialities taking place in the Jewish district had not reached us. Nor were we suffering from hunger. There was always some milk or an egg for the children, and some kasha for the adults.

We continued working for "our" Germans. Preparing for the winter, they brought in coal and wood, which had to be sawed and chopped. That was my responsibility. Ludwik and Tolek Kahane were building henhouses. Unfortunately, our Germans had decided to keep their own geese and chickens and a piglet to be fed on scraps from the kitchen – food that until now had been ours to eat or take home. Still, we never went home empty-handed, loading our pockets with food or coal, preparing for winter. Our Germans also managed to store a stock of potatoes in the cellar. We helped ourselves occasionally, taking them home in our pockets. The Germans must have noticed something because Ludwik and Tolck were ordered to secure the gates and install locks on the cellar. It was our last chance. The evening before the cellar was to be locked, Lusia walked past the house with Elżunia in her stroller and, at the right moment, Ludwik and Tolck scrambled out of the cellar with a bag of potatoes, which they quickly placed in the stroller. With Elżunia on top, her mother hurried on, disappearing quickly. We celebrated our success with some wonderful potato soup seasoned with stolen onions.

As time passed, there was less and less work for us. I was the first to be dismissed. Ludwik and Tolck continued working for a little longer since they had proved to be excellent workers and skilled in many fields. When finally, their jobs finished, our German boss recommended them to the army transport depot, the Heeres Kraft-Park, where they worked for a few months under the protection of a special armband bearing the letters *HK* and an excellent Ausweis. I remained without work, and the validity of my Ausweis was due to expire. I dreaded to think what would happen then. Raids on the unemployed had not stopped and the labor camp on Janowska Street was continually swelling with new victims. The thousands who had perished had to be replaced. Going out was dangerous, but sitting at home was even more so.

I was getting desperate. One day I met a young architect, Stamberger, whom I had helped years earlier with a technical problem in Kraków. Because I had refused payment for my services, he had sent me a beautiful vase with a sprig of wattle (mimosa), which in those days was imported from Italy. It was an exquisite gift. He was glad to see me and inquired how I was getting on. When I mentioned my problem, he asked if I would like to work as a builder's laborer. Naturally, I eagerly accepted.

Stamberger had graduated from a Kraków technical school with a certain Mr. Weglarski, a Pole of German origin who ran the Lwów branch of a building company. They had several building contracts, the largest being the reconstruction of the main railway station. Stamberger took me to the company's office and, after only a few minutes, I left equipped with a document certifying my employment by the Johann Pontess Building Company. Further, my papers stated that this building was important to the "war effort" and that the bearer of the document must not be molested or employed by any other organization.

Deliriously happy, I ran home to share the good news with the family. Everyone read and admired the precious piece of paper, typewritten in German on a most impressive German letterhead.

Early the next morning, I reported to the site office. The official supervising engineer was an elderly Pole with a gray goatee beard, but the work was actually managed by a Jewish engineer, Witold Markus. He received me rather coldly, but then in the course of conversation, it turned out we had lived in the same apartment block in Kraków – Lenartowicza 17. I remembered meeting him sometimes in the lift. He had always been reserved – silent and unsmiling. Now he sat behind his desk with a Jewish armband on his sleeve.

He directed me to the job foreman, Bednarski, who, with an unfriendly look, paired me with Stefan Gold, a young solicitor from Kraków. We were entrusted with the important job of carrying sand. With a wooden stretcher and two shovels, we labored for days at the monotonous task of loading sand, carrying it ten meters, then unloading it onto a heap of gravel while Bednarski shouted and threatened. Other slaves were entrusted with gravel or cement or mixed it into concrete to be carried in wheelbarrows and poured into formwork. The labor brigade was composed entirely of beginners like me, many of whom did not even know how to grip a shovel. Their hard work was inefficient, so they quickly ran out of breath while hoping Bednarski would not notice while they paused. The foreman watched with a hostile eye, but we were doing our honest best. For some he let us be, for others, he shared his ire. He might come running out unexpectedly, hitting with his whip.

His favorite victim was Preminger, a Jewish boy barely 17 or 18 who infuriated Bednarski whether he was working or not. Preminger had to carry heavy iron rods without protective gloves and only rags to protect his hands, which by then were rubbed raw. I could stand it no longer and approached Bednarski, suggesting this work was too hard for the boy. Bednarski heard me out, remembering a few days earlier I had drawn attention to a fault in the layout of steel reinforcement. I enjoyed that episode greatly. Bednarski had stared at me, surprised that I should have this kind of knowledge because Engineer Markus had not told him I was an engineer. He made good the mistake immediately, and from that time on, he behaved politely toward me, appearing almost embarrassed when giving me orders.

I tried to explain to him that among his laborers were people of various professions, as well as university and high school students, who had never done this kind of work and suffered hunger and constant fear – and that many were exhausted before they started.

While he and other Poles could use the trams, the Jews had to walk, often great distances, and so arrived already tired before starting their heavy work. I called Preminger over and asked him to take the rags off his hands. They were raw and bleeding. Bednarski said nothing, but after lunch he transferred Preminger to the store, tasking him with sorting screws and nails according to size. Bednarski kept him in the store till his hands had healed, then assigned him another easy job.

The next day, I brought Bednarski a box of cigarettes. He accepted and even thanked me. It was a precious gift. From then on, he stopped beating the Jewish workers, though his curses, *Kurwa twoja mac zydowska* [your Jewish mother is a whore], could still be heard all over the building site. The workers welcomed his scolding, since by hearing his voice in one corner, they could steal a few moments of rest in another.

Preminger always smiled with gratitude whenever we met and tried to be of help. Indeed, the time would come when his help would prove invaluable.

Speculators, railway workers, and guards – anyone who could – dealt in the black market. Food was smuggled in by train. The Jews of Lwów were starving. But the ingenious Preminger always managed to get something for me. Sometimes a loaf of bread, a few onions, or a cabbage, sometimes a chicken, a piece of meat, or cheese. I paid his price. If he made a profit, good for him. Sometimes I would give him a piece of clothing in exchange for food. While I rested during the half-hour lunch break, Preminger would run around the railway station looking for food. He never returned empty-handed. From time to time, Bednarski received a few cigarettes and so disregarded our activities.

After some time, I stopped carrying sand as I was needed for more "professional" work. I was ordered to take stock of all timber in the yard and given steel tape, a pencil, and a writing block. Relaxing my weary body, I took Stefan Gold as my assistant. Occasionally, I would sit down and work out the totals, keeping my writing block on my knees. This arrangement was considered not satisfactory for me to accomplish my work, so I was transferred to the office, making quite an advancement from laborer to white-collar worker. The pay remained the same, though, and as a Jewish laborer, it was trifling.

My desk was near the entrance, and during lunchtime, Preminger would appear discreetly in the doorway to deliver the smuggled food.

This was not unnoticed by my new colleagues. Joe Abrahamer, also from Kraków, was the company bookkeeper. He was married with a child and was also interested in buying additional food, as was Engineer Markus. Both, from time to time, happily used the services of Preminger.

Walking home after a long workday with a military satchel full of food was not easy. I dressed simply as became a laborer, wearing my Jewish armband, and walked on the roadway close to the pavement. This was safest as I did not obstruct the passage of pedestrians, among whom were Germans who would not hesitate to hit a Jew. I had to be continuously alert and prepared for police raids and document checks. A few potatoes or a piece of black bread in my satchel could perhaps be forgiven, but the presence of a piece of meat or lard posed an immediate threat of being locked up at Janowska. Buying on the black market was forbidden on penalty of death, even for Poles. So, on those walks home I remained tense and acutely observant, like a hare. At the sight of a stationary military truck or a gathering of people, I would stop until I could ascertain from passersby that nothing threatening was happening. Sometimes I would shelter in the entrance of a block of flats, disappearing from the street until it was safe, sometimes waiting there for up to an hour. My journey home lasted over an hour and a half, sometimes two hours. Every time I arrived it was with a racing pulse, wondering when I knocked on the door of our flat if everybody was all right. Was my family intact?

Many atrocities occurred over those weeks. The Ukrainian militia and the German gendarmerie were entering Jewish homes and taking away whomever they chose, an elderly father or mother, a wife with child. My family had documents certifying that I worked at the railway station. Lusia had a false work certificate. My mother had a certificate stating that her brother worked for the army and Elżunia's nanny, Zosia Janicka, worked in a military hospital from where she would occasionally bring some thin soup for Elżunia and Felix. But we still feared the raids. I knew of many cases where exhausted Jewish laborers had returned home to find their parents, wife, and children taken away.

One day, a huge, obese, heavily armed giant of a German gendarme entered our flat. Luckily, Lusia was at home. He inspected all the rooms, including the kitchen, which Lusia had just thoroughly cleaned as that was on her schedule for the day. The German investigated each corner, touching everything – the gas stove, the table, the cooking utensils. In the end, he declared that he was not taking anybody because of the exemplary cleanliness of the kitchen. Thus, did human life depend on the whim of a German gendarme.

Had we had such a visit today? Was everybody at home? These were my thoughts as I waited for our door to open. When at last someone approached the door, I would feel as if a stone had been lifted from my heart. We had survived one more day. How many such days were left for us?

Winter was unpleasant. The distance to work seemed to lengthen, but I was lucky to be working in an office where we had an iron stove and plenty of wood cuttings from the building work. The Jewish workers outside, malnourished and poorly dressed, froze. Human efficiency decreased and work progressed slowly. Consequently, the firm requested that the client, a company named Ostbahn [Eastern Railways] should supply more workers. Trucks arrived and unloaded work brigades from the Janowska camp. How miserable they looked! They were skeletons, eyes devoid of expression, with swollen, sore cheeks and feet wrapped in rags. Even Bednarski stopped shouting.

"How can I be expected to finish this building with these people?" he complained confidentially to me. "They are walking cadavers, and even shouting at them would be useless." At last, his humanity was stirred. "Those German sons of bitches! They will not escape God's punishment, and may it come soon!" he muttered.

"As soon as they finish with us, they will start with the Poles. That is Hitler's plan," I reminded him. He remained silent.

During the lunch break, the Janowska camp slaves sat down to some watery soup and crumbs of bread. They had their own tin plates and spoons. One poor creature settled near the entrance to our office. He looked terrible. His eyes watered, his mouth dripping saliva, as he wailed, "Hungry! Hungry! Hungry!" I gave him part of my lunch. He swallowed it in a second and then continued wailing, "Hungry!" Then one day he did not turn up. The Germans finished anyone off who ceased to be capable of working. They would squeeze the last drop of energy from a man, then put him on the train headed for the Belzec extermination camp or shoot him on the spot. They worked under the supervision of a Kapo, a Jewish supervisor, who had to watch to prevent their escape, as if there was any way to do so. Under German law, the penalty of death threatened anyone who helped a Jew. The Kapo's life was a bit better than that of the other slaves. He was slightly better dressed and did not have to work other than to dispense soup, and he looked considerably healthier than his charges.

At times, the Kapo would come to our office to warm himself. There, he would talk, describing life in the camp – shocking stories of the sadistic treatment of prisoners, shootings, tortures, and daily beatings. It was hard to believe. He was responsible, with his life, for the return of each and every man. Once he asked me to post a letter from Wilhaus, a famous assistant camp commander, to his mother in Germany. The temptation was too great and I opened it carefully and read. It was an innocent letter from a loving son to his mother. How tenderly he inquired about her health! About himself he wrote little, other than that he was well but had trouble with the Jews who were lazy and didn't show much eagerness to work. But, he wrote, he had shown them how to labor. That German mother must have worried about the troubles inflicted on her dear son by the wretched Jews. Perhaps she was never aware that his Jews were dying of hunger and exhaustion, and her dear boy was finishing them off with the butt of his pistol! "I kiss you, dear Mother. Heil Hitler!" were the closing tender words of this felon. We all read it. Then I closed it carefully and posted it. Why cause trouble for the poor Kapo should the letter not reach its destination?

With lightning speed, the German armies were progressing into the center of Russia, followed by the SS and SD (Sicherheitsdienst, the Nazi intelligence service) units trained for the mass murder of the Jews. The further east they moved, the bloodier became their methods. The Russian Jews were completely unprepared, paralyzed by the shock. Hundreds of thousands of defenseless souls perished during the six months of that German attack.

By December 1941, within sight of Leningrad and Moscow, the German offensive slowed down. They were far from their own country, in the midst of a severe Russian winter unforeseen by the German High Command, and they were not prepared. An order was issued requiring Jews, both men and women, to immediately surrender their furs because the Germans were freezing. "General Winter" had made himself felt. We heard the news with satisfaction. Should we give our furs or let them freeze? Of course, we had no choice! The furs were surrendered because withholding them was punishable by death, except I gave Lusia's fur coat to a Polish friend for safekeeping. There was a story circulating that while reviewing a military parade of frontline soldiers, Hitler was booed instead of receiving the usual military salutes. When the angry Führer inquired what the meaning of this was, his bodyguard drew his attention to the fact he was wearing a Jewish star on the sleeve of his fur coat. Jews were dying, but Jewish humor was still very much alive.

Working at the railway station enabled us to observe the movements of the German war machine. Heavily loaded freight trains were hurrying eastward with tanks, armored cars, and artillery. The Russian front was swallowing masses of war material. There were also transports in the opposite direction – long trains marked with the Red Cross symbol, full of wounded soldiers. There were innumerable cases of frostbite; the Jewish fur coats had been of little use. The Germans were starting to taste the hell of war. The blitzkrieg was over.

After giving up their fur coats, the Jews again fooled themselves that they would have some respite. They went to work and labored hard. They were optimistic and believed the German war machine needed those 100,000 Jewish workers, and that except for some chicanery and occasional beatings, nothing should threaten their lives. Nobody dreamed that Hitler's plans for a "Final Solution" – the murder of the entire European Jewry – was to be executed.

Yet by early March 1942, frightening stories started to emerge. Jews from small towns were being deported to an unknown destination. There were apparently messages that these deported Jews were working on the land and were in good health, but I knew nobody who had actually seen such letters. Special German commando units called *Einsatzgruppen* were handling the deportations. One gloomy day we heard these units had arrived in Lwów. Terror befell Lwów Jewry.

No one knew who the victims would be. Some said that the old and sick, incapable of work – the so-called unproductive elements – would be deported. The Germans demanded the cooperation of the Judenrat and the Jewish militia, who had no choice but to comply. Quotas were imposed, lists were drawn up. Each Jewish militiaman had to bring in a certain number of people or his own family would be deported. It was announced that the deportees had the right to take with them some clothing, food, and 200 złoty per person. We had Lusia's parents, both old and sick, and my mother at home. Deportation for them would equal death. We were panic stricken, listening in constant dread as the vicious roundups continued. There were new victims daily. The so-called "March action" was in full swing.

We lived on the mezzanine floor and one night heard knocking on our window. Carefully, we opened it. Below stood the Ferbers, parents of Anda Henzhaft, our friend from Kraków. With them were two Jewish militiamen. We were puzzled by such a visit but dared not go downstairs to the front door. There was only one other way to rescue them, through the window, but Mother Ferber was an obese lady and it took quite a while before the militiamen managed to hoist her to our window. Her husband was tall and lean and followed easily.

When we had calmed them a little, they told us what happened. Their names had been on the list of deportees, but they had bribed the militiamen. They could not remain in their flat so had requested the militiamen to bring them to us.

It was not uncommon for Jewish victims to retain their freedom through bribery. The Germans took bribes in all forms. Even members of the Gestapo took bribes. Sometimes they took the bribes and then made no effort to help those who had just bribed them. Sometimes they would take Jewish hostages, demand huge ransoms, receive the money, and still murder them. A friend of ours had been taken by the Gestapo and a $20 banknote was the bribe required to free him. His family begged me to help as I knew it was possible to buy gold or dollars on the black market. One Sunday afternoon, when the Germans were resting, I ventured into the Jewish district carrying my saw, the symbol of my work for the Germans. Many strange types strolled along the streets, mumbling softly in undertones, "Tea, coffee, tea, coffee," while others in a similar tone advertised, "Gold, dollars, ..." Some looked like brigands. Others I suspected to be conmen or simply criminals.

I regretted having undertaken the mission, but on the other hand, I thought I might learn things, as one day I might need to do the same. I came across a decent-looking Jew and heard the murmurings "Gold, dollars, gold, dollars." He spoke Polish quite well and seemed trustworthy enough. Yes, he had dollars and could sell me a $20 bill. When he quoted a price, I argued a little, and he agreed to lower it by a few rubles. He asked me to wait. I felt uneasy, fearing he might return with a German. But after a while, he returned and produced the money. Inspecting it, it seemed to me to be genuine, although I was no expert in the field. He then took it back quickly, folded it several times, and hid it in his palm so no one could see it. I started counting my money, and when I had almost finished, he skillfully squeezed the bill into a partition of my open wallet, advising me to leave the area immediately, because there might be a *razzia* [raid]. He disappeared, and so did I, grateful I had managed to purchase the dollars at a lower price than expected.

Suddenly, the price aroused my suspicion. I stepped into a house entrance to have another look at the bill. At first sight of the crisp, green, neatly folded bill, I felt relief, until, to my consternation, I unfolded the note and discovered that it was a $1 and not a $20 bill!

I returned immediately to the scene of our transaction, looking for the scoundrel, but, of course, in vain. I had been robbed of an enormous amount, about 4,000 rubles (my monthly salary at the mill was only 650 rubles). I did not want to admit my calamity to anybody but Lusia, who accepted it with her usual calmness. We pondered how we could obtain the money to make up for such a loss. In the end, we decided I would have to sell the rest of my stamp collection. The cost of my experience was high indeed.

The next day, I again went to the Jewish district. This time I was more careful. The Gestapo man accepted the banknote. My arrested friend, however, was not seen again. During the March roundup, according to German statistics, a further 15,000 people were deported. Lwów Jewry was rapidly dwindling.

There were rumors of a death factory in Belzec near Rawa-Ruska, but who wanted to believe such rumors? Even so, after the last "action," the Jewish community once again calmed down and their incorrigible optimism returned. "The Germans have cleared Lwów of non-productive elements. The remainder will live and work," suggested some Germans in private conversations, and the Jews believed them.

The building work at the railway continued normally. One day, I found a letter addressed to me on my desk, written in an unschooled handwriting. Whom could it be from? Opening it, I glanced at the signature – Preminger. For some days, he had been absent from work, but I had been too affected by the last action to notice. Intrigued, I began to read:

Dear Mr. Reiss,

I was captured in the last action and loaded with others onto a freight train. The train stopped after three or four hours at the Belzec station. We were unloaded and segregated. Old people, women, and children were taken away and led to a building. What happened there, I don't know. Together with a few more young people, I was taken to work. We had to sort clothing and load it into railway trucks. A gendarme supervised us. At a moment when his attention was distracted, I crept under the bales of clothing and froze motionless. As others continued to load, I felt an almost unbearable weight but somehow managed to withstand it. At last, the train moved. I managed to creep up from underneath the bales, break part of a wooden board on the wagon's side wall, and jump off the moving train. I don't know what happened to the people left at the camp. Do you think they were killed? Where were those masses of clothes from?

He had found a job with a local peasant and would not be returning to Lwów. I showed the letter to my friends and its contents left us speechless. So, the stories about Belzec were not a rumor. The transfer of people to work on the land was a callous lie designed to hide an awful truth – there appeared to be full-scale mass murder. Genocide.

Depressed, I returned home to share this ghastly news. What should we do to save ourselves? We wanted to believe these things would pass us by. Didn't the Germans need us, the workers?

I had made many contacts through my work at the railway station. Joe Abrahamer and I shared our many problems and worries, and even Engineer Markus lost his aloofness in light of our common danger. From time to time, I noticed he was visited by a young, pleasant-looking man whose name I learned was Emil Sawczyn. They conversed only in whispers. Sawczyn was Ukrainian. They knew each other from Kraków, where Markus had employed him as caretaker for his block of flats. After the annexation of eastern Galicia to the General Government, Sawczyn had moved to Lwów, while his wife had remained in Kraków, taking over the caretaking work. With the traditional respect for the house owner, Sawczyn remained loyal to Engineer Markus.

Thanks to my knowledge of the Ukrainian language, I had managed to become friendly with Sawczyn. His respect for Markus reflected, to some extent, on me being Markus's colleague. Sometimes I would give him small gifts such as cigarettes or a mechanical pencil and, after supplying Markus, he would sell me any surplus food he had. There were times he would bring something to our home, where he met Lusia and fell in love with Elżunia, then four years old and looking like a little angel. I spoke to him about my village that I had loved so much, about people who had worked for us and had taught me the Ukrainian language, songs, and customs. One day, Sawczyn assured me that, though his first duty was toward Engineer Markus, I would be the next to whom he would be glad to offer all possible help should it be required. I was touched by that expression of friendship, which he was to keep in a time of future emergency.

My second contact made at that time was Stanislaw Wilczek, my friend from Budynin and schoolmate at Sokal High School. We met by chance in the street and, since he lived nearby, he would occasionally drop in. Like many Poles, he was smuggling food to Lwów and sometimes would bring us some "spoils." We were delighted to see him and would buy whatever he brought.

Implementation of the ghetto ordinance of the previous October had been postponed from month to month. There were continuing negotiations regarding the borders of the ghetto. The Germans were receiving considerable bribes and so kept postponing the final decisions to close the ghetto. From day to day, we lived with suitcases and sacks ready, thanking God for every day we remained in our home. But we knew that our luck would run out any day and the gates of the ghetto could close behind us, too. We trembled at the thought.

ACTIONS AND THE JEWISH STAR

A fresh registration of workers was ordered. New work certificates, stamps, and armbands with the letter *A* and a serial number were issued. The Germans were trying to delude us and create an atmosphere of trust and stability while preparing further onslaughts. People believed that work, particularly in war-effort institutions, could save their lives. Fortunes were paid for a certificate bearing the letter *A*. Our office had been allotted a limited number. All technical workers and their wives were given the *A* certificate. It was a blessing – a miracle – in our situation. The *A* certificate gave Lusia and me the right to survive. Now it was imperative to find work for my mother so she, too, could have an *A* certificate. She was in good health, very diligent, and willing to do any work.

At that time, an extensive industrial center, the Städtische Werkstatt, or municipal workshop, was created for Jewish women. Salo Tremski (I think that was his name), a Jew from Rzeszow, had somehow established a friendly relationship with the Gestapo to the extent that he was permitted to walk about without his armband. It was with his assistance that the Städtische Werkstatt was established in the center of Lwów in a few empty department stores. The demand for a job was great. Acceptance was conditional upon supplying your own modern sewing machine. Lusia's mother used to sew and mend clothes for the children and had an old Singer that she put at Mother's disposal. The demand for machines was such that prices were exorbitant. At five o'clock one morning, Mother and I joined the queue outside one of the workshops, and on Elżunia's stroller rode the sewing machine. There was already a long line of people, and an even longer one was quickly forming behind us. A long wait had begun, and our mood was not helped by the pitying looks at my mother's old machine or the comments about her age. I realized our chances were slight, but we had to try – her life was at stake.

We moved slowly toward the office where our fate was to be decided. We could see two secretaries and two men sitting at the desks. The men were interviewing candidates and inspecting their sewing machines. They seemed familiar. Of course! One was Izaak Reisler, whom I had met in 1928 on holidays in Tatarow, a mountain health resort. I was then a young man of 21 and, as I had contracted pleurisy, Mother had sent me to the mountains. Reisler was a capable, confident, and ambitious young law student. We spent the holidays together, and though we did not subsequently keep any regular contact, we did meet on occasion at dance parties organized for Jewish students. On completing his law studies, Reisler had married the daughter of Dr. Laib Landau, one of Poland's famous criminal lawyers. His name was famous for the successful defense of the Jew, Stanislaw Steiger, who was falsely accused of an attempt to assassinate President Stanislaw Wojciechowski in 1924.[1] The other man at the desk was David Schechter, or Dudek, as we called him, who had been a member of Zakmik, the Jewish Academic Society of Bushwalkers, with me. We had acted together on the society's Arbitration Committee. I noticed both recognized me, but neither blinked an eye. At the sight of the machine, Reisler made a wry face, but Dudek Schechter quickly asked for Mother's name. The secretary took note, wrote out the Ausweis, and both directors signed it. It was another lucky coincidence. How often had our lives depended on these!

We returned home elated that my mother would now be employed to serve the German war effort. For the time being, we could then continue our "normal" life. I was working at the railway station, Mother at the Städtische Werkstatt, Lusia had her A certificate, and her mother was taking care of the household. My brother, Ludwik, and Anatol Kahane continued working in Heeres Kraft-Park, where they even completed a driving course. Our uncle, Joseph Tilles, worked in the Lwów branch of the Kraków Bank, and Zosia, our nanny, continued at the hospital. So far, the Germans had respected the Haushalt Ausweis, marked by the letter *H*. Each working family had the right to support one family member, an elderly person who managed the household. Based on my work for the railway, Lusia's mother possessed an *H* certificate, but Lusia's father had no valid document. The arrangement was that whenever there was a knock at the front door, he would rush out the back door to the courtyard and hide in the outside toilet.

Despite this "normal" life, sooner or later I felt the Germans would destroy us. Some Jews were fleeing to Warsaw, where they tried to live under false Aryan papers. I, too, had begun to entertain the thought of this alternative. Joseph Abrahamer, with whom we often discussed this subject, was a great supporter of the idea. Our continued stay in Lwów was, in our opinion, suicide. But it was much more difficult for me to consider this seriously. My mother and Lusia's parents were unfit to live on false papers. They were people of the old school, righteous and honest, brought up with centuries-old Jewish morality. None of them knew how to lie or even pretend, particularly Lusia's father, who was too proud a Jew to disguise himself as an Aryan Pole. Also, their looks would easily reveal their origins. It was unthinkable for us to run away and leave them behind. We were their shield, protecting and supporting them. Without us, they would have perished long ago.

The ideal solution would have been to find a Polish family who would hide us until the end of the war. But we had no such Polish family, nor the sum of money that would have been required. The two children also constituted a problem. When in danger, one could run carrying one child, but two? Impossible!

Felus had not been circumcised. Born in the Soviet Union, he had a birth certificate in the name of Felix Smirnow. I felt we could save him by placing him in a monastery. Surely, we could find a convent that would accept a lovely Russian child. But Lusia's father opposed the idea forcefully. "Things won't be as bad as you envisage," he said. "And if they are, he is Jewish and the fate of our people will be his fate, too." Thus, Felus remained with us.

May 1942. Another month was gone. One day, Zosia Janicka's cousin arrived unexpectedly from Kraków. He had come to take Zosia home. She had been with us for almost two years of Soviet occupation and this nearly full year of hell under the German occupation. She longed to be with her family. She had been so helpful and Elżunia loved her so much, but there was nothing we could do, and we parted tearfully. Lusia now took over all the duties relating to the two children, Elżunia, aged four, and Felus, five, in addition to caring for her sickly father and mother. But being Lusia, she managed it all.

Some weeks later, Joe Abrahamer informed me he had obtained Aryan identity papers and was preparing to escape to Warsaw. He offered to give me his contact for false papers, indicating that Engineer Markus and a few other colleagues had also secured some. He advised me to act promptly as obtaining permits for residence in Warsaw was growing more difficult daily. I met the supplier at the railway station during my lunch break. There were several kinds of documents available: genuine and false.

Genuine belonged to people who were either prisoners of war in German or Russian hands, or in the Polish army in London, or had been killed in the war. It was their families who were selling the papers. With genuine papers, if you were caught and your documents were checked, the parish of the birthplace would confirm that the name in question appeared in the register. Some people were lucky. They had access to a friendly priest they knew, and he would give them real birth certificates of deceased persons. Naturally, the purchaser of such papers would have to be transformed into an entirely different person, assuming not only a different name but a different date and place of birth, different names of parents, maiden names of mothers, and so on. Such genuine yet suitable papers were very difficult to obtain, especially for married couples, and therefore more expensive.

Alternatively, false papers were issued with typical Polish names. The advantages of such papers, fabricated to order, were that they could state the actual dates of births or marriage, which were much easier to remember. One could perhaps introduce parents' real names if they didn't sound too Jewish. Such papers were considerably cheaper. The producers had access to blank birth or marriage certificates and filled them out according to the clients' instructions.

After some careful consideration, I decided to buy genuine papers even though there was hardly a chance of obtaining real papers for a couple approximating our ages and with a child. Our supplier brought papers for a couple in the names of Piotr Daraż (born 1906) and Stanislawa Daraż (born 1908). So the dates of birth were approximately right; the birth certificate for the child could be prepared later. Our certificates cost 600 złoty, and for a child an additional 100 złoty. It was not cheap, but I felt had no choice.

On seeing the documents, I was not happy with their quality. The handwriting was careless and the writer had used purple ink, revealing that the certificates were recently issued, doubtless *after* the occupation of Lwów by the Soviets. Purple was the only color available in the territories occupied by the Soviets. I had expected to receive original documents from people who had been forced to sell them. All I got were two poorly falsified copies. Taking the papers home, I hid them carefully, determining to use them only when there was no other way to survive. Fortunately, there was no immediate need for them. At that moment, it seemed as if the Jewish situation in Lwów had somehow stabilized. Maybe the optimists were right. The letter A on the sleeve was being honored; apparently the German war machine did need us.

It was known that the German army was facing difficulties on all fronts. The Eastern Front had slowed down since the Russian defense had stiffened. In Africa, the British Eighth Army, under General Bernard Law Montgomery, routed the attacking Germans and forced their withdrawal. The Allied bombers continued to destroy the industrial centers of Germany. It was therefore difficult to imagine, with the German war machine needing endless supplies of labor and material, that the Jewish cadres of tens of thousands of workers could possibly be considered redundant. Millions of Germans were in the army and somebody had to replace them in the factories and workshops. The Jews were working hard and were efficient. What's more, their labor was nominally free – just slave labor. The Germans must have realized the great value of the Jewish working masses. After months of specialized work, they were now experienced in all kinds of jobs and excelled in them. In what became known as the TODT Organization, they built roads, bridges, and railroads following the paths of the army; in the east, thousands of Jews with the armband *OT* performed the most difficult jobs in this organization. Thousands worked in the *Rohstoffefassung* [the collection of raw materials], while thousands more, like me, worked for the Ostbahn, so important for the supply to the Eastern Front. How could it be imagined, we reasoned, that the Germans would ever relinquish such a cheap and essential labor force?

Such optimistic talks took place at every family table. Of course, there were cases where some people did disappear, but most people became used to such happenings – so long as they affected others. "It won't happen to us!" they hoped. For those who were targeted, it was a catastrophe, but for those not directly affected, it did not pay to dwell on it too much. Such is human nature; one gets used to anything. An earthquake in Japan or the starving people in Africa disturbed nobody's sleep in Lwów.

Life went on. People clung to their optimism, confident of their own survival, refusing to believe the alternative. Living with the Jewish star meant living legally. Very few would have been able to survive illegally, lacking the training for the necessary daily vigilance necessary to avoid betraying oneself by a gesture, word, look, or sigh. Living as Jews meant they were only threatened during German raids, whereas living on false papers would mean living in constant danger of being recognized and denounced. There was a death sentence for a Jew caught without a Jewish armband. True, we were aware of death camps. There were rumors of Jews being burned and their fat being converted into soap. A macabre joke was circulating of two Jews saying goodbye to each other: "See you on the shelf in the pharmacy."

Despite those deliberations and wishful thinking, I was convinced that our destiny had been sealed by the Nazis and I was glad to have false papers in reserve. One day, on my return from work, I found the family very agitated. Felus had been taken ill with a severe tummy ache. Up till then, both children had been well and we had no trouble. They were not hungry, although the food available was not always nutritious. We ate whatever could be obtained, sometimes substantial, sometimes less, and never adequate. We had endeavored to give the children some sugar, butter, and fruit, sometimes endangering our very lives in the search. We supplemented our diet with bits of dry bread that we had stored during the Soviet occupation, even if it was covered by mold, which Lusia's mother spent lots of time trying to remove. The children ate everything. Elżunia might sometimes leave something on her plate, but Felus – never! He would eat, sitting quietly and sadly. He never laughed or even smiled. In truth, I don't remember

Elżunia laughing either. No wonder! Our home was sad; our faces, our thoughts, our conversations were always sad. Did I ever embrace my child? I can't remember doing so. How do you embrace a beloved child when your thoughts are permanently, feverishly, preoccupied with concern for how to save that child?

Poor Felus was sitting over his plate, often in tears. He must have been longing for his mother. His grandparents loved him dearly, but their love was mixed with worry and sorrow. Looking at their grandson, they saw their own beloved son, who had probably perished in a Soviet prison. Everybody liked Felus and he clung to us, but we were too worried by everyday life to radiate that warmth so necessary for a child.

However, now he had fallen sick. He was trying not to cry, but we could see that he was writhing in pain. Jewish doctors, not having the right to practice, were unavailable. We thought of going to the Jewish hospital but rejected the idea. It was situated in the Jewish district, which was too dangerous. Also, it was full of typhoid fever cases, and the danger of contagion would have been high for the child and his visitors. The child was in agony. We suspected appendicitis. On making inquiries, we were recommended to Dr. Gruca, a very well-known Polish surgeon. He came immediately and diagnosed a bowel obstruction, requiring immediate surgery. But where? All hospitals were closed to Jews.

We told Dr. Gruca that a Russian couple, who occupied a room in our flat, went home just before the war, leaving their little son in our care. That story got Felus accepted to the hospital. Since Felus was not circumcised, the story was accepted, but the surgeon warned that no person wearing a Jewish armband could visit. Lusia pushed the boy in Elżunia's stroller, and I followed behind. It was evening and there were few people on the streets. After an hour's walk, we reached the hospital without incident. The poor child was in agonizing pain. Lusia took her armband off and entered the hospital. I stood outside for a while, then went home and waited. Three hours later, Lusia returned with the good news that Felus had a successful operation. Lusia visited Felus daily despite the risk. She didn't wish to leave the child alone among strangers. The hospital sisters were polite even though they probably suspected that Lusia was Jewish. After a few days, Felus returned home happy and well. Dr. Gruca didn't charge us either for his visit or for the surgery. Elżunia welcomed Felus's return and, as before, they played together, always alone.

There must have been some problems at the building site because the firm invited a specialist for consultation. To my astonishment, he turned out to be my old professor on the theory of bridges, Dr. Stanislaw Brzozowski. Recognizing me he greeted me heartily. "Ah, Engineer Reiss!" he exclaimed, and then smiled sadly. I was touched. My thoughts went back 12 years to the time of the antisemitic excesses at the Polytechnic. I recalled our dreams at that time: equality without religious, racial, or national discrimination. And what were my dreams today? To reach home safely, to find my family intact, to survive the war.

Enormous loads of war materials were passing through Lwów Station day and night heading east, while huge railway trucks loaded with broken artillery pieces and wrecked tanks were being returned to the Fatherland. Red Cross trains, full of wounded, were returning home. The German monster was bleeding! A Wehrmacht officer, on his way to the front line, entered our office and asked politely if he could use our telephone. We heard him speaking to someone, probably a high official, considering his respectful tone and manner. After passing on greetings from the family in Germany, his tone changed, as if he was too apprehensive to continue talking. All at once, having noticed our armbands, he told us to leave the room. We did so gladly, feeling that bad news was not for Jewish ears.

Joe Abrahamer, having good contacts with the Judenrat, was usually given reliable information; the morbid rumors that he used to bring to the office always came true. One day, again the horror struck. The previous day had been 24 June 1942, a memorable day for me: the eighth anniversary of our wedding. It had been a sad anniversary and I arrived at the office downcast. Glancing at Joe, I froze. I knew immediately that he had bad news. "An action against children is expected today," he said.

My legs refused to obey. The blood seemed to freeze in my veins. My stomach was in a knot. "Against the children? Are you sure?" I asked. Alas, it was from a most reliable source. A specially trained SS Sonderkommando arrived yesterday and an action was scheduled for today. Joe had already placed his son Witek with some Polish friends.

Realizing that my place was with my family and my children, and not in the safe Ostbahn office, I asked Joe to excuse me to the chief. I grabbed some office papers so I could have an excuse for going to our city office and left in a panic. The distance home was considerable. It normally took me over an hour, but on that day, it only took 45 minutes. I was lucky and nobody stopped me on the way. I arrived home breathless. The children had just gotten up. The whole family was shocked by my appearance. No, they knew nothing about a threat to the children. Our district had been quiet. I turned around and ran to the city office. The news was confirmed: an action had already taken place in the Jewish district. Streets were closed. Gendarmes in steel helmets and battle dress had burst into Jewish flats, spreading terror, shouting, beating mothers and frightened children, rounding them up in the yards, flinging them onto trucks, and driving them away.

In front of our office stood a few of our Jewish workers in utter despair. They had rushed to the office as I had, with the hope that our chief, Johann Pontess, might use his influence and intervene, but he was helpless.

One of our laborers, a young solicitor from Kraków, stood in the middle of the road weeping bitterly. He had married a very beautiful girl shortly before the outbreak of war, and they had a delightful two-year-old daughter. He was much in love with his wife, always carrying her photo with him. I looked at him, a broken man, weeping in the middle of the street. Approaching him gently, I led him away. We sat down on the pavement, our backs against the wall. He told me that when he went running home, he found the room broken into, wife and child taken. Some food remains were still on the table. He wept bitterly and I wept with him. According to witnesses, thousands of mothers and children were taken into Janowska camp that day and bestially murdered. There are recorded cases of small children being torn to pieces by specially trained dogs or their little heads smashed against walls, of kicking and trampling mothers who threw themselves down to beg mercy for their children.

The action lasted just one day, and then the Sonderkommando left to repeat the performance elsewhere.

Murderous actions took place in other towns as well. Anatol Kahane had received a letter from his parents, who hitherto had lived comparatively peacefully near Tarnov. They wrote that since they had had no holiday for quite some time, they were now on a "holiday trip" to our part of Poland, from where they would try to write again. "May God take care of you" were the last words written to their son.

News of a massacre in Stanislawów reached us through Uncle Efraim Seinfeld, husband of Aunt Teofila, where we had stayed during the Polish-Ukrainian war in 1918. He told us how the Germans drove all the Jews to the cemetery, where the SS units shot them. Aunt Teofila was killed and so were thousands of others. By some miracle, Uncle Efraim managed to escape and dared to come by train to Lwów, where he stayed with some family. The poor man didn't realize then that he had jumped from the frying pan into the fire. People fought for every extra day of life, running like mice from a sinking ship. Could we be the exception?

Inevitably, our time must come!

ACTION AGAINST MY MOTHER

Again, there was a lull as families who had been affected mourned their losses while those who had escaped returned to "normal" living. However, after the last action, I had no doubt that our lives were in mortal danger despite our excellent papers and the letter *A* on our sleeves. I realized that although the younger people, if they were capable of working, had a chance of carrying on a little longer, the situation for the elderly, women, and children was hopeless. The Germans would murder them according to plan. Our only chance of survival lay, as I could now very clearly see, in assuming an Aryan identity. But what about our parents? I knew they were unfit for such a transformation. What could I do?

There was a good chance of survival for Uncle Joseph Tilles, who was still with us. His wife, a Christian, was living in Kraków and in an emergency would surely come and take care of him. There was still a way to save Felus. Over and over again, I brought up this problem, saying, "What right do we have to decide the child's destiny? His life, like ours, is in danger. Why can't we place him in the safety of a monastery? Should we perish, he will live. Should we survive, we will take him back."

To my distress, Lusia's father stubbornly stuck to his decision. He declared that he would never agree to his grandson being placed in a monastery. As head of the family, he would decide and nobody else.

Apart from that, he still wouldn't believe that Hitler would murder everybody. After all, over the 12 months of Hitler's rule, not one member of our family had perished. Why then part with a child who had it so good with us? Besides, the war would soon be over! He would not discuss the issue any further.

The fact that the letter A had been respected during the last action confirmed the reasoning of the optimists. German authorities, who were chiefs of various organizations employing Jews, assured their employees they had nothing to fear. The deputy town commander, Dr. Reisp, who oversaw the Town Workshops, declared that the workers in his shops were under his personal care and no danger faced them. Similar declarations were made by other German bosses and even Gestapo officers, who spread encouragement to people willing to believe, people who refused to see the deliberate deception designed only to placate and provide a false sense of security. My apprehension remained undiminished. I felt that sooner or later we were bound to find ourselves trapped and our only chance of survival was to transform ourselves into Aryan Poles. Although I had birth certificates in the name of Daraż, I was worried I had been sold very inferior forgeries. Who knew how many identical copies that unscrupulous man had made and sold to others? This possibility nagged at me incessantly and finally prompted me to look for new papers. I was lucky; I met someone who offered me an authentic looking, undoubtedly genuine birth certificate in the name of Jan Sliwinski for 150 złoty. I bought it as a reserve in case the Daraż papers failed. The price was reasonable; it was apparent that the Daraż supplier had most certainly cheated me. Now I had two Aryan birth certificates. I hid them both.

The summer of 1942 was nearly over. June and July had been very hot. Still, day after day, six days a week, I rushed in the morning to the railway station, and every evening I retraced my weary steps back home, over an hour each way. While thousands of our people had already perished, we were still alive and together.

One day, Joe Abrahamer did not turn up at work. Obviously, he had escaped as planned. Some of his relatives had been in Warsaw for some time, so he had good connections to give him a head start. Before leaving, he had given me his Warsaw phone number. Lusia and I embedded this number in our memories. No written notes.

At the beginning of August, a disturbing change took place within the Judenrat. The Jewish Labor Department was dissolved, and the dreaded SS took over the management of the huge reservoir of Jewish laborers. Panic spread among Lwów Jewry; we nursed dreadful forebodings.

It was the beginning of a serious deterioration. One day, we were ordered to move out of our flat. A Romanian citizen presented us with a police order empowering him to take over the flat. Appeals and pleadings were useless. He was uninterested that we were a large family without alternative accommodation. Giving us six days to move out, he threatened to return on the seventh day with the Ukrainian police and, if necessary, throw us onto the street. There was no other solution.

Lusia's mother had two sisters in Lwów who were living on the border of the Jewish district. They were willing to take Lusia's parents and Felus. Aunt Pepcia agreed to take my mother into her Ossolinskich Street flat, which already housed some 14 people. In the meantime, Ludwik had obtained false identity papers as a Volksdeutscher, a person of German origins without German citizenship. Being in full command of the German language, he now waited. Lutek Kahane planned an escape to Tarnov where his parents had close friends in a Polish family. Cousin Bronck and Mother Rozia (who had been living with us since the Soviet occupation) moved in with a Polish family, doubtless in exchange for a generous sum of money. With Lusia and Elżunia, I planned to move temporarily to Edda Fishler's, our university colleague, who, still lived in Sykstuska Street in an Aryan part of town together with her child, mother, and some friends. She invited us to stay with them as long as necessary. We were determined not to be locked up in the ghetto.

For Uncle Joseph, we determined that the situation required his Catholic wife to immediately come to Lwów and rescue him. I cabled her. At the same time, I cabled Zosia Janicka, asking her to come at once. We knew that her help as a Pole would be invaluable and hoped that she would care for Elżunia in case of an emergency.

On Saturday, 8 August, we were still together. The town was quiet, the atmosphere loaded with fear. There were rumors of great concentrations of police, the arrival of special units of the SS Vernichtungskommando [Destruction Commando], and the mobilization of the Ukrainian militia. On Sunday, 9 August I left early to organize the removal of some furniture and belongings to Zolkiewska Street. Lusia's mother packed suitcases, boxes, and bags, not knowing what to take and what to leave. It was cruel. Naturally, she took the food we had, plus some pieces of wood and coal.

In the Jewish district, some poor Jews stood, offering their services to move expelled Jews into the ghetto. I paid 100 złoty to a couple of porters – a father and son – who helped load the handcart with mattresses, a few chairs, a sideboard, bedding, some pots and saucers, and odds and ends.

A huge, beautiful crystal mirror that Lusia's mother insisted on taking was carefully placed against the wall of the house, but suddenly, and without any obvious explanation, it fell, shattering into thousands of pieces. For the first and only time during all our war sufferings, Lusia burst into tears. I knew she didn't really care for the mirror, but I also knew the superstition that a smashed mirror foreshadows disaster. Alas, only a few days later, the portent was vindicated. It was a sad procession leaving that house in Chmielowskiego Street where Lusia's family had lived for so many years. The young porter led, pulling the cart while his father pushed from behind. Lusia's father, in dark glasses, leaned on his walking stick, supporting his small and prematurely aged wife, with little Felus clinging to her hand. We stood watching them leave, not fully realizing we would never see them again.

Yet there was more trouble to come. My mother developed a high temperature that night and was forced to stay in bed. The next day, Monday morning, I left for work as usual. Huge posters appeared on the city walls warning Lwów's Christian population that the harboring of Jews or offering them any assistance was punishable by death. Doubtless, some horrible action was imminent.

There was an air of terrible despondency in the office. Although we were equipped with the *A* armbands, rumors circulated that the SS intended to reassess whether our jobs were essential and restamp our identification cards with a different colored seal. I had only just started work when I was called to the phone. I never received phone calls at the office. Who could it be, I wondered? It was Uncle Joseph. He had also just received information about the restamping of identity cards with the new (green) color that day in the Städtische Werkstatt where

Mother worked. Whoever missed receiving the new stamp would be out of work. Knowing that Mother was at home sick, he had lost no time contacting me. I was terrified. There was no other way of informing Mother than by rushing home and taking her to the workshop irrespective of her illness. It was a matter of life and death. There was no choice; I had to leave the safety of the office, ignoring the perils of the walk home during an action. A Jew was not permitted to be in the streets during working hours. If caught, his life depended upon the whims of the Germans or the Ukrainian police. An alternative was to take the armband off, which was easily done but risky. The Ukrainians were masters in recognizing a Jew and handing them over to the German police. My colleagues considered my decision extremely risky and advised me to stay put and not endanger myself or my mother, for we were aware a big-scale action had already taken place in the Jewish Quarter. But my mind was made up. I informed my supervisors that I had to leave the office for an hour and rushed home. Mother was understandably frightened when I woke her. "What is it?" she asked, and I quickly explained. In a few minutes, she was dressed and we hurried off to her work. When we arrived there, the gate of the huge building was firmly locked, guarded by Ukrainian militiamen. I told them that I was escorting Mother to work and would leave the building within a few minutes. I showed them my work documents. They opened the gate and allowed us to enter.

Mother's forewoman, a pleasant, friendly person, was relieved to see her. It was obvious she liked my mother, such a calm and soft-spoken lady, a diligent, capable, and obedient worker. "It's lucky that your son brought you," she said, smiling at us. "We are getting a new stamp on our Ausweis."

I had no trouble getting out. Sneaking along the back streets, I arrived safely back at my office. "Well done, Henry!" my colleagues greeted me upon arrival. Before settling down to work, I phoned Uncle Joseph that all was well with Mother.

"Thank God!" he said, and I could hear his sigh of relief.

"Thank God," I replied and put down the receiver.

About two hours later, the horrifying news reached us: an action was raging within the Städtische Werkstatt. The whole block of buildings had been surrounded by SS men; streets had been sealed off, and all houses and shops were shut. Poles living there were forbidden to leave their homes. Everything was at a standstill. Police trucks had arrived. All the workers had been led out of the building and, to the accompaniment of beatings, kicking, and abuse, loaded onto the trucks and carted off to the Janowska concentration camp. My mother was among them. I was numb. I had led my own mother to her executioners.

We spent that evening in deep distress. Uncle Joseph blamed himself bitterly, but how was he to know? How was I to know? The noose was tightening around our necks and the neck of our precious Elżunia. My mother was gone. Most certainly, we would be next.

The following morning, I returned to the office devastated, desperately trying to decide what steps we should take. Few words were spoken. Everyone just sat and waited. Suddenly, the door to our room burst open and three SS officers entered. Was this it? Terrified, we scrambled to our feet and stood to attention. With the SS men was the chief of our firm, Johann Pontess, pale as a ghost. No one spoke. We hardly dared to breathe.

The SS men looked at us with penetrating eyes for a tortuous and unending moment. Pointing at me, one of them shouted, "Ausweis!" With a trembling hand, I gave him my work certificate. He examined it at length, staring at my photograph, and asking my name and date and place of birth.

With a final glance at my photograph, he returned the document. Then the three of them, smirking, turned and left the room. Pontess went with them. Perhaps they had their fun – managing to frighten the bloody Jews. And the frightened, bloody Jews collapsed back on their chairs and took a deep breath. We all received the new green stamp, a postponement of our death sentence. Our greatest anxiety now concerned our wives and children as they had no hope of getting new stamps. If they were caught, that would be the end.

With Lusia and Elżunia at home, communication was difficult since we had no telephone. When Marcus's Ukrainian friend, Sawczyn, came to the office to see him, I begged him to go to our flat (he knew where we lived) and take Lusia and the child away.

He went immediately, returning after an hour with good news. He had taken Lusia and the child to Tosia, Tolek Kahane's girlfriend. They were to stay there overnight, and hopefully by then the action would have blown over. Every day, every night, each hour of survival, was a victory. Again, I was called to the phone by Uncle Joseph. He rang to say that he was going to stay in the bank overnight. The bank janitor, a Pole, who went to town with the mail, had come across an action against women and older men, witnessing the barbaric loading of victims onto trucks. Quickly running back to the bank, he offered to keep Uncle Joseph there until the morning when he would open the bank early and bring him some food. Since Uncle was always the first to arrive and the last to leave, nobody would notice that he had never left the bank.

For several days, Uncle Joseph stayed in that safe haven behind locked doors. That wonderful man, a simple, honest Polish janitor, brought Uncle a clean shirt, shaving gear, and some food. But how long could he continue to do so? Things were getting worse by the hour. Fela, Lusia's younger sister, and her husband, Olek Ornstein, did not return home from work.

The company's chief engineer, Jan Spira, escaped to Warsaw with his wife and child. Ludwik left for Stanislawów as a Volksdeutscher. Mila Gold, an old friend from Kraków, left home on an errand and returned to an empty room; her parents had been taken away. She needed a place to stay for the night. Could I help her? With Lusia and Elżunia being cared for by Tosia, my next concern was young Felus. I approached Sawczyn again, asking him to find a place in a Ukrainian monastery for the child, telling him the story of the boy's Soviet parents. I was hoping that Lusia's father would not oppose the idea now, considering the present catastrophic situation. Sawczyn promised to deal with the matter after he had helped Engineer Marcus escape to Warsaw.

Both Aunt Stasia (Uncle Joseph's wife) and Zosia had arrived from Kraków and stayed in a hotel. I was hoping Aunt Stasia would rescue Uncle Joseph from the bank. Zosia called on Lusia, who was back at Chmielowskiego. Regretfully, Tosia could not keep Lusia and Elżunia any longer. Her landlady had started to ask awkward questions. What was I to do now? Where to hide Lusia and the child? What had happened to Lusia's parents? To Felus?

Finally, Sawczyn came back with good news: he had found a monastery that agreed to take Felus. Regrettably, he had no time to fetch the boy himself, so he gave me the Mother Superior's name and address. How was I to arrange it? Just then Zosia arrived at the office with news from Lusia that our district was quiet so far. I gave Zosia the address of the monastery and she hastened to Zolkiewska Street to get Felus. For the first time in days, I felt some relief, having at last found a safe haven for Felus.

When we finished work at five o'clock, I rushed home, eager to tell Lusia of the chance to save Felus. Together, we waited nervously for Zosia's return. At last, she arrived, dejected and tearful. She had been an hour too late. She had found the flat empty. Lusia's parents, uncles, aunts, and poor little Felus were gone, taken by the SS.

Polish neighbors had told Zosia that the child had cried so bitterly that it broke their hearts to hear him. But nobody tried to rescue him. A handwoven, woolen jacket of Lusia's Aunt Adela Fuchs had been hanging on the door handle. Zosia took it and gave it to Lusia. This was to be her only family souvenir. A pale Lusia listened in stony silence, unable to shed one single tear.

I was afraid to leave Lusia at home. Rumors had it that the SS were preparing attacks on Jews living in Aryan districts. I was still protected by the new stamp, but Lusia or Elżunia were not. How could I save them? Where should I turn next? The Wilczek family was living not far away. Maybe they would agree to give them shelter for at least one night. I had to take the risk. We spent a restless, sleepless night. Early next morning, Lusia took the child and left home, without her armband. I followed a few paces behind.

Lusia was not the only Jewish mother running with her child. People going to work looked at these desperate women, some with curiosity, others with pity, but the majority with total indifference. On the city walls, some posters were displayed: "Penalty of death for aid given to Jews."

Luckily, there were no Ukrainian militia on the streets. Lusia reached the Wilczek house without incident. Nodding in my direction, she disappeared into the entrance. For some minutes, I strolled along the street, wondering if the Wilczeks would give her shelter or shut the door in her face. Ten minutes passed and nobody left the house. Thank God, Lusia and the child must be safe! Thus reassured, I ran to Edda Fischler to pick up some of our belongings that were left earlier at her place.

Edda was preparing for her own escape. Her brother, Nulek Fischler, was already in Warsaw. A new industry had developed – the smuggling of Jews. There were Poles who, for a price, escorted Jews during the railway trip to Warsaw. Such escorts gave added encouragement and security during escapes. One such smuggler, a certain Mr. Wolski, had just arrived from Warsaw. He booked a room in a hotel for Edda as his wife and child. I had met him in Edda's flat. He was a handsome man in his thirties, but to me he did not look trustworthy. Yet he helped Edda and her child to survive the horror of the infamous August 1942 action.

With my new stamp, I felt relatively secure at Edda's. Tolek Kahane's girlfriend, Tosia, visited to inform me that Tolek, with whom she was deeply in love, had left for Tarnov. As her landlady had become very suspicious lately, she planned to escape to Warsaw.

Suddenly, a Ukrainian militiaman arrived and demanded our papers. He passed over mine because of the stamp, but Tosia's Aryan false papers must have raised his suspicion. He took her off to the police station. Poor, kind Tosia!

Zosia arrived in the afternoon. She brought me some food and the news that Aunt Stasia had somehow panicked, left Uncle Joseph in his bank, and returned to Kraków. I could not understand how a Polish woman who loved her husband so much could leave him locked up in hiding and return home without him.

I felt uneasy staying in the large empty flat at Edda's. Her mother, whom I had known for years, had been taken a few days ago. She was denounced to the Gestapo by a tenant while trying to hide some jewelry in a cellar. The block of flats in which they lived belonged to the Fischler family, and some nasty tenant took the opportunity of getting rid of one more dirty Jewish property owner. I decided to return to our flat on Chmielowskiego Street. The period of six days grace had not yet expired. Thus far, the action had not reached there; however, there were already some victims. I met my cousin Zofia Bambach on the street. Her parents had been taken from home that morning. She had escaped and was roaming the streets, homeless. She had lost her two small children some days earlier and her husband had perished at the Janowska camp. Aunt Mina, the beautiful wife of our favorite Uncle Joshua, was caught in the street with her daughter, my lovely 15-year-old cousin Johanna. Uncle Jacob Weissglass, who had not obtained the new green stamp, was taken from work. His wife, Aunt Malcia, and their son, Dolek, escaped with the help of their maid, Anna.[1] A Polish woman approached me. She was looking for a Mrs. Goldberg, once her good neighbor who had recently moved into Chmielowskiego Street. Mrs. Goldberg had a very lovely lounge suite and this Polish woman wanted to locate her solely because she wanted to take it into her custody. Regrettably, Mrs. Goldberg's address was not known to me.

I reached our flat at Chmielowskiego Street safely. Our Romanian "friend" had not taken it over as yet. Perhaps he was waiting for a better one. After this action, there would be a surfeit of empty flats. I decided to stay there overnight, closer to the Wilczeks and Lusia. An unexpected visitor called – Maria Ferber, a friend from Kraków. She was frantic. Her parents had been taken during their transfer to the Jewish district. She had managed to escape and was looking for a refuge for the night. Was our flat safe? How could I answer that?

Mila Gold, another friend from Kraków, called. Returning from work, she found her home empty, her parents taken, and had run away. Same questions. Could she stay the night? Was it safe?

Irka Haber's brother, Janek, who lived around the comer, arrived. His old, sick parents had been taken in the morning, his wife hadn't returned home from work, and he had failed to obtain the green stamp. He rushed away but had no idea where to go.

It appeared that the Germans had covered the whole city of Lwów with their murderous Einsatzgruppen. How could we survive this onslaught?

I was paralyzed with fear – alone in this flat, once so full of life I went to bed. How long was this action going to last? Would it move into our district, into our street? Would they leave the Wilczeks' flat alone? I didn't sleep a wink. In the early morning, I ran to the Wilczeks and knocked softly at the door. Mrs. Wilczek opened quietly and led me into a room where Lusia was sitting in an armchair in which she had spent the night. Mrs. Wilczek's mother brought us coffee. My gratitude was boundless. I fell on my knees and kissed both her hands. There was silence in the room. As the old lady left us alone, there were tears in her eyes. A noble Polish lady!

Lusia told me how on arriving the previous morning, Mr. Jan Ruszczynski, Mrs. Wilczek's uncle, had opened the door for her. Introducing herself, she had asked whether she and the child could remain there till the next morning. "Of course!" was the answer without a moment's hesitation. They had never met before.

The situation was complicated by the presence of a German, a subtenant of the Wilczeks. He was just leaving for work when he encountered Lusia in the entrance hall. He asked who the lady was. With great presence of mind, Mr. Ruszczynski said that it was his niece who had just arrived with her daughter to see a doctor in Lwów. "A good-looking woman!" said the German as he went out. Luckily, like many Germans, he could not tell a Jew from a Gentile. Nevertheless, Lusia, as well as her hosts, spent a sleepless night while Mrs. Wilczek's mother was on her knees all night praying in front of a picture of the Holy Mary.

The action continued for several days and nights. The SS beast raged. We lost our whole family: my dearest mother; Lusia's mother whom she adored; her father; her younger sister Fela and her charming young husband; and sweet little Felus. We lost all our aunts and uncles and all their children – our cousins.

Uncle Joseph was still in the bank, brother Ludwik was somewhere in the country. I was uncertain how much longer the lifesaving green stamp would protect me and was confronted by the desperate problem of how to protect my beloved Lusia and child from this mortal danger. I realized the moment of decision had arrived. We had to leave Lwów immediately and adopt a new name and identity.

There was nothing left to keep us in Lwów. Our parents were gone. Lusia agreed without hesitation, ready for our next move, our only move. It was easy to decide but much harder to carry out such a dangerous undertaking. Slowly we planned our escape.

The next day, I went to work as usual, hoping it would be the last time. Half of my colleagues, including the chief engineers, Spira and Markus, had already escaped to Warsaw. I asked the engineer in charge to provide me with a document on the firm's letterhead certifying that Mr. Piotr Daraż was a purchasing officer authorized to locate and purchase equipment for the company. I was asked to pay 1,200 złoty. When he saw my astonishment, he explained that the money was needed to free a colleague from the Janowska concentration camp. I paid the required amount and at his request left him my *A* armband and my Jewish documents carrying the current green stamp. Until then, I had not realized that these Jewish documents were used by people who escaped from the camp. Now I understood why, during their visit to our office, the SS men had sought verification of our names, birthdates, and other details. They certainly knew all the tricks. I gathered up a few illustrated catalogues of building machines, building materials and tools.

At the close of the working day, Sawczyn arrived to fetch me. Leaving with him, I was without my armband and naturally felt much trepidation. We took a tram and went to his friends, who lived far away from the Jewish center. He introduced me as Mr. Sliwinski so as not to endanger the name "Daraż" in case of trouble.

When suppertime arrived, I was invited to join the family, which consisted of his parents and two teenage sons. A decent Polish family, they were very excited by the latest BBC news bulletin announcing the Allies' unexpected landing at Dieppe on the French coast. I was also greatly excited and relieved that the news had diverted their attention from me. Was this the invasion we had been praying for these many months? Was it the Second Front of which Hitler had warned? Could we believe in the miracle of being saved?

Later that evening my guardian, Sawczyn, arrived carrying a sack, pretending it contained his belongings. He placed the sack in my room. Of course, it was filled with my things – how could I possibly have arrived at a stranger's place carrying a sack? I guessed they must have realized who I was, but behaved as if they didn't, speaking of everything but the Jewish problem. Great Polish people!

It was difficult for me to realize that while thousands of people were running in panic, looking for a safe place for a single night, this Polish family was sitting quietly in their tidy drawing room, sipping tea, and talking about the end of the war. And I, as Mr. Sliwinski, was sitting with them, participating in the conversation, fittingly dressed and relaxed, with a cup of tea in my hand and a napkin on my lap.

It seemed like Act One, Scene One of a drama in which Lusia and I were to play the leading roles. Would we be able to play our roles properly? The role of a Jew disguised in a false Aryan skin – the struggle of a family – a husband, wife, and a sweet little girl condemned to death for the crime of being born Jewish. Would we succeed?

PART IV

UNDER GERMAN OCCUPATION – AS AN ARYAN

AUGUST 1942-JANUARY 1944

PLANNING OUR ESCAPE

I found myself in bed in this Polish home enjoying a strange almost forgotten feeling: I felt safe. No threats of a night visit by the SS. It was hard to believe that I could have a calm and peaceful night.

Tomorrow, of course, was loaded with tension and danger. I was grateful I would have Sawczyn's assistance. His presence was reassuring. The sudden conversion from a Jewish slave into a free Pole required a great deal of determination and some courage, more perhaps than could be expected from a victim of years of oppression and terror. One needed to be a good actor, which I was not.

Our arrangements had been carefully planned: In the early morning, Sawczyn would arrive with an empty suitcase into which I would transfer my belongings from the sack. Under the protection of his company, we would take the electric tram to the central railway station, where he would buy my ticket. I had worked there for months, meaning I could easily be recognized if I bought the ticket myself.

Zosia, who had taken care of Lusia and Elżunia until then, would bring them to the station at about the same time and purchase their tickets. Of course, we would pretend not to know each other. After a hopefully uneventful journey, we would arrive that evening at Kraków Station. Zosia would take Lusia and the child, and I would proceed directly to my old boss, Mr. Elsner, hoping to obtain some sort of help.

This was the plan. Would it work? We would see. It took a long time to fall asleep. It was dawn when something woke me – the sound of heavy steps outside my window. It was only five in the morning – too early for Sawczyn. Who could it be? The flat was on the mezzanine floor. Clearly the steps were right below the windows. Heavy steps. Military boots! "*Wo ist er* [Where is he]?" It was a hateful voice. The steps seemed to stop in front of the entrance door.

"*Da ist er* [Here he is]!" The voice of a German. A moment's silence, then knocking on the door. More silence. Another knock.

I decided not to wait any longer. Jumping out of bed, I hastily donned trousers and jacket over my pajamas, put on my shoes, and waited. The moment I heard a knock on our door, I would jump out the window and run. Carefully, I opened the window and looked out. The street was empty. Silence. Nobody was outside. A nightmare? Quietly, I closed the window, undressed, and returned to bed with wonderful relief.

Sawczyn arrived at the set hour and we walked together to the tram stop. It was strange being able to mount a tram car after so many months of obeying "*Nicht für Juden* [Not for Jews]." Neither the driver nor the passengers gave me a look. Obviously, my appearance raised no suspicions. Thank God! My confidence, however, would be slow to return. At the railway station, Sawczyn purchased my ticket and stayed with me until, at the last moment, I noticed a few familiar railway men, but luckily nobody recognized me. They could not possibly have guessed that this decently dressed gentleman with well-pressed trousers and polished shoes had worn the armband just a few days ago.

I looked around for Lusia and Elżunia. There they were, on time. I turned my back to them so Elżunia would not recognize me; she could have cried out "*Tatuś* [Daddy]!" and run to me, compromising our plan. After a while, our train arrived. I occupied a seat in the same carriage, but in a different compartment than Lusia's. I was trying to behave casually like any ordinary traveler: calm and self-controlled. One passenger looked at me strangely. I recognized him immediately; during the Soviet occupation he was our Ukrainian caretaker. Luckily, he was sitting in another compartment and did not show any further interest in me. Maybe he hadn't recognized me or didn't want to. Not all Ukrainians were bloodthirsty. There was Sawczyn, there would be others. I sat in the corner, pretending to be asleep. The ticket inspector woke me and checked my ticket and did not give me a second glance.

Further pretense of sleeping was useless. I opened my elegant, prewar, kid-leather briefcase and started to study my catalogues in order to avoid exchanging glances with other passengers. My thoughts were completely detached from Lwów. I became one of the passengers who normally traveled by train. Some were reading newspapers, one a book. A woman was busily knitting. The man opposite was looking at my catalogues.

"Is it a good business?" he asked.

"Sometimes it is, and sometimes it isn't," I answered evasively. I didn't want to pursue the conversation. What for?

Sitting at the window, I could see the peaceful Polish landscape. It was a hot, sunny August. Fields, meadows, forests, settlements, and silhouettes of people and animals all flashed by. It was harvest time. We were passing crops of wheat and golden stubble fields of harvested rye. Certain plots were already plowed for the winter sowing. Fields of potatoes and clover were in full green. Occasionally, people were waving happily at the passing train. It all seemed like a dream. This wasn't... This couldn't be real! Reality was back there in Lwów. Reality was people living in the shadow of imminent death, humiliated, maltreated by the scum of the German and Ukrainian society. Reality was people fleeing from the brigands trained for genocide.

My thoughts returned to Felus. He could have remained among the living. Even at the very last moment, Lusia's parents could have placed him with some neighbors and explained his background. He hadn't been circumcised; he had a Soviet birth certificate and bore the name Smirnow. There would have been no risk in keeping him. Why had they not done it? Was their will paralyzed or had they believed, in their naivete, that things would be okay or hoped for a miracle?

Then my thoughts turned to Uncle Joseph. Who would take care of him now that his wife had returned home to Lwów, leaving him shut up in his bank, in the care of a strange caretaker? How long could that situation last without management becoming suspicious? After all, the director of the bank was a German, and all employees were Poles.

After an hour the train stopped at Przemyśl. The danger I dreaded all the time was the inspection of documents by the German police. True, I had a piece of paper from my firm, Pontess, but that was a far cry from an identity document. A normal document had to bear a photograph and a seal of some German authority. For almost three years now, the Germans had occupied this so-called General Government and presumably had already introduced some identity documents for the Poles. Neither Lusia nor myself possessed anything of that kind.

Our next stop was Jaroslaw. Looking through the windows among passengers changing trains for Warsaw, I noticed Edda Fischler with her escort, Mr. Wolski, leading her five-year-old boy by the hand. She noticed me too and nodded. That was the last time I ever saw Edda.

I wanted to have a glimpse of Lusia, so I went into the corridor. The three of them were sitting in an open compartment. Lusia noticed me but remained motionless. She appeared worried – not her normal self. I felt concerned.

The train was moving fast, passing Rzeszów and Tarnów, and soon was nearing our destination, Kraków. My excitement grew. What was awaiting us there? A police raid at the station or an action against Jews? Undoubtedly, we were not the only refugees fleeing the hell of Lwów. The Germans would certainly be informed and were probably preparing a reception for us. My heart was racing with fear. I collected my few things. People alighted quickly and rushed toward the exit. Noticing my family group, I tried to approach them, but Lusia gave me a sign to keep away. Again, she seemed worried. Something must have happened, but what? Everything was calm, not a single gendarme. I handed in my ticket and followed at a safe distance.

At last, they stopped and I approached slowly. There had to be a reason for Lusia's concern. Quickly she explained. She, Zosia, and Elżunia had taken their seats in an open compartment, unaware that in the adjoining compartment, behind the partition, a group of our colleagues from the Polytechnic were sitting. They had been speaking loudly about Jews. Lusia could hear every word. To her great terror, she heard her own name mentioned. "The Jewish problem regrettably will not be fully solved because many Jews drop their armbands and escape. Like, for instance, our colleague, Lusia Herman, who sits quietly in the next compartment, pretending to be a Christian! Yet I remember her at the Polytechnic as a Jewess."

Lusia had not reacted, but during the whole trip remained panic stricken. She was not sure if they would denounce her. Perhaps they would consider that immoral and it might even burden their conscience, but somebody else could have heard their revelation and made use of it. So Lusia had waited until her "colleagues" had left the station and disappeared before she dared to meet me.

According to plan, we separated. Zosia took Lusia and Elżunia to her family's home. Those wonderful people agreed to offer Lusia hospitality for a few days until we managed to find another place to stay.

I went to my prewar boss, Joseph Elsner. He opened the door himself. I noticed his astonishment at seeing me again after three years. He was obviously afraid and received me rather hesitantly. The reason became clear: I was not the only Jewish refugee from Lwów. Only a few moments earlier, his wife's brother, Dr. Glasner, who had also escaped Lwów on the same train, had come to the Elsners for help. Mr. Elsner's wife, a converted Jew, apparently had a permit to live with her Aryan husband. He was still glad to see me alive and we talked.

My reemployment was out of the question, he said, since he employed the same staff as before the war. It would be too risky. However, he would issue and sign any documents enabling me to live under my new name, Daraż. Asking me to keep in touch, he apologized for his inability to help further and politely accompanied me to the door.

In Emil Sawczyn's absence, his caretaker duties were carried out by his wife. He had given me her address and recommendation. I found her without any trouble and gave her news of her husband. She was very friendly and – aware of the accommodation difficulties – offered that I would stay at her place while in Kraków. We had a pleasant supper. I told her in Ukrainian about my life in our village, the harvest, and so on. I talked about Engineer Markus, whom she respected greatly. I did not mention a word about the extermination of Jews in Lwów. I felt that I was playing the role of Daraż well. I had a wonderful night's sleep on a comfortable couch in an Ukrainian home. Above me hung a painting of the crucified Christ with his crown of thorns and bleeding temples. I was well protected, absolutely safe.

The next morning, I set out for the Linguistic bookshop, owned by the Habers. Henry Haber was surprised to see me and shocked to hear my account of recent events in Lwów. He found it difficult to believe. Regretfully, I had to give him the bad news about his wife Irka's family. He, in his turn, told me of their life. It had been incomprehensible to me that while the Jews of Lwów were perishing by the thousands daily, Kraków's Jews were still able to lead regular, quiet lives. From Haber's report, his family was still intact, going to work daily and returning each evening to the ghetto.

The bookshop had been taken over by a *Treuhändler* [trustee], a decent type of a Sudeten- German, but Irka was actually managing it while the trustee just drew his salary and didn't bother them. Henry still had his job as an architect and from time to time would visit the shop. It had become a safe place for his friends to meet and talk.

I found this situation just as incredible as Haber found my story of what it was like in Lwów. Two cities, both occupied by Hitler's armies, yet two different worlds! I was most definitely convinced that this Kraków paradise could not last and I warned Haber accordingly. The Nazis' decision to totally liquidate Polish Jewry would not stop at the walls of Kraków. I advised him to prepare Aryan papers as the only possible path to safety and to escape from the ghetto as soon as possible. He was obviously shocked, unable to collect his thoughts, and committed only to discussing my suggestion with Irka.

Still of great concern to me was the fate of Uncle Joseph, hopefully still hidden in the bank. I telephoned his wife and arranged to meet her in the afternoon. Arriving a few minutes early, Lusia and I decided to fill the time by taking a stroll in the adjoining public park. I was pleasantly surprised to find that we were moving around Aryan Kraków with a growing sense of self-assurance. Was it the peaceful atmosphere or the climate? Kraków was lovely, green, warm and quiet, like before the war. The hated uniforms of German gendarmes and Ukrainian militiamen were nowhere in sight. Carrying within us such recent memories of Lwów's hell, Kraków calmed us and gave us hope.

It took over an hour before Aunt Stasia understood and agreed to accept the plan. My patience was sorely tested while I outlined it to her. She was to pack some clothing, a shirt, a tie, a pair of shoes, a decent suit, and, if possible, a straw hat with a large brim. Further, she was to prepare sufficient food for the return trip. She should leave Kraków on a night train, arriving in Lwów in the early morning. On arrival, she was to buy immediately two tickets to Kraków, take a taxi to the bank, and take Joseph back to Kraków by the first train available. Mrs. Halina, his loyal former Polish secretary, would help her get him home from Kraków Station.

I also suggested that he should pretend to have a severe toothache and bandage half his face, take a sleeping pill, and not speak to anybody during the trip. I had written it all down, and as I handed her the piece of paper, tried again to impress on her that every minute counted and that his life was in her hands. We were very upset as we left her, not knowing what she would do – if anything. Probably she did not fully realize the danger her husband faced. Many Jews wouldn't believe our words, so why should she?

It was in Haber's bookshop that we met Lusia's Uncle Emanuel Herman. He had settled in Kraków a few years before the war, working successfully as a representative of a well-known international pharmaceutical company. He was surprised that we had decided to live a dangerous illegal life on Aryan papers in Warsaw instead of settling in the Kraków ghetto, where his connections could help us get established. He lived there in quiet contentment with his wife, Genia, and his 14-year-old son, George.

Irka Haber was firmly opposed to living on Aryan papers. She thought it too risky and that their non-Aryan appearance would make living outside the ghetto more dangerous. On learning of our arrival, my cousin, Manusia Beckman, came to see us at the Habers. As a young girl, she used to spend her summer holidays in Oserdów where she fell in love with Ludwik. Now, she lived with her mother, my Aunt Andzia, and her brother Joseph, his wife Bronia, and their child, who was born in the ghetto, in a small but cozy flat. They all had good jobs and felt quite safe.

At the outbreak of war, I had left the keys to our flat with Manusia and asked her to save whatever she could. She had found my memorabilia and photo albums, which she had taken into the ghetto. I asked for them as I wished to deposit them with Uncle Joseph's ex-secretary, from whom I could collect them should I survive. But Manusia refused to part with them. She loved the photographs of Oserdów – the animals, the people, the orchards, and the fields – pictures that brought back the few sunny memories of her prewar life. I did not insist. After all, my main problem was saving lives, not photo albums.[1]

)

Manusia told me about other members of my large Kraków family, and I was glad to hear they were all alive and reasonably settled.

Again, I was puzzled how it could be that within this same felonious system, two such different situations could exist as in Lwów and Kraków. In the former, a total physical liquidation, in Kraków an oasis of calm and comparative security. I felt sure it was a perfidious policy of murder by installments to avoid putting the hunted animal prematurely on alert. The future was to prove me right. Time was running out. Our continued stay in Kraków didn't make sense. I decided to leave Lusia and Elżunia with Zosia while I went to Warsaw to prepare accommodation and attend to registration formalities with the police.

But first I went to take leave of Aunt Stasia. I was hoping that I would find Uncle Joseph there. Regrettably, she was home alone. She offered me tea and gave me a lesson on how to make the sign of the cross. She was a devout Catholic and did it with great pathos. She also wrote out the text of the Lord's prayer and advised me to learn it by heart. Actually, I still remembered the words from my time at secondary high school, when my Christian colleagues had recited it twice daily.

I dared not ask about Uncle Joseph, not wanting to hurt her. At last, she mentioned him. I should not worry on his account, she said. He was out of the bank with reliable care in a safe place. Despite my insistent questioning, she would not give me any details other than he was alive and in good health. I was convinced that he was dead and refusing to tell me for fear of our wrath.[2]

MOVING TO WARSAW

It was 9 a.m. when I knocked at the door of Joseph Abrahamer in Warsaw.

"Henry! How wonderful to see you!"

"And you, too, Joseph."

We had much to talk about: my horror story of Lwów and his description of life in Warsaw. He told me it was not easy to obtain a flat. Many Jewish – and non-Jewish – refugees from Lwów and other parts of Poland were frantically seeking accommodation. As a result of the expulsion of Poles from territories annexed to the German Reich, Warsaw was already overpopulated. The expelled as well as the political refugees constantly poured into this large city where it was thought to be relatively easy to disappear in the crowd. In addition to the housing crisis, it had become increasingly difficult to supply the city with food and electricity because part of Warsaw was still in ruins after the heavy bombardment of 1939.

Consequently, starting on 1 March 1942, the Germans closed Warsaw to newcomers. Only those with special permits issued by the local police were permitted entry. But Poles were not easily subjugated by the orders of the German conquerors.

Courageously defiant, they did whatever they could to frustrate the Germans' orders. There were clerks in the police registration offices willing to backdate registrations. For 700 złoty, the applicant's form would be predated to before the first of March and smuggled into the police records.

Remembering the shifty fellow who had sold me the Daraż birth certificates, I decided to check if a Piotr Daraż was already registered in Warsaw. I had never trusted my supplier; he could easily have sold several identical birth certificates to various people. Attempting to register at the local police where someone else with identical personal data had already been registered would be catastrophic for both parties.[1] I decided to lodge a request for the address of Peter Daraż. With great relief, I discovered he was not registered. Now I could go ahead. With a feeling of relief, I handed Joseph the backdated registration forms and the fees.

I started to look for a furnished room, tramping from one place to another, and finally obtained one in the flat of a pleasant-looking landlady. I phoned Lusia with the good news, asking her to come with Elżunia as soon as possible. I was somewhat concerned because this time they would have to travel without Zosia's escort. Still, our few days' experience of illegal living had given us some confidence, and little Elżunia with her blond hair and blue eyes was wonderfully convincing as proof of our Aryan identity.

The next morning, I met them at the central station and we went straight to our new flat only to be greeted with an unpleasant surprise. The landlady declared that her daughter was arriving from the country and would need the room!

There we stood, outside the door, Lusia and the child worn out after their night's travel, their suitcase on the doorstep. Did she suspect we were Jewish? I was certain she had not told us the real reason for withdrawing the offer. Perhaps another tenant had offered her a higher rent or she had found a single tenant, which was always preferable to a couple with a child. Well, it could not be helped. She returned the deposit. Unhappily, we returned to the guesthouse where I had spent the previous night.

We were lucky. They had a vacancy and the landlady agreed to accommodate us. As a rule, she did not accept families with children, but our little girl looked so lovely and well-behaved that she would make an exception. She stressed, however, that it was only for one night. That evening we went down to dinner. There were perhaps some 20 guests; half of them were surely Jews hiding on Aryan papers. We felt uneasy. We had been warned about sporadic document checks. From time to time, Polish police visited Warsaw boardinghouses and hotels and always picked up a few Jews. Sometimes this could be solved with bribes: a few thousand extra złoty were always welcome. It was easy to recognize a Jew either by suspicious-looking papers or reluctance to answer questions. Many victims were also caught at street crossings, where Polish policemen directed the traffic. A poor frightened Jew from the country, in Warsaw for the first time, might disregard the white gloves of the traffic policeman and try to cross the street at the wrong moment, giving himself away. At the four corners of a street crossing stood policemen in wait for such people. Unless able to bribe or talk their way out of trouble, they would be handed straight to the Germans.

In the dining room, a familiar face smiled at us. It was Aunt Mania Tilles from Kraków. She was an elderly lady, always elegant, who introduced herself as Mrs. Tarczynska. She lived permanently in the boardinghouse. With perfect command of Polish, she played her Aryan role very convincingly. We sat at her table feeling somehow relaxed. She warned us of Jewish informers from Lwów who collaborated with the Gestapo, denouncing refugees they recognized. Mrs. Tarczynska gave us further worrisome information: Polish blackmailers had become a great danger. By threatening denunciation to the Gestapo, these hoodlums extracted damaging sums of money.

Fortunately, the night passed peacefully without any unwanted visitors. In the early morning, I left in pursuit of a place to live. The boardinghouse was very expensive and dangerous. We had to get out quickly.

It was not an easy task. Good flats were let quickly; only dens in dirty and dangerous parts of the city were available. Landlords were suspicious and asked too many questions. Our Lwów accent was different than the Warsaw one. People were afraid.

In Żoliborz, I finally found a room to let with a telephone. I hurried there. The pleasant-looking landlady showed me a nice corner room with a balcony, once the drawing room of a four-room apartment. The price was 120 złoty a month, to which I agreed. We left the boardinghouse that same evening, hoping in the dim light of dusk that our not-too-Aryan features would be less noticeable. Disarmed by

Elżunia's appearance, Mrs. Baltorowicz, the landlady, seemed favorably disposed toward us.

The next morning, I went to the police to register our new address. I did so with trepidation. What would happen if my previous registration, for which I had paid the 700 złoty, had not been successfully recorded?

I handed in my completed forms and waited with the throngs in the waiting room. There were only two possible outcomes: All would be well, or the police would appear. Sitting and waiting was torture. Every second felt like an hour.

Suddenly, the entrance door opened and a Polish blue-uniformed policeman appeared. My heart skipped a beat. Expecting the worst, I decided to run should the policeman ask for Mr. Daraż. I stood up, ready to retreat, but then a voice from the window called out "Daraż!" With relief, but still cautious, I approached the clerk, who handed me the registration certificates, duly stamped and signed.

On my return home, I handed the registration certificates to our landlady, who promised to lodge them with the janitor, who would then take care of the formalities. That would save me the risk of facing another stranger who well could be suspicious. Janitors were notorious for working with the police. Afterward, I went to the local police to obtain our food coupons for bread, flour, sugar, marmalade, and the other basics of the Polish rations. To collect some of our luggage, which had been left with Zosia, Lusia decided to travel to Kraków since the danger of such a journey would be decidedly less for a woman than a man. I remained with Elżunia. Although only four years old, our daughter was mature for her age and did not whine, although, naturally, she kept asking for her mother. I told her stories to keep her quiet. It goes without saying that I was tense and restless awaiting Lusia's return. That day and night seemed endless, almost unbearable. After hiring a young lad at the railway station to carry her luggage, Lusia had walked with him all the way home. She didn't trust the adult porters.

We now faced another significant problem. The only documents we had were those questionable-looking birth certificates. Yet one could hardly present birth certificates to prove one's identity. We needed papers with a photograph and also some kind of work certificate. The only source I could think of was my ex-boss, Josef Elsner, so I decided I had to risk another trip to Kraków.

I took a night train, considering it safer, with less chance of curious fellow passengers. Sitting next to the window, I watched the city's glittering lights, considering that each light was a home with a family, mostly peaceful and secure. Where was God's justice, granting a safe haven to some while denying it to others? What sin had one committed by being born to Jewish parents? I could find no answer.

On my arrival in Kraków, I went immediately to the Elsner offices. I had no difficulty in obtaining a document certifying that I was employed as a commercial representative and that my duties were providing building materials for the firm of Josef Elsner Industrial Constructions throughout Warsaw and the districts of the General Government. The document was valid for one year and entitled me to travel all over the country. Equipped with two photographs apiece of Lusia and me, I went next to the Social Security Department, where I lodged the necessary forms and was told to report back in about ten days to collect the certificates.

While filling out the forms, it had occurred to me that it would be advisable to know a bit more about my place of birth. The name Śliwica, near Dubiecko in the Przemyśl district, indicated a small village and nothing more. How could I find out more?

I went to the bank in which Uncle Joseph had worked and asked his ex-secretary Mrs. Halina to let me have a look at the directory of Poland. With some apprehension, I turned the pages of that tremendous volume till I came to the letter S. I turned page after page but could not find the name Śliwica. It appeared that the village of Śliwica did not exist! I found a village Śliwnica in the same parish of Dubiecko in the Przemyśl district, as on my documents. The scoundrel who had sold me the birth certificate had omitted the letter *N* when copying! How careless, thoughtless, and irresponsible he was. I was worried and very annoyed with myself. I should have thought of checking before registering at the Social Security Department, not after. What should I do? In the end, I decided to let things go, because any attempt to correct the spelling of my birthplace on the already lodged form would certainly look suspicious. My next visit was to the German *Arbeitsamt* [Department of Labor]. Here I filled out the form correctly: Śliwnica. The clerk, a German woman, was pleasant and polite. I realized that it was easier to pull off my disguise with the Germans, but I had to be most careful in the presence of my fellow Polish citizens. I was also advised to call in ten days' time. Rather than travel back and forth, I decided to wait in Kraków.

By now, a month had passed since our escape from Lwów. I was moving around calmly, trying to feel and behave with self-assurance. I walked the streets of Kraków like everyone else. So far nobody had stopped me or stared at me, meaning my appearance, behavior and manners did not attract suspicion. Or maybe I was just lucky.

I visited Haber again and told him in detail what I had been doing both in Warsaw and Kraków. I also gave him my Warsaw address just in case, but he and Irka were not thinking of leaving. I called on my cousin Bronek Tilles, who owned a fashionable men's tie shop in the city center. Although the shop had been taken over (like all Jewish businesses) by a trustee, Bronek continued to manage it. The shop was doing well, and he even employed a young Polish girl as a saleswoman.

I expressed my concern. He had good Polish looks and was friendly with the saleswoman. Why didn't he think of some way of saving himself? I could not shake my astonishment at the easy lifestyle led by the Jews of Kraków. Surely this false paradise could not last long. Like many others, Bronek believed nothing would change. The situation had lasted for three years, his relationship with the Treuhändler was excellent, so why should he worry? "You were under Soviet rule for two years and the Lwów Jews were always closer to the idea of communism than the Kraków ones," he said. "No wonder the Germans, while liquidating communism, had to liquidate the Lwów Jewry! Here in Kraków, it is different!" Bronek invited me to dinner where, on the first floor of a block of nearby flats, a Polish family ran a small private restaurant. Using one room, a few tables, and chairs, they served a few regular customers. The food was homemade and excellent, although the prices were high. The place was like the headquarters of an underground movement. The doors were opened only with a password. All customers were Jewish, their stars removed. No questions asked.

After a few days, I went back to the Social Security Office. A box full of membership books was on the desk. The German clerk browsed through, picked up one, and checked the name Daraż. When I confirmed my name, he asked me to wait a moment, took the book, and left the room. I was alone with the box in front of me. Thinking quickly, I pulled one of the many membership books from the box and had a quick look. It was that of a boy of 18 years. Useless! I took another of a man of 35 and put it quickly in my pocket.

The German official returned and handed me the duly signed book equipped with my photograph and Lusia's and our particulars in the name of Daraż. The name of Elżunia was also included. It was my first proper identity document.

Three days later, I collected from the German Arbeitsamt a certificate of registration, signed, sealed, and stamped, with the impressive Nazi eagle and swastika. I was overjoyed. I had two excellent, genuine identity documents.

The certificate I had stolen I gave to Bronek Tilles. The photograph could be exchanged, and now an authentic Social Security identity certificate was in his hands. Bronek took it and hid it, though not with enthusiasm. He still believed he would never need it.

With heightened confidence, I strolled through the city until, suddenly, in a loud, clear voice, someone called. "Henek! Good Lord, what are you doing here? They may catch you!" Indignant and frightened, I recognized Marcel Gruner, whose bulky figure confronted me. We shook hands. Before the war, he was a friend of my cousin Genia Stillman. A tall, handsome, talkative man, working for an insurance company, Genia was an arts graduate from Kraków University. We had never been very close, but they had visited us once or twice for coffee and we had enjoyed each other's company.

Marcel was without the Jewish armband and behaved freely and with self-assurance. It looked strange to me: He was Kraków-born and, living there, surely well known to many people, yet still he moved around without an armband. When he asked me where I was staying overnight, I preferred not to tell him. He told me where I would find Genia at five o'clock that afternoon.

I arrived five minutes ahead of time to see Genia, also without an armband. She was waiting for Marcel. When she saw me, she burst into tears. She was shocked that Marcel had disclosed their meeting place and asked me to disappear at once, which I did. Our meeting had lasted no more than a few seconds.

The next day, Sunday, I intended to return to Warsaw by night train. I completed all my arrangements and vacated my room at Mrs.

Sawczyn's. It was a beautiful morning and, with nowhere to go, I wandered along the famous Kraków Boulevard. The people were well dressed and looked relaxed as they strolled along the thoroughfare, but I was uneasy, afraid of being recognized. After all, I had lived and worked in Kraków from 1934 to 1939 and many knew me. I had not been walking more than ten minutes when I encountered two prewar acquaintances. They were obviously surprised to see me in a Kraków street and greeted me nonchalantly. Then I met a young girl who had once worked for our firm. She stared at me as if I were a ghost. I hurried away as quickly as possible.[2]

The prospect of spending the remains of a Sunday walking the streets of Kraków was now a frightening one. What could I do with myself? Destiny came to my aid once more in the form of a saleswoman whom I had known by sight in Lwów. Recognizing me, she stopped. Yes, she, too, had escaped from Lwów just a few weeks ago and had found work as a housemaid with a German family. This was her day off. I told her my problem and she gave me the address of a Polish woman who had been recommended to her and with whom she had stayed temporarily until she found her present position. I went and found the woman just getting ready for church. I told her that friends I had come to visit were out and asked if she could provide a place to rest until my night train. I had spent a sleepless night on my travel to Kraków and needed a few hours' sleep. Hotels were overcrowded and very expensive. The good woman offered me tea and a piece of cake. She would be out for the day, she said, but would return in the evening. Meanwhile, she was happy for me to stay and rest. She left me some food and locked the door after her. On her return, she cooked some eggs and we ate together. I paid her 20 złoty, which was a lot of money to her. There's no doubt she realized who I was. After all, would any Pole need to spend a whole day closed up in a room? God bless you, good soul!

The night trip to Warsaw passed without incident. I was happy and confident, equipped with a few authentic documents in my pocket. Yet there was not a single check by the German police during the journey. Were they all busy in "actions"? My tension increased in the morning as we were nearing Warsaw. Somebody mentioned rumors of a raid at Central Station. Passengers were getting nervous. When we arrived at Warsaw station, I approached the exit with the other passengers, trying to look calm. There were plenty of people around. Handing in my ticket, I quickly glanced left and right. There was nothing suspicious – no gendarmes, no raids. What I did not see, however, was a man closely observing those arriving. I was unaware he had noticed my restless glances and was following me.

I left the station building again looking around. Everything seemed quiet. It was not until waiting at the tram stop for the number three tram to go to Żoliborz that I noticed him staring at me intensely, his eyes never leaving me. I tried to ignore him but could feel his stare. When I strolled along the tram stop, carrying my small suitcase, he followed. A secret agent? A police informer? A blackmailer?

I tried to persuade myself that I was imagining things, that he was simply waiting for a tram just as I was. Alas, that was not the case. I allowed several number three trams to pass. He didn't move either; he just kept staring. At last, I decided to mount a tram when it was already moving away, but he managed to jump on, too, and I felt his breath on me and his ugly, penetrating look upon me. We were nearing my destination. I could not allow him to follow me home. I confronted him.

"Why do you follow me?" I asked.

"You know well," he answered.

I suggested that we alight to continue the discussion as people were staring. The next stop was an open area, near a railway bridge. No houses, only fields on both sides.

"What do you want?" I asked.

"You are a Jew?"

"What business is it of yours?"

"I work for the police, and if you don't settle with me voluntarily, I shall take you to the station and that won't end well for you."

I was too inexperienced to realize he feared the police, too; the Polish police were fighting such extortionists not because they wanted to protect Jews but because they simply did not want to let Jewish money fall into the hands of blackmailers. I knew he was lying about working for the police, but what could I do? If I had been younger or stronger, I would have punched his face with great pleasure. But I was not. I would not win.

After some bargaining, we settled for 1,500 złoty. He then started apologizing – his father had been killed in the defense of Warsaw, his mother was sick, there were plenty of children at home. What else could he do? He had to live and support the family. He had tears in his eyes. I almost felt sorry for him. I gave him the money and he thanked me profoundly. We even shook hands. I was relieved it was all over. He was about to go when he turned and asked innocently, "What is the time, sir?" With unforgivable stupidity, I took out my gold Omega fob watch, my wedding present from Lusia's parents. The scoundrel tore it off with the chain and ran off. There I was, alone, poorer by the watch and 1,500 złoty, furious but relieved. After all, he could really have been a police informer and then I would have been in real trouble. I was glad that he hadn't robbed me of the additional 2,000 złoty hidden in another pocket. Making sure that the hoodlum had really disappeared, I mounted the next tram and arrived home a few minutes later. Lusia and Elżunia had been waiting for me anxiously and were relieved. I told Lusia my story, regretting the loss of the money and the watch.

"We are together, thank God!" she comforted me quietly. "What could be more important than that."

FIRST STEPS AS DARAŻ

Settling down in Mrs. Baltorowicz's small apartment in Żoliborz was relatively easy. However, pretending to lead a normal life turned out to be much more complicated. Each venture into the street was literally risking one's life. For a Jew hiding under false papers, the streets of Warsaw were especially treacherous. The Jews were exposed to perils that also threatened some Poles – roundups, blockading of streets, and sudden searches. Poles might be sent to German prisons or work camps. They could occasionally become hostages as a warning against future acts of sabotage by the Polish Underground. Yet fierce attacks against the Polish community were only sporadic. There were peaceful days when life seemed normal. In some neighborhoods, nothing dangerous or unpleasant ever seemed to occur. There were streets in Warsaw where no German soldier had been for many months. Of course, central areas were plagued with frequent German action – near the central railway station, on Marszałkowska Street, Aleje Jerozolimskie, Krakowskie Przedmieście, The Squares of Three Crosses, and in the vicinity of various historic buildings, movie houses, and parks. Thus, a quiet, politically non-active Polish citizen could survive the war years peacefully without being confronted by the despised German SS uniform or the threatening helmet of a German gendarme. If occasionally they did come across a patrol of SS or gendarmes – those murderous occupation forces in their gray, blue, brown, or black uniforms (depending on the weapons carried) – the citizen was neither accosted nor molested.

The situation was different for a Polish citizen who happened to be a Jew living under false Aryan papers. For them, danger lurked at every step – on each street, at each entrance, at every trolley stop, in buses or trolley cars. Any policeman, any Pole, could easily suspect a Jew by his demeanor, a sad expression, the shape of his nose, or a look betraying fear. Such danger cast a shadow of impending doom. Among thousands of daily encounters, just one evil-intentioned individual could cause a catastrophe.

Nevertheless, I could not stay home. What would Mrs. Baltorowicz think? I had presented myself to her as a business representative of a Kraków building firm – their Warsaw buyer of building materials. Mr. Jozef Elsner had given me the document, which I hung proudly on our door. From time to time, I had telephone conversations on behalf of my firm, making some appointments with clients. Needless to say, they were one sided. I would speak into the receiver, knowing my landlady could hear me since the telephone was in the hall. I would make fictitious appointments, get dressed, and leave the house. I tried avoiding my neighbors and the janitor as much as possible. I walked with a decisive step and was well dressed to look self-assured. I would take a streetcar. The carriages were overcrowded since quite a number of them had been confiscated and taken to Germany; others were not operational. Also, three-quarters of the seats were reserved for Germans: *Nur für Deutsche* [For Germans only]. These were usually nearly empty. We "Poles" were packed together like sardines. Generally, I attempted to push through toward the front where a chain separated the space reserved for the Germans from the rest.

I made a point of standing with my back to the Poles and facing the Germans, who were the regular employees of the occupation forces. They did not concern themselves with catching Jews, a business of the German police or Gestapo. I felt safer facing them, than facing my Polish compatriots.

Usually, I would get off at the Iron Gate Square, where there was a huge trading hall full of women vendors selling a variety of goods: meat, fruit, vegetables, shoes, rags, and various articles of clothing – new, used, smuggled, and stolen. Buying and selling, arguing and bargaining went on as if the war and mass murder did not exist. I walked around this magical world examining the merchandise, inquiring about prices, and even bargaining, simulating a normal existence. Learning to play the role, I laughed when others laughed, elbowed my way through the crowd with everyone else, and generally behaved like the Pole I was supposed to be.

I would search out a woman vendor who seemed decent and, smiling pleasantly, buy a few potatoes, vegetables, a piece of cheese. With these marvelous purchases, I would slowly make my way back home.

With time, I became more and more accustomed to this way of life, feeling a little more self-assured. Apparently, my appearance was not suspect. Nevertheless, I remained constantly on guard. My encounter with the blackmailer at the central railway station had unnerved me. I thought I saw blackmailers lurking everywhere in search of a victim. I avoided the central railway station for several weeks. Henry Reiss must cease to exist. In his place was Piotr Daraż, with his wife Stanislawa and little daughter Elżunia. Their lives were dependent on how well Piotr Daraż played his new part.

Time slowly assuaged my fears and I became more courageous and confident. One morning, while waiting for the tram, I felt a piercing stare. I knew that look. What was I to do? Just then the tram arrived. On a sudden impulse, I boarded it and sat down in the section assigned "For Germans Only." The tram moved on, leaving him stunned and disappointed, presumably waiting for another victim.

I took out a German newspaper from my briefcase and was soon engrossed in reading, carefully making sure that its huge masthead *Warschauer Zeitung* [Warsaw Newspaper] was clearly visible. None of the Polish passengers could see my face, nor would they suspect that in the section reserved for Germans sat a fugitive Jew. Occasionally the German police would run a document check on German citizens. Not only did I not possess the identity papers of a German national, but I also had no *Arbeitsausweis* [work ID] apart from the slip of paper from Elsner. It was such a scant document it would be of no value in an inspection. At the next stop, I moved very quickly into the section reserved for Poles, where, as Piotr Daraż, I really belonged.

Sunday mornings became a real problem. Lusia could not as easily pass for a Pole. Elżunia, with her blond hair and lovely blue eyes, looked typically Aryan. I decided that I would attend Sunday morning mass accompanied by my daughter. The reasons were twofold: first, it would not look right to Mrs. Baltorowicz if we stayed home and on Sundays and, secondly, if asked, Elżunia could testify that we had been to church.

At first, I would watch other people make the sign of the cross and kneel. I tried to imitate them, and Elżunia, who was only four, followed them in every detail. I was very pleased with her (and myself). I would carefully listen to the sermon, chant the hymns, kneel with the crowd, and leave the church with the others after mass. I always returned home feeling more tranquil as the church music and the choir had a soothing effect. Elżunia, too, enjoyed going to mass and was happy to accompany me. Slowly, I was creating a new life, albeit a frugal one. The food rations provided us with enough bread. Although there was just a mixture of flour, bran, and some unknown ingredients, it was edible and apparently harmless since we were not sick. We also were receiving small amounts of jam made of beetroot and other root vegetables. Rarely, we could obtain a little sugar. These were the rations for the Poles. Jews in the ghetto were entitled to half the Aryan ration, and even that was not always forthcoming.

Occasionally, I would go to see my friend Abrahamer to obtain the latest news from the outside world, including Lwów, where the situation was tragic. Only a small group of Jews had remained, confined to the ghetto. They were mostly young men working for the Wehrmacht along with a few young women. Nearly all the children had been exterminated. We realized the dangers of our present existence but knew we had been lucky to have escaped. Had we not left, Elżunia would definitely be dead, and probably Lusia also. The question now always in our minds was how much longer would Providence continue to protect us.

The news coming from the front was not good. The British victories in North Africa were keeping our spirits up, but we needed immediate help here in Warsaw, not in Africa. Only once did we experience cheerful excitement and joyful optimism – during a Soviet air raid over Warsaw. It must have been after midnight when we were woken up by the sharp hooting of the warning siren. It was long and awesome. The whole household jumped out of bed and we heard the terrified voice of Mrs. Bartolowicz calling out: "Run for shelter, quick!"

We hesitated a moment, then decided that we would not go down to the shelter. We reasoned that down there we would meet all the tenants of our large block of flats, and our small family, who until now had managed to keep away from other people, would suddenly have to face strange, perhaps hostile stares. It was common knowledge that many Jews were living on Aryan papers. A few hours among the tenants in the shelter could be more dangerous than spending the night in bed while Warsaw was being bombarded.

We pretended to be fast asleep, unaware of the alarm. Finally, Mrs. Bartolowicz could not stand it any longer and banged at our door. "Mr. Daraż! Air raid alarm! Run down to the basement! Quick!"

Pretending I had just woken from a deep sleep, I answered, "Ours is a corner room and difficult for the best pilots to hit. We'll be safe here."

Soon all was quiet. Everyone had gone down to the basement. We were left alone. The hoot of the siren was dying down. We could hear a few bombs being dropped far away. We felt calm and safe. We were no longer afraid of a sudden call by the Polish police, the Gestapo, a blackmailer, or any other hostile character. All of them, the whole hostile world, were at a standstill, terrified by the Soviet bombs.

For the first time in many months, while everyone around us, even the German "heroes", were trembling in the basements, we slept through the night. It was a moment of terror for all those from whom we usually hid. If a bomb did hit us, our death would be quick. No humiliation, no torture. Unfortunately, the Soviet air raids did not recur.

Although we were officially registered in the Warsaw Police Registry Office, we still had to go through the terrifying procedure of getting a *Kennkarte,* an official identity document issued by the General Government authorities that included one's photograph and fingerprints. Every person had to produce it as proof of their identity.

The inhabitants of many Warsaw suburbs had already been issued these identity cards. Finally, it was the turn of the suburb of Żoliborz. Large posters informed us of the various dates for lodging documents. The following were required: birth certificate, marriage certificate, certificate of registration, and two photographs. One had to personally present them at the local police station.

We had to face a very hard decision. Should we go there and wait in a long queue among other people who might recognize and perhaps report us to the police? Even if nobody did, we would have to face the Polish police official, present him with our poorly falsified documents, leave our fingerprints, answer some questions, and then wait nervously for four weeks, uncertain whether we would be issued our Kennkarte or arrested.

Another alternative would be to order a Kennkarte from a bribed clerk, who would come to our flat with the required forms, fill them out correctly, have our fingerprints taken, and on the following day bring it to us, duly stamped and signed for a fee of 500 złoty each! Almost all the Jews in hiding were resorting to this method as they were too afraid to go to the police themselves.

One thousand złoty was a lot of money to us. The price of a loaf of bread was 80 groszy. Besides, we were not sure whether we should trust an unknown clerk who would then learn our names and address and could easily give us away. After hours of deliberation, we decided to go there individually as together we could raise suspicions. My birth certificate was a serious problem because of the Soviet-made violet ink used and the missing *n* in Śliwnica. Thus, I decided to make a copy and have it certified by a Warsaw notary. The copy had to be made in such a way that it would be possible for me to insert the *n* after the notary had certified it. That's what I did. While copying it, I wrote "*SLIW I CA*," leaving double spaces between the letters *W* and *I* and between the *I* and *C*. The document was certified like that. Then, I used the spaces to convert the *I* to an *N* and insert another *I*, and so created the correct name: "*ŚLIWNICA.*"

I was too nervous to go to the notary myself. I did not know whether I would find a decent man or a scoundrel. My betrayal would be fatal. Lusia, being aware of the situation, decided to go to the notary herself. As a woman she could not be proven to be Jewish.

She was courageously confident and calm. I knew she could cope with any situation. The notary silently studied the documents. It was obvious they were false. Meticulously, he compared the copy with the original, hesitating at every little flaw. Finally, he asked the name and address of the person who was lodging the documents. Surprised, Lusia gave him the first name and address she could think of: Janina Drozdowska. She was cautious enough not to give her assumed name or her real address. Luckily, the notary did not ask "Janina

Drozdowska" for her identity papers. He just certified the documents signed and stamped them, only charging five złoty for each.

The marriage certificate was an original document from the parish registry in Lwów where the marriage between Piotr Daraż and Stanislawa Weżowska had taken place. I received that document directly from St. Andrew's Parish in Lwów in reply to my written request with which I had enclosed a 20 złoty note. It could have seemed suspicious that, of all the documents I was going to lodge with the police, two were certified copies and one was an original. To avoid any questions, I copied it as well. A photographer, recommended to us, took our pictures. He was a specialist in producing so-called Aryan portraits by retouching any characteristic Jewish features.

The time to go to the police station had arrived. Nervously waiting in the queue, we did not speak to each other, pretending to be strangers. Finally, we reached the official's desk. A Polish official interviewed us and took our documents. Another man took our fingerprints and gave us two numbered slips and told us to come back in four weeks' time. We were jubilant. Our appearance had not betrayed us. Lusia, despite her rather semitic features, passed the test well. That gave her more confidence, which was essential for survival in the difficult role of an Aryan.

Four weeks later we collected our *Kennkarte*. We were proud and elated. We took a risk and won. However, the acquired Kennkarte did not solve the problems of our everyday existence. Our finances were diminishing. From time to time, I would sell a pair of Lusia's stockings or a blouse and that money supported us for a time.

I was afraid to go out, yet I could not stay at home. I had to keep up appearances with our landlady. Sometimes, the janitor would come up to talk with her. We would be afraid that they were talking about us. Once, two gentlemen with briefcases called and spoke with her in the kitchen, taking notes. During those visits we trembled with fear.

CRITICAL NEED FOR EMPLOYMENT

The Germans on the Eastern Front were steadily moving forward swallowing Soviet land. They had captured the Crimea and Sevastopol and were progressing toward Baku and the Soviet oil fields. The German propaganda was triumphant. What was most on our mind was our chances for survival. We felt desperate. Could we find someone generous enough to hide us in a basement or attic and bring us bread and water if something went wrong?

During his teaching days, Lusia's father had been a close friend of a Professor Baley, a Ukrainian mathematics teacher who had taught her at the Karp-Fuchsowa High School. He had admired Lusia's exceptional talent, often complimenting her father on how quickly she solved the most complicated problems. Since then, he had been appointed professor at Warsaw University. Perhaps he still lived in Warsaw and might be willing to find us a nook in his house or garden in an emergency. His phone was not answering, so Lusia decided to visit. From the street directory, we carefully planned her journey. It was critical to avoid having to request directions.

I waited at home with Elżunia. Time was passing very slowly, my anxiety increasing with each hour. After several hours I was beside myself, and then finally I heard a key at the door. It was dark, but she was back. It had been a long trip, including a long walk from the tram stop to Professor Baley's house. He received her coolly and was obviously unhappy to see her. He seemed more concerned about whether she was followed or seen entering his house than her plight.

Lusia asked him if he knew anyone who might hide us in an emergency, even for one day or just overnight. No, he did not, it was too risky, though he offered one solution: "If you would like, you and maybe your child could stay here in my house with me, only without your husband, of course. You would be my housekeeper, my companion, the lady of my house. Neither you nor your child would come to harm. I have a good job, good German connections, and live in comfort. You would survive. After the war, you would be free to do what you want."

Lusia was appalled. She recalled his reputation as a ladies' man. He used to invite female students for private tutorials at his home. All kinds of stories were told about those "tutorials."

Disgusted, Lusia thanked him and quickly retreated. Luckily, she had not told him our new name, address, or phone number. Who knows what revenge the rejection might have precipitated?

She was tired, upset, and very disappointed, and we felt even more depressed. Was there no solution, no hope? Days were passing – hours of long, drawn-out anxiety. Going out was a tense, dangerous affair. When I went out shopping, Lusia, at home with Elżunia, was constantly worried if I would return.

The tension amplified when we heard our widowed landlady on the hallway phone. She was a cheerful and happy soul. The rent from leasing four rooms gave her financial security. Sensational events, gossip, and rumors made her days. Something was always happening in Warsaw. She was greatly excited by the Jewish problem and often shared that excitement with her Polish friends.

We had heard her discussing the profits one could gain by sheltering a Jew: "They buy false documents and then you can rent a room to one of them for 1,000 złoty per month (though our rent was 120 złoty). You can cook for him and claim another 1,000 złoty. He will be afraid to stick his head out in the street, so you will do all his shopping, for which he'll pay you another 1,000 złoty. Before you know it, you will have earned about 20,000 złoty from a single Jew in six months! Take five Jews and you've got 100,000 złoty.

"Should they get caught," she continued happily, "the Gestapo will take them away and turn them into soap and you will be left with all their possessions: their clothes, with dollars and gold jewelry sewn into them. It's an excellent business!" Then we heard in horror, "They pretend they have jobs and even make telephone calls holding the receiver and pretending they are talking to somebody, while in fact they are talking to no one."

We were struck dumb. Did she have an extension, had she been eavesdropping, or was it a guess? What should we do? Should we run? Now? But where to? Could we change our documents, our names, find other accommodation? But how? Where to start? I did not know a document forger in Warsaw. What about the new registration in Warsaw? What about a new identity card? Even if we could work it out, it would cost a great deal of money that we didn't have. I thought hard day and night trying to find a solution. Out of all this thinking, the name Poniż came to my mind and would not leave me.

Professor Venceslaw Poniż was my friendly senior tutor from Lwów Polytechnic. Since my graduation, I had lost all contact with him, although I had heard that he, too, was a professor at Warsaw University. I had a strong feeling he would be willing to help, although Lusia was not confident. After her disappointing encounter with Professor Baley, she had lost faith. I phoned him, but the number was disconnected. Still, I had to find him. I had already taken many risks, so why not another? Maybe he would permit us to spend a night, in a cellar in his house, should a sudden danger emerge at Mrs. Bartolowicz's place.

Poniż's last address had been 5 Bajonska Street in the suburb of Saska Kępa. I found the street on a map. It was a long way. I studied the map carefully. Changing trams would be necessary, increasing the risk of encountering someone dangerous.

I thought the best time to go was in the afternoon since the Germans usually carried out raids in the morning. I would take a train to Poniatowski Bridge, cross the bridge on foot, and walk along the Vistula Riverbank for the whole length of Saska Kępa until I reached Bajonska Street. It would be dangerous. One never knew who would be roaming along the embankment. I could be stopped, bashed, robbed, and thrown into the river. The weather was cold and it was beginning to snow. Should I go or not? Lusia left it for me to decide. She feared futility and danger, and I worried she was becoming depressed or indifferent. Yet an inexplicable force was propelling me toward Mr. Poniż. I had to go.

I reached the Poniatowski Bridge without trouble and started to cross it, keeping my gaze down to the water, which was gray, stony, and frightening. The bridge appeared very long to a desperate man walking alone on a gloomy November afternoon. Should I really be investing such risk hoping for a miracle?

After crossing the bridge, I walked fast, trying to disappear in the bushes alongside the riverbank, far from houses and people. I reached some stairs leading down toward the river. I was walking fast, though the distance seemed much longer than it appeared on the map. The path was winding and unpleasant. There were no street lights, only the river on one side and the silhouettes of dimly lit houses on the other. By the time I reached Bajonska Street, it would be dark. Would I be able to find Mr. Poniż's house? I was afraid. My fears increased when I saw two young men walking toward me. One of them stopped and asked the time. Politely, I replied I did not know because I had no watch. Should I have mentioned that his countryman had already cheated me of my gold Omega? I grew more and more frightened, feeling it would probably be useless and even unwise to proceed. I retreated, quickly retracing my steps, caught a tram, and returned home.

Lusia thought it was a warning, a bad omen, and did not want me to undertake the trip again. I felt differently. The strange compulsion to find Poniż meant I had to try again immediately.

The next day, I set off much earlier. The bridge did not seem so long, and the Vistula did not look so gray and overwhelming. The day before, the waves of the river had been splashing wildly against the banks; now the river was flowing calmly, almost as if leading me to the house of Mr. Poniż. The day before, the river had been warning me not to go; now the waters seemed to be encouraging, "Go on! Go on!" Finally, after two hours I found the street. I knocked at the door hesitantly, and then strongly. Eventually, it opened, and there he was – Mr. Poniż.

Recognizing me immediately, he let me in quickly, closing the door behind us. He asked whether I had noticed anyone following me. I assured him I had been very careful. Mrs. Janina Poniż appeared and they both were happy to see me alive. It was dark, there was no electricity, and their son, Duszan, a boy of 14, lit an acetylene lamp. Sitting with them in the dimly lit room, I told them all – the losses in Lwów, our narrow escape, and the dangerous situation now. I explained that I was here to discover if, in case of an emergency, they would be willing to give us shelter for a day or two. Mr. Poniż answered without hesitation. He wanted us to be sure we could depend on them for shelter. He did not trust his neighbors as some of them were quite unfriendly and could denounce them to the Gestapo. In a critical situation, we must come at night and tap three times on the kitchen window. With tears in my eyes, I tried to thank him. He had given me courage and hope.

Only those who know what it is like to live under the constant threat of betrayal, with no safe place to rest, can comprehend what that man's offer meant to me. An animal surrounded by hunters sometimes finds a hole in the ground, a bush, or some other shelter in which to catch its breath before running off again in another attempt to foil the scent of the hunters' dogs. Sometimes those animals manage to escape. Perhaps we would be lucky, too.

Mrs. Poniż served tea with bread and margarine and we talked about the war situation. With no access to a radio, I knew very little. I was thrilled to hear of the heavy fighting and the victories of the Red Army. Although Leningrad was surrounded, its people were defending it heroically. The German attacks on Moscow had stopped and the mighty German war machine was suffering enormous losses at Stalingrad. Although happening far away, we had new hope. Mr. Poniż was optimistic. He felt victory and liberation were near, which raised my spirits.

I was just getting ready to leave when suddenly we heard knocking at the door. Both Mr. and Mrs. Poniż grew pale as they looked at each other.

"What name do you use now?" asked Mr. Poniż quickly.

"Piotr Daraż," I said.

They repeated my name several times. "Sit here and don't be afraid," said Mr. Poniż. "You're my former student who has come to visit me after ten years." The knocking continued until Mrs. Poniż opened the door. To our relief, we heard a lively exchange of Polish greetings and the unexpected visitor entered.

"Your telephone isn't working," he said, "so I came by."

"This is Piotr Daraż, my former student from Lwów," Mr. Poniż introduced me. "He couldn't get through on the phone, either." The visitor was Wojslaw Bielicki. He, too, was a former student from the Warsaw University. He looked about 30, medium height, handsome, with a round face. Not having seen Poniż since graduation five years before, he told of his life during those years. He was divorced and had a four-year-old daughter. He was working as an engineer for a Warsaw building company owned by a certain Henryk Stolzman. The company had received an order for the reconstruction of the railway station in Skierniewice and Bielicki was in charge of the construction work.

The client for that contract was the Deutsche Ostbahn and the building inspectors were Germans. Unfortunately, neither Bielicki nor any of the company's employees could speak German, so he was looking for a German-speaking engineer who could represent the company in negotiations. So far, he hadn't been able to find anyone. Perhaps Mr. Poniż might be able to recommend someone.

Mr. Poniż did not hesitate. "This is your man," he said pointing at me. He turned to me and said, "You surely know enough German, don't you?"

"Of course I know German. In the years 1914-1918, I attended school in Vienna, where I spoke German. In high school, German was my second language and it was one of the subjects I passed in my matriculation. Just before the war, my last job was with the construction company owned by Jozef Elsner, who came from the Poznan region. He was a Pole of German origin. He had employed me because I could handle all the negotiations and correspondence in German with one of his clients, the Danzig Shipyard Co."

Mr. Bielicki listened keenly. When he heard I had experience in civil engineering, he said he would employ me at the construction site in Skierniewice as long as I was not afraid of contact with the Germans. One of the inspectors was an extremely unfriendly character, a typical Prussian. Even the other inspectors were frightened of him.

"I am not afraid of Germans," I assured him.

Bielicki gave me some details of the working conditions.

Work started on site on Monday morning and finished on Saturday at two in the afternoon. At two-thirty, I could return by train to

Warsaw. The offices of the Stolzman Company were in Kolejowa Street [Railway Street], while the German inspectors had their office on the first floor of the station building. It was called Bauinspection Skierniewice. The company premises consisted of a large room that used to be a storeroom. It had been partitioned off, with the front section used as the office and the rear as sleeping and dining quarters for the engineers. I was to sleep there with three other people, one of whom would be Bielicki. Was I interested?

I was stunned. My hope was to find a quiet nook where I could hide, and now I was being offered a responsible position as liaison officer between a Polish building company and the German railway. I had to think it over and advised I would let him know the following day.

Mr. Bielicki also shared a second problem. His mother, an elderly lady, had been evicted from her flat in Toruń, which was annexed into the German Reich. He had managed to find accommodation for her in Legionowo, a small town near Warsaw, in an empty house deserted by its owners. His mother was lonely and frightened at night and he was looking for a lady companion to live with her. Did Mr. and Mrs. Poniż by any chance know of anyone who would be willing to share the house with his mother? Since he was extremely busy in his work in Skierniewice, it was important to find someone quickly. In Warsaw for the weekend only, he had to discuss company problems with the management and also see his young daughter. He had little time for his own life and could not stay with his mother in Legionowo.

Mr. Poniż turned to his wife, asking, "What about Mrs. Glinska? Is she still looking for a flat?"

"She has already found something," replied Mrs. Poniż. "Besides she would never go to live in the countryside. She has a daughter living in Warsaw and she wants to be close to her. I can't think of anyone who would want to leave Warsaw."

"That's the point," said Mr. Bielicki. "One has to catch a train from Warszawa Gdańska Station and then travel for over an hour. People are afraid to be cut off from Warsaw."

"How about you?" Poniż asked me. "Perhaps your wife would like to live with Mrs. Bielicki. You mentioned you were not very happy with your present accommodation." He turned to Bielicki. "Mr. and Mrs. Daraż and their daughter live in just one room. It is very small and uncomfortable. Their daughter is only four. Would your mother mind that?"

"On the contrary!" exclaimed Mr. Bielicki. "My daughter is the same age. Sometimes I take her to visit my mother. Both girls could play together. Would you like such a change?" Bielicki was addressing me.

"I would be very happy and I am sure my mother would be, too," I said.

"I know Mrs. Daraż from Lwów," added Mrs. Poniż. "She is a very nice, quiet lady." Wisely, she did not mention that my wife had been a student or that she had never met her!

"'I can't decide myself," I responded. "I have to talk to my wife, then I will let you know about the job and about Legionowo."

Mr. Bielicki gave me the address and telephone number of the Stolzman company and asked me to contact the office the following morning by 10 a.m. As for moving to the countryside, perhaps my wife and child would visit Legionowo to meet his mother and then decide.

He was going to see his mother the following day. It was getting late. We said goodbye and Mr. Poniż winked at me in friendly reassurance that everything would be all right. Mr. Bielicki and I crossed the Poniatowski Bridge and caught the tram together. I felt safer in his company. We parted in the city, I took the number three tram, and in 20 minutes was home to Lusia, who had been waiting anxiously. Little Elżunia was asleep.

"I have been offered a job and accommodation for you and Elżunia," I told her.

Lusia quickly lit a cigarette. She always did when she was excited. We discussed the new situation; should we accept this extraordinary offer? Surely, there could be no better solution. But what would seem natural to Poles who lived normal lives could be madness for a Jew living under a false name. We tried to analyze the pros and cons. Danger number one was the necessity for me to travel by train to and from Warsaw. There were raids by the German police and blackmailers at the railway stations. Danger number two was the job itself, with the necessity of communicating with workers on the construction site. During 1937 and 1938, as mentioned before, I had been in charge of the construction of a boiler house and turbine house for a Warsaw cable manufacturing company. I might come across a worker from that time who remembered me. That was quite a possibility. Danger number three was the need to share living quarters with the other engineers. I would have to act my role of Mr. Daraż nonstop for 24 hours. I would have to eat with them, talk with them, play cards, and remain constantly careful not to say or do anything that would betray me. What if I said something in my sleep?

We considered each of these factors against the advantages, which were a steady job with the Ostbahn, an authentic and very creditable work document, and a wage of 500 złoty per month, which would provide a steady if modest livelihood. Besides, our life in Warsaw was not safe at all. How long could we live there without any job or authentic work documents, without money, just walking the streets watched by the police and the blackmailers? How long could we last like this?

Thus, I would go to see Mr. Stolzman. We went to bed late, but I could not sleep at all. I could not stop thinking about that inner force that had driven me to go to Poniż's house. I could not stop thinking about the luck of being delayed by a day, and the consequence and coincidence of meeting another student of Mr. Poniż – visiting the same day and hour as I, who had also not seen his professor for many years, a man who could offer me a job perfectly suitable to my qualifications as well as accommodation for my wife and child. Was this Providence? Could I ignore God's hand?

The next morning, I put on my best clothes and went to see Henryk Stolzman, an elegant gentleman. He had already heard about me from Bielicki and was willing to entrust me with the job in Skierniewice. Like any businessman, he was mostly concerned about profits and asked me to pay special attention to that aspect. Another engineer, a Mr. Kobylinski, was in charge of claims. I would be required to work with him and aim to extract as much money as possible from the Germans. I promised I would do my best. Stolzman seemed pleased with me, asking me to get in touch with him whenever I came to Warsaw.

I returned home happy and, naturally, very excited. It was Saturday, and on Monday morning, I was to start work at Skierniewice. Then suddenly, I got cold feet. Could I leave Lusia and Elżunia in Warsaw, would I be able to return home on Saturday? And if I did, would I find them safe and sound? As for moving to Legionowo, we decided to wait until the end of the first week in Skierniewice. We did not want to act too hastily.

There was one big problem – the name of the engineer Kobylinski, mentioned by Mr. Stolzman, seemed familiar. Didn't we have a colleague by that name? I asked Lusia if she could remember such a person. She did. "A tall, handsome man with blond hair," she said. "A certain enemy of the Jews. An active leader of anti-Jewish demonstrations at the Lwów Polytechnic."

I was terrified that this man would be the same Mr. Kobylinski. If so, he would surely recognize me. I had been very active in the Jewish self-defense organization and he knew me well. How could I find out whether he was the same Mr. Kobylinski? There was no choice but to proceed. There was no time. I packed a few necessities. Should I take a suitcase or a knapsack? We decided on the knapsack, which I could find secondhand in the marketplace and was more casual.

I was ready to set off on my journey to Skierniewice, mostly excited and happy. I was sick of sitting in Mrs. Bartolowicz's flat doing nothing. Fate had bestowed a chance on us and I had to take it. Maybe this new future for Piotr Daraż was a chance for life. Maybe it would end in catastrophe. Dig deep! I said to myself, pushing the doubts aside and remembering the Polish saying: *Do odwaznych swiat nalezy* [The world belongs to the brave].

LUSIA BLACKMAILED

I reached Warsaw Central Station without incident. Since my unfortunate arrival there from Lwów in August, I had tried to avoid the station as much as I could. But now I was more familiar with it and could not afford to be afraid. I stood in the queue with the others, bought my ticket, and located the right platform and train. At Żyrardów, I alighted and changed trains, and after an hour's journey I was in Skierniewice.

I was uneasy about meeting Kobylinski and kept in mind that there was a train returning to Warsaw in just an hour. I went to the office of the German railway inspectors to inquire about the location of Mr. Stolzman's office and ask permission to leave my knapsack for a short while. Five minutes later, entering the company's office, I waited anxiously. If, on first glance, Mr. Kobylinski appeared to be the same man I had known at the university, I would rush back to the station, grab my knapsack, and return to Warsaw on the next train.

The man at the desk advised that Kobylinski was in the adjoining room. I opened the door slightly and peered in. A slim, tall man was standing at the drawing table facing the window, but his hair was dark. I stepped closer, moving quietly, ready for an immediate escape. One glance at his profile brought relief. He was not the man I feared. I quickly introduced myself and he welcomed me courteously, having already heard about me.

Soon, Mr. Bielicki arrived and, after introducing me to the others in the office, showed me our sleeping quarters. There were two bunk beds, one along each wall. The two lower ones had been taken by Bielicki and Kobylinski; one of the upper ones was occupied by a young office clerk, Mr. Klim, and the other was for me. I reclaimed my knapsack from the office and returned to make my bed.

I had a blanket with me produced by a company called Leszczkow, which was in Belz, near Oserdów. The Leszczkow property produced textile and woolen blankets, and its special shops sold products in Lwów, Kraków, and Warsaw. It was my only possession that served to remind me of my village. Sleeping brought me a memory of Oserdów.

We lunched in the office on bread and butter, cheese, and tea, and afterwards, Mr. Bielicki took me to the inspectors' office, the *Bauinspection*, where he introduced me to two German inspectors. One was of junior rank. Johann Rudisch, a German from the Czech Sudetenland. He had a pleasant smiling face and could understand some Polish. He shook my hand, repeating my name, Daraż, before taking me to meet his superior, the *Oberinspector*, Herr Herman Hanewinckel. I had been warned. The Oberinspector was a tough, unpleasant man, capable of being rude to Poles. He was a typical member of the *Herrenvolk* [master race] and a committed Nazi.

When Inspector Rudisch introduced me, Hanewinckel was sitting at his desk and did not even bother to turn to look at me. Staring at the wall he snarled, "*Spricht er Deutsch* [Does he speak German]?"

"*Hie und da*," I answered quietly, deliberately using the colloquial expression for "here and there" that revealed my familiarity with the language.

"*Immer muss er Deutsch sprechen, nicht nur hie und da* [He must always speak German, not only here and there]," he answered angrily, showing a characteristic German lack of a sense of humor.

I quickly realized that my joking was out of place, but fortunately with a few courteous comments spoken in perfect German, I demonstrated my command of the language. He seemed satisfied and even tried to smile. He ignored Mr. Bielicki's presence completely.

Later, Mr. Bielicki shared that he was happy I had managed to establish a rapport with Inspector Rudisch and had satisfied Hanewinckel that my German was good. I was happy, too. So far, so good.

Bielicki took me around the construction site, Mr. Kobylinski showed me the accounts, and I met new people without fear. (Well, why would I, Piotr Daraż, need to be afraid?) Every Friday, Mr. Wojciechowski, Mr. Stolzman's business partner, would bring our pay from Warsaw.

I made it to Saturday without trouble. We got our wages and our share of bread. Each railway worker was entitled to one free loaf of bread a week. Some workers who did not collect their bread ration had no objection to me taking their share. Mr. Bielicki gave me his bread, too, so when I returned to Warsaw on Saturday, I had four huge loaves in my knapsack. I felt like a returning hero.

We were overjoyed to be reunited. I had to relate everything in great detail to Lusia, who listened eagerly as she smoked her usual cigarette. I gave two loaves to Mrs. Bartolowicz, which made her very happy.

As long as no one recognized me, it seemed I would be able to keep my new job. Lusia's situation had become much more dangerous as she had to take over the shopping and meet people who might view her looks with greater suspicion than they had mine. It would be best for her and Elżunia to take the one-day trip to visit Kazimiera Bielicki at Legionowo and evaluate. They did, and could see that she was a kind, reserved woman. Lusia was willing to live with her, although she was hesitant about moving to an unknown place. We decided to put off the final decision until after Christmas. It was already December and we were reluctant to spend Christmas with Mrs. Bielicki and her family as our poor knowledge of Polish religious customs could be risky.

More serious factors intervened. The workweek before Christmas was usually shorter as everyone got ready for the holidays. I was looking forward to spending days with my family. Then, unexpectedly, on Christmas Eve, the Skierniewice postman brought me a telegram from Lusia: "We are celebrating Christmas in Legionowo." A short but very significant message. I was shocked and worried. Something unexpected and threatening must have happened if Lusia had decided to leave Warsaw so suddenly. I concealed my anxiety and mentioned to Bielicki that since my family had already arrived in Legionowo, I would accompany him home and we would spend Christmas together. My news elicited no response; he was reserved as usual.

Before leaving Skierniewice, we bought some food to take home. There were two shops opposite our offices. On the left was a small cake shop whose telephone we used to make calls to Warsaw since we had no phone of our own. On the right was a grocery owned by Mrs. Biedkowska, who lived at the back of the shop. The shelves of her shop were mostly empty, but she would sell black-market goods from under the counter: butter, eggs, cheese, and sometimes meat, sausages, and sugar. She sold these things only to customers she personally knew like Bielicki, and thanks to his recommendation, to me. Thus, in addition to the usual black bread, I had some wonderful trophies: butter, cheese, potatoes, and a chicken.

For safety reasons, Bielicki and I alighted at Warsaw West following the warnings from passengers that Central Station was surrounded by Germans who were confiscating everything they could lay their hands on. We arrived without encountering trouble.

Lusia acted as if nothing had happened, but I could see through. Quickly she told me that one afternoon when she was returning home from shopping, she was accosted by two scums, one of them saying, "You are Jewish. You must come with us to the police station."

She defended herself. "I am not Jewish and I will not go with you. Leave me alone!"

"Then we'll go to your flat and talk to your landlady," one of them said. "We will check your documents and discover the truth."

Fearing a confrontation with the landlady, Lusia decided to chance her luck by bluffing. "All right," she said. "I'll go with you to the police station." And so they went. Lusia walked fast as she knew where the police station was. Approaching the police station, the two men began to slow down and talked to her in a less belligerent way. They were starting to obfuscate. "Why go to the police? You know what's awaiting you." Lusia did not answer but kept on walking. "Why all this trouble? It'll end in a disaster for you and your child." So they knew about the child. They must have been watching her for some time.

"You wanted the police," was all Lusia answered. "So we'll go to the police."

The men slowed down even more. The police station was near.

"Let's settle this matter privately. We don't want to have a guilty conscience because of you," they said, seeming to back down.

"I'm going to the police," Lusia insisted. "I'm in a hurry. My child is waiting, hungry at home."

As they came close to the police building, the blackmailers suddenly disappeared. Although the police themselves often blackmailed Jews, they did not like other blackmailers competing in this lucrative business. If caught, the two men would have been imprisoned, and they knew it well.

Despite her "win," Lusia returned home upset and frightened. The scenario could easily be repeated the next day. She packed her belongings and the following morning left with Elżunia for Legionowo. She sent the telegram from the station post office.

Carrying her luggage presented a problem of appearances, so she sought to hire a boy in Warsaw to help her carry the suitcase to the train, and then from Legionowo Station to Mrs. Bielicki's house. She would, of course, pay his fare, but it would not cost much. There were lots of boys around each station just waiting for such jobs. At the last moment, she decided against this plan, fearing that perhaps the boy who had helped carry her luggage before from the Warsaw Station was the one who later told the two blackmailers about her. How could they have known about her existence unless someone informed them? She felt quite sure that the young porter, perhaps 16 or 17 years old, was a member of one of the blackmailing gangs.

She decided to carry the suitcase herself. She packed her and the child's few things, carried it to the railway station, then up to Legionowo and Mrs. Bielicki's home, relieved that her new address was not known to anybody.

One's nerves were not always strong enough to withstand relentless challenges by blackmailers. A real Christian, even if they looked Jewish, would always react confidently. Hiding Jews, who could never be sure of themselves, were always on edge because of their lie. Only someone with exceptional personality and great mental strength could act as courageously and determined as Lusia did.

Often people would try to negotiate with their blackmailers, hoping that by paying some agreed sum of money, the problem would be solved. But the merciless criminals would often return in a few weeks' time to demand more money. Some victims would pay again only to find that the same blackmailers were back or had passed their address to another gang who started a fresh blackmailing game.

Ultimately, the victims might have no solution but to change their name and address and get new documents, which were extremely costly and sometimes impossible to procure. Every change in lodgings increased the risk of falling victim to the Polish police or being captured in a raid. Many Jews who might otherwise have survived lost their lives because of such unscrupulous ruffians.

Lusia had won that battle of wits and managed to get rid of them almost in front of the police station. In a few more seconds, she would have had to give in. It would have been too risky for her as a Jewish-looking woman to enter the police station. She had played poker for her life and won.

Just as Lusia was recounting her story, there was a knock at our door. The Bieleckis were inviting us to join them for Christmas supper. We were embarrassed and afraid. We did not know the Catholic customs. A gesture or an incorrect word could betray us and we would lose our new accommodation and the job in Skierniewice. We would have to return to our flat in Żoliborz, the address known to the blackmailers. We decided we had no choice but to smile and participate graciously. There was a white cloth on the table and a plate full of sandwiches prepared with tasty rye bread, butter, cheese, and herring. There was even a bottle of wine. We shared the Christmas supper, but the atmosphere was uneasy. We felt embarrassed and uncertain as we talked a little about the war and the battles on distant fronts and the job in Skierniewice. All the time we were nervous lest we betray ourselves. It was a relief when the evening came to an end.

The house in Legionowo was L-shaped and not big. There were three rooms and a kitchen and outside toilet. In our room, there was one single bed, a small wardrobe, and a chair. Elżunia slept on a blanket on the floor. I folded it many times and Mrs. Bielecki gave her a small pillow. It was a little hard for the poor child. but she managed to sleep while Lusia and I talked all through the night.

In the morning, Mr. Bielicki left for Warsaw. He spoke very little but smiled to Elżunia and said to me: "See you in Skierniewice on Monday." It meant my job was safe! What a relief!

Although Lusia farewelled Mrs. Baltorowicz, it was not as a final goodbye. She had told her that she was leaving for a few weeks to stay with her husband who was working for the Ostbahn (she had not left her our new address either), paid the rent a month in advance, and left her our food coupons. Almost all our belongings were left in the flat as Lusia took only the most essential things she could carry herself.

I had to think about some furniture for our new lodgings. We needed a bed for Elżunia and a partition for the middle room. A young carpenter, Jasinski, working for us in Skierniewice, agreed to make them to my design. The idea was to place a small hole in each end so a piece of string could go through, allowing me to carry it all home on the train. Somehow, I managed the two trains and two trams loaded with this heavy, bulky bundle as well as a knapsack full of food. I arrived totally exhausted but completely safe and unchallenged. In fact, I did not have to fear the Germans as they were not interested in the goods I was carrying. As for my Polish fellow travelers, they suspected nothing for I looked just like one of them, loaded up to my ears.

It was admirable to watch how inventive people were at hiding the smuggled food they brought into the city. Almost always, it was working-class women doing the smuggling, hiding slabs of meat and sausages by strapping them onto their bellies, around their waists, and under or between their breasts, which was not flattering, bulging so they could hardly move, sit, or stand. The carriages were packed, compounding the difficulties.

The Germans frequently raided the railway stations, robbing smugglers of their goods. Yet confiscated food was not a tragedy. The following day they could try again. Their lives were not threatened since they were Poles, not Jews. Nevertheless, illegally killing a cow or a pig could be punished by death, via a slave-labor-camp internment. Even so, some brave Poles still did, hence the meat. I have no doubt that the smuggled food helped thousands of Poles to survive the war. With enough money, one could in fact buy anything in Warsaw – white bread, chocolate, cakes, ham, butter, fat, and vodka.

Old, poor men also sometimes smuggled, but young men could not, as if they were caught they would be taken to Germany. A safe employment document – an Ausweis – provided some protection. The safest was issued by a German authority, a document with a round seal showing the German eagle and a swastika. Back in Lwów, to have such a stamp on documents meant to stay alive. People paid a lot of money for a piece of paper with such a stamp. Here in Warsaw, Mr. Stolzman's company issued only a small employment certificate written in Polish on ordinary paper without an official stamp. It was not worth much during a German document inspection.

I approached Inspector Hanewinckel about it. At first he did not understand. I explained to him that some of our workers, including Mr. Bielicki, might not be able to come to work should their present papers be inspected. They could even be sent to Germany as *Zwangsarbeiter* [forced laborers]. He agreed to sign the appropriate work certificates, the Arbeitsausweis. Of course it was not Bielicki I was worried about, but myself. Bielicki and the others would manage somehow, but if I were caught without a proper Ausweis, I dared not imagine what could happen.

With Hanewinckel's blessing, I designed an appropriate Ausweis document and presented it to him. He approved it immediately, and after a few days I received a number of printed cards that I filled out for our staff. Inspector Hanewinckel signed and stamped them across the photographs with the German eagle and swastika. The date of issue was 30 December 1942 and they were valid for six months. I had a fortune in my hands – a lifesaving document.

Should I fall into the hands of the Polish police, this document would be of no help. They knew how to recognize a Jew and how to check on him. But my card was excellent protection should I be caught in a German raid. The Germans did not look at one's face and they wouldn't recognize a Jew, relying only upon the seals on one's papers.

It was now 1943. January, February, and March came and went. Every Monday morning, I left for Skierniewice, and every Saturday afternoon I returned, loaded with food, my share of bread, and any special treats I had been able to buy in Mrs. Biedkowska's shop. I always returned by the same train, and Elżunia's greeting at the gate signified that everything was all right. Always neatly dressed, smiling, and with golden hair, she was very much the Aryan child.

Sometimes I forgot that I was not Piotr Daraż but a fugitive with a death sentence over his head. One Monday morning, on my way to work, I was caught in a German inspection at Legionowo. A crowd of German SS and Bahnschutz [railway] police in blue uniforms surrounded the station to inspect our documents. Many people were taken away as their employment cards were not good enough. When they checked Bielicki's documents and mine, with Ostbahn printed on them and the impressive round seal, they let us go. None of the railway workers were held, but news of the raid reached Lusia. She had to wait through six long days of not knowing until Saturday, the day I was supposed to come home. Another time I was caught at Warszawa Gdańska Station. Gendarmes, huge, well fed, and heavily armed, looking severe in their steel helmets, were doing the inspection. They stopped many people, but I was allowed to go as a worker of the Deutsche Ostbahn. Occasionally, they would inspect documents on the trains, but I felt safe with my Ausweis and was becoming less afraid. Maybe I could survive the war this way.

But I had to remain alert. Once I went into a toilet at Warsaw Central Station and suddenly recognized the face of the man who had blackmailed me in 1942. It was an ugly, unforgettable face. How I would have loved to punch it! He did not notice me and left me unmolested, but the important thing was that I was learning to live as Piotr Daraż, behaving like other Poles, not attracting special attention. Most importantly perhaps, was that I did not have the frightened look that could have betrayed me. I must have played my Daraż role convincingly for I did not encounter any difficulties in my work in Skierniewice, either.

But sometimes, there were tricky situations. It is well known that Polish workers love vodka. They drink to celebrate special occasions and they drink without any occasion. Our subcontractor, Mr. Jasinski, frequently asked me to join him. He earned good money and was always ready for a drink. "Let's have a drink, Mr. Daraż," he used to say. "Just one glass. To your health!" I can't tolerate alcohol and feared I might give myself away if alcohol loosened my lips. On the other hand, Mr. Jasinski might feel offended if I refused as it was very unnatural for a Pole not to drink. I decided to tell him that my doctor had forbidden me to smoke and drink so, reluctantly, I had to give it up. I hoped he would understand and leave me in peace.

I was conscientious in my work and generally everybody was satisfied, both the management in Warsaw and the German inspectors in Skierniewice. The reconstruction of the so called "Czar's Station" was part of our contract, though I considered it unnecessary, particularly for military purposes. No one could understand why the Germans were spending so much time, materials, and money on the building. It had been constructed at the beginning of the century especially for the Russian czar and his entourage when they paid a visit to Skierniewice. At that time, this part of Poland had belonged to the Russian Empire. The building was never used again by the Poles. Now the Germans had decided to renovate it, but no one knew why. Perhaps they expected the "German Czar, Adolf the Great," to pay a visit one day.

One part of the building was used at the moment as a mechanics' workshop, managed by a German boilermaker from Hamburg, a coarse but kind-hearted man. He would often shout at people and later give them cigarettes.

Once, he instructed me to carry out a small job for his workshop. I did the job better and quicker than he had expected, so he asked me to follow him to another part of the station building, a section that was not a part of our contract. We walked along a dark corridor until we reached a hidden door. Putting his finger to his lips to indicate silence, he opened the door, and we entered a large storeroom. I was astounded. The shelves were full of goods, anything you could wish for. When the Polish store man came up to us, the German said: "Give him a bottle of vodka. He did a good job and deserves a drink." The store man looked surprised, but he fetched a bottle of the best Polish vodka called Luksusowa [Luxurious] and gave it to the boss, who handed it to me, and putting his finger to his lips, he left.

Neither the storeman nor I knew what to say. I had no idea that a store like this existed. Nobody knew. I was not sure what to do with the vodka. I had told my workmates the same story: I suffered from ulcers and did not drink. If I took the vodka to the office, they would start asking questions such as where I had gotten it from and how much I had paid. And that information I must keep secret.

"Excuse me," I said to the store man, "but I am not allowed to drink. I've got ulcers and the doctor forbids me to touch alcohol. Perhaps you could exchange it for something else, some food?"

"What would you like?" he asked.

"Perhaps some fat, maybe a tin of lard?" I suggested.

"I don't have any lard, but there is melted butter."

"That's good. My wife will be very pleased."

The man disappeared behind the partition and soon returned with an impressive block of five kilos of butter wrapped in grease-proof paper. As he handed it to me, he asked me not to mention it to his German boss and took the vodka.

I was delighted. Five kilos of butter was a treasure. Lusia would be thrilled. But I had a problem – how to carry it home. I bought a few kilos of potatoes and some bread from Mrs. Biedkowska and covered the butter with them. The butter arrived slightly squashed, but it was still butter and tasted delicious. It lasted for a long time.

There had been no sugar for Elżunia for a long time. Perhaps I might be able to exchange a bottle of vodka for some sugar. I asked Mr. Jasinski for some good vodka, telling him I needed it for a present. He knew where to get good moonshine known as "bimber," produced illegally all over Poland. The store man smelled it, then exchanged it for two kilos of sugar and some semolina. It was like a lottery win. I bumped into him in the street, and he thanked me for the "bimber," asking for another bottle. I was loath to become involved in some "moonshine affair," but I couldn't help thinking what an excellent job it was to be a store man. Undoubtedly, many throughout German-occupied lands were living like kings.

The working days in Skierniewice were passing quietly. Bielicki, Kobylinski, young Klim, and I prepared our own meals, usually some bread and sometimes butter, a piece of cheese or some honey, anything that we could buy from Mrs. Biedkowska's shop. Sometimes, we would cook a pot of potatoes or a thick pea soup with plenty of bread. Once, after cutting a slice for myself, I placed the rest on a corner of the table in such a way that it overturned and landed upside down.

"In my part of the world," remarked Mr. Kobylinski dryly, "that is not the Christian way of putting the bread on the table."

"In my part of the world," I said calmly, "one does not place bread that way, either, but sometimes when a person is very hungry and his soup is getting cold, it happens."

I corrected the position of the bread and quietly went on eating my soup. I was disturbed by Kobylinski's remark. Was it a hint? Had he guessed something? Mr. Kobylinski's attitude toward me was always reserved. Generally, our relationship was not close. Everyone lived for himself. That suited me. I liked to keep my feelings and thoughts to myself.

At times, I discussed problems with the German inspectors. Inspector Rudisch was a pleasant, easygoing person who liked my sense of humor, and I could usually manage to talk him into accepting my suggestions, which was advantageous for our firm. Mr. Kobylinski didn't like that. He meticulously abided by the terms of the contract, which was not always profitable for our company. My bosses, Stolzman and Wojciechowski, were pleased with my actions, though.

Was it possible that Kobylinski suspected something? I was extremely careful not to repeat my faux pas with the bread. I took great care with my gestures, the way I sat, and how I spoke. But despite my caution, I once made a mistake that nearly betrayed me. As mentioned earlier, in our office there was no telephone and we used the one in the cake shop next door. Once, the lady owner rushed into our office, saying, "Mr. Daraż, you are wanted on the phone. Hurry!"

I picked up the receiver and said, "Hello, Reiss speaking," and was seized by terror, but luckily the connection with Warsaw was very bad and they could not hear me well. The lady from the cake shop was just serving a customer, so she did not hear me, either. It would only take one mistake to end it all – for all of us.

WARSAW GHETTO REVOLT

Our work usually finished at 5 p.m., after which we were free. There was no radio. Listening to the radio, particularly the London BBC news, was prohibited. There was a death penalty for just possessing a radio set.

Sometimes we had visitors – engineers from other companies. We would talk about many subjects but mainly about the war. We cracked jokes, exchanged gossip from Warsaw, and discussed the new German regulations, the raids at railway stations, and the food prices. Nothing was ever said about the Jews, as if that problem never existed, although I knew of other Polish quarters where the Jewish topic was frequently spoken about. Was I suspected? Were they being too delicate?

I tried to keep in mind that I was Piotr Daraż and would not allow myself to think about the ghetto. I dared not show emotions, either sadness or fear. However, the Warsaw Ghetto was not easy to forget as, on Saturdays, on my way home, my tram route ran down Nowiniarska Street along its wall. The tram rumbled along at great speed, but the ghetto wall imposed itself, huge and hideous, built of old bricks from buildings destroyed in the 1939 bombings. The wall was about four meters high, topped with broken glass and rows of barbed wire, ensuring no one could leave. I imagined what it must be like behind those walls, but my imagination never matched the terrible reality: over 500,000 Jews squashed into a few blocks of the poorest part of

Warsaw. They came not only from Warsaw itself, but also from other towns and included some who had been deported from Germany and other European countries. I imagined the dirt, hunger, illness, hopelessness, despair, and terror of those people who, with their families, were forced to squash into gloomy, cold spaces. What must it be like for the children who wandered those streets, where the sun never shone, without grass or trees, without schools and with no one to properly look after them? I imagined them poorly clothed, cold, sick, dirty, and hungry. The young and old, men, women, and children, were sentenced to a slow death in that hideous prison like the Christians in Nero's time.

The tram passed quickly, the driver hooting at people crossing the street too slowly, and the sound of the horn would disperse my thoughts. The tram and I were running from a world of indescribable suffering and death. For several months this was my usual route. Outside the walls, everything was quiet, although the quiet never lasted long. The Nazi murderers did not forget our existence and would not let us forget theirs. On Monday, 19 April 1943, I was traveling from Legionowo to Skierniewice as usual. Unusually, the tram slowed down while passing the walls of the ghetto and I could see people standing around in groups outside. I could hear explosions, and gunfire and thick smoke could be seen coming from the ghetto. The Germans had probably begun an action. Depressed, I reached work at Skierniewice. Colleagues mentioned the shooting, but no one was really interested. People were conditioned to such actions.

It was the week before Easter. We got to finish work on Thursday and have a few days off, and I was looking forward to that. Then, in the afternoon, someone arrived with news: "The Jews are fighting!" It seemed unbelievable. The Jews in the ghetto had taken up arms. There was a great commotion apparently. Truckloads of steel-helmeted police and SS troops as well as ambulances were apparently rushing to and from the ghetto. People were stunned. Everyone was talking about the fighting Jews.

In the afternoon, I took the train home, carrying some bread and other food from Mrs. Biedkowska. As usual, smugglers were returning to Warsaw loaded with goods. People were talking about the fighting in the ghetto, some even making jokes, though others kept silent, but most seemed delighted: The Germans are busy with the Jews. They won't have time to raid the railway stations. They were right. The stations were quiet.

When I left the station, I could smell the smoke. The crowded tram terminated prematurely in Krasinski Square. The Germans had blocked all traffic along Nowiniarska Street, needing quick and easy access to the ghetto. Without trams, heavy drays drawn by horses, such as those used for carrying beer barrels, set with rows of benches, drove along routes parallel to Nowiniarska Street. The ride cost more than the tram ticket, but it would otherwise have been difficult for me to get to Gdańska Station with my heavy knapsack. The platforms were crowded and we stood in long queues staring at the burning ghetto. We could hear shooting and explosions. I kept thinking and wondering, "God, how could you let this happen to your people?"

A tall block of flats visible behind the walls was burning. We could see smoke billowing from its windows. Silhouettes against the flames cowered and then someone jumped! Then two more! The crowd stood still, watching.

"Don't jump, Moishe, you'll break your neck," shouted someone, trying to be funny.

"Shut up! You should be ashamed of yourself," a woman said.

"Keep quiet, you scum!" said another, sharing her admonition.

Some people bent their heads in horror. One woman sitting next to me murmured, "God help you, heroes!" and another made the sign of the cross and wept quietly. I felt ashamed to be on this side of the wall. I knew my place should be among those who took up arms against the murderers of my mother, my family, Lusia's family. But how could I? When I finally arrived home, Lusia greeted me with a forced smile. Mrs. Bielicki was near so we could not show our true emotions. Piotr and Stanislawa Daraż had to act their roles. At night, when everyone was asleep, we went onto the open veranda and could see a red glow over Warsaw. The ghetto was on fire. Innocent people were being burned alive – men, women, and children. They were dying with guns or grenades in their hands or maybe just kitchen knives. All while we were enjoying the relative safety of a small suburban house. Our child was sleeping peacefully while other children were burning alive.

How long could this life last anyway? We had already had five months, which seemed like five centuries. What would be our end, or would we succeed and defend ourselves and our child to this war's end.

My work in Skierniewice continued as usual. The heroes of the ghetto were holding out for a surprisingly long time. Polish Underground papers were bringing wryly witty reports from the battlefields: "The High Command of the German Army reports that our brave units fighting in the Warsaw Ghetto have seized today one room and a kitchen using two tanks and two armored vehicles. We lost one tank and ten soldiers." In fact, the Germans were continuously bringing in new troops, which were meeting with strong resistance. More and more ambulances were entering and leaving the ghetto. Its defenders were being killed, but so were the "mighty" Nazis. Incredible!

The fighting continued right through April, although it had been expected to end in only a few days. It seemed unbelievable that defenseless, starving, and untrained boys and girls could rise against the strongest and best-equipped war machine in the world. My fellow workers made various comments. Some said, "Those are not Jews fighting but German deserters hiding in the ghetto." Others said that they were Soviet paratroopers who had landed in the ghetto when Warsaw was raided by Soviet bombers. The Poles did not want to admit that a few Jews – simple, ordinary Jews – were fighting a heroic, albeit suicidal war.

The Germans, too, were embarrassed. Inspector Rudisch took a keen interest in the events and I was glad to keep him informed. He tried to tease me. After 20 days, he joked that the Jews were fighting longer than the Poles had in 1939. He reminded me that the Poles had considered Jews as rag pickers and usurers, cowards who had shunned military service for hundreds of years. Poles were indeed ashamed to hear of Jews fighting with almost bare hands. Ten days later, Rudisch announced that the Jews were better than the French and the English in 1940. I asked him how it was possible that such a splendid, victorious German army could not cope with a few shabby, starving Jews.

The fighters had hoisted two flags on the roof of the highest building, visible from much of Warsaw. One was the Jewish blue and white, the other the white and red of Poland, and they declared they were fighting for the right to die with honor and dignity. I will not dwell much longer here on that heroic but hopeless fight. Much has been written about it, including by historians who describe the battle by the Jewish Fighting Organization (ZOB) as one of the most famous battles of the Second World War.

Unfortunately, Polish society, with very few exceptions, showed almost complete indifference. Everyday life continued. The black market flourished. In Krasinski Square, close to the walls of the ghetto, crowds of people waited their turn to ride merry-go-rounds, accompanied by loud but discordant music. Crowds of Warsaw residents came to Krasinski Square to watch the spectacle of the burning ghetto and Jewish children jumping into the fire. How bitter it must have been for those young fighters suffocating in smoke and flames to see the Polish people just across the wall having a wonderful time. I watched the laughing faces on the merry-go-round while before them burning alive were fighters for humanity, defenders of the honor of the Polish Jews and the honor of Poland: *Za wolność nasza i vasza* [For our freedom and yours].

The Germans made frequent announcements over the radio and in the press threatening the Warsaw population with death for helping Jews. Hiding with false Aryan documents was getting harder, and I felt I was being carefully watched on trams, buses, and in food queues. Blackmailers made easy profits and informers went on denouncing Jews. Many who had managed to survive on false documents until now were trapped. I was very worried about my brother Ludwik. I had lost contact with him during the action in Lwów in August 1942 but had met him once in Warsaw through Lutek Kahane, who knew my address. Ludwik told me that he had been sharing a flat with another family but had been blackmailed and had to change his name and address.

It was a rule among Jews living on false documents never to keep in close contact with one another. One Jewish face could blend in with the crowd, but two Jewish faces seen together could be easily recognized. I took great care to always be seen alone. I never walked together with Lusia, and I seldom got in touch with Ludwik or Lutek. Since I had started working in Skierniewice, I hardly ever stayed in Warsaw, so we lost all contact. Ludwik, Lutek, and Tosia knew my home and work address by heart. We never wrote down names, addresses, or phone numbers and we agreed to make contact with one another only in an emergency.

One Saturday morning, I was on the building site supervising some concrete work that had to be finished by noon. My train to Warsaw was leaving around two and I dropped into the office about 11:30 a.m. to see whether there was any news concerning our wages. To my astonishment, I found a letter in my brother's familiar handwriting on the desk. My brother never wrote to me. This was his first letter. Something unusual must have happened. I opened the letter with trembling hands and read:

Puławy, April 1943

Dear Piotr,
    I was shot several times and am staying now in the hospital in Puławy. I am writing this letter from the local post office and, at the same time, a similar letter to Tosia. She has my black wallet with money. My brown wallet was lost. I have neither money nor documents, so I can't come to Warsaw. Could someone bring me the black wallet. Please!

Fortunately, there was no one in the office to notice the effect of this letter on me. I looked at a map of Poland. Puławy was a small town between Warsaw and Lublin. There was a concentration camp in Majdanek, close to Lublin. Ludwik must have been caught in a raid and deported with other Jews to Majdanek. Probably he had jumped off the train and was shot. Somehow he must have reached the hospital in Puławy, from where he was writing this letter. I looked at the date on the letter. It had been mailed four days ago. Tosia had probably received his letter two days earlier.

Arriving in Warsaw in the afternoon, I rang Tosia immediately. We had an agreement that we never dropped in without previously making sure that the place was safe for the hosts as well as the visitors. There were incidents when people who dropped in unexpectedly were greeted by the Gestapo. Tosia was at home and told me the whole story. The Polish police, obviously alerted by informers, had entered a flat where a few Jews, including Ludwik, were living. They arrested everyone, robbed them of their money, and handed them over to the Germans. Ludwik, with a few hundred others, was put on the train, obviously for his last journey. The train was packed, but he had been able to push his way through to the wall. Being very strong, he succeeded in removing two planks and jumped through the opening of the fast-moving train. An SS man who was sitting on the roof shot him several times. Wearing a sandy-colored overcoat, he was an easy target. Had he thrown the coat out before jumping, the SS man might have focused on the coat and missed Ludwik.

In the morning, a passing farmer found him bleeding and unconscious. The farmer picked Ludwik up and took him to a hospital in the nearest town – Puławy. He was immediately put on the operating table and the bullets were successfully removed. When the staff realized he was a Jew, the Polish police were notified. They arrived and took his documents, leaving him in the hospital after the doctor advised that he would not be able to escape in his condition. The following morning, Ludwik told the nurse that he wanted to go to the post office to let his family know his whereabouts. He borrowed two złoty from her and bought envelopes, some paper, and stamps. Tosia, who received his letter two days before me, was friendly with a man, also a Jew, who had some connections with the Polish Underground. This man knew and liked Ludwik and decided to go to Puławy himself. Tosia had given him the black wallet with the spare set of documents, money, and clothes. At the hospital, he asked permission to see Ludwik, informing the reluctant director that Ludwik was a soldier in the Home Army with an important military mission to fulfill. When the director expressed surprise that a Jew could be assigned to such a task, his visitor told him: "My duty is to see our man, not to examine his racial origin." The director of the hospital conveniently disappeared and the nurses pretended not to notice when Ludwik changed his clothes and left the building, assisted by Tosia's friend.

He hired a *droshka* [coach] that took him to the river port on the Vistula. His escort thought it would be safer for Ludwik to travel by boat than train, where documents were frequently inspected. Ludwik's papers were not good and also, quite naturally after such an operation, he looked very weak, which would arouse suspicion. If the police were going to search for him, they would surely start at the railway station. His rescuer returned by train and related the whole story. I was grateful beyond what words could express. He smiled modestly. "We will talk about it after the war, if we survive," he said. Unfortunately, he did not.

Still, there was much to worry about. Ludwik should not have been left alone to return. Someone should have stayed with him or at least watched from a distance to act in an emergency. How could one help now? If he arrived back, we would need to find a safe place in a Polish home to stay a few days and recover from his wounds until hopefully the police forgot about him. There was no chance of that for a Jew. The riverboat was expected to arrive in Warsaw late Saturday evening. I always arrived in Legionowo on Saturday at seven. Were I not to arrive, Lusia would be extremely worried. To stay at Tosia's awaiting a phone call from Ludwik made no sense, although it would have been good to hear his voice and be able to go to Legionowo knowing that everything was all right, but unfortunately, I had to leave. The next day, I rushed to Warsaw. Tosia had no news. I phoned the port office. They told me that boats were arriving very irregularly. Sometimes they took a day, sometimes two to travel the distance. I waited all Sunday. There was no news on Monday, either. I returned to my normal duties in Skierniewice. There was nothing else to do and I needed to behave as if nothing had happened.

I waited with internal anguish all week and on Saturday rang Tosia to discover there had been no news. Her kind friend had gone again to Puławy to try to find out what had happened. Once more, he had spoken with the director of the hospital. He learned that about two hours after Ludwik disappeared, they informed the police and the search began. They found Ludwik in a restaurant, drinking beer with the carriage driver. The boat had been late and he had not wanted to wait alone, probably thinking a relaxed beer with a Pole was as good a disguise as any. The Polish police took Ludwik away. I was devastated and tormented. What dreadful tortures would my only brother be subjected to, with wounds still fresh from the bullets? What beastly or inhumane death did the Germans provide for him? How did the Polish police treat him before handing him over?

For a long time, I was haunted by visions of Ludwik's suffering and his last hours. As I write many years later, when the world already knows six million Jews and millions more others were murdered, it remains impossible for me to control my emotion over my brother's cruel death. Did that SS man escorting the transport have to shoot an escaping man? The gang of war criminals facing the Nuremberg trials claimed they had to obey orders. If they had refused, they said, it would have been disastrous for them. Perhaps. But did the criminal who shot my brother really have to obey that order? Was he being watched by his superior? Was he compelled to obey? No, he was not. He could have shot into the air. He need not have shot at Ludwik.

What about the Polish policeman who was searching for my brother and found him at the river port? Did he really have to find him, to recognize him? He could have pretended that he did not see him. He could have left him to his uncertain fate. A simple question I've asked myself many times is: If the escapee had been a Pole, would the policeman have found him, or would he have looked away? But the escapee was not a Pole.

Did the staff of the hospital in Puławy have to report their missing patient to the police? What consequences would the director, doctors, or nurses have faced if they had not let the police know? Would the police have arrested those responsible? Would it have been possible to establish who was responsible and therefore guilty? The hospital staff had plenty of other duties to attend to and could have easily overlooked that one of their many patients was missing. They could have explained this to their own Polish police, and nothing would have happened. The Germans did not know about the incident and did not have to know. It was entirely in the hands of the Polish hospital administrators and the Polish police. Would they have acted as they did had Ludwik not been Jewish?

The only person who showed courage and human feelings was the peasant who found the bleeding, unconscious man near the railway line. He must have realized that my brother was Jewish. The trains carrying Jews passed that way every day. The railway workers as well as the local people knew who the passengers were.

He could have ignored the wounded man. He could have reported him to the police, who would have taken care of him by their own ruthless methods. Such were the official instructions at the time. But that peasant stopped his horses and behaved as one man should to another. A true Christian.

The hunt for Jews in the Aryan part of Warsaw continued. The danger of getting caught in the street, at railway stations, and on the trams was growing. I decided to take a break from my regular trips to Legionowo and remain in Skierniewice for one Sunday. I asked Mr. Bielicki to tell Lusia so she would not worry. My excuse was that I wanted to catch up with my work on the company accounts as well as have a good rest. The Sunday visits were rather strenuous and nerve-racking.

Saturday came and at two, as usual, everyone left – the clerks, the workers, and my roommates. I was alone in the whole building, alone with my thoughts. I was sad but felt safe. I did not have to be afraid of the raids at the railway stations, the inspections of the documents, or the hunts for Jews. And I did not have to fear the frightening journey across Warsaw from Central Station to Gdańska Station and back. Locking myself in the office, I started working on my papers and drawings. I was looking forward to a quiet evening.

Suddenly, there was a knock at the door. I waited, but the person knocked again. I was not sure whether to open the door or pretend that no one was in, but the light was on. A good friend of ours, the father-in-law of Mr. Grabowiecki, the railway engineer for the *Bauinspection,* stood there. He had seen the light on and was curious why. Surprised to find me in the office, he invited me to have supper with his family. I was embarrassed. I knew I should refuse.

Mr. Grabowiecki and his father-in-law had known me for several months. They had grown accustomed to my Lwów accent. I was, however, afraid of meeting others. I did not know Mrs. Grabowiecki and did not want to meet others who might be there. Would they be equally friendly? Would they see through my act? I managed to excuse myself politely. Slightly offended, he left, but what could I do?

I slept all through the night. Sleeping while so many of my people were dying in gas chambers or burning alive in the flames of the Warsaw Ghetto. Should the police be looking for us in Warsaw? Our landlady there did not even know our present whereabouts. How wonderful.

I rose late on Sunday, feeling relaxed. It was a warm and sunny morning in the middle of May. I decided to take a stroll, not wanting to stay all day in an office, hiding, which itself could have aroused suspicion as Mr. Grabowiecki and his family already knew that I stayed in Skierniewice that weekend. As soon as I went outside, I heard someone calling out, "Hello, Mr. Daraż! Didn't you go to Warsaw?" It was our carpenter, Mr. Jasinski. He seemed pleased to see me and immediately invited me for a drink.

I could find no excuse. We went to his workshop, where he proudly showed me his equipment, stock of timber, and the windows he was making. There were no workers and he was alone. He took out two glasses and a bottle. "To your health, Mr. Daraż," he said.

"Cheers, Mr. Jasinski," I said, and we emptied two glasses.

"Dear Mr. Jasinski, I have work to do, let's leave the rest of the drink for tomorrow."

"All right," he said. "Let's go for a *mayowka*."

Good idea, I agreed. Many years ago, I often went hiking with a group of young students. We would take a few sandwiches, hard-boiled eggs, cheese, a bottle of milk or coffee, and, with our knapsacks and jumpers, wander through the beautiful Polish woods, singing, picking mushrooms and flowers, having our picnic by the stream – enjoying life and freedom. Since one went on such hikes in May, they were called mayowka.

Those were the good old days. And now in the year 1943, while this terrible war was raging and millions were dying, I was walking with Jasinski, a carpenter from Skierniewice, for a May picnic. I had to follow him. I could not refuse.

After ten minutes, I noticed other people of all ages, dressed in their Sunday best, walking in the same direction. As we came near a gate, I saw a small but beautiful church. Everyone was going there, and we followed. Then suddenly it all became clear to me: Mayowka did not mean a May walk, but a May mass.

I did not feel uneasy. I had already gained some experience since I had attended mass in Warsaw. I knew what to do in church, when to kneel, when to rise, how to make the sign of the cross, and to listen to the sermon. Later during mass, people began to sing accompanied by the organ. As mentioned before, when I was young, I had learned how to sing. Our music teacher, Mr. Golgier, organized us into a lively choir, which he conducted or accompanied on the violin. After a few weeks of practice, we were quite good. I enjoyed singing in that choir.

Twenty years before, the general animosity of the Polish students toward their Jewish colleagues seemed forgotten during singing class. We were one splendid choir; singing equalized us. We sang folk songs, national songs, and religious hymns. Now, at this May mass in Skierniewice, the congregation sang the familiar hymns. I happily joined in, singing loudly, perhaps even too loudly, but I wanted Mr. Jasinski, the priest, and the whole congregation to hear me.

Jasinski could not help but hear me. If he had harbored any doubts as to my origin, they would have been dispersed. As I sang along with the congregation, I looked at the faces around me, the faces of fathers, mothers, and children dressed in their Sunday best, and I thought of those fathers, mothers, and children who at that moment were burning alive. Why? Why, God, were the people behind the walls of the burning ghetto so different from those standing around me, singing to the same God, the same creator of all people? Then why were we, the Jewish people, chosen for such horror? But Piotr Daraż should not have such thoughts. He had to sing loudly so that others would hear him and see him. Piotr Daraż had to keep singing while the ghetto was burning, his family dying and his heart bleeding.

Slowly everyone left church. "You sing very well," said Mr. Jasinski, adding jokingly. "Like a bird."

"I used to sing in the church choir when I was young," I said modestly.

It was a splendid morning in May. The lawn in front of the church was lush and green and the lilacs were blooming. People seemed in no hurry to leave. After all, it was Sunday. I thought I saw Mr. Grabowiecki in the crowd. I was hoping that he had noticed me, too. I was feeling secure. As it turned out, it had been a very good idea to stay in Skierniewice that Sunday.

I worked through the following week in Skierniewice, so returning to Legionowo after a peaceful fortnight was a relief for me as it was a long time without news of Lusia and Elżunia. For Lusia. those were two long and apprehensive weeks.

Simultaneous to the uprising in the ghetto, there was a "clean-up" action in other parts of Warsaw. Some people tried to escape, but, although Warsaw was a big city, it was very difficult for a Jew on the run to find a spot where he could safely spend a night. I remembered the times when I was sitting in a night train between Warsaw and Kraków, looking at the thousands of little lights blinking in the darkness, thinking how each of those lights represented a home, a family, perhaps gathered round a table, eating, talking, and even singing. But for us, the outlaws, there was no home, no family, no shelter, no friends, and probably no God. I still had to travel each Saturday and each Monday, realizing the danger of being recognized. There was no choice. On one of my Monday morning trips, I had no doubts as to who the lady sitting opposite me was with a beautiful little boy about four or five years old. She was sitting by the window seeing no one, just looking out as if into some frightening void. I was certain she was a Jewish woman escaping from Warsaw. There were tears in her eyes and the boy, looking excitedly through the window, kept asking endless innocent questions. She did not answer; perhaps she did not hear him, seeming to concentrate only on holding her tears back. Maybe she was recalling terrible scenes whose consequence she could now comprehend.

I was afraid for her. She was so easily recognizable, such a typical Jewish woman with a beautiful and typical Jewish child. I tried to draw her eyes toward mine. I wanted to let her know that I understood and that she had to be strong and carry on to save herself and her boy. Her eyes did meet mine. but that only alarmed her. I turned my head away instantly. She got off the train at the next stop. I helped her with the suitcase. There were plenty of people in the carriage.

Thank God no one seemed to recognize her! Did she survive or was she caught with the boy?

It was spring, a splendid, green, Polish spring. I looked through the window at the orchards in bloom, the freshly plowed soil, and the fields of rye, wheat, sweet corn, potatoes, and sugar beets. I saw the hard-working peasants stooped over their land, a place of peace and tranquility, the land of their forefathers.

It was a different world, a fairy-tale land. For a moment I forgot that in this world, at any moment, the door of my carriage could open, and a band of German thugs could end my fight for survival in one instant. For a moment, I forgot. Then thinking of those warriors in the Warsaw Ghetto, I wondered what new chapter was being written for us. Written with the blood of those Jewish heroes. I felt proud yet ashamed at the same time. What was I fighting for? I and the others hiding on Aryan documents to save our skins – perhaps we were cowards. History would not take any notice of us. Yet someone had to survive, to pass on the story, to ensure the suffering, the courage, and the lesson of the Holocaust would go into tomorrow's history.

The train came to a halt. The station master called out "Skierniewice!" and I alighted. I moved along the platform with renewed purpose – determined to carry on doing the only thing I could do. Trying to live, fighting for my family's survival.

ONLY WITH AN AUSWEIS

After many weeks of heroic fighting by the Jews of the Warsaw Ghetto, the special SS squads under the command of the expert in Jewish extermination, General Jürgen Stroop, using artillery and tanks, destroyed the resistance, house by house. Firebombs burned remaining insurgents alive and the ghetto was leveled to the ground. Those remaining preferred mass suicide rather than to be captured and killed by the enemy. Warsaw was *Judenfrei*.

The remaining Jews still living in the Aryan districts of Warsaw on false documents were easy prey for blackmailers. I was conscious of the possibility of recognition and denouncement whenever in Warsaw, though I carried the mask of calm. One day, I met Nulek Fischler, the brother of our friend Edda from Lwów University. Because of Nulek's Aryan appearance, he had remained unchallenged so far, but he had the same fears as me. Edda had been living as the wife of Wolski, the Polish butcher, who had brought her from Lwów in 1942. She had become pregnant, but it had been impossible to find a qualified doctor or a place at any hospital as she looked very Jewish. Too frightened to keep the baby, they found someone to perform an abortion illegally, but Edda did not survive. Nulek could not hold back his tears.

Now he relayed some important news. The Warsaw Gestapo had received several thousand foreign visas for Polish Jews, mainly from South American countries and the United States, with some entry certificates to Palestine. It was too late for most, who by then had disappeared or been taken to concentration camps or killed. Apparently, the Gestapo offered to transfer those visas to other Jews in return for considerable sums of money. They would be treated as citizens of those countries, guaranteed the appropriate rights, and, we suspected, exchanged for German prisoners of war. According to Nulek's information, several hundred Jews had already been transported to a transit camp in Vittel in southern France and sent letters full of hope for their future exchange being negotiated by the Swiss Red Cross. That arrangement seemed trustworthy, as among the members of the organizing committee was the representative of The Joint (American Jewish Joint Distribution Committee) for Poland, Mr. Guzik, several Jews who used to work for the Gestapo, and other well-known citizens who had left their safe hiding places in friendly Polish homes to move into the "Polish Hotel" on Długa Street, where the Joint headquarters was located. Nulek had decided to take advantage of the opportunity and offered to put me in touch with the right people. He felt Lusia's ring (a gift from my mother) and our two gold watches (all the valuables we had) should be sufficient to buy a place on the list. I thought hard but ultimately decided I could not trust the Germans. They might take our gold and jewelry and then kill us. I advised Nulek not to risk it as he was doing well with his "Aryan" looks.

Sometime later, I learned that German trucks had collected all the candidates for foreign citizenship and delivered them to the Pawiak prison. Some were shot, and the rest were taken to Auschwitz and Bergen-Belsen. Nulek did not survive the war.

As the months passed, my Ausweis had to be renewed several times. I traveled to Legionowo carrying loads of bread and other food which, combined with tomatoes Lusia grew in the garden, fed us through the summer. Lusia had put a mother hen on about 18 eggs, and soon they had several chickens. The bread fed the chickens, too. I was impressed that Lusia, who was brought up in the city, could learn so quickly how to breed chickens and grow tomatoes.

The war situation was improving. The Germans suffered heavy losses on all fronts. By early 1943, they had lost nearly 300,000 men at Stalingrad. The tide turned against the campaign of Field Marshal Erwin Rommel in Africa. The Allies developed better protection for their sea convoys, so German submarines presented less of a threat.

American and British planes stepped up their bombing of German territory with the cooperation of Polish, Czech, and French squadrons stationed in Britain. These European airmen, particularly the Polish ones, became famous for their performance. The underground movement in occupied France, Poland, and the USSR and the forces organized by Marshal Josip Tito in Yugoslavia were causing disruptions and inflicting heavy losses on the Germans. The underground press was full of enthusiastic news about the German advance, halted on all fronts. Perhaps we might survive?

My travels to and from Warsaw continued, always with apprehension. One Saturday, there was a raid at Skierniewice station by the *Grenzschutzpolizei* [frontier police]. They surrounded the station just before the train to Warsaw was due to depart. As usual, many smugglers (heavily laden with food) were waiting for that train, and I was among them. The Germans, like a pack of vicious dogs, attacked us. They checked our documents and looked in our bags. They confiscated what they wanted. Women were wailing and the men looked on in grave silence. One of the *Grenzschutz*, an obese fellow, shouted at me "Ausweis!" He examined my pass and ordered me to open my knapsack, which was full of apples and other food. He ordered me to put it aside with the other confiscated suitcases and knapsacks mostly full of food.

I was very angry. I had been so pleased that Mrs. Biedkowska had sold me those apples, knowing how delighted Lusia and Elżunia would be. Now this German was going to steal them from me. I could not control my anger, raging at him in German, which for a moment stopped him in his tracks. He was unused to resistance and hesitated. I went on shouting: *"Ich bin der Leiter einer deutschen Baufirma hier, in Skierniewice. Wir arbeiten fur die Bauinspection. Jeder kennt mich da, fragen Sie doch, bitte!* [I am in charge of a German construction job in Skierniewice. We work for the railway. Everyone knows me. Ask them!]"

At that moment, a local *Bahnschutz* [railway police] officer was passing. We had seen each other many times. *"Kennen Sie ihn* [Do you know him]?" asked the Grenzschutzman, but the local gendarme looked frightened, grew pale, and did not answer. Was he afraid to say he knew me?

"Naturlich kennen Sie mich," I said. *"Ich sehe Sie jeden Samstag hier auf*

der Bahnstation und auch Montags wenn ich von Warschau züruck komme [Of course, you know me, you see me every Saturday going to Warsaw and every Monday morning returning from Warsaw]."

"*Sagt er die Wahrheit* [Does he speak the truth]?" asked the Grenzschutz.

"*Ja*," answered the guard. "*Ich kenne diesen Herrn; er arbeitet hier* [I know this man, he works here]."

Without saying a word, the Grenzschutz left me with my bag. The train arrived and the robbers proceeded to their next victims. My precious apples reached Legionowo.

One day, I was asked by Mr. Bielicki to accompany our accountant to the central office of the Ostbahn in Częstochowa to clarify some accounts and speed up payment from the Germans. Mr. Stolzman's accountant could not speak German. I was not pleased. I was familiar with the route between Skierniewice and Legionowo, but I was not keen for new travel experiences, this one another 250 kilometers. I was apprehensive to meet new people. Nobody asked whether it suited me to go and, of course, I couldn't refuse.

The next morning, I collected some documents and we left for Częstochowa. We arrived there without trouble and went by carriage to the hotel where the company had booked a room for us. My companion was about ten years older than me. He kept silent most of the time and so did I, though it was a social custom of those times to say very little.

We were to meet the Germans at nine the following morning. I had a look at the papers to make myself familiar with the problem. It appeared the Germans had underpaid by a considerable amount.

We decided to take a stroll before supper. The streets were almost empty. Częstochowa looked like a ghost town as we passed the empty shops still bearing Jewish names and crossed the square that used to be full of Jewish stalls. We came to what used to be the ghetto. A rusty, metal grating had been put up across the street, closing it off. We stopped and looked – empty houses, broken windows, open doors, miserable pieces of furniture on the street, an old mattress, a bucket lying upside down, a chair, feathers flying from a torn pillow – dead silence. It was a scene that evoked terrifying torment, suffering, and sadness. We stood there silent, just looking. "Perhaps it was inhuman and brutal, but with it, Hitler did solve our problem," said my companion. Returning to the hotel, we ate our supper and went to bed. My companion fell asleep quickly, but I continued to imagine the torment and suffering of these Jews of Częstochowa and the reality of my colleague's (and everyone's) satisfaction with the outcome.

The next morning, I settled the problem of the accounts with the Germans in our company's favor. Mr. Stolzman telephoned from Warsaw to thank me. Another small victory, another step toward survival. That trip to Częstochowa was my first one, but not my last. I received more calls from Warsaw and, whether it suited me or not, I had to collect my documents and travel. The Germans got to know me, and queries and disputes were quickly settled. I went there on my own now as Stolzman thought it was unnecessary for the accountant to accompany me. I never went to see the ghetto again, nor did I visit the famous Black Madonna, a holy place of worship for Poles.

Gradually, I became used to this new assignment. The danger of traveling to Częstochowa was no greater than that of traveling to Warsaw. Taking the risk was good training for me. I gained confidence, becoming more at ease acting my role as a Pole. I developed a better relationship with Inspector Rudisch, and Inspector Hanewinckel got to know me better and never refused to sign documents for me. That strengthened my position in the company, and it seemed my colleagues in Skierniewice respected me for my ability to talk so freely and confidently with the Germans.

The procedure for preparing invoices was the same as before the war. Engineer Kobylinski took the measurements of the finished construction and made out the invoices according to specifications. They were sent to Warsaw for typing and returned to Skierniewice. Then Mr. Bielicki would take it to Mr. Grabowiecki, who would carefully check it before taking it to one of the German inspectors for signing. The inspector, usually Rudisch, had to be sure the invoice was correct. If any discrepancies were discovered, the consequences would be unpleasant.

The signing procedure was not simple. First, he would have to stamp the document with each of the three seals he kept on his desk, one imprinting the date, another with the word "Inspector," and the third adding "Ostbahn-Bauinspection Skierniewice." Then the inspector would sign his name over the "Inspector" stamp before using the most important stamp with the eagle and swastika, a seal that was always locked away in a special safe, to which only the inspectors had keys, which he kept on his person.

One day, sitting before Inspector Rudisch's desk with Mr. Grabowiecki next to me, we waited for the inspector to stamp the signed invoices, but the telephone rang in the adjoining room. When he went to answer it, he left the powerful German seal with the eagle and swastika just in front of me. I could hear Rudisch speaking in the next room and knew such an opportunity might never be repeated. Quickly, I opened my briefcase and took out one of the several sheets of blank paper I always carried. Grabbing the seal, I quickly stamped my piece of paper with it. Immediately, Grabowiecki rose and retreated to his desk in a corner of the room. Obviously, he did not want to get involved. Rudisch was still talking on the telephone, so I took out three more blank sheets and stamped each one twice. The other stamps were also lying on the desk. Without those imprints, no document would be legitimate, so I stamped my papers with them all. Now, by cutting the sheets in half, I would have eight blank sheets on which I could type in any wording I wished. The stamped sheets were just back in my briefcase and all the seals correctly replaced back on the desk when Mr. Rudisch returned. He completed the stamping of the documents and handed them back to me.

"*Schönen Dank, Herr Inspector,*" I said and we parted in the usual cordial manner.

The inspector was locking the round seal back in the safe as I said goodbye to Mr. Grabowiecki, who looked at me with a strange expression. I was not bothered by it; he was a good Pole, and I was not afraid he would betray me. I was also a Pole. No doubt, he wondered why I would need false documents. Most likely he thought I was working for the underground or the Home Army. They could always use false German documents. From then on, I felt Mr. Grabowiecki looked at me differently – perhaps with some reverence, surely aware of the risk I had been taking.

After all, Rudisch could have reentered the room and found me holding the seal. What would have happened then? A call to the Gestapo would have been enough and they could have suspected both Mr. Grabowiecki and me. I well understood why he so quickly withdrew to his desk when he saw what I was doing. Grabowiecki did not need false documents; he had a quiet and steady job with the *Bauinspection* and did not need any false Ausweis. But I did; my situation was different. My job in Skierniewice was coming to an end. My Ausweis had been renewed several times already, but only for short periods each time. Living with the Ausweis was dangerous, but living without it was impossible. I had a treasure in my hands – eight lifesaving documents.

There was one problem – where to keep them before taking them home to Legionowo. I was afraid to hide them in the office lest someone find them. I could not hide them in the mattress because I was never alone in my room. So I decided to keep the papers in my briefcase, with which I never parted. In the same briefcase, I had company papers, sketches, and calculations as well as the invoices signed by Inspector Rudisch. It was full of documents.

The following day, I left for Częstochowa. I boarded the train as usual but found there was no vacant seat. The train was packed with smugglers and their goods. I stood in a corner where I could put my briefcase on the shelf beside me. We passed several stations and were crossing open country when suddenly the train slowed down, then stopped. As I looked through the window, I froze. A detachment of German police had stopped the train and were boarding.

I could feel the clamminess on my forehead as five or six men entered our compartment. Some began checking documents, while others searched the luggage. People were panicking when the Germans started throwing their bags out the windows. Women became hysterical, some hitting at the Germans with bare hands. After the Germans retaliated, the screaming subsided. In the silence, I could hear the agitated breathing of people shaken with terror. An officer was giving orders. He only had to point at a suspected person or a bag and one of his henchmen finished the job. A few young Poles were taken from the train. The officer's eyes moved from one face to another, from one shelf to another. Finally, his penetrating gaze rested on my briefcase. My heart stopped.

Picking up my briefcase he asked: *"Wem gehört das* [To whom does it belong]?"

"To me," I answered in a calm, controlled voice.

"Ausweis!" he ordered.

I passed my Ausweis to him.

"*Wohin fahren Sie* [Where are you traveling to]?"

I told him that I was working in Skierniewice and I travel every fortnight to the headquarters of Ostbahn with the invoices. I was hoping that my fluent German and my Ausweis would be enough for him and that he would not open my briefcase.

Unfortunately, he was not so trusting. My beautiful, prewar leather briefcase had two little locks. He opened both and took the folder with the documents out while the other policemen waited like vicious dogs, ready to attack. Everyone was silent, watching the German officer and me. He opened the folder and carefully studied every document, examining the seals and signatures, checking one after another.

I was not afraid anymore. I felt that in only a few seconds my stamped blank pages would be discovered, and it would be the end. But I suppose a miracle occurred. He simply discontinued his search, shut the folder, put it back into the briefcase, which he locked with German meticulousness, and returned it to the shelf, exactly in the same spot from which he had taken it. A perfect example of *Deutsche Ordnung* [German order]. Handing back my Ausweis, the despised pack of *Raubritters* [robber knights] left the train. Soon, we were moving again. The whole operation had lasted no more than 20 minutes, though to me it had seemed an eternity.

I visited Josef Abrahamer a few days after this latest narrow escape. To my surprise, I learned from him that there was a possibility of undergoing an operation that would rectify a circumcision. Two Jewish doctors from Kraków were performing such operations for 12,000 złoty – a lot of money considering that my monthly salary was 500. If successful, such an operation would be a miracle, making the dream of survival more likely. Josef would find out more about it for me.

He also mentioned the possibility of crossing over illegally into Hungary, where apparently the Jews lived a peaceful, normal life, without ghettos or Jewish stars. Some Polish Jews had written after crossing the border that they had been granted asylum and given financial assistance! It sounded incredible. I asked Abrahamer to make inquiries.

Conscious of my recently acquired forgeries, I asked him whether he had a safe Ausweis. "Yes," he replied, showing me a miserable document with obviously forged seals. He was delighted when I presented him with one of my "real" documents. I forged the signature of Inspector Hanewinckel, and with his typewriter he could do the rest. I explained how I had obtained the forgeries and related the story of my close encounter with the German border police on the train. Only in the retelling did it sink in how close I had been to death. I felt an angel watching over me. My mother?

"*Krowki* for sale, ladies and gentlemen. *Krowki,* two for a złoty." I opened my eyes. I was on the train to Legionowo. I must have fallen asleep. There was the Polish conductor standing in the doorway, but instead of checking tickets he was selling sweets – *Krowki* [cows] – made from milk and sugar with the picture of a cow on the wrapping. The passengers were buying them, and the Polish conductor claimed some extra money to add to his meager wages.

Then, under cover of darkness, the train came to a slow stop. I was afraid of those unexpected stops. Through the window, all appeared quiet except for some people crowding around the engine. I soon realized what was going on: The train driver and his assistant were hastily unloading coal, which was being quickly carried away in sacks. After a few minutes, the train moved on, leaving nothing but a large black mark on the snow-covered field as witness.

I bought two sweets from the conductor. I would have bought more, but others were only buying two and I did not want to attract attention. We shared the sweets after supper – Elżunia a whole, and we shared the other. When Elżunia went to bed, I told Lusia about the forgeries and the Germans on the train. I gave her the papers to hide. Once my job in Skierniewice finished and my current Ausweis expired, they would be useful for us and others.

Mrs. Bielicki, who would go to the village to do her shopping, buy newspapers, change library books, and hear the local gossip, shared some information with Lusia. The Jews were a favorite topic of conversation and the ghetto uprising revealed that the locals did not resent the killing of the Jews. What annoyed them was Germans destroying Jewish houses and shops – properties that the Poles considered should belong to them. Mrs. Bielicki was agitated by the news that German police had found Jewish families hiding in the village. Polish families were shot on the spot for hiding them. Mrs.

Bielicki's opinion was that monuments should be erected to honor Hitler for solving the Jewish problem. Such a statement from a cultured Polish lady – an artist, painter, and sculptor educated at the Sorbonne – was horrifying. Sharing a house with a person who expressed such views was unpleasant, but more importantly, we realized we could never hope for understanding or help if we needed it.

ACCUSED

An argument broke out between Mr. Bielicki and Mr. Kuhn (a Pole with a German name), who was in charge of the companies' mechanical problems. I cannot remember the reason, but Kuhn felt offended and refused to speak to Mr. Bielicki. The situation became very unpleasant as each felt their honor was at stake and demanded satisfaction. They must have been members of a student fraternity, actually believing only a duel could repair their besmirched honor.

I tried to mediate without success. Finally, Mr. Kuhn asked me to be his second for a duel! I was embarrassed and unhappy. Kuhn brought me the "Code of Honor" by Boziewicz, a kind of manual stipulating how such matters of honor be handled by members of the Polish academic fraternity. Despite reading, I could not find a solution. A duel? What nonsense! I invited them to consider mediation. "We are all trampled by a hated enemy. The whole nation – men, women and children – are suffering. Young people are being deprived of education. Our brothers are fighting in the underground or dying in concentration camps. The prisons are full of martyrs. Innocent people are being killed while you, gentlemen, are fighting for your individual honor instead of the honor of your nation (a subtle reference to the Warsaw Ghetto revolt). In my humble opinion, now is not the time for educated and proud people, keen patriots, to waste their strength, which must be saved to rebuild our destroyed country. In the face of national tragedy, I beg of you, forget your argument, forgive, and shake hands." It worked. They rose and actually shook hands, obviously moved and thanked me. Imagine if they realized who the real Piotr Daraż was...

Once, I asked Mr. Poniż if Bielecki might know I was a Jew. He admitted that Bielicki had queried him about it. He had replied that he knew Mr. Daraż in Lwów as his student, though without examining his bodily characteristics. I never learned whether Mr. Bielicki had considered that sufficient reassurance, but he never asked Mr. Poniż again and continued to accept my work and residence in Skierniewice and Legionowo.

I used to buy our food in Mrs. Biedkowska's shop. One evening, while Mr. Bielicki and I were shopping, Mrs. Biedkowska asked Bielicki to speak with him in private. Of course, I worried that the important and confidential matter concerned me. What should I do? I could already see myself without my job and without a home for Lusia and our child. I had to find a face-saving way to leave before being told to go. After ten minutes, Mr. Bielicki returned. He was taciturn as usual, but after an uneasy silence, I decided to preempt him. "I forgot to tell you," I said, "I know that the work in Skierniewice is coming to an end, but I have received a letter from my previous boss, Mr. Elsner from Kraków. He advised he would be pleased to take me back, as there was plenty of work there."

This was a face-saving exit from Skierniewice. If my situation became uncertain, I wanted to create the impression that I was leaving of my free will. It would look credible, and perhaps Lusia and Elżunia could even remain in Legionowo. I would stay in Warsaw – and maybe Poniż would help. "What do you think Mr. Bielicki? Will the Stolzman Company have more work for me?" I asked.

Mr. Bielicki listened quietly then replied that, in his opinion, I should stay in Skierniewice to finish the job unless I was in a hurry to take up a position now. I was relieved. Perhaps I was mistaken. After a while, my curiosity got the better of me and I asked, "What did Mrs. Biedkowska want from you, if I may ask?"

"Nothing important. She's obsessed with the Russian Revolution of 1917, during which she suffered from actions by Jews and warned me to be careful because you are, in her opinion, a Jew," he said calmly.

"What? How dare she accuse me?" I exclaimed. I left the office pretending outrage and intent to see her. In fact, I was terribly frightened. I did run to the shop, but it was closed.[1] I tried to maintain my calm, but after all, why should Piotr Daraż be upset? I went to bed thinking of what I could usefully say the following day, a conversation that could decide my whole future. Even the wisdom of initiating it made me uncertain.

The following afternoon, I did go to see Mrs. Biedkowska. Strangely enough, although I never felt nervous talking to Germans, I was trembling when I went to see that Polish woman. She was sitting behind the counter. There were no customers in the shop. She was surprised when I asked to speak with her in confidence. She had nothing to sell anyway, so she locked the shop. How to begin? I decided to appeal to her humane feelings, believing that nearly everybody was capable of kindness, understanding, and sympathy. It was only a matter of finding the right approach to arouse such feelings. I wanted to try to appeal to Mrs. Biedkowska, the only chance left to me.

"Dear Mrs. Biedkowska, you must have guessed why I want to talk to you," I began calmly, looking straight into her eyes. "Mr. Bielicki shared your opinion of me, one that could have grave consequences for me and my family. Before we try to establish its truth, I would like to ask you why you spoke to Mr. Bielicki and not to me?"

She was surprised but not embarrassed. She answered calmly, "Dear sir, I went through the Revolution in Russia in 1917. Jews were the organizers and the executioners of the Soviet Revolution. Russians were only their tools. Together they killed my father and husband. I escaped with my children, leaving everything behind, then my children were lost in the crowd, and I have been alone until today. It should not surprise you that I hate Jews. As to you, it seems to me that you are a Jew, and that is why I warned Mr. Bielicki."

"Dear Madam," I said, "because the Bolsheviks killed your father and your husband 20 years ago, you accuse me now. Yet if, as a result of your remarks, the German police become interested in me, my family and I will be in grave danger. Before I can prove to them that I'm not a Jew, the Gestapo will likely imprison me. My wife and four-year-old daughter who live with Mr. Bielicki's mother will be without support and may not survive. Will you, as a devout Catholic (under the cross hanging on the wall) allow your conscience to bear the guilt of deaths precipitated by your actions? Could you forgive yourself?"

She was listening in silence.

"As to the Bolsheviks," I continued, "I did notice in Lwów in 1939-1941 that Jews greeted the Red Army as their saviors. But I also saw many Ukrainians and Poles who entered the Russian service. I saw families of Polish officers deported to Siberia, including my own uncle and aunt, aged over 70, as their son was a Polish officer. Should I be subjected to an interrogation by German police or Gestapo, because of murders committed by Jews or Bolsheviks almost 20 years ago?"

Mrs. Biedkowska was looking at me, confused. "Mr. Daraż, don't be afraid. I don't know whether you are a Jew or not and I don't want to know. You seem to have many Jewish features, yet I know people, and I have the feeling you are a decent man. Keep on working. I'll always prepare something for you to take home to your wife and child."

I felt relieved. I could stay in Skierniewice and Lusia could go on living in Legionowo. For the time being, we were safe. Nevertheless, it was a warning. If I was recognized once, I could be recognized again. I decided to investigate the possibility of escaping to Hungary more seriously. Obviously, the illegal crossing of the Polish-Slovak and Slovak-Hungarian borders could be dangerous, but so was our daily life in Skierniewice, Legionowo, and Warsaw. Perhaps in Hungary we might have a better chance.

My Saturday trips through Warsaw were nerve-racking. Big posters in large print threatened death for any underground activities against the German forces. One day, however, a new type of poster appeared. It depicted a Soviet soldier with a stereotypical Jewish hooked nose and a bloodthirsty look holding a gun at the back of a Polish officer's head. The officer's arms were twisted and tied behind his back. This coincided with sensational headlines in the press of the German army's discovery in Katyn, near Smolensk, of mass graves containing bodies of Polish officers with bullet holes in the back of their heads. Photos on the front pages depicted their bodies, in full uniform, buried in layers.

In 1939, the Soviet NKVD had arrested large numbers of Polish officers and deported them to the East – my cousin, Józek, among them. The German army was now warning Poles of a Jewish-Soviet alliance and of barbarism in the event of an Allied victory. Josef

Goebbels, the infamous Nazi minister for propaganda, was expert at this. The criminals of the "New Order," who had by then killed millions of Jews and hundreds of thousands of others, were suddenly appalled at this sight of the murdered Polish officers and using propaganda to garner support.

The Germans invited the International Red Cross to investigate. Scientists from many countries examined the bodies and identified them. Every day new names were published. I regularly read *The Warsaw Courier* and one day found listed among the identified bodies: "REISS, Jozef, engineer, born 11 June 1907 in Budynin, lieutenant, employed in Expon-Bacon factory in Zloczów." My cousin!

Józek was not the only one in my family who lost his life wearing the uniform of the Polish army. Adolf Beckman, my cousin, the beloved son of my mother's sister Andzia from Kraków, was a poor scholar and unable to get his high school certificate. At age 21, he was called up for army service and spent two years being derided as a Jew. I remember one incident he related. Adolf (we called him "Dolek") had been an excellent marksman. To the surprise of the non-commissioned officers and soldiers, he would hit the bull's-eye with regularity and precision. A sharpshooter usually gained promotion and privilege easily and was the pride of a company. At one shooting competition, Dolek, the only Jew, entered the finals. He performed well, recording nine or ten after each round. A young second lieutenant was in charge of the competition. After eight of Dolek's excellent shots, he demanded his rifle. "I want to have a go," he said.

An order is an order: Dolek handed his rifle over. The officer aimed and, in the distance, up jumped the numbers three, then four. "I completed your round," said the officer. "That makes up the ten, and that's the end of the competition." As a result, Private Adolf Beckman did not qualify as a sharpshooter. He died in the first few days of fighting against German tanks.

Another cousin, Edward, the younger son of Uncle Salomon, finished his training at the military academy with the rank of second lieutenant. He was to be demobilized on 1 September 1939. Alas, the war broke out and so instead he went to the front line. In a battle he was taken prisoner to a POW camp for officers (*Oflag Offizierslager*) in Waldenberg. Among his "brother officers" was someone who informed the camp commander that there were Jews among the officers. This led to a physical examination. Fortunately, not every German approved of Hitler's racial theory and the camp physician managed to overlook Edward's Jewish "characteristics." Edward remained in the camp as a Pole. After liberation, the Polish People's Republic decorated him with the Order of Polonia Restituta, the Golden Cross of Merit, and the Medal of Victory and Liberty.

Three cousins, three Polish uniforms, and three different destinies. To one, a bullet through the skull at the hands of the Soviet NKVD – a soldier's death on the battlefield; to the second and the third, a medal.

Stalin vehemently denied the German accusations, accused the Polish government-in-exile of collaborating with the Germans, and broke off diplomatic relations.

The propaganda directed against the Żydokomuna [Jewish communists] caused even greater hatred by the Poles against the few surviving Jews. More bad news struck with General Władysław Sikorski's death in a plane crash near Gibraltar after his flight to inspect the Polish army units in Palestine. Sikorski (prime minister of the Polish government-in-exile) was a popular leader, and his tragic loss was deeply mourned by the nation. Our German "friends," Inspectors Rudisch and Hanewinckel, like all Germans, were pleased by the loss that Poland had suffered. "*Schöne Freunde habt Ihr, Ihr Polen* [Nice friends you have got, you Poles]!" teased Inspector Rudisch. I kept silent.

We, too, had our moments of joy when the Germans were forced out of Africa and the Allies landed in Sicily. We were especially pleased to hear the great news that the Germans had been betrayed by the Italians, who had suddenly joined the Allies. Everyone in Poland got drunk on that occasion. Poor Inspector Rudisch had a long face. "*Schöne Freunde habt Ihr, Herr Inspector* [Nice friends have you got, Herr Inspector]!" I could not refrain from a touch of sarcasm. He tried to cheer himself up by saying their Italian friends were not actually worth much and reminding that they had done the same during World War I.

Meanwhile, the work in Skierniewice was coming to an end. The bosses were expecting settlement of the final account, and Mr. Kobylinski prepared the invoice summing up the results of our many months of work. The figure was considered unsatisfactory by the owners, who had expected a considerably higher profit. One of the company directors, Mr. Wojciechowski, came to try to convince Mr. Kobylinski to alter the account in the company's favor. Mr. Kobylinski refused, concerned that changes were not supported by the building plans and might be picked up by the Germans. Mr. Bielicki took the same stand. Finally, Mr. Wojciechowski approached me, asking whether I had any ideas on how to increase the amount due from the Germans. It was, he said, the patriotic duty of every Polish citizen to extract as much as possible from the Germans. I took the same stand as both the engineers. The building was finished, and all measurements could easily be checked against the plans. "However," I added, after a moment of hesitation, "we could increase the dimensions of the underground structure. The Germans would surely not dig around the foundations to measure their depth!"

"That would not be possible," said Mr. Kobylinski. "Before we started work, the Germans made a survey, and after the excavations were completed, another was done. All measurements were shown on the drawings. We have the copies, and the Germans have the originals, so they could easily check the amended figures."

I suggested that the only way to carry out this forgery would be to obtain the originals from the Germans, alter them where necessary, and return them.

"That's out of the question," replied Mr. Kobylinski. "I would not undertake that."

"Nor would I," said Mr. Bielicki.

"What about you, Mr. Daraż?" asked Mr. Wojciechowski. "'Do you think it can be done?"

"I don't know. I'd have to think about it," I answered.

"The company will cover all costs if you would be willing to try." Mr. Wojciechowski said.

"I might if Mr. Kobylinski and Mr. Bielicki don't object," I responded, ensuring deference to the two men.

"Not at all!" said Mr. Kobylinski, stating they would be pleased.

I knew exactly how to do it from my past experience during the Soviet occupation in Lwów. The present problem was similar. The risk was great but excited me.

First, I had to get the original survey documents, which were kept in a safe in the inspectors' office. The next day, I called on Mr. Rudisch. I made no mention of my problem, simply asking him about his planned trip home for the holidays. Would he like something for his family that I could try to obtain in Warsaw? Pleased at my offer, he asked me to buy shoes for his four-year-old daughter, and perhaps a large goose. I was glad to take his order, feeling it would pave the way for my request. The following Monday, I handed Rudisch not only the shoes but also a little dress for his daughter. He was extremely happy and asked me about the price.

"It's a present from the company," I said. "I couldn't buy you the goose as yet, but I ordered one, and, if possible, I will bring it next week. You realize that your friends in the blue uniforms may also have an appetite for a goose dinner and take it from me."

"God forbid!" he said.

We both smiled.

Now was my opportunity. "In conjunction with the preparation of the final account, I may need to examine the original documents as the dimensions on our copy are barely readable," I said. "Could I have them for an hour?" He opened the safe, located the plans, and handed them to me, requesting I return them as soon as possible as it is forbidden to let anyone have the originals.

Returning to my office, I carefully entered all figures that needed to be amended on the original and our copy as well and returned the documents to him. Based on the new dimensions, I made corrections to the invoice prepared by Mr. Kobylinski. The final sum exceeded the originally claimed amount of 600,000 złoty by over 100,000 złoty. Mr. Wojciechowski didn't hide his pleasure and, when thanking me, asked about my costs. He appreciated that such a job had to be worth something and knew some bribery had to be involved. I told him 10,000 złoty, and he accepted it immediately. The invoice was approved by the German office in Skierniewice, but that did not guarantee it would be accepted by the Head Office of the Ostbahn in Częstochowa. Knowing how precise Germans were, I was worried they might look back into previously paid invoices and discover discrepancies. That could cause serious trouble for the company and Rudisch and have frightening consequences for me.

LUSIA BLACKMAILED AGAIN

Again, a request came from Warsaw to go to Częstochowa to hurry payment. An idea entered my mind. While in Częstochowa, perhaps I could pay a visit to the Habers, who were staying in a small town near Kraków. It was a gamble, but it was almost two years since we had seen them in Kraków on their way to Warsaw as they fled the September 1942 massacre in Lwów. Like many others, the Habers remained in the Kraków Ghetto. I had given them my address in Skierniewice.

One day, I received an unexpected letter. The sender was from an Adam Haberko. Henio had obviously changed his name. He wrote that they had managed to leave Kraków at 11.58 p.m. I knew what he meant – they had fled at the last moment. I was so happy they had made it. He had received a letter from his sister in Budapest, who wrote that life in Hungary was more or less the same as before the war and that he would like to visit her. He provided his new address and advised me how to find it so I could avoid asking passersby.

I knew that Haber did not have a sister in Budapest. I guessed he must have also heard about the situation in Hungary and was considering the possibility of escaping there. Perhaps he had some contacts there. Wieliczka was very near Bochnia, where the organized escapes to Hungary started many months ago. Although such escapes seemed extremely dangerous, I believed it was the only solution for our situation, which no longer seemed safe. As work in Skierniewice was coming to an end, being jobless in Legionowo was far too risky. I had to do something.

We also feared the approaching front – the unavoidable crush of two military giants. In addition to the normal dangers of war, the whole village might be resettled and we could be recognized. While we were considering whether to go, a grave incident involving Lusia finally decided it. She was blackmailed by the Polish police. It happened like this:

Mrs. Bielicki had a tiny, portable stove on which they could cook, using pinecones as fuel. They burned very slowly and kept the temperature high for a long period. It was difficult and too expensive to buy proper fuel, so the little stove was very precious.

About an hour's walk from the village was a huge, dense pine forest. Needing more cones, Lusia one day decided to go herself, trying to help Mrs. Bielicki, who usually supplied them. It was a beautiful autumn day. Lusia dressed Elżunia, brushed her hair, tied it with a ribbon, took Mrs. Bielicki's knapsack, and off they went. Soon they were outside the village amid fields and meadows dotted with wildflowers. It was a fairyland. The child was delighted. It was her first excursion ever. She skipped and ran about, gleeful and excited. They reached the forest and found plenty of dry cones, even small ones, which were best. Soon the knapsack was full. Lusia had sewn a small cotton sack for Elżunia, who filled that up, too. It was great fun.

After a short rest, they set off on their return. The dry cones were light and easy to carry. When approaching the village, Lusia noticed two men and felt uneasy, but there was no alternate route to escape. As they came closer, she recognized the navy blue uniforms of the Polish police. They stopped her and started asking questions: where was she coming from, what was she carrying, and for whom? They emptied her knapsack but found only cones, of course. They decided that Lusia was connected with the Polish Underground and that she had carried food for the Polish freedom fighters, who were hiding in the forests.

In vain Lusia denied the accusations. She explained that no mother would drag her child on such a long and dangerous journey deep into the forest. The policemen maintained their suspicions and then changed their accusation: "You are Jewish and carry food for Jews hiding in the forests." They followed her home and Mrs. Bielicki opened the door. "Do you know that you are hiding Jews?" asked one of the policemen. They entered our tiny room and searched it carefully. We had nothing except a few items of clothing hanging on the pegs – typical "treasures" of a Jewish refugee.

They demanded to see Lusia's documents. They had a careful look at her certificate stating that I was employed by the German railways. They looked at my photograph (in which I could pass for an Aryan). They wanted to see Lusia's birth certificate. Instead, she showed them the marriage certificate, which looked convincing because it was an authentic one. Again, they started interrogating her. Luckily, she remembered the parents' names and the mother's maiden name. She also remembered her supposed date of birth but unfortunately forgot the date of marriage. She did not want to blunder so said she could not remember.

The younger policeman left the room. The older one, about 50, stayed with her. Very politely, he asked her, "Was it spring, summer, or autumn?"

"I don't know. I can't remember," Lusia insisted.

The policeman was certain she was Jewish. "Can't you really remember whether on the day of your wedding you were wearing a summer dress or a winter coat?" he asked.

"No, I can't," Lusia replied. She realized she was trapped.

The policeman seemed to be a decent man. She tried to appeal to his human feelings. "My husband has been working for the railways since before the war," she said. "This is our child." He had already noticed the golden hair and blue eyes of our daughter, so typical for a Polish child. "If you arrest and hand us over to the Germans, it will be disastrous for all of us, particularly my husband, born a Pole. They will kill his child, a Polish child. What good will it bring you? You will have innocent blood on your hands."

He was looking at her sympathetically, she thought. She continued, "You probably have a wife and children, too. How would you feel if you came home from work to find an empty house, your wife and children gone? My husband works for the railways with Mrs. Bielicki's son. They come home every Saturday and stay for Sunday. Do you want my husband to come home and find that his child has been taken away? Why would you want to do that?"

The policeman was hesitating. "Look," continued Lusia calmly, "forget that we exist and I will give you 1,000 złoty. You can have a drink to our health and yours. All right?"

"All right," was the answer. Then, speaking loudly, the policeman said, "I'll take your documents to the police station to be checked. I'll come back tomorrow around three." He smiled as he left the room.

Outside, he said to Mrs. Bielicki, "We've taken the lady's documents to be checked. We'll drop in tomorrow." Mrs. Bielicki uttered not a word. Lusia went to the kitchen and started cooking soup for the child, making the fire with the cones she had just collected. The following day around three, the older policeman came on his own. He entered Lusia's room and closed the door. Lusia gave him 1,000 złoty in various denominations, from 500 złoty to several one-złoty notes. She had selected the mixed notes deliberately so he would not think she had plenty of 500-złoty banknotes.

Returning her documents he said quietly, "You need not worry. The matter has been settled."

"For good?" asked Lusia.

"Forever," said the policeman with a smile.

"One more thing," said Lusia as he was about to leave. "Could you please tell Mrs. Bielicki, who is very upset, that everything is all right?"

Mrs. Bielicki was nervously waiting in the kitchen. "Everything is all right, madam," he said, leaving the room. "We checked all the documents. We made a mistake. I came to apologize to Mrs. Daraż and return her papers. Goodbye."

Lusia finished telling me her story. I had listened trembling. We could not sleep that night, wondering whether the policeman would come back. He knew that I would be home on Sunday. But he did not return that night or any following night. Our policeman did not come back, but one day another might come. The decision was made. We were going to Hungary.

The same doctor from Kraków who was reversing circumcision had contact with the organizers of the escapes. My friend Mr. Abrahamer gave me the address. I went to see him in the apartment where he lived comfortably with his wife, Wisia. They had no landlady. He did not have to pretend. His nephew Jurek had been operated on successfully and lived next door with his mother. I was able to look at the result. Not a trace of Jewishness. Unfortunately, nature was not as kind to me as to Jurek. I did not have much excess skin to stretch. It would cost 12,000 złoty, which was good money, never mind the suffering.

We discussed the prospects of escaping to Hungary. A woman would come to Warsaw to pick up the candidates and escort them to Kraków. There, another woman would take them to Tarnów, where she would put them up for the night. The following morning, another person would escort them by train to a small place in the Carpathians near the Slovakian border. The doctor did not yet know the name of the railway station. From there, a mountaineer would take them across the Carpathians to Slovakia, where they would be cared for by the American Joint Jewish Distribution Committee. It all sounded very vague. The doctor said that some of his friends had already crossed the border, but he was waiting for a message from them. The cost, covering all arrangements, all escorts, was 10,000 złoty per person, regardless of age. There would be an extra fee for a small child who had to be carried. The amount was to be arranged directly with the guide.

I was quite shocked. It was a fortune. The doctor offered to reduce the charge to 25,000 złoty for our family of three. All our savings along with Lusia's gold watch, the bracelet, my gold Schaffhausen watch, Lusia's fur coat, and other pieces of wardrobe would not amount to the required sum. We decided not to sell Lusia's diamond ring until we received news from those who had escaped to Hungary.

We also decided to quickly visit Henio Haber, who had mentioned his plan to visit his sister in Hungary. The business trip to Częstochowa made my task easier. I left early in the morning, discussed the company problems with the German officials, caught the night train to Kraków, and then took the local train to Wieliczka early next morning.

Henio had described in detail the way to their house. There was an open meadow in front of the station with a path running across it that took me to the end of a short street. The last house was the Habers' hiding place. I found it without any trouble, walked up a few steps, and knocked at the door. Silence. After a few moments, I knocked again. This time, someone came and half opened the door: "Who is it?" asked a timid voice.

"My name is Daraż," I said politely, "and I wish to see the Haberko family."

The door opened and I entered a big kitchen. An elderly woman was standing in front of me. She looked frightened. "I'm Mr. Haberko's school friend," I introduced myself. "I had to travel from Warsaw to Kraków on business, and since it was not far from Wieliczka, I've come to see him."

"Mr. Haberko is not at home," said the woman uncertainly.

"What about Mrs. Haberko? Is she in?"

"No," she muttered, obviously wanting to get rid of me.

I was sure she was not telling the truth. As Irka did not look Aryan, she would have stayed home all the time. Their son, Rysio, was a lovely boy, but he looked very Jewish, too. With his dark eyes and dark hair, it was not difficult to recognize him. He must also have been at home. All this time I was standing near the entrance door. Nearby was another door. The woman indicated it with her eyes. I opened it and entered the room. Irka must have heard my voice and recognized me. She emerged from under the bed and Rysio followed her. Irka explained that when she saw someone carrying a briefcase and entering the house, they immediately hid under the bed. We were happy to see each other but sad as she told me of their last days in the ghetto. They had escaped at the last moment. This house belonged to the mother of Irka's school friend, a courageous Polish girl who had taken them here. I remembered that friend – a charming young woman working in the office of a German concentration camp in Plaszow, a suburb of Kraków. She had also helped get money to Lusia's Uncle Herman. He was working as a pharmacist in the camp, and so far, that had saved him and his family. I had given the girl 2,000 złoty, all I had with me, and asked her to give it to Herman from me. During my next visit, she had handed me a note in which Herman had written: "With the 2,000 złoty, I received two loaves of bread, which was how much bread cost in the camp, though my monthly salary was 500!"

I asked about Henio. He was still working as an architect on the renovation of the local tannery and would be home after 5 p.m. I had to return to Skierniewice by night train to be back at work the following morning, but no one was willing to take the message to Henio; people were afraid as a lot of German gendarmes had descended on Wieliczka the night before, so I had no choice but to go myself. I couldn't afford the luxury of being afraid.

The factory was at the other end of town. From the town center, one had to cross the marketplace and climb a steep street. I was lucky. It was quiet with no police in sight. Reaching the tannery, I knocked at the huge gate and a guard let me in.

"Who do you want to see?" he muttered, then showed me the way.

When I knocked at the door, Henio Haber himself opened it. He could not believe his eyes when he saw me. We talked only briefly. "I'll try to be home as soon as I can," he said and went back to his drawing board while I returned to Irka. We waited for him impatiently. Irka prepared something to eat, and we discussed the possibility of escaping to Hungary. The Habers had an address of a woman in Bochnia who used to escort people across the border. Henio knew more about it.

Suddenly, we heard shooting coming from somewhere around the market area. The terrified landlady ran in with the news that the Germans had surrounded the marketplace and were dragging Jews out of their hiding places. They had killed some on the spot as well as Poles who gave them shelter. Irka was afraid and insisted I leave immediately. In spite of my safe documents, I knew I could be in great danger. I left at once. Irka and Rysio slid back under the bed. I waited at Wieliczka Station for over two hours, all the while in fear that the Germans would surround it. Luckily everything remained quiet. I safely reached Kraków and was back in Skierniewice in time for work the following morning.

That afternoon on the way home to Legionowo, I dropped in to see the Abrahamers. He was in bed in terrible pain. He had been operated on by his doctor friend. Now, every time he had to pass urine, he suffered excruciating pain. It worsened during erection, which unfortunately he could not control. He wanted to howl out but was afraid their landlady would hear. His wife was applying cold compresses all the time. Despite the unbearable pain and cost, he suspected the stitches would cut through the skin and it would return to its original state – which is exactly what happened!

Everything had been fine in Legionowo. Lusia had been thrilled to hear from the Habers and was excited by the possibility of escaping to Hungary. Perhaps they would go together, she mused. They were closer to the Hungarian border and perhaps knew more than we in Warsaw did.

"Unfortunately, they can't write about that and Wieliczka is too far away," Lusia mused.

"It's not so far as it may seem," I said, surprising her with my news that I had just returned from there this morning.

As I expected, Lusia jumped with excitement. "What?" she said. "Don't tell me anything yet. Let me first get a cigarette."

I told her the whole story – about their escape from the ghetto, Henio's job, Irka hiding with her son under the bed, the shooting in Wieliczka, and even Mr. Abrahamer's operation. She listened, excited, full of enthusiasm and courage. We decided at all costs we would try to get to Hungary. Lusia was a gambler; she loved excitement, and the Hungarian adventure into the unknown was made for her.

The situation at the Eastern Front was deteriorating and a new order was issued – as of 1 January 1944, civilians were forbidden to use trains unless special permission was obtained from the police. The trains were needed to transport war equipment and soldiers, not civilians. A huge slogan was proudly displayed on all station buildings: *Die Rader rollen für den Sieg* [The wheels roll for victory]. Our journey to the border suddenly seemed doubtful.

The work in Skierniewice was nearly completed. There were only a few final jobs to do. Mr. Wojciechowski came to Skierniewice and gave me 10,000 złoty, as per our previous agreement, suggesting I share it with the others in whatever way I thought most appropriate. He thanked me for my masterpiece and for hurrying the payment from Częstochowa. The company had been paid every złoty they had claimed.

Then he told me privately that the company had received a big contract to build a rice mill for the Germans in Kraków. The contract was valued at around three million złoty! Would I take the position of construction manager at a salary of 2,000 złoty per month and, in addition, free accommodation and meals in the canteen? (My present salary was 500 złoty per month.)

I was flabbergasted! It was a difficult decision to make. The salary of 2,000 złoty was a lot of money, but I had worked as an engineer in Kraków for four years before the war. There was a real possibility that I might be recognized by someone who might remember me, so I could not accept his offer. The risk would be too great. How could I explain my refusal? Although I felt privileged to be offered the position, I told him I did not want to be separated from my wife and child in such uncertain times. "We've thought about that," he said. "We're prepared to cover the costs of travel for your family to Kraków and they could also have free meals at our canteen."

I did not know what excuse to make now. This was a time when it was not wise to be a good employee! "I will talk to my wife and let you know," I told Mr. Wojciechowski. As we parted, he asked me to keep our conversation confidential and in particular not to mention it to Mr. Bielicki.

I was considering how I should distribute the 10,000 złoty, which I thought should have been for me. I had taken a great personal risk. The whole thing could have been found out, and the only person who would have had to pay a price would have been me. No one in the firm would have done a thing to save me. Hence this was not the time for altruism. Nevertheless, Mr. Grabowiecki had been helpful to me and was always kind. I happily gave him 2,000 złoty on behalf of the firm. He was delighted. I bought a pair of shoes and a dress for Inspector Rudisch's daughter (800 złoty) and him a goose and brought it to Skierniewice myself, which was a stupid and risky undertaking. I didn't need to buy him the goose; it would have been easy to say I had not been able to get one. But I liked Rudisch. He was amicable and had helped me a lot, so I wanted him to have the pleasure of taking home that "war trophy." I also managed to get him half a kilo of coffee. He was very moved by my gifts, which must have cost me around 1,500 złoty.

I wanted to gain the favor of the difficult Inspector Hanewinckel as it was he who signed the renewals of our passes. I knew that he would not accept such presents as a goose, coffee, or a pair of shoes. He would have probably told me off or even suspected I was trying to bribe him.

However, one day I plucked up my courage and knocked at his door. "*Herein!*" he called and greeted me with restrained annoyance. "*Was Wollen Sie* [What do you want]?"

"*Ich habe fur Sie ein Geschenk im Namen unserer Firma* [I have a gift for you on behalf of our company]," I said.

Before his fury could explode, I handed him a book, *Taschenbuch für Bauingenieur* [pocket book for building engineers]. It was a huge and splendid encyclopedia of engineering knowledge, the latest edition, issued in 1942, which I had managed to buy in a German bookshop in Warsaw for the official price of 23 złoty (the cost of one loaf of rye bread on the black market was 20 złoty). It was an extremely useful book for engineers and difficult to come by. In hard cover, it was about 2,000 pages with a wealth of plans, drawings, graphs and tables – a unique collection of valuable information. He looked at it with great interest as if he were seeing such a book for the first time in his life.

"*Wie haben Sie das bekommen* [How did you get that]?" he asked with unusual politeness.

I answered that I had noticed it in Warsaw in a German bookshop and bought the last copy. "*Ich hoffe das Sie es brauchen können* [I hope that it might be of some use to you]," I said.

"*Ich glaube doch* [I think so]," he answered, muttering, "*Ich danke Ihnen und der Firma* [I thank you and your company as well]." No handshake, of course – a German superman and a Pole? Oh no!

I was glad he had accepted my *Geschenk* [gift] and did not throw me out of the room. A few days later he signed my Ausweis, valid till 31 December 1943 even though the work had to be finished in November. I also gave a Christmas gift to Mrs. Biedkowska. Once she had asked me if I could find her a pair of shoes, size seven, in Warsaw as she had none for winter. She would pay for them. Mr. Bielicki also traveled through Warsaw every week. I wondered why she didn't ask him to do her the favor.

She was sure I would do my best to find her the shoes (A Jew could do that!). She was right. Lusia had saved one pair of good shoes from before the war.

I took them to Mrs. Biedkowska. They would have been worth 800 to 1,000 złoty on the market. I charged her only 200. "That's how much I paid," I said. She knew they would have cost much more. She was familiar with the prices. But she occasionally sold me some butter, which was difficult to get, and sometimes a piece of illegal meat. But, most importantly, she had let me live. That was worth more than the several hundred złoty.

The rest of the money – 6,500 złoty – I gave to Lusia to hide. She was delighted with the money and so was I. Delighted, too, were the directors of the firm: Inspector Rudisch, Mrs. Biedkowska, and even Inspector Hanewinckel. Furthermore, I had fulfilled my patriotic duty: I had swindled 100,000 złoty from the cursed Germans.

PLANNING AN ESCAPE

I received another letter from Henio Haber. He was sorry he had not been able to meet me during my unexpected visit, but he had been "held up" and returned home very late. He had established new contacts that could be of interest and suggested we meet again.

I decided to go immediately to Wieliczka and stay at the Habers' overnight. I arrived in the evening as I found it easy to locate their house in the dark, and we spent almost the whole night talking. Someone had given Haber two contact addresses – one in Kraków and the other in Bochnia. He had been to Kraków and met a middle-aged man with a severe limp who offered to arrange the trip to Slovakia for 10,000 złoty per person. Haber accepted the price and gave him a deposit of the so-called "hard 20," that is, a $20 gold coin worth about 5,000 złoty.

By now, the Polish złoty and the German mark had almost no value. American dollars had become the real currency of the black market. One could buy everything with dollars – even a human life! The SS, the Gestapo – all those murderers never scorned American currency. There were dollar banknotes (so-called "soft" ones) and gold dollar coins ("hard" ones).

We decided I should go to Kraków, despite my fear of meeting old acquaintances, and talk with this man with the limp. He presented himself as the escort who takes his clients from Kraków and guides them personally over to the Slovak side. He had done this already very successfully.

He did not want to name the place at the border. It was winter and the Carpathian Mountains must have been covered with heavy snow. But how could a lame man walk through those mountains in summer, let alone winter?

I had very little knowledge of smuggling or the smugglers. I knew they were usually recruited from local people – mountaineers who lived by the border or had fields there. They knew every path, tree, and stone. But how could a man living in Kraków tell me that he himself had escorted people across the border? When I asked him what happened to those people after they crossed over, he told me to trust him and that everything would be all right. Did he think that Jews were so stupid as to believe him? I returned to Wieliczka disappointed. We concluded it would be wise to forget that man and as well the deposit given him.

The other contact happened to be a woman in Bochnia. She was said to know smugglers in a small mountain village and would deliver people from Kraków to them. It was a more reliable contact as people assisted by her were said to have already sent confirmation from Slovakia.

Unfortunately, Henio Haber did not know either the name or the address of the woman. We decided I would come back to Wieliczka the following week and that we would travel to Bochnia together.

I returned to Skierniewice by night train to Warsaw, where I again called on the doctor to find out whether he had any additional information. He was not home, though I spoke to Jurek's mother, mentioning that I was trying to establish some contacts in Kraków, Wieliczka, and Bochnia. She was very interested as the doctor did not have any definite information and asked if I would take Jurek with me should I succeed in establishing contact with the smugglers. Jurek could then help his family and other people. Of course, I agreed.

A few days later, I went back to Wieliczka. Unfortunately, Henio Haber had not managed to get the name or address of the woman in Bochnia. He only knew that she lived on Kolejowa Street (Railway Street), which ran parallel to the railway line. We were to walk past some 20 houses then look for a gray painted one with white windows and two tall poplars in front. The description was reasonably accurate and we hoped only that the woman was still living there.

I took out my timetable to plan the trip, but at that moment, Irka interrupted. "You can plan what you wish, but Henio will not go to Bochnia!" she said. "I'll not let him go!" Henio and I kept silent. "Piotr, if you want to take risks, it is your decision, but why should two people take risks? You will manage, Piotr, and if you don't, Henio will not be able to help you anyway, perhaps quite the opposite. Alone, Piotr, hopefully no one will pay any attention to you, but together, you'll be easily recognized. Actually, I think even you should not go to such an uncertain address, to look for a totally unknown person, whose name is not known to you. It's too dangerous."

Henio was embarrassed, but Irka had made up her mind. I knew she was right. Two suspicious-looking faces attracted more attention than one. How could Haber help me anyway? I left early next morning. Fortunately, there were no raids. Kraków was the seat of the German-controlled government in Poland. Whenever passing through Kraków, everything seemed peaceful and quiet, but passing through Warsaw was always nerve-racking. There was always turmoil, perhaps as the Polish Underground was very active.

I got off at Bochnia and started walking along Kolejowa Street and located the gray house with white windows. It had to be the one. I walked past a few more houses just to gain time and plan what to do next. How should I begin? If only I knew her name as she was bound to be afraid of me. Probably, she would not speak to me as to her it would be stupid to take such risks. Irka was right. She had advised me to return home and not to go to Bochnia. But here I was now. I buttoned up my jacket and with my briefcase under my arm, I knocked at the door. The door was opened by a woman of about 40.

"Good morning," I said with a smile.

"Good morning," she replied.

She led me into the kitchen. She was tall, well built, and attractive with a round and rosy-cheeked face. I was sure she was the woman I was looking for. I could easily imagine her courageously working with the smugglers – determined, responsible, and cheerful. A splendid woman. I asked if I could have a glass of water. She gave me the water, looking at me with interest. I smiled and so did she, but still, I did not know how to begin. It was a strange situation. There was no clever way to do this. "You must be wondering who I am and why I've come here," I started. She just smiled as if she knew. "I'll tell you the truth. I've come from Warsaw. I represent a group of people who want to go to Hungary." Was she going to report me and hand me over? Would she let the police know about me? She just did not look that kind of person. I continued, "I was told that you can organize such an undertaking and have experience and good results."

She became serious. "Did anyone see you enter my house?" she asked.

She went to the window and drew the curtains. I knew that I had found the right person. "No," I said, "nobody saw me. I walked past a few houses down the street and then returned here to check that I was not being followed. There was no one in the street."

"You're not going to believe me," I added, "but I don't know your name or the number of your house. I only had the description."

She smiled and said, "And weren't you afraid to enter an unknown house?"

"Dear madam, I've been living in constant fear since 1939 and I've become used to it," I answered.

She smiled again. "Perhaps you'll have some tea? You must be thirsty." I drank the tea and ate some cake. She confirmed she had helped many local people, but the contacts she had were no longer available, so she had to stop. She was very sorry, but she could not help me.

I was extremely disappointed. I had been so happy finding a trustworthy person. I begged her to consider another attempt. So many people were waiting for help. But she was determined. I asked her if she knew of anyone else in Bochnia who could undertake the task. There must be someone else. But, she said, she did not know of anyone. It seemed to me that she was not telling the truth. I explained to her that I came especially from Warsaw where people were waiting in despair to get out. How could I return to them without bringing some hope?

She relented and gave me the name of a man who at one time did escort people across the border. His name was Piotr Rawinski. But she did not know whether he was still doing it.

"I have one more request of you," I said. "Can I give your name for reference? It would help me a lot when talking to that man. I realize that you may feel apprehensive, but, believe me, you can trust me."

"Tell the man that Zula is sending you," she said. We shook hands and I went. What a wonderful person! A splendid Polish woman.

I started looking for Mr. Piotr Rawinski. "Zula" had given me the name of the street but not the number of the house. She said she did not know what the house looked like, "not even what trees are growing in front."

Although I was reluctant to talk to strangers, I asked a few people about Piotr Rawinski, and finally an old woman told me she knew his family. The street climbed to the top of a hill where the house of the Rawinski family stood. I found it without any trouble. After knocking for quite some time, an elderly man opened the door. He let me in only after I told him that a woman named Zula on Kolejowa Street had given me this address. He said Piotr Rawinski was his son, but he was not home.

"Can I wait for him or shall I come back later?" I asked.

"It's no use waiting for him or coming back later," the old man replied. There was a note of sadness in his voice.

I decided to approach him in the same way as I had the woman on Kolejowa Street. "Look, Mr. Rawinski," I said, speaking loudly as he obviously was a little deaf. "I came here especially from Warsaw to talk to your son, and I'll wait here until he returns. You probably guess what I've come here for. A group of people is anxiously waiting in Warsaw for my news, and you're telling me that it's no use waiting for your son. I have to see him. That's why I risked the long trip from Warsaw." I deliberately repeated the word Warsaw as it always impressed people in small towns.

Mr. Rawinski looked puzzled. Scratching his head, he remained silent. I tried to encourage him to talk. "You can tell me the truth, Mr. Rawinski," I said. "Is your son dead, God forbid?" I felt that he was hiding something that he was fearful to relate. "Tell me the truth so that I'll know what to do."

"I'll tell you the truth," he finally said. "I don't know whether my son is alive or dead. He left together with those people six months ago and has neither returned nor sent any message. Do you think he might have been killed on the border?"

The poor old man was living alone, was deeply worried, and had tears in his eyes. I was worried, too, but tried to cheer him up, suggesting that perhaps his son had crossed over to the Slovak side and decided to remain there. "Do you really think so? May God help him," he said.

Several changes had recently taken place in Skierniewice. Bielicki became the manager of the big construction project in Kraków. I politely turned down the offer of the position, explaining to Mr. Wojciechowski that as Mr. Bielicki had employed me, it would be unfair to him if I accepted a position to which he was more entitled. I added that Mr. Bielicki would surely manage very well, particularly as his command of German had greatly improved in the last 12 months. Mr. Wojciechowski accepted my explanation. However, he asked if I would help Mr. Bielicki if he needed assistance, particularly in preparing the final invoice (did they really think the war was going to last for years?). I promised him gladly.

Another change concerned Inspector Rudisch, who was promoted to the position of *Oberinspector,* adding one more star to his splendid German uniform, and transferred to Ostbahn Bauinspection Warszawa.

I finished our work in Skierniewice, lodging the last invoice for some extra jobs, packed my belongings in the knapsack, including the blanket from Oserdów, and left. I did not forget to say goodbye to kind Mrs. Biedkowska.

"Take good care of yourself," she said, a tinge of sadness in her voice. How can one convert an enemy into a friend? I was lucky.

It was the end of November 1943. I had started the job in Skierniewice in November 1942. For 12 long months I had commuted between Legionowo, Warsaw, and Skierniewice, mixing with the Polish workers of the Stolzman Company and the German inspectors of Bauinspection-Skierniewice. I had become used to my illegal status. I grew accustomed to my new name, living among Poles and Germans, buying and smuggling black market food. Nevertheless, I had lived in constant fear of being recognized while at the same time trying to appear calm, controlling my gestures, and imitating Polish manners. It was a responsible job that enabled me to keep myself, my wife, and my child alive. I had even managed to save money, which could help our next move. It was a miracle we had never dreamed of when we first found ourselves in Warsaw. And to think it was all because Professor Poniż's telephone was disconnected

What luck would come now? We needed some.

THE GESTAPO TAKE LUSIA

Life was dreadful in Legionowo after I finished in Skierniewice. Mrs. Bielicki insisted we register with the police as required by law. We suspected someone had scared her. A great advantage of living in Legionowo was that we did not have to register. To go to the police meant we could be recognized, which was terrifying. We had delayed, using the excuse that I was not in Legionowo during the weekdays (making sure I left early and returned late) and the office was closed on Sundays. But once I finished work, I no longer had that valid excuse.

Meanwhile, I went to see Joe Abrahamer, who had been in touch with his doctor. Something new must have developed regarding our escape to Hungary as the doctor apparently wanted to see me. I phoned and we met in the street. The doctor had decided to undertake a trip to the Slovak border himself to establish contacts with smugglers and perhaps even cross the border to discover what it was like on the other side. He asked me for 1,000 złoty to cover his costs, which would be deducted from the total amount to be paid.

With admiration for his courage and energy, I gave him the money. (I always had some money with me in case of emergency.) He advised me to make all the necessary preparations. First, I needed travel documents from the police, for which one had to go in person at the police headquarters, presenting acceptable justification for such a trip. The only other way of obtaining travel documents was on the black market for between 1,000 and 2,000 złoty, depending on how greedy the "middle man" was. Luckily, I was prepared. Before leaving Skierniewice, I had taken some blank Stolzman Company letterheads and envelopes. On one of those sheets I wrote a short letter to the police president in Warsaw advising that Piotr Daraż was required to make some business trips to the forests in the Carpathian Mountains to purchase timber necessary for the company's work for the Deutsche Ostbahn and thus asked for a permit to travel by train between Warsaw and Muszyna. I wrote another letter to the chief of the Warsaw police asking for a permit for the wife of Mr. Piotr Daraż – Mrs. Stanislawa Daraż – so her husband would not have to use the trains too often to travel home to his family in Warsaw, as his stay for business purpose would last several weeks.

With those letters properly typed, signed (by me) and genuine looking, I went to the police. There were two desks in front of the police building, one for ordinary citizens and the other for employees of German companies, behind which sat a German policeman who instructed a Polish-speaking official.

I was shocked when I saw the size of the queue on that frosty morning in January. I could only imagine how early they must have come to get their places. Polish police were keeping order. Everyone had to answer questions before each decision was made.

I was very concerned at my own prospect of waiting in the queue, exposed for so long to Polish people and police, and there appeared to be no way Lusia could do it. I did not have the right contacts or enough spare money to buy the pass on the black market. Then I had a brilliant idea: Rudisch! He was now in Warsaw, the chief of Bauinspection Warszawa-Wilno. I went to him immediately and found him at his desk. He was surprised and pleased to see me. After a short chat about things in general and his family (I had not seen him since he returned from his holiday in Germany), he asked about my family and my job.

I told him that my wife had an elderly aunt living in a small house in the mountains who was not well and had asked if my wife could stay with her there for a few weeks. I was keen to be with them in the country, where it was less difficult to get food and there were no air raids. I explained that our company had orders to construct a few wooden bridges in the area and that I had instructions to go there to purchase the necessary materials. I showed him the two letters.

After reading, he asked, "What's the problem?"

"The problem is that there are about 1,000 people waiting at the police to get a travel pass. I will have to wait till the end of the war to get my turn. I was wondering if you would be good enough, dressed in your coat and official railway inspector's cap, to accompany me to the police to assist. Perhaps afterward I could take you for a cup of tea and a cake, or perhaps a cup of coffee."

Without a word, he put on his coat and cap, and we left. Rudisch went straight up to the German policeman in charge of the manifold travel passes. I was standing just behind him. The policeman asked why I was not waiting in the queue like the others. Rudisch explained that it was very important that I leave Warsaw immediately. (Perhaps he was not as naive as he seemed!) The policeman looked at me, took the letters, and in a few minutes, I had two valid passes for travels from Warsaw to Muszyna. I was elated.

We then went to one of the few cafés in Warsaw where they served homemade cakes. Mr. Rudisch had a sweet tooth and showed a special liking for a type of shortbread cake covered in thick chocolate. They were known as "piano keys" and cost ten złoty each. A fortune! It was my first and only visit to a Warsaw café. It was great to be sitting in the company of a German official whose uniform protected me from blackmailers and other devious elements. I was not even afraid of a police raid. In a strange twist, his uniform was my security.

Before we left, I bought four of those piano keys. I gave two to Mr. Rudisch, which he quickly put in his pocket, and I kept the other two for Lusia and Elżunia. Getting those passes was an important step toward the realization of our plans. They were valid till the end of January 1944. As my *Arbeitsausweis* had expired in December 1943, Mr. Rudisch also extended my Ausweis, until 31 January 1944, stamping it with that powerful swastika and eagle seal.

Several days passed with still no news from Doctor S. It became apparent that he and his wife had gone for good. They had made fools of us and conned us into paying them 1,000 złoty. We were very angry.

Unexpectedly, Jurek came with the news that he had just received a postcard from someone who had managed to cross into Slovakia some time ago. In it, he advised that "Aunt Maryla" had changed her address. She was living now in Piwniczna. The name of the street and the house number was written on the card. We had new hope. Jurek left for Piwniczna immediately, returning two weeks later. He had contacted a forester in charge of a group of guides and determined a plan: My family was to be the first to try the new route. The Habers and Rysio, then my two cousins hiding in Warsaw, and Anatol Kahane were to follow. Anatol could hardly make ends meet, and I asked Jurek and his mother to charge him less. They agreed to take Anatol free of charge if I should succeed in establishing the route into Slovakia.

Jurek estimated that the cost of crossing to Slovakia would be 2,000 złoty, payable to him, and another 2,000 payable to the forester in Piwniczna. Altogether, it would be 4,000 złoty per person instead of the 10,000 demanded by the doctor. The mountaineer carrying the child was to be paid by negotiation. Jurek did not charge Kahane the 2,000 złoty due to him. Having a few matters to settle, we decided to leave around the middle of January. We had to sell most of our belongings, including our watches, and to exchange our złoty for dollars, which would be essential in Hungary.

With the excuse that Elżunia had outgrown her clothes, I passed some on to Mr. Rudisch, who accepted them happily. He was a good man, more Czech than a German. (I did wonder what his reaction would have been had he known my identity.) We had kept a few good things in our flat in Warsaw, including Lusia's fur coat. It was winter and a fur coat would fetch a good price. It was worth around 10,000 to 15,000 złoty, but it would require time and effort to sell. I went to visit Mrs. Baltorowicz. I had done so from time to time to pay her rent. Wanting to keep on good terms with her, I often brought her something from Skierniewice. This time I took a packet of tea and, over a cup, put forward a business transaction I hoped she might find attractive.

"As you surely are aware," I said, "the Russian front is coming closer to Warsaw. There will be fighting, air raids, bombing. A lot of buildings will be destroyed and windows smashed." She was listening and nodding her head. All of that made sense. She remembered well September 1939.

"It may be a good opportunity to do business," I continued. I was not afraid to talk about business. Although it was the Jews who had always talked business, during the five years of war, the Poles had taken over from the Jews and were doing well indeed. They had completely taken over the black market, smuggling food and other items. They were buying and selling goods stolen from the Germans or taken from the Jews. They traded in gold, valuables, and hard currency. They learned to buy cheap and sell at high prices. The very things the Poles accused the Jews of doing, they were now doing themselves, making money on a large scale as shrewdly as their predecessors.

Trading on the black market was so common that I did not feel embarrassed to talk about it with Mrs. Baltorowicz. She was listening carefully. "What business?' she asked.

I explained, "I have the opportunity to buy large quantities of glass. As I work for the railways, I have some contacts with glass suppliers."

She looked at me, surprised. "Glass?"

"Yes," I said. "After the liberation of Warsaw, there will be thousands of broken windows, and glass will be worth a fortune. That is, if we survive. That's the risk in this business."

"How much will it cost to purchase that glass?" she asked.

"Ten thousand złoty. I have 5,000 and I'm looking for a partner who would add another 5,000. After we sell the glass, we'll share the profit."

Mrs. Baltorowicz was clearly interested but hesitant. I knew she might worry I would secretly sell the glass and trick her, or simply take her money and disappear.

"I understand your doubts," I said. "You don't know me well. As a guarantee for your money, I'll leave you my wife's fur coat, her suit and dresses, everything that's in the flat. That's worth between 12,000 to 15,000 złoty." Mrs. Baltorowicz knew I was being honest about the value of those items as the door to our room in her flat was often open.

Mrs. Baltorowicz got up, left the room, and returned with the 5,000 złoty. She was pleased with the deal, and so was I. I had sold cheaply but without the risk of travel to the market of Żelazna Brama. That trip, with me loaded with a fur coat and other ladies' clothing, could attract suspicion. Even if she did sell at a big profit, she deserved it. In her flat, we had survived the first weeks of our illegal life in an unknown and hostile Warsaw.

I had already sold our watches. I'd tried to sell them through the dealers, but their offers were too low. Lusia had a beautiful gold

Omega, and I had a gold International Schaffhausen. In Skierniewice, I had offered my watch to Mr. Jasinski, the same man with whom I had gone to church back in May. He was happy to pay me the amount I asked. He had never dreamed of having such a beautiful watch. As for Lusia's Omega, I offered it to Mrs. Biedkowska, who bought it without haggling. My price was quite reasonable. I told them that I was selling on behalf of some friends. Both probably knew that they were likely Jewish watches, but no questions were asked. Such business deals were now commonplace. All Jewish possessions were slowly passing into Polish hands. Jews from hundreds of *shtetlech* and thousands of villages would have left their meager belongings behind. I was lucky to be able to sell directly to the customer, without a middle man, thus at a reasonable price.

To reach Budapest, we not only had to cross the mountains through snow-covered forests but also travel by train. We had to be dressed to survive snow yet at the same time look like city people. From the beginning of the war, we had worn our prewar clothes, as did most of the Polish population.

Lusia decided to go to Warsaw to have a recommended dressmaker alter her dresses and winter coat. It was a gloomy day in January when she set off early in the morning. It was safer to travel in a crowd of people going to work, making it less likely to be noticed. That was what we thought. I expected Lusia to return about noon.

Elżunia had a cold and was in bed. She was running a temperature and had a nasty cough. No wonder – it was very cold that winter and we had no fuel. I stayed by her bed, that primitive structure of my design, and played with her, making her tea – using the famous pine cones as fuel. Most of the time she slept. When awake, she was whimpering like all children when sick. We were both waiting for Lusia to return.

Twelve o'clock came, but Lusia did not. Since our house is close to the station, we heard the train arrive and depart. She did not come by the one o'clock or the two o'clock train, either. Trains from Warsaw were arriving every hour. I started to wonder what could have happened. Perhaps she had met someone and stayed for a chat? Maybe she had to wait longer at her dressmakers. Elżunia was whimpering and I was anxious. We had nothing to do, nothing to read. I played cards with her until she fell asleep, then sat at the table and played the game patience. Three more hours passed. I was becoming extremely anxious. Every hour, I heard the whistle of the train arriving, then leaving, and listened hopeful for Lusia's footsteps. A few people were coming from the station, and I stood hidden behind the curtain to watch the people passing. Our Lusia was not among them. She did not come. Good God!

Evening was approaching. Elżunia asked, "Where is Mummy? Why hasn't she come back yet?"

What could I answer? I could sense disaster, but I had to pretend in front of our child and Mrs. Bielicki. My fears grew. Now I simply stood at the window and waited. Six o'clock passed and more people were passing our windows, but no Lusia in sight.

"Where is Mrs. Daraż?" asked Mrs. Bielicki, clearly also anxious.

"Where is Mummy?" asked Elżunia.

I prepared some semolina for Elżunia. I could hear my heart pounding in agony. God, return our Lusia! Return our Mummy! But I started to fear the worst. In fact I knew! It was already eight o'clock, the curfew hour. Another train arrived and I could hear people rushing home, but no Lusia.

That was the end. Lusia must have been caught. I was alone with a sick child. We were to leave for Hungary in two weeks. Everything was ready – our passes, guides, money. But without Lusia? I despaired, clenching my fists in agony. I wanted to cry. I could barely keep sitting, playing patience, watching the cards to tell me whether Lusia would return or not. The cards sometimes said yes and sometimes no.

"What's the matter with Mrs. Daraż?" asked Mrs. Bielicki again.

"Perhaps she stopped overnight at her friends," I tried to explain calmly. But she could read my face and did not ask any more questions.

Elżunia was crying now. "I'm cold. I'm scared. I want Mummy!" she said. She was whimpering. I covered her with my jacket. It was the first time since we had left Lwów that Elżunia had been without her mother. She could feel that something was wrong.

"Go to sleep," I said. "Mummy will soon come." I felt numb. Elżunia fell asleep. I did not know what to do. The last train would arrive in two hours' time at ten o'clock. What was I waiting for? A miracle? We had been waiting eight torturous hours. Lusia would never let me wait like this if she could help it. She would know how much I would worry. Obviously, something had happened, yet I could not accept the truth, either.

Perhaps she had decided to stay the night in Warsaw. It was a possibility. We had our room and a bed at Mrs. Bartolowicz's flat. Maybe it had just become too late to return? Yet in my heart I knew that I was deceiving myself. I knew that millions were being killed, among them wonderful wives and loving, devoted mothers like Lusia. But Lusia was *ours* and *she* could not die. No, she couldn't!

Little Elżunia wailed and tossed in her dreams. I covered her better. "Sleep, my darling. Mummy will be back," I said. She was asleep. I was not talking to her but myself. I looked at the clock. The curfew was on. No one was in the street. The last train would arrive soon. Not even realizing what I was doing, I put on my coat and left the flat, closing the door quietly to not wake Mrs. Bielicki or Elżunia. It took only ten minutes to walk to the station. I was oblivious of the danger of going out after curfew. Why would I stay at home? I had the whole night before me and I was as if in a dream. I entered the dimly lit station. I could see its name: Legionowo-Przystanek. There was not a soul around, and then a station guard came out to check the signal. The train from Warsaw was coming. I saw two light points on the horizon, growing slowly, coming closer and closer. I could hear the wheels rolling and the whistling and puffing of the approaching engine. I went to the end of the platform, standing where the engine would stop. Why I chose to wait there, I did not know. Anything could have happened to me. I could have slipped and fallen under the wheels of the engine, but I did not think of that. I did not think of anything. I only stared at those two lights.

The train rolled into the station and the engine, blowing steam, stopped beside me. I stood, staring. It only stopped for one minute, and then the station guard gave the signal. The train moved off slowly, puffing steam. No one had gotten off. No one! I stood, staring at the carriages passing by. The train had left the station, but then a figure appeared out of the fog and steam of the train and my heart almost stopped beating. I recognized that familiar quiet way of walking: Lusia.

ELŻUNIA AT THE GESTAPO

"I had no trouble getting to the station," Lusia began her story. "I bought a ticket and traveled to Warsaw without difficulty. It was dark on the train, and most were wrapped up in winter coats. No one paid any attention to me. When the train arrived, everyone rushed to the exit. I followed, holding the ticket in my hand, though I felt very uneasy. I was not used to being among people and traveling by train. I haven't left Legionowo for a year. I handed over the ticket and left the station building. The whole area was surrounded by German gendarmes. Each gendarme was accompanied by a civilian. They scrutinized everyone. I felt faint, but I followed the other people, trying hard not to show my fear. I approached the row of blue uniforms. A civilian noticed me, and I could see him whisper something to the gendarme, who stopped me immediately. He called another gendarme, who took me away even though I tried to protest. There was nothing I could do. Terrified, I climbed into the German police van.

"It was one of those raids to catch Jews, and I had been recognized. I remembered that last time I left home to collect some pine cones in the woods and was accosted by the Polish police. Now when I left for a second time, I was caught again. The civilian who had identified me came up to the police van with five more people. He asked in Polish for our documents, which he kept. We tried to protest, but he paid no attention. Escorted by two more heavily armed gendarmes, we set off.

"Mrs. Bartolowicz's address was shown on my identity card. We stopped in front of the apartment house in Plac Inwalidow. The Pole and one of the gendarmes accompanied me to Mrs. Bartolowicz's flat, and when she opened the door, she was visibly frightened. 'Which is your room?' the civilian asked me. I showed it to him. The gendarme was guarding the front door while the civilian searched my room. Fortunately, Mrs. Bartolowicz had taken my Persian fur coat and put it into her wardrobe. That fur coat could have been proof of my Jewish identity.[1] He searched the drawers and wardrobes but did not find anything incriminating. I was very relieved at least that only our Warsaw address appeared on the identity card. If it had been our address in Legionowo, we would all have been caught.

"The civilian checked the two other rooms that Mrs. Bartolowicz rented. One was occupied by a German woman, whom he left alone. In the other, he found a couple still sleeping. He did not like the look of them and instructed them to get dressed immediately and accompany us. They were very frightened. We were all told to get in the van, and we drove away. In that way, we made a round of all the addresses shown on the identity cards. After about two hours, our van full of people stopped at the German police station.

"We were taken to a large room, where a civilian interrogated us in Polish. Our replies were typed. Two or three people were released. Under the escort of two more gendarmes, the rest of us set off again.

"After a while, we turned into a beautiful-tree lined street. I managed to read the name of the street: Szucha Avenue. It could not have been worse."

Here, Lusia paused. I had been listening to her, horror struck. Whoever lived through the German occupation in Warsaw, whether a Jew or a Pole, knew the meaning of that street – the headquarters of the dreaded Gestapo. The exit from Szucha Avenue was by way of Pawiak prison, and from there you went to either the Auschwitz extermination camp or immediate execution. Release was very rare.

Lusia resumed her story: "The van stopped in front of a huge iron gate. An SS man opened it and we drove into a yard full of police vehicles. We were taken to one of the buildings and told to wait in a large, cold waiting room. Nobody said a word. We were all paralyzed with fear. They started to call our names, and finally it was my turn. An SS man took me along several corridors until we reached a door on which was written *Rassen-Erforschung-Abteilung* [Department of Race Examination], room 404. He knocked on the door, nodded to me to go in, and shut the door. I was standing in a big, elegantly furnished room with Persian carpets, dark velvet curtains, and a huge desk with three people sitting behind it. There was a fat, bald, round-faced Gestapo officer in the center, next to him a young, important-looking SS officer, and beside him a civilian.

"All three looked at me. I was asked to sit down. '*Sprechen Sie Deutsch* [Do you speak German]?' was the first question. '*Ja*,' I answered. '*Dann brauchen wir Sie nicht* [Then we don't need you],' said the officer in the center, apparently the chief, to the civilian. He got up and left the room, looking at me with an unfriendly stare.

"The young officer inserted a sheet of paper into his typewriter and the older one started questioning me. First, he asked if I was Jewish, which, of course, I denied. Then he asked why I had been picked up? 'I would like to know that myself,' I replied.

"He looked at me with suspicion and asked for my handbag, which he emptied on the table. In it were keys to our flat in Warsaw, some cigarettes, a powder compact, a lipstick, and very little money. The Kennkarte and other documents (including the permission issued by the Warsaw police to travel by train from Warsaw to Muszyna and a card from the Medical Insurance Office in Kraków) were already on the desk before him.

"While the young officer was making a list of contents, the chief asked me to follow him. In a corner of the room behind a partition were some instruments and a scale. He wrote down my weight. I was glad I had lost my prewar weight. He measured my height and examined my skull with various instruments. He inspected my hair at the temples. It was not dyed. Jewish women living on Aryan papers usually dyed their hair blond, since Polish women were mostly blond. He seemed fairly satisfied with the results of his examination. He also looked at the color of my eyes. Again, I was glad they were blue. He returned to his desk, and I sat down in my chair. Strangely, I did not feel nervous anymore. He asked me the usual questions: my first name, surname, my husband's profession, and his place of work. He had a look at the Ostbahn document to which I drew his attention. He wanted to know where I had learned German so well. I told him the truth: born in the once-Austrian part of Poland, I had graduated from a German school in Vienna, where my father had been a teacher, and we also spoke German at home.

"He seemed satisfied. The young officer was writing everything down. The carriage of the typewriter was moving fast. He asked me if I had any family and whether they were alive. I said that my father was dead and my mother lived in Kraków on Lenartowicza Street number 17. I gave him my sister's address in Muszyna on Konopnicka Street number 3 and told him that since I was on my way to visit her, I had with me the pass for rail travel. Both addresses were our real prewar addresses in Kraków – in case of further questioning they would be easy to remember.

"By then I'd had enough. Pretending to be insulted, I asked why they were interrogating me. I am not Jewish and had nothing to do with Jews. I requested them to send a telegram to my mother and sister, who would come and prove it. I offered to cover the cost of the telegram. I could not stay here any longer, I said, because my child was waiting for me, hungry and anxious, at home. I told them to give me my keys and documents and let me go.

"'*Langsam, langsam* [slowly, slowly],' the officer smiled and asked me about my child, her name, sex, date of birth, etc. A good example of German thoroughness. They want to know and write down everything before they kill you.

"I answered all his questions. My interrogator made his decision: I was allowed to go home. He returned my keys but kept all documents. I was very surprised. He explained to me politely that my documents and the report of the interrogation had to be checked carefully. If the results were satisfactory, the documents would be returned to me. He told me to come back the following morning at eight o'clock and bring my child with me. He stressed again: '*Sie kommen mit dem Kind* [You will come with the child].'

"I asked him politely to let me have my documents. I needed my identity card in case of a control, as I might again be in trouble. In such a situation, he told me to refer them to him. I asked him his name, but he refused to give it. I should refer to his office, room 404, he said.

"'How can I get out of here?' I asked. 'The guard at the gate will not let me out.' '*Ich begleite Sich* [I'll accompany you],'" he said. We left together the office. An SS man opened the gate. '*Gute Nacht* [Good night],' said my 'friendly' interrogator. *'Gute Nacht,'* I answered, and heard the gate close behind me. I was free.

"It was seven o'clock. It was dark and I was alone outside the Gestapo headquarters. I felt stunned by the events of the day and by the miracle of being freed. I could hardly believe it. I felt weak inside.

"Wondering what I should do next, I decided to go to Mrs. Bartolowicz's. I wanted to keep that address safe in case our escape to Hungary could be unsuccessful. The sanctuary in Legionowo could become worthless and we might need our flat in Żoliborz, even if only for a few days. Mrs. Bartolowicz was very happy to see me, kissed me on both cheeks, and made some tea with bread and jam. After a short rest, I rushed to the railway station. I had to wait at home for the next train. I bought the ticket (the Gestapo officer had given me my money back) and returned to Legionowo on a cold and almost empty train. I was so happy to know that I would see you again. It was a wonderful surprise to see you at the station. How did you know I would be coming on that train?"

How could I explain that after eight hours of waiting in terrible fear I just found myself at the station? I could not explain that to myself, either. Her story finished and we both fell silent. She was exhausted, but the ordeal was not over. We needed those documents. We had only two alternatives: either we acquiesced and let Lusia and Elżunia return to the Gestapo the following morning or ignore them. If Lusia did report to the Gestapo, the officer who had interrogated her could take that as proof that she had told him the truth. He might close the matter and return her documents. But the same Gestapo officer or another on a whim could pack both Lusia and Elżunia into a van without any explanation and send them to Pawiak prison. If Lusia did not report, her documents would be held by the Gestapo and she would neither have her identity card nor the permission for rail travel, and we would not be able to use the flat in Żoliborz because that address was already known to the Gestapo. We would also likely have to leave our accommodation in Legionowo immediately, because the Gestapo would quickly learn, through the office in Skierniewice, that Mr. Daraż was living with his family in the house of Mr. Bielicki's mother in Legionowo and they would find us very quickly; the name Daraż would be "burned," as we called it, and we would have to find new contacts to procure new documents for a different name and a new address and identity cards, etc. etc.

We would have to look for new shelter, which would be almost impossible to find without documents and, finally, we would have to forget our plans of escaping to Hungary. All in the middle of winter. This could be the end of our "life story." We could not sleep at all that night, considering all the pros and cons, the alternatives, possibilities, and consequences. It was Russian roulette, but no game. I shuddered at the thought of letting Lusia and our child go straight into the lion's den, but Lusia felt it was the only reasonable solution. She instinctively felt that it would all end well. She hoped that the Aryan-looking features of Elżunia with her golden curls would avert any suspicions they may have had. Having no choice, I agreed to trust her instinct, her personality, her courage, and my lucky star.

We got up very early. It was pitch dark when we dressed the sleepy child, who did not understand why she had been woken so early. We went to the railway station and boarded the train undisturbed. We parted at Warszawa Gdańska Station. There was no police razzia this time. While Lusia and the child went to Szucha Avenue, I went to the Poniż's, remembering that his neighbor, the Polish general's widow, allowed Poniż to use her telephone in case of emergency. Mr. Poniż had told me her number, which I had memorized. I had given it to Lusia.

At 7:30 in the morning I knocked at the Poniż's door. He opened it, frightened, and let me in quickly. I told him my story. He and his wife listened intensely and were most upset. They were shocked that Lusia had gone back to the Gestapo in Szucha Street.

"Nobody ever does that," Mrs. Poniż exclaimed. "No Pole fortunate enough to have been released has ever gone back. Better to leave home and stay somewhere with relatives or friends in the country, or even hide in the woods! To return to the Gestapo voluntarily is madness."

Needless to say, hearing this did not help me. Perhaps it was crazy, but what other alternative did we have? We had no family, no friends with whom we could hide. It was a game of high-stakes poker – with the stakes extraordinarily high – our lives. I waited almost numb with anxiety. Minutes passed like hours. Mr. and Mrs. Poniż were with me, tense and upset. They made tea. Eventually, we heard knocking at the door and Mr. Poniż rushed to open it. It was the general's widow coming to say that there was a phone call for a man called Piotr. I rushed to the telephone. It was Lusia! Everything was all right and she was waiting for me in a small café. She gave me the address. Mr. Poniż had been standing beside me and Mrs. Poniż joined us. They could not believe it. They had never heard of such a miracle. Both had tears in their eyes. I composed myself quickly as there was no time for sentiments and took a tram to the city and found the café.

Lusia quietly related the experience. "I reached Szucha Avenue and approached the gate of the Gestapo headquarters," she said. "The SS guard stared at me. He could not believe that a woman with a child would voluntarily come to the Gestapo. He rang room 404. He opened the gate and an SS man took over. The chief was busy and I was told to wait in a big room next door. I felt very uneasy. Perhaps there was another raid in preparation as the room was full with heavily armed gendarmes wearing those threatening steel helmets. Pretending to be without any fear, I was looking at their ruddy faces. They seemed surprised to see a single woman with a small girl, neatly dressed in her white stockings and white woolen cap. I took off her cap and her golden hair fell over her shoulders. I could notice their admiring looks. One of them came near and patted her on the head. Others tried to make her smile, but Elżunia could sense their beastly instincts and was intimidated.

"After a while, an SS man came and took us back to room 404. The same senior Gestapo officer and young one were sitting behind the desk. The chief looked at me surprised as if he hadn't expected me to come. 'I've come to collect my documents,' I said as confidently as I could. 'I've brought my child along as I was asked.' 'She really does not look Jewish,' the chief said. I asked if I could leave, but was told by the young one to 'take it easy, we still have to check your statement.'

"But quite unexpectedly, the chief declared, 'There's no need. I have checked it all. Everything is in order.' He returned my papers and I carefully checked that everything was there. When I saw the travel pass, I sighed with relief. Before leaving, I turned to the chief asking, since my features must look somehow suspicious, would he mind writing a certificate that my documents had been examined and found correct. 'I would not like to go through this same experience again,' I added innocently.

"He smiled and assured me it was not necessary. Should such a situation occur, he advised me to refer to the statement, which would be recorded in his files. They do not issue such certificates. We left.

"Outside, it was bitterly cold. The streets were deserted, but I found a small café with a telephone. Luckily, I could still remember the telephone number of Mr. Poniż's neighbor."

We sat in silence while Elżunia finished her milk. That Gestapo man saved the life of my wife and child. Why? I had no doubt he was aware that Lusia was Jewish. Did she impress him with her courage, her calm attitude, her knowledge of German, or was he guilty of so many murders that he wanted to have one noble deed on his account before he faced the Last Judgment?

LEAVING LEGIONOWO
17 JANUARY 1944

We decided to put our plan of escaping to Hungary into action. Lusia returned to Legionowo, and I went to see Jurek to work out the details. I related Lusia's story and, like the Poniżs, he and his mother were amazed and full of admiration for her courage and self-control in her incredible decision to take our child straight into the headquarters of the Warsaw Gestapo. "Unbelievable!" he said.

We decided to cross the Slovakian border on the night of 21 January, and the Habers would follow us two days later. I had to let the Habers know, yet we could not relay word through the mail. Thus, I once again had to risk the journey to Wieliczka to talk in person.

I arranged for Jurek to be in touch with Anatol and my cousins, Frania Ecker (adopted name, Danusia) and Wisia Ecker (adopted name, Stasia). On the way to the Habers, I had to pass the document control of the German police. The document, which I had forged, was faultless. The gendarme read it carefully, looking at me searchingly. I was no longer afraid of his scrutiny. He could neither recognize a Jew nor was he looking for one. I passed all the details of our arrangement to the Habers. They had a few days left to dispose of their belongings, exchange złoty for dollars, and prepare their travel passes. We also had to plan a possible return to Legionowo should our escape fail. We decided to leave some of our clothes and books so that Mrs. Bielicki would think we had gone for only a short time. An unexpected event made our last days in Legionowo much more relaxed, allowing us to drop the Daraż masquerade. Poor Mrs. Bielicki broke her leg and had to stay in the hospital. For the first time in 13 months, we could be ourselves. We could freely discuss our plans without fear of being overheard. The day of our departure, 19 January 1944, finally arrived. Anatol Kahane had visited us the day before to discuss the final details. We were delighted to talk freely and even put him up for the night on the kitchen floor. We left Legionowo at dusk. We gave our remaining food to Anatol – not much, but a welcome supplement to his meager rations.

We did not know what to do with Mrs. Bielicki's hen, which she kept in the shed. We decided to put her in the kitchen, where there was more light and it was warmer. We put all the remaining chicken food into a dish and filled up a bowl of water. Whether the hen survived until Mrs. Bielicki returned from the hospital, I still do not know.

We walked to the station separately, Lusia taking the child and a small suitcase. I carried a knapsack, and Anatol had his bag full of food. Arriving in Warsaw, we said goodbye to Anatol. "See you in Budapest." It was eight in the evening when we found ourselves on the platform of Warsaw West. The station was dimly lit as we sat huddled together (the child already asleep) on the platform waiting for the train to Kraków. It was bitterly cold. A group of German soldiers were also waiting. They were nostalgically singing "*Heimat*" and other sad songs about their fatherland, followed by a cheerful song "*Schenk mir dein Lächeln Marie* [Give me your smile, Mary]."

Finally, two lights appeared. The train to Kraków was approaching. All its carriage lights were off, its windows dark. With the war still raging, the blackout regulations were strictly adhered to. I jumped onto the step of the third-class carriage and opened the heavy door. Lusia and Elżunia followed. It was overcrowded and full of cigarette smoke. How could I find a seat for Lusia and the child? We had a long journey before us: all night – 12 hours. I opened the door to the first compartment and asked politely if there was room for a mother and a child, but no one answered. When I opened the next door to ask the same question, I was met with the same silence. At the third attempt, to my utter surprise, I heard a familiar voice: 'Where are you going, Mr. Daraż?" It was the voice of Mr. Bielicki. Of all the people in the world, he was the last person I wished to meet. I had wanted to leave without him or his mother knowing. I had not wanted to find excuses or lie to them. What if we had to return to Legionowo?

In the darkness, I could not see who else was inside, but the compartment was full. I answered briefly that I was taking my family to the mountains for a few weeks but would be returning soon. He did not ask anything more and I closed the door. After a few more attempts, I finally did find a seat for Lusia and the child. I spent the night sitting on my knapsack in the corridor next to the toilet. I couldn't sleep as people walked to and from the toilet all night. Some days prior to our departure, we had sent a letter to Zosia, Elżunia's nanny, advising her of our arrival in Kraków and asking her to meet us at the station. We wanted to leave Elżunia with her so we could travel alone to Wieliczka and see the Habers, not wanting to expose Elżunia to unnecessary hardship and danger. We were not sure whether Zosia was still living at the old address or whether she had received our letter in time. Would she meet us? Was everything all right at their place or were we to be trapped?

The night journey was passing slowly, but we were getting closer to Kraków. People on the train were waking up. They collected their luggage and put on their coats. Nobody bothered to look at us and we did not look at them. Everyone to themselves, with their own worries and problems. Anyway, who would expect a Jewish family to still be alive in January 1944?

Faithful Zosia was waiting for us. She was happy to see us alive and gladly took Elżunia. We told her what time we would like to meet her the following day, said goodbye to the child, and started looking for the train to Wieliczka. The Habers were expecting us. We talked the whole day and night, discussing the last details of our plan. Two days after our departure, the Habers were to follow us. They were to look for Jurek, who would be walking along the platform holding a newspaper in his right hand. Henio Haber was to hold his gloves in his right hand; his mustache and glasses would make it easier for Jurek to recognize him. By that time, Jurek should have already had my report of our crossing the border. Depending on that message, the Habers would follow us or return to Wieliczka. It was easier for them to return since their landlord knew their identity.

The Habers needed two days in order to sell some silver

candlesticks and other objects of value. I left them a $20 note in case they could not convert their "wealth" into dollars in time. We went to bed late, Irka and Rysio sleeping in a small bed, Henio in the other, while Lusia and I slept on the floor. A hen spared for the "last supper" was running around us. After some incessant cackling, the hen fell asleep and so did I. The next day, Zosia and Elżunia were at the station on time. Elżunia had a lovely time with Zosia, who had fed her generously. She also brought us some food for the journey. Dear Zosia waved to us as the train pulled away. We were alone in the compartment. What a relief! The guard checking our tickets did not bother to look at us. He surely had his own problems. In Tarnów, we changed for the train toward the border of Slovakia.

There was hardly anyone on the train, and those we saw seemed to be relaxed. They did not rush the way people did in Warsaw. Yet *we* were very nervous. Some people might have found it an adventure to cross the German border the way we planned to, but we were conscious that the slightest mistake on our part would result in dire consequences.

The train was climbing slowly. We could see the snow-covered villages, the roofs, the fences, the trees. It was hard to believe that this old sleepy world still existed, one so different from that which we were trying to escape. I looked through the window in Stary Sącz. A few people got off or boarded. I looked around and noticed Jurek standing on the platform, pretending not to see me. As he boarded our train, he smiled very slightly and I let Lusia know that Jurek was with us as planned. My heart was pounding. There were now only a few people in our compartment – simple villagers. Lusia covered her face with her winter coat and pretended to be asleep. Elżunia gazed at the passengers with interest. She had never seen people like them, speaking Polish, although a little differently. A peasant woman opened her bag and gave Elżunia an apple. The little doll looked at me, waiting for permission. I nodded and she smiled. "*Dziękuję* [Thank you]," Elżunia said, delighting the whole compartment with her sweet voice.

We heard heavy steps along the corridor and suddenly the door opened. All smiles vanished and silence fell. Two heavily armed German gendarmes entered the compartment. Lusia was still pretending to be asleep. As they checked the documents, they did not pay any attention to the peasants but carefully inspected our papers, studying the photographs. Finally, they smiled at Elżunia and cast a quick look at Lusia but did not wake her. They had her documents. That was enough. They were satisfied and moved on to the next compartment. We sighed with relief.

At about noon, we approached Piwniczna station, our terminal. Collecting our things, we got off and slowly followed other passengers toward the exit. I glanced around quickly but could not see any Polish or German police. Piwniczna, a small village in the Carpathian Mountains, lived quietly as in the old days. I went to the exit and handed in my ticket. A few people were behind me, then Lusia followed with the child and gave her ticket. Jurek was pacing outside the station building. Our eyes met for one moment and he immediately left the station and started walking along the main road. Keeping my eyes on him, I followed at a distance of about 50 meters, Lusia and the child walking another 50 meters behind me. So we set off on our march to the unknown, guided by a brave young Jewish boy. We followed him with hope and trepidation. Were we really, at last, escaping the hell of the Nazis' Final Solution and those "friendly" compatriots who eagerly were ready to help in the implementation of this monstrous plan. Would we succeed? [1]

PART V
UNDER GERMAN OCCUPATION IN HUNGARY

JANUARY-DECEMBER 1944

POLISH GUIDES – GERMAN POLICE

The road that led through the mountain village of Piwniczna seemed endless. Jurek marched hurriedly as time was running out. It was noon and the sun overhead was unbearably hot. We were dressed for winter, naturally, in jumpers and coats, and loaded with a suitcase and heavy rucksack. The heat and fear made us perspire.

I was following Jurek, who moved ahead quickly, and Elżunia lagged behind, though no wonder since she was only five. Lusia was exhausted and kept slowing down behind her. I needed to keep sight of Jurek, who, from time to time, would stop to tighten his shoelaces to give us a chance to close the gap. We needed to leave the village behind and get out of people's sight, escaping their curious, sometimes unfriendly (though sometimes compassionate) stares. They knew who we were. Piwniczna was the destination for many who were trying to save their lives crossing the Slovakian border. The villagers could recognize that these "hikers" were no tourists. Who would head for the mountains in the middle of winter dressed in city clothes, carrying luggage while dragging a five-year-old? We tried to avoid their looks. What would happen if someone approached us, or if they notified a policeman who started asking questions? Our hearts were pounding. Soon there were fewer houses, yet Jurek continued hurriedly and could hardly be seen in the distance. The road was now covered with snow. A sleigh would pass now and then, drawn by fast, well-kept horses with bells attached to their collars. To let them through, we had to rush to the side of the road.

I kept walking but lost sight of Jurek in the mountain fog. There was only one route to follow, so I went on quickly despite exhaustion while at the same time worrying about getting too far ahead. A *Goral* [mountain man] passing by in his sleigh must have seen my tiredness because he slowed down, almost stopping. "Get in!" he invited. "Where to?"

I was embarrassed but didn't know how to reply. "It's not far now," I answered with a smile. "Just a few more meters. Thanks anyway." He passed and I braced myself and marched on. Lusia and Elżunia were way behind now. How did Lusia manage with a child and a suitcase? Jurek's silhouette appeared again on the horizon. He had stopped and, calling for us to hurry, pointed to a roadside shed. I entered quickly and collapsed on the straw, followed soon after by Lusia with the child, who both dropped next to me. Jurek joined us and quickly closed the door. We lay motionless, silent, breathing heavily, tense and utterly exhausted.

After a while, we heard a whistle, something like a wild bird's call. Jurek uttered a similar call and the door opened. A tall man appeared and Jurek greeted him warmly. We were told to stay in the shed until nightfall. In the corner, covered with straw, was a basket with some food – bread, a piece of cheese, some hard-boiled eggs, milk, and some water. Under no circumstances were we to talk, smoke, or go outside. In another corner, also covered with straw, was a bucket in case of emergency. After dark, this local forest ranger – who was, as it turned out, the organizer of our undertaking – would return. We bade a warm farewell to Jurek, who had done such a fine job.

Stealthily, they left the shed – first the ranger, then after a few minutes and a whistle, Jurek, too. We were alone, hidden deeply in the straw. Tired but excited, we ate and fell into a deep sleep. Suddenly we were awakened by dazzling torchlight cutting through the darkness. It was very, very cold. Elżunia was terrified and started to cry. Lusia hushed her. There were two men in the shed. The forest ranger, we already knew; Mr. Pavel Liber and someone else. They told us to collect our belongings and be ready to leave. We washed our faces with snow. From the road, we heard a whistle and started toward the road.

We had been told to follow at no closer than 50 meters and to keep to the side of the road. From time to time, they would shine the torch to show us the right direction. We were to watch them constantly. When there was danger, they would give us a Z sign using the torch. In that case, we should jump into the roadside ditch and hide in the snow. An O sign would mean that the danger was gone. We could continue. I thought they were only joking about any danger as the road seemed totally deserted in the dark freezing cold. Who would venture out from a warm house into the street? And what for? We were walking slowly, barely able to see our guides, though from time to time they gave us a reassuring sign with the torch. We followed in silence. Where were they taking us? The child's little hand was trembling in mine. "Don't worry, darling," I whispered, "just a little further and everything will be all right."

Then, suddenly, we recognized the Z sign. We jumped immediately into the ditch, which was deep and full of snow. We were almost covered, Elżunia much more deeply. Frightened, she began to cry. I covered her mouth hard and she was silent. Poor thing.

After a while, lights appeared on the road – a German jeep of the border police. They drove slowly looking around. The lights of the vehicle lit up the road and their powerful torches threw beams in every direction. Something must have attracted their attention because they slowed down, almost stopping near where we hid. Perhaps our footprints. The searchlights seemed to illuminate the very spot where we were hiding. We buried our heads deep into the snow and lay motionless. After a few moments (though they seemed interminable), the lights faded, and the jeep drove on.

We stayed hidden for a further few more seconds, watching the those dreaded German *Grenzschutz-Polizei* (border police) disappear. Soon our guides returned, also covered in snow, and helped us out of the ditch. We moved on without delay. The men had not been joking. Day and night, German border police searched for smugglers, spies, and runaway Jews. They had their informers, we presumed. They knew everything. How lucky we had been not to come across them in daylight, when we were passing Piwniczna. We could not have answered their "*Wohin gehen Sie* [Where are you going]?"

Making a turn into a side lane, we reached the ranger's house. It was warm and cozy, and the ranger's wife treated us to hot potato soup with fresh rye bread and butter followed by cheese and potato dumplings. It had been a long time since we had such a feast. Afterward, we settled for a short rest. Our frozen bodies began to warm. Elżunia fell asleep while still sitting at the table.

About seven in the evening, the other man reappeared. He had gone home to prepare for the mountain crossing. It was hard to leave that cozy house. The ranger and his wife bade a warm farewell. Kissing Elżunia, the woman said goodbye, obviously moved. "She's a little angel," she said, looking at her compassionately. Perhaps she could not believe this was a Jewish child. At the last moment, she gave me a small bottle of milk "for the child." We began up a hill, past farmhouses and fenced orchards. Our path was covered with deep snow. We passed the last cowshed of a mountain farm and entered the forest. Our guide knew his way. Lusia followed him, then the child, though by now she could hardly walk in the deep snow, so I took her onto my shoulders, securing her as best I could with towels tied together. The guide had taken my suitcase and Lusia the rucksack.

After half an hour of slow climbing through the deep snow, I could not carry her any further. Short of breath, I dropped onto the snow utterly exhausted. The guide rushed back and ordered me to get up immediately and keep walking. I begged him to carry the child, offering extra payment. He asked me if I had dollars. I said no, even though I did have some hidden in my coat. "I have 200 złoty in silver," I said. One hundred two-złoty coins at that time were still reasonably valuable. That satisfied him and he quickly took the child onto his shoulders, securing her.

I took the suitcase, tying it with belts to carry it on my back. The stars were shining in a clear sky and soon the moon appeared, brightening the surroundings. We could see trees bending under the heavy snow, dark green branches of the conifers, jet black in the darkness. It was a glorious night. At our feet, the snow was stark white, untouched by humans. All around was silence and not one German soldier! I felt like I was in the most beautiful of dreams. We were climbing, higher and higher, leaving the village behind. After two hours, we emerged from the forest. Yet the snow was not the same light snow of the Polish forest. This had an extremely hard but thin crust, twinkling in the moonlight, spotlessly white, lit by the big lamp moon above our head. We continued up the hill as if it was a huge mountain.

Our guide stopped to give us new instructions: The snow was about one meter deep and, although the crust seemed firm, it was not strong enough to withstand a person's weight. He showed how he could lift his leg out of the deep snow, leaving a deep footstep. He instructed us to follow only in his footsteps, yet I was not convinced. If he could pull out his foot, why couldn't I? I tried and got stuck immediately. My legs were hopelessly immobilized. The guide noticed my trouble and returned to pull me out. Humiliated, I obediently followed in his steps after that. Our eyes slowly adjusted to the stark whiteness. I stayed at the back, 20 meters behind Lusia, and another 20 meters ahead was our guide with Elżunia on his shoulders. The huge range reared ahead and, on its peak, the Slovakian border. Climbing up was extremely hard, every step a great effort. We were physically not fit and not prepared.

And then, suddenly my heart sank. Before us, on top of the hill, a blue uniformed German border guard appeared out of nowhere and pointed his gun in our direction. Other guards appeared on both sides. More and more blue uniforms appeared on the horizon, their guns pointing at us. Our way into Slovakia was blocked!

I heard a noise, then realized my face was wet from the snow. Leaning over me was the concerned guide and frightened Lusia. The Germans had disappeared.

"Where did they go?" I asked.

"Who?" was their reply.

Slowly, I regained consciousness. A hallucination? The guide allowed me a few minutes' rest and I drank some milk from Elżunia's bottle – milk had never tasted so good. My strength was returning. With the help of the guide, I rose to my feet still unsteady, yet he hurried us along. It was still quite a distance to Slovakia, and he had to go back to Piwniczna the same night. In the next two days, he was to make the same journey with the Haber family.

We continued pushing uphill. The guide carried Elżunia, who slept soundly. I followed, then Lusia. At last, we reached the top of the mountain. We paused for a moment and could see Slovakia ahead of us, Poland behind. Poland, the country of our birth, our parents' and our parents' parents; the country of our youth, our work, hopes, and dreams; the country we were no longer safe. A chapter of our lives was closed. A new one was beginning.

We started walking down, now on the Slovakian side. The conditions at first seemed similar. The guide was making holes in the snow, and we continued in his tracks. The snow had become firmer, but new troubles were emerging. Before leaving Warsaw, I had bought a pair of calf-high boots for Lusia made of sheep's wool with a leather sole. Being new, they were extremely slippery and Lusia was constantly falling. The child cried every time she saw her mother fall. The guide was rushing us – we had to hurry and be quiet, yet the quicker we descended, the harder it was for Lusia to manage. Each fall slowed us down further, Lusia was getting so tired that even getting up was getting hard and slow. I'd also bought myself a new pair of shoes in Warsaw, and it seemed they had been sewn with paper threads and the shoelaces of paper, too. Both shoes were dissolving in the wet snow, with the soles slowly coming off! I had to keep going and tied them together with some string, which I luckily kept in my pocket.

After about two hours descending, we could see the first Slovakian village in the distance in the slightly brightening sky. There was no movement. The village slept. It was just like any Polish village – the same thatched roofs, barns, and fences. We passed a mountain stream with weeping willows along its banks, a small wooden bridge thrown across, and water cascading over the rocky bottom, fresh white snow covering everything – the roofs, fences, the road, and the bridge. It was a beautiful sight, like a postcard. We hurried on and soon entered the village, quietly like thieves, not one sound uttered. Dogs started barking, which made us nervous, but we had no choice but to press on. We crossed the bridge and turned into a narrow path and passed a few cottages before stopping in front of one of them, though the barking was increasing.

Our guide knocked on the window once, and then, after a moment, a second time. The door opened and we followed him into a small dark warm room. A kerosene lamp, the glass black with smoke, was standing on a table. We put Elżunia into a bed still warm. An old woman lit the fire. We sat down by the warm flames trying to straighten our frozen limbs. I removed my soaking socks and shoes (what was left of them) and tried to warm my numb feet. On the range, the water began to boil.

SLOVAKIAN LATKES

Our siesta did not last long. Our host was already preparing to transfer us to another safe haven as soon as possible before dawn. He sent his 10-year-old daughter to reconnoiter while he began to harness the horses to a sleigh.

Our guide was also leaving to start the journey back, wanting to reach his home before sunrise. The trip would probably take him about four hours. He asked me to write a few words to Jurek and gave me a pen and paper. I described our journey, its profound beauty, and stressed the consideration and care shown by our guide and recommended him highly. The letter was copied and distributed widely, and I heard that some who followed could never forgive me for not saying a word about the difficulties. The beauty of the adventure must not have impressed them.

Our guide was happy with my letter and even more with the silver coins. We said a warm farewell, expressing our deep gratitude. We knew he could have robbed us in the middle of nowhere and left us at the mercy of the cold and snow. If only more Poles had been able to demonstrate such beauty of character, our whole Hungarian adventure might not have been necessary!

The sleigh was waiting. I was lucky to have brought (on Lusia's advice) a spare pair of shoes and socks. The Slovak asked us to lie flat on the sleigh, then covered us with a big blanket and a layer of hay topped with frozen manure, pretending he was heading for the fields in the early morning like most other farmers. Down the road, his daughter was signaling that everything was all right. The road was heavily covered with snow, making it easy and comfortable to travel. The air we were breathing through the hay was sharp but clear and lovely as the manure was frozen and odorless.

After an hour, we reached the next village. The Slovak drove into a farmyard and knocked on the door. Entering a large warm room, we were welcomed by a farmer and his wife, who had just risen. We were given something to eat and shown into a still-warm bed. Feeling safe at last, we fell into a deep, blissful sleep. Someone was taking care of us. No need to pretend, tell lies, make difficult decisions.

The three of us slept through the whole day. It was dark when we woke and found a splendid supper waiting for us. The farmer told us that he would escort us the next morning to a small town where we would be handed over to Jewish people. Lusia and Elżunia were to wear large head scarfs similar to those worn by village women; I was to wear a farmer's fur hat. We would leave at three in the morning and travel to the railway station – about an hour's journey. The farmer would buy the tickets and travel with us but sit separately. He asked us to remember the name of the town and taught us how to answer simple questions regarding our destination in Slovakian.

It was dark and gloomy the next morning. Everything went according to plan. We arrived at the station without "adventure." The farmer's wife took the horses home while he went with us. No one asked any questions. The railway guard checked our tickets in silence and did not even bother to look at the sleepy passengers. At six in the morning, we reached our destination and found ourselves on the street of a quiet little Slovakian town. The whole community was asleep. We quietly followed a few steps behind our guide. On reaching the marketplace, we approached a two-story brick house. Our guide knocked on the door of the first floor and a frightened Slovakian Jew opened it. Recognizing the guide, he let us in immediately. After only a few minutes, our companion left with our heartfelt thanks.

Our hosts were a Slovakian Jewish man, his wife, and her old mother and they received us gladly. When we asked who was responsible for these arrangements, either they did not know or would not tell us. It appeared the whole operation was secret. Our hosts were very poor; their flat was small and scantily furnished. The man might have been in his forties; his wife could have been younger, but her face was drawn, prematurely aged. They fed us with the little they had. They probably lived day to day, our presence likely a much-needed source of income. Only the poorest would offer their homes to illegal Jewish refugees from Poland.

One couldn't help but notice the difference between the living standard of the Slovakian peasant we had just been with and this small-town Slovakian Jew. How similar these contrasts were to those in Poland! Peasants had their own farmhouses, a shed, stable with at least two horses, a few cows and calves, pigs, and a flock of chickens, ducks, or geese. They had land. Some had less, some had more, but usually enough to live and work peacefully, providing for themselves, dependent only on the weather, nature, and perhaps God.

In contrast, in the shtetls of Poland, the Jewish folk had nothing, or close to nothing. They lived from hand to mouth and were happy if they managed to procure something for a Saturday meal. Our present host was such a poor town Jew. Every hour we spent under his roof was desperately needed income. There was scarcely food in the house. He put on his winter coat and went to the market to shop.

I was unnerved to see the yellow star on his coat. In the farmer's house, we had felt safe. For 14 long months, we had managed to avoid that sign, one we associated now with certain death. Suddenly, were we Jews again? Our host tried to reassure us. Despite the star, nothing had happened to anyone. The police did not trouble them, and townsfolk behaved as before. Everyone knew who the Jews were anyway. Officially, they were not allowed to shop in the market, but this restriction was generally ignored. The Jews would cover their stars and the police would look the other way.

In the corner of the room stood a brick oven, with a steel plate on top, similar to the one we had in Oserdów. I remembered my childhood years and those hotplates on which we used to fry fresh, crisp potato pancakes topped with an abundance of butter, rolled, and consumed in huge quantities. Our hosts kindly started peeling potatoes, which was probably the only food available in the house. The husband returned from the market with fresh butter. We had a feast. Now well rested, our thoughts were focused anxiously on the

Habers, who were supposed to join us soon providing everything went to plan.

And so, it was with relief early next morning that a knock on the door signaled their safe arrival. Our joy was overwhelming. Once they rested, we readied for the next stage of our journey. Two young Slovakians escorted us in two groups: Lusia, Elżunia, and I followed a young man, and behind us were the Habers. A policeman could easily recognize that our group was not local and demand documents. We kept some distance between us. If there was trouble, the only solution would be the hope that the Jewish Council would, with luck and money, free us. That was not guaranteed to work. There were reports of people caught and escorted straight back to the Polish border! A terrifying nightmare.

We were lucky and reached the railway station undisturbed. The guide bought the tickets and we sat separately. After two hours, we alighted at Prešov, a small town. There, carefully avoiding the main roads, we arrived at a big gray house. I shuddered on seeing huge Hebrew letters, the menorah, and the Star of David on the front of the building. Our guide, via a side entrance, led us into a synagogue – the last thing we had expected! Could they not have heard about roundups and massacres in synagogues, groups of people incinerated? Since June 1941, we had been successfully "dancing over a volcano," and now we were voluntarily entering a Slovakian synagogue!

The man who greeted us tried to calm us down. "Our synagogue," he kept saying, "is like the Vatican. Slovakian police have no right to enter. You will feel absolutely safe." We did not. After all, Slovakia was Germany's satellite and owed its very existence to Hitler. The president of the country was the priest Jozef Tiso, and naturally he would be anti-Jewish. How could we feel safe here under the Jewish star after all we had gone through in German-occupied Poland?

"It is true," Frank, our host, admitted, "that the first wave of the Jewish deportations took us by surprise. Thousands of our people were taken, but we learned our lesson. We are now on good terms with the government in Bratislava and 'friends' with the local police. We will be informed in time if there is another action. We have friends abroad who are very strong financially and a great help to us." He shared that the government and police were bribed, and so there was nothing for the Slovakian Jews or us to fear. We had no other choice but to stay in his shelter, his "Vatican"!

Other information from Frank was more disturbing. "Usually," he said, "Polish 'visitors' stay in Prešov no longer than two or three days. Unfortunately, the border guards to Hungary have changed and the Jewish Committee had not yet established contact. Negotiations are in progress but so far without result."

We would have to wait here a few more days. The only accommodation the committee could offer refugees was the synagogue – the only furniture there were two tables and a few stools. They could organize private accommodation with Jewish families in town, but such accommodation had to be paid for in dollars and, anyway, for our own safety, we would have to be back in the synagogue before daylight. We did not have spare dollars. The committee could provide very basic meals– enough for three meals a day. Coffee, potatoes, rye bread and butter, cheese or boiled cabbage could be provided if we had dollars. Yet, the only thing we needed was a safe place to wait until the situation with the guards was clarified. The committee advised us that the cost of transport over the Hungarian border was likely to be high, and we were expected to contribute a minimum of a hundred dollars per person – if we could afford it. We said we did not possess a hundred dollars even between the families. The way we looked and dressed convinced them we were telling the truth. Frank, our negotiator, was a kind of Shamus[1] in the synagogue – quiet and good natured, well dressed, and always with a friendly smile. We liked him. The head of the committee was a Mr. Schwarz, who had connections with the police and the border guards but was unapproachable and self-important. Frank did the talking, and Schwarz was the one to act and make decisions.

Prešov was a small town, and the news about two Polish families with children spread around the Jewish community. After dinner, two young people came to offer their parents' hospitality to our wives and children. We hated the idea of being separated, but Frank reassured us that it was close by, and the young men promised to bring them back early next morning.

So, Henry Haber and I were left alone in the gloomy synagogue. We lay on the tables to sleep. It was cold and we had a sleepless night. Early the next morning, our wives and children were back. Their

Slovakian hosts had treated them to an excellent supper and gifted them with fresh shoes and clothing. We spent that day in the synagogue, and in the evening, the same young men appeared again to escort our wives and children to their warm and comfortable homes. We shall never forget the hospitality of the Jews of Prešov.

Members of the Synagogue committee, six to eight people altogether, came to the synagogue every day. They sat at a neatly set table, while we sat at the other end of the big room. We watched with interest. Frank's wife cooked, and he served a delicious meal! We could not decide whether it was a duck or goose served with buckwheat or baked potatoes in a rich gravy – delicious, judging by the aroma. There was wine on the table and homemade cakes served with coffee. When he had finished serving the committee, we were served a modest soup with potatoes and cabbage and, on Friday nights, some gravy beef and the luxury of stewed prunes. But we were not that hungry and didn't feel unhappy. We were beginning to see the way the committee worked. Personal details including names, dates and places of birth, professions, and prewar addresses were all carefully collected. Slovakia was a neutral country, and as such, in contact with the whole world. Detailed reports of the transfer of Polish Jews through the country were sent to "the Joint" in Switzerland. For every Jewish "head," the committee received a payment in American dollars. The money, besides being used for bribing authorities and paying the village people to act as guides, also covered the "expenses" of the committee, including those splendid dinners. For every day we spent in Slovakia, American dollars were pouring into the committee's coffers. The longer we stayed, the more money was forthcoming. In fairness, they were doing an excellent job, and not without risk. Many Polish Jews owed their lives to those Slovaks and, of course, to the Joint. If their dinners seemed like feasts to us, it was only because we had not seen such an abundance of food for at least five years.

The young people offering accommodation for our wives became friendly. They advised us to buy watches in Slovakia where they were cheap because in Hungary they were almost unobtainable and thus much dearer. Slovakia was trading timber and brown coal against watches from Switzerland, hence their low price here. I took their advice and bought a chrome "Etema" for $20. (Unfortunately, later we discovered that watches were much cheaper and more abundant in Hungary!).

During this period of waiting, some Slovakian Jews did try to escape. One way was via the export of timber to Switzerland. Railway workers loading the timber would leave a space between the logs where the Jews could hide. Once in Switzerland, they had access to the free world. We heard a story that one time, the bearings of a carriage were running hot and the timber had to be reloaded while still in Austria. None of those Jews reached Switzerland and, after that, the solution was abandoned. Most local Jews were not that interested in fleeing to Hungary. They felt there would be plenty of time as it was so near Slovakia, and they had such a well-arranged warning system.

I was curious to discover if Doctor S and his wife had also gone through Prešov. They had, indeed, and were remembered for being well equipped and splendidly dressed in new shoes, leather jackets, and fur gloves, with brand new rucksacks. When approached to donate some money to the committee, they had refused yet showed great interest in arranging private accommodation and good home cooking.

Schwarz heard that after the border crossing had been arranged, Doctor S and his wife were caught by the Slovakian border guards. Paper dollars, gold coins, and jewelry, which had been sewn into their clothes, were found and confiscated. Perhaps the local police, and even the committee, shared the booty, as Frank's eyes were smiling at the story. I also could not help feeling some satisfaction, still smarting from the 1,000 złoty the "noble" doctor had stolen from me.

We stayed in the synagogue for some 20 days. Sleeping with Haber on the table was no fun, but sleeping alone would have been worse. The days dragged with the lack of activity and stress. Frank brought us a set of chess, and Lusia and Henry spent long hours over the chessboard. I was trying to read some old German books, and Irka was knitting. The children were restless, and it was difficult to keep them occupied without toys or books – just the gloomy, empty room in the synagogue.

At last, we received the longed-for signal from Schwarz. At seven in the evening, we were to be ready. A car was to take us toward the Hungarian border. After a half-hour drive, a guide would take over and lead us through the mountains toward the Hungarian border town of Kassa (today Košice, Slovakia).

We were served an excellent dinner to give us some extra strength for the trip. Would we make it? The die was cast; our peaceful existence at the "Vatican" was over. The little Czech Tatra car for four could barely accommodate the six of us and a driver. I sat in the front seat with Elżunia on my lap, Lusia and the Habers were in the back, Irka was on Henry's lap and 11-year-old Rysio (Richard) was on Lusia's.

The car belonged to the Ministry of Communication, driven by a high-ranking officer of the ministry. He admitted he was not earning enough money and was helping himself by helping (smuggling) people, and he was pleased to do so. The car dropped us on the main highway.

We were truly alone now, in pitch darkness, in a strange, snow-covered land. Out of nowhere, a man appeared and ushered us quickly off the road. Luckily, there had been no traffic in sight. We were advised to follow him at a distance of at least five meters and not to smoke, talk, or stop. Behind the guide was Henry Haber, then Rysio, followed by Irka, Lusia, and Elżunia. I was at the rear. We were walking quickly across the snow-covered fields and soon were away from the road. From time to time, we could see the light of a passing car.

Little Rysio could not help sharing his excitement with Elżunia. He would jump out of line and go back to where she was, whispering something into her ear, and then run back to join his father. Not for long, though, as he soon was back talking with Elżunia. Reprimanded by his mother, he would return, but alas, after a few minutes, he would rush to Elżunia again to tell her something very important. He stopped only when the guide berated him. By following each other, the guide said, we were leaving all footsteps in one line, rather than scattered. We did not want to suggest that a group was heading for the mountains. This might raise suspicion and endanger us or future escapees. With this understanding, Rysio stayed in line.

After we entered the forest, we were permitted to have a short rest. When we started to climb uphill, I again could not manage with Elżunia, and the guide immediately took her on his back, perhaps instructed by the committee in Prešov. God bless Mr. Schwarz.

We were climbing nonstop through the dense forest. The snow crunched under our feet, but luckily, we did not fall into it. We were perspiring profusely even though it was freezing cold. Elżunia fell asleep on the guide's back, but Rysio was already at the end of his tether. No wonder! His energy had been depleted greatly at the very beginning of the walk. Also, he was scared. The forest was dark and gloomy; ominous sounds could be heard. Wild birds or animals? Who knows?

We kept walking uphill slowly, in pitch darkness. There was no moon at all to help us this time. It was eerie. After many hours, we reached the top totally exhausted. We were frozen and our shoes were soaking wet. We leaned against the trees to rest. The guide was behaving strangely, looking around. Suddenly, the guide handed Elżunia to us and left us, running off. We had no idea what this meant and were scared but stayed put, not sure what else to do, waiting and hoping. Rysio started to cry. The guide returned but then almost as quickly ran off in another direction, again without explanation.

Despite the warning, Henry lit a cigarette, the flame of the match suddenly illuminating the area. The Slovak burst out angrily, "How can you be so stupid? Don't you know a flame could be noticed from far away?" Poor Henry needed the cigarette badly to calm his nerves. Now knowing a momentary flame had endangered us further, his fears were heightened, rather than reduced.

Finally, from deep in the darkness, we heard a strange whistle. It sounded like a bird. Our guide ran toward the sound and returned quickly with another man – our new guide, who was to lead us across the Hungarian border. He was late, hence our guide's apprehension. The new guide lifted Elżunia straight onto his back. My towels came in handy; she could sit comfortably and sleep.

WAITING AT KASSA, HUNGARY

We started on our way, this time downhill, first the guide with Elżunia on his back, followed by the Habers. Henry, totally exhausted, was still carrying his suitcase. Rysio, after all his running around with Elżunia, could hardly walk. Only Irka seemed to be coping. The guide, being late, was in a hurry. We could hardly keep up with his pace. This time, luck was not with us. Unfortunately, Henry twisted his ankle. Poor Irka had to carry their suitcase and support Henry while Rysio dragged along slowly.

At last, we were out of the forest. From the top of the hill, we could see Kassa, the Hungarian town. It was around three in the morning and the moon was spreading its light around. Our figures must have been clearly visible against the background of white snow. The Hungarian guide, who was nearly half an hour late, was trying to make up for lost time and moved ahead quickly. Suddenly, a strong wind started to blow forcefully, and it began to snow. Our field of vision suddenly blurred. Lusia could not keep up with the guide and the distance between them was increasing steadily, although she tried hard not to lose sight of him. The distance between Lusia and I also grew. I had to slow down so she could see me. Thus our "procession" grew longer and whilst Lusia could hardly see the gradually disappearing guide, I could also hardly see her. The Habers were following me in a haphazard way. The drizzle of white flakes became a snowstorm, with the strong wind and snow cutting straight into our faces. I could see almost nothing ahead of me. Lusia had disappeared, yet I slowed down even more to be sure I was seen by the Habers, who because of Henry's injury had fallen far behind.

It was blowing fiercely. Such a gloomy, threatening atmosphere of wind and snow I had only seen in films, never in real life. Being inside a snowstorm surrounded by complete darkness was frightening. I was only aware that the path led down a hill but was blinded, with no choice but to follow and keep walking.

The storm abated as suddenly as it had begun and Lusia reappeared. She had already caught up to the guide, and both were waiting for us. Once she spotted me she turned and followed the Hungarian into a shed. I stopped and waited until I could see the Habers. I waved till they waved back. Relieved, I entered the shed and was happy to find the guide with the sleeping child still on his back. We were in a cowshed, warm and smelling of fresh manure and hay. There were a few cows contentedly munching. What a change it was from the snow and wind! I was longing to lie down if only for a minute, but the guide gave a definite no. It was dawn and not a living soul must see us. We must leave this warm, friendly haven immediately.

The wind still blew, and it was snowing heavily again. Since we were approaching houses, we had to move quietly. Following the guide, we moved onward. Haber was heroically ignoring his twisted ankle as fear was stronger than pain. It was four in the morning. An early dawn slowly began to dissipate the grayness around us. Following some byways and jumping over a few ditches, we finally reached a small house. The guide quietly opened the gate and we stepped onto an open veranda. There were two doors on opposite sides of the veranda. The guide put Elżunia down, asking us to be quiet because everyone was asleep, and pointed at the door on the right to indicate where we should enter. Then, with a quick handshake, he was gone, not even listening to our whispered efforts to express our thanks. Dogs started to bark and then were as quiet. We had finished hours of exhausting walking across the Carpathian Mountains.

We were on the outskirts of the Hungarian town of Kassa. On that cold, open veranda, there was not even a bench to sit on. Exhausted and wet through, we lowered ourselves onto the floor, too tired to utter a word to one another, just waiting quietly for a door to open and for someone to let us in. But both doors remained closed without a sign of life behind them. We felt strange and feared the guide might have mistakenly taken us to the wrong house. So far, wherever we had stopped we had always been welcomed and good-hearted people had greeted us with smiles and hot tea.

I could not bear it any longer and quietly began to knock on the door. Nothing. Then, after a pause, another knock, a bit louder. Still no answer. We could not understand it. Time passed with us still sitting there on the floor – frozen to the bone; Haber in pain, Rysio half-conscious, and Elżunia asleep in Lusia's arms. And still nothing was happening.

I tried again, knocking louder – so loud that the dogs began to bark. It scared me and I stopped, but not for long. More and more nervous, I resumed my knocking. This time, we heard movements inside. Someone had probably just woken up. We waited to be let in, but no one opened the door. The noises inside the house diminished after I started knocking again, this time, aggressively. It worked. The door slightly opened, and a woman's face appeared. "Quiet! Quiet!" she whispered and closed the door quickly. We were puzzled, not knowing what to think.

For a change, I started knocking at the opposite door. The effect was the same. Even after knocking hard, no one answered. What did it all mean? Two hours passed. Two eternal hours. Then, at six in the morning, the doors opened, both at the same time.

The woman who had earlier opened the door took the females – Lusia, Irka, and Elżunia. The other took us men. We entered a small flat and were ushered into a room where a warm iron stove was already burning. Only one narrow bed was in the room. Totally exhausted, Rysio dropped onto it just as he was, fully dressed in his wet boots. Henry joined him. I lay on the floor by the stove, hot and glowing like a red lamp, its blessed warmth spreading all over me so I could feel the frost and snow on my clothes beginning to melt. Poor Haber couldn't even hold a glass of hot lemon drink the women had quickly prepared for us. Rysio was already fast asleep. After a while, I, too, fell asleep with my head on our rucksack, covered with my coat. The heat embraced my body, and even the hard floor didn't bother me.

After some four hours, we awoke and were permitted to see our wives, who were in much better accommodation. Their hostess had put them in her still-warm double bed, where they had slept blissfully. At about ten, she woke them with a warm and hearty breakfast. She explained why we had to wait for so long in the cold. It was a routine procedure to protect the women whose house was a stopover for refugees from Poland in case someone had noticed the strangers approaching from the Slovakian borders at such an early hour and followed them. Disclosure of the hiding place would have frightening consequences for the women. As long as the refugees remained outside, they could deny any involvement. If after two hours nothing happened, they knew everything was safe.

It was Sunday, and the women were getting ready for church. They drew the curtains and closed the door from the outside, leaving some food but warning us not to touch the curtains and to be as quiet as possible.

In the evening, two Jewish youngsters arrived to take us on to another place, which this time belonged to a Jewish family. There, after an extremely modest meal, we went into the bedroom. We had two single beds at our disposal, one for each family. The children slept crosswise at our feet. We were comfortable enough until our warm bodies woke armies of bedbugs. I could hardly believe that two small beds could house such numbers of those abominable creatures. The moment they attacked us, there was no way we could sleep again. After a sleepless night, two young men took us to the railway station. We were on our way to Budapest, the city we had dreamed of during the last few months.

We were, however, warned that documents could be checked during the journey and people without papers or acting suspiciously would be arrested and possibly sent back to Poland. There was no way we could get hold of Hungarian documents, so we were extremely scared.

Our guides bought our tickets and warned us to be sure not to speak. The guides would travel in another carriage. When (if?) we arrived in Budapest, they would guide us to a safe place to stay until our documents were legalized and political asylum granted.

Tense, we boarded the train. Our compartment was nearly empty, with only one man sitting by the window. He was well dressed and looked distinctively Jewish. A Hungarian couple joined us just before the train departed. The six of us sat quietly in one row; the train rumbled steadily on. We tried to catch some sleep, but fear kept us awake. Although already on Hungarian soil, the danger of being sent back to Poland was hanging over our heads. Without identification papers or the ability to speak a word of Hungarian, we could only pray to God to save us from any police inspection. The beautifully dressed Hungarian gendarmes alighted on our train, we had learned, while in Kassa. Our escorts had pointed them out to us as they walked slowly down the platform – two giants with their huge hats decorated with dozens of colorful long feathers. We were made to understand why our guides had been concerned. Heaven forbid they should ask for our documents.

The train stopped at every station. Life seemed normal, with people getting on and off as if the war did not exist. The people were well dressed and well fed. The man in our compartment had apparently become hungry. He opened his overnight bag, took out a nice piece of embroidered cloth, and covered the small folding table from under the window. Out of the bag appeared two hard-boiled eggs, a piece of sausage, some white bread, and a cucumber. The fragrance of fresh hot tea from his thermos reached our nostrils. His feast finished with a piece of cake.

We all were watching in amazement. How was it possible that in a country that was an ally of Germany, a man – clearly a Jew – could travel without fear and right before our eyes peacefully enjoy his meal? No wonder that, watching the man's performance, our children became more and more restless. They were getting hungry. We tried to explain to them, whispering that we, too, soon would have a fine meal in Budapest. The man must have noticed their hungry eyes since he pulled out two small apples and smilingly handed them over to the children.

We adults did not feel hungry, being too nervous at the frightening thought of a possible encounter with the gendarmes. Whenever the train stopped, I watched the gendarmes, who were moving from one carriage into the other at each station, coming closer and closer to ours. Lusia and the Habers were watching my face tensely for any sign that the situation was deteriorating.

The other people in our carriage sat relaxed. Our Jewish gentleman was already snoring. I remained constantly on the lookout with the gendarmes now only one carriage away. At the next station, they would inevitably approach us – which could mean the end of our adventure. Nice effort, I thought, but at least we had tried. Many people had tried to escape in different ways, and few made it. I felt most sadly for the children.

The train was slowly approaching a large town. One could feel it crossing various rails – and the passing of suburbia, typical of a city. Then I saw the name of the station – Miskolc. Looking through the window, I noticed gendarmes alight and remembered being told that Miskolc was where they might stop inspecting documents. We had been placed by our young guides in the middle carriage of the train – they had known that the gendarmes usually started checking from one end. Sometimes, they reached the center carriage before Miskolc, yet this time we had been lucky.

The train remained at the station for about 15 minutes. I was at the window all the time, watching the platform and people. I could not see the gendarmes, but I saw one of our guardian boys with a thumbs-up and a big smile on his face. The danger was over.

Without words, my smiling face showed the happy news to Lusia and the Habers. I grasped Lusia's hand stealthily so no one could see. My tension gone, I tried to sleep. Elżunia was already sleeping, leaning against Lusia. Rysio was asleep already, and next to him was Irka. The train was moving steadily toward Budapest, but too slow for our nerves – it was an all-stops train. We had been strongly advised to keep silent, but how could we expect that from the kids? How to keep them quiet? The moment they awoke, trouble began. Elżunia was quiet most of the time. Not Rysio, though. He had a lot to say to everybody. His tongue didn't stop for a second, and because he was not allowed to talk, he whispered – whispering into his mother's ear, then his father's, then back sometimes to Elżunia. We felt quite uneasy about it. Finally, Haber decided to put an end to it by taking Rysio out of the compartment into the corridor. There, he made sure that the boy understood that his behavior was putting all of us in a dangerous situation. The reprimand seemed to work and Rysio kept quiet and we reached Budapest without any further trouble. Near the exit, our guides were waiting for us. We felt safe at last.

CAMP KADARKÚT FOR POLISH FAMILIES

We left the station looking in amazement as we followed our guides. How different a world this was. We were dazed by the normalcy of life in this beautiful city. There were wide, clean, brightly lit streets with shops full of goods and well-dressed people.

Our young guides were in a hurry and we had to keep pace with them. For them, this wonderful Budapest was nothing special; they had seen it before. But for us, after five years of war, struggle, and deprivation, this city was something to marvel at. We couldn't take our eyes off the shop windows and the displays of food and goods we had almost forgotten existed. When we came to a tempting display of luscious chocolates, we had to stop for a moment. What an unbelievable sight! But there was no time to enjoy more than a glance. Our guides were well ahead of us. We walked for nearly two hours before we reached our destination, an uninviting apartment in a slummy part of town.

We were led into a small, dark, and unpleasant room by the landlady – an unfriendly, grubby-looking woman of about 40. She looked like a prostitute, and the furniture and furnishings added to that impression – the walls with faded red wallpaper, the torn upholstery, the threadbare carpet, the shoddy double bed. Off the room was a small alcove with another double bed. After pointing out that our stay there was illegal, the woman asked us to be sure we were quiet. "There are other tenants here, you know," she warned belligerently in a mixture of Yiddish-Slovakian jargon. "And see that those kids only talk in whispers. In fact, it would be better if they didn't talk at all. I'm putting myself in danger. I'm only doing this out of the goodness of my heart, so remember that." She made no mention of the money she was getting from the Jewish Committee for this service.

Before leaving, our Slovakian guides advised us that someone was going to take us to the Polish Committee, where we hoped to obtain temporary permits to stay in Budapest. We were also warned that people without documents could be picked up during a police roundup – or razzia, as they called it – imprisoned, and in many cases sent back to Poland. We should be watchful. Anxiously, we waited for the morning, when, indeed, someone did come to take us to the Polish Committee. We did not find out until later that the Polish Government-in-Exile, established in London, had representatives in Budapest whose office was at 11 Fö Utca. Their aim was to give financial and legal support to all Polish subjects, irrespective of religion or nationality. The head of the mission was General Dr. Jan Kollontay.

The Polish Committee was recognized by the Hungarian government and cooperated closely with the police. The strange aspect of the situation – something we could not understand – was that Hungary, while in a state of war with the Allies, still tolerated and even supported the activities of the Polish Committee. It had been established at the beginning of the war when quite a number of Polish army unit members had managed to cross the Polish-Hungarian border.

Since 1941, fewer Poles were attempting to cross the border. It was, after all, a risky venture and, difficult as it was living under German occupation, the Germans did not usually molest ordinary Polish citizens not involved in anti-German activities. However, it was in 1942 that the influx of Jews into Hungary began, reaching its peak in 1943. They were the ones with nothing to lose, as for many of them, staying in Poland meant a constant threat to their lives. The Polish Committee in Budapest was instructed by the London government in exile to assist all Poles running from the Nazis. In order not to embarrass the Hungarians, it was decided to give the Jews Polish names and register them as Roman Catholics.

We had no problems in this respect. Our name was Daraż and we kept it. The Habers also had no trouble, their name being Haberko. The officials, although they knew exactly who we were, gave us all the papers we needed without fuss. With these documents, we went to the police and were given permits to stay in Budapest for ten days. As refugees from Poland, we were also eligible for financial support –150 pengős for ten days for our family – quite a sum even considering the almost prewar cost of living in Hungary at that time. We couldn't believe our luck! This was the first financial help we had ever been given. It seemed incredible that we could now walk the street, ride a bus, enter shops, buy whatever we wanted – and not be afraid either of the Hungarians or of the police or blackmailers. It seemed like a wonderful dream to live in a city where neither a Pole nor a Ukrainian would point at us an accusing finger: Jew!

The first thing we decided to find better accommodation. The woman was, in fact, a prostitute, and whenever a client was expected, we had to leave the house, even in the freezing cold. She always had a good excuse – it was someone from the family, or the police, or whoever. No matter who was coming, we had to leave. It was not easy to find accommodation in a foreign city. With the help of the German newspaper *Die Budapester Zeitung*, we finally found a large room in what had been an elegant pension in one of the best districts of Budapest. It was owned by a Jewish lady, Mrs. Levayne, who now had to accept tenants of a different class than those before the war. She put both our families into one of her most luxurious bedrooms, the only vacant one. We paid quite a high rent but had little choice. One king-size bed had to accommodate all six of us. Use of the kitchen and bathroom was permitted only at certain times and under close supervision. Mrs. Levayne made sure we didn't use too much gas, electricity, or water. We were happy, all the same, to escape that dreary place at Kiraly Street.

Soon, we met other refugees from Poland who already had some experience of life in Budapest. We learned from them that while in Budapest we were not eligible for any sort of financial support after the initial ten days. If we wished to stay longer, we would have to pay out of our own pocket. The only other alternative was to move into a camp for Polish refugees. No one was particularly eager to go into a Polish camp and live among Poles, hence our people tried every possible avenue to prolong their stay in Budapest. Some were luckier than others.

My cousins Danka and Stasis, having successfully followed our route to Budapest, found accommodation with a Christian family on the outskirts. The landlady's son, Karci, fell in love with Danka at first sight, so their stay in Budapest was secured. Karci, his parents, and sister were friendly and hospitable. Many refugees stayed with them for a few days, receiving much needed help, especially those who had no money or documents.

This wonderful Hungarian family rendered their help to strangers at great personal risk – without financial consideration, on the contrary – and fed them at their own expense. There were others who were lucky enough to get help from the American Jewish Joint Distribution Committee. Those who had their own resources (and there were a few) could remain and live quite comfortably in Budapest.

Prior to leaving Poland, I had obtained a recommendation from Janek Spira, chief engineer at Pontess, to a Dr. Balla, the governing director of Wander Pharmaceutical Limited, a worldwide chemical company. Many years before, Janek was in charge of the construction of Wander's factory in Kraków when he met Dr. Balla, at the time the head of the Polish branch of Wander. He was excited when I rang him and invited me to come as soon as possible. He was interested in the well-being of Janek Spira and others he remembered from his days in Poland, but he could hardly believe the horror stories I told him. I was not surprised. Those stories were just unbelievable. As I expected, there were no job possibilities for me in Wander's factory even though I was ready to accept any manual work. It was beyond his comprehension for a qualified engineer to work as a laborer, although, due to the language barrier, I could not carry out any other work. Dr. Balla was helpful and advised me to see the friendly director of a building company. A letter of introduction was quickly prepared, but as expected, my visit at the builder's office was, for similar reasons, unsuccessful.

When our financial resources came to an end, we had to leave Budapest. The Polish Committee directed us to a camp in Kadarkút, a village next to Kaposvár in southern Hungary, some 50 kilometers from the Yugoslav border. Henry Haber and I went first in order to prepare accommodation for the families.

Kadarkút was an affluent village with tree-lined streets, brick houses, a large marketplace, a council building, and a beautiful old church nearby. The community had two doctors – one a Jew, at present a captain in the army – and the other the official government doctor, Balla. The villagers were mostly prosperous, the land was fertile, the village surrounded by acres of vineyards. The population totaled some 1,000 souls. The camp was not in an enclosure. We were considered civilians. We were internees, free to move around the village and to choose our own accommodation at our expense. There was a Polish school and a Polish priest. There were a Polish physician and dentist, both Jewish on false papers. There were a few similar camps for Polish refugees in various parts of Hungary, but the one in Kadarkút was mainly to accommodate families with children. The Habers knew a woman from Kraków with two children already living there. She introduced us to a Mr. Stern, who owned a large hardware shop selling building materials and agricultural equipment as well. One of the wealthiest people in the village, be had lived for generations in a beautiful two-story house with the shop on the ground floor. He was the only Jew in Kadarkút who could speak German. The rest spoke only Hungarian. Very friendly and wanting to be helpful, Mr. Stern began to look for accommodation for us. Everyone knew and respected him, and he knew everybody. He was a personality in the village.

Seventeen Jewish families lived in Kadarkút. Some were prosperous owners of vineyards, others had shops, and some had land. All lived in large houses. Since he had been recruited into the army, the young, good-looking wife and 17-year-old daughter of the local Jewish doctor lived alone in a big house. Stern approached her asking if she would rent a room to us or the Habers. She refused. She wasn't the only one to turn us down. Quite unlike Slovakian Jews, who had opened their doors and hearts to us, the Hungarian Jewish community was generally inhospitable. Wealthy people with houses of six of more rooms couldn't spare a corner for Polish refugees. It was unbelievable but true. While a husband and wife shared the main bedroom, daughters and sons would each have their own bedrooms and would not share with strangers. A lounge room was for receiving guests; a dining room was for eating not sleeping. The spare room had to be reserved for servants. No, they insisted, they had no room for strangers. This was the usual answer we received from our co-religionists. In Budapest, and now here in Kadarkút, the answer was the same: no. Nevertheless, thanks to Stern's popularity and powers of persuasion, he was able to talk two neighboring villagers into letting us have their bedrooms at a low rent. Returning to Budapest, we packed our belongings, collected our families, and the next day reported to the officer-in-charge of the camp.

Officially, the head of the local gendarme was in command, but the day-to-day running of the camp was entrusted to a second-in-charge, a Pole named Jozef Grylko. The camp secretary was a certain Wladyslaw Skonieczny. Polite and friendly, they registered us and issued us proper identification cards. They seemed quite happy to have new people in the camp and informed us of our rights and restrictions. Once a month, we were paid our allowance of 15 pengős per family per day. It was enough for all our modest needs. We could start a normal, peaceful existence, go to the marketplace, buy fruit, vegetables, milk, butter, eggs, cream, and chickens – which we had been unable to buy for the last few years in Poland but here were nothing extraordinary. Peasant women would sit on the stony ground of the marketplace and, like the good old days in Poland, sell their goods. Everybody would touch, smell, and bargain. A wonderful, wonderful, almost forgotten world! And here we were, after dreary Soviet occupation and Nazi terror finding ourselves in this land of milk and honey. We could not believe it! Was it a dream? We became friendly with Stern and would have long conversations. He couldn't believe our stories. "Horthy wouldn't allow that," he would say.

Once an admiral of the imperial fleet and a devoted subject of the Hapsburg family, Regent Nicholas Horthy was the head of state since the collapse of the Austro-Hungarian Empire in 1918. He was held in high esteem by the Hungarian Jews. They liked and trusted him and, although they knew that the country was too weak to resist Germany, they ruled out the possibility of anti-Jewish laws being imposed on Hungary. "Horthy would not allow that," was their absolute conviction.

We also met a few other Polish Jews who, like us, had crossed the border. Altogether there were 20, including six children. There were also about 200 Poles in the camp, living around their church and club, where they gathered to chat or read their newsletters. In the beginning, we visited the Polish club, too, but soon stopped as we became aware of the general animosity toward us. The conversations always revolved around the subject that was too painful for us. These Poles didn't even try to hide their satisfaction when discussing the wonderful work that Hitler was doing for them and their country.

We were, however, on good terms with Grylko, the camp commander, his secretary Skonieczny, and two other young Poles. We used to play cards, allowing them to win small sums and treating them generously with good Hungarian wine. So we lived in peace and hope. We had a place to sleep, enough money from the Polish government to support our modest needs in a friendly country, and, most important of all, we were legal residents. Hence we began to recover slowly from our trauma of the last five years.

As the days passed, we still found it hard to believe our luck. We quietly nourished the hope that Providence, which had guided us so far and kept us alive up to this day, would help us survive in this way until the end of the war. But our haven was not to last.

YELLOW STAR FOR HUNGARIAN JEWS

One morning, while having breakfast, Lusia and I heard a loud knock on our door. It was Irka Haber, her face ashen and terror stricken.

"What's happened?" we exclaimed.

She stammered out one word: "Germans!" She could say no more. We sat her down and haltingly she told us that her hosts, who were worked up after listening to the morning news, had tried to tell them something in Hungarian. The only thing they understood was that the Germans had entered Hungary. Some units were already in Kadarkút. We were speechless. Our beautiful dream had collapsed. Our trouble-free life in Hungary had come to a sudden end.

With the military situation taking a disastrous course on the Eastern Front, it was obvious that the Germans had to occupy Hungary. They could not trust their ally, especially after two Hungarian brigades surrendered to the Russians without a fight. The Germans were in retreat, and to secure the retreat, they had to occupy Hungary.

The question now was whether the murderous Gestapo would follow the military forces. But there seemed little hope they wouldn't. I could see the tragic future in store for us and the Hungarian Jews. Despite their deep faith in Horthy, I didn't believe they could escape the yellow star with all its deadly consequences. And what would happen to us? Would the Hungarian government still respect international law? After all, we were Polish political refugees who had been granted asylum. The Poles would probably be quite safe; either they would stay in Hungary or be sent back to Poland. The question was what would happen to all those who had entered Hungary illegally on false papers – Jewish people like us. I wanted to find out whether the Germans would stay in Kadarkút. I left home and reached the center of the village in a few minutes. The sight was terrifying. The place was packed with personnel carriers, trucks, and motorcycles and a mass of those well-known and deeply hated green uniforms of the German forces.

It was breakfast time and a field kitchen had just arrived with a truck full of fresh white bread. I could smell the strong aroma of hot coffee. I looked around and spotted a Polish man from our camp talking to some Germans. I waited. After a while he went off, waving his hand and shouting in Polish, "Till this evening. I will come back at six."

I followed him and while passing I remarked casually, "Germans speaking Polish?"

"Yes," he said. "Silesians know Polish very well. Quite nice guys. We are going to have a drink tonight. It will be fun!" He was happy and excited at the prospect.

Again, cautiously, I questioned him, asking whether he knew anything about their future plans.

"They don't know anything themselves. Just waiting for orders," he said. "They had to leave Yugoslavia suddenly this morning and are only staying here for the night."

Depressed, I went home. We spent all morning discussing the situation with the Habers and others. Our spirits were low; we had absolutely no idea what to do. Our children were affected by the whole atmosphere. We had neither time nor patience for them. Poor Elżunia kept asking: "Tatusiu, why are you so sad? What's happened?" How could I answer her?

After a number of meetings with our group, it was decided I should go to Budapest to obtain more information and perhaps some guidance on what to do since all government offices, as well as all Jewish organizations, were there. They would probably know much more than we did. Equally unhappy with the new situation, Commandant Grylko issued me the necessary travel documents, ignoring the new regulations that internees were not to be allowed to leave the camps anymore. He asked only that I return as soon as possible and when leaving the village try not to be seen by any Poles. He had been instructed that the gendarmes were to take over command of the camp. An atmosphere of depression and fear prevailed in Budapest.

German occupation had taken everyone by surprise even though the possibility had often been contemplated. The Hungarian Jews were completely unprepared. Within days, the Gestapo followed the army and began their usual operations. All Jewish charity organizations were suspended. Arrests followed. The Polish Committee at Fö Utca was liquidated. The Gestapo entered their office just as General Kollontay was burning documents. He kept on doing so and was killed on the spot. It was evident the Germans knew every detail of the activities of the Polish mission in Hungary. Apparently, some Gestapo members had passed as Polish Jews. Their attack on the Polish mission in Budapest was so sudden and carefully prepared that it was several hours before people knew about it.

After killing Kollontay and arresting the other employees, the Germans set a trap at the office. Unfortunately, many fell into their hands. Lutek Kahane was one of them. He and our two cousins from Warsaw, Frania and Wisia Ecker, had followed our route. They had managed to reach Slovakia, but Lutek had a stroke of bad luck while crossing over to Hungary. In the region of Bratislava, he was caught by the Slovak border police. Thanks to the intervention of the Jewish Committee, however, he was released. When on his next attempt he succeeded and, in due course, called at the Polish Committee, a Gestapo officer opened the door. He was arrested and taken with others to the Gestapo headquarters.

The situation in Hungary was becoming hopeless. Some people were already looking to flee toward Romania. Illegal ways of getting there had been previously established – a Jewish Welfare Committee existed in Bucharest and Constanța. The port city on the Black Sea was still a door to the world outside. Unfortunately, this door was open only to the wealthy. Still, a chance to save Elżunia was there. A young, courageous girl had been smuggled from Palestine via Romania into Hungary where she had organized a rescue operation of Jewish orphans. A member of a Jewish underground organization called

Brycha acted cautiously, sleeping in a different Jewish home each night, and was not easy to locate.

Finally, I succeeded in meeting her. We spoke Polish. I was struck by the young woman's determination, devotion to the cause, courage, and common sense that one would hardly expect at her age. Over the preceding weeks she had traveled between Budapest and Bucharest in charge of Jewish orphans, escorting them on to Constanţa, from where other young chaverim (friends) took them on illegal boats to Palestine. Her task was fraught with danger, the more so since the invasion of the Germans. Yet she was fearless, full of enthusiasm and hope – a real heroine![1]

I told her about our great concern – the frightful destiny of our eight children in Kadarkút. Although I wasn't authorized by the other parents, I felt I should speak on their behalf as well. The girl listened, not showing much enthusiasm. After the operation for the orphans has been completed, she said, "The organization will most certainly look at other children. They would be welcome in Palestine. She advised me to keep in touch with the Brycha liaison officer in Budapest and wait for future developments. Disappointed, I returned to Kadarkút. Yet I was relieved not to be parting with Elżunia for the time being.

The situation developed just as we feared. The Gestapo began to introduce their "new order." Posters with regulations restricting Jewish lives appeared. Jews were ordered to wear a yellow star, forbidden to use public transport, and forced to abide by all the other repressive laws we had experienced in Poland. However, Hungarian Jews accepted these laws calmly, so strong was their faith in Horthy and their belief that he would protect them. No, we knew what the future was holding for them. We knew that the yellow star was only the beginning and that the end would be their annihilation. Luckily, having identities as Christian and foreign citizens, we were not obliged to conform to these regulations. Not at the moment anyway.

We reasoned there were around 40,000 Hungarian Jews but only a small number of Polish Jews in the country. Provided that the files at Fö Utca had been destroyed, we hoped the Germans would not easily locate us unless helped by someone interested in solving the Jewish problem.

It surprised and even shocked us that Hungarian Jews didn't realize what this new situation meant for them. I felt it was my duty to warn them before it was too late. I cautioned Stern strongly against putting on the yellow star. "What can we do?" he asked helplessly.

"Pack up and go with your wife to Budapest, rent a room or flat, change your name to Kovacs or any other Hungarian name, and no one will ask you questions," I told him. I was sure he had enough money to do it. I offered to put him in touch with someone who would help him obtain the necessary Aryan papers – the refugees from Poland had their own ways. "Do anything, but for God's sake don't put on the yellow star."

He looked at me as if I were out of my mind. Leave his house, vineyards, animals, his enormous stock of food – everything? He would have to think about it and talk it over with his wife. There were still a few more days left. Over the following days, I spoke to Stern, warning him over and over again. Yet after speaking to other Kadarkút Jews, they all decided to put on the yellow star and stay. Orders were orders! They were confident Horthy would not let them be harmed. I was dismayed! They put their heads in the sand.

I couldn't allow that to happen. I asked Stern to organize a meeting of all the Kadarkút Jews. Henry Haber, Lusia, and I went along. I addressed them passionately, vividly describing my experiences, the persecutions, and my knowledge of the concentration camps and even the death chambers. I pointed out how only by resisting German orders and posing as Aryans had we managed to stay alive, while all who had obeyed were now dead. Lusia and Haber supported my arguments with further appeals. We spoke in German; Stern translated into Hungarian.

When we had finished, our audience was silent until the doctor's daughter, a teenage student, stood up and presented her viewpoint. She argued that by their insubordination, the Polish Jews had forced the Germans to use more drastic measures. If Hungarians were willing to follow orders obediently, she argued, nothing would happen. "After all, Germans are not barbarians." Two more speakers supported her. There was no doubt, Polish Jews were not much liked by their Hungarian brethren. Finally, the assembly decided to stay put in Kadarkút and put on the yellow star. Stern looked somehow relieved. He was simply unable to leave all his possessions behind. He acted the way we did in 1939. We left the meeting horrified.

When the deadline came, I went out into the streets, curious to observe how many stars were being worn. I had hardly left home when an unknown Hungarian fellow approached me and, speaking in Hungarian, pointed to my chest where the star should have been. He was asking why I wasn't wearing one. I knew, for I understood the word *Zsidó* [Hungarian for Jew, similar to *Żyd* in Polish].

He sneered when I said in Hungarian, "*Lengyel Vagyok* [I am Polish]." I wondered how he knew we were Jewish. Who had told him? Or was it that Stern, the best-known Jew in the village, had sought accommodation for us. Or maybe some Poles had told him. I was shocked by this sudden encounter. Although I was aware that the Hungarians "loved" their Jewish co-citizens as dearly as the Poles did theirs, I was not aware the local Hungarians knew who we were. We now realized that we were in even more danger than we had been in Poland, where at least by knowing the language and the people we could keep ahead of the danger by asking for help, appealing, pleading, convincing. We knew the Polish character, the Polish mentality. Of course, it would still be a matter of luck; there were blackmailers and informers everywhere, but there were also honest and courageous people among the Poles – real Christians. I could find them and approach them in the right way to touch their hearts and hope for results. Even if only out of hatred for the Germans, some would help. If all my arguments or pleading did not help, there was always money, a wedding ring, a watch – something to get us out of trouble for a night, for a few hours.

But how different it was here in Hungary. Here our situation seemed even more hopeless. Our biggest problem was the language, but even if we knew it, there was no way we could rationalize, argue, or plead with a Hungarian peasant. Yes, they were honest, hard-working people, but they were hard and cold and blindly followed the orders of the authorities. "*Nem szabad* [It is not allowed]," they would say. They would never act against the law. They would always do what they were told like the Germans did. Orders were orders. Trying to bribe the Hungarians would be futile – even dangerous. They would most definitely never lift a finger to help a Jew, let alone a Polish Jew who could hardly utter a few broken Hungarian words.

And why should they? Would a Polish Jew have helped a Hungarian refugee hide illegally in prewar Poland? We felt trapped and helpless, just hoping that the approaching Soviet army wouldn't give the Germans time to solve the Jewish problem in Hungary. Meanwhile, we had to go on with our normal lives, still receiving the allowance, shopping at the market, playing cards, drinking Hungarian wine with Grylko and Skoweczny, and just waiting.

We shared our fear with our Polish friends. But was there a traitor among the 200 Poles who knew us? That was our major concern. Without the fear of denunciation, we would have felt fairly safe. We could survive as other Poles, unmolested, for surely the Germans would not contemplate liquidating a few hundred Polish refugees! Unfortunately, our fears were justified. It wasn't long before the commanding officer of the Hungarian gendarmes received an anonymous letter informing him, in broken Hungarian, that among Polish refugees in the camp were Jews living under false names. Grylko was summoned and asked for an explanation. Without hesitation, he assured the commandant that everyone's documents were checked by Polish government officials in Budapest, that everyone was definitely Catholic, and that he himself had thoroughly looked through their papers. He invited the gendarme for a drink and somehow managed to get that anonymous letter from him and destroy it. News of the denouncer's letter alarmed us greatly. We all realized that whoever had written it would not stop until they saw us in a cattle truck on the way to Auschwitz.

THE MEDICAL EXAMINATION

We spent long hours talking about our situation. Night after night, we gathered at various places, discussing plans, and trying to organize our next steps. Going to Yugoslavia and joining Tito's partisans – rising up in arms to repay the Nazi murderers for all our sufferings – was seriously considered. Should we die, let's die with honor. Henry Haber volunteered to contact partisans regardless of how futile the whole undertaking seemed. The Yugoslavian border was about 50 kilometers away. It was the river Drava, deep and wide, which would be the most difficult obstacle. We had no contact with smugglers and no chance of establishing such contact. Even if there were an opportunity to contact the partisans, what would happen to our wives and children? That was our greatest dilemma. Tito was only taking men. Leaving the others behind to face inevitable death? The whole idea had to be dropped.

Lusia and I were worried about Elżunia. Could we place her in a convent? Then, we could simply run away and hide in the forests for weeks, even months, and wait for the Red Army. I was restless and had to act.

The Poles are a religious people and Sunday mass in Kadarkút church, conducted by a Polish priest, was well attended. I decided to talk openly to the priest. He was quite surprised to see me since I was not of his flock. When I told him the purpose of my visit, he was speechless. I went on to tell him about the Jews in Poland – the tragic fate of the three million. I told him of our flight to Hungary on false papers and our assumed names. He listened quietly, although I had a strong feeling he did not fully believe me. I was not surprised; without experiencing it, our story was unbelievable.

"That's impossible," he said. Then I mentioned the anonymous letter and he looked embarrassed. I asked of him only two favors – the first, to condemn during his sermons those who had made the denunciation, reminding them of the sinfulness of such an act; and secondly, to explain to the offender during a confession, if it came to that, of the commandment, "Thou shall not kill." Such a letter would bring about the death of innocent people. I hoped that such strong words from the priest would bring these shameful acts to an end.

There was one more thing I wanted to raise, though with little hope of success. "Our six-year-old daughter does not know that she is Jewish," I said. "In Warsaw, she went regularly to church and was brought up as a Christian. Could you use your connections to have her placed in a convent? This would save her from certain death. In return, should we perish, she would remain a Christian." I waited for his reply. After a silence, he said he would think it over let me know through Grylko.

I returned home downhearted. Lusia had anticipated that my visit would be fruitless, and so it was, for the priest never contacted us or Grylko.

The Hungarian Jews put on their yellow stars and life went on as before. The Hungarian people did not bother the Jews. The Hungarian authorities also did not interfere with the Polish or Jewish refugees. We lived as two separate communities. The Poles had their church and we had our friends. Grylko and Skonieczny played cards and drank wine with us as before. Later on, another young man, Kluska, joined our company. After the monotony of camp life, the time spent with us was stimulating and good fun and they enjoyed it greatly. Elżunia remained everyone's favorite. All seemed peaceful, but how long could it last?

As expected, the Gestapo had quickly infiltrated the country. To our distress, we learned that they had already established offices in Kaposvár, a district town only a few kilometers away. Horthy was still head of government and as yet there were no anti-Jewish activities by the Germans. Utterly helpless and constantly worried, we expected the worst. And one day lightning struck: It was Grylko who brought the news that another anonymous letter had been sent directly to the Gestapo. Not wanting to be involved in Hungarian affairs, the Gestapo forwarded the letter to the Hungarian police. It seemed likely the Germans preferred to maintain the Hungarian Jews' false sense of security rather than act against a small bunch of Polish Jewish refugees. Grylko again succeeded in assuring the police that there were no Jews in the Polish camp. Anxiety about our future was with us day and night.

We spent long hours trying to find a way to escape yet knew the sword of Damocles was hanging over our heads and sooner or later would fall. Then it did. An order was issued to Grylko by the camp commandant: After mass the following Sunday, all male camp inmates were to undergo a physical examination by the local government physician – Dr. Balla. Panic spread among our people. Nearly all decided to leave immediately for Budapest. Grylko issued everyone a travel permit. Regardless of the consequences, this wonderful man was ready to help.

Everyone except the Habers and us left Kadarkút. We were no longer capable of running. We no longer had the energy to flee for our lives and no money to start again in Budapest. We stayed to face whatever was to come. Left alone in Kadarkút, we determined we would not surrender. We had to think of another way out. To go for the examination and expose ourselves in the hope that the physician would make a mistake or ignore the circumstances was out of the question. We hated the idea of exposing ourselves before the Poles, feeling their smug looks, and hearing their derogatory remarks. Grylko advised that we should simulate illness, yet we were sure that sooner or later, the Gestapo, helped by our "friendly" co-citizens, would find their way to our door. No, we had to think of a more ingenious way of saving ourselves. With only two days to act, I considered the only thing to do now was to confront Dr. Balla directly, tell him the truth, and appeal to his humanity. Perhaps it would be fruitless, but what alternative did I have? According to Stern, Dr. Balla was known as a cold, unfriendly individual and an antisemite. Even though he thought my chances of success were one in a thousand, I decided to take a gamble. Together with a pessimistic and reluctant Haber, I went to see Dr. Balla on the

Saturday evening, leaving our wives and Polish friends waiting anxiously at home.

The office was closed. Dr. Balla was not available for patients at that time of night. However, in response to our knocking on the back door, he appeared. He did not understand what we wanted. "To save our lives," I said.

We had come to beg him to do just that. After a few words, I felt like I was talking to a stone. How could I get through to him? I referred to tomorrow's examination.

"The examination? What has that got to do with saving your lives?" he asked.

Briefly I told him about our exterminated families, the tragedy of the Polish Jews, and why we had come to Hungary. I tried to explain how he could save us by not noticing our Jewish body characteristics during the examination.

He reacted angrily. Did we ask him to lie? Did we want him to break the oath of a physician? "I will sign what I see," he said.

At this moment, poor Haber pulled me back. He'd had enough, but I had to try one last argument. "A doctor's duty is saving human life," I said. "I am sure that during your many years as a medical practitioner, you have saved many, many lives. Wouldn't it make you feel good if you knew that with your signature the lives of six innocent people will be spared?"

He was taken aback and did not answer at first, then he began to rationalize. "Nothing is going to happen to the Jews except that they will have to wear the yellow star," he said. "Don't exaggerate. No one is going to murder you. The worst thing that can happen to you is that you might be sent to a labor camp." Seeing what must have been despair on our faces, he asked our names. We told him. "I will talk to the mayor about your case," he said, anxious to be rid of us.

I made a last attempt to convince him. "Three million Polish Jews have already been murdered by the Germans. The same will happen to Hungarian Jews. Our lives are in your hands, sir."

"Whatever I see, I will state and sign," he firmly repeated. Returning home, we told the others what had happened. Lusia and Irka were most upset. Even Grylko, Skonieczny, and Kluska were affected and did not hold out much hope. Suddenly, an idea struck me. I recalled Dr. Balla's last words: "Whatever I see, I will certify."

What would happen if someone else went in our place? Then let Dr. Balla examine and certify what he sees. Everyone liked the idea, but where to look for volunteers?

"I will stand in for you," Kluska suddenly declared. I knew this young man liked us and wished us well, but his spontaneous offer touched me deeply. What a magnificent young Pole. Grylko was trying to think of someone who would stand in for Haber. He rushed and later returned with a suitable substitute.

It was Sunday morning, and as we waited, the tension grew. Finally, around noon, a grinning Grylko arrived. We knew everything had gone well even before he told us what had transpired. The Hungarian chief of police, Grylko, and Skonieczny were in the hall along with those waiting to be examined. A long line formed in front of the table at which Dr. Balla sat. Dr. Balla seemed surprised when he heard the name "Daraż" given by Kluska. He must have remembered Kluska's face when the young man, only a few minutes earlier, gave the name "Kluska." Dr. Balla looked at him and repeated the question. "Daraż" was the answer again.

"Do you know," the doctor said, "that there is an insect called *Daraźs*?"

"Yes," answered Kluska, dumbfounded.

"It looks like a bee and it stings."

In fact, "wasp" is the translation of the Hungarian word *Daraźs*. There was an uncomfortable moment of silence. At that moment, Skonieczny located the appropriate page of the register and Grylko pointed to the name Daraż, waiting for the doctor to sign it. Dr. Balla, hesitatingly and bewildered, looked at Grylko. As Kluska had been a patient of his for the past four years, he must have realized there was a conspiracy. He did not utter a word. He was a doctor, not a policeman. He placed his initials next to the name Daraż. He had kept his commitment, certifying only what he saw. Haber's double also managed to get through, and soon this *Schwanzparade* [genitals inspection], as they called it in the Austro-Hungarian Imperial Army, was finished. A parade of those who would live and those who would die, as dictated by the maniac who ruled over 60 million Germans and implemented his Final Solution, was accepted – and sometimes even welcomed by millions of others.

Later that day, we all celebrated with wine and sandwiches, which

Irka and Lusia quickly prepared. I gave Kluska my fountain pen and 100 pengős; the other man was given a cask of wine and some money. We wanted to show our gratitude yet realized only too well that Kluska and probably the other Pole would still have taken the risk without any reward. Of all nations, only a Pole would do it. Would a Jew do it for a Pole? I wonder. Strongly believing in the magic power of the round seal, I asked Grylko for a certificate confirming our Christian identity. The very next day, I received it, typewritten in Hungarian with the official stamp of the camp's authority. One more document – and a very important one at that.

Our friends, who had run away to Budapest, phoned Grylko and, after finding out what had happened, returned. They were given similar documents. For a while, we felt we could sleep safely, but for how long?

It was fortunate that the Habers were our neighbors because the children could play together. Henry Haber tried to encourage Rysio to play with Hungarian children as well but quickly changed his mind when Rysio informed him that the boys called him Zsidó.

Living alone in her huge house in which she had previously refused us accommodation, the wife of Kadarkút's doctor (now a major in the Hungarian Army) was having second thoughts. When the Germans began to force the Jews to wear the yellow star, she felt insecure living alone and offered to share her house with us. We also received a similar offer from a Jewish woman, a Mrs. Kantor.

She, too, had been living alone with her six-year-old daughter since her husband had been called up to Murka Tabor, the Hungarian forced-labor camp. Stern had thought when he approached her at the time that she would have been happy for someone to live with her as our Elżunia would have been company for her daughter. We did not know she was having an affair with the mayor's son and the presence of other people in the house would have been embarrassing. Now she came asking us to share her home.

We refused both offers, preferring to live in a Christian home. Our landlady was poor and her humble cottage with its clay floor and thatched roof was away from the center of the village. Should there be any trouble, we thought, the widow would hopefully help us. We felt more secure there than in a large Jewish house in the village center.

However, the Habers accepted Mrs. Kantor's offer. Their present

Hungarian landlords were quite well off and did not need their money. Not being able to communicate with their tenants, they didn't like having the Habers in their home and, when the Germans invaded Hungary, they gave them notice. True, communicating was difficult because of the language. In this respect, Lusia's linguistic talents were a great help. She had quickly learned basic Hungarian and communicated easily with our landlady, with whom she shared the small kitchen, whereas I had the greatest difficulty in putting together even a few short sentences.

After the Habers moved, we visited them every day, playing bridge while the children played in the garden. It was peaceful until one day an agitated Mrs. Kantor showed us a letter she had just received from the mayor.

The letter instructed her to pack her most essential belongings for herself and the child and be ready on a certain day when transport would be provided to take them to Kaposvár. The rest of their belongings were to be stored in one room of the house, which was to be locked, and the keys were to be deposited in the mayor's office. A list of all those belongings would be signed by the mayor and Mrs. Kantor would keep a copy of it. After the war, she and her husband would return to their house, which for the time being would be looked after by the police and the mayor, a close family friend.

On reading the letter, everything became clear. The Germans had begun their action against the Hungarian Jews. Henry went immediately to see whether Stern had received the orders. He had, as had every Jewish family in the village. People despaired at the thought of leaving their homes and going into the unknown, yet they did not know that Kaposvár was only a stopover and that their final destination would be Auschwitz. But we did! I tried once more to convince Stern that he should run to Budapest if he wanted to survive. He had enough money to do it, but he didn't have the willpower or the courage, and like others, still believed in the power and protection of Horthy.

They went to see the mayor to obtain more information. They believed him to be a decent, friendly person. He welcomed them warmly and assured them that their houses would be well looked after and that, upon their return, they would find them exactly as they had left them. He even suggested they check the locks and change them for new ones if not sufficiently secure. He also advised them to take enough food for the first few days in case the ghetto in Kaposvár was not organized to receive the new influx of people.

Reassured, they returned home to start packing. The mayor would not mislead them and probably did not. He could hardly have imagined that these Jews whom he had known all his life were being taken to be murdered.

We also urged Mrs. Kantor to leave everything and run. She did not look Jewish and neither did her daughter. No one would question them or ask for any identification. Like Stern, she would not listen. She continued with her packing, counting her silver, porcelain, furnishings, sheets, tablecloths, everything. She was systematic and tidy, documenting everything in her list. Her larder was full of stewed fruit, jams, and marmalade and she examined each carefully, offering us the ones that might not keep. It was a long time since we had eaten such delicacies.

The day of departure came. A number of horse-drawn wagons arrived and the Jews, with their suitcases and bags, climbed onto the carts and went on their way. In one cart, we saw Mr. Stern, his wife, and his elderly mother. Sadly, he waved. In another cart was the doctor's wife and their lovely 17-year-old daughter, then Mrs. Kantor and her child. Slowly, the long cavalcade of carts rumbled out of Kadarkút. The Habers remained in Mrs. Kantor's house[1].

How strange are the ways of Providence. The Jews of Kadarkút, who had lived on their land for generations, were gone, while we, strangers and refugees from this very fate, wandered around their village free. How sad it was to recall Mr. Stern proudly showing us her husband's military decorations from the First World War and to recall those Jews, so proud to be Hungarians, to speak only Hungarian after being settled there for centuries, becoming prosperous and assimilated. We looked sadly at their empty houses and watched village life go on as before. Just as usual, people thronged in the market, buying food and chatting together – the Hungarians, the Poles, and us. Yet we knew that this idyllic situation would not last for much longer.[2]

There was not a single moment when my mind was not occupied by plans of finding a hiding place. The house we lived in had a big backyard, ending in a dense bush that might serve as a hiding place.

On a rainy day, we could use the little lavatory shed, covered with a sheet of rusty tin. We realized, however, that without our landlady's help, the whole plan was useless, so as much as we could, we tried to make every effort to gain her friendship. The rent was always paid on time; I would assist her in the garden, clean up around the house, prepare the firewood, and occasionally buy her a bottle of good wine. Not one word was said about a hiding place yet. But even with her friendly cooperation, which one could hardly have expected from a Hungarian peasant woman toward some strange, unknown Jews, how long could we exist in the backyard and bushes? And what about the Hungarian neighbors? What about their children? We would be found and reported to the police in no time. Our situation was desperately hopeless. Could we expect one more miracle?

TASZÁR AIRFIELD EMPLOYMENT

As on several previous occasions, a solution to our problem came along unexpectedly, but not without initial hardship. Under German pressure, the friendly relationship between the Hungarian and Polish governments was abruptly severed, resulting in the cancellation of our financial allowance. Refugees, previously not allowed to work, were advised by the authorities to seek employment. For us, it was a catastrophe. What could we do to earn a living in a strange country with no connections, friends, or money and unable to speak the language?

To someone with a more rural background, the answer could have been in the large, luscious meadows around Kadarkút. It was harvest time. Since the young Hungarian peasants were in the army, most of the Poles found jobs as haymakers. My greatest wish was also to get away from the camp: "Out of sight, out of mind," as they say. Yet haymaking was not really my favorite pastime. Nor was it Haber's. I remembered when, as a young boy, I used to watch workers in the fields and sometimes grabbed a spade or sickle just for fun. But field work did not suit me. Haber's hands – those of a violinist – were even less suited. I used to tease him, saying he could not even distinguish a scythe from a sickle.

But what could we do? I kept pondering the question until an idea struck me. Why not organize a team of ironworkers, consisting of four or five men, and try to obtain work on a large reinforced concrete structure? Surely, there would be some large projects under construction in the area. Henry, Lusia, and I were well qualified not only to read but prepare reinforced concrete drawings.

I shared my plans with Skonieczny and Kluska and they were keen to participate, thinking how useful the job possibilities would be after the war in Poland. With the country completely ruined, there would be great demand for building workers. I was looking forward to being able to train them in a profession that would give them a sound base for the future. Strong and young, they would have no trouble cutting and bending heavy iron bars. Haber and I could carry out the easier tasks – cutting and bending lighter bars – something more suitable for us, unaccustomed as we were, to hard physical work. Lusia was excited, too, for with her engineering abilities and good command of the language, she could be of great help not only in checking the structure but in communicating with supervisors and other trades.

Grylko issued me a traveling pass, and I started the next morning to look for work possibilities, but wandering through the streets of Kaposvár, I found no sign of any construction work in progress. Tired and hungry, I went into a café. The waitress happened to be a Jewish woman from Poland. Her whole family had been exterminated, and only she had managed to escape. I asked if there had been a ghetto in Kaposvár. She told me there had been one for a brief period. Everyone rounded up from the neighborhood villages had been kept there in terrible conditions until they were packed into freight trains and deported. I thought about Stern. He must have finally understood what I had been trying to impress upon him. But it was too late. I thought about that beautiful young girl, the doctor's daughter. Obedience and humility had not helped her. Like Kadarkút, Kaposvár was cleared of Jews except for, ironically, a small number who had come from Poland.

The waitress did not know of any construction work in Kaposvár. She suggested I see the Polish-Jewish chemist nearby. He might know of something. I called on him and, indeed he knew that in the nearby village, Taszár, a huge military airfield was under construction.

I wasted no time and managed to barely catch a train arriving in Taszár 30 minutes later. The airfield was some two kilometers from the station. I walked through the village, entered the airfield, and located the office of the construction company.

I was interviewed by the engineer in charge, Mr. Selinger, who spoke German like all educated Hungarians. Regrettably, he told me, there was no work available. He seemed rather unfriendly and unwilling to talk to me until I showed him the letter of recommendation from Dr. Wander. Suddenly, he looked at me somewhat differently. Before, I had been just another Pole running from the Germans. Now I was a Polish engineer recommended by Dr. Wander. He indicated there would be some work for in about two weeks' time and suggested I come again to see him. He would not commit himself, but I felt there was a strong possibility of some work to come. I expressed my appreciation, shook his hand, and caught the next train home, feeling jubilant that at last, with my family, I would be able to leave the camp. Like a hero, I returned to Kadarkút to share the good news with Lusia, the Habers, and our Polish friends.

When I reported to Mr. Slinger two weeks later, he had bad news for me. On German orders, the construction of the airfield had suddenly been suspended, all workers had left, and only the office staff was still there. "Maybe you should try elsewhere," he said sympathetically.

Suddenly, I had a brilliant idea. "I think it is now that you really need me," I suggested rather excitedly, "now, when every single building has to be measured and assessed in order that the company can prepare a final claim for payment. You need drawings for each building. As I can see, they're all at different stages of construction. Although I don't know the language, I do know how to draw, how to measure, how to count." He looked at me in amazement. It had not occurred to him that he urgently needed a draftsman to prepare those drawings. He left the room, probably to consult with someone, and when he returned, he had only one question: "When can you start?"

Two days later, I was back in Taszár. My family was to follow as soon as I had found accommodation. Mr. Selinger introduced me to his partner, Mr. Topesh, a cold and unfriendly man. However, the people in the office were very pleasant to me. A man named Pishta Toch of Serbian origin was especially helpful. We communicated in a mixture of Polish and Russian.

He took me into the village, where he knew everyone, in search of accommodation. But the people were mostly prosperous and did not need extra money. At his persuasion, a widow agreed to let a room. She was poor and her house had only one room – a kitchen and a pantry. In a small stable behind the house, she kept a cow, a pig, about a dozen chickens, and a dog, She slept in the kitchen, so the room was available for us.

The Habers decided to stay in Kadarkút since Mrs. Kantor had left them a comfortable house with kitchen utensils, sheets, and towels. Besides, Henry felt tired and in need of rest after so many years of constant stress. He felt secure with the documents he had obtained from Grylko, documents clearly stating his Polish and "Catholic" origin.

Skonieczny, too, decided to stay, keeping his job as secretary of the camp, while Kluska and others found jobs as haymakers. They probably had reservations about working with us anyway. Maybe the Polish community wouldn't look with approval at a Jewish-Polish venture.

Thus began the next chapter in my life, the Taszár chapter, with just Lusia and Elżunia. We were a small and happy family. Once again, we felt safe.

The village of Taszár consisted of only one street about 500 meters long, with the church, school, town council, and post office at its center and the houses of the villagers lining both sides. The villagers were well off, their houses solid, built in brick and tile, clean and neat, each with its colorful frontage of well-tended flower beds.

The landowner's manor, with a cluster of farm buildings, huge orchard, and large vegetable garden was at the far end of the village, while our modest quarters were at the beginning.

The military airfield had been in a stage of rapid, large-scale development. Additional hangars, office buildings, workshops, and 24 houses for officers and staff were under construction, with some half-completed and some already roofed, while others were still at the stage of being excavated or foundations completed.

I had plenty to do. A desk, a drawing board, a sketch pad, and drafting implements were allocated to me. I would leave my office for two of three hours, accompanied by a young assistant, who would help me measure various parts of the uncompleted buildings. I felt great! Free again, I had a pencil and sketchbook in my hands! Back at the office, I transferred the sketches into the drawings, showing proper cross-sections, views, and elevations. Often, I had to return to check some missing dimensions. With the help of a German-Hungarian dictionary, I described my drawings, calculating areas and volumes from which to prepare the final account, with Pishta Toch helping me translate into Hungarian and spell the technical terms. The bosses seemed happy with my work and Selinger was friendly, but Topesh hardly looked my way. The office staff kept reminding me how friendly our two nations, Hungary and Poland, used to be. My Hungarian was haltingly comical, but my colleagues were tolerant, even amused by my "Hungarian" name. "Daraż" proved to be an advantage. My story was that Stefan Batory, a Hungarian king, who had also been a king of Poland, had a Darażs as a member of his court. Thus, according to my colleagues, I undoubtedly had Hungarian blood in my veins. I was well liked and happy. What's more, I was being paid. True, it was only a laborer's paycheck, but it was more than sufficient to satisfy our modest needs. I could not imagine a more serene and peaceful existence. Walking home along the main street, I would be greeted in a friendly manner by people who already knew me. "*Jo estét kivanok, mernok-ur* [Wishing you a good evening, Mr. Engineer]." The Hungarians hold all people with titles in esteem. "Jo estér!" I would answer with an equally friendly smile.

The Simmental cattle were meandering home from the pastures – beautiful, majestic beasts, contented giants. The pigs were returning, too – great boars covered in blackish bristles, fat sows happily squeaking. A young boy followed that big, orderly herd. At the front of each house, a group of two or three animals branched out and trotted to their stables, some stopping on the way for a drink of fresh water at the troughs. Then came a flock of sheep, some jumping about and bleating sadly for no obvious reason. They were followed by a huge flock of white geese marching in closed formation, like soldiers, and driven by a small lad armed with a long stick. A few of them separated at each cottage and waddled toward their homes.

Some village women awaited their flock at the gates. Sometimes, there was an elderly man. "Jo estét, mernok-ur!" Jo estér!" Is this a dream or reality?

On Sunday mornings, I took Elżunia to church while Lusia stayed home, The congregation greeted me with respect and friendly smiles.

Little "Erzika" was very popular. After mass (I did not understand a single word!), we returned home. Everything – the house and yard – was swept and cleaned. We had a light snack and would go to see the woman's vegetable garden. I introduced Elżunia to the world of botany, picking, dissecting, and explaining the miracles of nature. She remembered from Legionowo some of the plants; she recognized tomatoes, onions, and potatoes. Chirping happily, always clean and tidily dressed, with a bow in her neatly combed golden hair, she resembled a happy, carefree bird.

Would the world ever believe that Nazi Germany exterminated in a sadistic manner over *one million* such carefree birds – over one million innocent Jewish children?

Behind the vegetable garden was a small orchard with a few fruit trees, large, full of color and sunshine, the cherries just ripening, There weren't many on the lower branches. The landlady, who was too old to climb the tree herself, allowed me to pick the cherries. It is not good for the tree to have fruit left on the branches.

Slowly and cautiously, I climbed, trying to squeeze myself between the branches. The fruit grew mostly on the outer ends of the branches that were exposed to the sun, as I remembered only too well from the good old days when, as a young boy, I used to climb the cherry trees in my grandfather's orchard. One had to use a special branch with a hook, called a *klucika*, hook it to the end of a heavily laden branch of the cherry tree, and bend it toward oneself in order to be able to pick the ripe, beautiful fruit. The bending must be done carefully to not break the branch.

Elżunia followed my slow ascent with fear. "Tatus, please be careful!" she said. "Don't climb higher! That is already enough!" I dropped a few ripe cherries down on her head and she laughed happily. But, no! I was not high enough yet. The ripest and biggest cherries would be at the top. I could see them but could not yet reach them. Very slowly, and with utmost caution, I tried to climb higher, placing my feet in the joints of the branches, as I remembered from my childhood. One more effort, one more careful step up, and I reached the top: The choicest and most beautiful cherries were just in front of me. I held my breath afraid to touch the fruit – and afraid of destroying this beautiful dream.

Is this real? This July 1944? The fifth year of war! The fifth year of persecutions, deportations, concentration camps, and gas chambers! And, after five years of running, hiding, lying, and pretending – five years of fear, anxiety, sleepless nights, and despair – here I am sitting in a treetop, in a Hungarian orchard under the warm Hungarian sun, with luscious, magnificent cherries above and all around me.

I hardly touched those cherries. I was far away in my thoughts, back in our village, in our orchard, with my family, among our own cherry trees. I was with my people, who, at this very time, while I could touch and pick those beautiful cherries, were exposed to the cruelest sufferings.

I picked nearly all the ripe cherries, leaving a few for the birds, and climbed down. Elżunia was happy to set me safely on the ground. I took the fruit home, giving half of it to the landlady. I hardly ate any, telling Lusia that I had eaten enough on the tree.

The idyll was short-lived; the landlady gave us notice. As an elderly widow, used to being on her own, she tired of our presence in her house. We had to look for another place to stay. I knocked on many doors, but no one was interested. Pishta tried to help us but had no luck either. Lusia tried at the manor house. The resident administrator, a young Hungarian and a graduate of the agricultural faculty of Budapest University, lived there with his wife and two children. The wife, a former teacher, spoke some German and sold us milk. From time to time, she gave us some leftovers from her vegetable garden.

The manor house was huge; some rooms were always empty. A few cottages were occupied by farm employees, while others were vacant.

"Would there be by any chance a small room available?" Lusia asked shyly after explaining our situation. The answer was no, just as I anticipated. So once again we were without a roof over our heads. We were desperate.

But my guardian angel was with me again, inspiring me with a new idea. Since there weren't enough skilled laborers available locally, it was necessary to bring them from elsewhere and provide them with some kind of temporary shelter. The construction company had built a number of small huts for these people, but as construction had been stopped, they now stood empty. Would one of them solve our problem?

Inspecting a few, I found them in a dilapidated condition. After all, they were intended only as temporary summer accommodation, and the materials, such as bricks and timber, were to be reused. Consequently, the bricks were carelessly slapped on with lime mortar. There was no rendering, the wind was blowing right through the joints, and puddles of water had formed on the floors. How could I bring Lusia and Elżunia here?

Then, fortunately, I located a hut that had been used by bricklayers, and they had rendered and whitewashed the inside walls! The furniture consisted of solid, clean bunks with reasonably clean straw. A small annex was equipped with an iron stove, the electricity was still connected, and there was a light globe on the ceiling. My bosses not only gave me permission to move into this "castle" but assigned a laborer to help me clean it and put it in order.

But it was Lusia who turned it into a home. A small tablecloth covered the rough table, a colorful curtain covered the freshly washed windows; the floor was swept, and dust was wiped away. Searching through other huts I found two stools, some dirty pots, a teapot, tin plates, some cheap cutlery, jars with leftovers, two old blankets, some used sheets, towels, and even some flowerpots with dried-out plants. All those treasures were collected. Together, we cleaned, washed, and repaired them, fitted a padlock to the door, and adjusted the window to open and shut.

Once again, we had a roof over our heads, a key to our own home, and as a bonus it was rent free! Best of all, however, was the privacy to do whatever we liked, with no one to worry us. What more could we ask for? Our residence at the airfield was conveniently situated, only a few paces from the office. Rain or shine, I was always the first at work. There was a night watchman guarding the constructions, offices, and storerooms who would often come to sit in front of our house for a smoke and a chat. We also had neighbors; the gendarmerie had taken over one of the finished houses, although unfortunately, next to our hut. In accordance with the terms of my work permit, I had to report to them every month to get my document stamped and signed.

We happened to have a small, private "swimming pool" next to our house – a cement-rendered tank full of water. It had probably been used as a water tank for the building construction, yet the water was reasonably clean. One very hot afternoon, I took Elżunia for a dip. It was marvelous. We were enjoying it immensely until I noticed the approach of one of our neighbors, the chief of the gendarmes. Elżunia jumped out and went home. I stayed in the water. The gendarme came closer and then stopped. He nodded.

"A hot day," he said.

"Yes, a very hot day."

A short pause. "Is the water cool?"

"Yes, the water is quite cool, very pleasant."

I was standing in water up to my waist. He was two paces away, staring at me. Minutes passed and my limited Hungarian was exhausted. I'd had enough of that pool but was too scared to get out. He was still watching me, maybe waiting for me to come out of the water, seemingly curious. Was he wanting to see something? Was there something he was unsure about? Maybe – the thought hit me suddenly – there was a copy of that anonymous letter from Kadarkút on his desk! After all, the Kadarkút gendarmes knew my whereabouts.

He continued standing there, staring, until at last Lusia came and invited him for a cup of tea. He accepted, following her into our hut. Elżunia brought me a towel and my pants, and I went behind our hut to dress. With relief, I saw him leaving. His visit was worrying me, and that worry grew when, before I finished dressing, I saw him returning with something under his arm. Puzzled, I hurriedly finished dressing and went into the house to find an unexpected situation – Lusia and the gendarme playing chess. It was a chessboard he had been carrying! I glanced at the chessboard; he had lost quite a few pieces and had just been checkmated. He asked for revenge but lost again and left somewhat piqued, saying he would return the next day. And so started Lusia's war with the Hungarian police. She would treat him to a glass of tea, then beat him at chess. I pleaded with her, "Let him win from time to time."

"No, this is my only satisfaction; maybe he will stop coming," she said.

He did not stop, but his game improved. Lusia allowed him to win occasionally, and we became "friends": a Hungarian gendarme and the Jewish refugees from Poland.

ARRESTED BY HUNGARIAN GENDARMES

Five months had passed since we left Poland. The situation on the Eastern Front was deteriorating daily. Hitler's armies were in constant retreat and the Soviets followed close behind. We subscribed to the *Budapester Zeitung*, a German daily published in Budapest, and studied with increasing excitement the bulletins from German army headquarters. The Russians had crossed the old Polish border and were now approaching Warsaw. Just as well we were not there anymore. Who knows what might happen? Would the Germans defend Warsaw? The thought of Warsaw becoming the battlefield of two giants left us thankful that we were now far away.

Developments on the Western Front were, however, thrilling. One morning I was quietly working at my desk when Pishta approached me whistling "La Marseillaise." The Allies had landed in France. It was a memorable sixth of June 1944. I rushed to Lusia to tell her the great news. Attached to a wall in the hut, we had a large map of Europe with colored pins marking the positions of the front lines. The line of the farthest expansion of the Germans to the east was marked with white pins – Leningrad and Moscow at one end, Sevastopol and Crimea at the other. This line remained unchanged. Red pins showed the current positions of the armies, and it was always a great moment when these pins could be moved. Overjoyed, I jabbed a red-headed pin into a new location – the beaches of Normandy. The Germans were retreating on all fronts!

It was a bright, warm Sunday in July when Henry Haber unexpectedly called on us on his way back from Budapest. The mail was being delivered normally and, in case he decided to visit us, I had sent him a little map showing where we lived. And find us, he did. It was a joyous reunion.

Better still was the news he brought of an assassination attempt against Hitler. A bomb had exploded in German army headquarters deep in the forests of East Prussia. Several people had been killed, including a general and other high-ranking officers. But by some miracle, the Führer had escaped unscathed. Henry had heard his odious voice on the radio proclaiming: "*Ich lebe und Ich bin gesund* [I am alive and in good health]!" He then made a few caustic remarks about the "stupid generals" who had been behind this plot. Listening to Haber's report, we became very excited. It increased our hopes. Wouldn't the end of Hitler mean the end of our torment? Possibly Hitler was telling a lie? Maybe he was injured and would "die" in the hospital? Maybe somebody else would try again to kill the monster and be successful.

We were greatly excited when the news reached us about the uprising against Germans in Warsaw. We did not quite understand the situation. According to reports, the Red Army was already occupying Praga, a suburb of Warsaw on the east bank of the river Vistula, Why then the uprising? The Russians had taken all other territories without any insurrection by the civilian population. Why this unnecessary bloodshed? Weren't there enough victims by now? I was greatly concerned about the fate of our people. How many more were to die? The few who had managed to survive in hiding had now crept out of their shelters only to meet eye to eye the hostile elements of the population?

I shifted the red pin on our wall map into a new spot – Warsaw – with mixed feelings. But there was more thrilling news to come. Neighboring Romania had suddenly surrendered and opened its frontiers to the Soviet army without a single shot. The Russian army was expected in a few days to reach the river Tisa, the Hungarian-Romanian border! My office colleagues were also alarmed. Until now, they had been living peacefully without giving much thought to the fate of others. Now, with the approach of the Red Army, many became uneasy, Not Pishta. He was enraptured and so was the foreman Lukas whom I had befriended, a communist who also spoke some German. But others began to be afraid. Meanwhile, I behaved normally and kept working as if nothing was happening. But the red pins moved with one giant leap closer to our village. Was it possible? Were we really going to be saved? It seemed hard to believe, but ...

On the Western Front, one success chased another. The Allies were entering Europe like an octopus – from all sides. There were more landings in Italy. Heavy battles were being fought everywhere. The German armies were retreating. Thousands of Allied planes dropped bombs on Berlin day and night. The red-headed pins were all over Western Europe from the North Sea to the Mediterranean. It was a great joy to look at our wall, to watch the Third Reich shrinking slowly but steadily.

On Sundays, we usually went for long walks. I didn't bother going to church anymore. Without a landlady, such play-acting was no longer necessary. We would walk along the fields. It was harvest time. The crops were beautiful. How fertile this Hungarian soil was. The ears were bending under the weight of ripe grain. Each ear was long, thick, and full of beautiful, healthy grain. As in Oserdów, poppies and cornflowers were dotting the gold of the cornfield. The carts loaded high with sheaves of wheat were returning home, just as in Oserdów. Instead of horses, two huge oxen slowly pulled the carts. The carts were bigger and more fully laden than ours due to the better condition of the roads and the superior strength of the oxen. We had plenty of food. Lusia shopped in the village; the villagers knew her well and she never returned empty-handed. Sometimes she walked to the neighboring village of Homok, some three kilometers away. Walking along the paths between the fields, she felt safe. Homok was inhabited by the descendants of early German settlers called Schwabes. They were peaceful, diligent, and well off, and German was still their mother tongue.

Lusia became friendly with one of these German families thanks to her command of their language. Although they did not need to, they were selling her their products. Sometimes she could buy a chicken, a piece of pork, some lard. Once she brought some special grapes home, a gift for me from the Schwabes.

Some Sundays we all visited them, with Elżunia, as usual, the most popular guest. I showed great interest in their farms, gardens, and orchards. I admired their cattle and pigs. They were impressed with my knowledge and sought my "professional" advice. They treated us to homemade bread with fresh butter and sour milk and would present us with a large fresh loaf of bread and a bag of fruit to take home. We loved those Sundays and the friendliness of those people.

However, once again this dream-like way of life changed dramatically. It was morning, 15 October 1944. The day began with sensational news. Usually, I heard the early-morning radio news from Lukas. Today, he told me Horthy had been addressing the nation on the radio, declaring that he was breaking with Germany and joining the Allies! At that moment, Horthy's speech was interrupted. Listeners could hear some commotion in the studio, a few shots, and then complete silence. After a short interval, the odious German martial music so well known to us started to blare.

We understood the meaning of this only too well. The Germans had captured the radio station, shooting some of the people before establishing their control. They had answered Horthy's surprise coup. The next day, we went to Homok, not so much for food as for some news. We found a different village. Homok was packed with German troops, tanks, and personnel carriers. The hated green uniforms had reappeared. We felt most upset, as was our friendly farmer. The commanding officers had taken over their house, installed telephones, and were already speaking with their headquarters. We were sitting in our friends' kitchen when the doors opened. A burly officer walked in, saying "*Wir bleiben hier and kampfen weiter* [We are remaining here and will continue to fight]."

We left Homok as fast as possible. It was imperative that we disappear before they started asking awkward questions. We looked at the map, trying to figure out the next move of the Soviet armies. We knew their strategy well. They moved in giant paces, attacked, captured an area, and then stopped at the newly established front line for two or three months to consolidate their positions before making another big leap. Then a new front line and no further movement for another few months.

How long would they sit on the Romanian border? How much time would they give the Germans to liquidate us? We felt we needed information from the outside world. Every Tuesday morning, a horse cart would leave for Kaposvár for a shopping excursion and to send messages for the firm, returning about lunchtime. We decided that Lusia would secretly go on that cart without notifying the gendarmes as officially we were not to leave our abode without their knowledge. There were some of "our people" in Kaposvár, possibly in touch with Budapest, and they would know more about the present situation.

At about five in the morning, I went with Lusia to the cart and arranged with the driver for him to pick her up at about 11 o'clock from the restaurant where the Polish waitress worked. I returned home, prepared breakfast for Elżunia, and sent her off to school. At the beginning of the school year, Elżunia, now six years old, had started her Hungarian education and did very well. The teacher was delighted with such a promising student. It was nearly eight when I went to the office as usual. The office building consisted of a few rooms – an entrance hall leading to a large room containing three desks, including mine; three doors led to adjoining rooms – those of the bosses, the accountants (where Pishta was sitting), and the supervising engineers of the Hungarian air force. The chief engineer was Otto Hamping, a lieutenant in the air force. Aside from him were two other engineers. One of them, Karci (Charles), was a Hungarian Jew. Jews were subjected to forced labor in a *Munka Tabor* [labor camp]. They had to wear special armbands and sometimes special uniforms. The conditions were harsh, the treatment often brutal, and many of them perished because of hunger, cold, and cruel treatment. Some Hungarians were as efficient as the Germans in tormenting the poor Jews. Kari's wife, a Christian, succeeded in getting her husband a protected job as a supervising engineer at the airfield.

It was quite a surprise for me to meet somebody working there wearing a Jewish armband. We often talked about professional matters, but I remained rather reserved, as a non-Jewish Pole would have been.

On this particular morning, I walked into the office, sat down at my desk as usual, and looked at my sketches. I could hear somebody talking loudly on the telephone in the directors' room. The door was half open and I could see a gendarme. I was gripped by a strange foreboding. Since the gendarmes' telephone was not yet installed, they often used ours. Normally, I did not pay any attention to them, but today was different.

The gendarme finished his conversation and came directly to me, mumbling something of which I understood only one word: Toporów. Nothing more. Toporów was a township a few kilometers away where the gendarmes' regional headquarters were located. At that moment Engineer Topesch appeared. I asked him to explain what was going on and learned that the gendarmes had been ordered to take me, my wife, and our child immediately to Toporów.

"What for?" I asked calmly.

"To check your documents," was the reply.

This had to be a lie. One does not transport a whole family just to look at documents. I expressed my doubts to Topesch, who did not react to my remark. He just stood there silently, gloomy as usual. I asked him to inform the constable that my wife had gone to Kaposvár early that morning because of a sudden toothache and was due back about noon.

Topesch and the gendarme were both very annoyed. "It is prohibited to leave Taszár without permission of the constabulary," he said.

"I know," I answered calmly. "However, the gendarmes were still asleep when the cart was leaving, and the toothache was excruciating. What should we have done? Still, the checking of documents is not a matter of great urgency. My wife will return from Kaposvár, the child will come back from school, and then we will go."

Topesch translated my statement to the gendarme. Very angry, he went to the telephone and reported the situation. Obviously, he was being admonished, since he returned red faced and said something to Topesch, who translated it: "You are not allowed to leave the office, and after the return of your wife, the company cart will take you all to Toporów."

Topesch went back to his office, his stony face showing neither compassion nor concern. The gendarme took a chair and seated himself next to the entrance door, blocking the exit. All of a sudden, the nightmare we had been running from for so many years had caught up with us at last.

We were trapped!

ESCAPE

I sat down at my desk pretending to be calm. I looked at the drawings, but the lines were moving before my eyes and my thoughts were turbulent. What was to be done? First of all, keep my composure. I must be calm and collected before undertaking any action. I have to proceed very carefully.

One thing was absolutely clear in my mind: We must not let them take us to Toporów. But how to stop them? A myriad of confusing thoughts.

"Henry, compose yourself," I heard my voice saying to myself. I obeyed and started immediately to plan a step-by-step action. First, I must divert the gendarme's attention and get out of there as quickly as possible. Second, I had to find some sanctuary for Elżunia, possibly in a convent, since escape with the child would not be possible. Third, I would have to join Lusia before she returned from Kaposvár and flee into the nearby forest.

There were a few obstacles to this plan. Lusia was in Kaposvár and would be totally unaware of the situation, Elżunia was at school, and my gendarme was sitting at the door and would not take his eyes off me. Should I succeed with my plans, we had a slight chance of survival, providing the Soviet army arrived within the next few weeks and we did not die of cold or hunger or be discovered by local peasants, who would undoubtedly turn us in.

Slowly, and with composure, I began thinking. Lusia will be in Kaposvár until 11, so I had three hours. "Henry! Remain cool!" I told myself. Since the very beginning of our stay in Taszár, I had never stopped thinking what should be done in case of an emergency. The only solution would be escaping into the forest, which was fairly close. We often took walks in that direction, mainly to become familiar with the terrain. The main road from the village led to the highway, turning right to Kaposvár, left to Dombóvár. A narrow dirt track went straight through, evidently running through the fields of the villagers, gradually narrowing until it became just a path. About half a kilometer further was a small creek. Two heavy tree trunks joined together forming a pedestrian crossing over the water. The ground became hilly on the other side. Bushes were growing along the riverbanks. Should we succeed in reaching the creek and hiding in the bushes during the day, going out to search for food at night, we might have a chance. But what should we do with the child? We couldn't leave her with the gendarmes, but we also couldn't take her with us into the woods. We had often discussed the possibility of placing her in a convent but disliked the idea of being separated. So far, the conditions in Taszár had not warranted such a step. Now, the situation had changed drastically.

I stood up quietly and moved slowly toward the door. The gendarme's eyes followed me. There was a trash basket near the door next to him. I took my penknife out and started to sharpen my pencil above the basket. Very calmly, very slowly.

The gendarme watched. When my pencil was sufficiently sharp, I walked back to my desk and continued to draw. That first walk had been accomplished. A few minutes later, I got up heading to Pishta's room, the gendarme's eyes still following me.

On my way, I looked through the half-open door of the inspectors' room. My blood froze! Karci, the Jewish engineer was there, his face pale and drawn. Next to him was a fully packed knapsack with a blanket rolled over it. I went over to him.

Karci told me that early that morning, the gendarme had come requesting him to pack and brought him here in order to take him together with us to Toporów. However, as my wife wasn't there yet, he had to wait.

Now, I was certain that the action was aimed at the Jews. But why us, the Poles? Obviously, they knew; possibly there was some special information in our file. The anonymous denunciation from Kadarkút? What else?

I went to Pishta's room where he sat at his desk visibly upset. One could see the Serbian fury in his eyes. Bending over his desk, I told him of my plan. I made a sketch showing the footpath and the little bridge over the creek and asked if he would go there every few nights and leave some food for us on the other side of the creek under the bridge. He knew the bridge well and agreed but said he would leave the food on the village side of the bridge; he did not like crossing it at night. With this arrangement, I asked him to collect our child after school and place her as soon as possible in the nearest convent. He should tell them the whole "truth": the parents were Poles and had fled into the woods to escape the Germans, leaving the child in his care. Should they survive the war, they would ask for the child. Otherwise, she would remain in the convent.

Pishta agreed to everything and even offered to cover all expenses, if there were any. Wonderful, dear Pishta! I felt greatly relieved! The problem of our child had been solved. What remained now was to work out a way to escape and join Lusia.

But how, while the heavily armed gendarme sat at the door? And how to get to Lusia, who was still in Kaposvár and knew nothing of the situation? Composedly, with a drawing in my hand, I approached Engineer Topesch and pointed out a missing dimension. I need this measurement, I explained, to finish the drawing. Would he tell the gendarme that I have to go out to the site? Topesch, eager to get as much work out of me as possible, agreed and spoke to the gendarme. Permission was granted and I stepped outside. I pretended that I was measuring the wall and then returned to the office. That first attempt was successful. I worked for a while longer, then repeated the procedure a few more times, and finally the gendarme paid no attention to my excursions. Meanwhile, time was slowly running out. It was now 9:30 a.m.

My plan was to go out again and not return, reach the Kaposvár highway as quickly as possible, hide in the bushes along the roadside, and watch the road. On seeing the company cart with Lusia approaching, I would leave my hiding place, collect her, and run into the field. By the time the coachman told the office what happened and the gendarmes started looking for us, we would, I hoped, be hidden in some bushes.

À crazy idea perhaps, but there was no other way ... until miraculously an unexpected occurrence helped me. The postman came and there, among company letters, was a money order for me. I had not been aware that families of working men were still receiving their original allowance. Now – unbelievably – the payment for several months had arrived. The draft was for 700 pengős, a large amount at that time. I showed the money order to Topesch and asked for permission to go to the post office to collect it as it was close to the school. I told him I would ask the teacher to release Elżunia early and take her home so we could wait for Lusia's return. Topesch examined the money order carefully before giving me a nod of agreement.

The bored gendarme was sitting half asleep. He was already used to my little outings, and it would never occur to him that I might not return. The distance to the post office was about a kilometer. It gave me an additional half hour of legitimate absence and also brought me closer to the Kaposvár highway. At the post office, I collected the money from a polite and smiling girl, then went to the school and obtained the teacher's permission to see Elżunia. She ran out of the classroom like a bird, slight, golden haired, beautiful. Happy to see me, she rushed into my arms. I had to hold back my tears. Since we would not be home that afternoon, I told her, she had to go to Pishta after school and we would get her in the evening. She knew Pishta well and liked him. "Very well, Tatusin," she chirped and returned to the classroom in little hops. I thanked the teacher with a smile, then hurried toward the highway. My heart was pounding. Would I ever see my child again?

Nobody saw me as I neared the highway searching like a thief for a suitable hiding place. Some buildings were to be erected close to the highway, and for this purpose, stacks of bricks were stored along the road. Finding a gap between two stacks, I squeezed myself into it. I was well hidden and, after shifting a few bricks, I created a lookout through which I could observe the road.

They would be expecting me back at the office in about 15 minutes, while Lusia would not leave Kaposvár for another 30 minutes. Would I be able to intercept her and get us into the woods before they started the search?

This Hungarian autumn was exceptionally hot. A merciless sun burned from a cloudless sky, making an oven out of the piles of bricks in which I was hiding. Nervously, I watched the highway. Various vehicles were moving along, scared of pursuit, but luckily the gendarmes only had bicycles. Meanwhile, the heat began to affect me as there was not the slightest breeze. My head was bursting. I felt I could not stand it much longer. My hideout was so narrow that I could not move. Passing minutes seemed hours. Every moment, I expected the gendarmes. Should they catch up with Lusia before the cart reached my point of observation, the whole plan would fail. What to do? Maybe I should catch a lift on a cart going toward Kaposvár and meet her halfway! She could be on the road by now.

A peasant's cart was approaching. Without hesitation, I emerged from behind the bricks and jumped onto the cart as it rumbled past. The peasant, obviously surprised, looked at me questioningly. I pointed toward Kaposvár, asking whether he was going there? "*Igen* [Yes]," was his answer. Well, it was better here than squeezed between hot bricks. At last, I could breathe. I watched the road looking for the company vehicle with Lusia. After a few minutes' ride, a sudden bend in the road revealed in the distance the familiar figure of the maintenance man from the Department of Main Roads, working on the road. He knew me well, as I had often talked (in my broken Hungarian) to him about his work. There was no doubt that the pursuing gendarme would ask him about me. There was no other way but to quickly return to my sweltering hideout.

Fortunately, there was another cart approaching at full speed from the opposite direction. Making a split-second decision, I jumped off my cart and hopped straight onto the other vehicle. My peasant was stupefied and the second man more so by my boarding his cart so suddenly. However, I gave him no time to ask questions – I jumped off again a few seconds later and disappeared in the hot crevice between the bricks.

I was quite sure what both peasants must have thought, but who cared? I was cursing that innocent road worker who ruined my plans. Again, I watched the road. Precious minutes were passing, but there was no sign of the familiar vehicle. My tension increased as at any minute I expected to see the bicycle of the pursuing gendarme. I decided I must act, and act quickly. There was no other solution but to stop a passing military vehicle. But what type to stop? A car or a truck? I excluded a car, for I might be asked some embarrassing questions, while the driver of a truck was less likely to ask anything. It would have to be a German military truck. Why not a Hungarian vehicle? Because I knew Hungarians. With my limited knowledge of the language, the driver might be afraid to take me, whereas I could talk to a German driver in German and perhaps be able to persuade him to take me without asking too many questions. Even then, I had to be very careful in the selection of the truck I intended to stop. The registration plates with the sign SS – one had to dodge these murderers. Just as dangerous was the plate with POL (police), while SD was still worse.

I decided the safest would be a plate with WH (Wehrmacht). The German army was neither engaged in politics nor in the murdering of innocent people. That was left to the "specialists." Also innocuous would be the (Organization Todi), a huge organization used in building roads and bridges. I continued keeping a cautious watch from my hideout. I could not see Lusia or the gendarme on his bicycle. Military trucks were rolling by, but nearly all were marked with either SS or POL. It seemed that they were seriously busy in Hungary. Finally, there came a truck with WH markings. This was the truck I had been waiting for. I emerged from my hideout, and with my heart racing, rushed to the center of the road, frantically waving my arms. The vehicle slowed down and stopped. To my surprise and confusion, it was not a German soldier who jumped out but a Hungarian officer. The confrontation I had been trying to dodge was unavoidable. There was no choice, I had to risk it. In fluent German, I asked him to give me a lift to Kaposvár. "I am working as a draftsman on the construction of the airfield. I was going to Kaposvár to purchase some drawing materials and have just missed the train," I said. "Could you take me?" He pointed politely to the back of the truck and helped me to climb up. Unexpectedly I found myself in the company of a huge pig, which seemed just as surprised as I. The Germans had started their normal looting and the army had to be fed.

I looked back along the highway. There was not a gendarme in sight. What a relief! We quickly passed the road worker still busily picking at the road surface. What a fortunate man. He just calmly repairs the potholes, returning home after work and drinking his wine in peace. The driver accelerated. The truck was speeding and swallowing the kilometers. I watched the road, intensely ready to jump the moment I saw Lusia's cart. But there was no sign of it. It was good since I did not have to risk jumping and perhaps breaking a leg. About 20 minutes later, we reached Kaposvár, I knocked on the cabin window, the truck slowed down, and I jumped off. I waved goodbye and walked quickly toward the coffee shop where I was hoping to meet Lusia.

Suddenly, there was a shrill wail. An air raid siren! All traffic came to an immediate halt. I sat down under a tree, still watching the road, although I knew it was pointless; our cart had to be immobilized, too. So I sat quietly watching the sky. What a marvelous view. A large fleet of heavily loaded American bombers, originally from Italian airfields heading toward Germany, were presumably returning the same way, empty. The difference in the sound of the engines was quite audible. Day after day, about 200 bombers flew overhead, but not one bomb was dropped on Hungary. However, the air raid precautions were rigidly observed. Sitting and watching the sky, I had to smile to myself. Here I am resting peacefully under a tree while my poor gendarme sits at the door of the office, waiting for me, presumably getting more agitated with each passing moment. Gloomy Topesch, who gave me permission to leave, would also be wondering uneasily. There went the siren again. The air raid alarm was over.

I jumped from my seat and ran to the coffee house, startling Lusia as she sat drinking coffee and talking to the Polish waitress. They both stared at me as if I were a ghost. They listened with fear as I related what had happened over the past hours. The arrest of the Hungarian Jew filled them with panic. The Polish waitress left immediately to see if she could get more information. She had lived for two years in Kaposvár and knew a few people. Just that morning, on her way to work, she had met a gendarme who knew her well. She returned half an hour later after contacting some of the few Polish Jews still in Kaposvár. They were all registered with the police and the gendarmes knew their addresses, but no one had been bothered so far. Naturally, they were now greatly concerned. The Jewish chemist had telephoned a friend in Budapest, also a Polish Jew. All was quiet in Budapest – there was no action against Polish Jews or any other foreigners.

A sigh of relief and disbelief. We couldn't understand what had happened in Taszár. Was it some unauthorized move against Jews on the part of some provincial police bureaucrat or an overzealous gendarme? In the meantime, the company's vehicle had called but left Kaposvár without us. Sitting in the restaurant wondering what to do, I decided to take the risk and ring the office. Topesch usually went to lunch between one and two p.m. That would be the best time to telephone because I did not wish to speak to him. Pishta answered the call as if he had been expecting it. "Come back, Piotr, everything is in order," he said.

Lukas, the one who spoke German, was luckily in the office, too, and told me that the order for our arrest had been revoked and we could return home. I asked about Kari, the Hungarian Jew. He had gone home.

"And what about the gendarme?" I asked.

Lukas laughed. "He went home, too," he said.

What incredible news. After a while, I rang Engineer Topesch. He was cool and calm as always but began with a reproach. "Why did you run away? You should not have," he said. Also calm and collected, I explained to him that I had not intended to run away at all. I had merely wanted to join my wife. The experience of five years of war had taught me how dangerous separation could be. We were together now, and we were coming back. How could he suspect me of running away knowing that our child was there at school? Did he imagine that we would run away and leave her to the Germans? His voice softened. My argument sounded convincing.

He simply added that I had been "unfair toward, the gendarme by making a fool of him."

"All right," I said. "I will apologize to him and explain. I am sure he will understand, and we shall be friends again."

That same afternoon, Pishta arrived in his little cart to take us home as there was no train late in the evening. The reunion with Elżunia took place amid tears and laughter. Pishta treated us to a lavish meal of smoked ham with potatoes, hot tea, fresh bread, and homemade jam. Dead tired, we returned to our hut at the airfield. But we did not sleep that night. In trepidation we pondered the uncertain tomorrow. The order had been revoked, yes, but for how long? One day? Two days? We were totally helpless and exposed. We could only hope. If the gendarmes did not come back within the next two days, the order was truly revoked. Luckily, two days passed and a few more days after that, and the gendarmes did not reappear.

HABERS DEPORTED

I continued working at the office, but my relationship with my colleagues had changed. Perhaps they did not like my making a fool of a Hungarian gendarme – or maybe they had some other ideas. Yet I must admit that my action must have looked quite unacceptable to a normal, obedient Hungarian mind. A few days later, I met Lusia's chess partner. He smiled yet did not mention the episode of my "disappearance." On another occasion, I encountered "my" gendarme, who quickly walked over to the other side of the street, avoiding looking in my direction. Obviously, he was still nursing his deep resentment toward me. I fully understood his feelings.

Although our life had returned to "normal," we no longer felt safe. We lived continuously in anticipation of some dreadful fate. The Russian armies were still at the Romanian-Hungarian border, but there was no further movement. It was already November and starting to get cold. Would they stay there till spring while we were waiting, counting the days, counting the hours?

The postman brought us a letter from Henry Haber. It had been a long time since his last message. It was a short letter with strange postmarks and a return address of Vámosmikola, a POW camp for Jewish officers of the Polish army. What terrible news! They had been in this camp for some days, he wrote, and expected to be sent back to Poland in the near future. They were saying goodbye since they doubted they would ever see us again. They were allowed to receive letters and asked us to write. As if hit by a sledgehammer, we sat in stunned silence. Poor Habers! Poor little Rysio! What an irony! To go through the terrors of the Kraków Ghetto, to live in fear for so many years, witnessing countless tragedies, then to undertake and succeed in this Hungarian escape, only to be caught and sent back to certain death, especially now when hopes for survival started to flicker alive, with the Russian armies just a few kilometers away. What a terrible turn of fate! Lusia turned away so as not to let me see her tears.

We decided immediately to send a food parcel, ignoring the risk of it not being delivered. I do not remember the contents in detail except that we had a jar of lard, about a kilo, that we included, although the dispatching of fat by mail was prohibited. Lusia had sewn a special cloth bag. We filled it with flour and placed the jar in the center so it was padded all around, protecting it from human eyes and breaking. I took the parcel to the post office, where it would be inspected prior to being dispatched. My heart was beating faster as they felt the softness of the flour. It passed the inspection. Success!

The Habers were delighted to receive this parcel. We later learned that Irka was a little surprised to get a consignment of flour and gave it, without much thought, to the camp kitchen. Only much later, on their way to Auschwitz, did Haber open the packet of cigarettes also included in the parcel to find my brief note: "Open the flour bag with care because of glass." It was too late for regrets. They knew by then that their transport was headed for the gas chambers. Why worry about some lost lard? We learned of the Habers' arrest and deportation from the sister of one of our mutual friends in Kadarkút. The Klobs and the Habers had been the only refugees left in Kadarkút since all other Polish Jews, afraid of further action by some wicked characters, had left for Budapest. One evening, quite unexpectedly, gendarmes had called on both families to notify them that all male members should appear before the doctor for physical examination. There was no way to dodge it this time – Henry Haber, Klob, and young Rysio had to go. They were immediately arrested and, together with their families, deported under police escort to Vámosmikola. Klob's nephew, who was not circumcised, was left in Kadarkút with Mr. Klob's sister, who on papers was listed as his mother. The broken-hearted woman was left alone in Kadarkút with a small boy. It was from her that we learned the tragic story of these two families. How fortunate we were to have left Kadarkút in time!

Our life went on. I continued to work at the airfield while anxiously awaiting the Russian offensive. The Romanian border was so close! At last, something was happening. One evening, planes began to land on our small airfield – German planes. Flying low and quietly, they landed one after another, about 30 of them. The German air force took over the airfield of Taszár and, of all possible places, selected our office for their headquarters, removing almost everybody. Selinger, the engineer, had left Taszár a few weeks earlier. Topesch, still in Taszár, lived in a peasant's home and seldom showed up. The Germans kept themselves busy. They installed telephones, walked all over the airfield, and tinkered with the planes without a trace of their usual arrogance – a retreating, defeated army! I was pretending to perform some work. My presence at the airfield would not be justified otherwise. From time to time, I went out with my sketch book and took some measurements. On one occasion, I encountered an officer speaking in German to Lukas. He gave me an unfriendly look.

"Who is that man?" the officer asked suspiciously.

"A company draftsman," Lukas casually replied. "He is sketching and preparing drawings for the final account." Clever Lukas! He avoided any mention of my Polish nationality.

"Idiotic!" the German said. He was right, of course. The Soviet army was quite near and here we, the idiots, were worrying about some final accounts.

With a contemptuous wave of his hand, he walked away. I went up to Lukas and thanked him because he knew very well that as a Pole, I probably would have been asked quite a few embarrassing questions. Actually, he had been trying to find out from the German what was going on, but the only thing he learned was that they had left an airfield in Romania the previous morning. How long they were going to stay he did not know. As much as we enjoyed the thought of the Russian army coming closer, we were also afraid, living on a military airfield now occupied by the Germans.

Over 30 German planes and several anti-aircraft guns were just a few meters away from our hut. What an easy target for the Soviet air force. To survive five years of war only to be killed by Russian bombs – hours before liberation? What should we do? Run? Where to?

So we remained in our little hut, hoping for the best. There was a deep trench running between our hut and the gendarmerie. In an emergency, it could be used as an air raid shelter – very inadequate, but close to us. A more solid shelter was the cellar of a three-story-high reinforced concrete building some 100 meters away. I placed some straw (gathered from nearby huts) and some bread and water in the cellar, which appeared to be the safest place.

The waiting continued. It was well into November and getting colder. The days were windy and gray. Some snow fell. Our hut was very cold. I sealed the window cracks with newspapers and collected some firewood. Broken timber boards littered the ground. Not having any tools, saws, or axes, I managed somehow; the instinct for self-preservation gave me added strength. Lusia brewed some herbal teas, and so we lived from hour to hour. The nights were scary since it was more likely the Germans would bombard the airfield at night. The Germans also held this fear – their windows were blacked out, with not a ray of light shining through.

One night, someone knocked at our door. On opening, I was surprised to see before me a German gendarme in the familiar steel helmet, and his gun pointing at me. "*Bitte kommen Sie herein* [Please come in]," I said politely and opened the door wider. The huge German hesitating slightly, walked in. "Sit down, please!" I said, pushing a stool forward. He sat down heavily and took his helmet off.

Being on guard duty at the airfield and noticing a light, he wondered who was living there. "Who are you?" he asked. "Why is your German so fluent?" I told him that I was employed as a draftsman, and German was a language taught in all schools in the old Austro-Hungarian monarchy. Lusia offered him a cup of tea. Looking around, he saw the "decoration" on the wall – the large map of Europe with the front lines marked by color red pins. He went closer and studied it for a time in silence.

"Where are we?" he asked. I pointed at the position.

"The whole world is fighting against us," he said with resignation. We cannot win this war."

An uneasy silence followed. To change the subject, I asked whether he had received any letters from home, from his family. He answered with sadness that his home was in Hamburg, where he had worked as a welder. He was married with two children and, since the last bombing of Hamburg, he had not heard from them and did not know whether they were alive or dead or whether his house was in ruins. He rose, put on his helmet, thanked me for the cup of tea, and went. Before leaving, he warned us to make sure that the windows were tightly covered since there was the possibility of a Soviet air raid.

Today, writing these lines over 40 years later, I feel some sympathy for this man who was drawn into the cogs of Hitler's war machine, possibly quite innocently, whether he wanted it or not. Yet at the time, we were glad to see his sorrow and hear about the bombardment of Hamburg. At last, we had seen a scared German gendarme whose house was perhaps demolished, who was suffering. It was their turn. It gave us pleasure to see a German gendarme heavily armed, wearing his steel helmet, who had lost all arrogance, conceit, and aggression. Also, we did not know, and never would, how much innocent blood he had on his conscience – this sad and depressed German gendarme.

We strictly observed the blackout. Lusia patched an old blanket, which we used to cover our window. We removed it when going to sleep to see the approaching daylight in the early morning. One night, suddenly awakened by an extraordinary bright light, I jumped out of bed and rushed outside. A fiery ball was suspended in the sky, illuminating the whole airfield. It appeared the Russians were preparing for an air raid. I quickly woke Lusia and dragged Elżunia out of bed. The poor child resisted, not understanding the situation. I folded a blanket around her, and within seconds we left the hut and ran toward the nearby trench. We jumped into the one-meter-deep trench, keeping close together, the ominous fiery ball hanging above us. We waited. All around was silence. No sound of planes. Just this blinding, terrifying light. The ditch was like any ditch. Some grass, a few bushes, Wet and cold. Elżunia was scared and cried quietly. We were scared, too. Suddenly, Lusia grabbed my arm. There was movement behind us in the bushes. We held our breath and Elżunia stopped crying. An animal? A snake? A wild pig? A human head appeared. We recognized our "chess player" gendarme, and with him, "my" gendarme.

Like us, they had jumped out of bed frightened and ran to the trench, half-dressed, half-asleep, and scared. They were embarrassed. A gendarme without uniform and awe-inspiring plumed helmet ceases to be a gendarme. Like any other mortals, they were scared of bombardment. The gendarmes had become human. Strangely, we somehow felt safer being together. Suddenly, it ended – the fireball slowly expired and finally died. The darkness of the wintry night took over and we returned to our cold beds. Russian airplanes? They would return, no doubt. After illuminating the airfield, taking photographs, completing their reconnaissance, and examining the extent of German flak, they would come. Maybe not tonight, or the following night, but come they would. It was an easy and rewarding target – numerous planes and minimal anti-aircraft defense. In fact, the thought occurred to me that had I been born a hero, I could easily have destroyed the German planes myself. It would have sufficed to pour some gasoline over any one of them. Standing close together with full tanks, they would have exploded in seconds. I decided to let the Soviets do this job – it would be easier for them. I would not mind watching this spectacle as long as the flames did not set fire to our hut. I was not born to be a hero; of that, I was certain.

As usual I went out for a stroll in the evening, just a little walk around the hut. During the day, I mostly stayed at home. The Germans were around all the time, and we tried to avoid them. The nights were dark, moonless. On checking our blackout curtain, I noticed a strong beam of light coming from the direction of our office, now the German headquarters. Visible light in a blackout? Something was amiss. Cautiously, I approached the source of the light. One window was brightly illuminated. I moved stealthily toward it. Usually, the place was humming with noise, but there was complete silence. Peeping through the window, I was astonished to see not a single German. I opened the door and cautiously entered. I was amazed. There was nobody there. The Germans had fled. I walked from one room to another.

There was no doubt; the Germans had not just left the place, they had left in a hurry. It was obvious from the disorderly mess of papers, with the blackout curtain gone and the light left on. There was a small, improvised kitchen in the adjoining room. There, the light was also on. And I could see a dark, shapeless substance on the kitchen table. It proved to be a large piece of freshly minced meat, already prepared with onion, garlic, salt, and pepper, ready to be formed into hamburgers. Close by was a frying pan with some butter in it, a huge loaf of fresh Hungarian rye bread, and a German military field flask, full of *palinka* [apricot brandy]. It was obvious that the order to flee was sudden, that there was only time to run. It was hard to believe, yet it had happened – I was stunned. I returned to the office and put the lights out. A Soviet air attack would be the last thing I needed.

I took my booty – the mincemeat, the frying pan, and the bread – and rushed home. Opening the door, Lusia looked at my spoils and at me with astonishment. "Where did you get this?" she asked, smiling with wonder and admiration. How I loved that look!

"Do you remember," I asked, "how we fled from our flat in Kraków in September 1939 and left behind the hamburgers ready for cooking, on the kitchen bench?" Of course, she remembered. "Well, here you have the hamburgers." A questioning look. I paused. "Our friends have run away," I explained. She still couldn't comprehend. "The Germans have left." Her eyes widened. She was speechless.

Together, we went back to the office so that Lusia could see for herself. We hung the blanket back on the window and switched the lights on. There was no doubt that they had left in panic. The wireless was still playing. We looked around. We took a chair, a typewriter, and the wireless as our war booty. We also took the blankets from the windows. These were clean, high-quality woolen blankets, similar to those we had once had in Oserdów – possibly the same or looted from another Polish property. Looking through the drawings, I found plans of the airfield and took them. They might come in handy for some future authority. In the kitchen were potatoes, onions, garlic, beans, cabbage, coffee, and a jar of lard. We took the lot to our hut and had a feast. We drank some palinka and fell asleep in a wonderful mood. In the morning, we arose to face a different reality. Now, we were totally alone on the huge airfield.

The Hungarian gendarmes had fled, too. We knocked at their doors and windows, but nobody answered; frankly, we would have preferred their presence so we would not be so alone in that vast emptiness of a deserted airfield. Lusia went to the village manor to collect the milk as usual.

The administrator's wife, pale and scared, was trying to find out about the Russians and the Red Army. The stories and reports coming from areas already occupied were frightening – looting, rapes, arrests. The villagers were panic stricken. For the first time, the wife of the administrator did not even ask for money for the milk. It did not matter anymore.

The school was still open and Elżunia attended every day. Even now she went without fear, walking across the eerily quiet airfield. It was odd, but this child did not know the meaning of fear. Perhaps it was because in her abnormal childhood she was never told stories about monsters, devils, and wild animals, of which every six-year-old would be afraid.

Impatient, I meandered around this vast airfield, waiting for the Red Army. The half-finished buildings looked haunted. It was cold and the November winds whistled across the vast emptiness. In the distance, one could hear the incessant rumbling of slowly moving vehicles. Trucks? Tanks? Guns? Whatever, the rumbling continued. Nothing could be seen. The hours passed slowly. We just had to wait.

Suddenly, I noticed two men walking hesitantly across the airfield. Their uniforms were neither German, Hungarian, nor Russian. They came closer and I took them in. They were Italian. After Italy's capitulation in 1943, the Germans had put them into a POW camp. Hearing that the front line was approaching and not wanting to fall into Russian hands, they had managed to escape. Lusia quickly made them some hot tea. They were hungry, unshaven, and unwashed. They just wanted to stop for a quick meal and have a few hours' sleep. After sharing our "German" meal, I took them to our air raid shelter in the cellar of the concrete building, giving them some of our blankets. They sank into the straw thanking me many times: "*Gratia, gratia! Molto gratia* [Thank you, thank you. Thank you very much]!" We felt happy to be of some assistance to those Italian friends, to whom we were so greatly indebted for those moments of joy when they broke with their German allies.

As I was returning to our hut, I noticed someone moving fast in my direction, I was perplexed. It was an SS man with a gun in one hand and a huge dog on a leash in the other. It was too late for me to hide, nor was there a place to hide. Should I start to run, he would no doubt shoot. If I moved toward him, he might also shoot. I just stood still. I was dressed in an old pullover, old boots, and a workman's cap. I could pass as a laborer. He stopped. The dog was snarling fiercely and pulling on the leash in my direction. The SS man had a map in his hand. Running across fields, far from the main road, was he possibly a deserter? But why was he running? He asked the name of a never-heard-of village. I pointed with my hand without saying anything and he ran off in that direction. I sighed with relief. Who knows how many innocent Jewish children had been torn to pieces by him and his dog? Hopefully, it was my last encounter with the hated human monster. Hopefully, the approaching Russians would get hold of him. The evening was gloomy and filled with tension.

Suddenly, the darkness was lit up. A blinding flare was once again suspended from the sky. For what purpose? There were no planes or any sign of life on the airfield. To be prepared for any eventuality, we grabbed our new blankets and some food and rushed to the cellar in the concrete building. Our Italians were happy to see us again. It was reassuring to have the company of some other humans. We huddled together, warming each other, and waited. Again, there was no sequel to the flare. Did they want to ascertain that the German forces had left the airfield?

We spent the night in the cellar covered in blankets and straw. We could hear the Italians snoring. In the morning, they left quietly. We returned to our hut shivering with cold. Day and night, we heard the constant rumbling of vehicles, booming somewhere on the horizon. I walked around the totally deserted airfield, waiting.

Suddenly, I could hear roaring high above me the sound of a biplane coming down. The Russians called this type of plane a *Kukurudznik* [*Kukurudza* means corn] since it is small and maneuverable and can land between stalks of corn. It landed successfully a few paces from me. Two Soviet airmen jumped out. They had smart leather jackets, high boots, and fliers' leather caps with goggles. They diffidently walked toward me with revolvers in their hands. I didn't wait! I ran toward them with outstretched arms, and excitedly shouted, "*Zdrastvuyrye tovarishi* [Welcome, comrades]!" I called out as I gave each of them a hearty hug. They put their revolvers away and looked at me with curiosity. It was the first day of December 1944.

A wonderful day. We were intoxicated with joy. The war was finished for us! Finished for us as Jews. There had been many wars in the world's history. Armies against armies, artillery against artillery, tanks against tanks. In the end, the stronger ones won. This war was different. It was our war. Here it was just us – Lusia, Elżunia, and myself – one army. Against us was the strongest, most modern, and best equipped adversary – the German army. They had special troops superbly trained for their task: to murder us – the three of us – my wife, my child, and myself. Many European nations were fighting this war against the Germans. The Poles were fighting, with their underground forces supported by a loving and patriotic population. The French were fighting, with their Maquis (resistance fighters) backed by the entire nation. Tito and his partisans were fighting in Yugoslavia. So were the Belgians, Dutch, and Norwegians in their own homelands. The Allied countries supported them, dropping arms, food, and money from the sky. Their radios communicated encouragement and moral support. But we, the three of us, did not get any help – or support – during our fight. No arms, no food, no money was dropped for us from the skies. We had no encouragement or moral support through the radio. The BBC sent messages in all languages of the occupied countries, but there was not one word of hope for us. We had been left to our fate. True, there were some brave people we met during our struggle who held out their helping hands in times of need. But how many? No, Lusia, I, and the child fought our war practically singlehandedly.

I felt therefore, that at last for us, for Lusia, myself and Elżunia – this war, our war, the war against so many odds – was over. True, we could still be killed by a bomb or a bullet, like any citizen of the conquered countries, but we ceased to be the *chosen* people, chosen to die a martyr's death. And that's why I greeted our Soviet liberators with jubilation and love! I invited them to our hut, produced the field flask of Hungarian brandy "magnanimously" left by a German soldier, and we emptied it.

"A toast to the Red Army," I said.

However, the fliers wanted it differently: "*Za nashu pobiedu* [To our victory]!" said the charming young lieutenant, lifting his glass.

"*Za washu pobiedu* [To your victory]!" we responded and drank the toast.

The victory of the heroic Red Army was already a fact and the prize of their victory for us was our freedom. At least that's what we thought then, on that memorable first December day of 1944.

PART VI
UNDER SOVIET OCCUPATION IN HUNGARY

DECEMBER 1944-JUNE 1946

LIFE WITH THE SOVIETS

Quiet and peaceful so far, the airfield suddenly had come to life. Seemingly out of nowhere, Red Army soldiers began to appear.

I had encountered many different armies in my life. I had seen the Austrian army from the time of the Austro-Hungarian monarchy under the reign of Emperor Franz Joseph. During the 20 years between the two world wars, I had witnessed the Polish army rise from its humble beginnings to a well-organized, disciplined force. I remembered the German armies triumphantly marching into Lwów and the Hungarian army in Budapest. I hadn't, however, encountered anything like what I saw and greeted so warmly now in Taszár. I remembered the Red Army back in 1939 when, after the treaty with Hitler, it treacherously invaded Poland at the same time the Poles were suffering defeat from the concentrated German onslaught. Even then, we could not help but be surprised. They had shabby old uniforms, tattered coats, and a variety of caps of different styles. As we watched them march, we had felt amazed at those soldiers and somehow sad. Nothing about them resembled the marching order of the Polish or German soldiers. The Russians just shuffled in uneven steps with no discipline and no rhythm in their movements. When I was a cadet at high school, two hours a week were spent on military exercises. A sergeant from the nearest military unit used to visit our school in

Sokal and give us instructions on how to handle a gun. We were taught to march, and we learned the art in no time.

When we saw this famous Red Army, marching into Poland in 1939, we couldn't believe our eyes. What kind of army was this? And now, nothing had changed. Is this the army that brought us freedom? Except for the pilots, who were well dressed and looked smart, the rest looked like a bunch of stragglers. They were dressed in all kinds of clothes, differing in color and texture; some wore military clothes, some just ordinary clothes. They wore heavy leather shoes that probably had not seen polish since they left the American factories, with gaiters, once green but now gray, sloppily covering their legs. Some had high leather boots, others white or gray felt boots suitable for frosty Russian winters. Some wore fufaikas – cotton wool-quilted coats covered with gray denim. That was the outfit of a Soviet worker or kolkhoznik.

Some wore caps made of white or gray fur with earflaps others military denim caps. Some carried automatic guns sloppily thrown over one arm. I could not guess the origin of all those guns, but God only knew how old they were. The Soviets did not arrive in armored cars or the Ford trucks that the American government had sent them by the thousands under the Lend-Lease Agreement. Instead, they came in poor old carts pulled by small, piebald horses. They either sat on them or walked alongside, supporting the carts with their arms to help the tired animals.

We watched them in amazement – was this the army that not only stopped the well-organized German advance but also, in a series of counterattacks, pushed the Germans back? The army consisting of members of the collective farms was now strolling around Taszár airfield in small groups, unarmed or with rifles carelessly slung over their shoulders. There were women, too – young Soviets ages 18 to 25 called *wolno-nayomne* [volunteers]. Some were in uniform with red stars on their caps; others preferred to wear colorful blouses, if only for a short while. They walked around the airfield looking everywhere. It was not long before our little hut was discovered, much to their surprise. We opened the door and, with a happy smile, invited them inside in their own language. They couldn't understand how a Polish family with a small child was living in this remote part of the world, in a hut in a deserted airfield, and, what's more, spoke their language so well.

Because of our hospitality, which we gladly and spontaneously offered, they visited us whenever they could. At first, we were happy to have them and offered whatever we could afford, but after a few days, we began to tire of it. They would bring wine – not in bottles, but in buckets. There was plenty of it. The Hungarians had huge casks of wine from their own vineyards, heavy, well-aged, and famous throughout the world. The Russians not only brought buckets of it but drank it by the bucketful, too. They would wander around the village in search of wine, going from one basement to another, from one vineyard to another. Some would be in such a hurry they could not wait for the tap to be opened. A few gunshots and the wine would gush out. They would take two or three buckets. Huge casks containing thousands of liters were standing in hollow pits. It did not take long before the pits were full, sometimes with the floating corpse of a Red Army soldier. Perhaps he could never have dreamed of a more pleasant way of parting from the world. At home, his loving family would receive a short letter of condolence from the army, informing them that their son or father died a hero's death in defense of the Motherland and Stalin [*Za rodinu, Za Stalina*]. The villagers lamented the wasted wine, but the Soviet soldiers were happy. They enjoyed their life today because no one knew what would happen tomorrow. They drank and ignored the owners' protests. After all, the Hungarians had fought side by side with the Germans; even if not as murderous, nonetheless they fought.

Certainly, the Russians soldiers felt no pity for the Hungarians. It was impossible to restrain them. To the contrary, despite orders from the Russian High Command to curb misbehavior and win over the Hungarian peasant and working classes, rape was an everyday occurrence. There was no regard to age. They raped young girls, married women, mothers, and grandmothers, country girls and city workers, and they did not discriminate. A 15-year-old girl was not too young or a 60-year-old woman too old. Some tried to defend themselves; others gave in without resistance. People in the villages and small towns were panic stricken, and so was the manager of "our" estate.

There were several church properties in this wealthy district of

Hungary administrated by graduates in agronomy. The Baycsy, managers of the Taszár estate, were good friends with the administrator of the neighboring estate, who had a beautiful young wife. He was greatly concerned about how to hide her from those ravenous Soviet soldiers.

The vineyards were usually outside the village. There, on sunny fields, vines matured under the caressing warmth of the Hungarian sun and the vigilant eyes of those whose lives revolved around their produce. The harvest was a big event. Every member of the family would go into the vineyard, taking their food with them. They would bring rye bread as big as a wagon wheel, round and dusted with flour. To accompany it, they brought sausages, smoked ham, bacon, and lard richly sprinkled with paprika, and baskets full of vegetables and fruit. Casks of wine were in abundance.

People harvested from sunrise till dark, the shiny bunches of fresh grapes slowly filling huge barrels. The whole family took part in pressing the juice out of the grapes with their bare feet. Streams of dark red or light gold juice slowly began to fill the barrels – wine that would last them the whole year for everyday use or special occasions. There would even be enough to sell.

The whole family stayed for a few days in little huts in the vineyards, where huge casks of wine matured and were stored. There they had a small stove, a table with benches, and some stretchers on which to sleep. Every Hungarian farmer had such a vineyard – some big, some were smaller. Every vineyard had such a hut, large or small. When the harvest was over, families, went back to their villages and then, there was silence in the vineyards. Only the vines, stripped of their fruit, and the huts with the barrels full of young wine, were left behind.

Such a hut was a perfect hiding place for the beautiful young wife of a concerned young husband. Yet nothing could be hidden from curious Soviet soldiers. It might have been the aroma of the wine that led them to this particular little hut outside the village, where they found not only the wine but this beautiful young woman all alone. That night, when her husband sneaked across from the village to visit her, he found her unconscious and covered in blood.

Lusia went to the village as usual early in the morning to fetch some milk from the manor house and found the landlady, Mrs. Baycsy, deeply upset by what had happened to their friend's wife. There were similar stories from nearby villages. There was now panic in our administrator's family. Their carefree days were over. Mrs. Baycsy asked Lusia if our family would move into their house, where many rooms were empty, being used only in the summer by guests from Budapest. She even offered to give us her own bedroom. They had heard that we spoke Russian and were friendly with the Russian soldiers and that nothing disastrous had happened to us even though we lived alone in the secluded airfield.

Maybe, Mrs. Baycsy said, our presence in their house would save them from the frightening consequences of a Russian visit. With tears in her eyes, she implored Lusia in her broken German to accept the invitation. She would cook and wash for us. Food would be in abundance and, she added, we would not have to pay for anything. Suddenly, the Hungarians were aware of our existence. Previously, they had only sold us their milk for our child reluctantly. Today she wanted to feed and cook for us, and all free of charge! How the wheel of fortune spins.

Excited, Lusia returned home. We discussed the proposition. On the one hand, we did not really like the idea of living together with a landowner, the number one enemy of the working class. It could expose us to some unpleasant questions. In each case, we would have to prove that we just lived there and had nothing to do with the estate. On the other hand, it was December and the chilly winter was ahead of us. Would we survive in this flimsy little hut on the windy exposed airfield? And with the child, without winter clothes, no firewood, not even a stove?

Another consideration was the constant visits of the Soviet soldiers to our hut. So far everything was all right as our story was simple – the Germans had deported us to work on the airfield, a forced-labor arrangement. They had retreated a few days ago, as did the Hungarians, and we had stayed behind in this little hut.

No word had yet been spoken about our Jewish origin. Why would we? Would they love us more for that? On the contrary. I knew the Russian attitude. We had been asked no further questions. To them I was just Petro Michaylowicz [Peter, the son of Michael]. We moved into the Baycsy house, choosing a small room close to the kitchen. It had once served as a maid's room and was modestly furnished, though it was a palace compared to our airfield hut. As in every country home, the kitchen stove was always lit, and our little room was comfortably warm. We felt secure. Living in the servant's quarters should prevent any adverse reaction from the Soviets. We had our own key and kept the door locked.

Every day, I went to the airfield. There were a lot of building materials lying around – timber, bricks, cement, glass, sand, and so on. I was concerned that sooner or later these items would be stolen. Lukas used to come, too, wanting to make himself available to the Soviets. We talked about the new situation. He was sad and disappointed; a communist himself, he had expected something else. A few Kaposvár communists had approached the military authorities offering their services, but the commanding officer declined, referring them to civil authorities to be set up later. They felt insulted, wanting a role now, not after the war. I remembered the years 1939 and 1940 when the Soviet command of Lwów had not trusted local communists either and were similarly disappointed. Also, the communists had expected to see a well-organized, disciplined army but had witnessed robbery, rape, and hooliganism. People were afraid to come out into the streets, barricading themselves in their houses.

My friendly Hungarian, Air Force Lieutenant Otto, now in civilian dress, appeared in our office one day and told us of his uncle, a Kaposvár jeweler. One night, his shop had been broken into and robbed of hundreds of Swiss watches and other valuable jewelry. He was quite naive in his belief that strong steel shutters would protect his shop; before the war, among the peaceful Hungarians, certainly it did, but not now with the Red Army about. They were well organized, simply backing their truck up to the shop fronts, attaching a heavy steel chain to the shutters, and driving away. The shop was thus easily exposed, the windowpane smashed, and within minutes emptied. Otto's uncle rushed to the commanding officers to complain. They listened to him politely and expressed their regret, promising to find the robbers. The naive jeweler went back to them every day until finally he was advised the offenders could not be found. He should make a list of the articles stolen and hand it into their office. The poor man spent days compiling an accurate record of his missing stock, then went to the *Commandatura* [headquarters] to have it signed. He was promised the original would be sent to the General Command and assured that eventually (there was a war going on and the army did have other problems), all his losses would be covered. He just had to be patient and wait. That poor jeweler is probably still waiting. Similar events took place elsewhere and the Hungarian communists felt ashamed. This was not their dream of deliverance from capitalist rule. I was not surprised. War was war. The Russians were in enemy territory, and they loved watches.

At last, some kind of authority emerged. The Taszár airfield was taken over by the Soviet air force. A few Soviet officers appeared on the airfield. Among them were the two who had first landed in their little aircraft and whom we had so warmly welcomed with the Hungarian palinka. They recognized me at once and even remembered my name. "*Zdrastwvoyte Towarish* [Hello comrade] *Petro Michaylowicz* [Peter the son of Michael]!" he said. They asked if I would like to help them.

"With pleasure," I answered. "I am at your disposal." My feelings were sincere because I really felt obliged to them. They had liberated us. My duty now was to help the Red Army as much as I could, helping them on their way to total victory over the Nazis. They appreciated my eagerness, and the new friendship was sealed with some more Hungarian wine.

I received my first assignment very soon. I was to summon the local notary, who was also the village mayor. In half an hour he was there, and I passed the new orders on. Tomorrow at seven in the morning, the whole village was to report to the airfield in front of the hangar entrance. No further information was given. The man asked politely, "Women, too?"

"Yes, and regardless of age," I said in my broken Hungarian.

He understood and turned pale.

I was surprised, too. If they had been Germans, one would have feared the possibility of the whole village being executed. I ruled that out. Perhaps the people were to be sent away from their village and the empty houses allotted to the army, And why not? After all, the pilots, mechanics, workers, and cooks had to live somewhere. And hadn't the Germans emptied the Russian villages without pity and deported them to unknown destinations? It must have been a sleepless night for the villagers of Taszár. The fact they were not asked to bring any tools deepened their concern. I was trying to get some information from my Russian "friends" but to no avail as they either did not know or did not want to say anything.

Early in the morning, I went to the airfield and met the commanding officer. Gathered around us were the Hungarian villagers, waiting anxiously. The airfield was heavily guarded. Every few meters was a soldier holding an automatic rifle. There was no way that anyone could slip through. Thanks to my intervention, the Baycsys did not have to be there. I had explained that the estate with its livestock had to be looked after in case the army needed them. Mothers with small children were also excluded. Otherwise, all Hungarians, just like the Germans, disciplined and obedient, were present: the village notary with his wife, the shopkeepers, the clerks, the teachers. Also there, to my surprise, was Mr. Tepesch, who somehow had survived the Soviet invasion in Taszár. Dead scared, they waited for orders – the old and the young, men and women.

It was a freezing December morning. The surface of the runway, once a smooth and grassy lawn, was plowed over on the order of the Germans prior to their retreat. Obviously in a hurry, the workers had not done the job properly. Every few feet, the overturned layers of grassy furrows could be seen. It was, however, sufficient to render the airstrip useless.

The crowd stood tensely, expecting the worst. Suddenly, one of the officers blew a whistle for attention. The officer ordered some of the people from the first rows to move forward and watch him. He bent down, grabbed with his bare hand a big chunk of lawn, overturned it, and delicately brought it back to the previous position. With his bare hands, he again smoothed down the edges and proudly presented to the crowd the final job.

It fit perfectly. He took his time. Slowly, he stood up, with both feet on the reconstructed chunk of lawn and pressed it thoroughly down. He addressed the crowd with a friendly grin. That was what he wanted. After the whole airstrip was restored and made operable, the villagers would be free to go home. Until the job was completed and approved by the Russian officers, not one person would be permitted to leave. With the help of Mr. Topesch, I translated this to the crowd.

The people sighed with relief. Smiling, they eagerly went to work. They divided themselves into groups, and each group had its own piece of ground to work on. The Soviet soldiers stayed to watch but were friendly, relaxed, and smiling. The Hungarians were working conscientiously and the Russians were happy with their progress. The officer offered me the position of second-in-charge of the airfield. Politely, I refused. I did not want to supervise the Hungarians or get too close to the Soviets. I owed something to the Hungarians for the ten months of hospitality, during which I had eaten their bread and drank their milk. I was ready to work as an interpreter, helping both sides, but I did not want to act as a Soviet commissar. I recommended Mr. Topesch for the job. The officers accepted my proposal. Poor Topesch turned pale, but an order was an order. On the Russians' instructions, it was his responsibility to finish the job properly, ensuring a safe runway. Topesch was not too happy and it allowed me a just revenge on this cold-blooded character.

The airstrip was large, and the work proceeded slowly. Whenever necessary, I helped to press the soil down. It was good exercise in the cold. In the field, I noticed the beautiful young wife of the village notary. She worked with her mother, an old, sick woman who could neither bend nor lift the heavy pieces of turf. In tears, the daughter asked me for help. "You speak Russian," she implored. "Please help my old mother." I went to the officer and asked him to let the two women go home. I said that I knew the older one suffered from severe back pain and could not carry out this work. He agreed. Soon, however, they were back, looking very frightened. A guard had aimed his rifle at them and stopped them, shouting, "*Dawai nazad* [Go back]!" Desperate, they came to me again for help. Since the officer I had approached was at the other end of the airfield, I took my notebook and wrote in Russian that the two women had been granted permission to leave the airfield due to the sickness of the old lady. Her daughter was taking her home. I signed it Petro Michaylowicz, lieutenant.

Hesitating, the women took my note and approached the guard again. The soldier read it, saluted, and let them through. My authorization worked. I wrote two more such notes for Pishta's family and Elżunia's teacher. Again, the guard allowed them to pass. My prestige among the villagers rocketed. Suddenly, I became their protector.

Life in the village returned gradually to normal. Planes began to land at Taszár airfield. Some rooms in the larger homes of the village were requisitioned as officers' quarters. Ordinary soldiers were billeted in the less comfortable ones. "Our" estate served as a general kitchen and storeroom. I had another job as an interpreter thanks to my now-adequate knowledge of Hungarian in addition to German and Russian. That I could speak Russian helped me enormously, but even more helpful was my knowledge of Soviet mentality, gained while living under the Russians in 1939-1941.

There were problems. Not everything went smoothly. The soldiers did not always act according to the code of their high command. There were robberies and rapes. On such occasions I was often called, by the victims. The sudden appearance of someone who spoke their language, and spoke authoritatively, would confuse the offenders. They were scared because there were severe penalties for acts of hooliganism, and the offender, mostly young soldiers, would give up their ill intentions.

Very often, groups of soldiers from units stationed in neighboring villages paid us visits. On such occasions, the Baycsys would hide in the back of the house, and I would be delegated to greet the guests. Hearing me speaking Russian, they usually refrained from causing trouble. Very politely, I would insist on seeing the documents authorizing them to confiscate food. As they could never produce such documents, the conflict was usually resolved in a friendly manner with a few bottles of wine, which was never lacking in the house. I would explain that the Taszár estate was serving the needs of the air force units stationed in the village and would advise them to look for food in other villages where no army personnel were stationed.

My other duty was to help provide our flight squadron with provisions. The usual practice was for the manager of the store, Comrade Tolstykow, to give me a list of items needed, which I would pass on to the village notary and the property administrator, Mr. Baycsy. The two were to decide between them which villager's pig would end up in the cauldron. Every morning, either a pig or a calf was killed. Sometimes, it was chickens or geese. The farmers complained, but they knew they had to deliver the animals. The Hungarian workers would kill and clean them, and the Russians did the cooking. They were very good cooks. One of the Russians claimed he had cooked in the czar's palace. We enjoyed his cooking very much, especially after years of living on mostly bread and potatoes. He used to demonstrate the best way of plucking chickens. The dead bird, still in feathers, was placed in boiling water for a minute and then, with one quick twist of his palm, he would pull almost all the feathers out, leaving just a few around the wings. Lusia and I were amazed. We had our meals together with the Russians in the kitchen next to our little room. At the crowded table (without the Baycsys, of course), we used to talk and sing and have a lovely time. Lusia and I often looked at each other, our eyes asking the same question: "Is this reality or is it a dream?" The table laden with food, the friendly smiling faces of the soldiers, men and women around us. We were at the front line. The Germans had left. We felt protected. We could sleep in peace. However, I received a complaint from village representatives that if the killing of their animals continued at such a pace (the Russian appetites were huge), the people would soon have little to eat. It is true that the Russians lived comfortably at the cost of the Hungarians. Nearly every day, one large animal went to feed the soldiers. And why not? How many Soviet pigs were eaten by the German or Hungarian armies?

I recalled the day when the first pig was killed on our estate, a huge animal of around 300 kilos. I watched them open its abdomen, revealing a thick, white layer of fat. What a sight! Bacon, liver, heart – what a price it would have brought on the Warsaw black market only 12 months ago! Lusia particularly loved liver. The last time we had eaten liver was probably before the war. I don't recall eating it during the Russian occupation, let alone under the Germans. At the sight of a fresh liver just taken out of a pig's belly, I couldn't resist asking the "butcher" to cut a piece for my wife. I knew how happy she was going to be. After that, with every slaughter, Lusia would get a piece of liver. The news that she liked it spread quickly.

It was winter, which was the time the villagers slaughtered their pigs to last them for the coming 12 months. Barrels were filled with thick layers of lard, salted, and sprinkled with paprika. Huge pieces of leg hams, necks, bacon, ribs, and sausages were smoked in specially designed ovens and stored in attics or cupboards hidden from the Russians. But the liver was always for Lusia. People we did not even know would knock on the door and offer it to her. How different it was before the "liberation." Whenever she had asked to buy a piece of meat or lard, "*Nekem kell* [We need it for ourselves]" was the answer.

Now that I had become their "king" and protector, all my loyal "subjects" were coming to Lusia with their offerings. I used to laugh at her embarrassment, but she had to accept even though she had become quite sick of it. To have refused such gifts would have been considered an insult.

I had become friendly with the store man Towarish – his full name was Iwan Semyonowicz Tolstykow – but they called him Sybirak [Siberian] or *dal'nevostochnny* [Far Eastern]. A wonderful man. He told me the story of his life in Russia. Before the revolution, he had owned a medium-sized farm. He was a *Kulak*, as they called such people. He was a well-to-do farmer with more than ten hectares of land, a nice house, cows, horses, and even some hired daily laborers from time to time. With collectivization of farms, Kulaks were confiscated and their fields merged into *kolkhozes* (collective farms) or *sovkhozes* (Soviet farms). The Kulaks opposed the change forcefully, having owned their land for generations, guarding it like a treasure. Peasants the world over till their soil with love and devotion. Thanks to their diligence, they had brought their farms to prosperity.

The new system dealt with Kulaks ruthlessly. At night they were taken from their homes, loaded into trucks, and deported to Stalin's infamous Soviet concentration camps – the Gulags. These concentration camps took 20 million innocent lives. Alexander Solzhenitsyn and others described this nightmare. Tolstykow (I called him Comrade Tolstykow, of course) told me his sad story. He was among those who stood up against the cruel system and, caught with weapons in hand, was put in such a concentration camp with thousands of others. Being strong and healthy, he had survived the hard conditions for nearly 20 years until the beginning of the war. When the Red Army was being pushed back by the Germans and disintegrating, there were fewer and fewer young men to fight. The Soviet authorities gave prisoners in these camps a choice: stay on or "voluntarily" join the armed forces. Tolstykow chose to fight. Death by a German bullet, he thought, was better than a life sentence. He was given a uniform and issued an identity card documenting his release after serving 20 years for *oruznoje soprotywlennye protyw Sowierzkoy Wlasty* [armed resistance against the Soviet Union].

Tolstykow told me a lot about his experiences in the camp, his family, and his home. He trusted me, sensing I understood him and his problems. He did not carry a gun as the military probably did not trust him enough. He was assigned to run the store.

Like most Russians, he drank heavily. There was always food, uniforms, cigarettes, and vodka in the storeroom. Sometimes, he would disappear for three days only to be found in a ditch asleep and subsequently locked up. There were heavy penalties for drinking. It was considered an insult to the Soviet uniform for a soldier to be found in a ditch. I begged him to stop. I was concerned but could not convince him. I tried to scare him by suggesting that some Hungarians might kill him in revenge for a raped wife or daughter, or he might simply freeze to death. He would listen patiently, nodding his head and, looking at me with a friendly, tolerant smile, say, "*Ty charoshyj, paryn* [You are a good person, *Petro Michaylowicz*]. *Tak znajesh chto, daway wypijem* [So you know what? Let's have a drink]?" That was always the result.

He longed for freedom. It was the greatest treasure of mankind he used to say. "*Ty ne ponimajesh* [You don't understand], Petro Michaylowicz," he used to say. And he illustrated his conviction with a story from his past. One day, years before the revolution, he had been standing on the front veranda of his house watching a young bull walking around the paddock – a beautiful animal, born on his farm that was his favorite. Suddenly, God knows how, his three-year-old son appeared inside the paddock, slowly approaching the bull. Tolstykow grabbed a rifle and, just as the animal was about to charge, he fired and killed the bull. "It was my decision, my son or my bull," he said. "I had a choice. I was a free man." He finished, kept silent for a moment with sadness on his face, then gesturing with his hand, added, "You would not understand anyway." He never knew how well I understood him, but I kept silent and remained so for a long while. There was nothing that could be said.

In search of supplies, we visited various neighboring villages. One day, Tolstykow and I decided to go to Homok. He organized the sleigh and a pair of horses. Even a bell was attached to the shaft. Again, after all those years, I found myself on a snow-covered country road on a sleigh, a pair of horses in front, clouds of vapor streaming from their nostrils. A quiet whiteness was all around. Cottages and haystacks were covered with snow. Fences, trees, and bushes – everything was white. The road was empty, people leaving their homes only when necessary. There were instances of half-drunk soldiers confiscating horses and sleighs leaving people to reach home on foot.

Here I was at the front line with this strange Russian soldier, the future unknown to both of us. Two different worlds, and yet so similar. We did not talk. Our thoughts were far away. The Russian farmer, a sybirak, alone in the world, his land taken, his house burned, his family dead, and 20 years in captivity, and now in a strange country far from home in a soldier's uniform on the front line before the retreating Germans. No one knew what tomorrow would present – getting wounded, becoming crippled, or being killed. And then there was my world. The world of a Polish Jew, a refugee from his country, a fugitive from hell, his family murdered, his life ruined. I had no country, no home, no name. I was neither Jew nor Pole. My world had been in Oserdów, his in Vladivostok. We remembered and dreamed of those snow-covered villages with similar sleighs, horses, and bells tinkling. We remained silent all the way, dreaming. But I shouldn't complain. When this trip was over, I would return to Lusia and my child. And Tolstykow? To his loneliness and his bottle. Poor Tolstykow.

We stopped in front of the cottage where our friends the Schwabes lived. They were obviously frightened when they opened the door – the sight of a Red Army uniform would scare any Hungarian, not just Hungarians of German origin. I tried to calm them down, reassuring them no harm would come, explaining the purpose of our visit and my role as interpreter. They notified the village notary and Tolstykow handed him a list of food we needed to collect from the village. We treated our hosts to some cigarettes, which at that time were impossible to obtain. And then the food began to arrive – eggs, chickens, onions, garlic, capsicum, cabbage, beetroot, carrots, apples. The villagers could not hide their bitterness at having to give away the fruits of their labor. I explained politely that their suffering was nothing in comparison to what their own countrymen were inflicting on the villagers in Russia. They left unhappy. I was not sorry for them, those cold, heartless people. Nothing was taken from the Schwabes. At my suggestion, Tolstykow left 100 cigarettes and a small packet of Russian tea that made them extremely happy. During the conversation, they complained about visits by Soviet soldiers. I asked for a pen and paper and wrote a note certifying that this house was serving as temporary quarters of a unit of the Soviet air force stationed at the nearby village Taszár; hence the owners were not to be molested or their animals or food taken. The certificate was, as usual, written in Russian and signed *Petro Michaylowicz*, lieutenant. Tolstykow smiled when I showed it to him but would not countersign it.

Every second day we visited a different village. After two weeks we saw Homok again, and I was told that my certificate had proved a blessing; they had hardly been molested anymore. They were extremely grateful to me, and I was happy to have found a way to repay them for their kindness to Lusia. I wondered what their attitude would have been had they known the origin of their Polish visitors.

Usually, we visited the large estates. They had to supply us with pigs, calves, lambs, yearlings –whatever we could lay our hands on – and for which we always left a signed receipt.

The commanding officer of our squadron was a handsome, polite, young captain from Moscow. His name was Warszawski, a Polish name. His great-great-grandfather had come from Warsaw. We became friendly and I was able to help him solve some contentious situations with the Hungarians. I would represent the villagers, he, the air force. At my request, he provided me with a document confirming I was an interpreter and supply officer for the Red Army. It held my photograph and the all-important round army seal typed in Russian, looking quite impressive. I felt proud of being part of the army that had beaten the Germans. I also felt happy to be needed by this army, which had brought me freedom, and gave my most loyal service.

Captain Warszawski stayed in the house of one of the wealthier villagers. His office and telephone were also there. I went there every morning for instructions, and we would talk. He was amazed at the high standard of living of the Hungarian peasants and compared it with the life of his own people in a Soviet kolkhoz. He could not understand it. The rotten capitalism, exploitation of workers and poverty of farmers seen in all those gloomy pictures from the Soviet "bible" he had grown up with looked different in reality. Being an intelligent, educated person, it must have dawned on him that it was not the European workers and farmers who lived in slavery but the Russians; factory workers and kolkhozniks who had suffered under the Soviet dictatorship for the last 25 years. He inquired about my life as an engineer before the war. He had been a teacher. I answered all his questions, and he was obviously disappointed and sad at the true comparison between the two systems.

I also made friends with the two officers who had first landed in Taszár. We used to see each other often and talk about life in the West. This subject was of particular interest to them; they listened as if it were a fairy tale. Several times I took them to visit Hungarian houses, stables, and stores to make them appreciate the fruits of hard work by the Hungarian villagers. They could see for themselves that it was not capitalist propaganda and no doubt felt their own government had not been telling the truth.

From time to time, Soviet women would visit us. It was strange to see females in uniform. We never saw them in Austrian, Polish, Hungarian, or German armies. Even in the Soviet army in 1939, were no women. Two women used to come over and talk to Lusia. They would listen, fascinated. Our life was like a fairy tale to those pretty and intelligent women. We were surprised when they told us they shared quarters with the two officers who were our friends. To them, it was perfectly natural. Lusia tried to find out if any attachment was involved in those relationships. Without any embarrassment, the women said they lived for today and tried to enjoy every moment of it; tomorrow did not count, as tomorrow might never come. They knew they would lose their companions and surely would feel sad about it, but such was life for those female soldiers. Tomorrow? There would be someone else.

Gradually, I was becoming more and more involved in the daily affairs of the village. I was already in bed one evening when a young girl, in tears, knocked on our door sobbing that some soldiers were taking away their only cow. I jumped out of bed and ran to intervene. When I reached the cottage, the cow was about to be loaded onto the truck. I explained to the soldiers that they were depriving this poor widow and her children of their only source of milk and stressed that Comrade Stalin's firm orders were to avoid behavior that would undermine the image of the Red Army. They quietly returned the cow and went. My arguments did not always bear fruit. Sometimes, a few cigarettes or a bottle of wine, combined with some friendly words, would convince the Russians to abandon their plans.

On another occasion, Pishta's wife came running, greatly upset, asking for my help. Her husband had been arrested. Pishta's passion was to hunt in the nearby woods. He had a small collection of precious guns that he greatly cherished. After their invasion, the Germans had ordered the population to surrender all their arms, but Pishta, who hated the Nazis, acted otherwise. After oiling them, he placed them in carefully wrapped leather bags and buried them in the woods. He was not going to surrender them to anyone. Now, the Russians had issued similar orders. Pishta did nothing about it. Why should he? He had no guns anymore! They were somewhere in the woods under a tree known only to him. However, someone reported Pishta to the Russians. Pishta was arrested and put in the local prison, the same one that extended hospitality to Tolstykow. I ran to help. I declared I had seen Pishta pack the guns and hide them in the woods. His political convictions and hatred for the Germans were well known to me, I stated, pointing out that the guns were impossible to recover now since it was winter. I guaranteed they would not be retrieved and used against the Soviets. Pishta was released.

In my free moments, I would wander about the village. There was always something happening. In the middle of the village, the Soviets erected a workshop for the army blacksmith. I would often stop to watch him. A tall, young man, he would be shoeing horses, fixing wagons, or repairing tanks. With my usual gregariousness, I would strike up a conversation. One day, he told me his story. Although he spoke Russian and wore the Russian uniform, he was Bulgarian. His parents had escaped from Russia to Bulgaria during the 1917 revolution and received citizenship. Obviously, they belonged at the time to the so-called "Whites" [anti-Bolsheviks] who were fighting the "Reds" [Bolsheviks]. When the Russian army recently entered Bulgaria, all White Russian immigrants were scared, fearing reprisals. Surprisingly, the Russian authorities were lenient. They promised amnesty to all Russian emigrants who volunteered to join the Soviet army. The young blacksmith had signed up, giving his parents the right to amnesty. His problem now was that he had lost contact with his parents and Bulgarian wife. As a Russian soldier, he had access to the Russian field post, from where letters were sent to the Soviet Union, but not to Bulgaria. Hence his family could not receive any news from him, and he had no news from home. He had asked his superiors for help, but there was nothing they could do. I felt sorry for him and tried to work out a way he could communicate with his family.

An idea struck me. During my visits to Kaposvár, I had seen some men in strange-colored uniforms. Curious as usual, I had questioned one of them and found them to be officers of the Bulgarian army. After entering Bulgaria, the Russians made sure these officers became involved in the war against Germany; hence a few Bulgarian battalions were present in Hungary. I told the blacksmith I might meet one of those officers in Kaposvár again. I would explain the situation and felt sure they would send his letter through the Bulgarian field post. I suggested he write only a few words about his well-being, and not one word about his location or occupation. He enthusiastically wrote his letter and gave it to me. I told him I would keep it with me and pass it on when the opportunity arose sometime.

Occasionally I went to Kaposvár to gather the latest news and do some shopping – I always notified my Soviet friends, asking whether they needed me to buy anything for them. One of the officers asked me to buy *sulfidin*. I had no idea what it was for until my friendly chemist in Kaposvár opened my eyes. Sulfidin, like all other derivatives from sulfur, was an antibiotic used to treat infections, including gonorrhea. The venereal disease was widespread among the Russians, but the medicine was impossible to obtain. My friendly chemist had sold nearly all his stock of the various forms of sulfur in the first days of the Russian occupation but somehow managed to keep several vials under the counter. He agreed to sell ten sets of injections at regular price along with 200 cigarettes and a piece of smoked lard. I gave one set of six injections to my Russian friend. After a few days, he returned with a bottle of vodka, extremely happy with the result. I realized I had put my hands on a small fortune when it came to the cigarettes. They were virtually unobtainable, making them a most valuable commodity in resolving everyday problems.

I was able to procure these treasures from the army store. Every time I went with Tolstykow on a food-collection trip, I helped unload the carts and trucks. The storeroom was bulging with everything: flour (the Russians baked their own bread), salt, sugar, grains, tea, vodka ... and cigarettes.

Cigarettes were kept in large cartons, one of which was usually open. Lusia loved to smoke, but there was nowhere to buy them. One day, I succumbed to temptation. I grabbed a box of a hundred cigarettes and shoved them quickly into the pocket of my overcoat.

There was a huge hole in the pocket, so the box slid down to rest safely inside the lining.

That overcoat had a history – it was a short winter coat, made of thick woolen material. It was a type of car coat – the Polish word for it is *kurtka*. I had bought it back in 1932 in Leszczkow, a village not far from Oserdów. Its lining was of strong, camel-hair material also produced in Leszczkow. I had worn that coat in Oserdów as well as Kraków, mainly on inspections of building sites. When we left Kraków in 1939, I took it with and it survived two Russian winters in Lwów when I carried loads of kasha and flour on my back. Then, during the German occupation of Lwów, I hid food – smuggled from the railway station – in its deep pocket. Later, it accompanied me on my winter travel to Skierniewice and Legionowo. Still in good condition in the winter of 1944, it went with me across the Carpathian Mountains into Hungary, and now here in Taszár I was still wearing it. It was well tailored and still looked good despite all those years of wear.

The only worn parts were the pockets. The huge holes, developed over the years, had proven to be of enormous help. Whatever I put into the pockets disappeared deep into the lining, as did the box of cigarettes now. I glanced at Tolstykow, not sure whether he had noticed my crime, but somehow, he always seemed busy. After that successful episode, every time I visited the store, one or two packets of cigarettes would disappear into my bottomless pockets. Tolstykow never seemed to notice. He was always busy doing something with his back turned. Nonetheless, he must have noticed the cigarettes gradually disappearing. Later, I understood his behavior. He was not allowed to give me the cigarettes; in case of mishap, I could have given him away. Stealing was a different story. It was my own responsibility, and so good old Tolstykow just kept on turning a blind eye.

Eventually, I found it difficult to hide my treasures. I had become a rather greedy thief as there were more and more cigarettes to hide. In our room was a wooden stand, a sort of vertical box about 150 centimeters high and 30 centimeters square, covered with a loose piece of board. On top of it was an embroidered cloth and a small vase. I kept the plans of the airfield that I had taken from our office after the Germans' sudden departure inside it. I had offered them to the Russian officers after their first landing in Taszár, but they asked me to keep them in safe custody until the authorities had settled in. Keeping plans for a military airfield was not wise. If anyone had happened to search the room and found them hidden, we would have been in serious trouble. However, I did not want to destroy them. I felt I had to accept this risk and was happy to find a "secret" location. Inside that stand next to the rolls of plans, I placed the boxes of cigarettes.

Life in Taszár was slowly returning to normal. The winter of 1944/1945 was harsh, but we were quite warm in our maid's room, having everything in abundance. On several occasions, I went to Kaposvár, assisting the Russians in collecting various goods from their base. One day, we had a truckload full of fresh sausages. Two Russian soldiers were sitting in the front, and I placed myself at the back among all those sausages, which I kept nibbling. They were delicious – fresh and spicy with plenty of garlic.

Passing through the streets of Kaposvár, I suddenly noticed Klob's sister with her small nephew, the only survivor of the medical examination in the Polish camp. Food at the time was in short supply; fresh sausages were not obtainable at any price. On the spur of the moment, I began to throw sausages from the truck. Meters of sausages landed on the pavement. I called out to attract her attention. Klob's sister recognized me and rushed to retrieve the gift from heaven. Other people joined in, and as the truck sped away, I caught glimpses of people with their hands full of sausages. I could imagine their surprise and delight. The driver had not noticed a thing, and a few lucky people had a lovely Christmas.

Another time, I escorted the Soviet soldiers to an abandoned flat. We took mattresses, some pots and pans, and a few armchairs. I helped to load the truck, which was no problem for me after my experience in Lwów. Grateful for my help, the Red Army men suggested that I take whatever I wanted from the flat. There were beautiful Persian carpets, fine pictures, antique furniture, and a library of books – all in Hungarian, of course. Lusia had virtually nothing to wear – no clothes or shoes. Her last pair of shoes were worn beyond repair. Tolstykow had given her a pair of old army boots from his warehouse. They were huge and heavy, and Lusia had to wrap her feet with old cloth before she could fit into them. She was happy, however, at least to have dry feet. I looked around the flat for some sort of clothing and ladies' shoes. Unfortunately, there was nothing. Obviously, we were not the first ones to visit this flat. However, in one of the rooms, I found two old dresses on the floor made from heavy, dark, awful fabric, but I knew Lusia could make something out of them.

I was still unable to find a replacement for the heavy boots, but who cared? We were well fed, warm, and under the protection of the powerful Soviet army. The war was not over yet and people were still being killed, but it seemed that at last our hard times were over. We were happy just to feel safe and not see the Germans anymore. The Hungarians, however, were still afraid – of arrests and the NKVD, which kept sniffing around for fascists and traitors. It was the Hungarians' turn to have sleepless nights.

A GERMAN SPY!

The Allied forces were gradually advancing deeper into Germany. British, American, and other Allied bombers were flying day and night toward their targets. Hitler decided to defend his Berlin bunker to the bloody end. For the defense of Berlin, he had only 16- or 60-year-old soldiers – the rest were fighting a losing battle on all fronts. Our spirits were high, our joy indescribable.

One gray winter morning, an excited Soviet soldier rushed in, shouting, "*Liberator posadki iskaje!* [Liberator is looking for a place to land]!" Everyone rushed toward the airfield. Invited by my Soviet friends, I joined in. In a matter of seconds, the Soviets formed two rows along a snow-covered runway. High above, a huge American plane was slowly coming down. An airman with two red flags was guiding it. It landed smoothly, stopping a few steps away from the red flags. When the door opened, a small ladder appeared and 10 or 11 airmen descended. It was an exciting moment. The Soviets shook hands with each American, repeating, "*Sdrastwujte, sdrastwujte* [Be in good health, be in good health]!" while the US airmen, smiling broadly, answered everyone with "Hello!" I watched the two groups. On one side were the Americans – young, tall, and smart in their leather jackets, caps, and polished boots. On the other were the Soviet soldiers in their worn-out uniforms, quilted jackets, and felt boots, Even the Soviet pilots, whom I had always admired for their smart appearance, now looked poor in comparison with these clean-shaven boys who jumped out of this American silver bird. East and West had met. I, too, approached the Americans, They were surprised to see me – the only one in civilian clothes.

"How do you do?" I kept saying.

"Fine, terrific!" they answered, still smiling, happy at last to find ground beneath their feet.

The American captain had a sports cap on. Others were happily chewing gum. All formed a line and followed the Soviet airmen. I was angry at myself for having neglected my English studies. The Americans were taken into "our" house. Mrs. Baycsy, Lusia, and others rushed around preparing a meal. Everyone was excited. This American arrival was a big attraction.

When Captain Warszawski asked for advice on what we should do to honor the Allies, I suggested a banquet. Immediately, several turkeys and chickens were deprived of their lives, the main dining room was opened, and the big table, which had not been used for months, was quickly set. A large, white tablecloth was found, and we all sat down to an exquisite dinner. The Soviet cook had not been telling tales. His dishes most certainly could have graced the czar's table. There was a hot Russian borscht, consommé, goulash made from different kinds of meat, barbecued chicken, homemade sausages. and fresh bread accompanied by Russian vodka and delicious Hungarian wine. The atmosphere was great. We all were elated. After a few drinks, when spirits were high, Captain Warszawski stood and made a short speech, greeting the Americans on behalf of the Red Army, mentioning the friendship between the nations, and toasting the American Air Force and the president of the United States.

I was praying for his speech to be short – and possible for me to understand and translate into English.

Before dinner, expecting I would be asked to translate, I had asked Lusia for help. With her talent for languages and good memory (her English was much better than mine), she composed a few sentences for me. I stumbled through the translation and probably got everything wrong because I noticed the Americans delicately smiling. But somehow, I reached the last part: "Long live the heroic American Air Force, long live the great president of the United States!" after which I raised my glass. People were clapping and Lusia, sitting at the other end of the table, bestowed one of her unforgettable smiles on me.

Then came the American's toast. The captain was speaking too fast for me to understand. I could only pick up certain words like Stalingrad, Berlin, Hitler, Stalin, victory, and "Long live the Soviet Air Force and the Red Army." All applauded. Again, it was my turn to interpret. I stretched my imagination to the limit. I honored the heroic defenders of Stalingrad, promised to destroy Berlin, expressed hopes that Hitler would be severely punished, and so on. I finished by honoring the Red Army and Great Marshal Stalin. I put a lot of emotion in my speech, far more than was in the American's version. It was a good, strong speech in fluent Russian. Enthusiastic applause followed, then the Russians began to embrace the Americans. There seemed no end to the bear hugs and kisses. The Americans had not expected such a display of emotions – they smiled with embarrassment. I caught a few kisses. There was even a toast in honor of Polish-Soviet friendship, which I accepted with moderate enthusiasm. At the end of the festivities, my Russian friends, the pilots, Captain Warszawski, and others thanked me for my cooperation. Their admiration for my knowledge of languages was obvious.

After dinner, Captain Warszawski began to make arrangements for the Americans' accommodation. The village notary was called, and I was asked to pass on the order: The best homes were to be seized and every American was to sleep in a separate house. I didn't like the idea. I wanted them all to stay in the manor house. Their presence had brought new life, breaking the monotony of the gray Soviet atmosphere. It was not too difficult to convince Captain Warszawski that it would be safer to have all Americans under our roof. After all, Hungary was still at a state of war with America. Who would take responsibility if something happened to one of them during the night? Under his plan, the captain would need to place 11 guards, one at every house. Keeping them all together in one group was much simpler. A guard was already watching the manor house. I suggested that 11 mattresses, sheets, blankets, eider downs, and cushions be collected from the villagers and the Americans could sleep on the floor in the large lounge room comfortably. Warszawski agreed. The Americans were also much happier to stay together.

Early the next morning, two NKVD officers arrived. They were not pleased to see the Americans asleep on the floor and asked Warszawski for an explanation. Poor Warszawski turned pale and explained that he had suggested a different arrangement, but I had persuaded him against it. When the officers approached me, their suspicious, penetrating looks made me shudder. "A *ty kio takoj* [And who are you]?"

Trying to appear calm, I explained that I was Polish and had been deported to Hungary to work at the airfield, where the Red Army liberated me. Because of my knowledge of Russian and Hungarian, I was working as an interpreter for the Soviets. As for the Americans, I thought it would be safer to keep them in one house under Soviet guard instead of placing them in eleven different houses.

The NKVD man listened, closely watching my face. When I finished, he said, "You are clever. But how come you know Russian so well?"

Now I had to be cautious. If I were to disclose that I was under the Russian occupation in Lwów in 1939-1941. I could be in real trouble. Lwów and the whole district of east Poland had been annexed into the Soviet Union and all citizens had become Soviet subjects. As such, I would be required to complete military service in the Soviet army. The Russians would have every right to put me in uniform on the spot and send me to the front. I gave him a different story. I explained that I came from Warsaw, and since Warsaw had been part of Russia before the First World War, I had learned the language at school. The officer seemed satisfied and there were no further questions.

A few minutes later, the Americans departed in the NKVD truck. Disappointed, we bade them goodbye. The next day, while in Kaposvár, I heard knocking from a window I was passing. I recognized one of the Americans, who did not look happy. The house had guards at the gate and bars on the windows – it was the headquarters of the NKVD. I was told later by my Russian friends that, according to the Soviet-American agreement, every plane making a forced landing in a Soviet-occupied zone automatically became Soviet property, while the crew was to be sent back to their country. Indeed, after a few days, two specialists from Moscow arrived to repair whatever had caused the forced landing.

I was curious to see inside such a huge bomber. I now had an opportunity that probably would never occur again. I asked my friendly pilot whether it would be possible for me to look inside the cockpit. "It must be an interesting thing to see," I added.

He replied that unauthorized personnel did not have access to military planes. A few days passed. The specialists from Moscow apparently had problems in locating what was wrong with the plane.

One evening, a group of farmers came to see "Mr engineer," or "*mernok ur*," as they called me. The following day, a big transport of grain was to be delivered to Kaposvár. Such transports were often intercepted by Soviet marauders, neither reaching Kaposvár nor returning home. The villagers were afraid, so they came to ask me to escort them. How could I refuse my "subjects"? I, the "King of Taszár" agreed, and we arranged they would pick me up the next morning.

It was about seven a.m. when quite unexpectedly my friendly pilot arrived. The technicians had found and fixed the defect. One of the petrol tanks had been fired at and the petrol was leaking. It had taken two weeks for those two "specialists" to find that out! The holes were sealed, the petrol tanks refilled, and the plane was ready to take off. But they didn't know how to start the engine! All instructions were written in English, and they couldn't understand a word. I had no time to think about the farmers now.

My friend told them there was a Polish engineer in the village who knew some English and could be of some assistance. I was taken to the airfield and now had that chance to see the plane's interior. A group of ten Soviet officers and pilots gathered around, everyone very excited. It was to be the first American Liberator to be flown to Moscow by Russian pilots, where a number of experts were anxiously awaiting its arrival. I was excited, too. Would I be able to help? I knew nothing about planes or engines. Well, I could only try.

I climbed into the cockpit and took the pilot's seat, with one of the mechanics next to me, the other behind me. Before me was an enormous panel with a confusing array of instruments. There were glass-covered indicators, handles, buttons, lamps of different colors, rows of manometers, and horizontal and vertical gauges. I was completely lost. Slowly, I began to sort out the different groups of instruments, reading the names aloud: motor one, motor two, motor three, and motor four. Everything had on and off buttons. The Russians were taking notes; their faces lit up. Next, I located the buttons for air, water, oil, pressure, speed, temperature, and several others. My friend had climbed into the cabin, too, smiling proudly. After all, he was the one who had brought me here. As I kept reading the foreign names out, the mechanics diligently continued taking notes. I asked them if I was of some help. "*Ty kak wozduch dla nas* [You are like air to us]. We are now beginning to breathe," they said.

It took some time to decipher the electric clocks. "Volt," "amp," and other mysterious signs could only be understood gradually. At last, I had finished. The delighted Russians shook my hands ecstatically. "*Spasiba! Spasiba!*" they thanked me. My pilot friend beamed at me. I was proud to assist my Soviet friends, helping to put into their hands a wonderful piece of American technology – a warplane, a military secret that landed on Russian-occupied soil.

Half an hour later, I was on my way to Kaposvár, escorting a cavalcade of open carts. We moved slowly; the wagons laden with grain. I was in the middle cart so that I could observe the vanguard and the rear. The road led along the airfield. We could see the American plane quite clearly. It was still on the ground, but I could hear the engines revving. I was relieved. My English lessons had been useful after all. Listening carefully, I suddenly felt something was wrong. The noise was coming not from the Liberator but from the sky above. It was from another plane or planes. Two planes eventually appeared and I recognized them: German Messerschmitt. I ordered the carts to stop. We jumped off and ran toward the nearest trees and waited there.

The planes circled above the Liberator before opening fire. We could see the Russians running. One jumped out of the Liberator. After the next German attack, smoke appeared and then, suddenly, the magnificent American machine burst into flames. Within minutes, smoke obscured the whole scene. Their task completed; the Germans disappeared.

Why didn't the Russians fire at the German planes? Two fully loaded machine guns were on that Liberator, ready for use. Instead, the Russians jumped from the plane and disappeared into the bushes nearby. Perhaps, I thought sadly, they did not know how to use the American machine guns. I signaled to the farmers to come out of hiding and we continued our journey. I felt very angry. Such a beautiful plane! In the silence, only a cloud of black smoke indicated where, a few minutes before, it had stood so proudly. We arrived home late in the afternoon after an uneventful trip. On our return, we could still see the black smoke lingering over the burning plane. The farmers dropped me off and thanked me warmly.

Sad and tired, I opened the door to our room and stood there, stunned by what saw – Lusia, pale and obviously frightened, surrounded by several NKVD soldiers. They were awaiting my return. My pilot friend, who had taken me to the airfield, was also present. They started to search me and then turned the whole room upside down, examining every corner. When they turned the lower stand over, the boxes of cigarettes and the airfield plans fell out. "*Dawaj* [Come with us]," they said sternly.

They took me to the Commandatura and the officer in charge of the search triumphantly reported they had found plans of the airfield hidden under heaps of cigarettes. In short, I was accused of spying for the Germans. A long interrogation followed. I did not mention a word about my Jewish origin, thinking it would only make things worse, especially if they asked the usual: "How is it that millions of Jews are dead and you have survived? Perhaps you have been working for the Germans as a collaborator?"

After a period of questioning, I asked whether they had ever known a Pole who would stay with his wife and child while spying for the Germans. I reminded them of my enthusiastic cooperation and all the work I had done for the Red Army.

"But the plans! The plans were found in your house!" they said.

I was annoyed. "I did not hide them. I was keeping them only because the first two officers who landed in Taszár asked me to do so. From the very beginning they knew of their existence." I insisted that my officer friend be brought in.

In obvious fear, he entered the room. In the Soviet Union, everyone feared the NKVD; everyone trembled when they saw the blue cap. When asked if he knew about the plans, he remained silent. At that moment, I became really scared. They all were looking at me with hate. The noose was tightening around my neck. Trying to remain calm, I confronted the trembling pilot. "Was I the one who greeted you immediately after you landed in Taszár?"

"*Da*," he answered.

"Was it I who told you at that time about the plans for the airfield?

"*Da*," was the answer.

"Did I not want to hand them over to you, but your decision was to keep them until the new authorities settled in?"

His answer was "yes" again.

"Why do you keep silent then?" I asked reproachfully. There was no answer.

The NKVD officer had one more question: Why had I been trying to get into the plane in the first place and then, half an hour later, the Germans burned it?

"I only wanted to look at the inside of the plane because I had never seen anything like it before and probably never would again," I answered. "It was just curiosity. Had I been allowed inside earlier, the plane would have been ready for takeoff long before the Germans spotted it. They would not have had time to destroy it."

Why they bombed it right after I was there is a question neither I nor anyone else could answer. There was silence. I had the feeling that I had managed to convince them of my innocence. "Comrades," I said at last. "I spent all day transporting the grain for the Army. I am tired, greatly upset, and hungry. I am going home to my wife and my child. The loss of that plane hurts me as much as it hurts you. Do you have any more questions? If so, you know where to find me. I have no desire to run away and join my 'German friends.'"

Without hiding my distress and hurt at their accusations, I rose from my chair and left the room. No one stopped me. Lusia, who would not let me go alone, was waiting outside. Sometime later, my pilot friend confessed that after the German attack, everyone had been convinced that I had sent a message to the Germans. Luckily, the radio receiver I had taken from the office was still hidden in Pishta's storeroom. Had they found it in my room, nothing would have saved me. As for the officer who had arranged my visit to the plane, he had the fright of his life.

GERMAN COUNTEROFFENSIVE

I was greatly worried by the military situation so close to us. The Soviet armies had crossed the southern Danube, penetrating deep into the Hungarian plains, including our village, and as a result created a triangle, with Taszár most vulnerable. The Soviets had cut off ten German divisions in Yugoslavia, where Tito's partisans kept them under constant harassment. The bulk of German forces were in and around Budapest, and one did not need to be a military strategist to foresee that the German armies in Yugoslavia would be trying to push northward to join with their forces around Budapest. Should they succeed, it would be disastrous for our Russians and for us.

I stayed alert, waiting for the first signs of danger. I did not have to wait long. One day I noticed the Russians digging trenches all around Taszár. Acting naive, I asked why. There was no explanation except that they might be needed. More Soviet soldiers had also arrived in Taszár. When I made inquiries, I was told that they had just been released from an army hospital in Kaposvár and sent back to the front! So, we were now the front line!

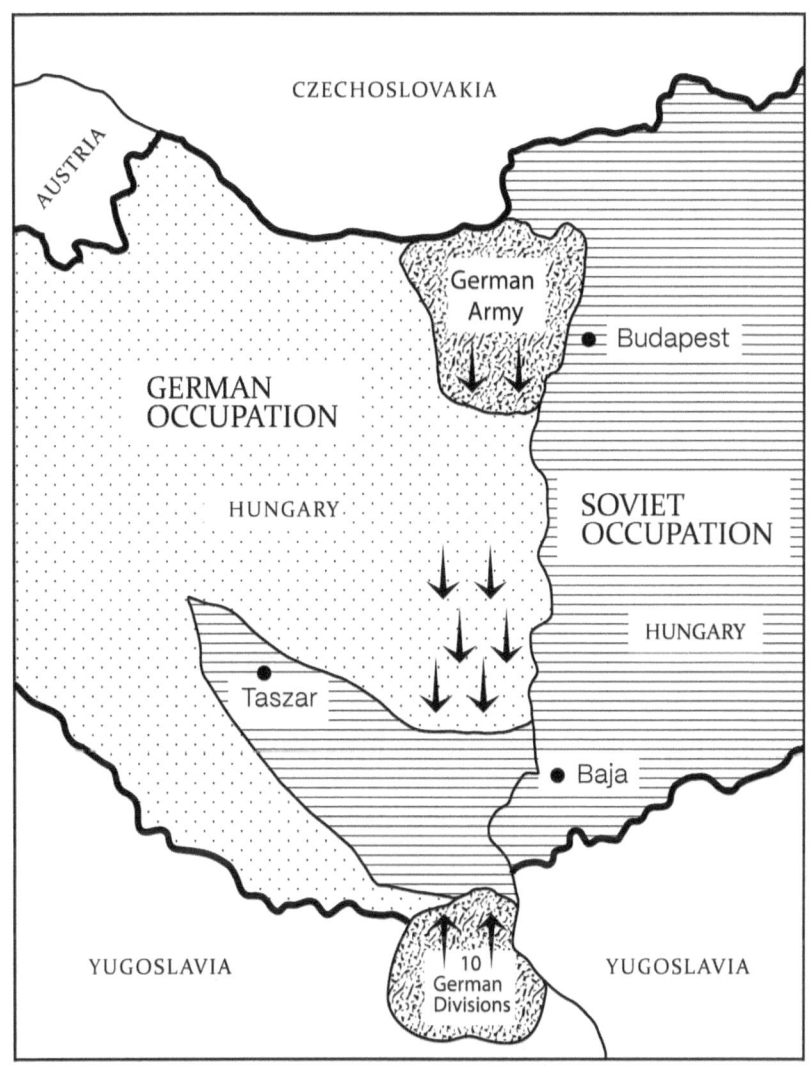

German attempt to rescue ten divisions, surrounded in Yugoslavia.

What most scared Lusia and I was not the expected combat but the terrifying thought of facing the Germans again. I urgently considered how to escape.

Sometime before, I had spoken with some Russians who had been collecting and packing machinery and equipment to send home. They were called the *"trofieyny"* squad, collecting the trophies or the spoils of war – an age-old tradition of conquering armies. I had become friendly with one of the squad's officers, who told me they were trying to get these trophies out as soon as possible – machinery, horses, cattle, farm equipment, cars, even furniture. I mentioned my plans to escape by crossing the Danube in case of a German attack and suggested that if he would lend me one cart and two horses, I assured him, I would deliver them to the Russians on the other side.

He agreed in principle and left the details to future arrangements. Now I tried to locate him, but unfortunately, he had already left the area, and with him my hopes for a "comfortable" escape. Yet, so far, there was no need for panic. Everything was quiet and we decided to stay put and wait. Generally, the military situation was good. The Allied forces had already crossed the German border and fighting was now taking place on German soil. Their air forces were steadily dropping their bombs day and night over German cities, particularly Berlin, their favorite target. It had been some time since Stalin ordered his troops to "destroy the German beast right in its lair – Berlin." The Allied armies were slowly getting there. On the Hungarian front, all remained quiet. The Germans had decided to defend their position in Budapest and, from what I heard from the BBC, there was heavy fighting in the Buda part of the city. The other part, Pest, situated on the eastern side of the Danube, had already been taken by the Russians. Naturally, I felt most uneasy. Living with and watching the Russians closely, I noticed a certain apprehension among them, too.

Then one night, all Soviet planes disappeared from the airfield and so did my friends, the pilots, and the women soldiers. There was only one unit left, stationed in our house.

We had decided to stay in the village so long as there were Soviet personnel. We had good reasons for such a decision. It was January 1945 – the middle of winter. We had a warm room to sleep in and food – as much as we wanted. To leave all this and run again with Elżunia, a six-year-old child? And where to, without money or warm clothes, and an insufficient knowledge of the language? Lusia and I discussed it night after night, but we could not make any other decision. After all, we reasoned, some Soviets were still in the village and right here in our quarters.

Why run? Nothing was happening yet. Maybe nothing would

happen? Let's wait and see. Unfortunately, again we didn't have to wait too long.

One night, the sound of heavy artillery fire woke us. The moment we had feared had come. It was war again. This time we were in the middle of it, the immediate target of German attacks. The German plan was simple and exactly as feared: They were trying to join up with their cut-off divisions in Yugoslavia.

Should they succeed, we would be in a most dangerous situation. We were not afraid of the Germans. They would not bother with us unless someone denounced us. We were afraid of Hungarians. As a well-known interpreter, always in the company of the Russians, I had been collaborating with the occupying army. No question about that. One denunciation and I would be dead, without trial. It did not matter how much I had helped the villagers, how many hopeless situations I had dragged them out of, day and night, always there, ready to help. There only needed to be one person to inform on me. The hope of being liberated by the Germans had lit up the faces of the Hungarians. They did not try to hide their happiness.[1]

One thing we knew – we had to avoid being cut off. We could not fall into German hands. But how? New military detachments were arriving in Taszár. They needed interpreters. Unexpectedly, I met two Poles – engineers working on bridge construction nearby. It took me by surprise because at the time we did not know of their existence. They were surprised when we met. I think they recognized me at once. They were officers of the Polish army and had crossed the border, as many others did, in 1939. Like us, they had lived in one of the camps until the Hungarian authorities allowed us to work outside the camps. One of them was called Klos; I do not remember the name of the other one.

One of the new Russian detachments now received orders to march out. They needed an interpreter and ordered me to come along with them. I was terrified. How could I go and leave my family behind? I explained that I lived in Taszár with my wife and child and was already working as an interpreter for another unit, stationed in Taszár, so I could not go. Luckily, after producing my work certificate, they let me off the hook and ordered the other Pole to pick up his things and join them. Klos overheard a conversation two days later between two

Russians and gathered that the entire squad had been attacked by German forces and killed. Once again, we had been very lucky.

Klos used to visit us now and then. He would stare with his penetrating gaze. Of course, he knew who we were, but not a word was said. He grew fond of Elżunia. A little chat and a cup of tea was sufficient excuse for a lonely man to visit us. He was most welcome.

The thunder of the artillery exchange was constant. We grew more anxious despite Russian reassurance that the situation was under control and that we had nothing to fear. They were in constant telephone contact with General Command, and should they receive orders to leave, they promised to take us with them. This somehow calmed us down. We only hoped they would not leave too late. Meanwhile, we packed some of our belongings so we would be ready at a moment's notice. I was always restless, especially in such a situation, and I decided to go to Kaposvár to gather some news. Maybe the Russians had already started to pack their equipment to get ready for the retreat? For me that would be an indication of the situation.

I left home early in the morning planning to return around lunchtime. A Soviet truck gave me a lift. I called in to see my friendly chemist. He could give me no information but was quite tense himself. He, too, was afraid of the Germans returning. Where to try next?

From my previous observations, I knew that in such situations, hospitals were always the first to be evacuated. On one of my previous visits to the chemist, I had met a Russian who used to work as a purchasing officer for the military hospital. We had a long and friendly conversation at the time. I assumed that he was providing the chemist with medications to which he had access at the hospital. It so happened that every time I had visited Kaposvár, I met him. I hoped I would meet him again this time. I circled the hospital buildings several times but without luck. The chemist had not seen him either for quite a few days. I walked around town closely watching for any sign of movements by the Russians. The artillery fire seemed much closer. Motorized columns of soldiers, accompanied by tanks, were moving. One could feel the tension. A few hours passed and I was beginning to regret I had ever set out on this journey. It must have been noon when I boarded the train and found a seat by the window. The train soon filled with soldiers. I was the only civilian.

Then, by an unbelievable coincidence, sitting right in front of me, was my Russian friend, the fellow from the hospital. We shook hands and exchanged the usual "zdrastwujta." The soldiers looked sad. The artillery fire was constant. The atmosphere was grave. I started to converse with my "hospital acquaintance," keen to find out whether the hospital was going to be evacuated. After a few clumsy questions, I eventually got the information I needed. The hospital was remaining.

I felt more relaxed, because that meant that the military situation was not so bad. I continued the conversation. There was not much time left as in a few minutes the train would be approaching Taszár. Then, just by chance, I noticed a soldier sitting at the door of the compartment handing over a note and whispering something to the soldier sitting opposite him.

The note went from hand to hand and soon reached my friend. His face turned white reading it. He rose immediately, took his backpack, and left the compartment, joined by the soldier who had sent the note. I realized something was wrong. All talk in the compartment had stopped; all soldiers were suddenly silent. They looked at me with undisguised animosity. The train approached Taszár and slowed down. I got up and left the compartment, making my way through the crowd of soldiers toward the exit. Once again, I had the premonition of something gone wrong, of facing a yet-unknown danger. Tense and apprehensive, I reached the exit, and there stood the soldier who had sent the mysterious note.

Young, inconspicuous, and rather poorly dressed, with blue epaulettes on his shoulders, a soldier of the Soviet Secret Police, the feared NKVD, stopping me from leaving. I tried in vain to explain my identity – my position of interpreter for the Soviet army, with my wife and child waiting for me in Taszár. He stood in stony silence.

Soon, the train was gathering speed taking me away from Taszár. I was in despair. Where were they taking me? The next large township was Dombóvár, a junction station. My guards got off and ordered me to go with them.

We walked along the railway platform, an armed NKVD man on either side of me. I was taken to the NKVD office at the railway station. The officer-in-charge had already left and was not expected before the next morning. What a prospect! It was now only about one in the afternoon. I was trying to say something to explain, but nobody was listening. My escort whispered something to the soldier on duty and left. I sat down and an armed soldier sat beside me. Still the artillery boomed. Minutes, then hours passed. Two o'clock, three o'clock. Lusia was waiting in Taszár and I was here in Dombóvár.

They gave me a piece of bread and a cup of *kipiatok* [boiling water]. The January night was closing in. At six, the soldier on duty waved toward me: "*Dawaj!*" I stood up, straightening my muscles after so many hours, and we went out into the snow-covered yard. We stopped in front of something that looked like a pigsty. The soldier opened the little wicket gate: "*Dawaj!*" he said. I stooped to enter the low shed and heard the gate padlocked behind me. Here I was, completely innocent, in a Soviet prison, right on the front line and amid a German offensive.

I lay down on the straw and closed my eyes, unable to think. It was after six in the evening and already very dark. The artillery sounded even louder than before. Probably Dombóvár was closer to the German lines than Kaposvár was.

Poor Lusia was waiting for me, worried and wondering what on earth could have happened. This was the first time since we left Kadarkút that I had been away at night.

How could she guess that I was imprisoned in Dombóvár, knowing I had gone to Kaposvár? I tried to move. I tried to stand up and my head hit the roof. Although the straw on the floor felt reasonably clean and dry, it smelled of pigs. The wicket gate was made of loose boards; after all, pigs need light and air, too. The night was freezing. I was shivering. I called a guard. After a while one appeared and I asked for a blanket [*harasho*], and after a few minutes he returned with an old army coat. I covered myself and felt a little better, not wanting to think of the fleas or lice it probably harbored.

I tried to sleep, but the thunder of artillery fire was too distressing. The front line must have been very close. Maybe the Germans had already broken through. What was poor Lusia doing? Still waiting, worried, and packed up ready to leave? Our Russians might have already gone and left her alone with our child and here I was, useless, locked up like a thief in this pigsty, with an armed guard marching to and fro outside my cage. What would tomorrow hold for me? Would the NKVD chief appear at all, or would he run away like Muraview in 1941, leaving me behind? Should I be fortunate enough to see him tomorrow, what would he do with me? Will he have time to interrogate me, or will he put me on a train and send me to a forced labor camp?

The Soviet Union always needed slave workers. The guard outside kept pacing. It was too cold for him to sit down. He would blow into the palms of his hands or keep hitting his arms against his back just like the peasants in Oserdów to keep warm. Poor fellow! The guards changed every two hours. They would point their torches through the gate slats right into my eyes, ensuring I was still there. Yes, I was still there, freezing.

It must have been around midnight when the gate opened, and two more men were thrown in. They were Hungarian gypsies, a father and son. Frightened, they could not stop trembling and crying. I tried but could not get any information out of them, yet I was quite glad to have company, some human beings, even though the pigsty was much too small for the three of us. We all had to lie in one direction, one close behind the other. It was impossible to turn over. However, I felt much warmer now that the gypsies' bodies were close to mine. Despite the constant exchange of artillery fire, I even fell asleep. The torch would wake me for a moment or so, but I would go back to sleep next to the snoring gypsies.

From time to time, they would wake up and cry bitterly, then they would go back to sleep, snoring heavily. In the morning, the gate was opened, and the gypsies left. I was alone again, sleepy, cold, and worried about myself, Lusia, and my child. The artillery started again. I began contemplating what fate would be best for me – the NKVD or the Germans. The NKVD would most probably send me to Siberia. What else could they do with a "German spy"? Would I survive there? And Lusia and Elżunia? If, on the other hand, the Germans broke the front line and found me locked up, they would set me free. It would be easy to convince them that a man imprisoned by the Russians could not possibly be their enemy.

It was early morning and nature was calling. I motioned to the guard to let me out. Naturally, there was no toilet. The soldier pointed his gun at a spot close to the fence. Despite the circumstances, I felt like laughing. Here I was with my pants down, bent most uncomfortably with my naked bottom just above the snow, and this Soviet guard was standing with his gun pointing at me! I asked whether he had a piece of paper. He looked at me in amazement. I should have known better. Paper, mainly old newspapers, was only used for rolling cigarettes and was a guarded treasure. At eight, I was called to the office. The officer-in-charge asked why I had been locked up.

"I have no idea," I said.

He kept searching through the papers on his desk but could find no report stating the charges against me. The soldiers who arrested me said I had been behaving suspiciously. I told my story to the NKVD officer and showed him my document, signed by Captain Warszawski. I also mentioned my wife and child back in Taszár.

Perhaps having other more important problems on his mind, he decided to release me. I caught a train almost straight away and reached Taszár within an hour. Just as I was alighting, I heard someone calling "*Mernok ur, mernok ur* [Mr. Engineer]!" It was the local postman, who told me that early this morning my wife had gone to Kaposvár to look for me. Instantly, I rushed after the already moving train and succeeded in jumping onto the last carriage. Short of breath, I fell onto a bench as the train reached full speed. I had to rush to Kaposvár to locate Lusia as quickly as possible so she wouldn't have to worry anymore. How happy I felt thinking of seeing her soon! How many women would have the courage to go looking for their husband in the midst of a German offensive, leaving their child behind with strangers? Looking for the husband who might already be locked up in a Soviet prison! It was nine a.m. when I reached Kaposvár. The first place I headed for was the military headquarters. The guard stopped me at the gate.

"I am looking for my wife," I explained.

He laughed, saying, "There was a woman in this morning looking for her husband, and now you are looking for your wife! Have you both gone mad?"

I was elated. It must have been Lusia. I asked when she had been there and where she had gone.

"It's none of my business, and you get out of here," reproached the guard.

I was sure that she would have next gone to the NKVD headquarters. Lusia was one of those people who always acted logically. She would doubt I had been in some kind of accident and would be certain I had been arrested. I could only be in two places – the military headquarters or the NKVD. I kept asking passing soldiers for directions to the NKVD headquarters. They looked at me with surprise. Whom could this fool be asking for the NKVD? Somehow, I got there at last. The guard had just taken over from the previous one. There might have been some woman looking for her husband, he said, but he did not know anything about it. After much pleading, he escorted me into the building and showed me the commanding officer's office. No one answered my knocking, so I opened the door. An officer was sitting behind the desk, dozing. He looked as if he had been drinking. When I shook his shoulders, he mumbled something. After shaking him harder, he opened one eye. In a loud voice, I asked: "Was there a woman here looking for her husband?"

"Yes, there was, but she left," he answered, then suddenly fully awake. "Who are you?"

"I am her husband," I said.

"Why did you desert your wife?" he asked before his head dropped onto the desk again.

As I was leaving, the guard asked, "Did you find your wife?"

"No!" was my reply.

"Don't worry," he said, "you will find another one."

Failing to find me, Lusia would by now have gone home, totally dejected. The artillery fire had started again. The wisest thing, I thought, was to return to Taszár. Anyway, there was nowhere else to look for Lusia. I rushed back to the station hoping to catch a train. If not, I would try my luck at hitchhiking on a Soviet truck. Nervous and excited, I looked around for the Russian stationmaster. Suddenly I realized that I had to get a hold of myself or I would find myself behind bars again. Very calmly, I asked about the next train to Taszár. He informed me that "trains ran irregularly in the present situation," pointing in the direction of the artillery. "The last train," he said, "has just left."

I emphasized that I had urgent business for my detachment. When I showed him my papers, he scratched his head for a moment, mentioning that a special train carrying a general to the front would be leaving soon but would not stop at Taszár. Indeed, a few minutes later, a locomotive with only one carriage arrived. A young officer standing on the steps took some papers from another officer of the platform. I rushed toward him and repeated my story. The officer glanced at my papers, then at me. "Dawaj," he said, letting me onto the steps of the carriage. I could hardly believe my luck. Since there were no stops between Kaposvár and Taszár, the ride would take some 20 minutes. Unbelievable but true, the train slowed down right before Taszár, enabling me to jump out, to the astonishment of the Hungarian stationmaster, who knew the train was not supposed to carry any civilians. It was now 11. I reached the village in no time and quickly headed home.

I still had about one kilometer to walk. There were no Soviet soldiers about. The villagers were standing in front of their houses talking. When they spotted me, they stopped their conversations, smiled happily, and greeted me warmly. Some approached me and shook my hand. Obviously, they must have heard about my disappearance and seemed happy to see me. "Thank God, thank God," they kept saying in Hungarian. Right in front of our house, I met our hosts, the Baycsys. The husband, always so reserved and composed, embraced me now. His wife raised her hands and excitedly rushed into the house to convey the good news to Lusia. In an instant I found myself in our little room, embracing Lusia, while Elżunia stood behind, awaiting her turn. To my astonishment, I saw tears rolling down Mrs. Baycsy's cheeks.

My first question was about the Russians. A silly question – I could see what happened. The house was empty, and the soldiers and trucks were gone. Early in the morning, the Russians had received their orders and left. They had offered to take Lusia and our child, but she refused.

She told me what occurred the day before. Since I had left for Kaposvár early in the morning, she had been expecting me back at lunchtime. When I did not return, she understood that something serious must have happened. Scared and worried, she counted every passing minute. Hours went by. The news of my disappearance spread quickly and reached the local priest, whom we had never met. At the request of the villagers, he opened the church to conduct a special mass to pray for my return. When the bells started tolling at this odd hour, all villagers – men and women in their sheepskin coats – headed toward the church. The Baycsys offered to take Lusia, and Lusia felt she had to go. She put on her old winter coat and army boots and a warm shawl that Mrs. Baycsy had lent her. The bells tolled solemnly, and the pounding of the artillery could be heard far away. When they entered the church, the people rose respectfully, while Lusia and the

Baycsys were ushered to their seats in the first row – Mr. Baycsy on one side of Lusia, Mrs. Baycsy on the other.

Six months ago, Mrs. Baycsy had been reluctant to sell Lusia a pint of milk and Mr. Baycsy would not even look at her. Yet on this day, kneeling before God, they prayed for my safe return. Sitting in the front row watching the priest, dressed in his special chasuble, conducting this special mass, Lusia could not help thinking how unreal the whole situation was. Under different circumstances, she would probably have been laughing. Now she sat quietly, shedding tears of deep despair.

When she arrived back home, she found an unexpected guest. One of the Russian officers was sitting at the table waiting. The Russians, too, had heard the news of my disappearance. They knew I had been detained by the Russian police. For them, this was a common occurrence; people often disappeared from their homes, farms, and the streets, not to return for years – if at all. Oh, yes, they knew how it was. Now Lusia's visitor had come to cheer her up. He asked for a cup of tea, which Lusia could not refuse to give. With a gentle smile, he reached into his pocket and took out a bag of sugar. "It's for you," he said. He was trying to be friendly.

He didn't even try to conceal his intentions. Lusia kept telling him that she had a husband and a child and was not interested in anyone else. He was trying to convince her that her husband was gone and she would never see him again and that he liked her and would look after her and the child. In civilian life, he said, he managed a *kolkhoz*, had a nice house, was earning good money, and had food in abundance.

The officer was one of those who had been friendly with us and promised to take us if they had to retreat from Taszár. He must have welcomed my disappearance. Why not? No harm in trying. He pulled out a bottle of vodka, inviting Lusia to join him. She refused, but he started drinking slowly. Lusia was alarmed, not only worried about me but scared of this drunken admirer, and yet she could not just run away and leave her sleeping child behind. She continued drinking her tea, trying to appear at ease.

Suddenly, someone knocked at the door. It was Klos, our newly acquired Polish acquaintance. Never had she shown him so much hospitality as on that evening. There was tea on the table and the sugar that the officer had given her. She treated him to a glass of wine, whispering in Polish to let him know that she was in trouble and asking him to stay. Time passed, and Klos was ready to leave. He was nearly falling asleep on his chair, but she would not let him go. At last, the Russian realized it was no use waiting. He yawned loudly, rose from his chair, and left. Right after him, Klos went, too.

Completely exhausted, Lusia locked the door behind them. "As you can well imagine, I could not sleep all night," she said. "Various thoughts raced through my mind. I was pretty sure you'd been arrested. After all, you'd gone to Kaposvár for some news and would probably arouse suspicion asking all those questions. I decided to look for you, hoping to get you out.

"Early in the morning, I told the Baycsys about my plan. Although they did not believe there was any chance of success, they offered me their cart. To find a driver was not easy; people were afraid. Tibor, for whom I had arranged a butcher's job with the Soviets, volunteered, perhaps out of gratitude for all those meat cuts he had been collecting for months. The Russians were quite generous. In Kaposvár, we went first to the military command. A few minutes passed until they let me see the officer-on-duty. He was quite polite, even helpful, although rather surprised. No one had been arrested, he said, but suggested I inquire with the NKVD. He did not know the address, though, or maybe he did not want to tell me. He indicated the general direction and that was enough.

"When I arrived, the guard at the gate stopped me and, although surprised, listened to my story. At long last, he beckoned me inside and I was shown into the commanding officer's office. I knocked on the door, but no one answered. I opened the door to a darkened room. Someone was sitting behind the desk, sleeping. I could hear him snoring. I tried to wake him, shaking his arm and calling, *Towarysz naczalnik, towarysz naczalnik* [Comrade commandant, comrade commandant]!" He stopped snoring, opened one eye for a moment, and closed it quickly, trying to go back to sleep. I kept shaking him until he was awake. He looked at me with surprise and asked me who I was. I explained my reason for being here. He was smiling. 'You are looking for your husband?' I said that you had gone away on business for the Soviet air force the day before but had not returned yet. He thought you were drunk and the police had locked you up. He asked your name and I told hi – Petro Daraż. He did not recall anyone by that name but said a man could have been looked up without his knowledge. He suggested we go and find out. Along the corridor, he opened a few doors flashing his torch. '*Smatry* [Look].' Some poor fellow was woken up, but it was not you. I thanked him and left. Arriving back in Taszár, I found the Soviets had left."

Now it was my turn to tell Lusia of my adventure.

With the Soviets gone, we faced a new situation. Our decision had been made some time ago that under no circumstances were we going to fall into German hands. We were determined to leave Taszár. We expressed our concern to the Baycsys, but they could not understand our fears. They strongly believed nothing would happen to us after all that we had done for the village. It was impossible that anyone would report us. Indeed, the villagers loved us. Nevertheless, we decided to leave. I only asked one favor – to give us their children's sled. It would make it easier for us to move –easier for our child, and we could take some food and belongings. The farmers watching our procession looked on in disbelief at Lusia in her army shoes holding Elżunia's hand and me pulling the fully laden sled. Of course, we could not take all our "treasures" – just a few packets of cigarettes, some sulfidin, and some food the Baycsys had given us. The rest of our belongings were packed in a bag and left under the bed in our room. A big container with lard (a present from the Russians), the remaining cigarettes, sulfidin injections, the typewriter, a calculator, and a few other items – all of these valuables were left in Taszár. I had written a note and stuck it on the bag, stating that the bag belonged to Lieutenant Petro Daraż from Red Army Unit No. 12023 (this number was on my document) and that he would pick it up after returning from leave. I put a similar note on the door of our room and left the key with the Baycsys, telling them that as soon as the military situation was clarified we would be back. They were sorry to see us leave, undoubtedly also fearing for their own security without our protection. After all, a lot of Soviet soldiers were still in the area and the possibility of a nightly visit by some marauders was still terrifying. We walked slowly through the village. Fresh snow had just fallen. It was difficult to pull the heavy sled. The sun shone strongly, and we felt very hot. Soon, we left the village behind and reached the highway.

My plan was to catch a lift to Dombóvár, followed by a lift to Baja, a large town on the other side of the Danube. Once we crossed the river, we would feel safe. Exhausted, we reached the highway and waited on the snow-covered roadside for a lift to Dombóvár. Elżunia was sitting on the sled, while Lusia and I stood leaning against a tree. Another chapter of our flight had come to an end. Behind us was Taszár, the village where we had spent six relatively peaceful months. Ahead of us was a new, unknown tomorrow.

CROSSING THE DANUBE

The road was unusually empty. From time to time a car would pass by, or a truck full of soldiers. We patiently stood there waiting for the next truck. A seemingly empty vehicle was approaching. It could be our chance. I stepped into the middle of the road, waving my arms. The Russian truck slowed down and stopped. Yes, the driver was going to Dombóvár and would take us. Lusia sat beside him (she wanted to make sure I did not talk too much again), and I climbed with Elżunia into the back, taking the sled with us. After a hectic half-hour drive, we reached Dombóvár.

The town was busy; transports of soldiers were heading in all directions. The market square was full of trucks and still more Soviet soldiers. I started to search for a truck going to Baja. It was freezing cold and Elżunia was crying. At last, I found a Russian truck driver who was willing to take us. Again, Lusia sat in the front, Elżunia and I in the back.

The driver was happy he had someone with whom to chat. The journey lasted nearly three hours. We passed trucks full of soldiers and heavy tanks in groups of five or six. The Russians were obviously preparing themselves for the defense of the "wedge." We were happy we had left Taszár and hoped to reach the other side of the Danube soon, where we imagined the Russians were well established. There would be peace and quiet. If there was to be a battle around Taszár, let it happen without us.

Soon, more and more tanks appeared. Their numbers increased as we moved closer toward Baja. And they were huge! I had never imagined that tanks could be so enormous. Our truck stopped. The driver had reached his destination and we had to get off. We could see the towers of some churches and roofs of higher buildings two or three kilometers away. We were at Baja. Yet the beautiful and powerful Danube, covered with ice and snow, separated us from the town. We could see trucks and carts crossing the river. The ice must have been strong enough, so there was hope.

All around us were tanks, only tanks. Heaven forbid a German attack! Such a huge concentration of Russian armor was an easy and attractive target. My only wish was to get out of there as quickly as possible. Harnessed to two beautiful horses, a sleigh came by, driven by a young Russian soldier who was hardly able to restrain them as we spoke. Yes, he would take us across the river to Baja.

Quickly we threw our belongings onto the sleigh. Elżunia was thrilled. It was the first time in her life she had ridden on a sleigh with horses and bells tinkling. In half an hour, we were in Baja, alone again in the midst of a strange city.

Where to go? Where to look for shelter, if only for the first night? Knock on doors? Who will let us in? A Hungarian? By now, we knew the Hungarians only too well. There was only one place to go – the synagogue. We might find some help there. It took us some time to locate the deserted building. A passerby told us of a Jew who lived nearby, so we found ourselves at the front door of a small house with a mezuzah[1] on the door frame. It was already getting dark. We knocked for some time before a voice asked who we were and what we wanted. Lusia did the talking, and after some manipulations of the locks, the door opened slightly.

A pair of frightened eyes looked at us. The man answered no, we could not stay. He had just returned from a forced-labor camp and found his family deported. He had no food, not even fuel to start the fire. He gave us the address of another Jew who had a bigger house and would probably have room to take us in. With that, he locked the door.

At the other house, the response was much the same. First a long silence, then the slow releasing of numerous locks: *No*. No room for us.

Unfortunately, the Hungarian Jews hadn't changed. Every time we were given a new address, we got the same reply. Finally, someone mentioned a Polish Jew who he thought could help us. He gave us directions and vaguely described the house. All the people we had approached thus far were men, just recently returned from the labor camps only to find their houses empty, their wives and children deported.

It started to snow. It was getting colder and we were getting wearier, particularly after our sleepless nights. We resumed our search, this time for the house of the Polish Jew. An old Hungarian woman was just closing her gate when Lusia made inquiries. Yes, she knew the Polish family and pointed at a big house opposite hers. We knocked gently on the door. Then again, a little bit harder. There was silence, but after another knock, we could hear some movement.

A male voice asked in Hungarian, "*Ki az* [Who is it]?"

Lusia answered, "We are refugees from Poland and have been told that a Pole lives here."

"Please wait a minute," the voice answered in Polish, which sounded like music to our ears.

Some time passed before the door opened and we entered, our coats covered with snow, pulling the Baycsys' sleigh in behind us. A young, good-looking man, about 25, ushered us inside and quickly locked the door, first with the key, then with a chain and some other complex security devices. He explained that Soviet soldiers used to break into houses, so it was necessary to take precautions. There were two women in the room, a lady of around 60 and her daughter in her mid-30s. They were just having dinner. The room was brightly lit. The young man looked at us in silence. When his eyes reached Elżunia, we noticed the tears welling. The women, although surprised by this unexpected visit, were most friendly. Strangely perhaps, we felt at home with this family.

We began to converse in Polish! What a relief it was to be able to speak and hear our beautiful language again! The young man introduced himself as Edward Stimler, a lawyer from Dobczyce (a small town near Kraków). The younger lady was a teacher from Warsaw, Wanda Latoszynska, and with her was her mother. A washbowl with hot water, soap, and fresh towels appeared in no time. There were spare chairs for us at the dinner table.

Edward did not rest until he seemed to have put all the food that was in their house on the table. There was plenty of fresh bread, butter, honey and cheese, a piece of cold meat, and sausage. We were given a bowl of hot soup – our first hot food in two days. Our hosts watched while we ate. Edward kept stroking Elżunia's hair, encouraging her to eat: "*Jed dziecko, jedz* [Eat, my child, eat]!" Soon, lollies and chocolates appeared. Then came the time for questions. We told our story of our escape from the front line up to the previous night. Our hosts were refugees, too.

Edward had escaped from the ghetto in Bochnia, where he had lost all his family – his parents and three brothers. Wanda and her mother and sister had run away from Warsaw. In Hungary, they had stayed in various camps for Polish refugees. They had met there by chance, and since then Edward had taken care of them. After the liberation, Edward, a very smart young man, had taken over the house, abandoned by its owners in Baja.

Speaking both Russian and Hungarian quite well, Edward had become friendly with some Russians at the army hospital and helped them with supplies – a career similar to my own in Taszár. It was very late at night when we finished talking. After that, the only thing I remember was a deep, uninterrupted sleep for many hours.

The cannonade of the German artillery was heard no more. Edward seemed well informed about the military situation. The Soviet army had already taken Pest, but the Germans were still trying to hold Buda in order to join up with their ten divisions in Yugoslavia. The German offensive was continuing amid heavy fighting. The military hospital in Baja was full of wounded. We were happy to have found shelter in the relatively safe town of Baja, far from the front line. We stayed in Edward's house for a few days. Every day, new supplies of food filled the cupboards. Edward was constantly bringing something home, including sweets for Elżunia.

We offered our cigarettes in a humble attempt to contribute to our board, but Edward wouldn't accept. He had good contacts in the hospital and, in exchange for some medical supplies, would obtain all sorts of food. After a few days, the Soviet High Command announced that the Red Army had crossed the Danube along the whole front and taken Buda, surrounding the ten German divisions in Yugoslavia, and were now heading toward the Austrian border. Surely, the war was practically over and the Nazi nightmare had finally come to an end. It was February 1945.

Hearing of the liberation of Budapest, I thought of going there in hopes of finding some friends who may have survived the heavy fighting. At first, Lusia did not want me to go but finally agreed, understanding we could not stay with Edward forever. There would surely be some committees in Budapest that would take care of us. If there was no possibility of moving to Budapest, we would go back, although only temporarily, to Taszár, where some friendly people, the Baycsys, were waiting for us.

Early in the morning, with a knapsack full of food, I set off for the Budapest highway. I had a few addresses with me of people we met in February-March 1944. It did not take me long to find a Russian truck to take me to Budapest. It was cold but sunny. I lay in the back of the truck, covered with an old army coat, excited at the thought that I might find some friends.

After three hours' drive, the truck slowed down. We had reached the outskirts of Budapest. It was a horrible sight – ruins everywhere. I remembered Warsaw after the German attack in 1939, but that was not comparable. During that half-hour drive toward the city center, I saw blocks of flats and houses totally destroyed, streets covered with rubble.

We stopped and, with the heavy knapsack on my back, I went in search of my first address. It took a long while to find, and when I did, all I saw were ruins. The same with the next address. Since there were neither buses nor trams, I had to walk. Before long I started to feel very tired, regretting I had ever set off on this trip. I should have listened to Lusia. Still, now I had to go on.

Slowly, I dragged myself to yet another address. By this time, it was around four in the afternoon, and if I found only ruins again, I would have to look for shelter in the basement of a bombed house. I was too exhausted to continue any further.

But I was lucky. Although partly damaged, the building still stood. I asked the caretaker about my friend Dombek and, to my delight, he pointed to a door. I knocked and Dombek appeared. It was wonderful for both of us. I opened my knapsack and invited him to lunch. While eating, he told me all he knew about our mutual friends. Some of them had been killed by the Hungarian Nazis (the Green Arrow brigades), while others had perished during the bombing. When I asked about the Habers, not really expecting any information, he told me they were alive and lived down the street. I couldn't believe my ears. When I repeated my question, he said, "Sure. Three houses away, at number four."

I couldn't wait any longer and rushed there. The landlady told me they had left not long ago, but she did not know when they would be back. I waited for some time, but they did not return. Before I left, I wrote a short note and went back to Dombek to finish my meal. I imagined their joy in reading my message.

It was getting dark. The huge entrance door was already locked, and no one responded to my knocking. I could not see a bell and was standing there when a Russian officer arrived and pulled a string that I had not noticed before. After a short while, the door opened. Both of us hesitated for a second, then I politely stood back to let him enter.

"Pozalusta," Russian for "please," I said, never dreaming what consequences that simple "pozalusta" could have for me. The officer stopped, looking at me with an expression I knew only too well.

"And who are you? Russian?"

"No, Polish," I answered.

"Where do you live?"

I truthfully replied that I lived in Baja but had come to visit my friends in Budapest. He looked at me suspiciously; there must have been something he did not like. He stood there thinking for a second, and suddenly he said, "Daway!" and took me into the building next door, number eight. A guard at the entrance stood at attention. We entered the building. He relaxed, but I was quite bewildered. The room we entered was full of soldiers.

Some were sitting on benches, others on the floor. Some were asleep and snoring loudly; others were talking. There was a nauseating smell of sweaty, unwashed bodies, and tobacco. The officer gave an order to a soldier and left. The men were looking at me with interest. Some asked what I had done. "I have no idea," I said. I asked myself if it could have been my innocent pozalusta. Anyway, it was no use telling them about it. A soldier took charge. He asked me to take my coat and jacket off, emptied my pockets, and carefully examined my clothes, trouser pockets, shoes, and socks. All my possessions were placed on a large, once-white piece of cloth, At my request, he left my handkerchief and watch. I sat on the bench, annoyed and furious, Such a stupid incident!

By now it was about seven in the evening. I felt hungry and asked for something to eat. I was given a bowl of thick pea soup, which was obviously what I had smelled on entering the room. I ate my soup with a piece of dark army bread, enjoying it greatly. I always liked thick pea soup.

The soldiers watched me; they were not so much interested in me as in my watch, a Swiss "Eterna" I had bought when we crossed Slovakia in 1944. They seemed to like it. "A good watch," they kept saying.

"Why don't you sell it? How much do you want?" one of them asked.

"Sell it to me," said another. "You won't need it anymore!"

Despite the whole situation, somehow I was not nervous. What could they have against me? Not spying for the Germans again? I had been in a similar situation twice before and each time I had managed to get out of it. I had to make it this time, too. Pity I could not sit down and talk to the Habers. There was so much I wanted to tell them, so much I wanted to hear.

"Daway," the soldier said in a friendly tone. The building consisted of three stories. It was a typical European type of block of flats with a gangway at the rear. We entered the top-floor gangway and the soldier opened a door. As a rule, there was a little closet where the caretaker used to keep his cleaning equipment – this was it.

Small and cold, the floor covered with straw, the place was dark with just a small glazed-in opening in the door. I asked the soldier for some blankets. He came back with an old military coat and a blanket, locked the door, and left.

Once again, I was under arrest. How ridiculous! I lay down and tried to think. It was too early to sleep, only eight. I was thinking about Lusia and Elżunia, whom I had left in Baja. At least they were under the care of some good, friendly people, safe and far away from the battlefield. My Budapest friends, the Habers and Dombek, were probably wondering what could have happened to me within the distance of only four houses! How could they imagine that I was right here, locked up by the Russian secret police? Slowly, I fell asleep. The guard in front of my door was changed every two hours. I knew the routine only too well. The light of his torch kept waking me every two hours. Still, I managed to catch some sleep.

Somehow, I got through the night. Around seven in the morning, I woke up and slowly rose from the floor to straighten up. I looked through the spyhole. It was already daylight. Another dull frosty morning. On the bench outside, I could see a soldier, apparently asleep. I was curious – who was guarding me? A Russian, Mongolian, or Ukrainian soldier?

I wanted to talk, get some information, do something. I knocked lightly on the door, and he turned in my direction. I saw the profile of a young, maybe 20-year-old man. His face was delicate. The nose was rather big and crooked. Jewish? I knocked again. With my face close to the window, I said, "*Shalom.*" His reaction was instantaneous surprise. My guess was right. Guards were forbidden to communicate with prisoners, but his curiosity was stronger than the rules. He was sitting with his back as close to the door as possible. We started a conversation in a mixture of Russian and Yiddish. He came from Bessarabia, a province that prior to World War I was part of Russia, afterward of Romania, and was annexed by the Soviet Union in 1939. During the German occupation, he was in a forced-labor camp. After the liberation, he was called up to the Soviet army. He had lost his family and was hoping eventually to immigrate to Palestine, where a few of his relatives lived. He was depressed, knowing there was little hope for him to obtain permission to emigrate. He asked where I came from. When he heard I was from Lwów, he smiled.

"At eight o'clock," he said, "a Jew from Lwów is going to guard you. His name is Jacob; we call him Yankel." I asked him not to mention anything about me to Jacob – I wanted to surprise him and enjoy watching his reaction. I realized that I still felt like having fun despite my absurd situation. My instinct kept telling me that somehow, one way or another, I would get out of this trouble. Much depended on the person who was going to interrogate me. I asked my guard about the man. He told me that the officer who had arrested me was firm, unapproachable, and antisemitic. All my night guards were Jews. Guard duty was hated by the soldiers, so why not employ the Jews for the job?

My conversation finished, I lay down on the floor feeling dirty, thirsty, cold, and miserable. My usual optimism was overcome by anxiety. Well, what will be, will be. The guard changed at eight as expected. After a few minutes, I approached the small window in the door. Another young man was sitting on the bench just staring ahead. I knocked. He moved but did not turn toward me. "Good morning, Jankiel," I said in Polish. I could imagine how surprised he must be. At first, he did not say anything. We started talking. He told me his story. Right after the liberation of Lwów, the Russians allowed him no rest; he was put in a uniform immediately. He and his sister had miraculously survived and she also joined the army, where there was food and clothing. I realized how wise it had been not to have disclosed that I was from Lwów because, surely, I would have been forced to join the army and fight for the Soviet motherland. I was also right not to have disclosed I was Jewish. Instinctively, I felt I better for not having done so. There was no need for it. On numerous occasions, listening to sarcastic remarks, I realized that the Russians' attitude toward Jews was not too friendly. All those Jews who after the liberation had revealed their origin had regretted doing so. I remembered Tolstykow telling me that Jews in the army had special guns, bent at a 90-degree angle. "They shoot around corners," he said – an inference to the cowardice imputed to the Jews by antisemites. The revolution had not changed the Russian people's attitudes. This guard feared his superior officer and was not too optimistic about my future.

At nine in the morning, a soldier ordered me out of my cell to follow him to building number ten, the one where Dombek lived. On the first floor, in a cozy warm flat, the officer who had arrested me the previous night was waiting. My guard remained outside. He ordered me to sit down, looking at me with unfriendly curiosity. The flat had once been owned by well-to-do Hungarians and was full of antique furniture, carpets, and paintings.

On the desk, in front of the officer, I could see the bundle containing my belongings. "Who are you, and why are you here?" he asked. He was staring at me. An intelligent look. I decided to answer as truthfully as I could. I would be in real trouble if he caught me in any lies. Everything had to be the truth – except my Jewish origin.

But how could I explain my escape from Poland? Illegally crossing two borders? As a Jew, I might have had good reason, but as a non-Jew? I decided to admit that Lusia was half-Jewish. That would make some sense. I told him that her looks, the comments of our neighbors, and then an anonymous letter making threats put us in danger. So, we ran from Warsaw to Polish Carpathian country, where we had some relatives. We met a smuggler there who agreed to take us over the border into Hungary, where we thought life would be better. Since we had no proper documents, the Hungarians put us in a camp, where we were sent to work at the Taszár airfield. The Red Army liberated us there. Right from the beginning, I had volunteered to work as an interpreter and help provide the unit with supplies. During the recent German counteroffensive, we moved on to Baja. Being active in my collaboration with the Russians, I was afraid of the Hungarians as well as the approaching Germans. I had come to Budapest yesterday for a few days only, to look for my friends and supply them with some food. I had found two families. One lived in this very house where I had left my rucksack, the other just two buildings away. He could ask them to check whether I was telling the truth. I was a Polish citizen, a devoted worker for the Soviets since liberation, had not committed any crime, and did not understand why I had been kept in the cell for the whole night.

While I was telling my story, he unpacked my bundle. First, he looked at the document issued by Captain Warszawski, confirming that I, Peter Daraż, had worked as a supplies officer. It was my identity card, the only document in Russian, with my photograph attached and stamped with the Soviet army's round seal – my most important and precious document. After studying it carefully, he stated that the document was false! How could Captain Warszawski confirm that the person in the photograph and you are the same? How could he know that you and Peter Daraż are the same person?

How right he was! I was most upset when I saw him tear the document to pieces and throw it into a bin. He said that if Captain Warszawski had indeed signed those documents, he must have been a fool and as such should have been reduced in rank. Although most unhappy to see my document destroyed, I had to admire his reasoning.

The next thing he found was the letter from the Bulgarian blacksmith. He read it and asked in a threatening tone, "What is this?" "I brought the letter to Budapest in the hope that I would meet a Bulgarian soldier who would send it on." I told him the whole story. He listened carefully and felt he believed me.

"Who, in times like these," he shouted, "would play postman between the Russian and Bulgarian armies?" He only said one word, "*Durak* [Stupid]!" and tore the letter to pieces. He was right again.

The next thing was money. I had with me Soviet rubles, Hungarian prewar pengős, Hungarian occupation notes issued by the Russian military authorities, prewar Yugoslav dinars, occupation notes issued by the Russians in Yugoslavia, and the $50 note I had hidden in my trousers. He couldn't conceal his agitation. "What is this?" he snapped. I explained that before we left Poland, we had some Polish money. Since the Polish złoty had no value outside Poland and dollars could be used everywhere, everything we possessed at that time was exchanged into dollars. He examined the Soviet currency next – the so-called *czerwiency* – three ten-ruble notes. Using it outside the Soviet Union was an offense. He asked in a sharp tone where I had gotten them. I explained truthfully that it belonged to a friendly Russian officer who had asked me to buy him something. He could not leave Taszár and had no chance of doing any shopping. The occupation rubles were given to me for the same purpose. The Yugoslav money was given to me by another officer who, after his unit crossed into Hungary from Yugoslavia, had found them in his pocket. They were now of no value to him and suggested I might be able to buy something for him, anything. The prewar Hungarian pengos were saved from my wages earned when working at the airfield. He listened without comment, then rising from his chair, he left the room.

I took the chance to look around. In the corner of the room, I saw several boxes with shoes, sheets of leather, a few lengths of fabric for men's suits, and colorful material for women's dresses – quite a pile in fact. My mood improved. This officer, like those I used to know, was speculating, buying in Budapest and selling in Russia. A black marketeer!

He came back, sat down, and looked at me with his penetrating gaze. We know everything about you," he burst out. "You are a German spy. You live on the front line to spy on the movements of our units. At the airfield, you watch the location of our aircraft. Then you come to Budapest where you have your accomplices and from there you send out intelligence through a radio." He was watching me triumphantly. He knew everything! I was struck dumb.

What should I say to that? On the tip of my tongue, I had

something like, "And you, the hero, are sitting here, safe, far away from the battlefield, speculating with leather goods and fabrics while your comrades are giving their lives for Mother Russia." However, such words would have been not only insolent but stupid. So I sat looking at him for a few seconds before I answered, slowly choosing my words: "And you, Comrade Lieutenant, are planning the assassination of Comrade Stalin."

The Comrade Lieutenant nearly jumped out of his skin. He looked at me, startled: "*Ty surria zayshol* [You are crazy]!" he gasped.

"You are crazy, too," I replied calmly. "Everything that I have told you about me and my family – our escape from the Germans – all that was true. And you accuse me of spying for the Germans! Such an accusation has as much truth in it as mine that you are planning to assassinate Comrade Stalin. Yes, I accuse you of that. Your intentions I can see in your eyes."

At this moment, my courage left me. Indeed, I might be crazy. He could easily force me to plead guilty. I remembered the famous Moscow trials of 1934 where the fathers of the revolution – old Bolsheviks, members of the Politburo, army generals – all accused of being foreign agents – had pleaded guilty of treason and went before the firing squads. I could see myself in the Soviet court or in the infamous *Lubianka* that housed Russia's security services. Silently, I awaited my verdict. Looking at me with amazement, he did not utter one word. He had not expected such a reaction from his prisoner.

Slowly, he collected my belongings, wallet, pocketknife, cigarettes, and all the Yugoslav, Hungarian, and American money and pushed them toward me across the desk. "Take them!" he said. I sighed with relief. I had won this battle. He was not looking at me anymore. He had returned everything except the Soviet money. I asked him to give it back to me since it was not mine, and I did not want the Russian officer to think that I had misappropriated it. "Tell your friend," he said, "that he is not allowed to carry this money outside the Soviet Union and he will be in trouble if he has more." The Soviet rubles remained on the desk. Obviously, he was allowed to have them!

He got up, opened the door, signaled to the guard to let me go, and closed the door without a word. I was free. Free again, I rushed to Dombek first, then to the Habers. They had been worried about my sudden disappearance and were greatly relieved at seeing me. I told them what happened. (For years afterward, Haber would tell the story of my disappearance in a Soviet prison caused by one friendly word: *pozalusta*.)

The contents of my rucksack were received with great excitement since the food shortage in Budapest was still acute. There seemed no end to our conversation. The Habers had their story of their escape from the transport that had been carrying them to Auschwitz. For all of us, that fear was now over.

After my return to Baja, we decided to go back to Taszár as we did not want to be a burden to Edward Stimler any longer. I could not see any chance of earning money and moving to Budapest was still too premature. Luckily, we had the alternative of Taszár, where we had a warm and secure place to stay, as much food as we needed, and would not burden our landlords. We knew the Baycsys would be only too happy to have us back; our help in handling the unexpected Soviet "guests" would always be appreciated.

We returned to Taszár at the end of March. The Baycsys were indeed delighted to see us again. Our room was waiting for us – even the note we had left on the door was still untouched. As before, various Russians were visiting the village, and every time a pig or calf would disappear. Some of the Russians who had been stationed there before were still in the village. Captain Warszawski gladly issued me a new identity card, this time without a photograph.

The officers who had given me the money for shopping received it back. They were disappointed when I told them that all the shops in Budapest were as empty as everywhere else. The officer who gave me the Soviet rubles had left. The one who had proposed to Lusia had gone, too. So had Tolstykow. I was sorry not to see him again. Artillery fire was not heard anymore. The front was by now far away, deep in the Third Reich. We lived from day to day, a safe but rather boring existence. Weeks passed. There in Taszár, we were cut off from the world. The war was coming to an end. It was high time for us to make a move, so we decided to go to Budapest.

LEAVING TASZÁR

It was a bright morning and we collected our belongings, including a can of lard (about 25 kilos, a gift from the Soviets), said farewell to Taszár, and left for Baja.

The journey this time was peaceful. It was early spring 1945. We found Stimler and the two ladies in good health and quite excited since they, too, had decided to leave Baja and go to Budapest. After a few days in their company, we were left alone. Edward left us whatever food he had collected but could not take with him. Dear Edward, we knew he could have easily sold it.

Not knowing anyone in town, it was difficult to arrange our daily life. I still had some Hungarian cigarettes, but even though they were in great demand, I could not risk selling them to strangers. I also had about ten boxes of sulfur ampules, and no doubt there were many potential buyers in Baja, but how could I find them? My Hungarian was still rather poor. Besides, I did not want to make any contact with strangers. Although I had some black-market experience acquired under the German and Soviet occupation, the Hungarians were different people altogether. Jews or not, they kept away from any illegal activities. They were simply afraid. As we had no money, I had to act.

One day, collecting my courage, I went to the local chemist to ask if he would buy a box of sulfur injections. He looked at me with suspicion, then examined the box carefully. I could see he was interested, but finally he decided no. He was afraid.

I left the shop feeling desperate when a young woman in a Russian uniform, who was in the shop when I'd been talking to the chemist, surprised me. She had seen the two boxes of sulfur injections, she said, and needed them for a patient in the hospital where she was a nurse. She seemed genuinely friendly, so I took her home and gave her two boxes in exchange for some sugar and a few American cans of meat. I suggested that if she ever needed some more sulfur, I could supply it. She was interested and we arranged the next visit when she would bring more food, coffee, tea, and sweets for Elżunia. I was delighted. I had established contact with a Russian hospital just by chance.

The next morning, I met my new acquaintance again. She was walking along our street, peering into every window. Since it had been quite dark on her first visit, she did not seem to recognize the house. She seemed extremely happy when she saw me. Two officers accompanied her, and all three entered our house. The higher-ranking officer asked politely about sulfidin, which he needed and for which he was ready to pay a good price. He was a doctor, and the nurse had told him I had eight boxes. He wanted to see them. There was nothing unusual in his manner, so I was happy to have found such a good client and took the boxes out. As soon as he had the drugs in his hands, he began to ask questions: "Where did you get this medication?" "How much did you pay for it?" "Why are you here in Hungary?" "Why aren't you going back to Poland?" "Where do you get the money to live on?"

He concluded that I had been speculating, which was forbidden in the Soviet Union. He confiscated my sulfur for the hospital and advised that I could complain to the military command if I wanted. I pleaded with him, telling my story of how I had to leave Poland with my wife and child, that I had to live somehow, and that a chemist friend had given me them as a present. But the officer was adamant; he would not return my boxes. He assured me the authorities would honor his receipt. He asked for paper and wrote a statement similar to those I had already seen many times while living under the Soviets in Lwów. Every theft by Russian managers, supervisors, directors, and others was always "legalized" by issuing such a document. The completed document was signed by the two officers, who asked me to sign it as well. Usually, a statement like this would be in duplicate. This one was not. We all knew I would not go to the Commandatura and expose myself to awkward questions or unnecessary investigations. My precious sulfur injections disappeared into their bags, but the officers had no intention of leaving just yet.

They asked if I had watches for sale. Angrily, I said I did not.

"Maybe the one you are wearing?" they asked. They offered to pay well for it.

"This is my watch and it is not for sale," I said.

"Let us listen to how it works." (By holding it to the ear, the Russians usually would assess the value of a watch.) But I refused. To give them the watch to listen to would mean saying goodbye to it for good.

"Perhaps you would like to buy one?" one of them asked, revealing five or six hidden under his sleeve, plus a few more from his pocket. They admired those treasures, excited like children, and invited me to have a closer look. I did not want to offend them, so I took one or two and inspected them, all the time afraid they would use force to take my watch. Luckily, Lusia, uneasy about the lengthy visit, entered the room and asked if they would care for a cup of tea. Feeling disturbed, they quickly collected their watches and my sulfur and left. I never saw them again.

One day, I met that nurse in the street again. There was reproach in my voice when I asked her how she could have brought such "clients" who unscrupulously had deprived me, a poor refugee, a citizen of a sister country, of my only means of support. She said apologetically that she had not known they would do something like that and assured me she had not received a single kopeck out of it. I did not believe a word!

The incident reminded me of what used to happen in Lwów. Aware that speculation and stealing were rife in all strata of Soviet life, the Soviets had established a system of dual management – a director and an accountant – each to control the other. Every document needed both signatures. To steal, both parties had to collaborate. I remember one of our mills had a few pigs fed by its waste. With Christmas approaching, the director and the accountant would sign a statement that a pig had become ill and, to avoid spreading disease, they had to kill it. To take additional precautions, there usually was a veterinary surgeon willing to sign the necessary certificate in return for a share of the spoils.

When purchasing goods required by the mill on the black market, the individuals would draw up a document justifying the purchase – an additional amount of rubles added to the black-market price to then be split among the supplier, intermediary, and signatories. "*Dokument sostawien wtom ca* [This document certifies that]" was the standard start of the statement.

I recalled occasions when I had to sign documents relating to repair work at the mills stating that the established costs given by various contractors were reasonable. I could only guess what the actual deal between the mill directors and the contractors was. Those generous donations of flour probably had something to do with my signatures. Judging from my current experience with my Soviet clients, the system was still flourishing.

Having no friends, we felt very lonely, totally cut off from the rest of the world. I made another trip to Budapest in search of the latest news (but this time decided to keep my mouth shut) and learned of some developments concerning Polish Jews. The new Polish government had established a repatriation commission to organize the return of all Polish citizens deported by the Germans all over Europe. The Habers, including Rysio, were among many who had already left. However, most Jewish refugees remained. They did not want to live among people who, with so little compassion and sometimes even with approval, had watched the massacre of three million Polish Jews. In fact, some Poles had helped in solving "the Jewish problem." The number of Poles who had shown compassion and given help was so small, and the bitterness and sorrow of those who survived so deep, that the reluctance of Polish Jews to return to their homeland was understandable. That's how many felt, and so did we.

For today, the more acute concern was that we had no money or shelter. Life in Budapest was slowly returning to normal. A union of Polish Jews had been established and worked alongside the Polish Repatriation Commission. Not wanting the Jewish aspect to be overexposed, they called themselves the Deportees Section, with the office at Magyar Street. While the Polish Repatriation Commission was serving all Poles who wished to go back to Poland, the Deportees Section took care of those who did not. Those under Soviet occupation had no chance of legally immigrating, meaning they had to wait patiently, hoping one day a small gap would open in the "Iron Curtain." I registered our family, received some financial assistance, and began looking for a furnished room. I found one with a shared bathroom and kitchen on Bezeredi Street, number ten. The landlady was a Hungarian Jew who seemed happy to have us as tenants. Her flat had only two rooms, one that would be ours, small but clean and comfortably furnished. Our needs were modest. The current tenants were to move out in two weeks. Hopefully, by then, the Hungarian railway would be operating. With my family, all our luggage, our typewriter, calculator, and a heavy can of lard, it would be out of the question to hitchhike in Soviet army trucks.

Returning to Baja, I started to prepare for our departure. One day, on my way back from the market, I heard two people speaking in Polish – a man and a woman, in their early twenties. The man looked very Jewish. I approached them and soon found out they were going together with a group of Poles to a repatriation camp, from where they expected to return to Poland.

"Do you have anyone in Poland?" I asked.

"No one, all our family was exterminated."

"Why do you want to go back then?"

"Where else can we go?"

I told them about the Jewish Committee in Budapest, where they could get some financial support and wait for a chance to emigrate. I suggested that they quietly separate from the Poles, wander into the nearest side street, then follow me. After a few minutes, we reached our house, where Lusia gave them a warm welcome. Quickly she prepared bowls of hot water – they had not washed themselves for several days – then a meal. Afterward, they fell asleep and slept the entire day.

The man's name was Elek Grossman, the son of a well-known merchant from Kraków. The young woman was his wife.

The next day, I brought two more young people home and, seeking out Jews from the Polish-speaking transports, I managed to collect one more young man. They were all happy to find a place to stay after breaking away from the unfriendly Poles since, as Jews, they were constantly the object of unpleasant remarks.

We decided to go to Budapest in one group. Until the day of our departure, we spent our evenings around the table, listening to each other's stories. When our group of eight reached the station, we were told that the trains were still not taking civilian passengers. What were we to do? A railway worker informed us that a train loaded with military equipment would be leaving soon. We located the train and, without asking, boarded and covered ourselves with a large tarpaulin. There we lay quiet and motionless for two hours until at last the train moved. At some point, however, we were discovered and ordered off. It was an impossible situation – seven people with luggage and a child. We decided not to move. We had what we thought was a good case. Our story was a sad one – we had been deported. We were coming back from the camps, absolutely exhausted, and were on our way home. I explained all this politely in Russian to the Soviet stationmaster who, unfortunately, had strict orders: no civilians on the trains. Then one of our young men began to quarrel with the stationmaster, shouting at the Russian. He was hot tempered, rude, and could not be restrained. To my surprise, without another word, the stationmaster retreated, leaving us in the carriage, and the train started on its way. The young protester felt triumphant. He clearly felt he had shown us how to settle matters with the Soviets. But then the train slowed down, stopped, and slowly backed off onto a siding. Our carriage was the last. It did not take long to disconnect and the train went on toward Budapest, leaving us behind. Night came, and we spent it huddled under the canvas, cold and irritable.

In the morning, our young "hero" politely asked me to go talk with the railway authorities. I found the stationmaster and apologized for my companion's rude behavior. I explained that the young people had spent their days in German camps, had no education, were treated like animals, and had gone through hell. They had lost their families and were desperate, acting under great strain. Apologizing, once again I asked him politely to attach our carriage to the next train to Budapest, appealing to him on behalf of my wife and child. Surely, he could not hold our group responsible for the behavior of one young person.

"We will see," he said emphasizing again that the trains were only for the use of the army, not civilians.

Nonetheless, after a while, he came to tell us that in half an hour another train would take us to Budapest. The young man who had screamed at him the day before now jumped out of the carriage, shook his hand, and embraced him gratefully. Soon, our carriage was hooked onto another train, also laden with guns and other military equipment. The stationmaster, an elderly Russian, waved and smiled as we moved off. He had given a lesson in good manners to the young ones. A few hours later we were in Budapest. The boys helped us carry the luggage to our flat. I gave them the address of the Jewish Committee and we said our goodbyes. It was April 1945. The parks were in full bloom, the trees already had new foliage, and in the sunlight, they shone like a promise of a new life.

CAPITULATION

But Budapest was not meant to be the end of our journey, just a stopover. The committee organized temporary residence permits in Hungary, which had to be renewed by the Budapest police every month. Obsessed with the need for proper identity papers, I prepared a suitable document for the committee in Polish, Hungarian, and Russian, typed, with photographs and all the necessary seals and signatures! It was a relief to be living legally again. But naturally, our name was still Daraż. We were in no hurry to go back to our original names. There was always time to do that once we settled down in the West. What would happen if we had to go back to Poland? Should we stay under the name Daraż for the rest of our lives for Elżunia's future, or live as Jews among the Poles, which we would never do?

Once a month we received our allowance, which came from the United States through Switzerland. The American dollars used to be exchanged into Hungarian currency before they reached us, but they no longer were. The pengő was devaluating rapidly, whereas the dollar was rising hourly. There were at least 200 Jewish refugee families in Budapest, and the fluctuations might provide significant sums of money to someone. I suspected the "honorary" treasurers' close guarding of their positions implied the rumors about their honesty were true.

People were speculating and the black market was flourishing.

Cigarettes, lighters, watches, currency, gold, leather goods, clothing – everything was being bought and sold. The Polish Jews quickly established contact with Russian officers who had access to factories, warehouses, and military vehicles. An international smuggling industry among Romania, Hungary, Czechoslovakia, and Poland was growing. Thousands of dollars changed hands.

However, among the Jews who remained in Hungary were many who had no talent for smuggling or black-market transactions. People like us – the remnants of the Polish intelligentsia – had to exist on those few devalued pengos handed out monthly. However, when we realized we could not survive on the subsidy, we, too, decided to go into business.

We remembered how empty the shops in Baja were. Why not try to deliver goods there? We began to look around the Budapest shops, bazaars, and particularly the famous Telekiter flea markets to see what goods were available. There were all sorts of products. Times were hard for the Hungarians, and they had to sell their possessions in exchange for food. We needed funds.

Our only disposable "wealth" was the can of lard brought from Taszár. The day after our arrival in Budapest, I called at a delicatessen in the neighborhood, offering the shop manager a sample of lard. He offered me 40 pengős per kilo. Having around 25 kilos, I made 1,000 pengős, which was a great help in those first few weeks. My lard was immediately displayed in the shop window marked at ten pengős per 100 grams. The next day it was gone. Quite surprised, I entered the shop and found it had all been sold. The shopkeeper asked for another delivery, offering me a much higher price this time, but unfortunately, I could not oblige. Taszár and my Soviet friends were too far away. I invested the rest of the 1,000 pengős.

We bought a variety of goods, such as women's underwear, stockings, lengths of fabrics, leather soles, needles, threads, fountain pens, flints for lighters, razor blades, mirrors, costume jewelry, and so on. When our rucksack couldn't hold enough, we bought two used suitcases and filled them as well. Although the railways were operating, most of the trains were fully loaded with Soviet army freight. Thanks to our friendly approach in Russian, we managed to get onto a train full of military personnel. After a most tiring journey, we reached Baja. Laden like donkeys, we reached the marketplace, sitting on our suitcases and wondering what to do next. Erect a stand in the middle of the market, open the suitcases, and wait for customers? Where would we get a stand? What if it rained? We decided to look for a shop. It had to be Hungarian, as all Jewish shopkeepers had been deported. Yet the Hungarian shopkeepers did not want to let us in – it was not legal, and they were afraid of anything illegal. They were Hungarians, not Poles, with total obedience to authority and respect for the law.

Luckily, we found a person who was willing to take the risk. In a room behind the shop, we unpacked our goods and displayed them on a table. The entrance door to the shop remained open. I stood behind the front counter, while Lusia stayed in the back room. I laid out a few handkerchiefs, new and colorful. All around me were empty shelves, empty cupboards, empty wardrobes, and empty drawers – a totally empty shop. A Russian soldier came in, looked at the empty shelves, and noticed my handkerchiefs. In a whisper, I told him there were more goods in the back room. The Hungarian shopkeeper opened the door slightly and the soldier entered the back room. After a while, he reappeared happy and with a parcel in his hand. Then a Russian woman came. The whole procedure went much the same. After that, once the shop doors were open, the Russians kept coming. To their amazement, they found goods unobtainable in the Soviet Union. They were buying everything without even trying to bargain. Everything seemed cheap to them. They had plenty of money and were happy to spend it. Our Hungarian shopkeeper, quite astonished, was forever opening and closing the door. I remained at my post behind the counter and, in less than two hours, we had sold all our merchandise.

Lusia was excited about our success. We had made nearly four times the amount of our initial outlay. Receiving his share, the Hungarian asked when he would see us again. We agreed to return in a week. From the shop we went to the market, where we bought potatoes, onions, a chicken, butter, and a loaf of bread. Before boarding the train, we hid our money deep inside the clothes we were wearing. Late that night, we were back in Budapest, exhausted but happy.

The next morning, I went to café Ostenda, where the black market operated, and changed some of my pengős into dollars. That same day, we started shopping for the next Baja trip. It was not easy; the shops were empty, and we did not know of any warehouses. In the beginning, Lusia was choosy and would examine the quality, color, and general condition of goods. It was time consuming. I tried to convince her that our Soviet customers would buy anything they found in "our" shop. After the next two trips, Lusia agreed. We paid whatever we were asked and would charge accordingly. Our Russian customers were happy anyway; they had the chance of exchanging the pengős that had no valve for them for something useful.

Business gradually increased. Lusia even began to take orders from Russian women who were extremely happy to receive fabric for a shirt, blouse, silk stockings, or a certain medication. Lusia was happy and our dollar reserve grew after each trip. Nonetheless, we knew this kind of business was risky. Any policeman could have arrested us and taken the merchandise and money. The Soviet authorities also could have made life difficult, charging us with smuggling and speculating. In addition, the soldiers could have robbed us and thrown us from the moving train. We had heard about such happenings. But we could not have survived on the subsidy from the Jewish Committee and were getting used to the "illegal" way of life. Besides, we did not lack courage. Lusia, in particular, enjoyed the excitement. The war had taught us that survival meant taking risks. If the game was dangerous, so be it. There had been many dangerous moments in our lives over the past few years.

The greatest danger we faced was on the crowded Russian trains. We were not the only ones who tried to get on trains full of Russian soldiers. I vividly remember a middle-aged Hungarian woman with a suitcase and a bag attempting to board one. Several friendly soldiers were ready to help her. Some grasped her arms to lift her onto the train, while others took the suitcase, passing it from one to another. Before she knew what was happening, the suitcase had disappeared somewhere in the back of the carriage, and then her bag did as well. Still holding her hands, the soldiers, helpful and friendly, carefully lowered her back onto the platform while the train slowly moved off. The poor woman was left on the platform without her luggage, helpless and desperate, while the smiling soldiers happily waved goodbye. We never let our suitcases out of our hands regardless of the "helping" arms reaching toward us. A warm *spasiba* [thank you] put the soldiers in their place. When asked where we came from, we always had a ready answer – we were from Poland and were going back home. After that, there was always a seat available and a cigarette, sometimes even a piece of Russian sausage. Someone would pull out a balalaika, and in this pleasant and friendly atmosphere we would travel to Baja. On the return trip, the situation would be the same and our *"Jediem domo* [We are going home]" always made the right impression, while Lusia's blue eyes, perfect Russian, and heavy military boots did the rest.

The Russians hated the Hungarians, but Poles were considered brothers. As to whether the way home was toward or from Budapest, they did not really care. *"Domoj"* meant "to go home," and that was that.

We did not always travel by trains carrying soldiers. There were times when we had to catch a train loaded with military equipment even though it was forbidden. Sometimes, we hid behind the carriages and boarded just as the train moved. We developed a special routine. First, I would help Lusia hop on, followed by the heavy luggage, and then myself. On one occasion, I was really scared. Lusia was going from an open carriage to another one. As the train gathered speed she had to sit down on the buffer. Her skirt got caught in the steely grip of the buffer and she was stuck. I took her suitcase to free her hands, but she had to sit motionless all the way to Baja, feeling every movement of the steel joint underneath her. To make things worse, it started to rain, and we were both soaking wet when we arrived. The train stopped, but Lusia still could not move. She had to jump, tearing the skirt, which was still in the grip of the buffer. The merchandise was still in good condition, unaffected by the rain. The skirt was neatly mended and later sold to a Russian lady at a discount!

In the center of Baja, in the marketplace, the Soviets had erected a huge map of Germany, showing the changing front line. Daily bulletins from the Soviet command announcing their progress inside the Third Reich could be heard over loudspeakers. We used to pass this map without feeling. For us, the war had ended in December 1944 when Taszár was liberated. The battles in Germany did not concern us any longer. The Germans were getting what they deserved. We were not alone. Very few looked at the map or were interested in the movements of the armies.

But one day, the speakers were louder than usual and a crowd had gathered. Something must have happened. We stopped and heard the news: "Hitler is dead. Germany has surrendered." It was the eighth of May 1945. We stood there, motionless. Were we supposed to be happy that the Germans had lost? We had lost. A tiny family of three, in a strange town, a strange country, alone in the whole world – with nowhere to go.

It was a warm Hungarian summer. We continued our business trips to Baja, but it was becoming more and more difficult. Our clientele was diminishing. The Russians were going home, and our shopkeeper eventually closed his shop, realizing that private enterprise was finished. Our Baja adventure had ended. We had to stay in Budapest, where we established some kind of social life within the Jewish-Polish community. Among the survivors were a number of intellectuals – a few solicitors, doctors, teachers, and so on. We would meet in the committee's rooms, which became a sort of club. Everyone was trying to establish contact with families and friends living abroad. Some lucky people managed to contact families in North or South America, New Zealand, or Canada. I managed to get the address of two friendly architects from Kraków, Messrs. Duntuch and Landsberger, who had left for Brazil before the war. I wrote to them describing our situation and asked if they might be willing to send immigration papers. I didn't attach much hope to my request, but there was no harm in trying.

THE YUGOSLAV REPATRIATION MISSION

While the living conditions of most of the Polish-Jewish community were difficult and it was hard to make ends meet, one group of our "brethren" indulged in lucrative black marketeering, buying and selling on a grand scale. In front of café Ostenda, they dealt in all types of merchandise. Huge quantities of goods were smuggled in Russian trucks to Poland. The Soviet military had the necessary documents to cross the borders, and these Polish Jews had the connections to sell them in Poland. They established an international trade and formed partnerships of two or three, but as often happens, there were arguments. One side often tried to cheat the other. The war, the ghettos, and the mass murders of their people seemed forgotten when making money was the order of the day.

A special section of our committee dealt with those problems. It acted like a court with three judges, with two solicitors and me appointed. We had quite a few interesting cases for which the committee charged a fee of $10 to $20, depending on the case. The speculators laughed at us sitting on cases for hours in an almost honorary capacity while they were making thousands of dollars.

During the court sessions, I encountered all types, and it was clear that human greed had no limits. Partnerships could be instantly created if money was to be made. One person might know where to buy half a million cigarettes, another might have contacts with Soviet truck drivers, while a third might know someone in Poland who would buy and distribute the cigarettes. There were still large amounts of goods available in Hungary, while after five years of Russian and German occupation, Poland was completely stripped of all necessities, making prices in Poland very high. The money exchange market was quite the opposite. In Poland, dollars were rather cheap, while in Hungary, the value of American currency was rising rapidly due to inflation. After successfully concluding such risk-laden contraband with gains reaching hundreds or sometimes thousands of dollars, partners would squabble over their share of profits. As the whole business was illegal, they could not settle their disputes in the Hungarian courts and hence would approach us. Our verdicts were respected.

As judges we also dealt with the activities of Jewish ghetto policemen, the infamous *Ordnungsdienst* (OD). Although the Germans finally liquidated the Jewish police, some managed to escape to Hungary. Our court sessions were open to the public and people watched the proceedings closely. We the judges did not have any authority to sentence, but our judgments were accepted as a moral condemnation. Not all OD were guilty. Among them were those who risked their own lives to save others.

As for the smugglers, they carried not only goods but passengers. The charge was $20 per person. With our trade in Baja finished and our money reserves shrinking, we began to wonder if it would a good idea for us to smuggle goods into Poland. One day, Lusia made the decision to go. Perhaps she would also find some survivors from our family!

I contacted a smuggler who looked more honest than the others and asked him to take Lusia to Poland and back. He refused at first. It was too dangerous for a woman, he said. No one had ever taken a woman on such a risky trip, and he did not want to be the first. Although he held excellent travel documents and if stopped for inspection could prove everything he was doing was legal, carrying passengers was illegal, increasing the risk. Up to now everything was going smoothly for him. At checkpoints, the Russians were only interested in documents; they never looked inside the trucks. A bottle of vodka or a few packets of cigarettes would satisfy their curiosity, but if they found a women passenger, it could create a dangerous situation.

Nevertheless, Lusia would not be discouraged. Despite my reservations, she persuaded him to take her along.

She took with her a few watches, fountain pens, cigarette lighters, and some women's underwear. Escorting her to the place of departure, I helped her settle into the back of the Soviet truck. She was given a place in the far corner and covered herself with a blanket. A wall of cigarette cartons and boxes of other articles were placed in front of her to conceal her from the curious eyes of Russian border guards. Only in the case of a total unloading of the truck would her presence have been exposed, and so far, that had never occurred. I believed in her instincts. I knew she could handle the Russians. Should the worst happen, they would probably take the merchandise and she would somehow talk her way out of trouble. After a few days, the truck arrived back with a note for me. Lusia wrote that the journey had been safe and she was already in Kraków with the Habers, who had given her a warm welcome. She had been to the Jewish Committee and put our names on the list of survivors. There was no one from our families on the list except Joseph Tilles, the only survivor of the Chmielowskiego Street community. I was delighted to hear Joseph was alive.

A few more days passed and Lusia arrived home. She had sold all the goods and bought dollars on the Kraków black market. Our financial position improved considerably. Her successful trip encouraged us to repeat the venture on a larger scale. We started purchasing the goods, but winter was approaching, early snow covered the streets, and the days became shorter. Trips to Poland became less frequent. The person who had taken Lusia was not ready; he had not collected enough cigarettes but promised to let me know in good time.

I wondered what kind of goods would sell best in Poland. Watches, lighters, and fountain pens were not in demand any longer and I had to find some different merchandise, something more original. Perhaps a collection of contemporary Hungarian stamps? This type of merchandise had probably never been considered by other smugglers. I would be without competitors. It really seemed an original idea, but would I find buyers? The country was hungry for everything. But stamps? I decided to take the risk. First, I went to the central post office hoping, that I would be able to buy larger quantities at face value. The stamps should be saleable if in complete sets.

The first issues, printed right after the war, would be in great demand by collectors, and Hungarians stamps were usually attractive and popular. The Hungarian Postal Department had considerable prewar stocks. On the stamps was the figure of St. Stephen, the patron of Hungary, as well as other historical personalities. Thousands of sheets of these stamps now had the year 1945 overprinted. The local wholesalers, informed well in advance, bought out the whole issue on the first day of sale. I had to approach the dealers. Fortunately, I managed to buy a few hundred sets in sheets. The cost was three times face value, but I considered myself lucky to get them at all. The stamps were indeed beautiful. There was also a new series called *Beke* [Peace] with a picture of Lajos Kossuth, the hero of Hungary. I bought them at a nominal price at the post office.

One afternoon, on returning from the market, I noticed two large canvas-covered trucks standing in front of our house. We had feared such trucks for the last few years. During the Russian occupation of Lwów, they had meant deportation to Siberia. During the German occupation, they meant a death sentence via a German prison, the Janowska Street camp, or the Gestapo headquarters at Szucha Street. What were they after now in Budapest? Why were they in front of our house? It was 1945! The war was over! Alarmed but curious, I looked at the trucks. On both sides was a sign saying Polska (Poland) in large white letters. On the bonnets were small white and red Polish flags. Growing ever more curious, I quickly climbed the stairs to our flat. I could hear a man's voice from inside. Someone was speaking in Polish. Who could it be?

The mystery was soon solved. The trucks belonged to the Polish-Yugoslav Repatriation Mission. They had stopped in Budapest on their way to Yugoslavia. The man in charge was Mr. Tadeusz Maczka, a charming gentleman. He had received our address from a mutual acquaintance in Warsaw, a member of the Polish Socialist Party. Mr. Maczka said there were still thousands of Poles scattered about Europe. The Polish government felt it was its primary duty to organize rail transport to bring them home. The trains would be going through Hungary, and I was being asked to help. My responsibility would be to establish contact with the Hungarian railway authorities and make sure the trains passed safely and without delay across Hungary, I accepted the assignment with pleasure, and we went for a splendid meal of Hungarian goulash with good Hungarian wine and delightful Hungarian gypsy music. All expenses were paid for by the Polish government! The very next day, I started talks with the railway authorities. My knowledge of German was quite helpful as all higher-ranking railway officials spoke German.

There was only one problem – coal. The Hungarians did not have any, whereas Poland had enormous reserves. Therefore, the Hungarians agreed to deliver the locomotives and the crew from border to border, but the Poles had to pay for the service with coal. I agreed. Mr. Maczka was pleased with my arrangements and before returning to Poland left an official document stating I was a member of the Yugoslav Repatriation Mission. The card was stamped with the emblem of the Polish People's Republic, of which I had suddenly become a representative. I was immensely happy with this "Yugoslav connection." It was good to hold such a "diplomatic" post in a foreign country as it would also help in extending our stay in Budapest.

WATCH SMUGGLING

Since my planned trip to Poland had been greatly delayed, and the trains between Hungary and Poland were already running, I decided to go by rail as a repatriate. My documents as a refugee would cover me, and my return to Budapest could be worked out later. There would always be a way, either legally as a delegate of the Yugoslav Repatriation Mission or illegally in a Soviet truck. It would be easy to bribe a Russian driver with a bottle of vodka. Crossing borders illegally had ceased to be difficult or immoral for me.

I bought a small suitcase, some cardboard, wallpaper, and a bottle of glue in the market to make a false bottom in the suitcase where I could hide my contraband – the stamps. Lusia was against the idea, but I felt it was the safest way to smuggle them. After the landlady, Lusia, and Elżunia had gone to bed, I worked till late into the night. The false bottom and the interior of the suitcase lined with wallpaper turned out well, and when Lusia looked at my masterpiece, she could not believe there was any concealed space.

Meanwhile she had purchased about 20 watches, which we decided to hide under the belt of my trousers. Lusia picked apart the lining and sewed them inside in a professional manner. Someone would have to look closely to notice anything strange about my waist. I would also have to rely upon luck, of course.

I packed some clothes, food, and a new pair of shoes. In Poland, such shoes would cost a fortune. I put some secondhand clothes to be sold on the "hungry" Polish market in my rucksack. I had a relaxed trip through Czechoslovakia as neither the Hungarian nor Czech border guards were interested in me. My identity card in three languages (Polish, Russian, and Hungarian) was enough to satisfy them. The train eventually stopped on the Polish border in Zebrzydowice. All passengers had to alight and proceed to the customs office. I have to admit I did feel rather uneasy.

It was a short queue and soon my turn came. A young customs officer asked me to open the suitcase and the rucksack. The latter was soft; he could feel only the clothes and was not interested. He then rummaged through the contents of the suitcase and became interested in the case's bottom. He looked at it with suspicion, knocked at it, and then suddenly pulled out a knife and made a hole in it. My heart raced. He removed the false bottom and revealed my Hungarian stamps. He looked at me in anger and triumph; he had caught a smuggler.

A senior officer took over. "What are these?" he asked sternly.

I explained that before returning home I had sold all my belongings, and with the money, I had bought the Hungarian stamps at the post office. I knew that Hungarian currency was of no use in Poland and was hoping to gradually sell the stamps or exchange them for things I would need. I used to collect stamps before the war and they had helped me to survive hard times. I was hoping they would help me again.

The young man was watching me angrily, but the officer in charge seemed to understand. Why was I hiding them? Knowing that Poles generally hated the Russians, I decided to gamble on those feelings. "I was warned against the Soviets," I replied. "They sometimes rob the passengers. The stamps are all I have to start a new life. I had to protect them, so I hid them."

The senior officer was sympathetic, but the other one distrusted me. Coming from behind his desk, he began to feel my clothes. I started to perspire. If he found the watches, I would be accused of smuggling and would lose them. What could I tell Lusia? I would be losing everything she had earned on her venture. On impulse, I took my jacket off and threw it on the table, angrily emptying the pockets. Two pens, two propelling pencils, a lighter, a packet of cigarettes, and a notebook fell out. I was trying to draw their attention to the contents of my jacket in hope they would not resume searching my trousers. I pretended to be deeply hurt and obviously upset.

"So this is the welcome I receive in my country?" I asked. "The Germans sent me to a labor camp, I worked like a slave, was mistreated and beaten, and now, poor as a church mouse, I come home and am treated like a thief? What have I stolen? Do these things belong to me or are they yours? Am I trying to smuggle out Polish stamps or am I bringing in foreign ones, bought with my entire savings? In Budapest, at the Polish Repatriation Mission, I was told I could bring anything into the country I wanted, and now you search my pockets? What right do you have to do that?"

My outrage was met with silence. The officer in charge explained that the Polish government in London was trying to smuggle reactionary literature into the country. He ordered a soldier to lead me to the soldier's mess, where I would be given something to eat. He was keeping the stamps until he could check with Warsaw. I put my jacket on, covering my bulging waist, and asked for the toilet. There, with a locked door, I pulled all the watches out, wrapped them in a handkerchief, and placed them at the bottom of my rucksack. I felt greatly relieved. The bulge on my waist had disappeared.

After a soldier's meal of fresh bread, thick pea soup, Polish sausages, and beer, I went back to the customs office. The officer was friendly, asking if I had enjoyed my meal and offering me a cigarette. He looked compassionately into my eyes and quietly uttered "*amchu*," Hebrew for "one of ours" – at the time a kind of password.

Obviously, the officer, a Jew, had recognized me. I am sure his enthusiastic deputy had also recognized me. Surprised, I answered yes. He returned my stamps, explaining that according to instructions from Warsaw, people returning home were fine to bring in everything belonging to them. However, in cases where the possessions were too excessive or pointed to speculating or smuggling, they were confiscated. With a wry smile, the officer said I was lucky to have encountered him and not his colleague. I would then have lost not only the stamps but everything else I was carrying. He mentioned a smuggler who had been intercepted a few days ago who had 20 lighters sewn into his trousers. He was allowed to keep two and the rest had been confiscated. I was quite sure that my watches would have met with a similar fate.

I caught the train to Kraków. As a repatriate, I was free to travel without paying for a ticket. Naturally, my first visit was to the Habers, with whom I spent the whole day.

They took possession of Irka's father's *Linguistic Bookshop*, a large stock of foreign language dictionaries, and *Teach Yourself* manuals and were already making a comfortable living. Since their war apartment was occupied by Poles who refused to move, they had to share accommodation with strangers.

I then visited Uncle Jozio. He had taken over their prewar apartment as soon as the Germans left Kraków. He had the same job as before the war – an assistant bank manager. He told me of his escape from Lwów during the massacre of August 1942. His wife, Stasia, had followed every step of the instruction I had given her during my brief stay in Kraków in 1942. She had gotten Jozio out of the bank, taken him to the station, and put him on a train. Everything had been all right until German police entered their carriage and began to check documents. Deadly scared, she gave them her papers, recently issued by German authorities and therefore in perfect order. Uncle Jozio had no documents. He was sitting in the corner of the carriage, his face covered with bandages, hardly visible, pretending to be asleep. The policeman looked at him and decided not to wake him up, waved his hand, and went. Poor Aunt Stasia could hardly breathe until the officer left, feeling how close death was for both of them. They reached Kraków safely and Joseph devoted secretary was waiting for them at the station. They brought him safely home. As mentioned earlier, Aunt Stasia came from a family of devout Catholics, and her mother would never forgive her for marrying a Jew. Only after long pleading did her mother agree to put Joseph in Stasia's room. The one condition, however, was that nobody must know. Hiding Jews was punishable by death. My aunt had to swear she would keep the secret. During our visit to Kraków in 1942 and again in 1944, Aunt Stasia did not even hint that he was safely hidden under her bed.

This time, Uncle Joseph and I talked for quite a while, yet somehow avoided the subject of our cruel experience in Lwów. Aunt Stasia did not show herself. I was told she had a severe headache. I guessed she felt ashamed that she required persuading to save her husband. A true Christian might have saved her husband and many more from our family. Uncle Joseph did not seem comfortable, either. He might have guessed my thoughts. Poles looked at Jews with thinly veiled resentment, sometimes even asking how it was that so many of us still lived. Quite a number of Jews who had been deported to the Soviet Union were also returning. They were trying to get their flats and houses back, and the Poles were reluctant to hand them over, even bringing cases to court. As Poles were forced to vacate the flats, their hatred toward the surviving Jews grew.

On her recent visit to Kraków, Lusia had gone to see our prewar flat at 17 Lenartowicza Street. We knew the Germans had taken everything, but she still wanted to look at the rooms where she had spent happy years. The current tenants received her coldly, maybe even with hostility, and only relaxed after she assured them that we had no intention of moving in.

"I'm sorry that I am alive," was the correct apology. Poles had hoped that Hitler would have solved the Jewish problem for them for good, yet now more and more of these unwanted creatures were drifting back – from Russia, Germany, camps, and from hiding. They were few and all very poor, without families or friends, in pain and scared. Yet somehow, they were embarrassed that they were still alive, almost asking forgiveness for their existence.

In fact, while the massacre of Jews had ended with the death of Hitler and the fall of the Third Reich, something appalling followed. Some Polish groups undertook to finish Hitler's work and carried on their extermination. An underground Polish organization called the National Armed Forces (NSZ) soon became infamous. Their ideology was to fight not only the Germans but the communists and Jews. With great enthusiasm, they continued the work of the Nazis. There were many incidents where they stopped trains in the countryside and checked documents. Jews were dragged off trains and executed on the spot. Their bodies were found along the railway lines or in the fields. Some of my distant relatives and friends died this way. Nicholas Huttner, a cousin of the Eckers, once an officer in the Polish cavalry, and his brother-in-law, Seweryn Steiner, with whom I went to high school in Sokal, were killed this way.

Jack Abrahamer, who luckily managed to survive the war on Aryan papers, took over his mill in Wieliczkanear Kraków. The mill had belonged to his family for the last hundred years. Afraid of the NSZ raids, Abrahamer used to take a coach every day to go to the mill from where he lived in Kraków. One morning, NSZ members stopped him and, right before the coachman's eyes, killed him. It sounds unbelievable, but it was a fact. Jews in Poland lived in mortal danger again.

Lusia had given me the address of a young watchmaker in Lodz. He had bought watches from her for a much better price than she had been offered in Kraków. As Kraków and Katowice were close to the border of Czechoslovakia, the market was saturated with smuggled goods. While on the train, Lusia met a young Jewish woman who had given her the address of her brother in Lodz, a large city about 300 kilometers from Kraków. Smugglers did not go that far, the black market there was hardly active, and watches were in demand. Friends advised Lusia not to go to Lodz because of the danger of NSZ raids, but she had not traveled from faraway Budapest to Poland just to give the watches away for next to nothing. Courageous as she was, she had taken the risk and succeeded.

I, too, decided to go to Lodz. While I still had my documents in the name of Piotr Daraż, I felt confident. Jews returning from Russia had Soviet identity cards with their original Jewish names. Others, after surviving under false names, returned as quickly as possible to their original ones. It was not difficult for the NSZ to identify Jews by their names. I could only hope that Piotr Daraż might be lucky, as he had been on his many trips during the German occupation.

After an eventless night's sleep on the train, I got off at Lodz early in the morning and headed straight to the watchmaker's. The man was hospitable, even offering me a hot breakfast. He lived in a two-bedroom unfurnished flat (all the furniture had been taken away by the Germans). In one bedroom, he put a mattress on the floor; clothes were hung from nails in the walls and doors. The living room was his workshop, consisting of a worktable, a stool with a worn-out seat, a lamp, and a few tools brought back from Russia. Along the wall was a huge pile of firewood. It was still winter and still cold. I unpacked my "treasures" and laid them out. They were quite a sight – glistening gold, silver, and chrome, with red, yellow, or black faces, Arabic or Roman numbers, modern or classic designs. We argued over the prices. He wanted to buy as cheaply as possible; I wanted to sell at the highest price. Our negotiations were interrupted by a customer coming to collect a watch he'd left for repair.

The watchmaker gave it to him for 20 złoty. When the customer left, we continued our bargaining. Perhaps 10 or 15 minutes passed when we heard an insistent knocking on the door. The watchmaker quickly grasped the tray with the watches and hid it under a few pieces of wood. The watchmaker's young wife opened the door and an armed policeman entered the workroom.

"Where are the watches?" he blurted out.

"What watches?" the watchmaker asked calmly.

"The watches that only a few minutes ago were laying on this table!"

"Oh, those!" the watchmaker said. "Their owner took them away and left a little while ago. He wanted to sell them to me, but they were too expensive. Some people think they can get a fortune for rubbish. It is my business to know the value of things."

The policeman gazed around the empty room, approached the wood pile, and picked up two pieces of wood. My heart nearly stopped. Suddenly he seemed interested in me.

"Documents!" he demanded.

I handed him my Hungarian identification card. He looked it over and said, "Follow me to the police station."

"Why, what have I done?" I asked politely.

"You will find out when we get there," he said, pulling out his revolver. I had no choice. He was armed and watched me all the way to the police station, not hiding his hostility. He reminded me of the character who had robbed me in Warsaw back in 1942. The commanding officer at the police station received me coldly but politely. He asked if I knew anybody in Lodz. Unfortunately, I could not give a single name.

I was thoroughly searched, but nothing compromising was found. I had left all the pens with the Habers, hoping to be able to sell them later. The watches were at the watchmaker's, hidden in the wood pile. I was calm. The face of the officer suddenly brightened; he had found in my purse a hard little object wrapped in paper. "Diamond?" he asked, smiling happily.

"Yes," I responded calmly.

He unwrapped it slowly. "What is it?" he asked, taking a magnifying glass out of his drawer.

"To me, a diamond," I answered, smiling. "To you, officer, just my little daughter's tooth." It was, in fact, the first tooth Elżunia had lost. I had kept it for luck. I had forgotten about it.

Disappointed, the policeman had to release me, and I found myself on the streets of Lodz free again. I sighed with relief, wondering how many more times I was going to be questioned at police stations. How many more times would my freedom depend on the moods and whims of Soviet, German, Hungarian, or Polish police officers?

I wanted to take a look at the city. I had visited Lodz several times before the war when working for Jozef Elsner in Kraków. I remembered those times as I walked along Piotrowska Street, the main street in Lodz. Before the war, the street had been full of Jewish shops and Jewish people. Then, one might have thought that only Jews lived in Lodz, no Poles. I even recall Jews walking to and fro on the street whose job was to persuade passersby to visit the shops. It was not an easy or a pleasant job for a poor man, on his feet from morning till night, who might walk the same stretch of the street, backward and forward, approaching the window-shopping Poles. Paid by one or more shopkeepers, he needed results to be paid. There were many days without any reward, without one client. How many of those small shops had earned just enough to pay the rent or the electricity, or to bribe the police to avoid paying fines when one more customer was let in after closing time?

Back then, Piotrowska Street had been full of black robes, black skull caps, black beards, and black side-curls. How different Piotrowska Street looked now! The Jewish shops had disappeared and so had the black robes and somber Jewish faces. It was new, different people now. The street was quiet, business was slow, and no one troubled me. I was thinking about all those dark, mysterious people in their attire from the Middle Ages. Where were they all? Who had solved this once insoluble problem for Lodz and Poland – the Jewish problem? And how?

Suddenly I heard someone yelling, "Henek, what are you doing here?" The friendly voice belonged to our close friend from Warsaw, Lutek Szulkin. We embraced. What a wonderful coincidence! What a wonderful surprise!

"What I am doing here, you ask? I am just out of the police station," I said. He did not believe me. He remembered my sense of humor and thought I was joking. I did not have time for a long conversation as I was on my way back to the watchmaker's flat. Lutek briefly told me that his wife, Elżunia, after whom our daughter had been named, had survived and they were living with her mother, Mrs. Medres, in Lodz. He gave me his address, and I promised to drop in as soon as possible.

I arrived at the watchmaker's finding he and his wife had been worried about me and were happy to see me again. They apologized for the unexpected and unpleasant incident. They had not realized that the client who came to collect his watch was a police informer.

The watches were safe and well hidden. I decided it was best to get rid of them as quickly as possible. The price of $20 a watch, which I had previously rejected, I now accepted. He could have kept the watches and I would not have been able to do anything about it. There had been no witness and I could not have gone to the police. Fortunately, he was an honest man. I had paid $15 to $18 per watch, so there was no loss. That the profit was not a bit bigger was bad luck. From under the mattress, he pulled out a bag full of Polish, Russian, and American notes. He gave me a choice – Polish złoty or US dollars. The dollar notes were in twenties, fifties, and hundreds and were plentiful. I took $400 in 100-dollar bills, which was the best denomination for smuggling. I was amazed how easily he paid such a large sum of money considering his poor living conditions. He explained that he lived this way to avoid jealousy from neighbors and customers. Jews were always the object of jealousy and were often robbed these days, so he preferred to sleep on an old mattress on the floor. No one would suspect him of being wealthy.

I admired the shrewdness of this young watchmaker and his understanding of human nature. If only all those Jews who had made their fortunes before and after the war could have lived more modestly, maybe the hatred of others would not have been so deep or antisemitic feelings so widespread. Quickly, I said goodbye, wishing them all the best for the future, and rushed to see the Szulkins. The smiling face of Elżunia Szulkin appeared first at the door, then Mrs. Medres and Lutek. There was no end to hugs and kisses. We were so happy to see each other and under such unexpected circumstances.

Our stories went on and on. I spent the night in their home just like before the war when visiting Warsaw on company business.

They quickly told me the news Elżunia was pregnant. It wasn't the best circumstances for bringing up a child, but many faced a similar situation. People felt compelled to expand their families quickly to replace the missing ones. Lusia was pregnant, too. We did not want our Elżunia to start a new life all alone. We did not want this for her or us. Maybe it was madness, maybe not.

I could not stay longer with the Szulkins as I had to leave for Warsaw. I managed to run to the market to buy a bathtub as a gift for the expected baby. Lutek asked me to write and send him some "Letters from Budapest" for his daily paper. He was the editor. He gave me a letter certifying that I was the Budapest correspondent of the *Kurier Popularny*, and I was proud of this new honorary post. Indeed, after returning to Budapest, a few of my Letters from Budapest were published.

The train to Warsaw was full, but luckily there were no raids by the NSZ bandits. I was greatly moved by memories when I was approaching Warsaw Station. How many times had I been there in 1942, 1943, and 1944? I was struck by the destruction I saw. Warsaw was in ruins. The once beautiful station building of Warsaw Central was no more. A temporary wooden building now accommodated the offices. The beautiful Marszalkowska Street and Jerozolimskie Boulevarde – the once beautiful center of the city – had disappeared. I could not believe so many streets I had known so well were now in ruins. Hitler's order had been carried out to the last letter, with the usual German precision – they had razed Warsaw to the ground. I remembered the ruins of Budapest right after liberation, but there was no comparison.

Yet the city was alive. Out of nowhere, new shops had sprung up and new stands appeared. Transport was slowly being reestablished. It was January, and the ruins were covered with snow, but the Poles of Warsaw had trodden a pathway among the ruins. They followed it like ants, laden with goods, backpacks, and suitcases, pulling carts and wheelbarrows, and driving trucks and cars. They kept moving, trying to survive in the Warsaw ruins. Yet there was enthusiasm and determination. Warsaw lived! The people of Warsaw lived! Hitler had succeeded in murdering millions of Jews, Russians, Poles, and other nationals, but he had not succeeded in stifling this living force – the soul of Warsaw!

I had a hot breakfast at one of the little stands – fresh bread, eggs, and coffee. Then I set off to locate Professor Poniż. He was happy to hear my voice so unexpectedly. The outer suburbs were in much better condition. Buses and cars were working. Even trams, once the power station was repaired, were moving in certain areas.

The Ponizes were at home and delighted to see me. Although I had let them know of our successful escape to Hungary in 1944, much time had since passed. Their house was intact – the whole Saska Kępa neighborhood had been spared. They told me about themselves and the Warsaw uprising. Professor Poniż had been given back his position with the Polytechnic and was about to go on a trip to Sweden to finalize with the Swedes the purchase of some of their famous little Swedish houses to temporarily accommodate government offices. I had a sudden idea. Perhaps he would take my stamps and sell them in Stockholm?

He was greatly interested and agreed. He himself was a keen collector. I told him my initial outlay and that any profit would be split equally between us. He welcomed the idea of additional income. This undertaking would not in any way affect his obligations toward the country. These were not Polish stamps, and the Polish People's Republic was not going to lose anything on such a transaction.

I had other business to attend to in Warsaw as well. I had to report to the chief of the Yugoslav Mission, Mr. Maczka. Perhaps, he could assist in getting me back to Budapest via diplomatic routes. Maybe I could even be given an official passport to travel abroad!

The next important matter was to obtain copies of my degrees, which had been lost during the war. Some professors would still remember me from the Lwów Polytechnic. I wrote out the details of our studies and degrees and needed two signatures for verification. Professor Poniż applied his signature immediately. He suggested I ask Jan Grubecki, another professor, for the second signature. Before the war, Grubecki had been a tutor at the Polytechnic. I remembered well my confrontations with him in those student days. Once a member of the Polish National Democratic Party, this known antisemite was now Poland's attorney general and a personal friend of President Bolesław

Bierut! How easy some could convert from the ultra-right to the far left!

Grubecki received me politely in his luxurious office. "I remember the face, but forget the name," he apologized but signed my document without hesitation. This document, now signed by both Poniż and Grubecki, also confirmed that Henry Reiss and Piotr Daraż were one and the same person.

Both Professor Poniż and Professor Grubecki urged me to come back to Poland. The country was in ruins; there would be plenty of work for qualified engineers, great opportunities, and access to the highest positions. "We need people like you, dear colleague!" Grubecki encouraged me. "With our cities in ruins and plans for restoration already underway, you could choose to do whatever you like. Any position would be open to you!"

"No, thank you," I replied. "I don't feel like rebuilding a country which did not recognize me in the past and probably will not recognize me as a full citizen in the future." An armed soldier, Grubecki's bodyguard, escorted me to the door and saluted respectfully.

I went to the Jewish Committee to register our names on the list of survivors. I doubted if anyone would look for us but, just in case....

The committee ran a dining room for repatriates who were constantly arriving. I sat at one of the tables and had the standard meal – a plate of hot, thick soup, and a slice of bread. Opposite me was a young man in Soviet uniform, and as usual I started a conversation. His Polish was quite good, although he was mixing it with Jewish jargon. What was he doing in a Soviet uniform? He said he was going back to Russia to bring his family back to Poland.

"Where is your family?" I asked.

"Far away, in Kazakhstan."

"Where exactly in Kazakhstan?" I persisted, becoming more curious.

"Not far from Semipalatinsk," he answered, surprised by my curiosity. "In a kolkhoz."

"What is the name of that kolkhoz?"

"Min-Bulak," he replied.

Hearing that, I nearly jumped off my chair. In that same kolkhoz lived my Uncle Samuel and Aunt Rozia who, at the beginning of the war, had been deported by the NKVD. Amazed, the young man said he knew Aunt Rozia; all the people in the kolkhoz knew her because she was always ready to help the sick or the children, and, as in Budynin, everyone liked her. He thought that my uncle had died. When I asked him to take a letter and money to my aunt, he agreed. Quickly, I wrote a few words to let her know about the tragedies of our family, and then I put 500 złoty in an envelope, adding the address of Uncle Joseph in Kraków where she could stay on her return to Poland. What a coincidence! How small this world was! It was a good feeling to have found a way to send help to my dear aunt. I imagined how thrilled she would be.

My meeting with Mr. Maczka proved successful. Happy to see me, he gave me all the necessary papers to apply for a passport. I went on to the Ministry of Foreign Affairs, lodged my application, and was advised to return in a few days to collect the passport. I could not believe my luck. I decided to spend my time waiting by attending theaters in Kraków. Before I left there, I bought a secondhand kangaroo fur coat at the market. It was the middle of winter and my old coat was already coming apart. I felt magnificent, like a Polish nobleman. (I did not dream that within three years I would be living in the country of free-roaming kangaroos!)

Looting of the conquered German territories was growing into a big industry that time. The Poles invented a name for it – *szaber*! Hundreds of speculators were following the victorious Polish army into Germany while the Nazi rulers were running away in panic, leaving behind their mansions and possessions, The most beautiful collections – pieces of art, silver, antique furniture, porcelain, books, even heavy, expensive curtains, could all now be found on the Polish black markets. They were being sold for next to nothing as people had little money and were struggling for necessities such as bread, meat, and fuel, not the luxuries left by the Germans.

Among the stolen goods were valuable stamp collections. In their ignorance, people were selling them to stamp dealers for a pittance. Just by glancing at the first page of an album, dealers knew the value of the collection, but would offer only the price of a kilo of sausage or bottle of vodka. The hungry and unaware vendor would accept the offer without quibbling.

It was surprising how quickly the Poles learned the methods that throughout centuries they had accused Jews of practicing. The Jews had always been accused of cheating or buying goods below their real value, making profits at the cost of the Gentiles. Now that the Jews had disappeared, Poles took over that role – and very successfully.

Stamp collecting was my hobby and I had purchased mine from a respectable dealer named Kadluczka, who used to have a philatelic shop not far from Eisner's offices. I would buy valuable Austrian, German, and Polish stamps. During my stopover in Kraków in 1942, I had gone to see him again. He remembered me and was most surprised to see me alive and without the Jewish star. While I was in the shop, a German officer in a brown *Sturmabteilung* (SA) uniform had come in. Kadluczka had served him immediately and the man left. I had with me several envelopes with mixed franking of Polish and Soviet stamps from the time of the Soviet occupation of Lwów. They must have been of some interest to him and he purchased them all (except one I kept as a souvenir). The badly needed cash was a godsend at the time. Now, back in Kraków, I decided to visit him again. He seemed happy to see me and remembered my last visit. When I thanked him for not giving me away to the German officer. He appeared offended by such a suggestion. Mr. Kadluczka was a decent man.

The loss of my prewar collection had hurt me deeply, especially the loss of the Austrian stamps, which I now wanted to replace. Kudluczka showed me his stock. I could not believe my eyes – stacks of albums full of the most valuable stamps. Most of them were German – complete series carefully set out on special pages. One could see the precision of a German collector. One album contained beautiful Austrian stamps, old and new: a jubilee set with Emperor Franz Joseph I and an 1830-1910 set with valuable five- and ten-kroner stamps – all rare, expensive, and almost impossible to buy in prewar Poland. I bought them, and very cheaply at that. Kadluczka was happy; he had such a large stock but hardly any customers. He charged me the lowest prices in the catalogue, which, in US currency, amounted to $50 or so. Kadluczka was interested in the current Hungarian issues and promised to deliver some on my next visit. Unfortunately, that next transaction did not happen. In March of the same year, when visiting Poland again and going to his shop, I found his door closed and window sealed. Kadluczka had been murdered a few days earlier.

Returning to Warsaw, I found my passport waiting for me. Again, I visited Poniż, who had just returned from Sweden. The Hungarian stamps had been snapped up for a good price. The dealer had asked for another delivery as soon as possible. He had contacts with America and my stamps were apparently the first to reach the Western world! I could imagine the ecstasy of Hungarian collectors in the US. I received my share of the American dollars and was delighted.

The chief of the Yugoslav mission told me there would soon be transport to Hungary from Kraków and I was welcome to join it. I hastened back to Kraków. Luckily, my train was not stopped by the NSZ during that journey. It was about time to go home. I was missing my family in Budapest. Also, the chunk of meat I had bought on the black market a few days ago, which Irka Haber was keeping in a bucket in her bookshop and sprinkling with fresh vinegar every day, would not keep forever. It must have been about ten kilos without bones. In Budapest, such high-quality meat was unobtainable, while at that time in Poland, there was a lot of meat on the black market.

Tired, but satisfied with my mission, with a rucksack full of meat, sausages, and bread, I arrived home, welcomed by Lusia and Elżunia, who had been starting to worry. I had been away too long. Lusia was now four months pregnant. A fresh supply of food was much needed by her and the expected baby. A few days after my arrival, I organized a meeting at the Hungarian Ministry of Railways. Those present were Mr. Bolesław Kocznur, a Polish delegate from the Ministry of Foreign Affairs; four representatives of the Hungarian Railways; and I as the representative of the Yugoslav Repatriation Mission.

The talks lasted for three days and concluded with the signing of a three-page document. Agreement was reached on the date, transit procedures, and all details of the coal deliveries. I had done a good job for the People's Republic of Poland. Encouraged by the success of my last venture, I started preparations for the next trip to Poland. This time, I decided to concentrate on stamps only. They were more difficult to buy now as prices had risen. The dealer who used to sell them to me, Mr. Benedek, liked me. One day he invited me to the "stamp exchange," which took place once a week in the evening. I have never seen anything like it.

There was a big hall full of tables with one or two stamp dealers at each table, on which were great quantities of stamps in albums, envelopes, boxes, and folders. Benedek introduced me to some wholesalers as an importer from Poland. I was buying in sheets of a hundred and paying in US dollars. Soon dealers knew me. The moment I appeared in the hall, the prices went up; the moment I finished buying, the prices dropped. I spoke in German. For the Hungarian intelligentsia, it was the second language. I was known under the name Daraż. In my new fur coat, with a leather briefcase, I must have looked like a great exporter. I became a steady visitor to the hall, never leaving empty-handed.

As Budapest was still recovering from the heavy shelling, electricity was in short supply and streets were ill lit. Transport was poor, with trams appearing only after a long wait. Crime and hooliganism were widespread. Robberies increased, particularly in dark side streets. Marauders from the Soviet army – small groups of soldiers – were best at getting an extra income. They considered Hungarians as enemies, so their conscience was clear. One evening, after a very satisfactory purchase at the stamp exchange, I was returning home, as usual following the same familiar and hitherto safe route, which was a short cut. The quiet side lanes were covered with snow, poorly lit, and full of rubble left after the siege. Normally, there would not be a soul in the street; it was always peaceful. This time, suddenly, as if from out of nowhere, there appeared in front of me a Soviet soldier with his gun pointing at me. Simultaneously I felt an invisible hand seizing me by my fur collar. "*Zabrat portfel* [Take the briefcase]!" The command was issued and a third person grabbed my precious briefcase.

On impulse, I exclaimed in Russian, "*Snimaj oruz* [Remove the weapon]!"

"*A ty kio tako* [And who are you]?" a bewildered voice asked.

"I am a thief like yourself, and that briefcase I just stole for myself, not for you. Go away!"

My assailants, obviously surprised, did not pursue the matter any further, and as if by some invisible signal, disappeared. I returned home, still with my briefcase and my fur coat, but shocked by this experience. After that I was more careful. I began avoiding dark side streets and limited my purchases.

STAMP SMUGGLING

The smuggler who had taken Lusia to Poland notified me he was ready to go again and for $20 would take me. He was amazed when I came with only a small suitcase. He was traveling in a heavily laden contraband truck carrying some three million cigarettes. What kind of merchandise was I taking? I opened my suitcase and showed him the stamps. He glanced at them with contempt.

The border crossing went smoothly. The Hungarians and Czechs hardly looked at the Soviet documents. The truck was never examined – a couple of hundred American cigarettes were opening all doors, including Poland's.

It was nearly six in the evening when we arrived in Katowice. My industrious smuggler and the Soviet driver got off the truck and disappeared. I was told not to leave and to wait until they returned. I was left alone, hidden under a cold, stiff tarpaulin. The truck was parked on a busy street, just under the streetlamp. It was snowing. Shifting my uncomfortable position on top of the contraband, I noticed through a small tear in the canvas a man standing under the streetlight, looking intently in my direction. Had he noticed my movements under the tarpaulin? With the covering over my head, I sat motionless. He looked quite agitated as he watched me and, smoking cigarette after cigarette, went on walking around the streetlamp.

The truck belonged to the Soviet army and was out of bounds to the Polish authorities. As long as I was on the Soviet vehicle, I was safe. The moment I put my foot on Polish soil, I would be subject to Polish law. The individual who was watching me so intently was obviously waiting for me to make that move so he could immediately come after me. To fall into the hands of the Polish militia and have to explain again about my stamps was too much for me to risk – far too much!

So I remained motionless, my limbs frozen. An hour passed – a long, seemingly never-ending hour. The man was still circling the lamp, smoking cigarette after cigarette and staring persistently at the shape on top of the Soviet truck, lying in wait like a dog for a rabbit. When would those characters return? After another hour, my smuggler and the Soviet driver finally reappeared, both slightly drunk. They got into the truck and drove off. I sighed with relief as the man under the streetlamp disappeared from view – surely disappointed. I decided never again to undertake any more smuggling adventures: How many more risks should I take?

Within two hours, we reached Kraków's marketplace, where I parted from my companions. They had tried to justify their long absence, saying they had problems selling the merchandise in Katowice. Perhaps.

I hurried to the Habers, and it was good to see one another again. There was much to talk about. There was some news, too. Their prewar best friend, Masia B., who had survived in the Soviet Union, had just left for Warsaw to go on to the US to join her husband, Poldek (who spent the war years there and succeeded in making a fortune). Following my example, Henio Haber had bought a small collection of valuable stamps worth about $1,000. A small envelope with stamps had been given to Masia to take to the United States so that, one day, when the Habers left for the West, they would have some money abroad.

Excellent thought! I knew Masia very well from the bridge parties given by the Habers before the war. Why shouldn't I visit her in her hotel when I was in Warsaw? She might take my stamps, too, or at least some of them. The Habers gave me her address.

Masia was glad to see me, but the idea of smuggling numerous stamps did not appeal to her. Immigration regulations in the United

States were strict. Poldek had made strenuous efforts to get her out of Poland, and she was reluctant to take any risk.

I did not insist, but suggested she allow me to buy her a suitcase that she could inspect before deciding. She agreed and even asked me to purchase another as well. She had a lot of clothes to take, she said, and one suitcase would not be enough. I bought two identical suitcases at the market – there were no shops in Warsaw yet – together with the necessary cardboard, patterned paper, and glue. I was already experienced with this pastime. While I worked on the cases in the hotel room, a friend took Masia out to dinner. When she returned, I gave her the two suitcases. She examined them thoroughly but couldn't detect any difference and agreed to take them both without hesitation. One of the suitcases had a false bottom filled with stamps worth about $1,000 – quite a fortune in those times. The rest I left for Poniż to take to Sweden. The next day, I took Masia to the railway station, helped her find a seat, and gave her a large box of chocolates, the best I could obtain. I appreciated the chance to be sending a valuable investment overseas. I did not suspect then that I was parting with my stamps forever. Masia joined her husband without any problems, with the Habers and my stamps. Poldek confirmed their receipt, and that was the last we ever heard from either of them. Being a stamp collector himself, he must have found the temptation too great to resist.

I decided to visit Mrs. Baltorowicz. She lived at the same address in Żoliborz and was delighted to see me. She asked me teasingly what had happened to all that glass we had been trading in and that after Warsaw's uprising would be the basis of a splendid business. We both smiled. For her, I was still Daraż. We didn't talk about the past. To confirm being Jewish? What for? She knew it anyway.

Unexpectedly, on the corner of Marszalkowska and Aleje Jerozolimskie streets, I ran across Wojslaw Bielicki. I didn't feel comfortable. The last time I had seen him was on the train en route from Warsaw to Kraków in January 1944. He had been on his way to his new job, the construction of a rice mill, while we were about to flee to Hungary. Two years had passed since and so much was different. He was in a hurry, and I didn't feel like talking, either. He only managed to tell me that his mother, with whom we had lived in Legionowo, had been killed during the Warsaw Uprising, as had his girlfriend. His daughter Marzenka, the same age as Elżunia, had survived.

I called on the Yugoslav Mission's principal, Mr. Maczka, and brought him up to date on my activities in Budapest. He was delighted. I needed an extension on my passport to return to Budapest, and he gave me the necessary references. I also visited Bolesław Kocznur of the Ministry of Foreign Affairs, my partner in Budapest in negotiating the transit of Polish citizens returning from Yugoslavia. He promised to phone the passport section at the ministry on my behalf. I didn't want to wait for the next convoy of trucks to go to Yugoslavia; I needed to have my passport as quickly as possible to get back to my family in Budapest. Despite my position at the Yugoslav Mission, confirmed by Mr. Maczka, and the urgency of my presence in Budapest, my passport was still not ready, even with the intervention of Mr. Kocznur.

A woman in charge of the passport section created many obstacles. Day after day, I had to see her, yet every time the passport was not signed. One day, I decided to take a risk and asked her what she would like from Budapest. Without any embarrassment, she handed me a list of cosmetics that she understood one could get in Budapest but not Warsaw. I promised her that once in Budapest I would attend to this matter and bring all her requirements the next time I came to Warsaw. In no time, I received my passport and a friendly smile. I replied with a smile, too, knowing I would not be returning to Warsaw.

I returned to Kraków by train. I was afraid of that journey. One often heard of trains being stopped by NSZ gangs and of Jews being executed. On the route to Kraków, the Radom-Kielce section was known to be the most dangerous. Luckily, the journey was uneventful and, as usual, Kraków was peaceful.

I again spent long hours with the Habers discussing our future. They were established in Poland, while we had neither settled in Budapest nor intended to settle in Poland. We didn't live in constant fear in Budapest and there was no danger from the Hungarians. Unfortunately, in Poland, the situation for the Jews was entirely different, and the Habers lived in fear due to the strong antisemitic feelings evident among the locals. It was sad. Even so, the Habers had gradually managed to settle in. They had taken back their bookshop and the family's spaghetti factory. How could they leave this comfortable existence for the unknown? They did not feel strong enough anymore to start a new venture.

Our decision was easier. We were outside Poland, meaning our emigration had already started. I was prepared to find out what life would be like in the West. I was in good health, full of energy, and I was blessed with a wonderful, resourceful, and equally enthusiastic partner in Lusia. I was about ready to return to Budapest when frightening news reached us. A pogrom was taking place. Jews were being slaughtered in Kielce, Lublin, and other small Polish towns. Panic spread among the Jews of Kraków, and they were afraid to go out. This small remnant of the Jewish community in Poland suddenly found themselves confronted with the nightmare of being killed by their own countrymen, slaughtered with an axe, spade, or pitchfork.[1]

The Jewish community in Kraków panicked. Irka forbade me to go out. Although I was scared, I nevertheless decided to go to town to find out what was happening since my appearance was not obviously Jewish and I was practiced at living as a Pole under the Nazi occupation. The city was quiet, but I decided to leave Kraków right away. It was quiet today, but what about tomorrow and the day after? The Habers were so sad when I said goodbye. They questioned their decision to stay in Poland. They realized their lives and that of their son was in danger.[2]

I went to the railway station alone as the Habers would not risk seeing me off. The money I had earned selling stamps was hidden in my clothing. It was a good thing I knew how to use a needle and thread. The journey was without mishaps, and I safely reached Cieszyn, a town on the Czechoslovakian border. I felt uneasy approaching the Polish customs office, but I passed without trouble. I had my passport to Hungary and a document stating my position with the Yugoslav Repatriation Mission in Budapest. The officers looked at my backpack and waved me on in a friendly fashion.

As I crossed the bridge over the river Olza, from Poland to Czechoslovakia, I felt my spirits lifting and a feeling of freedom engulfing me. I was nearing the middle when I heard someone running behind me. It was one of the Polish guards. "Sir," he called, "the officer wants to see you. You have to come back!" I knew I had to obey, being on the Polish side of the bridge. The soldier was armed. I turned back and was escorted to the officer to whom only minutes ago

I had been talking. Then the man had been friendly and smiling. Now he was looking at me in an unfriendly, even hostile, manner. "Passport, please!" he said.

I handed my passport to him.

"Name?"

"Piotr Daraż."

He looked at me with a triumphant smile and said, "Is it really?" Then a door opened and a colleague from the Lwów Polytechnic entered the room. His name was Kozdon, a Silesian. I remembered him well. He must have remembered me, too, and he gave me a malicious look. He turned to the officer, and they exchanged smug smiles. They had caught a Jew with false papers trying to escape! Who knew what offenses he had committed? Two soldiers standing on either side of me were also smiling.

Remaining calm, I opened my wallet and pulled out the document that I had drafted in Warsaw and luckily had with me. It stated that Piotr Daraż and Henry Reiss were one and the same person. Recognition of my degree from the Lwów Polytechnic was endorsed with the stamp of the Polish eagle – and the signatures of Professors Poniż and Grubecki!

The lieutenant read the paper and showed it to Kozdon who was standing behind him. Their smiles faded. They looked embarrassed, especially Kozdon. The officer returned the document. I asked if he had any more questions. If not, I said, I would be ready to go. He gave a sign to the soldiers, whose smiles had also vanished. Without another word, I left the room.

A few minutes later I was in Czechoslovakia, receiving a friendly welcome from the Czech border guards. They stamped my passport and opened the door to their country. Behind me was Poland, the country that had once been my homeland. Behind me were people who were capable and willing to repeat "Kielce" in every corner of their land. Unfortunately, I had missed the train to Budapest. There was only one train a day, early in the morning. Ahead of me was a lonely day and a long night.

I was still upset after my Polish experiences and went into a small café. At the adjoining table were two women. They looked Jewish and spoke an excellent, educated Polish. (Cieszyn had a mixture of Polish and Czech citizens.) I approached them and introduced myself. When they heard I had just come from Kraków, they showed great interest. We had coffee together and, assured of my identity, one of them, the wife of a local solicitor, invited me home. There, I met her husband and children. We spent nearly all day talking. I stayed for supper and for the night, grateful for the warmth and generous hospitality extended to me, a complete stranger. A typical example of the wonder of belonging to one nation – the Jewish nation – even in the Diaspora. We were just *Amchu* – one people, our people. We talked about Kielce. I gave my point of view, trying to be impartial and understand both sides, the Jews and the Poles. During the war, the Poles had moved into the houses of Jews whom they believed to be dead, and here they were coming back and demanding the return of their properties. Evictions were taking place. Resentment, even hatred, was growing. Most of the Poles had gladly accepted the Final Solution, and now here the Jews were back from the grave demanding the return of their homes.

Yet where else could the Jews have gone? For five years, they had dreamed of returning to their hometowns, small houses, and little gardens, hoping to find someone who would help them, maybe a friend or neighbor. Where now could the survivors go? They obviously had not realized that during those years of Jewish persecution, changes had taken place in the Polish society, and for the worse. The antisemitic attitude had deepened. And now those unwanted, despised elements were back, demanding their rights.

The Jews, despite their "wisdom," had not realized that for hundreds of years, they had made a serious mistake. They had forgotten they were Jews. They lived among people who hated them – including ordinary folk, working class, intelligentsia, and clergy – the great majority of Polish society. The Jews had forgotten and dug their heads in the sand. Now they were starting new lives, some even taking high positions in the government of a People's Republic that the Poles had not rushed to take part in building. Behind that People's Republic stood the hated Russian, and the Jew was his tool. The Poles still remembered arrests and deportations to Siberia; they remembered Katyn. They remembered the Soviet attack in September 1939. They remembered the partitioning of Poland and 123 years of occupation by the hated Russian Empire. They saw the new Polish People's Republic as a vassal of the Soviets, governed by the Jews.

A story was circulating. A Pole meets a Russian and complains, "In

Poland, we Poles are governed by Jews. You enter an office. In the first room, a Jew is in charge. He sends you to a higher authority, where again a Jew is in charge. You go further up – another Jew. And in the last office, that of the department's head – there sits a Russian." The Russian replies sadly, "In Russia, it is quite the opposite. You enter an office and in the first room you meet a Russian; in the next one, a Russian. Only in the last one, that of the department head, you find a Jew."

Could a Pole, who as the saying goes sucked antisemitism with his mother's milk, accept such a state of affairs? No. But the Jews could not see it. Why should they not accept positions offered to them, positions in the government never before accessible to them? So they jumped at the opportunity without thinking. They took the highest positions in government, education, foreign service, foreign trade, internal security, justice, and the coal industry – many as deputy ministers or even ministers and as directors of various departments as well as planners and managers of the rebuilding of Warsaw. They were seen as somehow ruling the country.

To make their appointments easier, they often took Polish names. They pretended not to be Jews. While in Warsaw, I had met a few of my old colleagues who had changed their names and held high positions in the government. Yet the Poles hated them.[3]

The massacre in Kielce and the cold-blooded murders by the NSZ reflected a general atmosphere – a consequence of the Jews' shortsightedness and short memory of Jewish history.

In this discussion with my hospitable hosts, they asked, "Why can't Jews work according to their education and abilities? Why can't they accept high positions when they are suited for them and can do a good job for their country? Are they not citizens of that country? Why should a Polish citizen be accepted joyfully as a minister in his country and not a Jew who considers himself a Pole, an equally loyal citizen who loves his country, loves Poland?"[4]

I parted with my new friends, happy to be outside a country where, after the massacre of three million people, a Kielce was still possible. My Czech friends stayed behind, sad and worried, uncertain of tomorrow, asking themselves over and over again that age-old Jewish question: What should we do?

The next evening, I knocked at the door of our little flat in

Budapest, happy to be welcomed by Lusia and Elżunia. Lusia was now seven months pregnant. I told her about Kielce. It strongly reinforced our decision not to return to Poland. But where to go and how? How to get out of the Soviet Empire? Run again across the border? Again, risk freedom, even our lives?

NEW LIFE: MAY 1946

Elżunia was nearly eight years old. She was still small, delicate, quiet, and well behaved. With her lovely golden hair and blue eyes, her fine features and dimple in one cheek, she was arrestingly beautiful. During our stay in Taszár, she went to the local school. She had mastered the language and was an excellent student. The name Erzika (Elizabeth in Hungarian) was popular in Hungary. The last empress of Austria, the wife of the popular Franz Joseph I, had also been the queen of Hungary and was named Elizabeth. She had been assassinated at a young age. The people of both nations, Hungary and Austria, had loved the popular empress. Our Erzika was loved by everyone, too.

Upon arriving in Budapest, Lusia had immediately enrolled her in a Hungarian school. Her teacher admired her quiet, good behavior. Elżunia was gifted. She finished first grade with very good marks and topped the second grade. The teacher congratulated Lusia. "I'm very happy," the teacher said. "Erzika is the best in the class, and if it was not for her, the best one would be a Jewish girl." That friendly teacher would have been astounded had she known the truth.

Elżunia's birthday was in April. Did we organize a big birthday party for her? No! There were no children, no playmates. Elżunia had no school friends, no one visited her, and she was not invited anywhere. She was well liked everywhere, but only by adults. Not by children. She never played with them, never felt like it. It was difficult for her to establish a rapport with her peers. This was understandable. From an early age, she had been isolated. At 18 months, she had been taken by her nanny to the village in Oserdów. During the Soviet occupation of Lwów, we stayed with Lusia's parents without opportunity to contact other families with children, in constant fear of arrest and deportation by the Soviets. That was followed by the horrors of the German occupation. She grew up in an atmosphere of unrelenting fear experienced by her parents. That fear must have affected the child's psyche.

Our family was unable to provide her the much-needed atmosphere of tenderness and warmth necessary to overcome the fears that enveloped us all the time. When little Felus was with us, the two children played together. Their grandmother could always find something to play with among her "garbage," as she used to say. But little Felus had been snatched from Elżunia's life and murdered by the Nazis. Whether he died in a gas chamber, was trampled by other victims in an overcrowded railway carriage on the way to Belzec extermination camp, or had his skull crushed by a German boot, we don't know and never will. From August 1942 until our flight to Hungary in 1944, our child had been hidden under the protective wing of Lusia. Elżunia was comfortable, safe, and warm, but without contact with other children. She must have thought this was normal and became used to solitude, without playmates. She had lived this way through Taszár and Budapest, too. Hence she was always shy and reserved. Well behaved and smiling, lovely with those dimples in her cheeks, but timid and lonely. A child of war.

While in Poland I had visited the Jewish committees in Kraków and Warsaw and searched the lists of survivors to no avail. We had no family left. Our child had no grandmother or grandfather, no aunt or uncle, no cousins. One day she would be alone without one close and loving family member. I was happy Lusia was pregnant. A new life was beginning for Elżunia and us.

Rumors were spreading about the possibility of leaving Budapest for the West. An underground Palestinian-Zionist organization called Bricha was in charge of arranging transports of Jews from Romania,

Hungary, and Czechoslovakia to the West. Officially no one knew anything. Everything was kept secret. We were waiting. How lucky I was to have that document from the Yugoslav Repatriation Mission! I could prove that I was needed here in Budapest, and we could stay on. So far, no transport from Yugoslavia had reached the Hungarian border; everything was proceeding very slowly. Each day of delay was a gain for us.

Yet, one day it started. The postman brought me a telegram: "The first transport for Poland left on the 20th. Intervention ... Locomotives ... etc." It was signed: Polish Mission Maczka. The monotony of my idleness was broken. Going shopping and helping with the housework could not fill my day anyway. I suddenly was busy rushing back and forth between the Department of Railways and the Soviet and Hungarian authorities. The Hungarians delivered the locomotives and the Poles their coal, but the Soviets had their special requirements: I had to send a telegram to Maczka for "a list of repatriates with names, places and dates of birth, including two copies, to obtain passes." The telegram cost me 1,062,500,000 pengős. (I still have the receipt in my folder of documents from that period.) I sent the cable in two languages – Polish and, for the benefit of the Soviet censor, Russian. It was certainly a busy time for me until the first train reached Budapest, which after the checking of documents by the Soviet authorities was allowed to continue toward the Polish border. I was glad we were not on it!

Without my "diplomatic" intervention in Budapest, that train, with hundreds of women and children, would have been held up by the Soviet bureaucracy for several days. The first transport was followed by two more. The last was much easier. It was escorted by Maczka himself. He expressed his deep gratitude for my help, energy, and initiative for which, he said, I would get a separate letter of thanks from the Polish government. He also extended the validity of my documents for the next six months, which made it possible for me to stay in Budapest unmolested by the Polish and Hungarian authorities. (As for the thank-you letter from the Polish government, it never arrived.)

Slowly, our chances of leaving Hungary started to look realistic. Our committee had established contact with Bricha and drawn up a list of candidates. I put my name down: Piotr and Stanislawa Daraż –

two adults – plus one child of eight and an unborn baby. Lusia's delivery was expected in May and indications were that the next transport to the West would take place in May or June. If only she could make it! We knew how unpredictable the Russians were. They could suddenly stop the transports, and should we miss this one, we would be stuck in Hungary as Polish citizens. How long would the Hungarians tolerate our presence? On the other hand, to leave in the last weeks of pregnancy and deliver somewhere on the way ... what a frightening thought! The gynecologist looking after Lusia was a Hungarian Jew, recommended to us by other expectant mothers. There were a lot of pregnant young women among the migrants, mostly for the same reason – family members had been murdered and they wanted to fill that emptiness.

Lusia felt well all the time. Everything was all right until one day, late in her eighth month, she slipped and fell on her tummy in the street and was unable to get up. People had to help her home. We were both frightened. The doctor had looked grave before pronouncing the baby's little heart was working normally. "Hopefully, everything will be all right," he said calmly. His calmness did not reassure me much. It was not his wife or his baby, it was my wife and my baby. On 24 May, Lusia started having pains. The private hospital I had booked some time ago was not far away. The next morning, she was taken to the delivery room while I nervously paced up and down the corridor.

My thoughts went back to the past. In April 1938, some eight years earlier, I had been pacing the corridor of a Kraków private hospital feeling just as nervous as now. Lusia had been in great pain, and there was no medication to speed up the delivery. I was up all night. In the morning, Elżunia was born, a tiny baby weighing just 2.65 kilos. Lusia's mother had been with me. She had come from Lwów to be at this important event. In Oserdów, my family was waiting for the news. In Lwów and Kraków, both Lusia's and my families, including uncles and aunts, and our friends were waiting, too. We were the first of our generation to have the courage to get married and have a child. Out of more than 20 cousins, I was the first, hence the interest of all our family and friends. Today, I was again nervously pacing the corridor but far from home, in the city, in a strange country. Neither in Kraków, Oserdów, nor Lwów was there anyone waiting for news. The child I was awaiting so anxiously would come into a family of only three.

For us, our number of children would double. Two children! One saved from hell. This next one would, if needed, comfort the first when both are alone in the world. My thoughts were interrupted by our friend, Dr. Brudner, the chairman of our committee who, with his wife, had dropped in to get the news. Our gynecologist peeked his head out of the door of the delivery room to say that labor was progressing slowly and it would be another two to three hours. We just had to wait. Accompanied by the Brudners, I went next door for a cup of coffee. Unable to calm down, I rushed back to the hospital after a short while. To my surprise, I was greeted by the doctor smiling broadly. He spoke in German: "You have a lovely healthy daughter – three and a half kilo! My congratulations!" I was ecstatic.

After an hour or so, I was allowed to see Lusia. She gave me the sweet happy smile that I loved so much during the 12 years of our marriage. Her eyes were glittering. By her side lay a sleeping baby, pink and plump. Beautiful! It was 25 May 1946. Later that afternoon, I took Elżunia to introduce her baby sister to her. Her mother received a bunch of lilies from the valley. I looked at my family, at Lusia whom I adored, and my two children and suddenly felt strong and capable of building a life of security, happiness, and love for my precious family, somewhere in this vast unknown world, knowing that with the cooperation of Lusia, no obstacles would be too difficult to overcome.

I started preparing for our journey. First, it was necessary to equip our baby with everything she would need. We had been thinking for a while about a name for her. We did not want a name from the loved ones we had lost. That would have been too painful. We did not want a name that would sound Jewish because we were still not sure whether we would succeed in going to the West, and the possibility of having to go back to Poland was unfortunately still very real and very frightening. Would we be forced to go back? Would we have to go as Daraż? We decided on Christine. Should we succeed in going to the West, the name Christina?? would sound all right in any language just as would Elżunia; Elizabeth was an international name. When little Christine?? came into this world, we had literally nothing for her and could not buy anything from the shops. The only possibility was again the black market. On the Telekiter, I managed to buy a black pram for $10. With the help of some black Indian ink, I was able to cover the stains and scratches and Lusia polished it to a high gloss. I bought a new mattress, and now the completed pram looked like new. I also managed to get some baby clothes and friends organized some nappies. We had only half a dozen, but still that was better than none.

We lived, this small family of four, in happiness and hope. It was the beginning of June and Budapest was warm and green all over. Elżunia was still attending school. Lusia went for walks with the baby. The Polish Jews were still smuggling on a large scale. The international trade now included Romania. Goods were smuggled out of there through Hungary to Poland. The smugglers risked their freedom, even their lives. One such smuggler, a well-known man from Kraków, was said to have fallen from a loaded Soviet truck onto a railway crossing and been killed on the spot. There were rumors that Russian truck drivers had murdered their "partners," taking their dollars, and left their bodies on the railway line.

Fortunes were not made easily. One day I met our old "friend," the doctor who in 1943 took us for a ride, taking 1,000 złoty as an advance payment for our transfer to Hungary and then disappearing. I saw him standing next to a Soviet Red Cross truck. He recognized and welcomed me cordially. "In the past, we were deceiving people," he boasted. "Now we are cheating countries." He was smuggling huge quantities of medication from Bucharest to Poland, where there was a great shortage of this lifesaving commodity. He had the foolproof documents of a Soviet Red Cross doctor and was traveling legally, without any risk at border checkpoints.

I delicately asked, considering that he was now doing so well, if he would be inclined to give me back my 1,000 złoty taken in Warsaw. He politely refused on the grounds that the money had been taken away by the Slovak border guards. He turned his back on me, obviously not wanting to discuss the matter any further.[1]

16 June 1946 was an important day in Elżunia's life. On that day, she was to take part in her first Holy Communion. We received a note from the school advising that the child should appear at school correctly dressed and with a bunch of white flowers. How Lusia managed to organize a white dress for that occasion, I don't recall. We had thought a lot about whether Elżunia should take part in the ceremony. We finally decided that because our chances of immigrating were still slim and our return to Poland could not be ruled out, it would be sensible to conform to this custom. Elżunia was bound to ask why she was not

taking part in the ritual like all other children. She could have been asked questions at school for which she would have no answers. She was unaware of our family history and did not know anything about the catastrophe we had experienced. The longer we could postpone telling her, the easier it would be for her to cope now. So Elżunia took her Holy Communion, looking like an angel. She brought a picture of the Holy Mother and a confirmation certificate home.

Secret talks with Soviet authorities were still being held and we lived in constant apprehension. Obviously, not a word about our plans to live in the West had been mentioned to our landlady. She could not help noticing that we were already packed and would be wondering. We explained there was a chance of our returning to Poland. Having seen large trucks marked "Poland," she was neither suspicious nor surprised. It was common knowledge that candidates for immigration had to keep silent. Should the Soviets suspect something, the whole operation would collapse.

Twice a day, I went to the committee for news. We were expecting a final decision any day. Excitement was increasing, but there was still uneasiness. What if something changed at the last minute? It was not easy to leave the Soviet Union. Soviet authorities would not let their citizens out of their protective grasp so easily.

Then at last! The long-awaited signal! Early in the morning, 23 June 1946, a truck would come for us. At six in the morning, we were waiting downstairs. Elżunia was quiet as usual but wondering where we were going. Baby Christine was asleep after a large breakfast. Nature helped Lusia to satisfy her child's healthy appetite. The rosy cheeks and contented smile of the baby rewarded Lusia's efforts. The hooded military truck arrived on time. We were not the first; others were already there, sitting silently in the vehicle. Our modest belongings, the sleeping baby in her pram, and a drowsy Elżunia were put onto the truck, and within seconds we were on our way, leaving our landlady in tears behind.

We had spent over a year with her in that small apartment, sharing her kitchen and bathroom. There had never been any misunderstandings, and she loved Elżunia and adored Lusia. We left all our food for her and, as I was a good provider, there was quite a lot.

We also left our pots and pans and some clothing. There were quite a number of things we had managed to acquire during our 2½ years stay in Hungary that we could not bring. We left her all our remaining Hungarian pengős, the equivalent of two months' rent. That made her especially happy.

Arriving at the railway station, we were quickly hustled onto a goods train. During the next hour, the carriages filled up. We had some friends with us: Dr. Brodner and his wife, Celina; Dr. Kneller and his wife, Szymon Szop, the tailor and his wife, Helena, and their two boys; and the ex-solicitor Samuel Gelles. We were advised that we belonged to a group of Greek deportees returning to the country from Romania and were told to be silent, "unless of course you can speak Greek," joked the transport leader, a young man in his early twenties. He was a member of the Bricha. We were silent as the heavy doors of the carriage closed slowly. We left just a narrow gap for air.

Some Soviet soldiers appeared. They conferred with our transport leader. Everyone was smiling. The Soviet soldiers were happy to see the "Greeks" going home. They didn't need Greeks. The Jewish leader was happy, too. We were all happy.

Slowly the train started to roll – toward where? We only knew we were heading to the "West," and the West meant freedom. Freedom! What were we leaving behind? The Soviet Union, and its despotic leader, Stalin. What were we taking with us? Painful memories of our families, cruelly murdered for being Jewish.

What might be in front of us? An unknown future in an unknown land.

PART VII
AFTER THE WAR

EMIGRATION

Nothing extraordinary happened to us, which had not happened to thousands of other would-be emigrants. After three weeks' stopover in Vienna, we again boarded a goods train and arrived in Ulm on the Danube, in the American-occupied part of Germany in Sedan-Kaserne, a Displaced Persons (DP) camp for Jews. Not having any overseas relatives, we were faced with a potentially hopeless stay in the camp with no clear end. I was frustrated and asked the camp commandant for a job. He put me in charge of the camp's food store. I found that quantities of nearly all articles listed in the stock records were fewer than actually was in the storeroom. This could only mean that the surplus had yet to leave for the black market. I didn't want to be the policeman or judge of the store man and resigned from the assignment.

Having the great urge to write down the history of our survival, I started to collect some notes but quickly realized that my mind was not able to relax and concentrate and gave up. Anyway, I was busy with problems of everyday life in the DP camp.

Then one day, a note from the Munich office of the American Jewish Joint Distribution Committee unexpectedly arrived stating that a certificate from Brazil confirming my employment offer with a building company as an engineer.

While in Vienna I had also applied, alas unsuccessfully, to the

Belgian Military Mission for a visa to the Belgian Congo, seeing myself directing Africans to build a road across the desert, in a tropical helmet, riding a huge camel, drinking warm water from a leather pouch, and perspiring profusely under the scorching African sun.

Well, the Brazilian alternative seemed more attractive. After six months of living in the misery and monotony of the DP camp, the Joint sent me to Paris while Lusia stayed in Ulm, taking over my job of teaching mathematics classes for the Or – an organization aiming at giving the Jewish adults some basic schooling missed during the war years. In Paris, some bad news was awaiting – the Brazilian Consulate was closed for Jewish migrants, and there was no transport whatsoever available into any overseas country. Even people with families overseas, and with all necessary affidavits, landing permits, and visas, had been waiting for months. It was 1946 and chaos reigned everywhere. Luckily, the Joint extended its helping hand and accommodated us (Lusia and the children had arrived in the meantime) at the Hotel Mirabeau, where we stayed for 12 long months with many other Jewish families with similar problems, "enjoying" our lunches and dinners, which consisted nearly every day of clear soup and boiled beef (read: bones) with boiled potatoes and cabbage.

Still, we greatly appreciated the help. It was a wonderful feeling to know that somewhere, far away, were people, our people, who cared about us, and did their best to support thousands like us through these difficulties.

During this period, I took lessons (with Alliance Française) in Portuguese for my future life in Brazil, and in French to be able to spend our 50 francs' daily subsidy in the fruit market and the *boulangerie* [bakery] buying fresh baguettes.

Having doubts about whether I would be able to earn a living as an engineer with my newly acquired Portuguese vocabulary of some hundred words, I enrolled in a technical college. I finished a course in *maroquinerie* [leather goods] to have another qualification that I could put to use while not being able to speak the language of the country of our final destination.

At the same time, Lusia took a course in dressmaking from a Polish lady, who for years had been running her own *haute couture* salon in Paris. Lusia must have been gifted, as the proprietress offered her a 50 percent partnership in her salon and a promise to arrange French citizenship for us.

Nevertheless, we decided to continue with our plans to emigrate from Europe, away from the danger of communist dictatorship. Realizing the difficulties with Brazil and not being keen on converting my family into South Americans, I looked for other emigration possibilities. Israel as such did not exist as yet. The few entry certificates to Palestine were reserved for younger people. It occurred to me that perhaps Peter Daraż, a Christian, would be allowed to enter. Yet my application to the Department of Immigration in Jerusalem was not accepted. The British were no fools.

In the meantime, after months of struggling with the French and Polish bureaucracies, we succeeded in returning to our original names – Henry and Lucy Reiss. People talked about Australia, a dreamland far away from Europe. As an English-speaking country with a good climate and being a Member of the British Commonwealth of Nations, it was at the top of the list for prospective emigrants. In Adelaide, we found Lusia's colleague from the university, Mr. Simon, whose friend, a local pastor, had agreed to sponsor us. We waited. Week after week passed without any news. Then we remembered that Mr. Eisner, whom I had met in 1937 in Warsaw, had migrated to Australia.

After finding his address, I wrote him and, to our indescribable joy, we received by return mail a huge registered air letter with two landing permits – one for us, and one for the Haber family, who were still in Poland. Two months later, we left unforgettable Paris, the city we learned to love, and boarded a small Egyptian military transport boat, the El Sudan, in Marseilles.

After a journey of seven weeks, under the most difficult and primitive conditions, surviving extreme heat, thirst, and seasickness, we landed in Sydney.

We felt relaxed and happy to have left El Sudan, where our Egyptian doctor didn't care about the Jewish passengers. One of them, Yankel, a sweet little boy of three, died because the ship's hospital did not have any antibiotics except for a few cartons of outdated drugs. The Egyptian captain surely felt uncomfortable watching, in his splendid gold-trimmed uniform, the small coffin sliding gently into the sea that early morning.

We were warmly welcomed by the Eisners, who took us to

temporary yet most comfortable accommodation. After a few days' rest, I started a job at Arcos, a steel factory established and developed by our friend Eisner. I was lucky – Eisner's wife, Giza, and her brother John Kuner, my boss and manager of Arcos, spoke German and were most friendly and helpful. My first drawings were accepted by the management and the workshop. By sheer chance, steel structures happened to be my best subject at the Lwów Polytechnic.

Lusia (now Lucy), the first female engineer in Australia, had no chance of obtaining a job in her profession. Since Arcos had more orders than could be handled in the drawing office, I had been asked to take some drawings home and Lusia joined me in performing this extra work, which was gradually followed by many more subcontracting orders. After moving into a small two-bedroom flat, I put a huge drawing board into the larger room for Lusia to use, while on weekends it was my domain. When our children outgrew the small second bedroom, we purchased a three-bedroom cottage in Chatswood and converted the sunroom into a drawing office, where Lusia had her own drawing board for her verification work, at which she was faultless.

As a result of those drafting jobs, our savings grew, and when approached by some enterprising friends to join a building venture, we were able to take part in the construction of a block of home units, where our professional knowhow was instrumental in its financial success. Those were extremely busy times for us. At 5:30 in the morning, I would leave home to meet our foreman at 6:30 on site to discuss the work program for the day. At eight, I would be at my desk at Arcos. During my half-hour lunch break, I called Lusia to sort out any drafting or building problems. Finishing at four, it took me 1½ hours to get home by public transport. After purchasing my first car, a Holden, my traveling time greatly reduced. After a quick dinner, I would retreat into our drawing room for a few hours and was often up until midnight as our drawings were always urgently required for production. We loved being together all the time on our weekends. I would devote my Saturdays to inspection of building sites and Sundays to the drawing board, sharing all problems with Lusia and enjoying every moment of it. During those periods, I would spend some 80 hours per week in intensive work and Lusia not much less. The growing girls also needed their mother, who would assist with schoolwork and do all the sewing and altering as well as attend to the housework.

At this time, I was also trying to dispose of the stamps I had bought in Poland and Hungary for resale. Only after mixing them with some African and New Caledonian stamps, bought cheaply from a friendly dealer, Mr. Kugel, was I able to sell them at one shilling a packet, paying one-third commission to the old Australian lady who owned the street kiosk. (I think I still have a few unsold packets left.) During a period of two years, I managed to put over 500 pounds into savings. Luckily, we did not always have those private contracts to keep us busy. Once the pressure was off, I could devote my free time to my most passionate love – my garden.

Having installed a special lighting system through the garage window, I would work late into the night at my beautiful vegetable plot, digging, hoeing, weeding, watering, and watching with love and excitement how strongly the vegetables would grow in the virgin soil of our backyard under the Australian sun. During those leisure periods, Lusia would take subcontracting dressmaking jobs and spend many hours each day at her sewing machine in addition to her other activities, increasing our savings with each hard-earned pound.

Our girls grew up in this most wonderful part of the world and developed into young, healthy, and happy teenagers. After leaving Budapest, where Elizabeth had attended primary school with excellent results, and a few short months in Germany, where she attended the French *École pour les filles* [school for girls] and was in the top ten in her class, she completed her primary and secondary schooling in Sydney. Her name was engraved in gold letters on the honors board at Cremorne High School, having been Dux in each year including the final.

After completing her Leaving Certificate, she studied medicine at the University of Sydney and later specialized in microbiology. She is currently the chief microbiologist at St. George Hospital, where she has been for over 20 years. Christine, eight years her junior, after finishing primary school in the "Opportunity" class, entered North Sydney Girls High School. She subsequently qualified as a medical technologist and is working at the Royal Prince Alfred Hospital in the pathology department. They were always delightful and promising youngsters, joining their parents' happy togetherness.

Then one day, disaster struck. Lusia had an appendectomy that developed into a major cancer operation. Once again, my life became a nightmare. To be with Lusia as much as possible, I left Arcos after ten years of service, from now on concentrating on drawings and buildings only. Luckily, Lusia recovered and joined me with her former energy.

We enjoyed a great moment of happiness when Elizabeth married Bernard Levy, a young, good-looking solicitor, and moved across the road into a lovely corner house with a row of beautiful flowering peach trees in the front. Lusia was thrilled to have them living so close by, but this happiness was short lived.

Another malignant growth attacked her brain, and medical science was helpless. She passed away on 8 August 1964. At that moment, I lost my lifelong companion, school friend, and courageous co-fighter for our survival, a wise professional partner and an utterly devoted, deeply loved, and loving wife and mother.

With her passing, the most beautiful part of my life came to an end. Two months later, a baby girl was born to Elizabeth and Bernie. They named her Lucy. My joy was deeply marred by Lusia not being with us to celebrate this happy event. I was lonely, depressed, heartbroken.

POLAND REVISITED: 1967

Two years passed. Elżunia and Krysia (Christine) insisted it was time for me to stop mourning for Lusia and to take a break, go abroad, and visit the old places, old friends, and remnants of our families dispersed all over the world. In the middle of May 1967, I landed in Israel around three in the morning. I felt greatly moved to be in a Jewish country.

It was early morning. The city was asleep. From the balcony, I could see the Mediterranean Sea. I went down to the beach to see and hear the waves, to touch and feel them. It is hard to describe my feelings standing at that shore. It was high tide. Strong waves were rhythmically crashing against the shore, the waves of the Jewish sea. Was such a miracle possible? The Jewish land, the Jewish sea, and all around, Jewish houses with Jewish families, sleeping peacefully. Nothing was threatening them; they were safe. The Jews were at last at home in their own country. It was hard to believe, but it was true.

Unfortunately, the political situation was tense. Egyptian President Gamal Abdel Nasser, supported by the Soviet Union, had concentrated large numbers of armed forces on the Sinai Peninsula, at the same time demanding that the United Nations remove the peacekeeping trooped stationed on the Egyptian-Israeli border. The Arab world would not accept the existence of the state of Israel. A hundred million Arabs were determined to reach "a simple solution" – driving all the Jews into the sea.

Following my itinerary, I had to leave the country of my forefathers, although with great anxiety. Stopping for a few days in Germany, I was impressed by the unexpected reaction of the German youth. There were pro-Israeli demonstrations, leaflets, and appeals to the people to donate money and blood. It was incredible. German blood to save the Jews! Without a command or threat, but voluntarily and spontaneously. It was indeed a different world and a different Germany.

My next stop was London. I managed to see *Fiddler on the Roof* with Topol in the lead role. I was lucky to get an excellent seat and watched the beautiful performance for three hours with enchantment. The scene of the lighting of the Sabbath candles by Jews scattered all over the world was moving. I was thinking about the Polish Jews. The tense situation in Israel was constantly on my mind.

On 4 June 1967, I landed in Paris. Paris was the same as always – beautiful. I found some old university friends, and we returned to the memories of our days at the Lwów Polytechnic. I went to see all the beautiful spots of Paris, the same ones that 20 years earlier I had seen with Lusia. Now I was alone.

The dangerous situation in Israel worried me greatly. What was going to happen? The answer came on 6 June: The Arab-Israeli war broke out. I was at a duty-free shop belonging to a store called Freddie, which came recommended and was owned by a Jewish woman from Poland. I was buying gifts for Sydney when the disastrous news broke. *War!* Freddie's shop employed several Jewish saleswomen, but none were attending to customers anymore. They were all glued to their transistor radios and shedding tears. For us, the clients, they were no longer saleswomen. They were children of a nation that was in deadly danger. The owner, Freddie, was also in tears, and so were we, the tourists. We had become one big family united in anxiety about Israel. There were demonstrations in Paris. The streets were in turmoil – cars, taxis, trucks, young people on foot, bicycles, and motorbikes were moving in the streets of Paris amid the noise of horns and pro-Israeli shouting of protesters. It was my last day in Paris as I was to fly to Poland the following morning. In the evening, I met some of my old friends in the Café de l'Opéra. All were concerned and unanimously agreed that I should not risk going to Poland. Nobody knew how the situation would develop. There could be conflict between superpowers and the outbreak of a Third World War! I could be cut off! No, I should not take that risk.

I hardly slept that night my mind, confronted by the dilemma of "to go or not to go?" The commotion of the pro-Israeli demonstrations could be heard late into the night. The following morning, the Air-France minibus turned up, as planned, to pick me up from the hotel. I decided to continue my trip according to my original itinerary. I had set out on this world trip particularly to see Poland, and I was not going to turn back halfway.

It was a long way to Orly Airport. The French newspapers carried banners screaming "*La Guerre!*" I could not get an English newspaper so early in the morning. A middle-aged passenger was sitting next to me with an English newspaper sticking out of his pocket. He was the manager of a Swiss branch of a big South African export company. He was tense. He had received a cable from his head office urging him to leave Europe immediately and was not sure whether he would be able to get a flight to London. When he learned I was going to Poland, he was amazed. "To Poland, in these circumstances!" he said. He thought I was mad.

I began to wonder whether I had made the right decision. Bravery was out of place in that situation. At the airport, one could feel the excitement and confusion. The newspaper stands were crowded, with people buying a magazine featuring the popular commander of the Israeli army, General Moshe Dayan, on the cover. Waiting for my flight announcement, I was again wondering whether my decision had been the right one even though I had already checked in, with my luggage probably deep inside the plane.

There were five passengers on the plane altogether. I felt quite uneasy. The plane was to take off in a few minutes but was still empty. Where were the other passengers? Had I boarded the wrong plane? I approached the steward. "Is this plane flying to Poland?" I asked.

"Yes," he replied.

"Is it taking off in five minutes according to schedule?"

"Yes."

"Is it always so empty?"

"No, it's always full," he said, "but in the present political situation, every sensible person stays home."

A few minutes later, we were flying over the roofs of Paris. At

Warsaw Airport, I collected my luggage, went through customs, exchanged some dollars for złoty, and opened the exit door. Someone called out my name. There were Lutek and Elżunia Szulkin, my old friends, who had moved from Lodz to Warsaw. They looked pale and frightened.

"I rang you in Paris this morning, but they told me at the hotel you had already gone," Lutek said. As Lutek was working as an editor of *Kurier Polski*, he was able to make direct calls all over the world.

"Did you want to warn me against coming here?" I asked.

"Indeed," he said. "I thought you were taking a great risk. There's a danger of a Third World War. All the shops are already empty, the shelves bare. There is no flour, rice, sugar, or oil. You name it, there is absolutely nothing."

Now I was terrified. Although an Australian citizen, I was born in Poland and hence might not be protected by the Australian Embassy in Warsaw. Also, I only had a little cash, with the rest in traveler's checks, which in case of war were probably worthless. I realized I had made a mistake and the consequences could be disastrous. But should I worry in advance? The Szulkins and I got into an elegant black, chauffeur-driven limousine, the property of the newspaper, and we went to their flat.

I experienced hours of anxiety. What was happening in Israel? Would they be able to defend themselves? The whole Arab world was united against them. Their ultimate aim was declared – to liquidate the Jewish State and the Jewish Nation. In short, to finish off Hitler's work.

After a few days, we received incredible news: the Arabs were defeated on all fronts. The war was over in six days. The Israeli forces had reached the Suez Canal and occupied Sinai, the Gaza Strip, the West Bank of the river Jordan, and the Golan Heights, from where the Syrians were shooting at kibbutzniks working peacefully in their fields.

We were overjoyed, but to our amazement, the whole Polish nation was celebrating, too. The people of Warsaw were drinking gallons of vodka to the Israeli victory over the Arabs, the allies of the hated Soviet Union. The Jews in government positions, who had been hiding their origins under Polish names and Aryan identities, were receiving congratulations from their Polish colleagues. Still, they were embarrassed and worried. Their incognito had been unmasked.

Cousin Edek Reiss took a week off from his job at the hospital in Katowice and we went by car to the family property in Budynin. We were driving through the townships and shtetlechs feeling sad. There was no life. The Jews – bearded men rushing, shouting, and gesticulating – once a part of the Polish scenery – had disappeared. There were empty markets, empty streets. Hitler had solved the Jewish problem for the Poles.

Our cousin, Dolek, his Polish wife, Zula, and two children from his first marriage welcomed us in Przemyśl. (Dolek's first wife, Anna, who had been a nurse looking after Uncle Jacob, had hidden him in her bedroom and saved his life. Grateful, Dolek had married Anna after the liberation.) We were very warmly received. Zula cooked lots of pierogies, the favorite dish of us, the "Galicianers." The following morning Edek, Dolek, and I went in a hired taxi to Budynin, which was the main purpose of my Polish visit. It was a lush, green Polish June. We were passing through villages with familiar names – Dyniska, which had once been the home of Isaak Reiss, and Potoki, which had been the home of Laib Reiss, both brothers of our grandfather, Nuchim. We did not stop, What for? Further along, we passed another small township and at the railway station read the name of Belzec, one of Hider's notorious extermination camps.

I stared at that name in silence. Edek, Dolek, and the driver were silent, too. I wanted to take a photograph. "It's forbidden to take photographs of the railway stations," my companions told me. But I was not going to give up easily and went to talk to the station master. After a moment's hesitation, he permitted me to take a photograph, but only the name on the railway building. I complied, and afterward, he directed an employee to show us the monument of the Martyrs of Belzec. There among the trees of the beautifully maintained park was an impressive monument inscribed:

"On this site there was a Hitlerite extermination camp. Between February and December 1942, over 600,000 Polish and European Jews died a martyr's death, as well as 1,500 Poles for helping Jews."

We stood in silence at the grave of our families. The sad thought crossed my mind: How could so many die without many, many denunciators? How else would the SS have known of the many Jewish hiding places?

We continued our journey in silence, passing through fields and villages, until the sign "Budynin" appeared in front of us. I looked at the familiar name of the village where I had spent my childhood. I was excited and tense. We came close to the familiar fields. The road was turning, and I could see the beautiful building of the Budynin Greek-Orthodox Church, the most prominent spot on the horizon.

Before the war, the church had been hidden behind the huge trees of the Budynin Park. But now the trees were gone, and the church was clearly visible. We were slowly approaching the village and stopped among some houses. I tried to discern our location but couldn't. Everything was so changed. I noticed that the once beautiful park had disappeared and the tall, old trees that remembered many generations of the owners of Budynin were gone, too. So was the beautiful orchard – not a single fruit tree left. The house in which my family had lived, a gracious country manor, was gone, too. In its place stood a number of small cottages with gardens separated by small fences. A different Budynin, no longer the Budynin I had dreamed about for so many years.

It was Sunday morning. A few people gathered around our car looking at us with curiosity. I asked, "Where's the manor, the park, and the orchard?" They looked at me in amazement. They did not understand what I was talking about. They were new people, strangers. I remembered there had been a well in front of the manor, the only one in the village, operated by an iron pump with a metal pipe reaching deep into the groundwater. It would have been easy to demolish the house, but not the iron pipe. "Where is the well and the water pump?" I asked. But the people did not know what I meant. Then a little girl, maybe seven or eight years old, mentioned there was a piece of metal pipe sticking out from the ground in their garden. We went to look and, sure enough, I had found the well. I also found the statue of St. Florian who, according to local beliefs, protected the village from fire.

With these landmarks, I could establish the position of our house. We found some remnants of foundations and a few broken bricks around a hole in the ground that once used to be the cellar. Everything else had disappeared. The whole area was overgrown by weeds. We continued the inspection tour of "our" property. I was walking along familiar paths to the center of the farm. The whole area was bare, not a single tree or trace of a building. The 14-hectare beautiful orchard was completely cleared. The big brick building, including the high chimney of the distillery, the three-story brick granary, stables, sheds, and huge barns had all disappeared. The whole center of the once dynamic farm was gone; an empty space overgrown by weeds remained. We stood in silence. During the many years of exile, this was not how I had dreamed of our family property in Budynin.

Our silence was broken by the approach of an agitated man about 40 years old. "People told me that some gentlemen had come who knew more about the village than we do," he said.

"Who are you?" I asked.

"My name's Leskiw. I used to work as a farmhand on the Reiss estate in Budynin and then for a few years at Philip Reiss's property in Oserdów. And who are you, gentlemen? Do you by any chance belong to the Reiss family?"

I felt my heart beating faster. Someone who used to work for my father was standing right in front of me. Should I admit who we were? What would be his reaction? Would he be angry or friendly? All three of us kept silent – Edek, Dolek and I – the remaining members of the family he knew and for whom he had once worked.

"Would you know what happened to the Reiss family from Oserdów?" I asked evasively. Dolek and Edek kept silent.

"Filip Reiss died before the war," said the man. "He had two sons, Henek and Ludwik. I don't know what happened to them."

Words choked me. Finally, I regained my composure and after a moment's silence, I answered, "Ludwik perished, and Henek is standing right in front of you." He was obviously moved, and so was I. We shook hands in silence.

Many questions followed, and then he gave us a brief outline of the village's history. After the war, the new Polish-Soviet border was established some two kilometers from Budynin. Ninety-nine percent of the population of the area was Ukrainian, while in this part of Poland, which now had been incorporated into the Soviet Union, were many isolated settlements of Poles. Then, he told us, an exchange of population had taken place. One day trucks arrived, collected the Ukrainians, and deported them into the Soviet Union, while their cottages and fields were taken over by the Poles who came from the east. It was sad. For hundreds of years, many generations of our villagers lived in their whitewashed cottages with the thatched roofs and toiled on their land, dreaming of an independent state of Ukraine. Today, they were under the hated Soviet system in the kolkhozes of the Soviet Ukraine. What irony! I felt sorry for them.

He also explained what happened to all the trees in the park and the orchard. One winter after the war was extremely cold, and there was such a shortage of fuel that all trees were chopped down and burned. Our large 14-room house, which could easily have been converted into a community hall, a school, or a library, as well as all the farm buildings and even the high factory chimney stock of the distillery, were pulled down by the new inhabitants of Budynin and used as building material for their own houses. Slowly, we returned to our car. Soon a group of villagers gathered around. Cousin Edek asked me shyly not to reveal our identity. But Leskiw excitedly announced that "the gentlemen who were with us are the former owners of the village."

During my talk with Leskiw, I found out that another inhabitant I knew was living next door. It was Jan Wilczek, the brother of my friend Stanislaw Wilczek. As a Pole, he remained in Budynin. That day, he was sick in bed, but when I knocked at his door and introduced myself, he jumped out of bed and soon joined our group just as Leskiw was inviting everybody for a drink of vodka. We all went into Leskiw's house. There was a big table covered with a white cloth, a huge loaf of bread cut into thick slices, and a big bowl of honey. Leskiw opened a large bottle of vodka and proposed a toast: "To the health of these members of the Reiss family who survived the war!" The room was crowded with people looking at us with interest and happily joining in the drinking. The taxi driver watched in silence, amazed by the warm welcome extended to the former Jewish owners of the estate by their former employee.

Afterward, Leskiw and Wilczek volunteered to take me to Oserdów. A cart was harnessed by two well-fed horses, one belonging to Leskiw and the other to Wilczek. Unfortunately, it started drizzling and it was cold. The Leskiws lent me a big winter overcoat and a cap, and we set out. Edek and Dolek left the village as the taxi driver was afraid that the dirt roads would get muddy, and he wanted to get onto the paved road as soon as he could. We were going to meet at the crossroads. We were traveling along a field track slowly approaching Oserdów. It was only three kilometers away. How well I remember that track! I was a young, perhaps 14- or 15-year-old, boy. We were still living in Budynin, but Oserdów, according to the last will of my grandfather, had already been allocated to my father. My father entrusted the building of our house to a local carpenter. Every two or three days, I would run across the fields to Oserdów and watch the growing walls of our future home. Now, after 40 years, I was approaching Oserdów again along the same fields, toward the same trees on the hill – a view I had longed to see again for so many years.

Driving slowly, we entered the area of our estate. We stopped and I climbed down from the cart and went to see our house. My companions stayed behind. I made my way through the bushes and stood in front of an empty piece of land overgrown with weeds – the place where our house once stood, where I had spent many happy years with my father, mother, and brother, sharing their joys and worries. With sadness, I paid my respect to that spot in Oserdów so dear to my heart. Wiping my tears away, I returned to the cart. Neither Wilczek nor Leskiw broke the silence. We reached the waiting taxi and said goodbye. I was overwhelmed by their warm welcome and understanding.

Passing Lublin, we paid a visit to Majdanek Museum, once the infamous extermination camp, where I assumed my brother Ludwik was murdered. We visited the barracks now holding the usual remnants of the thousands of exterminated victims – caps, shoes, spectacles, and so on. Once a death factory, today a sad museum.

Upon my request, the women in the office carefully searched through Nazi files, and surprisingly the name Rudolfina Reiss (my mother's name) was found. According to their records, she was deported to Ravensbrück on 13 April 1944. Number 3820. Could that have been my mother? The name Rudolfina was extremely rare. Her parents gave her that name to honor the successor to the throne of the Austro-Hungarian Empire, Archduke Rudolf von Habsburg. So the name Rudolfina coupled with the surname Reiss could surely only refer to my mother. I was shattered by that discovery. It appears that my mother was not killed (as I had assumed) in Belzec in August 1942 but taken to the concentration camp in Majdanek, where she apparently survived until April 1944. It would be quite possible, as she spoke German well and looked young for her age (55). Efficient and precise in her work, she could have been kept by the Nazi killers for two more years of hell. Three months after her deportation, Majdanek was liberated by the Polish and Soviet armies! I went to Auschwitz and again saw the piles of shoes, glasses, and suitcases with labels on which you could still read the owners' names. I felt dismayed seeing children's shoes. Could one have belonged to little Felus?

"Arbeit macht frei [Work sets you free]" was written in huge letters above the entrance gate to the death camp, a familiar sight from so many photographs and film shots.

I went to Auschwitz, courtesy of the Polish government – not directly, of course. A colleague from the Polytechnic, once Salomon Mermelstein, now Zbigniew Moron, occupied a high position in the coal industry, with a huge office, government flat, and chauffeured car at his disposal. The car took me there, waited for many hours, and then returned to Katowice. The same chauffeur-driven shiny black limousine took us, the Morons, my cousin, and me to spend the next weekend at Zakopane. I didn't like this arrangement, with Polish taxpayer money spent to entertain friends of the upper hierarchy, particularly that it was for Jews in high positions. They especially should behave differently from their Polish colleagues in that respect.

One had to remember that the wheels of history might revolve again against them as they had happened before. It was not normal for so many Jews to be in high and responsible government positions in a country like Poland. It would never meet with the approval of the Polish populace, which was basically antisemitic, now even more so than ever.

I warned them against it. The policy of Poland in those days, as well as the other countries of the Soviet bloc, was directed against Israel. My friend Lutek Szulkin's experience was an example. As editor of *Kurier Polski*, he was asked to write an editorial condemning Israel as a fascist and imperialistic country, condemning the acts of Israeli "aggression" in severe terms. Although basically an assimilated Jew, he refused and lost his job. Twelve months later, not a single Jew remained in high positions in Poland. Many of my Jewish friends considered themselves devoted, patriotic Poles, totally disconnected from their Jewish past. They, who had for many years honorably and loyally served the country they loved, found themselves refugees scattered all over the world.

A small number of Jewish people, sick, unwilling, or unable to emigrate, remained – around 8,000 people altogether. One Jew per 6,000 Poles compared to the prewar proportion of one Jew per eight Poles. Some Jews that remained were married to Poles, with children brought up as Catholics and who had nothing to do with their Jewish origins.

I left Poland in sadness, leaving remnants of a once proud and great Jewish family that was now just a handful of people. They do not belong to the Jewish faith anymore. They are Roman Catholic Poles. For their Jewish parents and grandparents, that would have been a tragedy, though to me it is understandable. I do not condemn them for a decision guided by past experiences and history, and for the benefit of their children and future generations, to reject the burden of belonging to the Chosen People.

SENTIMENTAL JOURNEY: 1988

The year 1988 has arrived. I have reached the age of 80 – not a young man anymore. Once again, I have had the urge to visit the country where I was born, spent my childhood, my youth, and half of my life – years of happiness and peace, years of struggle against human vileness and cruelty. I decided to take both my daughters and wander through the places that were so deeply embedded in my memory. I wanted my children to see the part of the world they hadn't known and would probably never see again, to take them to their roots – to Poland. I wanted them to see Lwów, Kraków, Warsaw, the family farms in Budynin and Oserdów, and the death camps where their families perished, and to follow our escape route to Hungary – up to the little Hungarian village Taszár, where we were liberated by the Red Army in December 1944. I was happy to see their eagerness and enthusiasm in accepting my plan.

I was also planning to have the manuscript retyped of the Polish version of my memoirs, which by now, after over ten years of work and over 1,000 pages, needed Polish typewriters operated by Polish typists. After a two-week stopover in Israel, where we met some old friends and relatives, followed by a few days in Paris, where again we met some relatives and visited Hotel Mirabeau and Elizabeth's school, we landed in Warsaw.

Our reservations in a hotel were not kept. Fortunately, we were able to stay in the most comfortable home of a taxi driver at a fraction of the hotel's cost. Then, after staying overnight in Lublin with Cousin Dolek, whose Polish wife, Zula, welcomed us with dozens of traditional pierogies, we left the following morning for Budynin. The Leskiw family, whom I had met 20 years ago and had kept in touch with ever since, prepared a royal reception for us there.

I was surprised to see their new two-story brick house with a tin roof, large rooms, timber floors – some polished, some carpeted – modern furniture, divans, a large paneled wall unit, a radio, a TV, electricity, a bathroom, hot and cold running water, a separate toilet, a laundry room, and a summer kitchen in the basement. It all seemed unbelievable. My parents and grandparents had been considered wealthy property owners, yet they could never have dreamed of such a luxurious house. My poor mother had darned socks by kerosene lamp late into the night. There was a primitive wooden toilet about 100 meters away from the house – it had been quite an "excursion" to get there on a rainy day or in stormy winter weather, when you had to dress in an overcoat, a hat, rubber boots, and take an umbrella. It appears the Leskiw's house was not unique. On our way across the country, we saw many houses like theirs, some smaller, some bigger. It seems to me that the farmers in the Polish People's Republic have no reason to complain about the system or the government.

We looked around and visited the old Greco-Catholic church, including the figure of St. Florian, the only remnant of the Budynin I remember. Once again, like 20 years earlier, our host borrowed a horse from a neighbor, and we went on a cold and windy morning to Oserdów. The only familiar things were a few shrubs growing on the border of the former orchard. I stepped toward them, and there in front of me were the fields of Oserdów – our fields. Once, its huge area had been covered with just one crop and was one color. Now the field was subdivided into multicolored strips belonging to various small landowners. Good luck to them!

I kept gazing in silence at the familiar and unforgettable outline of that land tilled with love by my grandfather, father, and brother. Next to me were my daughters, Elżunia and Krysia. Could they understand my feelings, follow my thoughts? Our next destination was to be Lwów. Przemyśl was on the border crossing into the Soviet Union. Before the war, both cities had belonged to Poland and the journey from Przemyśl to Lwów took one hour. Now it took three. The customs clearance on the Polish side was only a formality, but on the Russian side, it was a fascinating experience. Six customs officers, including one woman, carefully but politely checked our documents and searched the contents of our luggage, not omitting our toothpaste. The train remained stationary, waiting. After an hour, the customs officers politely said goodbye, and two hours later, we arrived at Lwów Central Station. There we were received by a smiling Russian lady from the Hotel Intourist with a waiting car. We drove along familiar streets where I had walked for months almost 46 years ago, going to and from my work at the central railway station, with the blue Star of David on my left arm, afraid of meeting a Ukrainian policeman who would have had the right to search my bag and beat me up should he find as much as a piece of bread, some potatoes, or any other illegal "treasures" hidden.

We were staying at the Intourist, formerly the Hotel George, on Akademicki Square. A friendly Polish-speaking maid exchanged some of our dollars for black-market rubles. The hotel was clean, although the furniture and carpets were neglected and worn. The hotel restaurant was lively, with a modern band, and the meals were tasty and cheap at the black-market rate of exchange – five rubles for one dollar. We unpacked our suitcases and set out to find our apartment at 3 Chmielowskiego Street, where we had lived during the war and left during the most savage of the German Einsatzkommando raids in August 1942.

Obviously excited, I knocked at the door. A Russian woman, surprised by the unexpected visit, appeared, and I explained in my half-forgotten Russian the purpose of our visit. She occupied one of the front rooms in the flat, which had been subdivided. When we admired the beautiful parquet floor that Lusia had liked so much, the woman became suspicious, not believing that three people – a father and two adult daughters – would travel thousands of kilometers just to inspect the old flat and the beautiful flooring. "Is there something special under the floor?" she asked with a smile. No wonder. According to popular belief, all Jews were supposedly rich, and they had kept jewelry, gold, and diamonds hidden under floors. I quickly assured her we were not going to demolish her floor.

It was already late in the evening when I shyly knocked at the door of the other apartment. After a while, it opened slightly and a man's head appeared, surprised by such an unusual group of visitors. When I repeated my story, the door was opened and we were invited to enter. His wife, who had been asleep, quickly donned a dressing gown and joined us. The man was a Ukrainian scientist working at a geological institute, and his wife was a Polish schoolteacher. They invited us to look around the flat. The front room, which Lusia and I had occupied, was now theirs. One part of the other room was occupied by their eldest son, his wife, and baby, while the other part belonged to the other son, still single. The kitchen and bathroom were shared by all, but their households were kept separate. We were sitting in the kitchen, talking and drinking freshly brewed coffee. The lady, a lovely, friendly person, presented me with a book about Lwów she had been reading. She wrote a dedication: "To Dear Visitors – after 45 years." How nice. The following evening, we went to say goodbye and brought them a large cheesecake we had received from our friends in Budynin and three packs of Swiss chocolate. As there was a shortage of sugar at the time, our gift was greatly appreciated. She insisted that we stay for dinner and in no time produced a platter of pierogies, the favorite dish of the host as well as mine. The following day, we left Lwów, the town of my youth, student years, dreams, loves, and despairs.

We arrived in Przemyśl in time to board the express train to Kraków. I had the feeling that Zosia would be waiting for us at the station and I carefully scrutinized the people on the platform. And, indeed, an elderly couple was standing there, watching the incoming passengers. Yes, it was our former nanny Zosia and her husband, Henryk Maj. Our meeting was emotional. Tears were choking me. Unable to utter a word, I embraced this 75-year-old lady whom I remembered as a vibrant 25-year-old, the only person remaining who knew Lusia's and my family so well.

For many years, I had been trying to find Zosia Janicka. I had written the Kraków and Krzeszowice councils and advertised in the local papers, but to no avail. Shortly before we left Australia, I had the idea of writing to the parish in Krzeszowice, remembering that was where she came from. I also wrote to the parish of Piwniczna looking for the mountaineer who in 1944 escorted us across the Carpathian Mountains to Slovakia. Since I did not know his name, I did not think I had much chance of tracing him. Throughout the ensuing years, I maintained a strong urge to find him and Zosia and thank them for their great help during that tragic period.

Shortly before leaving Australia, I received a letter from the priest in Krzeszowice, whose church announcement had been answered by one of his parishioners, Zosia.

We had dinner together. Zosia gave me a linen towel from Oserdów, hand-embroidered by our kitchen women, the same type as those that had tied Elżunia to the back of the guides escorting us across the borders. Zosia remembered how she sewed those memorable three towels by machine into one to reinforce Lusia's handiwork. She also remembered the cupboard under the window in Lwów where we had hidden her to save her from being deported by the Soviets to Siberia in 1940. Our memories were sad.

On the way to Budynin, we visited the death camps in Belzec and Majdanek. I wanted Elizabeth and Christine to see the horrors of the Nazi period. Now, while in Kraków, they went alone to see Auschwitz. I didn't want to see it again. We went sightseeing in Kraków, the beautiful hometown of many generations of my mother's family. We located the house where I was born and where my mother, grandmother, and grandmother's mother were born, and then we went to the house where Elżunia was born. We saw the exhibition of "The History of the Polish Jews" at the Jagiellonian University, a sad reminder of Jewish life in Poland. I was amazed by the changed attitude that could be felt everywhere in Poland. A strange phenomenon had taken place. The Poles had become very polite toward Jews, talking and writing positively about them and their valuable contribution to Polish culture. One could admit to being Jewish without shame or fear. It was all so new and different to me. We went to Katowice to visit the last branch of the Reiss family, Jurek Reiss, the son of my late cousin Edward, and his family. We met him, his charming wife, Lilka, and son, Dominik. They were now a Christian family.

The next morning, a Polish driver arrived in his Mercedes to take us on our tour to Hungary.

Since we were already in the area of the Polish Carpathians, I once more wanted to see and show my daughters the magnificent Polish Tatra Mountains and the heart of the area, the picturesque village Zakopane. The next stop on our journey was Piwniczna, the border village where we had crossed the Carpathians in January 1944. Once again, I wanted to see those mountains, the village, and what seemed the endlessly long road we had walked in terrible fear of being recognized and handed over to the Germans. Staying overnight in a small guesthouse, we learned that the local priest had made several announcements in the church on behalf of a Jewish woman looking for a mountaineer who had carried her on his back across the border to Slovakia during the war. The Jewish woman was Elżunia! I was pleased to learn that my letters had not been ignored. The next morning, we crossed the border and reached Prešov. I wanted to locate the synagogue where we had stayed and had to sleep on a wooden table with Henry Haber, waiting until the newly installed unit of border police had been bribed not to "see us" as we crossed the Slovakian-Hungarian border. It was raining heavily. I inquired at the restaurant, where we had an excellent Czechoslovakian lunch, and was told there were no Jews in Prešov and no synagogue. So, we left heading toward Budapest and, because of the heavy rain, decided to stay overnight in Miskolc, the town where during our flight in 1944 our fate had been in the hands of two Hungarian gendarmes who had stopped checking documents just before reaching our compartment and left the train.

We had our first Hungarian dinner, goulash and wine, and were entertained by a Hungarian band with a violinist playing his soulful gypsy music close to our ears. I was happy to be able to entertain my two children but sadly regretting the absence of Lusia, who would have so greatly enjoyed this trip. Arriving the next morning in Budapest, we located our flat in Bezeredi Utca and looked up the school Elizabeth had attended in 1946. Our visit caused a sensation among the girls and staff, particularly when Elizabeth tried to communicate with them in her broken Hungarian. During our few days in Budapest, we visited the largest and most beautiful synagogue in Europe and the Jewish Museum, where we met other "pilgrims" who like us were seeking their "roots." Together, we shared many sad memories. Everyone had a story to tell.

We went to Taszár, about 300 kilometers south of Budapest. In anticipation of this visit, I had written from Sydney to inform them of our intended arrival; hence we were expected. Two council officials accompanied us on the tour of the village. Elizabeth, as a former pupil of the local school, received a beautiful bunch of white lilacs, a wonderful and moving gesture. Unfortunately, the old school building no longer existed.

Next, we went to the house of Pishta, my good friend who was so helpful in those days, but who unfortunately had died in a car accident. We were welcomed by his wife. I told her that I had come to express my gratitude for the friendship her husband had shown during that dangerous period. I then admitted we were Jews.

"We thought so since your dramatic escape from the hands of the gendarme," she said. She gave us Pishta's photograph. Leaving some money and gifts, we departed from Taszár, the Hungarian village where we had spent the last months of the war and had the pleasure of seeing the Germans flee.

The next stage of our journey was Vienna where we had dinner at the Rathaus Keller, greatly enjoying the show: Austrian dancers in the colorful uniforms of the officers of the Austro-Hungarian Imperial army performed to Strauss music with beautiful girls in folk dresses. At my discreet request, a handsome young "officer" asked Elizabeth to dance. Was she thrilled!

The next day we spent some time at the Schönbrunn Palace, which during our stay in Vienna in 1914-18 had not been open to the public. Now 300 of the 1,400 rooms were open to visitors. I listened nostalgically to the personal history of my beloved Kaiser and his family, looking at the rooms where they had lived, worked, played, and received visitors. I drew my children's attention to the parquet floors – identical to the flooring I showed them in our flat in Lwów of which their mother was so fond.

We spent the evening in Grinzing, the famous district of Vienna popular with Austrians as a venue for music and singing while drinking their young wine, the Heuriger. The restaurants were crowded and people were drinking, eating, smoking, and singing. The noise was overwhelming, and so was the tobacco smoke. Ordering some wine and something to eat, we sat quietly, just watching. My mind returned to the past, 50 years back, to 1938. Hitler had annexed Austria and the Viennese were hysterical with joy. Here, in Grinzing, in this as in many other *Bierhalle* [beer halls], the Viennese had celebrated Nazism. At the same time, thugs in brown uniforms with swastikas on their sleeves were breaking windows of

Jewish shops and heads of Jewish people. Jewish blood was beginning to spill.

"What are we doing here in this place?" I asked, disgusted with myself. I expressed my thoughts to my daughters. A group of three musicians approached our table. The mother, playing the guitar, the father, on the accordion, and a teenage daughter all were singing. They asked if we would like them to play for us. My daughters welcomed the offer, hoping to break the thread of my memories and disperse my sadness. "What would you like us to play?" the musicians asked as they sat down.

I suggested a few songs I still remembered from my childhood in Vienna during World War I. Ordering another carafe of wine, I tried to forget 1938. The trio was playing and singing. I joined in. My daughters were pleased and rather surprised that I knew and remembered so many German songs, but soon I was back in 1938. Deep inside me, I was churning old anger, old anguish. The words *"Spielen Sie mir bitte das Horst Wessel Lied* [Please play the Horst Wessel Song]" burst unsummoned from my lips. It was more a command than a request. The musicians fell silent.

"Wenn Judenblut von Messer spritz [When Jewish blood squirts from knives]" the song began. It was the Nazis' national anthem. No one spoke. I repeated my request. The musicians' embarrassment and my hardening persistence were noticeable. I repeated: *"Spielen Sie Bitte* [Please, play]!" Reluctantly they began to play, but they were not singing. I stopped them with a gesture of my hand, asking, *"Warum singen Sie nicht* [Why don't you sing]?" and they looked uncomfortable. The father and the daughter were dead silent. Only the mother found the courage to say they did not remember the lyrics. I listened while they continued that hateful tune, but after a short while, I had enough. I paid the bill and after leaving a generous tip ("Jewish money"), we left, followed by hostile looks from the confused musicians and the astonished waitresses. I did not bother to look at anybody. I didn't care. I'd had enough of Austrians and decided to cut short our sightseeing and shopping in Vienna.

The following day, we landed in Warsaw and were welcomed at the home of Eva Poniż-Parandowska, the daughter of Professor Poniż. Elżunia and Krysia did some sightseeing and shopping, and two days later, on 10 June 1988, they left Poland, while I remained in Warsaw for another three weeks. During that time, after many changes and corrections, the Polish version of this book was typed up by five Polish ladies.

My search for people involved in our survival did not cease. I wanted to find Jurek, the young Jewish boy who had arranged the border crossing to Slovakia in that unforgettable month of January 1944. A coincidence helped me. Eva had studied architecture with a Jurek Nowakowski, who she knew had smuggled some people to Slovakia during the war. Eva invited him and his wife for supper. The shock of this meeting was moving. Jurek remembered me well as I was his first client to risk the new route. After reading my enthusiastic report, we were followed by another 47 people. Some perished at the hands of the Hungarian Nazis. The majority, luckily, survived.

I spent some time with Mrs. Kazimierz Bielicki, the widow of the late Wojslaw. We talked about Wojslaw, who died some years ago, and about Skierniewice and Legionowo. There were details she did not know, and others that were unknown to me. At the time I had often been greatly perturbed wondering whether Wojslaw was aware of our identity.

"Of course, he knew," she answered. "'Since God has entrusted the lives of those people to me,' he said to me, 'I considered it my duty to help them to survive. It was God's will which I carried out.'" That was Wojslaw's attitude. He put us up at his mother's place knowing she hated Jews. He ignored the warning from the shopkeeper in Skierniewice and fulfilled his mission to the end. There is no doubt in my mind that due to his bravery and his sincere religious beliefs, we survived the Holocaust. A great, noble Pole!

I wish I had the answer to another question: Did the other people who lived with me in Skierniewice know my identity? Actually, it would have been hard for a Pole not to guess. I remember the remark made by Mr. Kobylinski at the breakfast table one day, "In the district of Sandomierz, where I come from, it's considered not to be the Christian way to place a loaf of bread upside down on the table." I am sure he knew. Mr. Kobylinski was being tactful. He could have said, "Only Jews would put the bread that way on the table." He also could have said nothing but turned the bread the correct way without any comment. He could have saved me a few sleepless nights. By some miracle and with God's will, I had survived for over a year living under the same roof for 24 hours a day as a "Pole" among Poles.

Prior to my departure from Poland, I left my retyped manuscript at the Polonia Publishing Company, with little hope of seeing it published. It was therefore a most exciting moment for me when I received a contract from Polonia, dated 25 July 1989, confirming the conditions of publishing my memoirs, accompanied by a sum of over five million złoty, paid into my account with the Polish National Bank. Hopefully, one day the Polish reader will learn more about a Polish Jew he never saw.

On my way home, I stopped in New York to see the only living member of Lusia's family, her cousin George (Jurek) Herman, his wife Miriam and their children, Rena and Lynnie. His survival story was traumatic, a boy of 14 with indescribable experiences in a number of Nazi extermination camps. Her survival story no less so: twelve years old, working 18 hours a day as a dairy maid and a general farmhand, pretending to be homeless, a lost child of war; she raised some suspicions in the mind of a local priest who put her through a religious examination; maybe, God forbid, she might be one of those responsible for the crucifixion of Christ. Luckily, she knew all the answers and was allowed to live. Those few days spent in the warm family atmosphere of their hospitable home gave me great pleasure.

I also visited our prewar friends, the Uberalls, who were now living next door to their daughter, Magda, and her family in a lovely rural area an hour's drive from New York City. We reminisced about their overnight stay in Oserdów in September 1939 when they shared our bedroom and inhaled the wonderful fragrance of thousands of apples from our orchard stored at the time on the floor in the spare bedroom.

My sentimental journey ended in Sydney on 12 July 1988 at 6 a.m. I doubt I shall ever see the country where generations of my family lived and toiled, the country I consider to be my fatherland, the country where I spent my youth and which became the cemetery of my family, friends, and dreams. I shall keep on longing for Lwów and Kraków, for Budynin and Oserdów. I retain an aching longing for my beautiful village, the home of my family, and know I shall carry that ache for the rest of my life. I would not want it otherwise.

MY THOUGHTS ON ANTISEMITISM

Before closing, I would like to comment on the problem of antisemitism, having encountered it personally during my life in Poland before and during World War II.

I have often asked myself why we Jews through the centuries have attracted so much hatred from the people amongst whom we have lived since Israel lost its independence in 70 A.D.

I have tried to understand why people who, whilst claiming to be followers of Christ's teachings of love and forgiveness, have acted with such hatred toward Jews – their pious older brothers and peaceful neighbors.

Much has been written and published on this topic, and there are numerous essays and historical works analyzing the cause of the tragic experiences of the Chosen People.[1] Often, it is the same sad explanation. In the beginning, there was poverty, hard work, and a very modest way of life. Later, due to diligence and skill, the Jews became prosperous, which attracted envy, jealousy, and ultimately hatred from their Gentile neighbors. This animosity was compounded by the different way Jews behaved and dressed.

Pope Honorius III in 1218 issued a decree ordering Jews to wear special clothing so they could be distinguished from Christians. It was from this that the long black coats and characteristic hats emerged setting Jews apart from the rest of the population. Rumors were also spread about Christian children being killed for blood for the making of matzos – the so-called "ritual killing" – and because Jews seemed to have lower death rates, they also were suspected of poisoning the wells and rivers. In fact, by following the teachings of the Talmud, Jews lived more hygienically than their neighbors. The rules of washing hands before each meal, taking a hot bath before the Sabbath, and not eating pork or seafood were strictly followed. Perhaps the deaths from various epidemics were fewer amongst them for these reasons. The Jews were accused by the Catholic Church of black magic and were held responsible for the spread of disease and epidemics.

Simple uneducated peoples believed these rumors and took revenge, through persecution and pogroms. To save their lives, the Western European Jews were on the run and in the years 1100-1200 found refuge in Poland.

The Polish King Casimir III, later called the Great, invited the German Jews to settle in Poland in the years 1330-1340 basically for economic reasons. As the Bible story goes, a beautiful Jewish young lady, Esther, became the mistress of the unmarried king and probably had some influence on his decisions since great masses of Western Jews arrived in Poland during his reign. In those times, Poland as well as other Slavic nations had existed mainly on agriculture, forestry, and animal husbandry in contrast to the nations of Southern and Central Europe, which had fairly well-developed industries and trade. The Western Jews had their own well-established business connections all over the world and the Polish magnates and princes were keen to utilize the Jews and their connections. Being much more educated than the simple Polish *shlachta* [gentry], the Jews were entrusted with the most responsible positions. They held leases on enterprises and were instrumental in establishing mines, custom houses, mills, sawmills, and breweries. Even the first gold coins were minted by Jewish experts, with the lettering on the coins in Hebrew. One can assume that the Polish populace, working for the Jews in so many diverse fields, must not have felt enamored of their Jewish bosses. There must have been episodes of violence to explain the special laws – issued by Polish princes, dukes, and kings – protecting the Jews and even creating some "Christian-free" districts reserved for Jews only.

One can also assume that these Western Jews, already highly skilled in numerous trades, unknown to the Poles were badly needed and therefore welcomed by the ruling class. Yet they were not always welcomed by the populace at large.

Polish historians are quick to point out the special privileges granted to the Jews by the Polish rulers. I would be prepared to risk the assumption that those privileges must have been handsomely reciprocated by generous donations. The financial needs of the Polish ruling class were great. It should be noted that at this period of history, a respectable nobleman had to have his own military detachment, and its upkeep was costly.

The Jews settling in the towns fulfilled the duties imposed on them loyally and efficiently yet remained singularly unpopular with the Gentile masses. Jews were also employed as tax collectors. Where can one find people who like their tax collectors?

The Catholic Church also forbade Christians to lend money to one another. Jews were used for that purpose by a simple arrangement: The Church, always affluent, lent money to the Jews at high interest and, in turn, the Jews were forced to lend it at higher rates to the Gentiles. In that way, the character of the Jewish usurer was created – hated by the Poles, Ukrainians, Russians, Lithuanians, and others. It is true that where there are moneylenders there will be some ruthless characters, and the Jews were no exception. There was a story about a Jew who charged 100 percent interest per year payable in advance. The story circulated that a peasant asked him for a loan of ten rubles. The usurer agreed on condition that the peasant would leave his sheepskin coat as security. The peasant did so and received ten rubles. "And now you have to pay me in advance the 100 percent interest, which comes to ten rubles," the Jew said.

The naive peasant paid the ten rubles and went. On the way home, he began to think about it. "I don't understand," he said to himself. "I was wearing my sheepskin coat when I went to borrow ten rubles. Now I'm going back home without my coat, without ten rubles, and on top of that I owe the Jew another ten rubles."

It was a sad joke, but in every tale, there is a grain of truth. That the Jews were dealing in usury was well known, but few were aware that behind the Jewish usurer stood the Catholic Church, which had already financed the Jews at excessive rates of interest. It is commonly known that the Polish aristocracy frequently used to borrow money from the Jews and spend it lavishly on parties, women, hunting, or gambling. Sometimes entire estates were lost in games of cards, as I well know from the history of Oserdów. As I mentioned in my story, my grandfather owned a large country estate in Budynin and some years later bought the neighboring estate of Oserdów from Count Grocholski. A separate piece of land of about ten hectares belonging to the Oserdów estate was registered in the records of the neighboring village of Chłopiatyn. Curious to know why, I discovered that one of Count Grocholski's ancestors had won that land in a game of cards from the previous owners of Chlopiatyn. Such happenings were not unusual.

Polish noblemen were known to be good at drinking, but they were not greatly interested in running their estates. For this, they willingly used Jews, who managed or leased the properties and supplied money to the always needy noblemen. While dukes, counts, and other noblemen were enjoying themselves on the French Riviera, their Jews always had to be ready to put cash at their disposal. The Jews, with their wives and children, had to work hard to meet the demands of their masters, and so too, did the peasants. It needs to be remembered that in a feudal country, the magnates not only owned the village but its inhabitants, too. In fact, every nobleman had "his" Jew, a devoted adviser and a loyal servant. There were cases when a Jew belonging to one nobleman was beaten up by another. That was considered an insult and the "owner" nobleman would act in defense of his Jew. He would warn the offender, "Should you again beat my Jew, I will beat your Jew." Thus, a Jew might be beaten up either way. These circumstances would not generate compassion amongst the workers or peasants toward the Jews. Throughout Polish history, the peasants never felt friendly toward their masters and naturally hated the executors of their masters' wills – the Jews.

Writing this today, I can understand the feelings of the Gentiles – these poor and simple people who, being exploited by their Polish masters, could not appreciate that the Jews were also at the whims of those masters.

A typical example of the exploitation of Jews was the Jewish innkeeper. Wealthy Polish landowners usually owned distilleries that produced spirits from their own potatoes and barley. They also owned the village inns that they leased to the Jewish innkeepers, often at exorbitant rentals. An innkeeper was also obliged to purchase all the spirits produced in the distillery at a price dictated by the owner. Polish, Russian, and Ukrainian peasants love vodka. It is their national drink. All their worries, problems, failures, and illnesses are drowned in alcohol. Their wives and children, often hungry, would wait for their drunken fathers and husbands to come home, and whom did they blame? The Jewish innkeeper. From their pulpits, priests threatened the peasants with all imaginable punishments of hell for drinking and primarily blamed the Jews for leading their flock astray. The hatred grew, but was it justified? The Jew had to sell the landlord's vodka. Otherwise, he would lose the roof over his head.

I was told by my grandfather a little anecdote he heard from his father Moshe, who came from Russia. In his village was a Russian Orthodox priest who was a very greedy man. He would not perform any religious services for his parishioners – weddings, funerals, or christening of newborn babies – without payment. Yet not every peasant had the money. So, the priest devised a scheme. He left the key from the church with the Jewish innkeeper, who was instructed to open the church after ten rubles had been paid to him. The deal was kept secret. The villagers just knew that the Jew was taking money for opening the church and naturally hated him.

I remember another anecdote from those days. An estate owner called his innkeeper to his manor. When the frightened Jew came, the landlord gave him his dog on a leash and ordered him to take the dog home for a year and teach it to speak. If he failed, the master would give him a good bashing and throw him, his wife, and his children out of the inn. The Jew had no choice but to take the dog home. "Have you gone mad?" cried his wife. "How are we going to teach the dog to speak?" And the Jew answered calmly, "A year is a long time. Who knows, maybe, with God's will, the dog will die, or the master will die. We'll see. God is merciful."

Perhaps this story was supposed to express Jewish optimism and belief in God's help, but, in fact, many Jews barely managed to exist. There were cases when the masters did beat them or set their dogs on them. The masters must have greatly enjoyed seeing a Jew running, the tails of his long black coat flying while desperately trying to keep his *yarmulke* [skullcap] on his head since he was not allowed, in accordance with his strict religious beliefs, to move with his head uncovered.

A poor Jew, scared and bleeding, would often return home to his crying wife and children. To meet the demands of his despotic master, the Jew might add water to the vodka or increase the interest on money he lent to peasants. That was the only way he could meet the demanded ransoms and delay his sentence for another few months, during which he would pray to God to send the Messiah and save him. Such a Jew attracted the anger and hatred of those to whom he was selling the vodka on credit and whose overcoats he was taking as security. The population would also turn its anger against his wife and innocent children, and against all the other Jews in the district – even the pious Chassid who studied Talmud in a rabbi's house, who did not sell vodka or even know of the existence of the Jewish innkeeper or his problems with his master.

As known from history, the Church greatly added to the hatred against the Jews. The village population was very pious. Holy pictures hung on the walls of the cottages and candles were lit in front of the holy statues. The crosses and holy shrines standing along the roads were always whitewashed and decorated with flowers. Statues of the crucified Christ gave people a sense of security and God's protection. Peasants driving their wagons or walking past piously took their hats off and made the sign of the cross. They believed in Jewish witchcraft and that the Jews killed Christian children at Passover, and they deeply blamed the Jews as responsible for Christ's crucifixion. In Catholic or Orthodox churches, these false accusations were repeatedly made and naively accepted by the devout and trusting but uneducated people.

Jews were blamed for Christians' poverty as well. Jews' ability to work and handle money increased their wealth but also the ostracism felt by the local people, a theme that recurred throughout the centuries and in various countries. The more prosperous Jews were, the greater was the hatred by the Gentiles. In medieval Poland, Jews organized industry and trade since they had the contacts with foreign countries to which they could export raw materials. While running the mints, collecting taxes, and making profits for their masters, they advanced their own prosperity, too.

Of course, not all Jews were successful. There were great masses of poor Jews living in the towns who were struggling. But the small proportion of successful Jews was sufficient to stir feelings of envy and hatred amongst the Gentiles. Along with their growing prosperity, the number of Jews studying in tertiary institutions increased. The hunger for knowledge is one of the characteristics of this "nation of the book." Gradually, Jews were becoming part of society at all levels and succeeding in literature, music, art, medicine, law, banking, trade, and industry, as well as in the political life of the country. The greater the number of Jews successful in the economic and cultural life of the country, the stronger the hatred against them. Yet Jews hoped that by reducing the ignorance of the masses, or by assimilation or even baptism, they would eventually be accepted by the better-educated classes of society. They were bitterly disappointed. In 1889, the Polish writer Klemens Junosza Szaniawski wrote about this on page 124 of his treatise entitled *Our Jews in Towns and Villages*:

"As for the Jewish problem, the Polish society turns around in a vicious cycle and cannot free itself. An ignorant Jew wearing a dirty coat who takes advantage of the peasants by poisoning them with vodka is hated and called a scoundrel. The Jew who separates himself from his people, who discards the dirty coat and instead of studying Talmud achieves a European style of education and wishes to live amongst the Gentiles, is also detested and considered an arrogant intruder. Finally, the Jew who has ceased to be Jewish by adopting the Christian faith and entering our society is called a convert and also detested. Our hatred does not refer only to a particular Jew, but also to his children, and to future generations who have nothing to do with Jewishness."

The hatred was directed at both poor and rich Jews. I can understand that the prosperity of some, especially if they were rightly or wrongly considered strangers in the country, could evoke hatred. But amongst those strangers – the three and a half million Polish Jews – over three million people were living in poverty and struggling to make ends meet.

Since I myself came from the country, I was able to observe the life of the poor Jew in the villages, the so-called *shtetlach*, and small towns. In our village, there were three poor Jewish families who quietly toiled their small plot of land next to their houses. In the neighboring villages, there were also three or four Jewish families. On Saturdays and during holidays, they would gather in the house of one of the families for common prayer to God, in whose existence they firmly believed. For the prayer to be valid and to reach the throne of the Almighty, at least ten adult men must be present. (A boy of 13 years who has gone through the ceremony of a bar mitzvah is considered an adult.)

Usually, a single village would not have ten adult Jewish men, so men from neighboring villages would join to make the necessary quorum. I remember them dressed in the traditional black coats, white stockings, and fur hats (whether in winter or summer) hurrying from one village to another to be in time for morning prayer.

Sometimes, they would walk several kilometers – the use of vehicles on holy days was not allowed. For safety's sake, they walked in small groups. I can well recall them taking shortcuts through our fields – sad-looking men who had thin pale faces and were undernourished, their appearance exaggerated by their black clothes, beards, and side curls of varying color and length. They presented a grim, almost frightening sight against the colorful outfits of the peasants, who hurriedly crossed themselves when they met such a somber procession. Mothers threatened their disobedient children that "a Jew would take them and sell them to the devil if they didn't behave." The children grew up in fear of the Jews and passed it on to succeeding generations. There was a well-known saying in prewar Poland: "The babies sucked antisemitism with their mother's milk."

And what was the life of the Jews in their shtetlach like? Mostly misery. Some Jews would make their meager living walking as hawkers from village to village. Early Sunday morning, the poor creature would leave the shtetl carrying two bags. One was his "shop"; the other was empty. The stock he carried would consist of items needed by the villagers. There would be a can of kerosene; a packet of marches; white, black, and colored cotton; needles; a few dozen buttons of various sizes; aluminum spoons, wooden spoons; salt (crude black salt as white salt was expensive); a few meters of ribbons of various colors; and so on. The peasant women would not have any money but had their gardens. So, the empty bag would slowly be filled with onions, garlic, green peas or beans, a few cucumbers, a head of cabbage, or a few apples, depending on the season. If lucky, he would return home the same day carrying food for the family for the whole week. If unlucky, he would go to the next village to continue his bartering. He would always be home Friday night. If he was lucky, a small chicken would be amongst his trophies, or a piece of cheese or butter, which not being kosher would be sold to a Christian neighbor. Was he popular with the villagers? Some felt sorry for him, offering a slice of bread and some milk, while others would make fun of him. They never robbed him. They were angry if a few matches were missing from the little box. One has to remember that the villagers were poor, too, the farm workers particularly. The match was sometimes split into four – an art very difficult to perform. Every cent, every kopek or złoty, was money.

The center of our district was the shtetl Belz, the seat of the famous Rabbi Rokach, commemorated in this beautiful song that, whenever I hear it, moves me deeply: "Belz, my shtetl Belz."

As in hundreds of other Polish shtetls, around 80 to 90 percent of the population was Jewish, the rest being Polish or Ukrainian. I often went to Belz, the economic and administrative center of the district. The marketplace, a big square surrounded by small shops, was the heart of the town, and almost all shops, except perhaps the pharmacy, belonged to Jews. These tiny, poorly equipped shops sold cheap goods, affordable to the mostly peasant local population. The dirty shop windows displayed handwritten, misspelled signs saying *Towary Miezane* [mixed goods] or *Towary blawatne* [textiles], where they sold cheap calico, colorful dress materials, scarves, and so on. The owners lived at the back of their shops or, if they were more prosperous, had their primitive, poorly furnished flats above them. Usually, women managed the shops while the men studied Talmud. Obviously, there were no cinemas or theaters and no daily local papers in town. International and local news came from the barber, who somehow always knew what was going on.

The Jews in these Polish towns lived in poverty. Their profits from the shops were meager, and the earnings of the tradesmen were equally miserable. The shtetl came alive only one day a week – usually a Thursday, which was market day, when the peasants from surrounding villages came to town. Some came by horse and wagon, others walked barefoot, carrying their boots on their shoulders. They would bring their produce for sale. The peasant women would sell a goose or a chicken, butter, cheese, cream, eggs, vegetables, and fruit while the men traded grain, pigs, cows, and calves. The town Jews usually bought goods for resale. From stalls erected for the day in the center of the marketplace, they would sell materials for dresses, red cotton for pillowcases, leather boots, farm tools, hardware, and buckets. The Jewish proletariat would rush around trying to earn whatever they could as peddlers, hawkers, go-betweens, porters, beggars, thieves, and even water carriers for people or animals for just a few groshy per bucket. There was great confusion and noise. People were haggling, squabbling, and shouting. The visiting peddlers were also shouting to attract customers to their merchandise. Chooks were cackling, the piglets wrapped in the cloth sacks were squeaking, excited dogs were barking, and agitated Jewish mothers were screaming at their children. The town was alive. On market days, Poles, Ukrainians, and Jews seemed to live like one big family.

But on Saturdays, the town was dead. The cleaned-up streets were empty, not a soul was to be seen, and the synagogue was full, with people praying to God. In the evening, it was time for pleasure and entertainment – for which both the old and young had been waiting all week.

In 1988, during our journey into the past, my daughters and I passed through the Polish towns, so quiet, now so still, as if they had died. There was no life in them. The Jews who were once an integral part of the Polish scenery have disappeared and with them much of the color and character of the little towns. To think that three million people, strongly believing in God, died the death of martyrs only because they were born Jews! To think the world saw and allowed it. To think that God saw and allowed it – allowed men dressed in the smart uniforms of the German army, with the words "*Gott mit uns* [God is with us]" engraved on their buckles, to murder those innocent Jewish men, women, and children.

"Love your neighbor as you love yourself," the Bible teaches. Will there ever in human history come a moment when people find enough goodwill and understanding to coexist according to God's commandments? Will that include coexisting with the people of Israel?

In May 1991, Lech Walesa, the first democratically elected president of an independent, free Poland, in an impassioned address to the Knesset, the Israeli Parliament, implored Israel to forgive Poland for its centuries of antisemitism – and admitted the regrettable activities of "some Poles" during the German occupation. It was a historic moment. The first star in the dark skies of the Polish-Jewish relationship appeared.

Let's hope that many more stars of brotherly love will appear over the skies of Poland – as well as all other countries in the world.

KINDNESS

We survived only with the kind help of these men and women:

The largest museum in the world commemorating the death of six million victims of Nazism is Yad Vashem in Jerusalem. Around Yad Vashem, the people of Israel have founded a beautiful park called the Garden of the Righteous Among the Nations to honor those heroic Gentiles who, by risking their own lives, saved some thousands of Jews from the hands of the Nazi murderers.

In front of the trees planted in the garden are marble plaques bearing the names of those heroes. We also owe our lives to such people. I feel a deep sense of personal fulfilment for having been able to carry out my sacred duty to express my immense gratitude and deep respect by having their names inscribed and by arranging the recognition of the following people:

Venceslaw and Janina Poniż had already been honored and a tree was planted by their daughter Eva in 1987.

The following Poles are honored in the Golden Book, Righteous Among the Nations: Wojslaw Bielicki, Zosia Janicka, Stanislaw and Janina Wilczek, Jan Ruszczynski, Michalina Brzezanska, and one wonderful Ukrainian, Emil Sawczyn, who regrettably died soon after the war.

I also wish to express my gratitude to the following:

Mr. Józef Elsner, my prewar employer in Kraków, who by issuing me false employment certificates enabled me to start a new life as Piotr Daraż. Irena Bartolowicz, our landlady in Warsaw, who undoubtedly knew our true identity but nevertheless allowed us to live in her flat and did not take financial advantage of us. Mrs. Biedkowska, the shop owner in Skierniewice, who although aware of my real identity was selling me black-market food at moderate prices, even sometimes adding sweets for my child. Johann Rudisch, a German from Sudetenland and Building Inspector of the Deutsche Ostbahn, for helping me obtain a railway pass to the Slovakian border. Jurek Nowakowski, who risked his life by guiding us in bright daylight from the Piwniczna railway station to the smugglers' chief – the forest ranger. Pawel Liber, the forest ranger, who risked his life by organizing the escape into Slovakia for many desperate people like us and coordinating the Polish gorals, trusted mountaineers, and reliable guides.

Those courageous unknown mountaineers – one Pole, one Slovak, and one Hungarian – who during the freezing nights of January 1944 guided us across the Polish-Slovakian-Hungarian borders.

The unknown villagers, both Slovak and Hungarian, who exposed themselves to arrest and persecution by giving us shelter, food, and transport during our escape to Hungary.

The Jewish Committee in Presov (Slovakia) who took care of us from our entry into Slovakia, keeping us safe in their Synagogue, and then escorting us across the border to the safety of Budapest, Hungary.

The head of the Polish Committee in Budapest, General Dr. Jan Kollontay, who was responsible for the legalization of our stay in Hungary and who was shot by the Gestapo while destroying compromising documents. I have recently submitted his name to Yad Vashem to be inscribed in the Golden Book of Righteous Gentiles.

Jozef Grylko, commander, and Wladyslaw Skonieczny, secretary of the Polish refugee camp in Kadarkút, Hungary, who gave us guidance and advice, provided us false documents, and helped us and others at great personal risk.

Mr. Kluska (I can't recall his first name), who courageously presented himself and appeared on my behalf before the Hungarian medical examination.

Pishta Toch, our Hungarian friend in Taszár, who offered to take care of us and our child should we have to go into hiding.

I also feel thankful to the following: The Polish policeman in Legionowo who, satisfied with the ransom of 1,000 złoty extorted from Lusia, never harassed her again. The SS-Obersturmführer of the Gestapo headquarters in Aleja Szucha, Department of Racial Matters, Room 404, who although undoubtedly aware of Lusia's racial identity let her go free. The blackmailer in Warsaw, who extorted from me half of my money and my gold watch but unwittingly taught me how to avoid similar criminal encounters on the streets of Warsaw.

I wish to thank my friend, Michael Eisner, who guaranteed us financially, and arranged all the documents required to enable us (and many others) to immigrate to this country. He also employed me in his business and continued to help us with encouragement, support and advice which greatly helped us to settle in this new country.

I would like to acknowledge the help of the Joint (American Jewish Joint Distribution Committee) who in addition to contributions mentioned in my memoir, funded our migration to Australia after the war.

Finally, I wish to express my deep gratitude to Australia for opening its welcoming doors to us. For welcoming homeless refugees and giving us a chance to start a new life as full-fledged citizens. Under your sunny skies our children have grown up in an atmosphere of freedom, equality, and respect toward all people, regardless of race, origin, or religion.

Thank you, Australia!

NOTES

Return to Budynin

1. Legions under Haller's command were inspired by the National Democracy movement. Recruitment of Jewish volunteers ceased in 1918 and the legions were later involved in pogroms.

High School: Oserdów and Sokal

1. This is not supported in the current historical references describing ARA work, where Jewish dietary restrictions were even considered to ensure supply was kosher. Yet as it is his memory, perhaps this was true in the school he attended, due to local manipulations.

German Army arrives

1. Rabbi Dr. Levin happened to be our relative. He was married to my father's first cousin, Hela Reiss, daughter of Laib Reiss. After his murder, Metropolita Szeptycki did take care of his widow and her children, saving their lives and those of some 40 other Jews in the sanctuary of his church.
2. The history of the Janowska camp victims has been described in detail in *The death brigade: (The Janowska road) / Leon Weliczker Wells*. Publication | Library Call Number: DS135.U42 L862 1978, The Holocaust Library, New York.

Working for the Gestapo

1. Dr. Filip Friedman, *Zaglada Zydow/wowskich* (The extermination of the Jews of Lwów), Lodz 1945

Actions and the Jewish Star

1. Izaak Reisler survived the war to become Attorney General in the Polish Democratic Republic, serving under the name of Jerzy Sawicki, as a prosecutor in the Nuremberg Trials.

Action against my mother

1. Anna had secretly saved Dolek who married her after liberation.

Planning our escape

1. In the end, the albums perished, along with Manusia and her whole family.
2. It was only after the war was over that I learned she was not lying. Her rather peculiar behavior during these tragic events was because her mother, a devout Christian, was not on speaking terms with her since she committed the unforgivable sin of marrying a Jew. Yet when the Germans entered Kraków and evicted her from her lovely flat, the great sin was forgiven and she moved into her mother's flat. She became aware of the grave situation of her husband in Lwów in 1942 only after receiving my telegram. She had returned home to obtain her mother's agreement to hide him on condition of her absolute silence. So, while I was discussing his fate, he was hidden under her bed.

Moving to Warsaw

1. There was a sad story of Tolek Kahane's friend, Tosia, who helped us greatly during the August action in Lwów. She worked as a maid in the home of an SS officer. The children of the German family liked her. Although it was compulsory, she kept putting off her police registration. Finally the SS man, a law-abiding German, offered to do it for her. He took her documents and returned very puzzled. "How on earth," he asked, "is it that another person with an identical first name, surname, and date of birth has already been registered under a different address?" Within minutes, poor Tosia left the house in which she could have safely survived the war and was never heard from again.
2. Some months later, a Polish Underground newsletter fell into my hands. In it, I was amazed to read: "The traitor, Marcel Gruner of Kraków, was sentenced to death by the court of the Polish government for collaboration with the occupying forces against his coreligionists hiding under Aryan documents in Kraków. Gruner and his wife were shot in their hotel room and the verdict of the court was pinned to his jacket." I understood now why she had panicked. Obviously, she had feared that some Gestapo man set up by Marcel would follow me and take care of me and my hosts. Did they carry out this shameful activity in order to save their own lives and those of their parents and families?

Accused

1. In fact, Mr. Bielicki was aware of our identity. As I was told years later by his second wife, he devoutly believed that the Lord had placed our lives into his hands and considered it to be his sacred duty to fulfill God's wish. Regrettably Wojslaw Bielicki died before having given me the opportunity to express to him my profound gratitude.

Elżunia at the Gestapo

1. The Poles usually didn't wear Persian coats.

Leaving Legionowo

1. I do not want to be misunderstood. I do not wish to imply that all Poles were happy to see the Jews exterminated or that all Poles were capable of blackmail and denouncement of the Jews to the Nazis. However, it was difficult for the Jews to know and be sure who among the Poles would be willing to act in such a shameful way. Consequently, we, the Jews, were quite simply afraid of all Poles.

Slovakian Latkes

1. An official carrying out all sorts of jobs at the religious service as well as others.

Yellow Star for Hungarian Jews

1. Like a heroine, she was caught by the Gestapo and tortured to death.

The medical examination

1. After discussions with other Jewish survivors from Poland, we found similar stories of the responses by most Hungarian Jews. Polish refugees had spread out in a few Hungarian villages, and when the Hungarian Jews were informed of the German plans, they were warned against obeying Nazi orders. Unfortunately, and repeatedly, the friendly advice was usually ignored. Many Hungarian Jews (just like the Polish Jews) went, like sheep to their slaughter, to Auschwitz. Why? Maybe they too were attached to their lives, prosperous and in large homes, with successful businesses? They were totally deaf to our cries of warning.
2. Most of the Jews who stayed in Budapest survived, saved by a heroic Swedish diplomat Raul Wallenberg. The only Kadarkút Jew who survived was the doctor who had spent the war in the army. When he returned, the mayor handed over the keys to his house – his empty house. His wife and daughter had perished.

German counteroffensive

1. I am sure my fears were justified. While on a sentimental visit to Taszár in 1988, I disclosed to Pishta's widow (Pishta was killed in a car accident) that I was Jewish. She was not surprised – she had known it since my clash with the gendarme in 1944 – as did the whole village.

Crossing the Danube

1. This Hebrew word, meaning doorpost, is actually a small case containing a rolled parchment inscribed with several passages from Deuteronomy. The case is attached to the right doorpost of the entrance and of each room in Jewish homes in accordance with Biblical commandment.

Stamp smuggling

1. This was a prelude to a pogrom that took place in June 1946 where many Jews were killed. Some time later, while in Australia. I talked to Mr. Herman, a lucky person who had survived this pogrom. He told me this story: Out of several thousand Kielce Jews, only a few had returned home after the war and started to rebuild their lives. Then one sunny morning, rumors were spreading among the local people: "Jews are slaughtering Polish children to collect blood for their religious rituals." "A bucket of Christian blood was found in the synagogue!" "Corpses of murdered children were in the river; some Polish women fished out the severed children's heads!" Stories of the "outrages" spread quickly. Masses of people armed with axes, pitchforks, spades, hoes, pieces of pipe, and so on set off to finish what Hitler had started. The attack was unexpected; the Jews completely unprepared. Caught in the streets, shops, and homes, unarmed, they fell victim to the mob. There were over 30 dead and many injured, yet the police did not act. Either they were afraid of the mob or did not want to interfere. Mr. Herman told me a fearful story of how, thanks to a miracle and common sense, he was spared from the massacre. When he heard the screams of the approaching crowd, he ran from his house, took off his coat and tie, pulled a piece of piling from a nearby fence, and joined the mob. He saw how large groups of people attacked the Jews, who were knocked down by enraged "avengers." Luckily, he remembered a shoemaker who before the war used to live in his grandmother's house. He managed to turn into a small side street and found the shoemaker, who recognized him at once. Quickly, the man hid him in his workshop behind a cupboard. He spent two days there, after which the shoemaker asked the police for help. In the evening, an armed policeman came and took him to the police station where other remnants of the Kielce Jewish community were locked in the cells, protected by armed security guards. When the street riots finally subsided, not one Jew remained in Kielce. Out of a total of some 140,000 remaining in Poland, over 100,000 left as quickly as they could.
2. A few months later, the Habers decided to leave Poland, prompted by a frightful incident. Their son, Rysio, stayed in a children's home in Rabka, a mountain resort near Kraków, to cure some respiratory problems. The Habers went over for the weekend, as did two more couples who had their children in the same home. All three couples arranged to meet in the local tearoom for supper. One couple didn't come. They were murdered by the NSZ, with their bodies found the next morning. The Habers decided then and there to leave Poland.
3. All of my friends who held the highest positions in the country at that time are now in Israel, America, Canada, or Sweden. They paid a high price for their loyalty, devotion, and love for *their* country.
4. I did not answer. There are people who would never understand the problem unless they woke up in a Kielce experience. Sometimes this kind of awakening comes too late.

New Life: May 1946

1. I met him again in Sydney where he was carrying on his medical practice while his wife became prominent in Australian high society.

My thoughts on Antisemitism

1. The Jews were chosen by God to spread the Ten Commandments amongst the nations of the world; hence the name the Chosen People.

PHOTOS

Filip Reiss (Henry's father), officer of the Austro-Hungarian Empire.

Henry (left) with his mother and brother 1911.

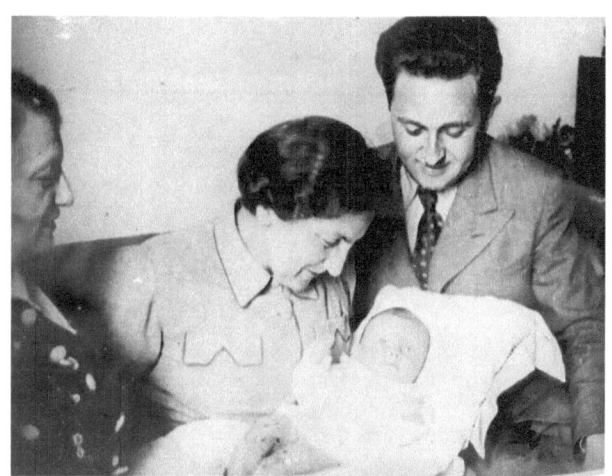

Baby Elżunia with Lusia and Henry, Krakow 1938

Elżunia with nanny Zosia, Lwów, 1941

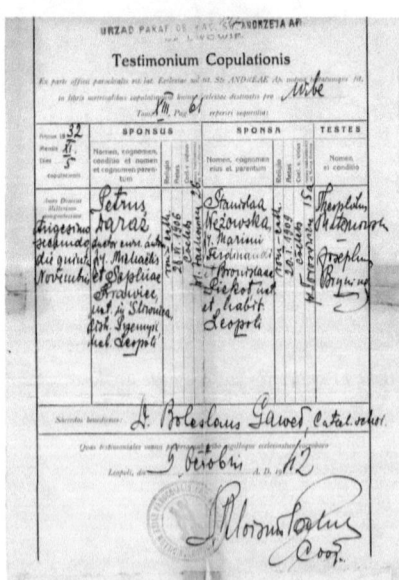

Falsified marriage certificate of Peter and Stanislawa Daraż, 1942.

Photos in Falsified document of a Health Fund membership for the Daraż family (with incorrect spelling of the town), 1942

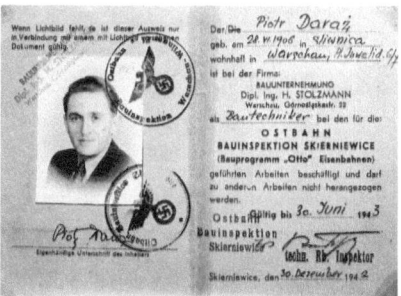

Employment certificate Deutsche Ostbahn (German Eastern Railway) with renewals December 1942-June 1943.

Cousin Józef Reiss who was later confirmed to have been murdered in the Katyn Massacre of Polish Officers by Soviets Union in 1940.

Opening page of diary commenced in Ulm Displaced Persons camp, 1946.

Lusia teaching math in Ulm Displaced Persons camp, 1946.

Bathing on the El Sudan (Christine on the left).

Family holiday shortly after arriving in Blue Mountains, Australia, 1949.

ACKNOWLEDGMENTS

I would like to thank my wife, Irene, for her great understanding and patience, which enabled me to devote so many hours of our life to this work.

I also wish to thank Joan Clarke and Irene for their contribution to the English translation, Shelley Gorn for typing an almost unreadable manuscript, as well as many of my friends for their favorable comments and encouragement to proceed with my story.

The original of this book, written in Polish, has been accepted for publication by Polonia, a leading Polish publishing house, yet due to the constant changes within management, the exact date of publication cannot be assessed. I wish to thank those Polish ladies who, while retyping my manuscript, expressed their enthusiastic comments in a most friendly and encouraging way.

Finally, I wish to thank my daughter Krysia and her husband, James, for their efforts in coordinating various participants in this work, never sparing their time and goodwill during all those years.

Henry Reiss, 1991

I would like to thank Liesbeth Heenk of Amsterdam Publishers, without whose commitment and skill this publication would not have been possible. Liesbeth capably supported the refining of the manuscript whilst preserving the wonderful voice of Henry Reiss. I thank those who helped me to realize this publication, particularly those family and friends who offered encouragement, support and advice whilst I spent time refining the original text. Special thanks to my husband, David Williams, my sister Lucy Levy, my mum Elzunia, and particularly my Aunty Krysia (Henry's daughters) who did so much on the original memoir and again was an exacting proofreader. Their enthusiasm and our discussions helped resolve some key decision points.

Special thanks to my artist and niece, Ilana Bodenstein, one of Henry's great-granddaughters, who created the powerful book cover imagery and produced the maps.

Miriam Levy, 2023

AMSTERDAM PUBLISHERS HOLOCAUST LIBRARY

The series **Holocaust Survivor Memoirs World War II** consists of the following autobiographies of survivors:

Outcry. Holocaust Memoirs, by Manny Steinberg

Hank Brodt Holocaust Memoirs. A Candle and a Promise, by Deborah Donnelly

The Dead Years. Holocaust Memoirs, by Joseph Schupack

Rescued from the Ashes. The Diary of Leokadia Schmidt, Survivor of the Warsaw Ghetto, by Leokadia Schmidt

My Lvov. Holocaust Memoir of a twelve-year-old Girl, by Janina Hescheles

Remembering Ravensbrück. From Holocaust to Healing, by Natalie Hess

Wolf. A Story of Hate, by Zeev Scheinwald with Ella Scheinwald

Save my Children. An Astonishing Tale of Survival and its Unlikely Hero, by Leon Kleiner with Edwin Stepp

Holocaust Memoirs of a Bergen-Belsen Survivor & Classmate of Anne Frank, by Nanette Blitz Konig

Defiant German - Defiant Jew. A Holocaust Memoir from inside the Third Reich, by Walter Leopold with Les Leopold

In a Land of Forest and Darkness. The Holocaust Story of two Jewish Partisans, by Sara Lustigman Omelinski

Holocaust Memories. Annihilation and Survival in Slovakia, by Paul Davidovits

From Auschwitz with Love. The Inspiring Memoir of Two Sisters' Survival, Devotion and Triumph Told by Manci Grunberger Beran & Ruth Grunberger

Mermelstein, by Daniel Seymour

Remetz. Resistance Fighter and Survivor of the Warsaw Ghetto, by Jan Yohay Remetz

My March Through Hell. A Young Girl's Terrifying Journey to Survival, by Halina Kleiner with Edwin Stepp

Roman's Journey, by Roman Halter

Beyond Borders. Escaping the Holocaust and Fighting the Nazis. 1938-1948, by Rudi Haymann

The Engineers. A memoir of survival through World War II in Poland and Hungary, by Henry Reiss

The series **Holocaust Survivor True Stories** consists of the following biographies:

Among the Reeds. The true story of how a family survived the Holocaust, by Tammy Bottner

A Holocaust Memoir of Love & Resilience. Mama's Survival from Lithuania to America, by Ettie Zilber

Living among the Dead. My Grandmother's Holocaust Survival Story of Love and Strength, by Adena Bernstein Astrowsky

Heart Songs. A Holocaust Memoir, by Barbara Gilford

Shoes of the Shoah. The Tomorrow of Yesterday, by Dorothy Pierce

Hidden in Berlin. A Holocaust Memoir, by Evelyn Joseph Grossman

Separated Together. The Incredible True WWII Story of Soulmates Stranded an Ocean Apart, by Kenneth P. Price, Ph.D.

The Man Across the River. The incredible story of one man's will to survive the Holocaust, by Zvi Wiesenfeld

If Anyone Calls, Tell Them I Died. A Memoir, by Emanuel (Manu) Rosen

The House on Thrömerstrasse. A Story of Rebirth and Renewal in the Wake of the Holocaust, by Ron Vincent

Dancing with my Father. His hidden past. Her quest for truth. How Nazi Vienna shaped a family's identity, by Jo Sorochinsky

The Story Keeper. Weaving the Threads of Time and Memory - A Memoir, by Fred Feldman

Krisia's Silence. The Girl who was not on Schindler's List, by Ronny Hein

Defying Death on the Danube. A Holocaust Survival Story, by Debbie J. Callahan with Henry Stern

A Doorway to Heroism. A decorated German-Jewish Soldier who became an American Hero, by Rabbi W. Jack Romberg

The Shoemaker's Son. The Life of a Holocaust Resister, by Laura Beth Bakst

The Redhead of Auschwitz. A True Story, by Nechama Birnbaum

Land of Many Bridges. My Father's Story, by Bela Ruth Samuel Tenenholtz

Creating Beauty from the Abyss. The Amazing Story of Sam Herciger, Auschwitz Survivor and Artist, by Lesley Ann Richardson

On Sunny Days We Sang. A Holocaust Story of Survival and Resilience, by Jeannette Grunhaus de Gelman

Painful Joy. A Holocaust Family Memoir, by Max J. Friedman

I Give You My Heart. A True Story of Courage and Survival, by Wendy Holden

In the Time of Madmen, by Mark A. Prelas

Monsters and Miracles. Horror, Heroes and the Holocaust, by Ira Wesley Kitmacher

Flower of Vlora. Growing up Jewish in Communist Albania, by Anna Kohen

Aftermath: Coming of Age on Three Continents. A Memoir, by Annette Libeskind Berkovits

Not a real Enemy. The True Story of a Hungarian Jewish Man's Fight for Freedom, by Robert Wolf

Zaidy's War. Four Armies, Three Continents, Two Brothers. One Man's Impossible Story of Endurance, by Martin Bodek

The Glassmaker's Son. Looking for the World my Father left behind in Nazi Germany, by Peter Kupfer

The Apprentice of Buchenwald. The True Story of the Teenage Boy Who Sabotaged Hitler's War Machine, by Oren Schneider

Good for a Single Journey, by Helen Joyce

Burying the Ghosts. She escaped Nazi Germany only to have her life torn apart by the woman she saved from the camps: her mother, by Sonia Case

American Wolf. From Nazi Refugee to American Spy. A True Story, by Audrey Birnbaum

Bipolar Refugee. A Saga of Survival and Resilience, by Peter Wiesner

Before the Beginning and After the End, by Hymie Anisman

Malka Owsiany recounts, by Mark Turkow (editor)

I Will Give Them an Everlasting Name. Jacksonville's Stories of the Holocaust, by Samuel P. Cox

The series **Jewish Children in the Holocaust** consists of the following autobiographies of Jewish children hidden during WWII in the Netherlands:

Searching for Home. The Impact of WWII on a Hidden Child, by Joseph Gosler

See You Tonight and Promise to be a Good Boy! War memories, by Salo Muller

Sounds from Silence. Reflections of a Child Holocaust Survivor, Psychiatrist and Teacher, by Robert Krell

Sabine's Odyssey. A Hidden Child and her Dutch Rescuers, by Agnes Schipper

The Journey of a Hidden Child, by Harry Pila and Robin Black

The series **New Jewish Fiction** consists of the following novels, written by Jewish authors. All novels are set in the time during or after the Holocaust.

The Corset Maker. A Novel, by Annette Libeskind Berkovits

Escaping the Whale. The Holocaust is over. But is it ever over for the next generation? by Ruth Rotkowitz

When the Music Stopped. Willy Rosen's Holocaust, by Casey Hayes

Hands of Gold. One Man's Quest to Find the Silver Lining in Misfortune, by Roni Robbins

The Girl Who Counted Numbers. A Novel, by Roslyn Bernstein

There was a garden in Nuremberg. A Novel, by Navina Michal Clemerson

The Butterfly and the Axe, by Omer Bartov

To Live Another Day. A Novel, by Elizabeth Rosenberg

A Worthy Life. Based on a True Story, by Dahlia Moore

The series **Holocaust Heritage** consists of the following memoirs by 2G:

The Cello Still Sings. A Generational Story of the Holocaust and of the Transformative Power of Music, by Janet Horvath

The Fire and the Bonfire. A Journey into Memory, by Ardyn Halter

The Silk Factory: Finding Threads of My Family's True Holocaust Story, by Michael Hickins

Hidden in Plain Sight. A Journey into Memory and Place, by Julie Brill

Winter Light: The Memoir of a Child of Holocaust Survivors, by Grace Feuerverger

Join the AP Review Team

Reviews are very important in a world dominated by the social media. Feedback for Holocaust books is more than just a customer review; it also shows the relevance and importance of such books in today's society.

Please go over to the AmsterdamPublishers.com website (top of page) if you want to join the *AP review team,* showing **at least one review on Amazon** for one of our books. You will get updates about new releases and will get the chance to read and review.

www.ingramcontent.com/pod-product-compliance
Lightning Source LLC
LaVergne TN
LVHW091651070526
838199LV00050B/2148